Local Government in Ireland

Local Government in Ireland
Inside Out

Edited by
MARK CALLANAN
AND
JUSTIN F. KEOGAN

INSTITUTE OF PUBLIC
ADMINISTRATION

First published 2003
by the Institute of Public Administration
57–61 Lansdowne Road
Dublin 4

ISBN 1 902448 93 6

British Library cataloguing-in-publication data
A catalogue record for this book is available from the British Library

Cover design by Butler Claffey, Dún Laoghaire
Typeset in Times New Roman by Carole Lynch, Dublin
Printed by Future Print, Ireland

Table of Contents

List of Contributors

Pauline Byrne is an urban planner with Murray Ó Laoire Architects, Planners and Urban Designers and has been involved in a considerable number of urban planning projects.

Mark Callanan works and lectures at the Institute of Public Administration and is editor of *Local Authority Times*. His research interests include local government and EU governance.

Tony Davis is director of finance in Louth County Council.

Gerard Dollard is a director of services in Clare County Council.

Maureen Doyle was formerly secretary to Comhar – the National Sustainable Development Partnership and is currently pursuing a BA in Archaeology and History in University College Dublin.

Liam Gleeson is an assistant principal in the Water Services Policy Unit of the Department of the Environment and Local Government.

Peter Greene is a principal officer with the Department of the Environment and Local Government.

Berna Grist is a member of An Bord Pleanála and is on leave of absence from her position as senior lecturer in the Department of Regional and Urban Planning at University College Dublin.

Richard Haslam, former county manager of Limerick and member of the Advisory Committee on Local Government Reorganisation and Reform (1990), lectures on local government at University College Cork and at the University of Limerick.

P. J. Howell is a director of services in Fingal County Council.

Liam Kenny is director of the General Council of County Councils and previously worked in the local media and local government.

Justin F. Keogan is pursuing a PhD in Trinity College Dublin. Prior to this, he worked in the Local Authority Unit of the Institute of Public Administration.

Jack Keyes is a director of services in Offaly County Council.

Colin Knox is professor of comparative public policy at the University of Ulster.

Joe MacGrath is a director of services in Kerry County Council.

Mrs **Terry Madden** is chief welfare officer in the Housing Welfare Section of Dublin City Council.

Nicki Matthews is an accredited conservation architect and conservation officer with Dublin City Council.

Michelle Norris is director of the Housing Unit, which was established by the Department of the Environment and Local Government and local authorities to improve management in the public and social housing sector.

Gerard O'Beirne is a director of services in Carlow County Council.

Donncha Ó Dúlaing is heritage officer with Dublin City Council.

Seán O'Riordain is director of ERM Ireland Ltd and formerly worked with the Local Authority Unit of the Institute of Public Administration.

Terry O'Sullivan is a former assistant town clerk with Waterford City Council.

Bríd Quinn is a lecturer in public administration at the University of Limerick. Her research interests include local governance and EU regional policy.

Edward Sheehy is county manager with Wicklow County Council.

John Tierney is city manager with Galway City Council.

Foreword

It is a privilege to have the opportunity to write the foreword to a book which is likely to become the definitive text on local government in this country. It is a worthy successor to Desmond Roche's *Local Government in Ireland*, published over two decades ago, and reflects the scale and pace of change in the intervening years.

New themes such as social inclusion, sustainability and social partnership have emerged while the impact of others like EU membership has greatly intensified. At the same time key local authority services including planning, environmental, housing and roads, together with a renewed emphasis on engaging with local communities, remain centre stage. Funding too continues to feature on the agenda. All are covered among the various contributions along with a description of how the system works – local elections, members, staff, management and the financial process. There is a look back to the evolution of local government from Norman times, right up to such recent developments as constitutional recognition, consolidation of the law and the ending of the dual mandate. And there is a look further afield to local government systems in other countries and to the future. All in all an essential source of reference for students and those involved in local government or concerned with local communities or public affairs generally.

I would like to commend the Institute of Public Administration and the editors, Mark Callanan and Justin F. Keogan, who undertook the task of bringing this book from a good idea to a reality. Likewise to the twenty-five authors of the individual chapters (among them the editors), who each played their own part in shaping this book which fills a major gap in the literature and provides a comprehensive overview of local government.

Martin Cullen, TD
Minister for the Environment and Local Government

Acknowledgements

Local Government in Ireland: Inside Out owes a great deal to Des Roche, who completed *Local Government in Ireland* in 1982 – itself an adapted version of John Collins' *Local Government* (2nd edition, 1963). Since 1982, *Local Government in Ireland* has been regarded as the authoritative textbook on Irish local government. However, Ireland has experienced considerable changes over the last twenty years as a result of socio-economic developments and a programme of reform. These have had a significant impact on local government's structures, functions and environment.

This book aims to be a worthy successor to Roche's *Local Government in Ireland* by providing a comprehensive reference on local government in Ireland at the beginning of the twenty-first century. *Local Government in Ireland: Inside Out* discusses the many developments in local government that have taken place since 1982 and provides new insights into the theory and practice of modern local government. Some of Roche's original text has stood the test of time and has been used to provide historical background for some of the chapters. However, we have added considerably to the 1982 publication in order to provide up-to-date information and analysis and to address contemporary issues such as sustainable development, social inclusion and local government's relationship with the European Union.

The contributors include local government practitioners, civil servants and academics and bring a variety of different perspectives on local government. It goes without saying that this book would not have been possible without the assistance of all the contributing authors, who kindly agreed to give their valuable time and expertise towards the completion of the project. Our thanks go to them for bringing their knowledge to print.

Many colleagues within the Institute of Public Administration, local government and central government assisted our endeavours with helpful guidance and commentary on early drafts of different chapters – there are simply far too many to list here. Special mention, however, must be made of the generous assistance of Kevin Cullen of the Local Government Policy section in the Department of the Environment and Local Government, who kindly agreed to provide up-to-date information and comments on a number of areas in light of recent legislative and other changes.

We are indebted to the editorial and publications staff in the institute, in particular Jennifer Armstrong, as well as our colleagues in the IPA library, all of whom were an endless source of assistance and advice.

We would also like to thank Tony McNamara and Willie Carroll, who originally took up this project in 1998, for preparing much of the groundwork for the book. Tony has since retired from the institute and moved on to further study (truly in the spirit of the IPA). Sadly, Willie Carroll passed away suddenly in 2002. As a part-time lecturer with the IPA, his contribution and long-standing commitment towards the study of local government in Ireland was much appreciated. We would like to acknowledge Willie's involvement in this book at its early stages and dedicate it to his memory.

It should be noted that any opinions expressed in this book reflect the views of the respective authors of each individual chapter and should not be taken as representing the views or policies of the organisations they work for or of the Institute of Public Administration.

Structure of this Book

This book groups different chapters together under common themes. First, an outline of the background and traditional role of local government is provided, covering the historical development of local government, its structures, the process of reform, local elections, the role of councillors and of the manager and so forth.

Second, the various services are discussed: housing, roads, water, planning, environmental services, recreation and amenity, the residual functions in education, agriculture, health and welfare, and the community and enterprise function.

Third, a number of cross-cutting issues applying to a range of local authority functions are addressed. These include chapters on finance, personnel and human resources, social inclusion, sustainable development, spatial planning, regional structures, and how Ireland's membership of the European Union has impacted on local government. Such horizontal themes often represent a challenge for organisations as some of them are not easily located within existing structures and sections.

Fourth, a comparative perspective is introduced, benchmarking Irish local government vis-à-vis systems of local government elsewhere in Europe, as well as the different path taken by local government in Northern Ireland.

Finally, an assessment is made on the current state of local government, looking at some of its limitations, central–local relations, changing trends and the evolution from local government to local governance. Some potential themes for the future are also highlighted.

We are conscious of the fact that readers may dip in and out of this book as a reference resource rather than reading it from cover to cover. For this reason, we have endeavoured to make each chapter as self-contained as possible. Inevitably, this led to some limited overlap in content between chapters, although we have attempted to minimise this through cross-references to other chapters where appropriate.

Changes to Names, Titles and Currency

Readers should note that the names of a number of local authorities were changed under the Local Government Act, 2001. As of 2002, county borough corporations became city councils, borough corporations became borough councils, and urban district councils and town commissioners were renamed town councils. In addition, Tipperary North Riding and Tipperary South Riding County Councils became North Tipperary County Council and South Tipperary County Council respectively. In general, references in this publication are made to the new titles, although the older names are used in an historical context.

Readers should also note that the Department of Local Government became the Department of the Environment in 1977, which became the Department of the Environment and Local Government in 1997. At the time of going to print, it was expected that a further name change would occur during 2003 with the department being re-titled the Department of the Environment, Heritage and Local Government.

Following the introduction of the euro on 1 January 1999 and its subsequent introduction as a cash currency in 2002, monetary values are expressed in euro; although, where considered necessary for historical reasons, the equivalent in punts is also given.

Mark Callanan and Justin F. Keogan
May 2003

Background, Operation and Structure

1

The Role of Local Government

Mark Callanan

At a time when the phenomenon of globalisation dominates much of the political agenda, it seems more important than ever for people to retain their sense of local identity. Despite the fact that people are more mobile, that communications are easier and that events on the other side of the world can have profound consequences on our lives, surveys show that the feeling of belonging to a locality is as strong as ever – often just as strong as the feeling of 'belonging' to a nationality.[1] Even in a global society, people attach a high value to their locality and to localness.

Virtually all countries have systems of local government. To a greater or lesser extent, these are designed to give expression to local identity, to identify local concerns and to set local priorities.

Roche (1982b, p. 1) provides a straightforward definition of local government as 'a system of administration in political subdivisions of the state, by elected bodies having substantial control of local affairs, including the power to impose taxes'. Elected bodies, known as local authorities, operate within a specific geographical area within a state, are locally elected or selected, have some discretion and autonomy from central government and generally have the power to levy taxes (as a precondition for autonomy).

There is, increasingly, an assumption that local authorities should be invested with a wide range of functions and powers allowing them to work towards the improvement of their communities. For example, the European Charter of Local

---

[1] In a survey carried out in 2002, 96 per cent of Irish people felt they were either very or fairly attached to their country. This compared with 95 per cent who were very or fairly attached to their town/village and 94 per cent to their region/county. The corresponding figures across the EU were 89 per cent, 87 per cent and 86 per cent (European Commission, 2003, Tables 3.1a, 3.1b and 3.1c).

Self-Government (see appendix 1), agreed in 1985 and signed by the Irish government in 1997, states: 'Local self-government denotes the right and ability of local authorities, within the limits of the law, to regulate and manage a substantial share of public affairs under their own responsibility and in the interests of the local population' (Council of Europe, 1985a, Article 3.1). This implies that local authorities have not only the right to manage a broad range of functions, but also the capacity and resources to do so effectively.

The charter goes on to say: 'Public responsibilities shall generally be exercised, in preference, by those authorities which are closest to the citizen. Allocation of responsibility to another authority should weigh up the extent and nature of the task and requirements of efficiency and economy' (Article 4.3). This is an allusion to the principle of subsidiarity – that services, where they can be provided efficiently and effectively, should be provided and decided on at the level closest to the citizen, that being the level of government the citizen is most able to influence. The assumption therefore is that issues are dealt with locally and that a convincing case must be made for functions to be transferred to regional or central government. Functions should only be delegated upwards where objectives can be better achieved at regional, national or indeed supranational level for reasons of scale, efficiency or effectiveness.[2] In many countries, the autonomy of local communities is jealously guarded against excessive encroachment by higher levels of government. In Ireland's case, the history of Irish local government shows that a different approach is taken to the 'burden of proof' – the presumption would seem to be that functions should be handled by central government departments and agencies wherever possible (see chapter 8).

While there are many similarities, the exact range of functions dealt with by local authorities varies from country to country. Local authorities remain for the most part multi-purpose bodies, although increasingly they work in an environment of single-purpose agencies at regional or national level. The application of the subsidiarity principle led to a widespread devolution of functions in many Western European countries during the 1970s and 1980s, with Ireland and the UK being notable exceptions (see, for example, Batley and Stoker, 1991).

This chapter sets out the different reasons given for local government. Chapter 28 of this book discusses some of the more recent challenges local government has faced, challenges that have resulted in changes to its role. Local government can have a number of different roles. It can be:

- an instrument of local democracy
- a provider of services

---

[2] For a discussion of subsidiarity as it applies in the EU context, see chapter 24.

- an agent of central government
- a local regulator.

Each of these roles is examined below in an Irish context.

Local Government as an Instrument of Local Democracy

One of the primary purposes of local authorities is to give expression to the right of local self-government. In a democracy, people have a right to have their say in the determination of affairs and the setting of priorities. This occurs at national level through the election of a national parliament and a national government. However, in addition to central government, where the opportunities for public participation will inevitably be limited, the importance of local democracy is also emphasised as part of a nation's democratic system. It is no coincidence, for example, that after the fall of the Berlin Wall in 1989, the process of renewing local democracy and local government has played a key role in embedding the democratic tradition in many Central and Eastern European countries after years of totalitarianism. Local government creates additional opportunities for public participation and political activity within the democratic process to influence events and local decisions. In fact, one of local government's greatest virtues is that it is closer and therefore more accessible to the citizen. In that regard, local government is seen as a vital element of a nation's democratic system.

Article 21 of the Universal Declaration of Human Rights states: 'Everyone has the right to take part in the government of his country, directly or through freely chosen representatives' (United Nations, 1948). This sets out general democratic rights, although it makes no specific mention of local democracy. The European Charter of Local Self-Government, which has been signed by most European countries including Ireland, goes further. The beliefs underlying the charter, as stated in its preamble, include a recognition of local government as part of the foundations of any democratic regime, the right of citizens to participate in the conduct of public affairs and the fact that this right can be most directly exercised at the local level. The preamble establishes local democracy at the heart of the rationale behind local government and asserts the need for:

> . . . local authorities endowed with democratically constituted decision-making bodies and possessing a wide degree of autonomy with regard to their responsibilities, the ways and means by which those responsibilities are exercised and the resources required for their fulfilment . . . (Council of Europe, 1985a).

The text makes the case that local government is a vital factor underpinning a nation's democracy (see appendix 1).

The continuing debate over local government, its link with democracy and the extent of local autonomy is a long-standing one. Rousseau held that in a true democracy, if the general will can find expression, there is no role for partial societies within states. In the early nineteenth century, a number of emerging movements, including utilitarianism, looked at new approaches to local government in Britain. The utilitarians, led by Jeremy Bentham, were concerned with central powers and argued that while local 'sub-legislatures' could be elected, they would be subject to central control. The emphasis was on national sovereignty centralised in a single source of authority. It should be borne in mind that local 'government' in Britain and Ireland was at the time diagnosed as corrupt, inefficient and dominated by a small number of the landed aristocracy.

Bentham, and later Edwin Chadwick, argued for the centralisation of powers, good administration and the abolition of inefficient and corrupt local government. They argued that local government as it was then constituted was the enemy of both democracy and efficiency in administration. Their centralising zeal reflected a trend in many other European countries where local (and often feudal) interests were overrun by the assertion of central control from national capitals through a process of nation building. This process was in many cases accompanied by a ruthless suppression of local cultures, regional languages and dialects in an effort to homogenise a national culture to fit within national boundaries.

The views of Bentham and Chadwick on efficiency and central control were challenged in Britain by Joshua Toulmin Smith and the mid-Victorian romantics who, on the basis of a tradition of local elites, argued that local self-government was part of the Anglo-Saxon heritage and therefore had a role to play in government.

A third view was provided by John Stuart Mill, who held that democracy and local self-government are inter-related, given that local democratic institutions widen the opportunity to participate in government, and that therefore local populations should be free to determine local issues as a pillar of liberty. Mill argued that local government could be a vehicle for political education, a training ground for citizenship and a mechanism for promoting fraternity. He therefore attached a high value to it regardless of what functions it carried out (Hill, 1974, p. 23). Mill also argued that local bodies would have an advantage in achieving efficient and effective service provision because of their local knowledge (Stoker, 1996, p. 5). Many of Mill's arguments provided the basis for the development of representative local government in Britain and Ireland. Some of the early socialists in Britain argued that local government, through accountability to the electorate and the provision of services, could embody the notion of civic responsibility and civic pride.

Beetham (1996) argues that there is a strong case for elected local government supporting the democratic principles of political equality and popular control involving all citizens. This argument is based on the following concepts:

- popular authorisation of decision makers through election
- accountability to the people for policies and actions undertaken while in office
- responsiveness of government to the range of public opinion and assessment of public opinion on issues in between elections
- representativeness, whereby all individuals possess a vote of equal value and have the opportunity to stand for office.

Beetham (1996, p. 33) also argues that elected local government needs to be complemented by an alert and active citizenship to ensure that it is accountable and remains responsive.

In the Irish context, the importance of local government as part of the nation's democratic system has often been overlooked. This can perhaps be traced to a political culture inherited from Britain, whereby democracy and sovereignty are seen as being almost exclusively vested in the national legislature. Hesse and Sharpe (1991, p. 607) comment that Irish local government belongs to the 'Anglo' group of countries, where the emphasis tends to be placed on local government's functional capacity and efficiency as a service provider rather than on its role as an instrument of local democracy. Despite this, the importance of local government in Ireland in representing the interests of the community has been highlighted a number of times.

The 1971 White Paper on local government reorganisation makes the link between local government and local democracy. It marks out local government from other local agencies of the state by noting:

> The real argument . . . for the provision of local services by local authorities . . . is that a system of local self-government is one of the essential elements of democracy. Under such a system, local affairs can be settled by the local citizens themselves or their representatives, local services can be locally controlled and local communities can participate in the process and responsibilities of government (Government of Ireland, 1971, p. 9).

An alternative viewpoint is to relegate local authorities to the status of local administration, delivering services but with little discretion or real decision-making responsibilities. The Devlin Report (Public Services Organisation Review Group, 1969, p. 159), while acknowledging the extent of central control on local government, reflected on a widespread view within the public service in Ireland that 'local authorities should be regarded as Executive Agencies, with elected boards, reporting to the Minister for Local Government'.

However, the 1996 blueprint for local government reform, *Better Local Government*, re-asserts the link between local government and local democracy, by stating:

Local authorities are the only bodies outside of the Dáil whose members are democratically elected by all of the people. This gives local government a status which distinguishes it from all other agencies – public, private or voluntary. In contrast to functionally organised government departments and other public agencies . . . it is locality-based, has a broad range of functions and has a concern and identification with its area. This concern goes beyond the particular services delivered by local government to encompass the general welfare and overall development of the local area and its community (Department of the Environment, 1996, p. 14).

Since 1999 local government and local democracy are specifically provided for in the Constitution (see below), again underpinning the separate status that continues to be assigned to local government.

The Local Government Act, 2001 (section 63) also notes that local authorities have a role 'to provide a forum for the democratic representation of the local community . . . and to provide civic leadership for that community'.

The strengths of local government as a democratic instrument are therefore its closeness to the population, its elected status, its accessibility and the opportunities it provides for participation in the democratic process.

Local Government as a Provider of Services

In addition to providing a forum for local decision making, Irish local authorities also have responsibility for the provision of a number of key services. These functions are largely concerned with development and the physical environment. The following list of the traditional programme groups illustrates the various local government competencies in Ireland:

1   housing and building
2   road transportation and safety
3   water supply and sewerage
4   development incentives and control (planning)
5   environmental protection
6   recreation and amenity
7   agriculture, education, health and welfare
8   miscellaneous services.

These functions are expanded on in later chapters. At first sight, the list seems to represent a reasonable devolution of functions to local government. However, it should be noted, as it is elsewhere in this book (for example chapters 8, 26 and 28), that Irish local authorities have a comparatively narrow remit. The only significant social service remaining with local government is housing. In contrast, many other local government systems encompass responsibility for primary and secondary education and management of schools, social welfare, care of the elderly, childcare provision, public transport, policing, local economic development and so on.

Notwithstanding these limitations, local government in Ireland does have important responsibilities that impinge directly or indirectly on the communities it serves. In general, local government functions are local services, including the provision of housing, the maintenance of local roads and drainage schemes, planning and development control, refuse collection and the provision of parks, libraries and other community facilities. Some commentators, such as Sharpe (1970), argue that local authorities are in the best position to provide local services on efficiency grounds, through their role of co-ordinating delivery, judging what is deemed desirable and necessary in the locality and representing all interests in the community rather than specific groups.

The services provided by local authorities are of course a visible area of activity and dominate the debate about the effectiveness or otherwise of local government. Increasingly, local authorities are being encouraged to improve the quality of the service they provide, to make services more responsive to consumer demands and to ensure value for money. For some functions, local authorities are contracting out service areas to private contractors (see chapters 4 and 28).

Local authorities in Ireland and elsewhere operate within the framework of national policy. Thus, local authorities would often decide on local policies and the level of local services within a broad national framework, in line with the principle of local self-government. While overall objectives and targets might be set at national level, local authorities would in principle have some discretion on how to meet these objectives, adapt policies and services to suit local needs and priorities and come up with innovative methods and new ways of tackling issues.

In this context, local authorities were given a power of 'general competence' under the Local Government Act, 1991. This replaced the earlier doctrine of *ultra vires*, which had prohibited local authorities from any action that they were not specifically authorised to undertake and effectively restricted actions to areas where local government had a statutory responsibility. Section 66.3 of the Local Government Act, 2001 (which repealed and replaced the 1991 Act) states: 'A local authority may take such measures, engage in such activities or do such things in accordance with the law (including the incurring of expenditure) as it considers necessary or desirable to promote the interests of the local community'.

Promoting the interests of the local community can include promoting social inclusion or the social, economic, environmental, recreational, cultural, community or general development of the local community or area. However, under the provisions of the Act, local authorities must take care to avoid duplication of the activities of other statutory bodies and should not engage in what the Act terms 'wasteful or unnecessary expenditure'.

Local authorities in most EU countries enjoy the power of general competence. This power can of course be purely hypothetical if it is not accompanied by sufficient staff and financial resources to allow local authorities to strike out in new directions. However, Blair (1991, p. 51) argues that the significance of a general competence for local government lies not so much in its operational implications, but in its symbolic value. It encourages the citizen to see the local authority as the representative body for the whole community and offers opportunities for local authorities to pursue innovative solutions to local problems.

The power of general competence also recognises local government's interest in the development of the locality and in promoting its concerns, which might sometimes imply action outside of its own statutory functions. It also reflects local government's role in giving expression to local interests. Elected members are sometimes criticised for debating issues, proposing motions and passing resolutions on matters that are outside the competence of local government. However, this has to be seen in the context of local government providing a voice for local concerns,[3] and the fact that Article 28A of the Constitution recognises 'the role of local government in providing a forum for the democratic representation of local communities'. The concept of general competence recognises that local government should not limit itself to speaking out on a restricted number of statutory functions.

Local Government as an Agent of Central Government

Some services are provided by local authorities on an 'agency basis' on behalf of central government. In these cases, local authorities do not enjoy the discretion referred to above, but are simply acting as an arm of the state in delivering a national policy. Essentially, central government makes use of local authorities as a resource and finances them to engage in particular activities. In France, for example, while local government responds to local needs in the delivery of some local tasks, there is also a tradition of local authorities acting as local offices of the state for delivering certain central government services.

A particular example of this role is in the area of pensions and child allowances in Denmark, which are paid to individuals by the local authority acting in its role as an agent of the state. Local authorities administer payments on behalf of central government but do not have the power to vary levels of payment, which are decided at central level. Central government in Denmark reimburses local authorities for the costs associated with the service. This lack of discretion contrasts with many other services provided by Danish local authorities, where national policy is outlined, rather than detailed, to allow for local discretion.

A clear distinction is therefore drawn in Denmark between those services where local authorities have some discretion and can decide on local priorities

---

[3] This tradition of local elected members discussing issues outside the remit of local government is well established. Meghen (1964, p. 198) reports that Daniel O'Connell used elected local authorities 'to stimulate interest in the Repeal movement. Complaint was often made by English writers that the local elected bodies in Ireland spent too much time debating national politics'.

and those services that are simply administered by local authorities on an agency basis on behalf of the state. In Ireland this distinction can be rather hazy. The collection of motor tax or the administration of higher education grants might be regarded as examples of Irish local authorities acting as agents of the state.

Local Government as a Local Regulator

Local government's role as a regulator is often overlooked and yet it plays an increasingly important part in local authority activity. This regulatory role is probably most manifest in local government's planning and development responsibilities, where local authorities adopt development plans and process planning applications. However, it is also illustrated through the power of local authorities to adopt bye-laws on areas such as environmental pollution and litter control. In some cases, local authorities regulate national standards, for example fire safety standards in buildings where they inspect premises, serve notices and ultimately take court actions.

The regulatory role involves the specification of standards (either at local or national level), checking whether standards are being met/complied with (often through inspections or examination of applications) and the enforcement of standards where necessary through the application of sanctions. However, as Stewart (1997, p. 17) points out, the regulatory function can pose challenges for a number of reasons, for example where standards cannot always be clear and unambiguous or where adequate resources for inspection are not available.

The regulatory function requires decisions to be taken about how to best ensure that standards are met – through either rigorous enforcement or through influencing, educating and preventing, which in many cases can be an effective method of meeting standards. Different situations might merit enforcement or influence and table 1.1 illustrates the criteria suggested by Stewart (1997, p. 23) for determining the appropriate approach.

There is a potential for tension between local government's role as a service provider and local government's role as a regulator. As service providers, local authorities are looking to continually improve services to 'customers' – they publish customer action plans and consult users on better methods of provision. As regulators, local authorities are required to take a somewhat more detached position and make potentially unpopular decisions (at least for the individuals involved) such as whether to grant or refuse planning permission or whether to prosecute for litter offences.

While it is general government policy to eliminate unnecessary and excessive regulation, some elements are likely to remain necessary for the foreseeable future, for example in areas such as physical development, protection of the environment and fire safety.

Table 1.1 Criteria for Determining Regulatory Style

Influence:		*Enforcement:*
standards and rules vague	←•→	clear standards and rules
complexity	←•→	simplicity
subjective/qualitative judgement	←•→	objective judgement
a lot of regulatory resources	←•→	few regulatory resources
few to be regulated	←•→	many to be regulated
harmful impact not obvious	←•→	harmful impact obvious
link of regulatees' actions and failures obscure	←•→	link of regulatees' actions and failures apparent
cost of failure low	←•→	cost of failure high
offenders not identifiable.	←•→	offenders identifiable.

Local Government and the Constitution

Until 1999, there was no specific constitutional provision for local government in *Bunreacht na hÉireann* (Constitution of Ireland). Local authorities were only mentioned in passing in the original 1937 Constitution, in particular with regard to the provisions for nominating candidates for the presidency of Ireland. Article 12.4.2 provides that a candidate for the office of President of Ireland must be nominated by twenty or more members of either the Dáil or Seanad or alternatively by four or more county or city councils. Until the presidential election of 1997, no candidate had ever been successfully nominated by the required four local authorities. In 1997, local authorities across the country added two candidates – Dana Rosemary Scallon and Derek Nally – to the ballot paper for the election ultimately won by Mary McAleese.

Two other articles of the Constitution make passing reference to local authorities. Article 15.2 makes provision for the possible establishment of 'subordinate legislatures'. Article 22.1, when defining money bills, excludes any taxation, money or loans raised by local authorities or bodies for local purposes. The absence of a specific reference to local government must be regarded at best as a curious omission, given their status as elected bodies and the fact that the Dáil and President (the only other directly elected offices in the country[4]) were provided for in the original Constitution.

---

[4] The members of Údarás na Gaeltachta are also largely directly elected. Although Údarás is not formally part of the local government system, it has a local remit in promoting industrial development in Irish-speaking areas in a number of counties.

Those advocating a renewed system of local government often made the point that the importance of local government and local democracy should be recognised in the Constitution as part of the democratic structures of government (Barrington Report, 1991, p. 17). It was argued that a constitutional provision on local government would be appropriate, given that local councillors, in the same way as the President and members of the Dáil, are directly elected and responsible to the people. Furthermore, constitutional recognition would end the hypothetical possibility of central government abolishing the local government system through an Act of the Oireachtas and require any such proposal to be put to a referendum.

A commitment was made in *Better Local Government* (Department of the Environment, 1996, p. 15) to give constitutional recognition to local government. The document acknowledged that this would be in keeping with the European Charter of Local Self-Government and would bring Ireland into line with established practice in other countries where local government is a partner in the overall system of government.

A constitutional referendum was held in June 1999, in conjunction with local and European Parliament elections, and produced a 77.8 per cent vote in favour of including a new Article 28A entitled 'Local Government'. The turnout was 51 per cent. The text of the constitutional provision reflects local government's role in defining local priorities and promoting the interests of the community, as well as providing statutory services (see appendix 2). The constitutional provision for local elections every five years also ended a long history of local elections being deferred by central government.

2

The Origins of Irish Local Government[1]

Richard Haslam

This chapter provides an overview of the origins of local government in Ireland. It includes a brief outline of the development of local territorial areas, the evolution of municipal government, the roots of local government and the development of local taxation and legislation dealing with local government. It also provides the founding context for local government as it exists in Ireland today, including an account of local government during the early years of the state and the principal developments and reforms that took place within the local government system. As the history of local government functions is covered in other chapters, an attempt has been made to avoid repetition here.

Local government in Ireland is largely a product of nineteenth-century statutes of the British parliament modelled on those enacted for England with some variation to meet Irish conditions – for example the Poor Relief (Ireland) Act, 1838, Municipal Corporations (Ireland) Act, 1840 and, of course, the foundation statute of Irish local government, the Local Government (Ireland) Act, 1898. The concept of the medieval town wall, segregating urban and rural, still exists. The walls are all but gone, but the mentality of distinction remains and asserts itself vehemently when issues such as boundary extensions are being considered.

The establishment of the county as an administrative unit developed slowly in individual cases over a number of years, if not centuries, dating from the definite existence of Dublin, Cork and Waterford counties in 1216 to the final emergence of Wicklow in 1606. It should be noted that the effectiveness of county administration varied with the acceptance of royal authority in areas hitherto under Irish rule or where English authority was merely nominal. For this reason the

---

[1] In the main, this chapter is based on extracts from Roche (1982b).

origins and development of the county system cannot be traced with absolute certainty but the outlines are clear enough.

Counties were formed principally as units for the territorial administration of justice. The king's judges visited each county (including counties of cities and towns) twice yearly and held assizes of the hearing and adjudication of cases with the assistance of grand juries. Grand juries foreshadowed county councils in the provision of many services taken for granted today. Efforts at reform, especially in 1836, were not very successful and their abolition in 1898 was inevitable. Members were chosen, twenty-three in number, by the high sheriffs, from among property owners – the biggest landholders in the counties and the higher bourgeoisie in cities and towns. From the seventeenth century onwards, this piece of judicial machinery began to accumulate certain administrative functions, which came to be known as the fiscal business of the grand juries.

The first statute giving a clue to the course of the fiscal business was an Act of 1634 'concerning the repairing and amending of bridges, causeways and toghers in the highways', authorising the justices of assize, with the consent of the grand jury, to levy the cost of road and bridge works on the county or barony according to the importance, one assumes, of the road or bridge affected. The levy came to be known as the county cess. The names of those liable, by ownership or occupation of land or other property, were inscribed in a roll and collectors were appointed for each barony and parish.

The system took little hold until settled conditions, of a sort, began to appear towards the end of the seventeenth century with the total victory of the Protestant cause. An Act of 1705 authorised the grand juries to take the initiative in making presentments or proposing works for financing by the cess-payers. The types of work gradually expanded and services began to be included until the grand juries were dealing with a large body of miscellaneous tasks. These included roads, paths and bridges, the maintenance of lunatic asylums, the cost of extra police, courthouses, conveyance of prisoners, salaries of county officers (for example secretary, surveyor), contributions to county infirmaries and fever hospitals, dispensaries, loan repayments and compensation for malicious injuries. Two assizes were held each year, in spring and summer.

By the early part of the nineteenth century, the volume of law dealing with the fiscal work of grand juries had greatly increased and reformers, in addition to clarifying and consolidating the law, made an attempt to curb the more flagrant malpractices that had developed. Inefficiency and corruption were widespread: grand jurors exerted themselves to secure presentments for works of benefit to themselves and their friends. As early as 1816 a parliamentary select committee recommended the separation of civil from criminal business, and an Act of 1817 established the office of county surveyor with the aim of bringing some control into the disorderly business of making presentments for roads and other works. Valiant efforts were made also to cope with the centuries-old problem of equitable valuations for cess-payers, and the Valuation Act, 1826 began the process of rectifying anomalies. An Act of 1833 (later incorporated in the Grand Jury Act, 1836) democratised the system in some small degree by requiring the high sheriff to include at presentment sessions one resident £50 freeholder or £100 leaseholder from each barony, the remainder to be chosen from men of like qualifications in any part of the county. Catholics had been eligible to become grand jurors since the Catholic Relief Act, 1793.

The Grand Jury Act, 1836 instituted a system of presentment sessions in counties and baronies. The baronial presentment sessions (dealing with expenditure for the benefit of the barony) were conducted by juries composed of officers of the peace and cess-payers – the latter numbering from five to twelve were chosen by a complicated formula. Cess-payers were in practice slow to attend because they could not be sure of selection and the business of the session tended to be left in the hands of the justices.

County presentment sessions dealt with expenses of benefit to the whole county (they also handled baronial presentments for the barony where the courthouse was situated). In addition to the justices of the peace, one cess-payer nominated by each baronial session figured on the county body. The function of county and baronial presentment sessions was to take over the initiation of expenditure from the grand jury. The initiatory role, that vital step in the local administrative process, was thus transferred to a somewhat more representative body.

The 1836 Act had little real effect and dissatisfaction with the fiscal operations of the grand juries persisted. The system was fully investigated by a royal commission from 1840 to 1842, but no action ensued. Twenty years later, Isaac Butt and other members of parliament were still trying to reform the grand jury system by means of private bills. But the system remained unchanged until its abolition in 1898.

The pressure – it was never an agitation – for better county government was low key and had little popular support. O'Connell was more or less indifferent. The torch was carried by Whig reformers like Lord Monteagle, an Irish landlord whose family name of Spring Rice recurs from time to time in Irish history.

The counties have remained substantially as delimited in the sixteenth and seventeenth centuries. An early departure, in the local government context, was the division of Tipperary into north and south ridings in December 1838. The two grand juries so created each dealt with fiscal business under general grand jury law. The grand juries, in their fiscal capacities, became the two county councils that continue to operate in Tipperary. Much later, the Local Government Act, 1991 provided for the establishment of three new county councils in the Dublin area to replace Dublin County Council and Dún Laoghaire Borough Council and to be known as Fingal, South Dublin and Dún Laoghaire-Rathdown county councils. These were established in 1994.

Cork County was divided into ridings in 1823, but for quarter sessions only, and thus retained its single grand jury, and in due course its single county council. Galway County had an east and west riding in the nineteenth century for certain administrative purposes such as the appointment of county surveyors and police management.

The Evolution of Municipal Government

Ireland had towns before the Normans came, some of Irish origin but most of them Danish creations. Dublin, Cork, Limerick, Wexford and Waterford were among those of pre-Norman source; others emerged shortly after the invasion. All of these were given charters by Henry II, his son John, or by their barons, and became boroughs on the Norman pattern with their own courts (principal among them the hundred court), chief executive officers (generally titled mayors) and councils. The charters vested the land on which the town was built in the general body of citizens or burgesses; and the grant of land might also include additional acreage in the adjacent territory. The idea of creating bodies corporate – by incorporating the mayor, burgesses and commonalty of citizens, which landholding on this scale would seem to necessitate – did not in fact emerge until the Tudor period, when clauses to this effect began to appear in the charters.

The mayor, portreeve, sovereign or other chief executive was an early type of city manager with wide powers, more authority and even greater prestige. He was chosen by his fellow citizens through the hundred court and held office for one year. The numerous bands of similarly selected officers – recorder, coroner, town/city clerk, treasurer, town sergeant and so forth – made up the management team, which conducted the military, judicial and much of the economic affairs of the town. The town council, a universal feature of the municipal structure, exhibited a tendency to evolve into two forms of organisation: a small inner council consisting in the main of former officers who, with the mayor, ran the town; and an assembly or common council, with some representative character, whose powers were mainly legislative. Revenue required for the expenses of defending and managing the town came from customs, tolls and rents charged for municipal properties. Local taxes in the modern sense were not levied.

The larger towns enjoyed freedom from the supervision of county authorities, had their own courts to administer justice, and regulated their markets and trade. Towns also asserted a large measure of independence of the crown in civic affairs from the twelfth to the sixteenth centuries. With the recovery and growth of royal authority, the central government took advantage of grants of incorporation to confer municipal powers not on the general body of the townspeople but on close corporations. In the many new boroughs created during the seventeenth century, civic authority was centralised in small, self-perpetuating oligarchies. This practice opened the way to the corruption and decay that infected virtually all boroughs in the eighteenth and early nineteenth centuries both in Britain and Ireland.

During this period the corporations, while flagrantly neglecting town services, concentrated on the important political function of returning members of the right persuasion to parliament. But even before the tide of reform finally overtook them, thirty boroughs were wiped out by the Act of Union, twenty of them close corporations of Stuart creation.

The first sign of reform of this early form of local governance was the growth in the latter half of the eighteenth century of bodies of commissioners in many towns. The commissioners undertook such matters as public lighting, street cleaning, paving, water supply, drainage and the police. These services, demanded by rising urban standards, underlined the inadequacy and failure of the old municipal system. A series of Acts creating bodies of locally elected commissioners culminated in the Lighting of Towns Act, 1828, a general adoptive statute under which sixty-five towns either bypassed their inactive corporations or attained new municipal status. The Act introduced a modified form of local democracy whereby liability to the new rate and the privilege of voting were limited to householders occupying houses of annual value of £5 or upwards. Eligibility to stand for election as a commissioner required occupation of property of £20 valuation at least. Commissioners held office for three years and could run for re-election.

In 1833, a royal commission was established to examine the municipal corporations of England and Wales and similar inquiries were set up for Scotland and Ireland. The English report was presented in 1835 and the Municipal Corporations Act, 1835 (to reform and restructure the whole system) was introduced in parliament and passed without much difficulty or delay. The report for Ireland was also presented in 1835 and a Bill along the English lines was introduced with commendable speed. But the Irish Bill had a much rougher and slower passage. It took five years to reach the statute book and, despite the pressure for reform, the Benthamite ideal of household suffrage (embodied in the English Act) was severely modified to require a £10 valuation for Irish householders aspiring to the municipal franchise. Also, in Ireland the power to appoint sheriffs and resident magistrates and the control of the police (vested in the municipalities under the English Act) were reserved to the lord lieutenant.

The Act of Union wiped out thirty decayed corporations and left sixty-eight standing, in varying conditions of maladministration and civic distemper. Sir Robert Peel, in opposition in 1835, urged the total extinction of the Irish corporations, to be replaced by town commissioners under the Act of 1828 – although the Irish corporations were not shown by the investigators to be notably worse, on the whole, than their English counterparts.

In the end, the Irish Bill followed the lines of the 1835 Act for England and Wales. Of the sixty-eight surviving corporations, fifty-eight were dissolved by the

Municipal Corporations (Ireland) Act, 1840. The remaining ten continued under a new constitution and name. The surviving corporations were Cork, Dublin, Limerick, Waterford, Belfast and Londonderry (all to become county boroughs in 1898) and also Clonmel, Drogheda, Kilkenny and Sligo. Their charters were annulled so far as they were inconsistent with the new Act; and corporate property, over which the old corporations had absolute control, was diverted to public use. The new councils, which were elective, were restrained by treasury control in the disposal of this property. The new borough fund had to be used for the public benefit and the councils were empowered to raise a limited borough rate. The councils were also given the powers of the 1828 Act, but only in so far as they related to public lighting. Wexford, exercising a right to petition, obtained a new charter in 1845. Galway became a borough by private legislation in 1937 and achieved county borough status in 1986. The remaining borough of Dún Laoghaire was created in 1930 by absorbing a number of former urban districts and became part of the new administrative county of Dún Laoghaire-Rathdown in 1993. In 2002 borough corporations became known as borough councils.

The powers conferred under the 1840 Act were, in fact, curiously restricted. They amounted to little more than a power to make bye-laws for the good rule and government of the borough, and the abatement of nuisances; with limited powers of sale and leasing the corporate estate and rating. It appears that the corporations had inspired such distrust that, even in their reformed state, parliament was unwilling to give them a wide range of duties. And besides, improvement commissioners under either private legislation or the 1828 Act were already operating in the boroughs and elsewhere.

Although the Municipal Corporations (Ireland) Act, 1840 was passed two years after the Poor Relief (Ireland) Act, 1838 it did not follow the same principle. The Benthamites had hoped to see all local government organised along the same lines as poor relief, but this hope was not realised. The new poor law was detested in England and Ireland and the urge for reform had slackened. Governments were not prepared to incur the unpopularity that the extension of Bentham's ideas would involve and, therefore, no root and branch reform was attempted. The old system was patched up and the old historical areas of county and borough preserved.

Under the 1840 Act, the accounts of the corporations were to be audited by locally elected auditors, whereas the poor law commissioners appointed the auditors of poor relief expenditure. The borough councils, as already noted, had very few powers or duties; and the borough rate was limited to one shilling or, if the Lighting of Towns Act, 1828 was in force in the town, to three pence. In time and by means of private legislation which they promoted in parliament, the borough corporations obtained new powers including the ability to strike improvement and other rates. This private legislation dealt with water supply, drainage, markets, rates and other matters that became increasingly the subjects of general legislation.

The outburst of private or local legislation in the early part of the nineteenth century inspired a series of reformist measures that went some way to bridging the gap between local initiatives and general legislation. These were the Clauses Acts, notably the Towns Improvement Clauses Act and the Commissioners Clauses Act, both of 1847. The Clauses Act was a device, invented by a noted Benthamite, Joseph Hume MP, for helping local legislators with a package of ideas from which they could pick or choose; and at the same time for saving parliamentary time. The clauses were drawn from private legislation and brought together in an Act that could be incorporated wholly or partly in subsequent legislation. The Towns Improvement Clauses Act was a collection of provisions found in earlier private Acts dealing with paving, draining, cleansing, lighting and so on. The Commissioners Clauses Act dealt with the constitution and regulation of public bodies. In addition, there were Clauses Acts on such subjects as land acquisition, waterworks, markets, harbours, electric lighting and railways.

Various sections of the Towns Improvement Clauses and Commissioners Clauses Acts were incorporated in the Towns Improvement Act, 1854, which was in essence an expanded and updated version of the Lighting of Towns Act, 1828. It had much the same procedure for local option in putting the Act into force in the town, or leaving it alone. The public health provisions (later replaced by the Public Health (Ireland) Act, 1878) reflected a substantial advance on the somewhat rudimentary enactment of 1828. And there were more elaborate and, one supposes, more effective police clauses. It is curious perhaps that despite these improvements a number of towns where the 1828 Act had been adopted did not take advantage of the opportunity of changing over to the 1854 Act and remained unreconstructed until the Local Government Act, 1898 forcibly placed them all under the later code. The Towns Improvement (Ireland) Act, 1854, although antiquated and to a large degree ineffective, was operative in over twenty towns until its repeal under the Local Government Act, 2001. Since independence this Act has been brought into operation in four towns: Tramore (1948), Shannon (1982), Greystones (1984) and Leixlip (1988).

The somewhat haphazard emergence of municipal towns took a small step forward with the Public Health (Ireland) Act, 1874, which was one of the first measures following the establishment in 1872 of the Local Government Board for Ireland. The 1874 Act set up a nationwide network of urban and rural sanitary authorities, but no new bodies were called into being as the Act made use of existing bodies and gave them new titles. Borough corporations and commissioners of towns with populations over 6,000 became urban sanitary authorities. Commissioners in smaller towns could apply to the Local Government Board for sanitary powers. Poor law guardians became rural sanitary authorities (for areas not covered by an urban authority). This Act conferred no new powers, but four years later under the Public Health (Ireland) Act, 1878, the new authorities were given a comprehensive and, for the time, updated code of sanitary law.

The work of system building culminated with the Local Government (Ireland) Act, 1898, which converted urban and rural sanitary districts into a second tier of local government under the new county councils. Urban and rural district councils endured as a complete second level covering the whole of the country until restructuring in the 1920s, when rural district councils were dissolved by the Local Government Act, 1925. Urban district councils continued to operate until the enactment of the Local Government Act, 2001, which replaced urban district councils and town commissioners with town councils.

The Roots of Local Government

Poor relief in Ireland hardly existed as a system before the nineteenth century. There was nothing in Ireland comparable with the Elizabethan poor law – the national system of parish relief and rating in England from 1601 onwards. In order to address extensive levels of Irish poverty, an outburst of legislative activity in 1771 and 1772 resulted in modest success but fell short of the general measure of poor relief that most thoughtful observers regarded as essential in the Irish situation.

The Union of 1800 brought Irish social and economic problems directly to England's door and by the 1830s the Irish poor law had become a national question in the United Kingdom. Malthus, Ricardo and other classical economists joined in rejecting the case for poor relief, arguing that a public provision would aggravate Ireland's traditional failings, described as improvidence, idleness, pauperism and lack of enterprise. But influential opinion in the radical and other elements of the Whig party was beginning to move powerfully against the experts. The pressure was generated mainly by a widespread conviction that the absence of a poor law in Ireland caused Irish paupers to descend in droves onto the backs of English ratepayers.

After a series of commissions and reports, which ranged from the visionary to the reactionary, the Poor Relief (Ireland) Act was passed on 31 July 1838. The Act was a version for Ireland of the reformed English poor law of 1834. However, there was to be no separate body of Irish poor law commissioners; the English commission would supervise the work provided for under the Act. By 1841, the machinery was in operation: 130 unions had been defined and poor law guardians elected. Design and construction of the workhouses remained in the hands of the central commission. By 1845, 118 workhouses were ready for occupation and about 40,000 paupers were getting indoor relief. There was no outdoor relief under the Irish scheme until a relaxation in 1847 authorised relief to be provided outside the workhouse.

The expenses of poor relief were entirely a local charge, assessed originally on district electoral divisions according to the numbers of paupers originating in each – on the absurd reasoning that the sin of poverty could best be expiated by the unfortunate reprobate's neighbours. The rate was payable by the occupiers of the houses, lands or other rateable property, but tenants could deduct half of the rates from their rents.

Boards of guardians were the first representative local bodies in Ireland, but they were only part elected: after 1847 a major proportion, up to half, were *ex-officio* members, justices of the peace. The electors were owners and occupiers of property liable to pay the new poor rate, and a system of plural voting ensured that property had its rights as well as its duties.

The unions were formed from aggregations of townlands, but with small regard to any other historic local boundaries that then existed such as counties, baronies, boroughs or parishes. The underlying principle was utility: geographical and administrative convenience. An area averaging about 250 sq. miles was centred on a market town containing the workhouse with its boardroom, offices and so forth, the idea being that the guardians could attend both meeting and market on the same day without much trouble or loss of time. It was the first and, to date, the last attempt to settle local government areas on some rational foundation. The guardians of the poor were invested with wide statutory powers, acted through paid officers and were under the direction and control of a central department for which at first no minister was directly responsible to parliament. The administration was under the control of the three poor law commissioners sitting in London, until 1847 when their powers were vested to commissioners appointed for Ireland.

The secretary of the commission of 1832, Edwin Chadwick, had been at one time Bentham's literary secretary. Consequently, Bentham's ideas of local government organisation permeate the report of the commission and the Acts of 1834 and 1838 based on it. Under Bentham's plan, the country would be divided into districts, each of which would have a popularly elected assembly with salaried officers. Both the assemblies and officers would be subject to government departments that would be newly created. It has been argued that Bentham's notion of local government was not local government at all, at least in the English sense. It was a continental concept with adaptations. His centralism was anathema to English traditionalists. But Ireland was not England, had no tradition of local self-government and was in a smouldering condition of sporadic disorder and anti-government feeling. All things considered, the introduction of local administration on the scale described was a brave experiment in local decentralised administration – firmly directed and controlled it is true, but with a fairly strong, while not dominant, admixture of local democracy.

The impact of the Great Famine on the new system was crushing: famine and disease on the appalling scale that developed after 1845 were burdens that the service was simply not designed to carry. Parliament reacted in somewhat arthritic fashion. Such were the combined effects of famine, fever and emigration in the three years after 1846 that more than two million people perished or emigrated. Shortly after the worst of the famine was over, the Medical Charities Act, 1851 expanded the work of poor law authorities by transferring responsibility for the dispensary system to boards of guardians. Two members were added to the three-man Poor Law Commission, one of them a medical commissioner.

Developing Local Government by Extending the Guardians' Functions

The guardians of the poor were not long in existence when parliament began to extend their functions beyond poor relief. In 1846, they were required on the requisition of the commissioners of health, a temporary body appointed by the government, to provide and equip hospitals and dispensaries for the sick poor. Sanitary administration was becoming intimately bound up with the administration of the poor law. In 1851, the poor law commissioners were given the central administration of the Nuisances Removal and the Diseases Prevention Acts (an early form of environmental legislation) and in the same year, under their direction, a dispensary system of medical relief for the poor was organised as part of the administration of the guardians. In 1856, the guardians became the burial ground board for the rural parts of the union areas.

The remit of the guardians was extended further to take on more and more local government functions. These extensions included civil registrations (Births and Deaths Registration Act, 1863); housing agricultural labourers, where existing housing was unhealthy or deficient (Labourers (Ireland) Act, 1883); and public health (Public Health (Ireland) Act, 1878). It was inevitable that the boards of guardians and the sanitary authorities should be used for these functions. They had an organisation of officers and institutions in every part of the country. Unlike the grand juries, they were permanent bodies holding frequent meetings.

The development of the English local government system in the nineteenth century has been described as primarily a response to the problems of urban growth following the Industrial Revolution. Outside of Belfast, Ireland had no industrial revolution. It did have, partly in consequence, a formidable problem of poverty, both urban and rural, and the efforts to cope with it stamped the Irish system of local administration with an indelible mark of Benthamite centralism and gave it a strong bias towards the alleviation of distress and various other aspects of poverty.

But Ireland was not without its urban problems, since the endemic diseases typhus or famine fever, cholera and other water borne infections, with various other contagious diseases, ravaged both town and country. When therefore the Royal Sanitary Commission of 1866 to 1869 resulted in the formation of the

Local Government Board in 1871, a similar body for Ireland was set up in the following year. The Local Government Board for Ireland absorbed the poor law commissioners and assumed certain other public health and local government functions. But while some emphasis was laid on the public health aspects of its work, the predominance of the poor relief side was not threatened in any appreciable way.

Local Taxation

The first of the annual summaries of local taxation was made for the year 1865. These returns show that the principal local taxes were the grand jury cess, the poor rate and various rates raised in boroughs and other towns. The grand juries in Ireland raised a total of one million pounds and spent the money principally on roads and lunatic asylums. The boards of guardians spent less than three-quarters of a million pounds on poor relief. Town taxation for paving, lighting, cleansing, water supply and drainage did not in the aggregate reach half a million pounds. The grand jury cess remained until the grand juries were relieved of their powers as county fiscal authorities by the Act of 1898. It was then merged in the new poor rate, which has since been renamed county rate, by the Local Government Act, 1946. Rates in towns were assessed under various names, that is boroughs had a borough rate and other towns a town rate. In addition, separate rates were raised for purposes such as water supply, bridges and general improvement. Under the Local Government Act, 2001 all local authority rates are known as the annual rate on valuation.

Before 1865, the government did not view the taxpayer as being under any obligation to help the ratepayer through regular financial assistance. The Irish parliament had given help to the county infirmaries and annual grants to hospitals in Dublin. These had been continued after the Union. Money had been advanced to build lunatic asylums, but it had to be paid back by the grand juries. The workhouses had been built by the poor law commissioners, in whom they were vested, and the loans, for the most part, had to be written off. From 1822 to 1846, half the cost of the constabulary (then a local charge) came out of government funds, and from 1846 the entire cost was government-funded – an arrangement which according to Sir Robert Peel was intended to compensate Ireland for the effects of the repeal of the corn laws. Local police and the watch lingered on in a few places before finally disappearing. The government controlled the Royal Irish Constabulary, which took over police duties. Local prisons passed to the government in 1877.

The first of the annual grants in aid of poor law expenditure was voted in 1867 for half the salaries of medical officers in workhouses and dispensaries and the whole of the salaries of workhouse schoolteachers, but there was no general system of grants in aid of poor law or public health expenditure. It was not until 1898 that a general grant in relief of ratepayers was introduced, confined to those liable for rates on a particular kind of property – agricultural land.

Local Government (Ireland) Act, 1898

For twenty years after the passing of the Public Health (Ireland) Act, 1878, no major change was made in the structure of local government. Since 1840, parliament had been giving new functions to local authorities and many towns were themselves obtaining new powers, but parliament had not produced a comprehensive system of local government. Instead it had adopted expedients to meet difficulties as they arose or as the political complexion of parliament changed. There was no unifying conception running through its local administrative legislation. The principle of representative institutions had been applied in the towns but not in the counties, although some efforts had been made during the nineteenth century to reform county government. The grand jury system had little to recommend it, but nationalist opinion, though officially favouring reform, conserved its energy and passion for the Home Rule struggle. The two issues became entangled in 1884 when Joseph Chamberlain, under the mistaken impression that Parnell would accept local administration under an Irish council as a substitute for Home Rule, brought his local government scheme to the cabinet. It was rejected. This confused episode, involving Parnell, O'Shea, Cardinal Manning, Dilke and Gladstone, had a decisive influence on the fate of Gladstone's first Home Rule Bill in 1886.

There were other attempts at reform, none of which were successful, and the nineteenth century drew towards its close with local administration still in a chaotic condition. The principle of suitable areas was adopted for poor law and public health purposes and the principle of strict central control had only limited application. The picture that local government presented was of independent authorities operating in overlapping areas. In the counties were the grand juries assisted by presentment sessions; in the boroughs were the town councils; in the smaller towns were the town commissioners, some of which were urban sanitary authorities. In the poor law unions that covered counties, cities and towns, the board of guardians acted as poor law authority and in the rural part of the union area also as sanitary authority. In asylum districts, which were either single counties or combinations of counties, boards of governors nominated by the government and bound by the rules of the privy council managed the district asylums. In addition, there were trustees for drainage districts and navigation, harbour and pier authorities, burial boards and governors of the eighteenth-century system of county infirmaries. Some of the authorities were subject to control by the central authorities and some were not.

The first step in reducing this jumble of authorities to order was taken in 1898, when the Local Government (Ireland) Act was passed. The key to rationalisation of local bodies lay in solving the problem of county government, which meant overcoming or bypassing the reluctance of landowners to abandon the virtual monopoly of local power that they enjoyed under the grand jury system. In England, the Local Government Act, 1888 had transferred to county councils the administrative functions of justices of the peace in quarter sessions, but reform in Ireland was delayed for a further decade by unionist fears of nationalist ambitions and spendthrift councils. The stalemate was eventually resolved by extending the new agricultural grant to Ireland, which meant that the exchequer paid half of the rates on agricultural land, and at the same time landlords were relieved of their liability for half of the poor rate. As a result of this piece of legerdemain, for which Tim Healy claimed the credit, the occupiers of land (in effect the nationalist farmers) remained financially more or less as they had been but with vastly enhanced political power, at least in local affairs.

The primary purpose of the Local Government Act, 1898 was to put county government on a representative basis. It transferred to elected councils that business of the grand juries and presentment sessions unconnected with the administration of justice. Here again, as in 1838, 1840 and 1878, legislation for Ireland followed that which had been enacted for England, after a time lag and with some variation to meet Irish conditions. Administrative counties with county councils were created. Six of the larger cities were made county boroughs in which the corporations had almost all the functions of a county council as well as the functions of a borough corporation. Kilkenny, Drogheda and the town of Galway were merged in their respective administrative counties. In Tipperary, two administrative counties were formed, one for each riding. Elsewhere each county was one administrative county.

The administrative county was divided into county districts, which in a few counties were all rural districts and in the rest rural or urban. The part of a rural sanitary district formed under the 1878 Act within a county became a rural district with a rural district council, and the urban sanitary district became an urban district with an urban district council. The district councils took over the business of the baronial presentment sessions and the business of the grand juries in relation to roads and public works, the cost of which was borne by the district. The rural district councils were assigned the sanitary functions of guardians. The towns under town commissioners that were not urban sanitary authorities remained part of the rural district.

The boards of guardians were confined to poor (including medical) relief, but their power to levy the poor rate was transferred to the county council. The district asylums were handed over to the county councils, which were required to appoint committees of management for these institutions. The financial relations between the counties and the exchequer were revised and a grant, the agricultural grant referred to above, was given in relief of rates on land outside the county boroughs, boroughs and other urban districts.

Political Aspects

Democratic local government, of which county councils were the central example, was a virtually unwanted gift from the Conservative government to the Irish people. There was no agitation in its favour. The Irish Parliamentary Party's feelings about county government were soured by the belief, widely held, that the English Local Government Act, 1888, which was the model used for the Irish Act, was a reward to Chamberlain and the other liberal unionists for their help in defeating Gladstone's (and Parnell's) first Home Rule Bill in 1886. Therefore the new Act was met with suspicion and grudging acceptance. The Irish Parliamentary Party looked on it as no substitute for national self-government and as another Conservative attempt to kill Home Rule with kindness. But once the Bill was passed, nationalist opinion quickly adjusted to the new situation and made the most of it, particularly in political terms.

There was indeed a small minority who favoured the use of local councils as a foundation on which to build up a substitute for Westminster. The idea was developed by Sir Thomas Esmonde MP (a member of Wexford County Council) in conjunction with John Sweetman (vice-chairman of Meath County Council and second president of Sinn Féin). The immediate result was the emergence in 1899 of the General Council of County Councils, but the more ambitious plan of a council of three hundred, despite strong backing by Arthur Griffith and its adoption as an item of Sinn Féin policy, was never realised. Its attractions faded with the revival of the parliamentary party after 1900 and the brightening prospects of Home Rule.

Up to 1899 the right to vote in local elections was confined to those who were ratepaying occupiers or owners. The qualification varied. In the boroughs it was £10 yearly value; in other towns it was £4 or £5. In the poor law unions, the guardians were elected by ratepayers on a system of plural voting: the more property occupied, the greater the number of votes. One vote was allowed up to £20 valuation. The number of votes increased by stages to six at £200 valuation, and if the occupier paying the rate was not entitled to deduct any part of it from his rent the number of his votes was doubled. Voting by proxy was allowed.

The Local Government (Ireland) Act, 1898 made the parliamentary electorate (plus peers and qualified women) the local government electorate. Householders and persons occupying part of a house then had the vote. Multiple votes proportionate to the amount of rateable property were abolished. Women, incidentally, could become guardians and district councillors but were debarred from county and borough councils until the Local Authorities (Ireland) (Qualification of Women)

Act, 1911. The next stage in enfranchisement was reached in 1918 when married women of thirty years of age and over got the vote. Proportional representation was first introduced in Sligo Borough in 1918 by a local Act and was applied generally to local elections by the Local Government (Ireland) Act, 1919.

The 1898 Act made the last major change in local government before it came under the control of an Irish government. Except for the merging of the rural districts within a county into one enlarged county health district and the abolition of the poor law unions, the areas remain as formed by that Act with some adjustments of boundaries. Notwithstanding great disparities in size, population and topography, the historical counties were retained (apart from Tipperary, divided into north and south ridings). The Act did not deal with the poor law except in some minor matters such as removing the *ex-officio* justices of the peace from the boards of guardians and widening the area of the expenses of relief by spreading them over the union area.

The councils that began to function in 1899 brought new people into local government. In the counties, the landlords, from whom the grand juries were mainly drawn, virtually disappeared from local bodies. In the towns, the councils became more fully representative of all classes owing to the broadening of the franchise (for further details on this see Travers, 2001). The county councils did not at first have much to do other than maintain roads and mental hospitals and collect rates. The main business was carried out by the district councils, the guardians and the mental hospital committees. In the towns there was a relatively progressive spirit; water and sewerage schemes were undertaken, a beginning was made with technical instruction, some houses were built for the working classes and labourers, and in a few towns public libraries were provided.

Early Twentieth Century

In the early twentieth century, the arrival in increasing numbers of mechanically propelled cars raised a problem of road improvement, the solution of which was beyond the resources of local authorities. The motorcar had a direct effect on the roads and a remote effect on other branches of the administration. When motorbuses began to operate in the 1920s, the small administrative rural areas were already disappearing. The union was the first to go and the rural district followed. It was not alone on the ground of convenience that they were no longer needed; larger areas were required to give scope for the proper organisation of services, particularly hospitals and homes, and to secure adequate financial resources.

After 1900 the idea of the state as the promoter of social welfare began to manifest itself in numerous statutes. The first Old Age Pensions Act and the first Tuberculosis Prevention Act were passed in 1908 and the National Insurance Act in 1911. They were followed by the first School Meals Act, 1914 and the

Notification of Births (Extension) Act, 1915, under which mother and child welfare schemes were put into operation. The Public Health (Medical Treatment of Children) Act came in 1919 under which provision was made for attending to the health of school children. Under the Blind Persons Act, 1920, arrangements could be made for looking after the blind. Local authorities were concerned in a number of ways with the administration of all these Acts.

In the first decade of the twentieth century the working of the poor law was twice investigated by government commissions. The first, a three-man vice-regal commission (1906), recommended the abolition of the workhouse system and segregation of the various classes of inmates in separate institutions. The second, a larger royal commission (1910), covered Britain as well as Ireland and proposed the abolition of the boards of guardians and the transfer of their powers to the county councils. The system of relief that had sprung from the Acts of 1834 and 1838 was now universally condemned. The trend was moving away from the idea of a deterrent poor law with its workhouse test. But before anything was done, World War I broke out and the question of legislation on this topic was shelved.

Local Government (Ireland) Act, 1919

The last piece of British legislation on general aspects of local administration reflects the unsettled post-war condition of Ireland. The Local Government (Ireland) Bill became law in June 1919. It made the system of proportional representation, inaugurated in Sligo the year before, universal in local elections, mainly in the hope that it would preserve the interests of minorities. The Act also attempted to protect local officers from vindictive action on the part of nationalist councils by guaranteeing their pensions against dismissal or refusal to vote allowances. The Bill, incidentally, included a provision empowering the Local Government Board to get rid of recalcitrant local bodies, but the clause was dropped in deference to protests by Sir Edward Carson, who thought that action of this kind would be undemocratic.

The impression of gathering storm clouds, of slow retreat broken by last-ditch stands, is conveyed vividly by a brief succession of legislative blows aimed at recalcitrant ratepayers and rating authorities: Criminal Injuries (Ireland) Act, 1919; Restoration of Order (Ireland) Act, 1920; and Criminal Injuries (Ireland) Act, 1920. These strokes were met by Dáil countermeasures in circular letters outlining a defensive strategy, all of which may be found in the introduction to the *First Report of the Department of Local Government and Public Health* (1922 to 1925).

Early Years of Self-Government

In 1920 the underground Dáil Éireann set up a local government department which assumed the functions of a central authority while the Local Government Board for Ireland was still active and, nominally at least, in control of affairs. At the second session of the first Dáil on 2 April 1919, W. T. Cosgrave was appointed Minister for Local Government, thus giving encouraging recognition to local government when the new state was merely in gestation. After some hesitation a majority of the local authorities recognised the control of the new department and broke with the Local Government Board. For a time there were two central authorities in Ireland.

The conflict between the Dáil department and the Local Government Board was the occasion of the Dáil setting up, in June 1920, a commission of inquiry into local government. The chairperson was the assistant minister, Kevin O'Higgins, and the commission was required to report, in only four weeks, on the problem of survival without the sanction and countenance of the Local Government Board. Its report therefore was limited mainly to the severe economic measures necessary for the system's continued existence. A few general policy initiatives were also recommended such as the pooling of contracts under a scheme of combined purchase and the sale of labourers' cottages to occupants.

As the *comitats* did in Hungary in the preceding century – Arthur Griffith's *Resurrection of Hungary* was then a Sinn Féin manual – local authorities in Ireland played a valuable part in resisting central government and both councillors and property suffered from British terrorist attacks. In Cork, for example, the City Hall was burned in December 1920, and two of its lords mayor died in the struggle for independence (MacCurtain and McSwiney). But once the battle was won, local autonomy began to lose its attractions. The concept of a tightly centralised modern state took hold and governed the shaping of the new state. One of the first symptoms of the trend was the direction taken by the constitution committee in 1922. Of the three drafts submitted to government by the committee, only one (a minority document drafted by Alfred O'Rahilly) recommended a decentralised administration with regional autonomy. It sank with hardly a trace. The Irish Free State started life under a constitution lacking all but incidental mention of local government.

Nothing new in this perhaps, since most earlier constitutions (for example the American constitution) overlooked this aspect of administration. But the newer note struck by the Weimar constitution and some other post-war constitutions found no echo in the Irish document. As the Devlin Report (1969, 3.3.5) put it:

> One of the first acts of the new Government was to extend to all local authorities the fullest of the central controls exercised by the Local Government Board over poor law guardians although the local government system was maintained with some degree of autonomy. Local administration was brought under the control of the new Government. Thus was established a highly centralised system of both central and local government.

Public administration under the new state exhibited marked differences of approach and treatment in different sectors. The civil service was handled with diffidence and caution and there was no attempt at innovation. Michael Collins's determination to replace 'an alien and cumbersome administration' with 'fresh, Gaelic' instruments died with him, insofar as it had the civil service in mind. However, some originality began to show itself in the creation of the earliest of the state-sponsored bodies such as the Electricity Supply Board in 1927. The attitude to local government was bold and confident from the start.

Adapting the Old System – Poor Relief

The first enactment of the Oireachtas relating to local government was the Local Government (Temporary Provisions) Act, 1923. This was an interim measure, while the civil war was in progress, to confirm the work already done by the Dáil in placing public assistance on a county basis. The Act also removed the statutory restrictions on relief being granted to certain classes outside the workhouse. Four years earlier, in January 1919, following the declaration of an independent Irish Republic, the democratic programme of the first Dáil called for, as part of its objectives, the abolition of the 'odious, degrading and foreign poor law system, substituting therefore a sympathetic native scheme for the care of the nation's aged and infirm, who shall no longer be regarded as a burden, but rather entitled to the nation's gratitude and consideration'.[2]

These ideals were not easily realised, but the republicans set to work at once on the task of demolishing the old system and assembling the pieces in the order sketched by the vice-regal commission of 1906. In 1923, schemes that had been hurriedly adopted for placing poor relief on a county basis were reviewed and redrawn on a uniform pattern with some local variations. County boards were appointed to administer relief, except in a few areas of Dublin where the old union areas remained in being. The principal institutions under the new arrangement were normally the county home, which received the old and infirm and classes other than the sick that were formerly in the workhouse, and the county hospital. For the rest, the government set up a commission in March 1925 to inquire into and make recommendations on the relief of the sick and destitute poor. The commission reported in 1927, recommending, *inter alia*, the replacement of county boards of health and assistance by paid officials.

Sinn Féin policy on local government, from which much of the reform thinking of this time derives, was aimed at clearing away most if not all of the undergrowth of small local bodies at sub-county level. Boards of guardians were the first to go – a clean sweep (outside Dublin) was made by the county schemes to which the 1923 Act gave statutory effect.

Rural district councils set up under the Act of 1898 were abolished by the Local Government Act, 1925 and a new and enlarged rural sanitary district was created which generally extended over the whole county excluding the urban

---

[2] Parliamentary Debates, vol. 1, 21 January 1919.

districts. The functions of the abolished rural district councils, which related mainly to road maintenance and sanitary matters, were transferred to the county councils which were required to discharge the new sanitary duties through boards of health. These boards, except where there were joint arrangements for the administration of public assistance, had the same membership (ten) as the body entrusted with the administration of poor relief.

The county boards of health and public assistance survived until August 1942, when the administration of public assistance (except in a few districts) and sanitary matters came under the direct control of the county council acting through the new county managers (see below).

The heavily reinforced apparatus of control over local bodies, which was a feature of the new government, had two impelling forces behind it (apart from the ideological reasons cited above). One was a general feeling, amounting almost to a tradition, that local councils could not be trusted to fill jobs fairly; the other was the administrative disorder caused by the civil war. Hostilities between republicans and the Free State government broke out in June 1922 and local government, already badly shaken by four years of war, deteriorated in some places to near disaster. A number of local bodies ceased to hold meetings and rate collection lapsed. It was essential to restore the situation and it was decided to make use of the drastic armoury of poor law powers designed originally for use against recalcitrant Irish guardians.

The principles of 1838 were given extended application in two directions: the minister was given the same power over other local officers and employees as he had over poor law officers and he was empowered to dissolve bodies that were not duly and effectively discharging their duties or were neglecting to obey lawful orders or not complying with judgments of the courts. This power of dissolution appeared first in the Act of 1838. The Public Health Acts following the Sanitary Act, 1866 also provided a means, although rarely if ever used, of enforcing the performance of certain duties by a defaulting sanitary authority; a *mandamus* could be sought from the High Court or a person could be appointed to perform the duty in default.

The power of dissolution was used freely at first and with a breathtaking disregard for the antiquity and prestige of the victims. In May 1923, Kerry County Council was first to fall, soon followed by Leitrim. The corporations of Dublin (May 1924) – the oldest public body in Ireland – and Cork (October 1924) were not far behind. Whether dissolution was a deserved or appropriate fate is debatable, but the surprising thing was the quiet acquiescence of the citizens in these violent assaults on their civic privileges such as they were. A number of ex-councillors (eleven, including Seán T. Ó Ceallaigh, later Tánaiste, Minister for Local Government and Public Health and President) published *A Vindication of the Municipal Council of the City of Dublin,* but it drew little notice. President Cosgrave offered the chairmanship of the three Dublin commissioners (P. J. Hernon, Dr W. Dwyer and S. Murphy) to the dismissed lord mayor, Laurence O'Neill, who refused out of loyalty to his colleagues. O'Neill became a senator and at least once (28 May 1930) vigorously defended the old city council. A total of twenty bodies were replaced by commissioners in the first three years of the new regime.

City and County Management

The first decade of native government saw the introduction of professional management firstly in the city of Cork (1929), then Dublin (1930), Limerick (1934) and Waterford (1939). The system was subsequently extended throughout country in 1942 when the County Management Act, 1940 was brought into operation (see chapter 7). This was one of the most far-reaching changes in post-independence local government in Ireland, leading to the dissolution of boards of health and significant reductions of membership, especially in cities. County council membership was also reduced but not on quite the same scale.

Local Appointments Commissioners

Another significant departure from the traditional role of the central authority took place in 1926. The minister's powers over the appointment, continuance in office and removal of local officers had been extended in 1923 but the benefits of this extension were negative rather than positive. Whilst the minister could refuse to sanction unsuitable nominees, there was little opportunity to provide suitable candidates for appointment. There was no power to require a special examination except in an appointment to the office of county surveyor.

The earliest solution, for which there was a respectable body of support, was to extend the scope of the new Civil Service Commissioners to include the local service. This idea was put forward in 1923 by Professor Eoin MacNeill, then Minister for Education. But the commissioners were reluctant to take on both tasks and the novel alternative of a separate local commission emerged in 1926 and was quickly put into legislative form. The Local Authorities (Officers and Employees) Act, 1926 established a three-man commission with the duty of selecting and recommending to the local authorities persons for appointment to the principal offices.

The categories specified in the Act were chief executive, professional and technical offices; to these could be added any other offices to which the minister applied the Act. The commissioners are not tied to any one method of selection. They can use competitive written examinations or selection by oral examination or interview, or a combination of both or any other method. The local authority is bound to appoint the candidate recommended or one of the candidates if more than one is recommended. This mode of selection has become part of the normal machinery of local administration (see chapter 17).

Local Government Acts, 1925 to 1994

Once the civil war ended (May 1923) and peace was restored, the building up of a new state began to take shape at local level. The first local elections under native government were held in June 1925 and the Local Government Act of that year, best known perhaps for the abolition of rural district councils, put in place a properly organised local government system including the establishment of boards of health and assistance with separate arrangements in Dublin and Cork areas.

More significantly, the powers of dissolution of local authority, introduced on what was originally intended as a temporary device in 1923, were made permanent by the 1925 Act. They were subsequently re-enacted more permanently in the Local Government Act, 1941 when the original, possibly offensive, term 'dissolution' was replaced by the euphemistic and legally more correct phrase 'removal of members from office'.

The 1941 Act embodies the very considerable changes that followed the County Management Act, 1940. It is a curious fact that although the 1940 Act completed the process of professionalisation over the whole range of local administration (with the exception of vocational education committees and county committees of agriculture), there was little evidence of heightened confidence in local institutions on the part of the government. There was, on the contrary, a substantial increase in the already formidable powers of central authorities in relation to local authorities and their staffs and services.

The principal features of the 1941 Act were a clarification of the position of various 'appropriate' ministers vis-à-vis local offices and employments, the inauguration of a new code of law and regulations for personnel, and a set of provisions on the constitution and procedure of local authorities. The latter included a reduction in the size of county councils by about one-third and empowered the Minister for Local Government and Public Health to fix the number of members of local authorities. The minister's ultimate power to 'dissolve' local authorities by removing the members from office and appointing commissioners was re-enacted in more elaborate form. Part VII of the Act had the merit of novelty: it furnished a procedure for establishing some kind of relationship between county councils and the numerous voluntary self-help bodies then springing up under the spur of Emergency conditions. Parish councils and the like became 'approved local councils'. However, the relationship between official local government and the bodies remained an uneasy one and the wartime movement faded out with the return of peace in 1945.

The Local Government Act, 1946 contained some elements of reform but they were confined to financial measures and concerned solely with the machinery of local authority expenses. Rating was tidied up – the poor rate became the only rate leviable in counties, where it took the new name of county rate, or in urban areas, where it became the municipal rate. Apart from genuine improvement, the new names sounded better. Town commissioners took one more step towards what seemed inevitable liquidation, by losing their old rating powers. They were to be funded by way of demand, on county councils, which recovered their outlay in the form of a charge on the towns. A new provision for dealing with 'insufficiency of rates' was added to the growing catalogue of crimes for which a local authority could be suspended by the minister. A different aspect of expanding ministerial authority gave rise to great controversy in the Dáil and Seanad – this was an extension of central control to minor employments and servants of local authorities.

The recital of general statutes dealing with local authorities continued with the Local Government Act, 1955. Though its size and intricacies are evidence of great industry, the Act is little more than a ragbag of minor improvements and reinforcements to a system that, in spite of the brief rejuvenation effected by the county management injection, was already showing signs of age. The 1955 Act did not continue any of the lines of reform sketched, however tentatively, by the Acts of 1941 and 1946. Nor did it break any new ground or hint at any novelties of attitude or thought.

The extension of universal suffrage to local government did not take effect until 1935. The Electoral Act, 1923 legalised adult suffrage for parliamentary elections, thus removing the thirty-year age qualification for women voters enacted in the Representation of the People Act, 1918. The thirty-year age minimum was retained however for women local electors as was the requirement that voters (male or female) should have occupied, as owners or tenants, land or premises in the electoral area for a period of at least six months. The wives of local electors were also entitled to the local vote, provided they had reached the age of thirty.

The Local Government (Extension of Franchise) Act, 1935 gave a vote in local elections to every Irish citizen over twenty-one who was not subject to legal incapacity. Registration could be claimed either at place of residence or in respect of property occupied elsewhere, but only one vote was allowable. There was considerable opposition to the Bill, despite the seemingly compelling arguments advanced in support – for example that a person entrusted with a vote in Dáil elections should be able to shoulder the added responsibility and that, in any event, some 50 per cent of local expenditure was met by central taxpayers. Introduced in May 1933, the Bill took two years to pass through the Oireachtas. The Seanad rejected it in June 1933, partly on grounds of principle and partly with the 1934 local elections in mind. The Bill was sent again to the Seanad after the constitutional delay of eighteen months and passed finally in March 1935.

An attempt in 1947 to change the electoral system for county councils is worthy of mention. The Local Elections Bill of that year proposed to substitute single-member constituencies for the multi-member electoral areas created by the Local Government Act, 1919. The object was 'to re-impose upon the members of county councils that peculiar personal obligation which attaches to a single individual who does not share with others the responsibility of representing a particular district' (Dáil Debates, 26 November 1947). The single transferable vote was to be retained and would operate in the reduced constituencies. The Bill lapsed with the dissolution of the Dáil and Seanad early in 1948 and was not subsequently reintroduced.

The Local Government Act, 1991 provided for a general competence for local authorities, limited the period of office of a county manager and provided for the regional authorities. The Local Government Act, 1994 limited the possibility of holding certain national positions and retaining membership of a local authority, provided for the extension of the local authority remit in recreation and amenity activity and made a number of changes to the making of bye-laws.

Principal Developments in Local Government Functions since 1922

Agriculture

On 1 July 1980 the agricultural advisory and training functions previously discharged by the Minister for Agriculture and the twenty-seven committees of agriculture were transferred to An Chomhairle Oiliúna Talmhaíochta (ACOT) the body established under the National Agricultural Advisory, Education and Research Authority Act, 1977 (amended). These functions included the operation of the four state agricultural colleges and the advisory and training services in agriculture, horticulture, poultry keeping and farm home management provided by the county committees of agriculture. The effect of this was to transfer to ACOT 840 staff of the committees of agriculture, 280 staff from the Department of Agriculture together with the property and other assets formerly owned by the committees of agriculture, consisting chiefly of some fifty agricultural training centres and also the four state-owned agricultural colleges at Athenry, Ballyhaise, Clonakilty and Kildalton.

So whilst the advisory and training functions of the county committees of agriculture were transferred to ACOT, the reconstituted county committees of agriculture retained the balance of their existing functions in relation to schemes and so forth until 1988 when they were dissolved under the Agricultural (Research, Training and Advice) Bill 1987, which established Teagasc. Teagasc took over the advisory and training functions of ACOT and the research functions of An Foras Talúntais (AFT). The dissolution of the county committees of agriculture in 1988 marked the end of a 57-year period of involvement by locally elected public representatives in the development of agriculture at county level. For further details on the agricultural function, see chapter 15.

Health Services

In 1922 the new government inherited a tangle of authorities – county councils, urban and rural councils and boards of guardians – each with powers in relation to health. By the cumulative effect of a series of statutes, the county council became by 1942 the public assistance authority for the county and the sanitary authority for the rural area of the county. It was then dealing with health services in three capacities: as public assistance authority, as sanitary authority and simply as county council. In urban districts the urban councils were also administering some health services.

The Health Act, 1947 made the county councils and county borough corporations health authorities for their respective areas. The effect of this was to take from sanitary authorities as such, including urban district councils, responsibility for health administration. This resulted in particular in the transferring of responsibility for preventive services to counties and cities – a function which had previously rested with local authorities generally including urban district councils.

Under the Health Act, 1953, county and district hospitals and other institutions were reclassified as health institutions under health authorities, thus detaching from public assistance the treatment of the sick and breaking with the old poor law tradition.

In 1960, the Health Authorities Act established a joint authority in the cities and counties of Cork, Dublin, Limerick and Waterford with comprehensive authority for health services.

A 1966 White Paper entitled the *Health Services and their Future Development* reflected the growing view that the county had become too small a unit for the administration of health and hospital service. This led to the Health Act, 1970, which established eight regional health boards, each covering a number of counties and so removing all local health administration from the local government system as from 1 April 1971. For further details on the health function, see chapter 15.

Housing

Housing is at the forefront of public services. It was responsible for more legislation than any other topic over most of the twentieth century. Separate legislation catered for urban and rural areas – the foundations of the code are to be found in the Housing of the Working Classes Act, 1890 and the Labourers Act, 1883.

Progress was far from satisfactory, due to many factors including both the War of Independence and World War I, so that the new administration in 1922 faced a housing crisis. This was tackled by various measures such as the Million Pound Scheme in 1924 under which that sum was made available by contributions from rates, short-term bank loans and the Department of Local Government and Public Health. Despite these measures, a serious problem still existed.

New legislation in the form of the Housing (Miscellaneous Provisions) Act, 1931 and the Housing (Finance and Miscellaneous Provision) Act, 1932 was required to simplify archaic procedures of the nineteenth century and provide for annual subsidies to local authorities rather than lump sum grants and the simplification of the compulsory purchase procedure. Many improvements to the housing code were enacted subsequently. One measure of note was the Labourers Act, 1936 – following the report of a commission – which placed an obligation on boards of health to prepare schemes for the sale of cottages.

Despite the successes of the 1930s, demands for improvement of the situation continued and two White Papers were issued. The legal changes and White Papers led to the phasing out of the different approach between urban and rural codes. This was effected by the Housing Act, 1966 – a most elaborate measure which replaced more than fifty earlier Acts updating and consolidating relevant provisions. For further details on the housing function and later developments, see chapter 9.

Planning and Development

Apart from city and county management, one of the most significant (and subsequently controversial) issues in the local government system since independence has been planning and development. Indeed when introducing the Local Government (Planning and Development) Act, 1963, the then minister stated that the Planning Act 'was one of the most important acts bearing on local government to be enacted in our generation'. The Third Programme for Economic and Social Development for 1969 to 1972 commented that local plans are the means by which expression and effect could be given to the role of local planning authorities as 'development corporations', as suggested in the 1971 White Paper on local government reorganisation.

The failure from many points of view of previous legislation in the Town and Regional Planning Acts of 1934 and 1939 led to the introduction of the Local Government (Planning and Development) Act, 1963 (partly amended in 1976, 1982, 1983, 1990, 1992 and 1993). In the words of the then Minister for Local Government, Kevin Boland, in a circular to each member of every planning authority in March 1967, 'new ground' would be broken in local government.

Basically the system operates around a development plan, made by elected members, with individual permission or refusals being a function of the city or county manager. A new planning code was introduced in the Planning and Development Act, 2000, which consolidates all previous Acts and much of environmental impact assessment regulations. For further details on the planning and development function, see chapter 12.

Finance

Local government finance and its major component, the rating system, has been a recurrent theme certainly since the mid-nineteenth century. It has been the subject of many reports, enquiries, study groups and so forth. It is also given significant political attention. In the early years after independence, adjustments in the agricultural grant were a regular feature – the annual budget of 1929 saw the establishment of a commission on de-rating, in which the majority defended the status quo. Non-payment of rates figured prominently as an instrument of protest during the economic war in the 1930s. Intermittent protest and annual denunciations continued on a regular basis leading eventually to a White Paper in 1972 on local finance and taxation, which held for reform rather than abolition. Political events then intervened and a new government in 1973 of a Fine Gael/Labour composition brought about the removal of health and housing charges from the local exchequer.

In a further change of government at the next election in 1977, Fianna Fáil abolished domestic rates. Subsequent developments, in a departure from the full recoupment of the rates remitted in 1977 by successive governments, forced local authorities to look to other sources of income to make up the loss of revenue. There was widespread organised opposition to charges and eventually the government surrendered and the power to charge for supply of water for domestic purposes was withdrawn in the Local Government (Financial Provisions) Act, 1997. However, in keeping with the polluter pays principle and the EU Water Framework Directive, the implementation of full cost recovery for water services is being advanced gradually (see chapter 11).

An effort to impose a farm (land) tax was abortive – lasting but one year, 1986, another surrender to organised lobbies. Proposals to solve local authority financial problems emerged in 1996 as part of the government's re-organisation proposals entitled *Better Local Government*. This involved assigning the proceeds of motor taxation to local authorities. The original proposal was altered somewhat but not in principle after a change of government. A new system was put in place on 1 January 1999, involving the establishment of an independent Local Government Fund consisting of motor taxation receipts and additional money (approximately €592 million in 2002) ring-fenced in legislation. This arrangement should help enormously from a purely financial standpoint but the view has been expressed that the independence of local government may be lessened by greater central involvement. For further details on local government finance, see chapters 18 and 19.

Re-organisation

Local government re-organisation in the fullest sense has not always enjoyed the highest priority from central government. Apart from limited changes such as the abolition of rural district councils in 1925, the creation of three county councils in Dublin (Fingal, South Dublin and Dún Laoghaire-Rathdown) in 1994 and of course the removal of all health administration from the local government system, successive governments failed to produce any significant developments.

After the 1989 general election, the new coalition government (Fianna Fáil/Progressive Democrats) nominated an advisory expert committee under the chairmanship of Tom Barrington, former director general of the Institute of Public Administration, which reported in 1990 (see chapter 4). This committee reported widely on many aspects of local government, including structures and functions (although not on finance, which was curiously excluded from its terms of reference, other than recommending criteria for putting contributions from central funds on a statutory basis). A number of significant recommendations of the Barrington Report were implemented in the Local Government Act, 1991, such as the introduction of a general competence for local authorities, the establishment of regional authorities, an amendment of planning legislation limiting the use of section 4 of the City and County Management (Amendment) Act, 1955 (now section 140 of the Local Government Act, 2001) in relation to the granting of planning permission, as well as some relatively minor items such as allowances for chairpersons, entertainment expenses, civic honours and twinning of towns.

Two more novel items relating to allowances for members of local authorities and a code of conduct for the local government service, as provided for in the Local Government Act, 2001, have come in to operation. Of some significance, and also of some controversy, is the decision to end the dual mandate – whereby members of the Oireachtas could also be members of local authorities – in 2004.

Conclusion

The development of local government in Ireland can be characterised as both ad hoc and imposed. Irish local government never recovered from Benthamite ideology. The degree of centralism, due to the status of Ireland in the British Empire (not entirely colonial for there was representation, but not trusted enough to have power devolved) and mistrust of localism, is an enduring inheritance. Successive legislation dealing with local governance in Ireland weakened democratic input into substantive decision making, though its logic could be understood in certain instances such as the need to take power away from the grand juries and the abuses in the recruitment process that took place in the period immediately after independence. The instrumental role of local government in the fight for independence in the years preceding self-determination did not accrue reserves of esteem when independent statehood was achieved. Despite bold attempts such as the creation of the Local Appointments Commission (1926) and the introduction of city and county management (1940s), reform of local government did not extend to trusting it with substantially more functions in general.

3

Local Areas and Structures

Terry O'Sullivan

Article 28A of the Constitution was inserted by way of national referendum held in 1999 and provides for local authorities, elected every five years, to provide a forum for the democratic representation of local communities, to exercise certain functions at local level and to promote through its initiatives the interests of local communities (see appendix 2).

Following on from the 1999 constitutional amendment, a Local Government Bill was published in May 2000 and subsequently enacted as the Local Government Act, 2001. This Act is now the basic legislation governing local government structures, operations and functions. The Act provided for the reconstitution of local authorities – as corporate bodies known as city councils, county councils, borough councils or town councils. The Act, *inter alia*, provides that each local authority has an elected council with a cathaoirleach and leas-chathaoirleach, provides for the holding of local elections and for the filling of casual vacancies, and also sets out a statement of local authority functions, including a representational role and the promotion of the interests of the local community.

Under the 2001 Act, the state is divided into thirty-four areas (29 counties and 5 cities) for the purpose of local government. Together these cover the entire land area and total population of the state. The twenty-six historical counties which make up the Republic of Ireland translate into twenty-nine local government counties because County Tipperary has two local government counties (North Tipperary and South Tipperary) and County Dublin has three local government counties (Fingal, South Dublin and Dún Laoghaire-Rathdown). The five cities are Cork, Dublin, Galway, Limerick and Waterford, each of which is entirely separate from its home county. Each of these thirty-four counties and cities has its own local authority elected by the local population and known as the county council or the city council. These thirty-four authorities are the primary units of local government with responsibility for the full range of local authority functions.

Within most counties, and forming part of them, are other local government areas known as towns. There are eighty such local government towns, each of which elects its own local authority known as a town council. Five towns (Clonmel, Drogheda, Kilkenny, Sligo and Wexford) are titled borough councils.[1] About 13 per cent of the total national population resides within the local government towns as legally defined (in many cases, the built-up area of a town extends beyond the legal boundary). The residents of a local government town vote in two separate elections held simultaneously, one for the town council and one for the county council.

Town councils exercise functions to varying degrees within the towns concerned. This ranges from a fairly extensive role for some to a largely representational role for others in which the county council provides practically all local government services. The county council has responsibility for some functions within the entire county, including the towns, for example library, motor tax, and usually national roads, fire services and environmental services. There are many towns without a separate town local authority (over fifty of such towns with 1,500 population upwards are shown in the 1996 Census).

Prior to the 2001 Act, the town local authorities were titled as borough corporations (of which there were five), urban district councils or UDCs (of which there were 49) and town commissioners (of which there were 26). The borough corporations and urban district councils exercised the same range of functions. Both urban district councils and borough corporations were planning, housing, road, sanitary and rating authorities and exercised functions under a range of other enactments. The main distinction between the two was largely ceremonial – the boroughs had mayors while urban district councils had a chairperson or cathaoirleach. By comparison, the town commissioners were largely representational bodies with very limited functions.

Under the 2001 Act, all the town-based local authorities (borough corporations/urban district councils/town commissioners) became known as town councils (see above regarding borough councils) and all have a basic range of functions: representational, adoption of local bye-laws, promoting the community interest and the possibility to introduce a community initiative scheme. However, the former borough corporations and urban district councils retained all of their previous functions under housing, planning, roads and other legislation, with the exception of water services which is to transfer to county level from 1 January 2004.

---

[1] A reference to a town council under the Local Government Act, 2001 includes a borough council [section 11(4)].

Terminology

Prior to the Local Government Act, 2001, the local authorities as corporate entities were known as:

- county borough corporations – now city councils
- borough corporations – now borough councils
- urban district councils – now town councils
- town commissioners – now town councils
- county councils – still county councils (however, North Tipperary and South Tipperary replaced the former titles of Tipperary North Riding and Tipperary South Riding respectively).

The elected councillors were collectively known as the city council, county council, urban district council or town commissioners and individually as councillors or commissioners. Under the 2001 Act, all local authority members are known as councillors – the term commissioners no longer applies and the term alderman for certain members in city and borough councils will cease in 2004 (see below).

For the purposes of reading legislation prior to the Local Government Act, 2001, schedule 2 of that Act provides a useful ready reckoner for interpreting the older terminology by reference to the new.

Incorporation

County, city, borough and town councils are corporations aggregate, that is, bodies of persons which are recognised by law as having a personality distinct from the separate personalities of the members of the body. A corporation aggregate is defined as:

> . . . a collection of individuals united into one body under a special denomination, having perpetual succession under an artificial form, and vested by the policy of law with a capacity of acting in several respects as an individual, particularly of taking and granting property, of contracting obligations, and of suing and being sued, of enjoying privileges and immunities in common and of exercising a variety of political rights more or less extensive, according to the design of its institution, or the powers conferred upon it, either at the time of its creation or at any subsequent period of its existence (Keane, 1982, p. 37).

As with every other corporation, the individual corporators, or members, of which the local authority is composed are something wholly different from the corporation itself.

The enactments which conferred corporate status on local authorities are: article 13 of the schedule to the Local Government (Application of Enactments)

Order, 1898 for county councils and urban district councils; that article as extended by section 65 of the Local Government Act, 1955 for town commissioners; various royal charters, recognised and confirmed by section 12 of the Municipal Corporations (Ireland) Act, 1840 for borough corporations, including the county boroughs. Every county council and every urban district council was a body corporate by the name of the county or urban district and every borough by the style and title set out in the Municipal Corporations Act; all have perpetual succession and a common seal.

A local authority, being a corporation incorporated by legal statute, can only have its legal existence terminated by statute. The continuity of the existence of a local authority by its appropriate title is not affected by the removal from office of the members of the local authority. The Municipal Corporations Acts distinguished between the council and the body corporate (the corporation) but in the case of county councils the term council applied to both the corporate body and the elected members. This led to confusion in the early years of the state when the Acts of 1923 and 1925 referred to removal of members from office as the dissolution of the local authority. The legal position was clarified by the Local Government Act, 1941, which substituted a ministerial power to remove the members of a local authority from office.

The 1941 Act also specifically provided that the continuity of the existence of a local authority by its appropriate title is not affected by the removal from office of the members of the local authority (see now section 216(2) of the Local Government Act, 2001). Section 11 of the Local Government Act, 2001, which repealed a major portion of the Acts mentioned above, continued the county, city, borough and town councils as bodies corporate with perpetual succession and power to sue and be sued in their corporate name and to acquire, hold, manage, maintain and dispose of land or any interest in land.

The city and county management system introduced a second element to the legal character of local authorities: the county/city manager, a full-time salaried chief executive officer. The manager has responsibility for the day-to-day running of the local authorities within his or her administrative area and in that role discharges the executive functions, that is all functions other than reserved functions (which are defined by law and exercised by the elected members – these consist mainly of decisions on important matters of policy and finance). It is notable that the manager's power to exercise the executive functions of the local authority is derived directly from statutory provisions and is not dependent on delegation by the council. The operation of the management system including the checks and balances implicit in the system are discussed in chapter 7. The functions of a local authority are performed for or on behalf of the authority and in its (corporate) name by the elected council or the manager as may be appropriate in accordance with the law.

Administrative Counties and County Councils

The administrative county, either a county for which a county council is elected or a city for which a city council is elected, is the principal area of local government. Administrative counties covering the whole country were formed in 1898 from pre-existing judicial counties. The area of every administrative county other than a city (formerly known as county borough) is as laid down in the Order of the Local Government Board of 1 November 1898, with such changes as have since been made by statute or provisional order confirmed by statute. The Local Government Act, 2001 establishes local government areas known as cities and counties, which are the administrative areas of city and county councils. The 2001 Act replaces various local government enactments dating back to the nineteenth century dealing with the establishment and operation of local authorities. Among the enactments replaced are some or all of the Municipal Corporations (Ireland) Acts, 1840 and 1843; the Commissioners Clauses Act, 1847; Towns (Improvement) Act, 1854; Local Government (Ireland) Act, 1898; various post-independence local government Acts and the city and county management code.

The geographical county of Tipperary forms two local government counties: in 1838 it was divided into two ridings, north and south, each being made a separate county. The Local Government Act, 2001 changed the administrative county names from Tipperary North Riding and Tipperary South Riding to North Tipperary and South Tipperary respectively. The Local Government (Dublin) Act, 1993 made a radical change in the Dublin area by abolishing Dublin County Council and Dún Laoghaire Corporation and replacing them with the only county councils to be established since the foundation of the state: Dún Laoghaire-Rathdown, Fingal and South Dublin. The Dún Laoghaire borough area now forms part of the administrative county of Dún Laoghaire-Rathdown. For the full list of county councils see appendix 3.

Each of the twenty-nine county areas has a separate elected council, known as a county council. The divide is based closely on the twenty-six historical counties to which there are strong ties of local identity, with the two county councils in Tipperary and the three in Dublin accounting for the variation between twenty-six and twenty-nine.

For electoral purposes, each county is divided into a number of local electoral areas. These electoral areas include all towns (with the exception of city councils) located within the county. The combined electoral areas cover the whole county. The county council is thus elected by the entire population of the county. Local authority town electors have a vote in two separate elections, one for the county council and one for the town or borough council.

The number of members of a county council to be elected from each county electoral area is fixed under statute by Orders of the Minister for the Environment and Local Government. The Orders in force in 2003 were made under the Local Government Act, 1994 and incorporated the recommendations of two 1998 reports (Dublin Electoral Area Boundary Committee, 1998; Electoral Area Boundary Committee, 1998). The recommendations were effective for local elections held in June 1999. The terms of reference, as advertised by the boundary committee in seeking submissions from interested parties, note that the committee would take due account of the desirability of preserving natural communities or the hinterlands of population centres in recommending changes to local electoral areas. The number of councillors representing an area in a county or city was not to be less than three and not more than seven. There was no provision for any alteration of the overall membership of an authority.

The council of a local government county consists of councillors, one of whom is elected, on an annual basis by the members, as a chairperson/mayor. The Local Government Act, 2001 had provided that from 2004 the chairperson/mayor would be directly elected by the population of the area for a five-year term, but this provision was repealed in 2003.

Total county council membership ranges from twenty to forty-eight (see appendix 3). The total number of members of each county council is set out in schedule 7 to the Local Government Act, 2001. Section 22 of that Act also provides that, following public consultation, a county council may apply to the minister for an alteration in the number of members. A report and recommendation from a local government commission must be obtained by the minister before deciding on the application.

County councils operate subject to law in the discharge of a full range of services for the entire county excluding those towns that were formerly boroughs or urban districts – the county less such exclusions was previously known as the county health district. County councils in most cases operate services such as national roads, waste, fire services, library services and civil defence for the whole county (including the towns). For accounting purposes, local authority services are classified into eight programme groups as follows:

1 housing and building
2 road transportation and safety
3 water supply and sewerage
4 development incentives and control (planning)
5 environmental protection
6 recreation and amenity
7 agriculture, education, health and welfare
8 miscellaneous services.

See later chapters for details of each programme group. Certain functions such as health or vocational education have been assigned by law to separate, independent regional or other authorities and are not exercisable directly by the county councils, but the councils appoint representatives to these bodies as specified by law.

Although the subject will be dealt with in more detail later, note should be taken that in recent years legislation has widened and generally strengthened the position of local government in Ireland. These measures include the introduction of a power of general competence for local authorities to act in the interests of the community, thereby relaxing substantially the archaic *ultra vires* rule. Section 6(1) of the Local Government Act, 1991 (subsequently replaced by section 66 of the Local Government Act, 2001) states that a local authority may take such measures, engage in such activities or do such things in accordance with law as it considers necessary to promote the interests of the local community. This involves promoting, directly or indirectly, social inclusion or the social, economic, environmental, recreational, cultural, community or general development of the administrative area of the authority or of the local community (or any group consisting of members thereof). Part 9 of the 2001 Act, which deals with the functions of local authorities, provides broad powers for a local authority to take action to promote the interests of the local community. Section 63 provides a general statement of local authority functions, which are to:

- provide a forum for the democratic representation of the local community
- provide civic leadership
- carry out the functions conferred on the authority by the Act or any other enactment, for example under the housing, planning, roads, fire and other codes
- carry out ancillary functions
- take action to promote the community interest.

County Districts

Every administrative county for which a county council is elected consists of one or more county districts. A county district may be either an urban county district or a county health district. The urban county district is an urban sanitary district and the county health district a rural sanitary district. The rural districts, formed in 1898 within every county, were combined in 1925 to form one enlarged sanitary district, which was given the name county health district. In a county that has no urban district the administrative county is the county health district; there are seven such counties. Under the Local Government (Amendment) (No. 2) Act, 1934, a county health district may be divided by an order of the minister on the application of the county council. The area of County Cork that is not included in town councils has been divided into three county health districts. Cork is the only county that has availed of this procedure at the time of writing. The urban county districts include the boroughs and every town council that became an urban sanitary district under the Public Health (Ireland) Act, 1878.

The Local Government Act, 2001 provides for the consolidation of water supply and waste water treatment and related functions at county level – these functions will transfer from borough and town councils to county councils to form a single sanitary district. The three divisions in Cork are not affected by this provision. This will take effect in January 2004.

Cities and City Councils

The county borough (redesignated as a city under the Local Government Act, 2001) was an area which ranked both as a county and a borough. County boroughs were created by the Local Government (Ireland) Act, 1898, which borrowed the idea and the term from the English Local Government Act, 1888. The notion has however an earlier ancestry, nearer home. In the eighteenth and nineteenth centuries (to go back no further) ten cities and boroughs were counties and had their own grand juries. Of that group, the 1898 Act constituted the cities of Cork, Dublin, Limerick, Waterford, Belfast and Londonderry as county boroughs but merged the county of the city of Kilkenny and the counties of the towns of Drogheda, Carrickfergus and Galway in their adjoining administrative counties. Since 1922 the county boroughs of Belfast and Londonderry and the borough of Carrickfergus are in Northern Ireland. Galway was constituted a county borough under the Local Government (Reorganisation) Act, 1985. Since 2002, Cork, Dublin, Galway, Limerick and Waterford have city councils.

The city councils have equal status with the county councils. They have a similar range of functions and a similar right of representation on regional or other authorities. The city council operates independently from the county council, each having its own council and manager. Membership of the city councils is 52 in Dublin, 31 in Cork, 17 in Limerick and 15 each in Waterford and Galway. The total number of members of each city council is set out in schedule 7 to the Local Government Act, 2001. Section 22 of that Act also provides that, following public consultation, a city council may apply to the minister for an alteration in the number of members. A report and recommendation from a local government commission must be obtained by the minister before deciding on the application. Each of the cities is divided into local electoral areas for election purposes. Dublin and Cork have lord mayors, while Limerick, Waterford and Galway have mayors. The (lord) mayor is elected on an annual basis by the city council members and is chairperson of the city council. The Local Government Act, 2001 had provided that from 2004 the mayor would be directly elected by the population of the area for a five-year term, but this provision was repealed in 2003.

The law relating to the election of cathaoirleach and leas-chathaoirleach of local authorities and the designation of the offices as (lord) mayor in the cities is contained in part 5 of the Local Government Act, 2001. At the time of writing, council membership was composed of aldermen and councillors. The local election regulations specify: 'at an election for a local electoral area in a county or other borough in which a poll is taken, the first and every other candidate successively elected for the area until the number of aldermen for the area is completed shall be an alderman and the remaining candidates elected for the area shall be councillors'. The Local Government Act, 2001 provides that each elected member of a local authority shall be known as a councillor, which effectively removes the title of alderman in city and borough councils following the local elections in 2004.

Boroughs and Borough Councils

The boroughs are areas to which the Municipal Corporations Acts, now replaced by the Local Government Act, 2001, applied. They numbered ten, of which five were county boroughs (now city councils). Ten boroughs (two of them in Northern Ireland) survived the dissolutions of 1840. In these the municipal corporations owed their origin to charters. Three came into existence post 1840 – Wexford by the grant of a charter in 1846 and Dún Laoghaire (1930) and Galway (1937) by Acts of the Oireachtas. The Local Government Act, 2001 in effect repeals charters, save for civic and ceremonial purposes. The Municipal Corporations Act, 1840 defined the boundaries of the boroughs in which the corporations were not dissolved. As regards boroughs created since 1840, the boundaries of Wexford were delimited by the Wexford charter, Dún Laoghaire consisted of four pre-existing urban districts in County Dublin, and Galway had the same area as the urban district which was the area of the town as defined in the Galway Town Improvement Act, 1853. Dún Laoghaire as a borough was abolished in 1993 and subsumed into Dún Laoghaire-Rathdown County Council and Galway was created as a county borough in 1985 (now titled city council).

At the time of writing there are five borough councils: Clonmel, Drogheda, Kilkenny,[2] Sligo and Wexford. The council of a borough comprises twelve members, fixed by statute (formerly the Local Government Act, 1941, but now the Local Government Act, 2001). Of the twelve, four are aldermen elected as for the city councils (see above in relation to the changes envisaged after the 2004 local elections). For electoral purposes, Drogheda and Sligo are divided into local electoral areas. Each of the other boroughs constitutes a single electoral area.

The councils of the five boroughs have the same classification of functions as for county and city councils – housing, roads, water supply and sewerage,

---

[2] For historical reasons Kilkenny has used the title 'city' for tourist, heritage and other promotional purposes – this is recognised under section 10(7) of the Local Government Act, 2001.

planning and development and so forth (see above). However, for certain
operations/activities under these programmes, the parent county council is the
responsible statutory authority. For example, subject to some exceptions, the
borough councils are not empowered to grant shared ownership loans. As road
authorities they have no responsibility for works on the national and regional
roads in the town (which is the responsibility of the county council). With one
exception they are not the fire authorities for their town. They are not building
control authorities, they are not library authorities and so on.

While borough and former urban district councils are equivalent in that for all
practical purposes they have the same range of functions, the former in addition
have such powers as are vested in borough corporations and councils by the
Municipal Corporation Acts and any private acts relating to the town. These
additional powers are of little practical consequence, the difference between the
boroughs and the town councils having been in the main a difference in status
rather than powers. For example, boroughs had mayors rather than chairpersons,
a ceremonial rather than a practical distinction. However, under the Local
Government Act, 2001 every council regardless of classification was allowed
adopt the title of mayor and deputy mayor for its cathaoirleach and leas-
chathaoirleach respectively – and a large number of county councils and town
councils adopted this title during 2002.

Towns and Town Councils

Town Councils (formerly Urban District Councils)

Besides the boroughs, seventy-five towns have municipal government. Prior to
the enactment of the Local Government Act, 2001 (which created the single title
of town council) these towns fell into two categories: forty-nine urban district
councils and twenty-six town commissioners. Originally town, township or
improvement commissioners were constituted either under the Lighting of Towns
Act, 1828, the Towns Improvement (Ireland) Act, 1854 or in the case of Bray
under a special Act of 1866. Most of these acquired public health or sanitary
powers under the Public Health (Ireland) Act, 1878 and became urban sanitary
authorities. The residue remained as towns with attenuated functions under
boards of town commissioners.

Boroughs, towns with a population of 6,000 and having town commissioners,
towns under local Acts having commissioners and towns separated from the rural
sanitary district by provisional order became urban sanitary districts under the
Public Health Act, 1878. Under the Local Government Act, 1898 these towns
became urban districts and where they were under town commissioners, the
commissioners became the urban district council for the town. This Act repealed

the Lighting of Towns Act, 1828 and replaced it in the towns in which it was in force by the Towns Improvement (Ireland) Act, 1854.

A town that was not an urban district could petition the minister to separate it from the rural sanitary district. This separation was effected by means of a provisional order, which, if the town had a population over 1,500 and at least one-quarter of the electors did not petition against it, took effect without confirmation by the Oireachtas (1898 Act, section 42). The Local Government Act, 2001 now makes provision for the establishment of new town councils (see below).

A reverse process, introduced by section 74 of the Local Government Act, 1925 provided that an urban district not being a borough could relinquish urban status by applying to the minister to be added to the rural sanitary district. If this was done, the council ceased to be an urban council and the members became town commissioners. This transition took place in four towns: Belturbet (1950), Cootehill (1950), Granard (1944) and Passage West (1942). The Local Government (Dublin) (Amendment) Act, 1940 dissolved Howth urban district council and the area of the urban district was detached from the county and added to the city. The Local Government Act, 2001 provides that a town council may by resolution apply to the minister to dissolve the town council. The full list of town councils is contained in appendix 3.

Each town council consists of a chairperson/mayor and councillors. All town councils have nine members each with the exception of Bray, Dundalk and Tralee, which have twelve each. Only Bray and Dundalk are divided into separate local electoral areas; the others each constitute a single electoral area. Their powers and functions, as stated above, are equivalent to boroughs with regard to planning, housing, water services, rating, amenity and other miscellaneous functions in their areas. In practice, some functions statutorily vested in boroughs and town councils are actually carried out by county council staff and resources on an agency basis. This can be effected either by informal arrangement or by formal agreement provided for in the local government acts.

Arrangements vary between individual authorities and for different services, with in some cases a very substantial county council input, while in others this is limited or may be absent. *Better Local Government* noted particularly the overall thrust of the 1996 report, *Towards Cohesive Local Government,* for greater cohesiveness in the delivery of services between town and county and for customer service to be the central determinant in the way the town and county system is organised and operated (Department of the Environment, 1996, p. 70; Local Government Reorganisation Commission, 1996). Both reports saw the provision of major services, such as water and waste water facilities, being consolidated at the county level, with the town council concentrating on town and community development measures. The Local Government Act, 2001 provides for such consolidation from 1 January 2004.

Town Councils (formerly Town Commissioners)

Of the seventy-five municipal towns, twenty-six remained at, or opted to return to, the basic level of towns under commissioners. Eighteen were constituted as towns before 1922, but did not proceed any further up the municipal ladder. Four urban districts chose to revert to town status under the 1925 Act (as mentioned in the section above). Four towns, Tramore (1948), Shannon (1980), Leixlip (1988) and Greystones (1984) have been constituted since 1922.

Prior to the Local Government Act, 2001, when a town having a population of 1,500 and upwards desired to have a form of municipal government, the electors to the number of at least twenty-one applied to the minister to carry the Towns Improvement (Ireland) Act, 1854 into execution in the town. The proposed boundaries were specified in the application and prescribed notices published. If the minister approved of the boundaries, the county manager was directed to convene a meeting of the electors of the town to decide whether or not the Act should be adopted. If adopted in whole or in part, and the minister approved, arrangements were made for an election of town commissioners. Such commissioners when constituted had not only powers under the Towns Improvement Act, 1854, but all other such powers conferred on commissioners since the 1854 Act was passed.

Note that the three most recent town commissioners to be established, Shannon, Greystones and Leixlip, each had a population of 8,000 and upwards. The 1996 report, *Towards Cohesive Local Government,* recommended that a figure of 7,500 population upwards would be a reasonable minimum level of eligibility for the establishment of a new elective local authority (Local Government Reorganisation Commission, 1996, p. 75). This is the population figure now specified in the Local Government Act, 2001, sections 185 and 186 of which set out the requirements and procedures for the establishment of a new town council and the holding of first elections.

Formerly, a board of town commissioners could be dissolved by the minister under section 74 of the Local Government Act, 1925, and its powers, property and functions transferred to the county council. Five boards have been so dealt with: Callan (1940), Fethard (1936), Newcastle West (1941), Rathkeale (1926) and Roscommon (1927). These areas continued to exist as towns, but without a town local authority, for which separate local authority estimates were prepared until 1994 when the Local Government Act, 1994 provided for the cesser of the Towns Improvement (Ireland) Act, 1854 in respect of them. Tullow, a town which had remained dormant since 1902, was similarly treated. As stated earlier, the Local Government Act, 2001 allows for the dissolution of a town council, at its request.

The number of elected members on each town council (that was formerly a town commissioners) is nine. The councils have a very limited range of responsibilities as practically all local authority services in the town (for example housing, roads, water, waste, planning) are now the responsibility of the county council. Towns with town commissioners had been described as 'archaic and almost powerless' (Local Government Reorganisation Commission, 1996, p. 3). These towns are no longer rating authorities and they obtain financing from the county council by means of an annual demand – the county council levies an additional rate on the town for this purpose. *Towards Cohesive Local Government* recommended however that town commissioners should exercise an enhanced role in local development and promotional functions, including representation of the local community, liaison with local groups and input to relevant public and other agencies, particularly with a view to promoting development and social/community objectives (Local Government Reorganisation Commission, 1996, pp. 67–8).

In light of these recommendations, the Local Government Act, 2001 provides such town councils with powers to promote the community interest, provide minor amenities, exercise a representational role and make local bye-laws, and makes the cathaoirleach an *ex-officio* member of the county council area committee in whose area the town is located. Such town councils also have the option to raise finance in co-operation with local interests by means of the community fund and associated community initiative scheme.

Non-Local Government Towns

There are many towns administered by county councils without a separate elected local government town structure, for example Celbridge, Kildare, Mitchelstown and Roscrea. The Local Government Reorganisation Commission, as provided for in the Local Government Act, 1994, considered criteria and procedures for the possible establishment of new town authorities. The commission's 1996 report noted that the question of sub-county local government structures had been on the agenda for at least twenty-five years and had been reviewed in the course of various studies of local government. These included *Local Government Reorganisation – White Paper*, 1971; Local Government Reorganisation Discussion Document, 1973; *Reform of Local Government, A Policy Statement*, 1985; *Local Government Reorganisation and Reform – Report of the Advisory Expert Committee*, 1991 (Barrington Report); and a 1991 government statement indicating proposals for a phased programme of local government reform in the light of the expert committee's recommendations.

The government statement, while accepting various recommendations of the expert committee and providing for them subsequently in the Local Government Act, 1991, noted the committee's failure to agree on a sub-county structure and considered it necessary to examine the matter further with a view to formulating acceptable and realistic sub-county arrangements.

The Local Government Reorganisation Commission (1996, p. 71) was of the opinion that the creation of new town authorities on a wide scale was totally unsustainable. It stated that the powers, procedures and structures provided for in the Towns Improvement (Ireland) Act, 1854 were largely obsolete and recommended procedures which should apply for the establishment of new town authorities in towns with a minimum population of 7,500. While any new town to be established should exercise a reasonable range of functions and play a meaningful role to the benefit of the town and its residents, the commission cautioned that development of its role should be on a gradual and suitably phased basis, without disruption to the county council's services and organisation. This recognised and underlined the county council's position as the primary unit of local government.

The establishment of new town councils is provided for in sections 185 and 186 of the Local Government Act, 2001. New town councils will not have responsibility for mainline functions such as housing, roads or planning and will not be responsible for setting rates. They will however have powers relative to minor works and community development (see above).

Townlands

Townlands are ancient areas that were used under the Poor Relief (Ireland) Act, 1838 to form electoral divisions into which the poor law unions were divided. The poor law commissioners had power for the purposes of that Act to declare any place to be a townland. A comprehensive index to the townlands was published in 1901. The poor law union electoral divisions became district electoral divisions under the Local Government Act, 1898. They ceased to be used for electoral purposes in 1919 but are, however, still retained for purposes incidental to parliamentary and local elections and for administrative convenience. The populations of the district electoral divisions are shown in the census. They are the basic building blocks used for the construction of local electoral areas.

Parishes

The civil parish is now obsolete as a local government area. In the seventeenth century an unsuccessful attempt was made (Highways Act, 1612) to persuade the parishes to maintain highways. Damages for malicious injuries were sometimes assessed on parishes and for the collection of the county cess the parish was part of the barony. The barony was a sub-division of the county that ceased to be used for administration purposes after the Local Government (Ireland) Act, 1898 came into operation.

United Sanitary Districts

United sanitary districts are districts that have been combined for any purpose of the Local Government (Sanitary Services) Acts of 1878 to 1964. Seven united districts have been formed and six joint burial boards and one joint burial committee constituted for them. One of the joint burial boards, the Deans Grange Joint Burial Board, established by the Local Government Board (Ireland) Provisional Order Confirmation (No. 4) Act, 1899 was dissolved by the Local Government (Dublin) Act, 1993 and Dún Laoghaire-Rathdown County Council became its successor.

Drainage Districts

Drainage districts were originally constituted under Drainage Acts of 1842 and 1863. These districts were under the control of trustees or drainage boards which had the care and management of the drainage works. After 1898 some districts were transferred to the county councils. Provision was made in the Arterial Drainage Act, 1925 for the formation of new drainage districts. Existing districts may be taken over by the Commissioners of Public Works but until such time they remain with the existing drainage authorities. The Barrington Report (1991) recommended that drainage committees and burial boards should be merged with the relevant county council or with directly elected district councils if established. The Local Government Act, 2001 allows for such mergers.

Navigations made in connection with drainage were vested in trustees on behalf of the counties and other areas affected. Galway County Council, Mayo County Council and Galway City Council are empowered to appoint trustees for the Corrib.

Fishery Districts

Boards of conservators were formerly elected for fishery districts, of which there were seventeen. The Fisheries Act, 1980 established seven regional fisheries boards to replace the old fishery districts. The Central Fisheries Board, under the same Act, has responsibility for the co-ordination and direction of the regional boards in the protection, conservation, management and development of Ireland's inland fisheries and sea angling resources. The Central Fisheries Board has thirteen members, seven of whom are the chairpersons of the regional boards, with the remainder nominated by the Minister for Communications, Marine and Natural Resources. In 2003, the Department of Communications, Marine and Natural Resources announced that it was undertaking a review of the seven regional fisheries boards; this could result in a rationalisation of structures.

Alteration of Boundaries

The boundaries of counties, cities, boroughs and towns may be altered. Statutory authority and procedures for these were contained in: Application of Enactments Order, 1898 for counties and boroughs; the relevant City Management Acts for the cities; Application of Enactments Order, 1898 and Local Authorities (Miscellaneous Provisions) Act, 1936 for urban districts (the former where the proposed action is at the initiative of the county council and the latter where the initiative is that of the urban district council); Towns Improvement (Ireland) Act, 1854 for towns with town commissioners.

From September 1996 the Local Government Act, 1991 replaced these acts for the purposes of boundary alteration and set out new procedures to be effective from that date. Part V of the Act and the Local Government (Boundary Alteration) Regulations (SI No. 217 of 1996) set out in detail the actions to be taken to progress an application to the minister for boundary alteration. The proposal for alteration of the local authority boundary must be by resolution of the relevant council. The county council may by resolution also make such a proposal in relation to any borough or town in its county area. The Act outlines the circumstances for the setting up of a boundary committee by the minister to prepare a report with respect to the boundary of the local authority and the minister must have regard to such report in making a decision.

The minister also has power to alter the boundary of any county, city, borough or town where he or she considers such an alteration ought to be made in the interests of effective and convenient local government. Before deciding whether to make such an order the minister must request a boundary committee report and must have regard to the report in deciding whether to make the order. Under section 17 of the Local Government Act, 1994 the minister took power to alter on a once-off basis the boundary of any borough or town for the purposes of the elections to be held in 1994 and subsequently. Where such alteration of a boundary breached a county boundary, such county boundary stood altered for the relevant election.

The minister could also request a boundary committee to prepare a report with respect to the boundary of any administrative or geographical district or other division based on a local government boundary and used for any purpose of public administration connected with or related to local government or any such district which it is proposed to establish; or a report with respect to any matter relating to local government that the minister specifies. The establishment of a boundary committee and appointment of the members of the committee (not less than three or more than five), in accordance with the terms of the Act and regulations thereunder, is the function of the minister.

The Local Government Act, 2001 replaced earlier law and set out new arrangements for the alteration of local authority boundaries by order laid before both Houses of the Oireachtas. The Act provides for the establishment of an independent local government commission to make recommendations on a range of boundary, local electoral and other matters arising under the Act. Its members are to be independent in the performance of their functions. The local authority proposing the boundary alteration must complete a consultation process with other local authorities concerned and with the public before making application to the local government commission for a report on the proposed alteration. The commission may either prepare a report or notify the local authorities concerned that for stated reasons it considers it is not appropriate to deal with the application. The minister may only make an order for boundary alteration following a report by the commission.

Changing of Place Names

On the application of an urban district or town, the government may change the name of a district or town (Local Government Act, 1946 as amended by the Local Government Acts of 1955 and 1994). The relevant county council's consent to the application is required. There is also a prescribed procedure for changing the names of non-municipal towns, townlands, streets and localities. In all proposals to change the names of areas mentioned above there must be prior consultation with the qualified electors, a majority of whom must consent to the change. A qualified elector for this purpose is defined in the Local Government Act, 1994 as every person who in relation to the area concerned is registered as a local government elector in the register of local government electors for the time being in force, or not being so registered is the rated occupier of a commercial property. Part 18 of the Local Government Act, 2001, which replaced the earlier legislation mentioned, provides for the changing of names of towns and areas and empowers the appropriate local authority to carry out such changes subject to specified consultation procedures.

Local Authority Committees

A local authority may, under part 7 of the Local Government Act, 2001, appoint such and so many committees as it thinks fit for purposes connected with the exercise or performance of any of its powers. In the case of a county or city council, the committee may be in relation to the whole of the county/city or a local committee empowered to exercise or perform powers, duties and functions in relation to a limited portion only of the county/city. A committee may include non-councillors. Provision for committees was previously contained in the Municipal Corporations Act, 1840; Consolidated Clauses Act, 1847; Local Government Act, 1925; County Management Act, 1940; Local Government Act, 1955; and Local Government Act, 1991.

Prior to the introduction of the county/city management system, the larger urban authorities and to some extent the county councils and other elective bodies had developed the system of working through committees. This was necessary where executive functions could not be delegated to an officer of the council and remained to be performed by the elected council. To achieve prompt discharge of the decision-making process, the work was allocated to committees. This enabled business to be dispatched without making excessive demands on the time of the members of the parent body. Discussion in committee, being usually less formal and freer than in council, ensured fuller detailed consideration and less likelihood of hasty decision making.

The management system, which placed the responsibility for the discharge of executive functions on a whole-time paid manager, removed the necessity for committees as executive bodies. Some authorities, notably Dublin City Council, continued committees in an advisory capacity. Area committees operated in many counties for road programmes and other purposes. In some this area system was well developed, dealing with many local issues which were generally ratified at meetings of the full council.

Committees are of two kinds, optional and obligatory. Examples of the former are local library committees or economic development committees. Under the City and County Management (Amendment) Act, 1955 a local authority had discretionary power to appoint a special estimates committee to prepare the annual estimate of expenses (however, this function is now the responsibility of the corporate policy group under the Local Government Act, 2001). Obligatory or statutory committees include, for example, vocational education committees. There are other bodies, such as burial boards, which although called boards are in their nature committees.

Strategic Policy Committees and Corporate Policy Groups

Better Local Government, in a chapter on enhancing democracy, sets out proposals for a radical overhaul of the existing committee structure and this was given effect in part 7 of the Local Government Act, 2001. Each county and city authority is required to establish strategic policy committees (SPCs) mirroring the major functions of the local authority. The number of committees is tailored to the size of the local authority. Each SPC is supported by the relevant director of services, who operates under the general direction of the committee and submits policy review papers for the service(s) in question. This is intended to give a clear focus to the work of the committee and allow it to play a major role in policy development.

To assist councillors in their corporate role, to foster a high degree of community relevance and local participation and to draw on the expertise of the various sectors, not less than one-third of the members of the SPCs are drawn from sectors relevant to the committee's work. The involvement of non-councillors in this way is not new. It has applied for many decades in the case of VECs and for some types of local authority committee such as library or national monuments. The SPC system, and arrangements for broader community involvement, should greatly strengthen the capacity of councillors to fulfil their policy development role. The 2001 Act also provides that a town council may establish a municipal policy committee. The new system was introduced to facilitate the elimination of most other committees relating to specific functions of the local authority.

Local authorities are increasingly seeking to decentralise decision making through the creation of committees based on the electoral area (see below). The creation of area committees, provided for in the 2001 Act, enables operational matters to be discussed at the area level leaving the full council free to discuss issues affecting the whole area and policy decisions emanating from the SPC system.

The 2001 Act also introduced, for county and city councils, a form of committee known as the corporate policy group (CPG), comprising the cathaoirleach/mayor and the SPC chairs. This was envisaged as a Cabinet-style structure, working with the manager to deal with corporate and other overarching issues. The annual budget and corporate plan are to be prepared in consultation with the CPG. It remains to be seen if the CPG will in practice develop as a key interface between the elected council and executive, and so establish a central role within the overall system. For further details on the SPC system, see chapter 4.

By 2003, a review of the operation of SPCs was underway.

Area Committees

The 1971 White Paper, *Local Government Reorganisation*, recommended new arrangements in counties in place of small town authorities. This would involve area committees of county councils, consisting of councillors, representatives of local development associations and other bodies concerned with the economic, social and cultural development of the area, with minor functions related to local needs delegated to them (Government of Ireland, 1971, pp. 45–6). There were to be approximately 130 areas in all, an average of five to a county. Elected members did not welcome the idea and it was not proceeded with.

Reform of Local Government, A Policy Statement (Government of Ireland, 1985a) outlined a proposal for a new category of local authority: a town council for towns with populations of 2,000 or more to replace existing town commissioners. These councils would not have executive functions in relation to works or services. Their role would be to represent the social and economic interests of the town community; promote works of a community, recreational or amenity nature; encourage initiative within the community; and provide a forum to discuss local needs and make them known to outside bodies.

The Barrington Report (1991, pp. 32–7) recommended that district committees of the county council should replace the town authorities. The districts would be based on one or more local electoral area. The committees would consist of the members of the county/city council elected for the relevant local electoral areas, would handle all district matters and would meet locally and interact with local voluntary and community groups. The report noted that where such an arrangement already operated it appeared to work well.

In 1996, *Better Local Government* held that elected councillors in their role as community representatives had the right and the duty to ensure that policies were translated into the effective delivery of services. It noted that while local authorities were seeking to decentralise decision making to the area level through the creation of committees based on the electoral area, and while this process should be encouraged, it would not be appropriate to be prescriptive about it, since much depended on local circumstances (Department of the Environment, 1996, p. 22).

An electoral area boundary committee was established in February 1998 under the Local Government Act, 1991 to review and make recommendations on the division into local electoral areas of all counties and county boroughs outside of the Dublin area and of the boroughs and certain urban districts. Its terms of reference required that the committee would have as an objective the drawing up of electoral areas which (alone or in combination) would, as far as practicable, have an urban or neighbourhood focal point and be of such size as would facilitate the decentralisation of local authority and other services. The committee, in its report published in June 1998, stated that insofar as practicable the areas proposed, or a combination of them, are of a suitable size from the population and geographical viewpoint to facilitate the local organisation and delivery of services. A separate committee reviewed electoral areas in the Dublin region (Dublin Electoral Area Boundary Committee, 1998).

The Task Force on Integration of Local Government and Local Development Systems in its August 1998 report stated that, to facilitate co-ordination of state agencies, there is a need for common areas and any move towards a more integrated framework at local level must see the introduction of common areas. It suggested that the local electoral areas should be used as the basis to build the framework for service delivery and for interaction with communities. The task force proposed that city and county councils would operate all but their major policy services through area committees based on the local electoral areas or a combination of these (Department of the Environment and Local Government, 1998e, 9.6).

Section 50 of the Local Government Act, 2001 authorised county and city councils to establish, by resolution, area committees in respect of single or two or more adjoining electoral areas. It also provided that where the cathaoirleach/mayor of a town council is not otherwise a member of an area committee within whose area the town is situated, the cathaoirleach/mayor by virtue of office is a member of that area committee.

Vocational Education Committees

There are thirty-three vocational education areas based on twenty-seven county areas, five city areas and the Dún Laoghaire Vocational Education Committee area (former borough area). The regulating act is the Vocational Education Act, 1930 as amended in 1944, 1970 and 2001, and as continued for Dún Laoghaire by the Local Government (Dublin) Act, 1993. Each vocational education committee (VEC) is a body corporate.

Until January 1998 there were thirty-eight VECs, comprising five city committees (Dublin, Cork, Limerick, Waterford and Galway), six town committees (the scheduled urban districts of Bray, Drogheda, Sligo, Wexford, Tralee and Dún Laoghaire) and twenty-seven county committees (including North Tipperary and South Tipperary).

Since January 1998 there are thirty-three VECs, following the amalgamation of Bray, Wexford, Sligo, Tralee and Drogheda with their respective county committees. As mentioned above, the Local Government (Dublin) Act, 1993, which provided for the division of the administrative county of Dublin into three administrative counties, continued the existence of the County Dublin and the Dún Laoghaire Vocational Education Committees.

The Vocational Education Act, 1930, as amended by section 7 of the Vocational Education (Amendment) Act, 2001, specifies that a vocational educational committee should consist of:

- in respect of a city VEC, nine members elected by the relevant council
- in respect of a county VEC, nine members elected by the county council (and where appropriate allowing for representation from town councils from the area)
- representatives of staff of the VEC and parents
- members representative of other interests, such as students.

The committee is elected in every council election year and holds meetings at least once a month (except in July and September). Its annual meeting is held before 1 December each year. The Minister for Education and Science has power to make regulations governing procedures of the VEC. An inspector of the Department of Education and Science is entitled to be present at and address meetings.

A VEC is required to establish and maintain a suitable system of continuous education in its area, provide for its progressive development and supply technical education. There is flexibility within the Vocational Education Act to allow the VEC to respond to local educational needs and to adapt national policies and programmes to local needs. In practice, this has led to the establishment of vocational schools, institutes of technology, community colleges, adult education centres, vocational training opportunity schemes, youthreach training programmes, post-leaving certificate programmes and so forth. VECs also assist in the provision of educational services such as school transport and student grants.

Each VEC has a chief executive officer. While the VEC is technically deemed to be a local authority for the purposes of certain local government acts, it was never brought within the county and city management system. Activities of the VECs are mainly funded by the Department of Education and Science, although local rates still make some contribution. Local authorities can contribute the produce of up to ten pence in the pound from local rates.

The Vocational Education (Amendment) Act, 2001 is the first major review of the legislation governing VECs since 1930. The purpose of the Act is to:

- revise the composition of the VECs to include representation for parents of students registered in VEC institutions and staff of VECs
- help modernise accountability structures by classifying the functions exercised by VECs into reserved and executive functions (along the lines of the local government model)
- provide for additional functions for VECs in areas such as the preparation of education plans
- provide for revised reporting, accounting and financial procedures.

Regional technical colleges (as a number of institutes of technology used to be known) operated under the control of the VECs prior to the implementation of the Regional Technical College Act, 1992. These bodies are now independent of the VECs and are under the direct control of the Department of Education and Science. The first five colleges were established in 1970 and were located at Waterford, Carlow, Dundalk, Athlone and Sligo. An additional eight colleges have since been established at Letterkenny, Tralee, Cork, Galway, Limerick, Tallaght, Dún Laoghaire and Blanchardstown. Following the report of the Steering Committee on the Future Development of Higher Education (1995), the title of regional technical college was changed to institute of technology.

The principal function of the institutes of technology is to provide vocational and technical education and training for the economic, technological, scientific, commercial, industrial, social and cultural development of the state with particular reference to the region served by the institute. Each institute has a governing body consisting of a chairperson, seventeen ordinary members and the director of the institute. At least three members of the governing body must be members of a local authority. The members are appointed by the Minister for Education and Science on the recommendation of the relevant VEC.

Committees of Agriculture

In 1899, county councils were empowered to raise a limited rate for the purposes of agriculture and to appoint a committee to administer it. These committees were succeeded by county committees of agriculture appointed under the Agriculture Act, 1931. The committees, composed of members with a suitable agricultural background, were appointed by the county councils, which were required to contribute towards their finances up to a limit of the produce of forty pence in the pound on the local rates. Management of the committees was separate from the local authority management system.

The responsibilities of the committees were substantially reduced by the Agricultural Advisory Education and Research Authority Act, 1977, which transferred the agricultural advisory service to the newly established state-sponsored body An Chomhairle Oiliúna Talmhaíochta (ACOT). The main function of the committees in relation to the advisory and training services was to submit to ACOT each year a programme for the county which the board of ACOT was required to take into account in preparing its statutory programme of activities. The committees were finally abolished under the Agriculture (Research, Training and Advice) Act, 1988, which set up Teagasc to provide advisory, research, education and training services to the agriculture and food industry.

School Attendance Committees

School attendance areas, as determined by the School Attendance Acts of 1926 to 1967, are the cities of Dublin, Cork and Waterford, the former borough area of Dún Laoghaire, as continued by the Local Government (Dublin) Act, 1993, and areas into which the Minister for Education and Science, in consultation with the Minister for Justice, Equality and Law Reform, has divided the rest of the country for the purposes of enforcing school attendance as prescribed by the Act.

Under the School Attendance Act, 1926, as amended, parents are required to ensure that children in their care, who are aged from six years up to fifteen years, attend a national school for full-time education, unless there is a reasonable excuse either of absence through illness or where the child is receiving suitable elementary education other than attending a national or other approved school. Until 2002, the enforcing authority was the school attendance committee in the cities of Dublin, Cork and Waterford and in the former borough area of Dún Laoghaire; outside these areas, the enforcing authority was An Garda Síochána.

School attendance committees were appointed by the respective city councils for the cities and by Dún Laoghaire-Rathdown county council for Dún Laoghaire. Membership was ten, or eleven if there was a juvenile advisory committee in the relevant administrative area. The Minister for Education and Science appointed five members and the council the other five or six. Provisions required that school managers and teachers were represented on the committee. School attendance officers were appointed by the committees and funding was provided by the local authorities.

The 1995 White Paper, *Charting Our Education Future*, stated that a task force had been established in the Department of Education to consider and make recommendations as to future action required to address the problem of truancy at first- and second-level education. At the same time, the process of reviewing the existing legislation was underway. It stated that, taking account of the findings, the regional education boards proposed in the White Paper would be given statutory powers and responsibilities in regard to the monitoring and enforcement of school attendance. Following a change of government, the regional boards did not proceed.

In 2002, under the Education Welfare Act, 2000, the National Education Welfare Board (NEWB) was established. It took over the functions of school attendance committees and has responsibility for the enforcement of school attendance for children aged from six to sixteen years. The NEWB has a chairperson appointed by the Minister for Education and Science and a chief executive officer appointed by the board. The board comprises representatives of parents, school management organisations, teacher organisations, education welfare officers and relevant voluntary or other bodies; and appointees of government departments with a special interest or expertise. The education welfare officers, appointed by the board, will be required to make all reasonable efforts to ensure the continued education of a child to whom the Act applies.

Joint Bodies

Under section 38 of the Local Government (Application of Enactments) Order, 1898, any county council, including councils of county boroughs, may from time to time join in appointing out of their respective bodies a joint committee for any purpose in respect of which they are jointly interested, and may delegate to such joint committee any power which such council might exercise for the purpose for which the committee is appointed. The council is prohibited from delegating a power of making a rate or borrowing any money. As stated earlier, burial boards can be formed for united districts. Ordinarily the sanitary authority is the burial board but under the general power to form united districts and constitute governing bodies of such districts and the power to appoint joint committees a number of joint burial boards and one joint burial committee were set up prior to the foundation of the state.

The provisional order forming a united district is made under the Local Government (Sanitary Services) Acts and defines the scope of the board's powers and contains regulations as to elections, continuance in office, meetings and other matters. Section 52 of the Local Government Act, 2001 allows for the establishment of joint committees by two or more local authorities and for the delegation of functions. Subject to the sanction of the minister, a joint committee may be set up as a separate corporate body. The use of joint committees has not been widespread in recent years.

Harbour Authorities

The Department of Communications, Marine and Natural Resources administers harbours legislation, which provides for the constitution and functions of commercial harbour authorities and port companies. The relevant acts are the Harbours Acts of 1946, 1976 and 1996. The 1946 Act provided a new legal basis for harbour authorities and for the control, operation and development of the specified harbours. Kilrush and Youghal urban district councils were the only local authorities which were harbour authorities under the Act. The Act did not affect the state harbours of Howth, Dún Laoghaire and Dunmore East for which the Commissioners of Public Works had responsibility or numerous small harbours, piers and quays under the control of the county councils. The Harbours Act, 1976 authorised the establishment of separate harbour commissioners for Bantry Bay following local agitation for greater powers of control of an oil terminal sited in the area.

Harbour authorities constituted under the 1946 and 1976 Acts are elected in the year in which local elections are held, under the general supervision of the Minister for Communications, Marine and Natural Resources. They include representatives of users of the harbours, local authorities and commercial and labour interests, some members being nominated by the minister. Harbour authorities are responsible for the operation and maintenance of harbours, but the minister exercises certain controls in the areas of finance, appointment and qualifications of certain officers, the fixing of certain harbour rates and charges, the acquisition or disposal of property and the preparation of superannuation schemes. It is government policy that harbours should be operated as commercial undertakings and should be self-supporting. The majority of fishery harbours operate under the control of the relevant local authority, but five are administered directly by the Department of Communications, Marine and Natural Resources under the Fishery Harbour Centres Acts, 1968 to 1980. These are Castletownbere, Dunmore East, Howth, Killybegs and Rossaveal.

The Harbours Act, 1996 introduced major changes in relation to twelve commercial harbours: Arklow, Cork, Drogheda, Dublin, Dundalk, Dún Laoghaire, Foynes, Galway, New Ross, Shannon, Waterford and Wicklow. The Minister for Communications, Marine and Natural Resources was authorised, with the consent of the Minister for Finance, to cause a private company conforming to the conditions laid down in the Act to be formed and registered in respect of each named harbour. The Act in its 105 sections and six schedules sets out in detail the constitution, objectives, general duties and powers of the new company, including a power of compulsory acquisition of land for harbour development schemes. The board of directors is to be representative of employees of the company, relevant local authorities, and one or more persons to be appointed after the minister has consulted with the Chambers of Commerce of Ireland, the Irish Business and Employers Confederation and such other persons as the minister considers appropriate.

The company is charged with the general duty to conduct its affairs so as to ensure that the revenues of the company are not less than sufficient to meet all charges properly chargeable to its revenue account and to generate a reasonable proportion of the capital it requires, to conduct its business in a cost-efficient manner, to regulate operations within its harbour and to have due regard to the consequences of its activities on the environment, the heritage relating to its harbour and the amenities generally in the vicinity of its harbour. The Harbours Acts, 1946 to 1976, were repealed in relation to a harbour in respect of which a company is established under the 1996 Act. Under the 1996 Act, the minister also has power to establish, by order, companies in respect of harbours other than the twelve listed above and section 87 sets out a further thirteen harbours in respect of one or more of which the minister is empowered to make such an order.

Regional Authorities and Regional Assemblies

A great deal of public authority business is conducted at the regional level. Formal statutory regional bodies for health, tourism promotion and fisheries development have been set up. Also a considerable number of government departments and state agencies operate through regional offices – IDA, FÁS, OPW and others. The Barrington Report (1991, pp. 26–7) noted that different regional areas are used for different purposes and recommended that there must be standard regions if regions are to make sense to people and if regional loyalties are to develop. Standardisation was also considered by the committee to be essential for collecting data, for planning and for relating the activities of different agencies. However, at the time of writing, the prospect of standard regions across different agencies looks remote.

Local government also has a regional dimension in addition to the two levels of county/city and towns described above. In 1969, regional development organisations (RDOs) were established in nine regions to co-ordinate development programmes. RDOs were non-statutory and had a membership representative of local authorities, central government and state-sponsored and other bodies and had a co-ordinating role for development in the regions. These organisations continued to operate on an informal basis until they were disbanded by the government in 1987 at a time of public sector retrenchment. Subsequently it was found necessary to establish regional structures in the context of the national development plan for 1989 to 1993 (Government of Ireland, 1989). These were called sub-regional review committees and they operated under the control and supervision of the Department of Finance.

Section 43 of the Local Government Act, 1991 provided that for the purpose of promoting the co-ordination of the provision of public services the Minister for the Environment and Local Government may declare by order, made with the consent of the Minister for Finance, that an area consisting of specified counties or cities shall form a region and shall establish in respect of the region a body to be known as a regional authority.

In pursuance of that power the minister, by the Local Government Act, 1991 (Regional Authorities) (Establishment) Order, 1993, which came into operation on 1 January 1994, established eight regional authorities. The eight regions are Border, Dublin, Mid-East, Midland, Mid-West, South-East, South-West and West. For details of the area constituting and the number of members of each region, see appendix 4.

Membership of a regional authority is restricted to elected members of the constituent county/city councils. The establishment order specifies the number of persons to be appointed to be members by each constituent local authority, ranging from fourteen in the case of Dublin City Council to five each from smaller counties such as Leitrim and Longford. Other conditions of appointment such as tenure, disqualification, resignation, casual vacancies, attendance at meetings and election of the cathaoirleach are covered in detail in the order.

In 1998, a proposal was made for the establishment of a new regional tier with two new regional areas, one comprising fifteen counties in the western seaboard, border and midland areas, and the other made up of the remaining counties. The purpose behind the proposal was to seek to retain EU Objective 1 designation for the newly constituted fifteen-county region on the grounds that, at the time, it had not exceeded the specified per capita income threshold for Objective 1 status.

Following discussions at EU level and the agreement of the European Commission and Eurostat, two new regional assemblies were established by the minister in 1999. The assemblies – the Border, Midland and Western (BMW) Regional Assembly and the Southern & Eastern (S&E) Regional Assembly – are based on the existing regional authority structure. For details of the constituent city and county councils and number of members of the two regional assemblies, see appendix 4.

The regional assemblies have been assigned functions relating to the management of regional programmes under the national development plan for the period 2000 to 2006 (Government of Ireland, 2000a), and are to monitor the general impact of all EU programmes of assistance in their areas. The assemblies also have a co-ordinating role for public services within their regions. Membership is drawn from the elected representatives of the eight existing regional authorities. Each assembly has a chief executive officer.

For further details on the establishment and operation of regional authorities and regional assemblies, see chapter 25.

Regional Health Boards

Eight regional health boards were established under the Health Act, 1970. This was the culmination of a long process, which had commenced with the Health Act, 1947, towards a reduction in the numbers and types of authorities operating in different branches of the health services. The changes made by the 1947 Act meant that, in most areas, the county/city council was to administer most of the health services, thereby reducing the number of administering authorities from ninety to thirty-one. Local consultative health committees were set up under the Health Act, 1953 to advise the city/county managers on the operation of the general health services. The effect of the changes of the law on health under the Health Acts of 1947 and 1953 was that the county council, as health authority, administered all the health services, apart from the mental treatment service, in most parts of the country. The administration of mental hospitals continued, under the Mental Treatment Act, 1945, in the hands of special joint boards.

The Health Authorities Act, 1960 established unified health authorities with comprehensive responsibility for all the health services in the Dublin, Cork, Limerick and Waterford areas. These four unified authorities were joint bodies within the local government system, the membership being made up of local councillors nominated by the county and city councils involved in each case. The number of local authorities responsible for the health services was thus reduced to twenty-seven (4 unified authorities and 23 county councils). This position obtained until March 1971 when the eight health boards set up under the Health Act, 1970 took over administration of the health services in their respective regions.

Membership of the health boards ranges from twenty-seven to thirty-five. The majority of the members must be appointed by the local county and city councils and the remainder of the membership must include persons elected by medical practitioners and members of ancillary professions. The Minister for Health and Children also has three nominees. Each board is a body corporate, with the usual authority to hold and dispose of land. The 1970 Act and regulations contain rules relating to membership and meetings of the boards and committees. The boards have authority to set up joint bodies, to act jointly in providing services, to co-operate with local authorities and to enter into arrangements with other bodies such as voluntary hospitals to provide services on their behalf. The 1970 Act also provided for the establishment of local health committees to maintain contact at county level with the operation of the health services. There was one committee for each county, local councillors were in the majority and the function of the local committees was mainly advisory. The committees ceased to function after a period and were dissolved under the Health (Amendment) (No. 3) Act, 1996.

Under the 1970 Act, each health board is required to have a chief executive officer. In contrast with the local government management system, the reserved powers and functions were those of the CEO, comprising a limited range mainly relating to eligibility of individuals for services and to personnel matters. All other business rested with the board. In practice virtually the whole of the day-to-day management was delegated to the CEO by the board. The Health (Amendment) (No. 3) Act, 1996 changed this and set out specified functions to be known as reserved functions, which were to be carried out directly by the members. Any function that is not reserved to the members is a function of the CEO. This re-statement of functions mirrors to a large extent the position which obtains in the local government management system.

The 1996 Act also required health boards to develop and adopt annual service plans which are to include a statement of services to be provided by the board consistent with the financial and indebtedness limits determined by the Minister for Health and Children. While the board exercises a supervisory/monitoring role, implementation of the service plan is an executive function. Each health board is also required to prepare and adopt annual financial statements and an annual report.

In 1999, the delivery of health services in the Eastern Health Board region of Dublin, Kildare and Wicklow was re-organised. Responsibility for the funding and management of health and personal social services was transferred to the new Eastern Regional Health Authority (ERHA), which came into operation on 1 March 2000. Three area health boards (Northern, South Western and East Coast) have delegated responsibility from the ERHA for the delivery of health services in their respective areas. The ERHA monitors and evaluates the services provided by the three area health boards and has responsibility for strategic planning of services for the region and the commissioning of those services from both the statutory and voluntary sectors.

Following a review of the state's health services during 2002 and 2003, it was expected that proposals would be made to reduce the overall number of health boards and also to reduce the number of elected representatives from local councils and increase professional health and consumer representation on the boards. A further possibility was that the funding and planning for hospitals would be transferred to a national agency and the health boards would be abolished.

The 1991 Barrington Report recommended that the regional health boards, or whatever new structures might emerge from the government review of health services then ongoing, should allow for adequate input by the local democratic system and be linked to the regional authorities proposed in the same report. It recommended too that the community care programme of the health boards should be linked with local government at the district level and integrated with the social welfare system with the aim of moving to a geographic base for planning and delivery of personal services, drawing together the various public support services and the voluntary bodies (pp. 21–2).

The interim report of the Devolution Commission (1996, pp. 27–8) included public and community health matters and operation of the supplementary welfare system in relation to housing on an indicative list of functions to be examined. The 1995 Report of the Review Group on the Role of Supplementary Welfare Allowances in Relation to Housing (p. 35), in recognising that supplementary welfare allowance housing supplements were now a mainstream housing support mechanism operating outside the framework of overall housing policy, welcomed the commitment in *A Government of Renewal* (Fine Gael, the Labour Party and Democratic Left, 1994, p. 33) that all forms of social housing assistance would be administered by the local authority.

Regional Tourism Authorities

Bord Fáilte, the Irish tourist board, set up regional tourism organisations in 1964. These are public companies limited by guarantee. Each company has responsibility for the promotion of its region and its products in conjunction with Bord Fáilte and the travel trade. Membership is open to all persons within the region, especially those involved in tourism, as well as local authorities, clubs and associations. The companies are financed by Bord Fáilte, local authorities and subscribing members.

They operate through a network of tourist information offices within the region, linking into the national system, and provide services to visitors including making room reservations, supplying accommodation listings, informational brochures and other publicity material, promoting visitor entertainment, liaising with transport authorities and surveying tourism resources.

Each organisation has the task of preparing a tourism development plan for the region and each county within its region in concert with county tourism committees. These latter committees, of which there are twenty-five, have on average twenty members drawn from tourism and related sectoral interests including local government. Administration of the regional tourism organisation is the function of the regional tourism manager.

County and City Enterprise Boards

County development teams were established in thirteen designated western counties in the mid-1960s with the principal aim of fostering economic development in less-developed areas. The counties designated were Cavan, Clare, West Cork, Donegal, Galway, Kerry, Leitrim, West Limerick, Longford, Mayo, Monaghan, Roscommon and Sligo. The teams consisted of the county manager (chairperson), county council chairperson, county engineer, chief agricultural officer, chief executive of the VEC and regional manager of the IDA. Each team had a county development officer, an official of the Department of Finance. Other non-designated counties also set up development teams and appointed county development officers out of their own resources. The county development teams continued in operation until they were superseded by the thirty-five county/city enterprise boards (CEBs) set up in 1993.

The CEBs were given clear enterprise and job creation objectives with responsibility for business areas not already covered by the state's industrial development agencies. They were to complement the work of existing state agencies and were not to displace or duplicate local enterprise initiatives. CEBs also provide direct support for services employment and their responsibilities include developing enterprise action plans covering all sectors in the county/city, creating local enterprise awareness and developing an enterprise culture to ensure community-based enterprise activity, providing grant support to individuals and local community groups to assist commercially viable small enterprise projects, and influencing the allocation of resources for small enterprises from EU, private and public funding sources.

CEBs comprise a chairperson and thirteen members. The composition reflects a balance of interests embracing four elected representatives from the relevant local authority, and representation from the main public sector agencies (including the county/city manager or other local authority official, who in many cases acts as chairperson of the board), business, farming, trade union and community interests. Specialist evaluation committees assist each board and make recommendations on the most appropriate level and form of assistance for projects, having regard in particular to the prospect of attracting other sources of funding.

These evaluation committees include persons with banking and accounting experience and expertise in assessing the quality, local relevance and cost-effectiveness of project proposals. Projects with investment costs in excess of €127,000 or with an employment potential of more than ten persons are not normally eligible for assistance. Each CEB has a chief executive officer, who is responsible for its administrative and day-to-day activities. Overall co-ordination and supervision of the CEBs is exercised by the Department of Enterprise, Trade and Employment, and their activities are jointly financed by the exchequer and the EU Structural Funds.

LEADER Groups

LEADER is an EU Community Initiative which supports the development of local rural areas in countries across the EU. The title LEADER comes from the full title in French: *Liaisons Entre Actions de Développement de l'Économie Rurale* (or Links Between Development Actions for the Rural Economy). LEADER began in Ireland in 1992 as a pilot programme (known as LEADER I) under which sixteen

Irish groups implemented local business plans and supported projects in a range of areas. For the period 1994 to 1999, a second programme (LEADER II) to support capacity building and encourage local people to become involved in the development of their area supported thirty-four local action groups, as well as three sectoral bodies (Irish Farm Holidays, Irish Country Holidays and Muintir na Tíre). LEADER II operated in virtually all rural areas of Ireland.

The third LEADER programme, LEADER+, runs for the period 2000 to 2006. As before, funding is channelled through local action groups, which are responsible for implementing the business plans they have drawn up for the development of their areas. In 2001, details were announced of the various groups around the country that are to be funded to implement LEADER+ and the complementary area-based national rural development programme until 2006. These programmes (the first being part-financed by the EU, the second being wholly financed by the exchequer) are run in tandem and are aimed at promoting rural development and improving the economic environment to create job opportunities.

LEADER groups have supported a wide variety of actions in different areas including training, rural tourism, supporting small firms and local services, marketing of goods, improvement of the environment, and technical support. LEADER companies have played an important role in promoting rural development in the areas covered and have (through both the county strategy groups and later the county/city development board structures) sought to co-ordinate their action with other bodies active in the area concerned.

The Department of Agriculture and Food had responsibility for the administration of LEADER in Ireland until 2002, when rural development was allocated to the newly established Department of Community, Rural and Gaeltacht Affairs. Local business plans are agreed between the local action groups and the department. However, decisions regarding support for local actions are the responsibility of the board of each LEADER group. Board membership comprises representatives from local communities, state agencies, local authorities and the social partners (which include farming and rural organisations, employers and trade unions).

According to the operating rules for LEADER II (Department of Agriculture, Food and Forestry, 1995, p. 5):

> . . . it is not the intention that LEADER Groups operate as the exclusive development agencies in their areas nor compete with the official State bodies. Accordingly, Groups must operate in harmony, and maintain close liaison, with all State agencies and local authorities and other official structures within their operational areas. The Group is required to participate fully in the activities of the County Strategy Group(s) which are to be established in each county.

A number of the LEADER groups also act as area partnership companies (see below).

Area Partnerships

Area-based partnership companies (often referred to as area partnerships) were established by the government in 1991, under the Programme for Economic and Social Progress (PESP), in an attempt to replicate at local level the perceived success of the social partnership arrangements at national level. They were designed to provide a local response to the problems caused by unemployment and social exclusion.

Area partnerships involve state agencies, the social partners, local elected members and the community and voluntary sector and operate in designated disadvantaged areas around the country. Financed on the basis of multi-annual integrated local area action plans developed in consultation with local people, the actions pursued by area partnerships have ranged from supporting enterprise, education and training to community development and environmental initiatives. Many initiatives are directed at specific target groups such as the socially excluded, the long-term unemployed, Travellers, the disabled, disadvantaged women, the homeless and young people at risk. In many cases, the area partnerships also work to source financing for their specific area.

During the 1991 to 1993 period, a total of twelve area partnerships were financed on a pilot basis. For the 1994 to 1999 period, this figure was increased to thirty-eight. Until 1999, area partnerships received part of their financing from EU Structural Funds. However, since 2000, they have been wholly financed by the exchequer. From 2000 to 2006, thirty-eight area partnerships (as well as thirty-three community groups) are implementing local area action plans. Overall responsibility for the area partnerships rested with the Department of Tourism, Sport and Recreation until 2002, when this was transferred to the newly established Department of Community, Rural and Gaeltacht Affairs. However, local plans are evaluated and funding is allocated by Area Development Management (ADM) Ltd, a national body, which acts as an intermediary for the administration of the programme.

Each area partnership has a board of directors made up of representatives from the local community and voluntary sector, local representatives of the social partners (trade unions, employers, farmers), elected members of local authorities and representatives of state agencies at local level. Area partnerships are independent companies limited by guarantee.

A number of area partnerships also act as local action groups under the LEADER programme (see above).

Community Councils and Local Development

The Local Government Act, 1941 gave authority to county councils in instances where the inhabitants of a locality within a county health district established a council, committee or other body for furthering the interests of such inhabitants, to declare such a body an approved local council. The county council was given authority to provide a building for use by the approved local council for meetings, lectures, exhibitions and general recreation or other similar social projects. It could also assist with furniture, office equipment and caretaking costs. If it so desired, the county council was authorised to delegate any of its powers and duties which it felt would be better regulated or managed by or through the approved local council.

The sections of the 1941 Act on approved local councils had their genesis in a 1940 Department of Local Government circular, the purpose of which was to encourage the formation of parish councils in view of the then existing emergency (Street, 1955, p. 303). There was a fair degree of activity during the war years although only a minority of parish councils became approved local councils. With the return of peace, the sense of purpose and the ardour and spontaneity evaporated. Muintir na Tíre worked hard to keep the spirit alive but in the early 1950s only fifty-four approved local councils were active, thirty-five of them in County Limerick.

The Local Government Act, 1955 extended the powers of approving and helping local councils to the corporations of county boroughs. This Act also authorised county councils to give grants for community halls.

The 1971 plan for local government reorganisation contained a modest set of proposals for establishing local councils, particularly in counties and major cities where identifiable communities existed with their own interests, needs and aspirations. The plan stated that:

> . . . development in all its forms, and at all levels, requires the active participation of all sections of the community; if economic and social activity is to be advanced in all areas of the country, the initiative, skill and energy of every community must be harnessed. This can best be done through voluntary bodies. But there must be a partnership between bodies and the statutory local authorities (Government of Ireland, 1971, p. 45).

The proposals were not pursued. However, in the intervening period there has been major growth in the number of voluntary and community organisations, some flowing from initiatives taken by local authorities. The Barrington Report (1991, p. 42), presumably acknowledging this, recommended that there should be structured arrangements to facilitate contact between local authorities and community groups and that a contact officer be designated for this purpose. In 1995 the government asked the Devolution Commission to make recommendations on how local authorities could become the focus for working through local partnerships of community-based groups, voluntary bodies, the private sector and public agencies.

In *Better Local Government*, the government confirmed its acceptance of the principles, set out in the Devolution Commission's preliminary report published in August 1996, that the existing local authority and local development systems should be brought together and simplified, that people should be provided with the best possible opportunity to participate at local level and that there should be maximum co-ordination between agencies at local level to benefit from the experience and work of others so that gaps can be identified and addressed (Department of the Environment, 1996, p. 26; Devolution Commission, 1996, p. 18).

The report of the Local Government Reorganisation Commission in April 1996 dealt comprehensively with this subject and pointed to the desirability of positive, structured and inclusive partnership between local communities and the local authority. It instanced the need for new responses arising from the increased focus on local development, with its strong emphasis on local community initiative, area-based approaches and integration of action across different sectors. In acknowledging that local authorities had become increasingly involved with other local interests in development activities related to their traditional functions such as the improvement of the physical appearance and general attractiveness of local areas or the provision of amenities, it said that such activity is central to the local authority's role in local and community development.

The commission was of the opinion that a more proactive approach by town authorities to helping community capacity building, establishing appropriate community structures and implementing arrangements such as neighbourhood watch or community alert schemes could be a major contributor towards the creation of self-sustaining local structures. It suggested that some existing voluntary community councils, particularly in non-local authority towns, should be accorded recognition through a suitable form of linkage with the local government system to provide a means of direct input in support of local needs and aspirations. The commission set out in some detail its recommendations for providing the enhanced linkage, a reading of which is recommended (Local Government Reorganisation Commission, 1996, chapters 10 and 14).

The report acknowledged too that while many local authorities recognised the potential and had developed links with local groups to considerable beneficial effect, there was still a degree of reticence on the part of some local authorities to become closely involved with, or to appear to accord significant recognition to, non-local government groups, as such recognition might tend to weaken the position of elected local authorities. The committee, in rejecting this approach, said that the interests of local democracy would be poorly served by a failure to come to terms with the aspirations and activities of people and groups at community level outside of, but often very relevant to, the formal local authority structure. It must be said too that there is a degree of reticence on the part of some community groups to become too closely involved with local authorities, fearing loss of independence to what can be perceived as unresponsive political and bureaucratic bodies.

The *Report of the Task Force on the Integration of Local Government and Local Development Systems* (Department of the Environment and Local Government, 1998e) recommended movement towards a more integrated approach to local government/local development and the local delivery of services generally through a number of steps. The measures proposed included the appointment of a director of community and enterprise by each county/city council to support and strengthen the county/city strategy, with the subsequent establishment of county/city development boards (CDBs) to replace the strategy groups and to work towards the implementation of a strategy for economic, social and cultural development within the county/city. CDBs were established in each county/city council in 2000 and ten-year strategies had been agreed by 2002.

For the purposes of this sub-section it is sufficient to note that one of the nominated tasks of the director of community and enterprise is to reinforce, promote, and guide local authority activity related to community development in its broader sense. The new model of community development should provide an outlet for local communities to be fully involved in, to influence and to shape local decisions. Any new model of local governance will have to be constructed along partnership lines, allowing local communities, the state sector and the social partners to have meaningful involvement in the design and delivery of local services.

For further details on the community and enterprise function, partnership initiatives and the CDB process, see chapter 16.

Central Authorities

Government Departments

Government departments exert an important influence on the local government system. They play a crucial role in the formation of policy, the preparation of legislation and statutory instruments, the provision of finance for local services and the stimulation and control of local authorities in their various operations. Central agencies may also provide services to local bodies or directly to the public. Table 3.1, although not comprehensive, gives some idea of the areas of local administration that different government departments have responsibility for, including interaction with local authorities.

Table 3.1 Local Responsibilities of Central Government Departments

Central department	Local responsibilities
Agriculture and Food	diseases of animals, abattoirs
Arts, Sport and Tourism	arts, sports, regional tourism organisations
Communications, Marine and Natural Resources	regional fisheries boards, harbours, coastal protection, forestry
Community, Rural and Gaeltacht Affairs	local development, LEADER, area partnerships, drugs task forces, community development support programmes, Gaeltacht, Islands
Defence	Civil Defence
Education and Science	VECs, higher education grants
Enterprise, Trade and Employment	county/city enterprise boards, consumer protection, safety health and welfare
Environment and Local Government	local authorities
Finance	EU monitoring committee, arterial drainage and flood relief (OPW), valuation for rating (Valuation Office)
Health and Children	regional health boards
Justice, Equality and Law Reform	coroners, pounds, courthouses, childcare
Social and Family Affairs	supplementary welfare
Transport	national roads and road safety

State-Sponsored Bodies

Some state-sponsored bodies are concerned directly with local government and may legitimately be regarded as part of the structure or at least as having a strong local dimension. They include the Arts Council, Bord Fáilte, An Bord Pleanála, Central Fisheries Board, An Chomhairle Leabharlanna, Environmental Protection Agency, Fire Services Council, The Heritage Council, Housing Finance Agency,

Local Government Computer Services Board, Local Government Management Services Board, National Building Agency, National Roads Authority and Teagasc. It is not intended here to give an account of how each of these bodies interacts with local government, but it would be remiss to omit special reference to the following:

- *Arts Council:* established by the Arts Acts of 1951 and 1973 to stimulate public interest in the arts and to promote knowledge, appreciation and practice of arts and culture. In addition to providing grants for specific projects, it assists local authorities through funding of county/city arts officer posts, subject to the adoption of a satisfactory arts plan.

- *An Bord Pleanála:* originally established under the Local Government (Planning and Development) Act, 1976, it operates under part VI of the Planning and Development Act, 2000. It deals with appeals, references and other matters under the Planning Acts, Water Pollution Acts, Air Pollution Act, Building Control Act, Roads Acts, confirmation of Compulsory Purchase Orders, and so forth.

- *An Chomhairle Leabharlanna:* established by the Public Libraries Act, 1947, as continued by the Local Government Acts of 1994 and 2001. It advises local authorities and the minister on the development of public library services and provides financial assistance for such development under the public libraries grants scheme. It also provides an inter-library lending system for the whole of Ireland.

- *Environmental Protection Agency:* established under the Environmental Protection Agency Act, 1992. It has wide-ranging powers and functions to promote improved environmental protection in Ireland. In relation to local authority activities it has an overseeing role in the monitoring of the quality of drinking water, the management of sanitary authority treatment works, the management, operation and licensing of landfill sites, the functions of local authorities in relation to environmental pollution, and the environmental monitoring of activities of public authorities generally.

- *Fire Services Council:* established under the Fire Services Act, 1981. It advises the minister in relation to the educational and training needs of fire services personnel and provides courses for these and other persons as required.

- *Housing Finance Agency:* established under the Housing Finance Agency Act, 1981. It lends money to local authorities for their housing loan functions under the Housing Acts.

- *Local Government Computer Services Board:* established in 1975, its functions are to organise and provide a service to local authorities in the

IT area and to co-ordinate and secure compatibility in such development. It provides training, education and research for local authorities.

- *Local Government Management Services Board:* originally established as the Local Government Staff Negotiations Board in 1971, it was reconstituted as the Local Government Management Services Board in 1996 to provide a broader range of services for local authorities including industrial relations negotiations, labour court proceedings and management services, particularly in the light of the significant increase in legislation relating to personnel and human resource issues. It also seeks to promote best practice in these areas amongst local authorities. The Local Government Act, 2001 provides that local authorities shall have regard to guidelines or codes of practice issued by the Board, and that the Board may identify the necessary employment qualifications for certain positions within local authorities.

- *National Building Agency:* established in 1960, it is a consultancy firm specialising in housing, architecture and construction management. It specialises in urban design and renewal and undertakes redevelopment work bringing together local authority, private and voluntary interests. It has provided over 30,000 housing units for local authorities.

- *National Roads Authority:* established under the Roads Act, 1993. Its primary function is to secure the provision of a safe and efficient network of national roads. It has overall responsibility for planning and supervising the construction, improvement and maintenance network of national roads including the access routes to the principal ports and airports. It generally discharges its functions through the agency of the county/city councils, which are the designated road authorities for their administrative areas, and makes grants to these authorities for that purpose, but it also has the powers to carry out these works itself, where it considers that this would be more convenient, expeditious, effective or economic.

Further details on how these organisations interface with local authorities can be found in subsequent chapters.

Local Government Associations

The Local Government Act, 1994 statutorily recognised two associations of local authorities, namely the General Council of County Councils and the Association of Municipal Authorities of Ireland. The Act also provided for recognition of any other body which may be established in place of either or both of those bodies. Their general function is to represent the collective interest of the local authorities which constitute their membership. The 1994 Act provided for a constitution, election of delegates and annual contribution by local authorities. The minister could specify the nature of contributions which might be made or make regulations for the purposes of any matter arising from membership by a local authority of an association of local authorities. The decision to hold or to cease to hold membership of an association of local authorities is a reserved function. It is notable that the provisions of the 1994 Act did not prejudice the right of any member of a local authority to be a member in his or her own right of a local authority members' association or the right of any group of such members to appoint a person to represent them on such an association.

The Local Government Act, 2001 re-stated the provisions of the 1994 Act in relation to the two named associations and also gave statutory recognition to instances where a member of a local authority in his/her own right holds membership of the Local Authority Members' Association (LAMA). It authorised the members of a local authority to appoint a person to represent them on that association, and applied the provisions of the Act in relation to procedural rules, accounts, expenses and general functions representing the collective interests of its constituent authorities. The Act states that nothing in the sections approving membership of the associations should be read as preventing the establishment of a unified body to replace the three bodies mentioned in those sections and to represent local government and its elected members – not an unexpected or demanding provision in an era of integration.

The General Council of County Councils (GCCC) was established in 1899, soon after the Local Government (Ireland) Act, 1898 came into operation. It was given statutory recognition by the Local Government (Ireland) (Amendment) Act, 1902. County and city councils are authorised to pay affiliation fees and to allow travelling expenses to delegates attending meetings. All county and city councils are members and may each nominate up to three members to the general council, which meets six times a year. The business of the council is managed by an executive committee assisted by a full-time director and support staff.

The Association of Municipal Authorities (AMAI), formed in 1912, is the corresponding body for urban authorities. The association adopted a written constitution and rules of procedure and set out in its objectives the duty to watch over the interests, rights and privileges of the affiliated local bodies as they may be affected by legislation, to take action on any matters affecting the members and to safeguard the interests of the ratepayers or other interests affecting the public welfare. The Local Government Act, 1941 provided that, subject to the minister's approval, an urban authority may contribute to the funds of an approved association. The AMAI was approved for this purpose in 1942. Membership includes the city councils, borough councils and all but two town councils.

Members of the AMAI meet in annual conference and resolutions submitted by member authorities are considered. This conference has been convened each year, with the exception of the period 1921 to 1923 during which no meetings were held in protest at the arrest and imprisonment of the then president of the association, Terence McSwiney. The 1916 conference was held in Belfast and the 1919 conference venue was Derry. An executive committee, chaired by a president who is elected annually, meets regularly and deals with the association's affairs between conferences, including meetings with relevant ministers, representatives of the state and local authorities. The day-to-day business is handled by a part-time secretary.

For further details on local government associations, see chapter 6.

4

Reform in Irish Local Government

Justin F. Keogan

As demonstrated by other chapters in this book, Irish local government is experiencing significant change. This is evident in its environment, its structure, its operations and to a lesser extent in its functions (see chapter 28). This chapter focuses on organisational and structural change and, following a brief history of previous attempts at reform, will concentrate on the set of reforms presented in *Better Local Government – A Programme for Change* (Department of the Environment, 1996).

History of Reform in Irish Local Government

The history and development of the Irish local government system is set out in chapter 2. The basic structure of local government in Ireland remained largely intact from its restructuring in 1898 after the Local Government (Ireland) Act until the late 1990s. The only notable changes were the widespread introduction of the management system in the 1940s and the abolition of domestic and agricultural rates in the late 1970s and early 1980s. However, before *Better Local Government*, there was a veritable industry at work reviewing the local government system and issuing recommendations for change.

Local Government Reorganisation – White Paper

The government published *Local Government Reorganisation – White Paper* in 1971. This was consistent with the trend for local government reviews in these islands at the time. The reports of the Redcliffe–Maud Commission (England), the Wheatley Commission (Scotland) and the MacRory Review Body (Northern Ireland) had been published prior to this. The 1971 White Paper advocated no real change in the services delivered or administered by local government. It favoured a single-tier system for the delivery of services, with the county to remain the basic unit of the local government system. It advocated the abolition of all town commissions and many of the urban district councils and recommended instead that area committees of county councils would be established to which local services could be delegated. The proposals had not been implemented when the government left office in 1973.

McKinsey Report

The McKinsey Report, *Strengthening the Local Government Service*, was also published in 1971. McKinsey and Company had been asked to review the staffing and management of the local authorities and to take account of the changes proposed by the White Paper. The McKinsey Report recommended a number of changes, some of which are echoed in *Better Local Government*.

It advocated the establishment of management posts under the county manager for each of the major services, thus integrating technical/professional and administrative responsibility for service delivery. It recommended the appointment of:

- a planning and development officer responsible for preparing county development plans and facilitating economic development
- a personnel and administrative officer responsible for recruitment, training and co-ordination of all administrative services
- a finance officer responsible for all financial and management accounting services and the development and installation of systems and programme budgeting approaches.

Under *Better Local Government*, the issue of a personnel and administrative officer has been addressed in the appointment of a director of corporate affairs and the probable professionalisation of the personnel officer post which was the subject of a study by PA Consulting for the Local Government Management Services Board. All local authorities have appointed a head of finance and implemented an accruals-based accounting system with the support of appropriate accounting information systems. This has been achieved almost thirty years after being proposed by the McKinsey Report.

There were no attempts at local government reform in the period from 1973 to 1985. Nevertheless, local government did go through one of the most significant changes since its inception with the abolition of domestic and agricultural rates. An attempt to alleviate the financial pressure on local government finances was made in the dark economic days of 1983 when the minister introduced a general power for local authorities to levy charges.

Reform of Local Government, A Policy Statement

In 1982, the government set up a Department of the Public Service. Public service reform was on the government's agenda and a policy paper, *Serving the Country Better* (Government of Ireland, 1985b) was published. As part of the public service modernisation programme, the government also issued *Reform of Local Government, A Policy Statement* (Government of Ireland, 1985a), which advocated: the consideration of a major devolution of functions, that every town with a population over 2,000 be granted an elected town council, that town commissions having a population of less than 2,000 be abolished and that a boundary commission be established. Only minor changes resulted from the policy statement including the redesignation of Galway City from a borough to a county borough (now city council) and the division of Dublin County into three county councils and the first steps towards a metropolitan council.

Barrington Report

The Advisory Expert Committee on Local Government Reorganisation and Reform, chaired by Tom Barrington, was appointed in 1990 and reported in 1991. The Barrington Report identified a number of problem areas for local government including:

- absence of reform. Although governments elsewhere in Europe had reformed their democratic institutions in response to demands for participation in the process of government, Ireland had not yet responded to this demand
- congestion at central government level. Central government was expending far too great an effort on operational rather than strategic issues, and was not responsive to local needs in any meaningful way. Local government was much better suited to operational matters of government
- lack of integration of public services at sub-national level
- very narrow range of local government functions
- absence of a local taxation system, which limits local discretion
- inhibited local stimulation of social, economic and cultural development due to central control and restricted functions
- no meaningful links between local authorities and local community groups
- limited role of councillors and the frustrations inherent in the system which prevented otherwise public-spirited people from becoming involved in local politics.

The principal recommendations of the Barrington Report included:

- constitutional recognition of local government
- devolution of functions to local authorities to include areas such as housing grants, group water schemes, driver testing, heritage and

amenity, standards and control of safety at work
- expansion of local government's role in education, health, community care, social welfare, transport and traffic, tourism, policing, courts and justice, consumer protection and social employment schemes
- establishment of eight regional authorities primarily for the co-ordination of public services
- at county level, boundary changes to facilitate certain urban areas
- division of Dublin County into three counties
- an option for either directly elected district councils or district committees of the county councils replacing the existing town authorities
- significant financial independence of local authorities from central revenue, having local taxation with accountability and a wide dispersal of liability
- abolition of the dual mandate
- establishment of a single representative body for local government in order to influence national decision making
- greater attention to the policy role of councillors
- modernisation of the law in relation to local government
- local authorities to be more responsive to the public
- staff development to be facilitated by exchanges with central government departments and other state bodies
- a substantial relaxation of the *ultra vires* rule
- making the post of manager subject to a ten-year contract
- press and public to be allowed to attend meetings of the council.

The Barrington Report was certainly more visionary than anything that went before it and represented the most comprehensive examination of local government since its establishment in 1898. Moreover, it heralded an era of change within local government with subsequent legislation delivering on some of its recommendations and it had a significant influence on *Better Local Government*.

Local Government Acts 1991, 1993 and 1994

In generally accepting the findings of the Barrington Report, the government enacted the Local Government Acts of 1991, 1993 and 1994, giving effect to a number of the recommendations. The provisions of the Acts can be summarised as:

- extending general competence to enable local authorities to act in the interest of their areas
- power to devolve functions from central to local level and to transfer powers between local authorities
- allowing the minister to dispense with statutory controls over local authorities where he or she considered it appropriate

- modernised and amended law in relation to committees and joint committees
- amended and updated law in relation to the alteration of boundaries
- greater powers were given to local authorities to make bye-laws without recourse to the minister
- reorganisation of Dublin County
- establishment of eight regional authorities
- county managers to be appointed on a fixed-term contract of seven years
- miscellaneous matters such as civic honours, twinning, payment of allowances and designation of functions to be reserved functions.

The legislative reaction to the Barrington Report was conservative, but it was a response that marked the beginning of a sustained change process.

A Flurry of Reports

The Fine Gael, Labour Party and Democratic Left coalition government that came to power in 1994 made a commitment in its programme for government, *A Government of Renewal*, to reform local government and to settle the finance question. In preparation, a number of reports were commissioned.

The Local Government Reorganisation Commission, set up by the previous (Fianna Fáil and Labour Party) coalition government, published a report in 1996 entitled *Towards Cohesive Local Government – Town and County*. The commission, prevented by its terms of reference from making recommendations on fundamental rationalisation or with financial implications, advocated:

- a single classification of town authorities, all to be titled town council with an office of mayor
- developing the role of town authorities in new directions with particular emphasis on representational, developmental and community-related aspects
- town authorities to be a key focus of civic and community leadership with an increased role in social and community development
- a joint town improvement programme to provide a framework for co-ordination and input by both town and county authorities
- at operational level, town and county authorities to have a joint staffing organisational structure subject to deployment by the city/county manager
- an increased linkage between town and county elected members, with a structured system of joint meetings
- joint (town/county) service centres through a merger of county council area offices with town authorities where possible
- the transfer of full responsibility for water services and certain regulatory environmental functions to county councils

- town authority involvement in local development and other community-related activities to be complemented by a structured linkage with local communities including joint meetings with representatives of appropriate local groups
- towns with population of 7,500 or more to be eligible for local authority status subject to appropriate procedures and rigorous assessment of need and demand.

Some of these recommendations were adopted as part of the *Better Local Government* process and will be expanded upon below.

A second report produced in 1996 was *The Financing of Local Government in Ireland* by KPMG. The report reviewed existing sources of finance and potential options for future funding. KPMG also carried out a review of local government financing in other countries. The report found that the system was too highly centralised, limited discretion, had too narrow a base and had no natural buoyancy. Having examined a number of options, the report concluded that service charges, a local property tax, a local income tax and domestic rates would be the preferred options for the future funding of local government. At the time of writing, none of these measures have been introduced. The report's findings and recommendations are discussed further in chapter 18.

The *Interim Report* of the Devolution Commission was also published in 1996. The commission was established in 1995 to make recommendations on functions to be devolved to local authorities, the policy role of local authorities, local authorities as a focus for local partnerships and the co-ordination of local authorities and local development bodies. It recommended that the local government and local development systems be integrated and simplified and that the development remit of local government be widened through a number of measures that would strengthen linkages between the two. *Better Local Government* addressed this issue (see chapter 16 for further details). The report also made a number of indicative suggestions for devolved functions similar to those in the Barrington Report. There followed some minimal devolution to local authorities in the areas of housing grants and sanitary services.

The Devolution Commission's *Second Report*, published in 1997, recommended the devolution of functions in the social, economic, development, environmental, infrastructural and transport services. It also recommended a mechanism for local authority input into national decision making similar to that enjoyed by the social partners. Government departments were requested to examine their operations with a view to identifying additional functions to devolve to local authorities and to involve them meaningfully with policy development and the administration of functions not devolved. Local government still awaits substantive devolution and meaningful engagement in national decision making on issues that affect local authorities.

Better Local Government: A Programme for Change

Better Local Government (BLG) has its origins in the wider public service reform programme: the Strategic Management Initiative (SMI). SMI was promoted as being different from other reform attempts of the civil service due to the fact that it was largely driven by the civil servants themselves. BLG also emanated from the civil service, a product of the then Department of the Environment, with little input from the local authorities.

The aspiration behind BLG was that it would give local authorities the chance to reassert themselves as the local discussion forum and be the origin of local action. It is a comprehensive effort at local government reform and is at times more radical than its parent, SMI. Much of BLG is consistent with, and was probably borrowed from, Barrington and subsequent reports. It contains four core principles or pillars on which a series of proposed changes are founded:

- enhancing local democracy
- serving the customer better
- developing efficiency
- providing proper resources for local authorities.

Enhancing Local Democracy

BLG seeks to enhance local democracy through a number of measures including constitutional recognition, strengthening the role of the councillor, reorganising the committee system and including local interests relevant to the committees' work. In 1999, a referendum was held to provide for constitutional recognition of local government. The extent of debate on the issue was minimal. The amendment was voted into the Constitution (for text see appendix 2). Accordingly, local government now has constitutional recognition, but, unlike the constitutional instruments of some other European countries, there is no guarantee of functions or power. The principal contribution of the amendment is that it prevents the deferral of local elections as happened in the past.

Another promised measure to enhance local democracy was Ireland's ratification of the European Charter for Local Self-Government in 1997. The charter, an international treaty of the Council of Europe, sets out principles to underpin local government in Europe. Ireland signed the charter in 1997 and ratified it in 2002. A rapporteur from the Council was appointed in 2001 to review Ireland's progress towards adherence to the principles laid out in the charter. While the report welcomes the many developments that were taking place in Irish local government, it recommends that:

- the role of Irish local government be increased, especially in the areas of health, education, economic development and social matters

- local government in Ireland become more financially independent
- consideration be given to direct election to council vacancies rather than co-option
- the proposed position of directly elected cathaoirleach/mayor be given greater executive function than envisaged
- the political and policy-making role of elected members be strengthened in general
- councillors be salaried and resourced
- a more balanced representation be achieved through support structures to provide for greater representation for women, youth and wage-earners
- the possibility of holding a dual mandate be restricted
- a greater balance of power be established in the relationship between the manager and the elected members in favour of the elected members
- the strategic policy committees do not take over the decision-making role of the elected council
- the Irish parliament explicitly accepts and recognises the concept of the principle of subsidiarity.

Two features of BLG that were to be central to enhancing local democracy were widening the remit of local government and strengthening the position of the councillor. The integration of the local government and local development systems was one of the mechanisms used to broaden the remit.

The introduction of strategic policy committees (SPCs) and corporate policy groups was designed to enhance the role of councillors. It was felt that councillors should be more involved in policy making and in order to develop this policy role, a radical overhaul of the committee system was instituted and the SPCs were established. The provisions (Department of the Environment and Local Government, 1997) for establishing the SPCs include:

- each county and city council is required to establish SPCs mirroring the major functions of the local authority
- the number of SPCs is to be tailored to the size of the local authority
- each SPC is to be supported by a director of services for the relevant service, operating under the general direction of the committee and arranging for the submission of policy review papers on the service(s) in question
- SPCs are to identify particular policy areas for special consideration and to report to the full council on necessary changes
- SPCs are to meet at least quarterly and submit a written report to the full council, with the chairperson to present the report to the council
- local people (or rather organised groups) are to be involved in relevant committees as they are seen as a potential major resource available to

councillors in carrying out their functions. To promote local participation and draw on the expertise of the various sectors, not less than one-third of the members of SPCs are to be drawn from bodies relevant to the committee's work.

The cathaoirleach of the local authority and the chairpersons of the SPCs form the corporate policy group (CPG) and it was envisaged that this group would have a key function in developing a wider role for councillors. This group links the work of the different SPCs, acts as a sort of cabinet and provides a forum where policy positions can be agreed for submission to the full council. The CPG is also responsible for overseeing the preparation of corporate plans (provided for under the Local Government Act, 2001); monitoring performance of the authority, overall and in specific areas such as customer service; and preparing the annual budget.

In order that councillors could ensure that policies are translated into the effective delivery of services, the development of area committees of the council was recommended (Department of the Environment and Local Government, 1999c). In some cases these were already in existence.

Strategic policy committees and corporate policy groups have been established in all county and city councils. In some local authorities the process has progressed very quickly, while in others it has yet to take root. The potential of the SPCs for handling difficult and contentious issues has been recognised. This can be built upon, making the SPCs the central policy-making instruments of the local authorities. Ultimately the success of the SPCs will depend on the commitment of the councillors and officials. The evidence, if only in terms of attendance, is not altogether encouraging in all local authorities and in 2003 the department commissioned a review of the operation of SPCs.

There has been some criticism of BLG's proposals to enhance the role of the councillor. There has been no change in the balance between reserved and executive functions. Councillors have not been given additional powers and some would argue that their influence has been diluted. It has been suggested that the involvement of interest groups on the SPCs detracts from the direct involvement or influence of directly elected people as representatives in the deliberative process and transfers some of this power and influence to others whose accountability to the public is at best ambiguous and at worst absent.

Serving the Customer Better

The second pillar of BLG involves improving the quality of service. The main areas of activity include:

- quality initiatives to be undertaken by local authorities
- participation in quality award schemes

- performance indicators to be developed for local authority activities
- efforts to be made to establish one-stop-shops for local government services
- promotion of the public's right to information and the general public to have the legal right to attend council meetings.

In preparation for this, customer action plans were drawn up by each local authority with measures relating to the following:

- quality service standards
- equality/diversity
- physical access
- information
- timeliness and courtesy
- complaints
- appeals
- consultation and evaluation
- choice
- official languages equality
- better co-ordination
- internal customer (staff).

Progress has been made and local authorities are more aware of their clients and customers than they had been previously. Significant efforts have been made to upgrade public service areas within local authorities, staff have received training and methods of communication have improved with proactive rather than reactive approaches being adopted. Local authorities engage with the public through consultation (more than is required by legislation) and many local authorities have tried to offer multiple methods for service delivery. A significant number of local authorities have developed one-stop-shops and more are on the way. More progress should be made when service level indicators are introduced and divisions are restructured within local authorities in order to configure them more closely to service delivery.

Developing Efficiency

The third pillar of BLG involves the achievement of greater value for money or efficiency through measures such as corporate planning, reorganisation of personnel and structures and the introduction of systems to improve decision making by management.

The local authorities were charged with the production of corporate plans, provision for which is made in the Local Government Act, 2001. The Act (section 134) states that the corporate plan shall include:

- a statement of the principal activities of the local authority
- the objectives and priorities for each of the principal activities and strategies for achieving those objectives
- the manner in which the authority proposes to assess its performance in respect of each such activity, taking account of relevant service indicators and of the need to work towards best practice in service delivery and in the general operation of the local authority

- human resources activities (including training and development) to be undertaken for the staff of the local authority and, where appropriate, for the elected council
- the organisational structure of the local authority, both elected council and staff, including corporate support and information technology and the improvements proposed to promote efficiency of operation and customer service and in general to support the corporate plan
- a recognition by the local authority of such policies and objectives in relation to any of its functional programmes as are set out in any other plan, statement, strategy or other document prepared by it.

The introduction of strategic planning to local government, through the corporate plans, is a significant development and has the potential to result in extensive changes to the way local authorities approach their business. This author reviewed the corporate plans of the local authorities for the period from 2001 to 2004 using a set of criteria that included the quality of environmental analysis, specificity in performance measurement and level of focus on citizens and clients. A deficiency in any of these areas will at best delay, or at worst prevent, effective implementation. The quality of the corporate plans varied considerably. Some local authorities have grasped the opportunity of the corporate planning process with full vigour. However, many plans suffer shortcomings of sufficient magnitude to impair their potential for implementation.

The environmental analysis in the majority of corporate plans was not sufficiently rigorous for operational purposes. Many local authorities simply outlined elements (such as legislative change, demographics and economic activity) in their environment and failed to link the relevant factors or developments to the pursuit of their goals and objectives, to how they would act as facilitators and barriers and so forth.

Many plans failed to state the internal changes (staff, resources, processes) that would be needed to achieve their goals and objectives and in some cases there is no evidence of the local authority having given consideration to the organisation's ability to deliver the plan. The treatment of performance measurement varied significantly: some plans failed to address this issue, while some included well-developed performance measurement frameworks. However, most local authorities were poor at articulating outputs and outcomes, which are essential to any performance measurement framework.

One of the areas where local authorities perform well is in their focus on the citizen and on their clients. Local authorities have always been superior to their civil service cousins at recognising the importance of their clients (Keogan and McKevitt, 1999), and especially the citizen, in their corporate planning. This may be explained by the fact that policy and decision making takes place much closer to the level of delivery, and therefore the citizen, in local government than it does in central government departments and offices.

Turning to the reorganisation of personnel and structures, measures under the Local Government Act, 2001 include:

- the devolution of decisions on personnel matters to local authorities
- an increase in the level of resources devoted to staff training and development
- the creation of a new management structure to facilitate the development of a capacity for policy
- the multiplicity of clerical and administrative grades and separate professional administrative structures to be simplified and the dual structure to be abolished
- more open recruitment for local authority positions.

The Local Government Act, 2001 effectively removes the role of the minister in relation to local authority personnel matters. It removes the distinction between officers and non-officers in the local authorities: all become employees of the local authorities and subject to the normal employment and industrial relations legislation. However, the department still retains considerable influence in the area either directly or indirectly through the control of resources.

There were also proposals to strengthen the human resources function, to examine recruitment practices and to develop flexible working relationships within local government. As part of this, it is proposed that the posts of personnel officer and training officer be professionalised. The assessment of training and development needs and the identification of suitable training providers was recognised as a priority area for the Local Government Management Services Board. Investment in staff training should be at least 3 per cent of payroll cost.

Under the BLG reform process, a considerable number of staff have been moved within the system and there are concerns that institutional memory will suffer. However, others point to the opportunity to clear institutional baggage and the fact that internal promotions offer some continuity.

Views on the abolition of the dual structure differ. Many suggest that it is still very much in existence and that it will take years of cultural change to provide for easy working relationships between technical/professional and administrative staff. The new management structure involves a new tier, directors of services, over functional areas such as roads, environment, corporate affairs and so forth. The new posts provide policy support to the SPCs and allow local authority managers to concentrate on strategic issues. The posts were primarily constructed in order to provide a focus on service delivery rather than on process and procedure, the traditional concern of administrators.

Providing Proper Resources for Local Authorities

The fourth pillar of BLG involves the provision of proper resources for local authorities. It acknowledges that local authorities were without funds to respond to worthwhile community projects and were finding it increasingly difficult to maintain services at acceptable levels. It states that a locally available, independent and buoyant source of finance is vital in the renewal process.

Taking into consideration the various options put forward in the study carried out by KPMG in 1996, the government opted for a new local revenue system to replace the rate support grant and the revenues generated from charges for domestic water and sewerage facilities. From 1 January 1997, the full proceeds of motor taxation became a dedicated local government revenue source. However, the basic rates were set nationally and after a short period of allowing local authorities to vary this revenue source within limits, this flexibility was abolished.

The Local Government (Financial Provisions) Act, 1997 abolished charges for water and sewerage services to domestic users. These were services which the local authorities were having particular difficulty in meeting due to considerable investment in new and upgraded plants designed to provide better services. While the Act went against the spirit of BLG in abolishing certain charges, it also gave effect to elements of the new financing system by assigning the proceeds of motor tax to local authorities with provision for equalisation of financial resources between local authorities and giving statutory effect to value-for-money auditing in local authorities.

Local Government Act, 2001

An important element of BLG was the modernisation and consolidation of local government law. The Local Government Act was finally passed and signed in July 2001. The central aims of the Act are to:

- enhance the role of the elected member
- support the involvement of local interests in local authority policy making
- modernise local government legislation
- underpin generally the programme of local government renewal.

More specifically, the Act makes provisions for:

- renaming local authorities as county councils, city councils, town councils and, in some cases, borough councils
- a revision of the election process and the direct election of a cathaoirleach/mayor in county and city councils in 2004
- general, ceremonial and other functions for a local authority

- more flexible arrangements for joint service provision between local authorities
- a formalised strategic management process in local authorities which requires a corporate plan to be produced for the life of the council
- a general ethics framework for staff and elected members
- new rights of media and public access to local authority meetings
- the establishment of an independent local government commission to deal with boundary changes and electoral reviews
- other provisions relating to the new financial management framework, operational procedures, local government audit and the making of bye-laws.

The Act emphasises the policy-determining role of councillors and the inclusion of the legislative basis for the strategic policy committees and the corporate policy group gives this emphasis effect.

Two provisions in the Local Government Bill that received considerable attention before being amended and passed were those relating to the payment of councillors and the dual mandate. The then minister stated a preference for not paying local public representatives two representational payments should they hold two representative positions. Therefore, in the same way as the preference for not paying councillors who held two representative positions at local authority level (county and town councils) had been held, so the same applies to members of the Oireachtas. Representational payments were introduced in 2002 (see chapter 6). The Department of the Environment and Local Government paid them for the first year but charged the local authorities with funding them thereafter.

An original provision of the Bill was the disqualification of members of the Oireachtas from local authority membership. Due to pressure from government backbenchers and independent deputies, the minister removed the proposed bar on the dual mandate. However, the Local Government (No. 2) Act, 2003 abolishes the dual mandate, disqualifying Oireachtas members from membership of a local authority from the 2004 local elections onwards. It also repeals the provisions of the Local Government Act, 2001, which provided for the introduction in 2004 of the direct election of county/city cathaoirligh.

Unfinished Business

Irish local government has been the subject of considerable change over recent years. But, as Edmund Burke stated, change does not equal reform. For change to be regarded as reform, it must result in something better than before: it must result in improvement. Irish local government still has a number of issues to address including: the competency of management to manage better, developing an in-depth understanding of outputs and outcomes, achieving a greater definition between what the local authority provides as an agent of central government and what it does in response to its local mandate, increasing the flexibility of staff resources, creating a voice for local government which seeks to develop and support local autonomy, and the promotion of co-operation between local authorities. Many other issues to be addressed are considered in other chapters of this book.

Local authorities have spent considerable time and effort responding to Better Local Government. However, for local government to be genuinely reformed, a devolution of substantial functions and decision-making powers would have to take place, and an independent source of finance would have to be granted in order to guarantee greater local discretion. In order to resolve these two issues, there needs to be a genuine commitment to the process by the principal actors, especially the central government departments.

In its attempts at reforming the civil service and state agencies, the SMI tinkered with the existing system rather than looking at the system *de novo* or from a first principles basis. The various programmes of the SMI – strategy statements, quality customer service, value for money, new financial management systems, performance measurement, and information technology systems – have been superimposed on existing operations and structures. These changes have not led to less congestion in the civil service; indeed they may in fact have led to more congestion. In the majority of cases, they have not radically changed delivery methods or led to the better co-ordination of services at the local level. In essence, departments and offices of state are still overly concerned with operational rather than strategic issues.

The opportunity to resolve these issues lies in meaningful devolution to local government both of function and, where possible, decision making. Since local authorities already offer devolved central government services such as the administration of higher education grants, the administration of the national roads scheme and the collection of motor tax, why is there a need for parallel localised services such as district veterinary offices and social welfare offices? If it does not play an important role in services such as health, social welfare, policing and education, the importance of the local government system diminishes in the public eye. To date no devolution of substantial functions has taken place.

Local government finance is the litmus test for central government's commitment to local government. Since domestic rates were abolished in 1977, successive governments have failed to address the resulting shortfalls. In the meantime, local authorities are charged with meeting commitments agreed at national level such as the payment of councillors and benchmarking.

5

Local Elections

Peter Greene

Article 28A of the Constitution requires that elections for membership of local authorities are held no later than the end of the fifth year after the year in which they were last held (see appendix 2). This provision was approved in a referendum on 11 June 1999. The law governing the conduct of local elections is set out in part 4 of the Local Government Act, 2001 and the Local Elections Regulations, 1995 (SI No. 297 of 1995). The law relating to the questioning of a local election result by means of an election petition is contained in the Local Elections (Petitions and Disqualifications) Act, 1974.

Local government electors vote for councillors by secret ballot on the principle of proportional representation using the single transferable vote. A local government elector is any person, irrespective of nationality, entered in the register of electors. A person must be at least eighteen years old and be ordinarily resident in a local electoral area in order to be entered on the register. Each county and city council compiles a register of electors annually for its administrative area.

Subject to certain disqualifications outlined below, any citizen of Ireland (whether or not he or she is resident in the state) and any other person ordinarily resident in the state who is at least eighteen years old is eligible for election or co-option to and membership of a local authority.

Frequency of Local Elections

Prior to 1953, local elections were held triennially. Since then, the law provides for the holding of local elections every fifth year. However, due to a variety of factors, local elections have been postponed on fifteen occasions since 1923.

Between 1973 and 1994, local elections could be postponed by order of the minister; such an order did not come into operation unless and until a copy of the order had been laid before both Houses of the Oireachtas and the order had been confirmed by resolution of each House. Local elections were postponed by such orders in 1984 and 1990. The Local Government Act, 1994 repealed this provision and reverted to the provision that applied prior to 1973, whereby amending legislation was required to effect a postponement of local elections.

However, the 1999 constitutional amendment referred to above now guarantees the maximum interval between elections. Under the Local Government Act, 2001, local elections are to be held in 2004 and in every fifth year thereafter; they are held in the month of May or June on a day fixed by order of the minister. The 1999 local elections were held on 11 June, along with elections to the European Parliament and the referendum to afford constitutional recognition to local government.

Local Electoral Areas

The administrative area of a county, city, borough or town may be divided into local electoral areas by order of the minister under section 23 of the Local Government Act, 2001. Such an order may also fix the number of members of the relevant local authority to be elected for each electoral area. A local electoral area is a constituency for the purposes of an election to a local authority and every county and city is divided into a number of such areas from three to thirteen.

Of the town authorities, only Bray, Drogheda, Dundalk and Sligo are divided into local electoral areas; each of the others constitutes a single electoral area for the purpose of local elections. At local elections, the residents of a town exercise two votes – one for the election of the town/borough council and the other for the county council.

Before deciding whether to make an order dividing the administrative area of a local authority into electoral areas, the minister is required to request a boundary committee to make recommendations relating to such a division. Two boundary committees were established in February 1998 to prepare, respectively, reports on the division into local electoral areas of local authorities in the Dublin area and local authorities outside Dublin. The committees furnished their reports in June 1998. The recommendations of both committees were accepted, implemented by orders of the minister and applied for the local elections held in June 1999. In 1999, a total of 266 separate elections for 268 local electoral areas elected 1,627 members to 114 local authorities (a poll was not necessary in two areas).

An independent local government commission is provided for under the Local Government Act, 2001 to replace the former boundary committees and to make recommendations on a range of matters including local electoral areas and the number of members assigned to each. It is also open to a county or city council to make application to the minister, following public consultation, for an alteration in the total membership of that authority. Town councils of 15,000 population upwards may likewise seek an increase from nine to twelve members. Before altering the total number of members of a local authority, its local electoral areas or the numbers assigned to them, the minister must request a report from the commission which must be published. The relevant statutory order must set out reasons in the event of any material variation from the local electoral areas as recommended.

Reviews of local electoral areas before the 1999 and 1985 local elections took account, *inter alia*, of significant population change between local electoral areas within the same county or city. There is no constitutional or statutory requirement as regards councillor:population ratios between different counties and cities – in fact these vary quite significantly. The total number of members of each county council and city council is fixed by schedule 7 to the Local Government Act, 2001 (see also appendix 3).

Disqualifications

Under sections 12 and 13 of the Local Government Act, 2001 a person is disqualified from membership of a local authority if he or she:

- is under eighteen years of age
- is a member of the European Commission or a member of the European Parliament
- is a judge, advocate general or registrar of the European Court of Justice
- is a member of the EU's Court of Auditors
- is a government minister or a minister of state
- is the chairperson of Dáil Éireann (ceann comhairle) or the cathaoirleach of Seanad Éireann
- is appointed under the Constitution as a judge or as comptroller and auditor general
- is a member of An Garda Síochána or a wholetime member of the permanent Defence Forces as defined in section 11(4) of the Electoral Act, 1992
- is a civil servant who is not by the terms of his/her employment expressly permitted to be a member of a local authority
- is employed by a local authority (certain grades are, however, exempted from this disqualification [section 161 of Local Government Act, 2001])
- is undergoing a sentence of imprisonment for any term exceeding six months imposed by a court of competent jurisdiction in the state
- has not paid any part of any sum due by him or her under a charge or surcharge made by a local government auditor

- fails to comply with a final judgment, order or decree of a court of competent jurisdiction for payment of money due to a local authority
- is convicted of, or has had a conviction confirmed on appeal for, an offence relating to fraudulent or dishonest dealings affecting a local authority or an offence relating to corrupt practice or acting when disqualified.

While dual membership of town and county councils is common (19 per cent of county councillors), simultaneous membership of more than one county, one city or one town council is not permitted (section 14, Local Government Act, 2001). Up until 2004, councillors who were members of either House of the Oireachtas were also disqualified from the post of cathaoirleach and leas-chathaoirleach (or mayor and deputy mayor, as the case may be) of a local authority. Under the Local Government (No. 2) Act, 2003 the dual mandate was abolished entirely, so that any member of the Dáil or Seanad is ineligible to be a member of a local authority (see chapter 6).

Procedure at Elections

Candidates at a local election may nominate themselves or consent to be nominated by a proposer, who must be a local government elector in the area of the relevant local authority. A non-party candidate is required to have his or her nomination form assented to by fifteen electors from the local electoral area (section 3, Electoral (Amendment) Act, 2002). The name of the political party, if any, which a candidate represents may be included together with that political party's emblem alongside the name of the candidate on the ballot paper/screen for voting. A photograph of a candidate may also be included.

Polling takes place on the same day throughout the country, but a returning officer may arrange for advance polling on the islands if he or she considers it necessary due to weather or transport difficulties. Postal voting applies at local elections on the same basis as at other national elections and at referenda. Similarly, special voting arrangements are made for voters resident in hospitals and similar institutions who cannot vote at their local polling station due to physical illness or disability.

The single transferable vote system is based on the principle of an electoral quota. The quota is the number of votes necessary to secure the election of a candidate and is calculated in such a way that it can be obtained by the number of candidates to be elected but not by more than that number. The quota is determined by dividing the total number of valid ballot papers by one more than the number of seats to be filled, and adding one to the result, disregarding any fraction that may arise.

Each elector has a single vote which is capable of being used to rank the candidates in the order of the elector's choice by marking the ballot paper 1, 2, 3 and so on. The vote is credited in the first instance to the elector's first choice. If that candidate does not need the vote, because he or she has obtained the quota of votes necessary for election or has so few votes that he or she has no possibility of election and is excluded, the vote is transferred to the elector's second choice and so on. In the 2002 general election, electronic voting was piloted in a number of Dáil constituencies. Electronic voting is due to be extended to all parts of the country for the 2004 local elections.

Any candidate who receives the necessary quota of votes is elected. If a candidate receives votes in excess of the quota, the surplus is transferred to the continuing candidates in accordance with the next choice indicated by the electors concerned. If, at the end of any count, no candidate receives the necessary quota of votes, the candidate(s) with the lowest number of votes is/are eliminated and the votes are transferred to the continuing candidates in accordance with the next preference of the electors concerned. This process continues until the necessary number of candidates is elected. Candidates can be elected to fill the last seats without reaching the quota where it is clear that they would be elected if the count continued.

Table 5.1 displays the percentage voter turnouts at local elections from 1967 to 1999. For details of the voter turnout in individual counties, cities and towns, see appendix 7.

Table 5.1 Voter Turnout at Local Elections, 1967 to 1999

Local authority	*% turnout*						
	1967	*1974*	*1979*	*1985*	*1991**	*1994***	*1999*
County councils	72	68	67	63	58	–	53
Dublin City Council	52	40	48	43	43	–	35
Other city councils	67	57	59	51	54	–	46
Borough and town councils (including former urban district councils)	69	65	64	62	–	59	54
Other town councils (including former town commissioners)	73	70	70	66	–	56	52
Average for all local authorities	67	62	64	60	56	59	51

*   elections were held in 1991 to county and city councils only
** elections were held in 1994 to borough and town councils only

Source: Department of the Environment and Local Government (2000e, vol. 1, p. vii)

Disclosures of Donations and Election Expenditure

Candidates at a local election are required to provide a statement of election expenses and donations received over a specified limit within ninety days from polling day in accordance with the Local Elections (Disclosure of Donation and Expenditure) Act, 1999. The donation limit for disclosure purposes is €634.87. The 1999 Act, as amended by the Electoral (Amendment) Act, 2001, provides that a candidate at a local election is required to open and maintain an account in a financial institution in the state if he or she receives a donation for a political purpose in any particular calendar year which exceeds €126.97. The Act provides that a candidate is a person who, on or before the date of the making of the order appointing polling day in relation to the local election, is declared by himself or herself or by others to be a candidate at the elections. A maximum limit of €2,539.48 on a political donation from any one source in any one year operates and there is a prohibition on accepting certain foreign donations and anonymous donations over €126.97.

Term of Office of Members of Local Authorities

Newly elected members of a local authority take up office when the outgoing members of the authority retire on the seventh day after polling day. Each member remains in office until the day fixed for the retirement of members after the next election, unless he or she dies, resigns or becomes disqualified in the meantime.

A casual vacancy caused by the death, resignation or disqualification of a member of a local authority is filled by co-option by the authority concerned. A co-opted member retires in the same way as other elected members of the authority. Co-option was introduced by the Local Government (Ireland) Act, 1898. Section 19 of the Local Government Act, 2001 provides that the co-optee must be a member of the same party as that for which the person causing the vacancy was elected. Where the person causing the casual vacancy was a non-party member, the vacancy is filled in accordance with standing orders.

6

Local Government and Politics

Liam Kenny

Commentaries on Irish local government tend to concentrate on the legal, operational and service-delivery facets of the units within the system. There has been comparatively little attention focused on the fact that the policy-making leaderships of local authorities consist of individuals who have come through a democratic electoral process and are therefore involved to a greater or lesser degree in a political environment.

Indeed, with some valuable exceptions, there has been little recent study of the factors that influence political activity at local government level.[1] This is all the more regrettable given that the individuals in question, the elected members or councillors, make decisions and shape policies which impact on every household and business enterprise in the country. But who are these occupants of the seats of local power in county council chambers, city halls and town halls, and what is their linkage with the currents and trends of the national political process?

Councillors – Local Activists or Foot Soldiers for the Political Parties?

Taken as a whole, the memberships of the local authorities could be characterised as a kind of standing army of supporters for the main political parties. The thirty-four local authorities at county and city level have a combined total of 883 seats. To give an illustration of the value of this political reserve force available to the parties, it is worth looking at the breakdown of this 883 component among the larger parties. Following the local government elections of June 1999, Fianna Fáil

---

[1] Collins (1987) presents an impressively comprehensive picture of council chamber dynamics and a number of articles such as Zimmerman (1976) and Carey (1986) provide valuable analysis of the role of councillors.

accounted for 382 councillors, a further 277 were Fine Gael members and Labour accounted for 83.[2] A more detailed breakdown appears in table 6.1.

Table 6.1 Party Shares of Seats in County and City Councils, 1999

Party	No. of seats	As % of 883
Fianna Fáil	382	43
Fine Gael	277	31
Labour Party	83	9
Progressive Democrats	25	3
Workers Party	3	1
Green Party	8	1
Sinn Féin	21	2
Non-party	81	9
Other	3	1

Source: Kenny (1999, p. 14)

At town level, Fianna Fáil account for 289 councillors, Fine Gael for 159 and Labour for 87 out of a total of 744 seats in eighty town councils (see table 6.2).

Table 6.2 Party Shares of Seats in Town Councils, 1999

Party	No. of seats	As % of 774
Fianna Fáil	289	39
Fine Gael	159	21
Labour Party	87	12
Progressive Democrats	7	1
Workers Party	0	0
Green Party	5	1
Sinn Féin	40	5
Non-party	156	21
Other	1	0

Source: Kenny (1999, p. 151)

---

[2] Unless otherwise stated, all statistics in this chapter are derived from Kenny (1999).

Again, like any reserve force, party headquarters may pay little enough attention to the routine activities of the local members but are happy to mobilise them at times of crisis – and at election time when the local councillors become directors of election, canvassers and poster-erectors (although, of course, many non-elected activists in parties also take on similar tasks).

Gallagher (1989, p. 28) and Coakley (2001, p. 86), in comparing national and local elections in Ireland, observe that non-party/independent candidates and minor parties tend to do better at local elections than at national elections. Coakley remarks that this is not so surprising, as 'it is precisely at local level that one expects non-party and local party candidates to make the biggest impact'. Non-party candidates seem to do particularly well in elections to town councils (this may be because town councils are generally nine-seat constituencies, which can make it easier to get elected).

Although eighty-one independents were elected among the 1999 to 2004 cohort of county and city councillors, when one discounts those who are perhaps temporarily disgruntled members of political parties but still support that party in voting situations, the number of 'true' independents is much lower. It is also the case that most independents find themselves engaged in the uncompromisingly political process of supporting candidates for chairs and committees within newly elected councils and therefore become blooded to the machinations of politics although not carrying any specific party label.

Party Loyalties and Council Chamber Realities

It is important to consider councillors with regard to two distinct but related meanings of the word 'politics': what might be called the macro level of councillors and their affiliation to political parties and the micro level of the negotiation, compromise and brokering needed within council chambers so as to secure support for sought-after positions and memberships of influential committees.

It is a common sentiment uttered among councillors, especially at the final pre-election meetings of outgoing councils, that 'there is no politics in this authority – we only speak for the good of the locality'. This is certainly true when councillors unite to protest to some agency outside of the area at some perceived neglect of their locality. For example, there will be cross-party unity on deputations to ministers for more grant aid for local projects. Equally, there will be cross-party agreement on protests against conservation organisations that object to what are perceived locally to be desirable planning applications.[3] In most of these cases there is a threat to the locality from an external source – the

---

[3] See, for example, 'Council calls on Government to abolish An Taisce', *Sligo Champion*, 12 December 2001.

fact that it is external allows parties latitude to ignore political differences and construct a populist show of unity.

However, apply the 'no politics here' assumption to the dynamics within the council chamber and a very different picture emerges. This is most vividly seen in the weeks after a local election when the bargaining for control of major positions and committees reaches a level of intensity matching anything to be found in the proverbial Tammany Hall. Coalitions and alliances are formed of a complexity and variety seldom experienced at national government level. The patchwork of committees, largely unknown to the public, to which county and city councils make nominations provides ample ground for contention between individual council members.

The major prize is the mayoralty or chair of the local authority, followed by the chairs of subsidiary committees and then membership of outside bodies to which the local authority has nominating rights. All give councillors an opportunity to extend their legitimate range of influence and most provide an extra income by way of expenses and allowances to supplement the modest income from holding a council seat.

Occasionally, politics arises at the macro level within council chambers over policy positions based on a party's deep-seated political convictions or on a more pragmatic assessment of public acceptability of a given course of action. For example, during the 1990s the controversies over service charges, particularly in urban areas, saw left-wing ideological arguments at the fore. No less important was a political assessment by the major party of the likely reaction of the electorate. These forces combined, no doubt, to create a situation where Ireland became the only EU nation not to have a charge for domestic water supply.

The complex interaction of macro and micro political influences becomes particularly fascinating when policy issues and the internal chamber politics become intertwined, with one party offering another support for a particular policy position on the basis of its members being granted access to various positions of influence. This was visible for example in Sligo Borough Council in December 2001 and January 2002. A pact arrangement between Fianna Fáil and Sinn Féin broke down over the acceptability of a major increase in the household refuse charge. Attempts by Fianna Fáil to reach an alternative agreement with Fine Gael proved highly problematic when the latter demanded the mayoralty for the two remaining years of the council. The intractability of the political impasse was such that the councillors held a meeting on 26 December in an attempt to find a resolution before ministerial intervention removed them from office – council chamber politics at its most intense and probably the most unusual date on which a public body has ever held a meeting.[4]

---

[4] *Sligo Champion,* 2 January 2002.

It is therefore clear that there are two strong currents of politics which intermingle within the council chamber: the councillor's affiliation to his or her national party and its policies, and the equally potent current of practical interpersonal relationships within the body of the council. It is this dual context that can profitably be borne in mind when analysing in more detail the factors which shape the composition, concerns and impacts of the cohort of councillors.

Trends in the Electorate

The ultimate basis of all political activity is of course the public from whom all councillors and parliamentarians receive their mandate. Since the foundation of the state, local government elections were held at five-yearly intervals except at times of national emergency. However, even this interrupted pattern began to break down from the 1960s onwards when election intervals extended to periods as long as eight and nine years (for example 1985 to 1994 for urban councils and 1991 to 1999 for county authorities). The severe decline in voter participation over the same period cannot therefore be attributed to electoral fatigue. This decline began quite sharply, with the 1974 elections recording a drop of 5 per cent on the previous local poll in 1967. There was a slight rally in 1979 but decreases in each of the following three elections to 1999 reduced turnout to 51 per cent of the electorate (see table 6.3). Taken together these decreases reflect a decline approaching 20 per cent over a period of thirty-two years; in other words, in the space of one generation public participation at local government elections declined by one-fifth.

Table 6.3 Voter Turnout at Local Elections, 1967 to 1999

Year	1967	1974	1979	1985	1991	1994	1999
% turnout	67	62	64	60	56	59	51

Source: Department of the Environment and Local Government (2000e, vol. 1, p. vii)

A detailed investigation of the factors behind such a decline is beyond the scope of this chapter but some considerations need to be outlined. It should be noted that there has been a noticeable increase in voter apathy at all levels of election. For Dáil elections over a comparable period (1969 to 1997) the turnout fell from 76 per cent to 65 per cent (Donnelly, 1998, p. 5). This represents a significant deterioration in participation for national parliament elections, but it is still much healthier, both in absolute and proportionate terms, than the local government election trend within a similar timeframe. Gallagher (1989, pp. 28–9) observes that a lower turnout at local elections compared to national elections is common to most countries.

Further pointers to the reasons for diminishing voter participation can be identified through a regional analysis of the declining figures. It is broadly true to say that turnout in the 1999 local government elections was at its highest in rural areas of the north midlands and the west and at its lowest in cities and suburban counties (see appendix 7). The ten electoral areas (out of 180 county electoral areas in the state) with the highest turnouts were in Leitrim and adjoining counties (all over 70 per cent); the ten electoral areas with the lowest turnouts (all less than 33 per cent) were in Dublin City and neighbouring suburban districts.

Three distinct factors can be interpreted from even this preliminary analysis. First, electoral areas with small populations have much better turnouts than more populated areas. Second, there was a strong west–east downward gradient in terms of turnout. A tentative explanation for this phenomenon may lie in the high profile campaigns in the Connacht-Ulster constituency for the 1999 European Parliament elections which were held on the same day as the local government elections. Third, there was nonetheless a marked urban–rural division, with voters in Galway and Cork Cities for example polling at least 10 per cent less than their county counterparts. However, the fact that an area was a rural area did not prevent weaker polling; for example some rural areas in Louth and Wexford had less than 50 per cent turnout.

It is plausible to suggest that the differences are due to the western rural constituencies having an older and more settled electorate compared to the younger and more restless populations in the cities and suburbs. Equally, anecdotal evidence would suggest that there is a class factor, visible particularly in the city areas but quite possibly also underpinning the higher rural turnouts. Compare a 41 per cent poll for coastal Clontarf with just 34 per cent for neighbouring Donaghmede in the Dublin City area or, in the case of Fingal County, 40 per cent for maritime Malahide contrasting with 30 per cent for Mulhuddart in the newly residential west of the county, and the impression that class is a factor becomes more solid.

Smaller populated electoral areas in rural areas, a tradition of farmer involvement in politics and a sense of alienation from the system in marginalised communities in the cities may all explain the quite major variations in the turnout. But whatever the reasons behind the decline in turnout in recent decades and their local composition, concerns have to be raised over any system which delivers a turnout of barely 50 per cent with, in some districts, less than 35 per cent of the electorate choosing to exercise their franchise.

Candidates

The political system depends on people willing to put themselves before the electorate so as to contest elections. It is a tribute to the enthusiasm of the section of the Irish population most committed to the democratic process that there is still a healthy pool of candidates willing to contest local elections, despite the pervasiveness of apathy among the wider electorate as outlined above. However, the number of candidates who contested the 1999 local elections at 1,838 was 135 less than the previous elections of 1991 – a decline of 7 per cent. And it is certainly likely that the drop in candidates may reflect the difficulties in finding people willing to put themselves through the rigours of the electoral contest. However, it is also possible that the decline in the number of candidates reflects more efficient election strategies of party organisers – a factor in the case of the Progressive Democrats fielding exactly half the number of candidates in 1999 in comparison to 1991.

What is surprising is that the number of non-party candidates who declared in 1999 was down by thirty on the contest eight years previously. The drop in non-party/independent candidates was unexpected, given that protest-based politics have become a feature of the local political rhetoric. If claims made by local groups protesting against plans for incinerators, halting sites or motorways to run candidates had materialised, there would have been a plethora of protest activists and single-issue candidates. The highly visible success of a number of independent TDs at national level in terms of their influence, if not a degree of control, on government policies also raised expectations of an increase in the number of non-party contenders.

A shortage of candidates generally led to an effortless election campaign for the four candidates in the Kilbeggan electoral area of Westmeath, where the number of nominees equalled the number of seats. A similar situation occurred in the municipal setting of Loughrea, with nine candidates for the nine seats. However, these were very much the exceptions, and throughout the country there was an average of two contestants for every seat with the record going to a Galway City ward which had fourteen candidates for four seats making it, arithmetically at least, the most competitive local poll in the state.

Arrivals and Departures

Every election brings two distinct forms of change: changes in the personalities who take seats in the council chambers and, in most cases, changes, however slight, in the political party strengths on councils. One party may gain a seat at the expense of another thereby introducing both a new face on the council and a change in its political composition. Or the change may occur within a party's ranks, with both voluntary retirements and involuntary departures providing openings for a constant if limited regeneration of the cohort of elected councillors.

A survey of the figures for selected counties suggests a turnover of approximately 33 per cent at each local election. This is confirmed by Donnelly's detailed study of the 1991 local elections (Donnelly, 1992). However, this level was exceeded in the 1999 local elections, which saw 351 new faces among the 883 county and city seats or a turnover of almost 40 per cent. Some of the new councillors occupied seats taken from defeated sitting members but the majority took seats vacated by those who retired voluntarily. It is estimated that some 210 sitting councillors retired of their own volition prior to the 1999 poll, compared to 125 sitting councillors in 1991. The long eight-year interval between elections was a factor in prompting retirements. However, many decisions to retire were influenced by an unprecedented retirement gratuity (indeed unprecedented by international standards) announced in 1998. Sitting councillors qualified for the gratuity by not contesting the June 1999 elections and undertook not to contest elections for any local council in the future (see below).

The declared ministerial intention behind the scheme was to give long-serving councillors recognition for their years of commitment. However, it was clear that an equally important motivation was to give an incentive to long-time occupants of seats to make way for new faces. Anecdotal evidence suggests that the scheme was modestly successful in this regard, but the absence of age data on either the outgoing or incoming councils in 1999 makes it difficult to pronounce definitively on the impact of an innovative but expensive scheme.

A Cold Chamber for Women?

The low level of participation by women in Irish elected office is starkly illustrated at local government level. Women form just 15 per cent of the elected cohort at county/city council level. The situation is only marginally better with the town councils where female councillors form less than 18 per cent of the total. Recent trends indicate little sign of change in this imbalance.

It had been expected that the 1999 local elections would see a significant advance by women in the local political process. There was no shortage of impressive role models: the decade had seen two women elected by popular vote to the presidency; the nation's first female Tánaiste; and a number of high-profile female ministers and MEPs. The signs were pointing to a significant uptake by women in the opportunities to sit at the council table. However, such expectations were to be frustrated. When nominations closed women made up just 16 per cent of the candidates offering themselves for election. In the event, 132 women were elected to county and city councils, an improvement of just twenty-nine on the number elected in 1991. At town council level, just one more woman was elected in the 1999 poll than in the previous town elections in 1994, bringing the total number of female town councillors to 133.

The reasons for the lack of participation are many: more pressurised lifestyles, leaving less time and energy for voluntary commitment, is a factor affecting both genders; the perception of a 'closed-shop' in many local branches of parties militates against the selection of new candidates; and the apparent growth in apathy towards politics generally is a significant factor.

However, there is a theory, possibly valid and certainly a challenging indicator for the future of local government, that women have found alternative channels in which to influence the national political process. Women, for example, founded and led many of the community development groups that have challenged the role of established local government in recent years. Seeing little scope for making an impact through the structures of traditional politics in the council chamber, it seems that many women have found value in alternative but effective groups which although highly political in terms of lobbying and organisation manage to avoid partisan political labels. That said, it must be noted that there are some 250 women involved in Ireland's councils, with many of them having had experience at chair or mayoralty level.

Juggling Politics and Work

If council memberships are seriously out of balance with the gender realities of the population, such anomalies are equally present in the kinds of work experience that councillors bring with them to their involvement in public life. A survey of the occupations declared by councillors on their ballot papers shows that those with flexible work timetables dominate.

The dominant job descriptions are public representative and farmer, accounting for 196 and 156 councillors respectively in 1999. The former description would, of course, include the 116 Oireachtas members who were also councillors in 1999. It also includes an unquantified number of councillors who are in early retirement and have the opportunity to arrange their schedules so as to maximise their participation in local government activity. Similar reasoning would apply to farmers who, while busy people, at least can set their own timetables.

At the other end of the scale there are just a handful of councillors who work in factory or office situations. The realities of production-line work or pressurised office schedules make it next to impossible for workers to get time off to attend to council business, and particularly to take part in council meetings which often take place during the day. While some councillors have informal arrangements with their employers as regards time off, there are few enterprises which could cope with the kind of repeated absences of an employee involved in the increasingly intensive round of council and committee meetings. This marked imbalance in the job background of elected members, with the emphasis heavily leaning towards the self-employed and farming sectors of the economy, is hardly representative of the make-up of the general working population.

Unequal Representation

If the occupational background of councillors is well out of line with the distribution of occupations in modern Irish society, an equally problematic mismatch occurs in the degree to which suburban Ireland is under-represented in the national cohort of councillors.

The number of council seats in each county has not been revised to reflect the massive shifts in the Irish population that have occurred since the 1970s. Electoral area commissions have revised electoral areas within counties about once per decade, but there has been no exercise to try to balance up representation on a nationwide basis. In fact the number of seats per county is not very different from the pattern set out under the Victorian local government code. As a result, rural Ireland is relatively over-represented but suburban Ireland is comparatively under-represented.

For example, Kildare has one councillor per 6,500 population, whereas Longford enjoys one councillor per 1,480 of its population. In South Dublin each councillor represents 9,200 people; by contrast, in Monaghan the ratio is one councillor per 2,600 population. In other words, the concerns of the citizens of rural Ireland have a much more accessible outlet than is available to the suburban dwellers.

This mismatch is more serious than just a statistical exercise. It points to a question mark for the relevance of Irish local democracy if the reality of life for a very great section of the population – those living in suburban commuter belt settings – is not being represented by a local political process still occupied with issues of farming and the land.

Committee World

An influential but little-known facet of local government is formed by the layers of committees, boards, authorities and partnerships to which councils have nominating rights (see chapter 3). This array of bodies might be termed 'secondary representation' in that councillors take part on the respective boards as an extension of their primary local authority mandate. Indeed the activities of some of the organisations are little known within the local government sector and often escape the attention of an otherwise knowledgeable local press.

Some of the bodies involved consist entirely of councillors; others bring elected and non-elected people to the boardroom table. Some are statutory; others in the partnership area are non-statutory but with a high level of official recognition. Yet again some committees are mandatory (for example strategic policy committees), while others are discretionary (for example historic monuments committees). Some of the bodies are internal to the council such as the strategic policy committees and area committees; others are nominally separate bodies but in fact are essentially under the council's auspices such as the drainage boards. The most sought after by councillors are those that are external to the council such as the health board, vocational education committee, regional authority and regional assembly. The local government representative bodies (AMAI, GCCC and LAMA, see below) provide further representational outlets for members. As an extreme example of the number of bodies concerned, the 2002 Fingal County Council Yearbook lists twenty-five external boards, committees, partnerships and representative bodies to which the council nominates members.

The existence of these bodies was made more transparent by ministerial order (SI No. 129 of 1999), when councils were obliged to publish notices of the committees to which they had nominating rights – this heightened awareness in particular of committees to which the council had the right to appoint individuals who were not elected members (the drainage boards being a case in point).

An understanding of the extent of this secondary representation leads to an appreciation of the workload on individual councillors. Perhaps even more importantly, it helps the observer to appreciate the significance of such appointment opportunities – as a way of sharing out the spoils among the dominant party or parties in the process of deciding the political control of a newly elected council and their role in the council chamber negotiation process.

Dual Mandate

It is a decisive indicator of the intense localism of the Irish political system that 138 of the 226 members elected to the Dáil or Seanad in 2002 were members of local councils. By 2003 this example of political double jobbing, or the dual mandate as it has been termed, had become one of the most contentious issues in ministerial attempts to reform local government and give it a distinct political identity.

The argument has been made cogently that if national politicians are to focus on national issues, they must be removed from the localised minutiae of the council chamber. Equally, councillors must be free to engage in policy issues at local level without their deliberations being taken over by the political concerns of representatives to the national parliament. In addition, removing national parliamentarians would help break the stranglehold of clientelism – responding to a series of individual issues rather than concentrating on policy improvement – which, say its critics, has impoverished political debate in the state. In other words, Oireachtas members should be concentrating on how to improve, say, Ireland's road network rather than pursuing council administrators over repairs for every secondary road in the county.

The dual mandate had its defenders. Some councillors have remarked that the presence of a strong channel of communication between them and central government is an asset, particularly when deputations and submissions have to be arranged to central government.

However, there has long been general agreement that, even on the practical level of workloads, there is ample reason for separating out the national and local mandates. The Local Government Act, 1991 barred TDs who became ministers or ministers of state from holding a seat in a local authority. The Local Government Act, 1994 also banned Oireachtas members from holding the chair or mayoralty on local authorities from June 1999. However, in a portent of things to come, a parallel measure, which would have prohibited TDs who are councillors from chairing Dáil committees, had to be repealed from that legislation under pressure from non-party TDs.

The Local Government Bill published in May 2000 included a provision to introduce a complete ban on the dual mandate. However the minister was forced to abandon his attempt to ban the dual mandate in the face of overt opposition from a quartet of key independent TDs and covert but equally effective resistance from government backbenchers.[5]

In the immediate aftermath of these developments, and judging from the increase in the number of TDs to the Dáil in 2002, it appeared that the dual mandate would remain a feature of the Irish local government profile. Nevertheless, the debate continued and a Local Government Bill published in February 2003 provided that members of the Oireachtas would be ineligible for local authority membership. By this time the arguments in favour of abolishing the dual mandate had been well rehearsed. It would allow councillors to focus on an increasing number of local demands and would mean that local authority business would not be affected by Oireachtas timetables. At national level, it was hoped that TDs and senators could focus on their legislative role through a more developed Oireachtas committee system. In a concession to TDs and senators, however, the Bill gave quite explicit facility for TDs and senators to have continued access to local authority documentation and information. While this may be acceptable in pragmatic political terms, it does raise the question as to whether the ban on the dual mandate is creating a situation of 'access without accountability' by giving Oireachtas members a continued means of intervention in council administrations. This legislation was adopted as the Local Government (No. 2) Act, 2003.

Political Control of Councils

Ultimately, all analyses of the composition of councils and assessments of statistics take second place to the ability of political parties to win control of individual councils. Control is achieved in two ways: by winning an outright

---

[5] See, for example, *Sunday Business Post*, 26 November 2000; *Irish Independent*, 15 December 2000 and 'Cabinet to drop dual mandate ban', *Irish Independent*, 11 June 2001.

majority in the number of seats in the council or by negotiating a power-sharing arrangement with one or more other parties or independents. Typically, the fortnight between the declaration of the results of the election and the first meeting of the new council is marked by the most intense period of negotiation, bargaining and deal making, as the party groups compete to maximise their results. In the process, patterns are set which will determine the dynamics of the council for the following five years.

Control of the council means that the councillors belonging to the majority party have access to sought-after positions such as the chairs of committees and membership of a plethora of committees and external agencies. Control of the council also means that the party in question has the dominant influence on the council's policy making in areas such as planning and infrastructure and can take public credit for initiatives achieved during the life of the council.

In the 1999 local government elections, the control of councils shifted in favour of the main government party. Fianna Fáil's dominance by outright majority in four councils was extended to eight. A useful indicator of a party's control is to pinpoint its ownership of mayor or chair positions and the respective deputy positions in the thirty-four county and city authorities. Of the sixty-eight mayor or deputy positions, Fianna Fáil occupied thirty-nine (57 per cent) in 1999, thus indicating it had full or shared control of over half of the county and city councils. Fine Gael occupied 22 per cent of the chair positions, indicating a controlling influence in about seven councils. Significantly, non-party/independent candidates accounted for 18 per cent of the mayor or deputy positions, indicating the extent to which they are drawn into coalition arrangements with other parties in the deal making for council control (see table 6.4).

Table 6.4 Party Control of Councils through Access to Mayoral and Deputy Office, 1999

Party	No. of mayors/ deputy mayors	% of 68 chairs	% of 883 seats
Fianna Fáil	39	57	43
Fine Gael	15	22	31
Labour Party	4	6	9
Progressive Democrats	2	3	3
Sinn Féin	2	3	2
Non-party	6	9	11

Source: Kenny (1999, p. 16)

This process of deal making for the position of mayor would have been curbed in a significant way with the proposed introduction of the directly elected mayor for county and city councils, which had been legislated for under the Local Government Act, 2001. As a result, the first position in the county and city councils would have been taken out of the post-election bargaining process. However, this provision was repealed in 2003.

The advent of a directly elected mayor, albeit without executive powers, would have introduced a new political actor to the local government sector. For some, it would have presented an opportunity to invigorate local government with personalities who would possess a strong mandate, and provide highly visible democratic leadership for their locality. However, the proposal for directly elected mayors was not unanimously welcomed by councillors, many of whom regarded it as depriving them of an opportunity to fill a much-coveted position from within the council chamber. There may also have been a fear of the election of a number of single-issue or 'personality' candidates to the position.

Councillors and the Wider Political Process

The point was stressed at the beginning of this chapter that councillors were not isolated in their respective localities but had links of various degrees of formality with the wider currents of political activity. These links are realised in various ways. First, by their memberships of political parties, councillors subscribe to national rulebooks and become subject to the party whip at local level, although this does not prevent members from rebelling against party policies. The parties have various channels in place for engaging with the concerns of councillor members. In a number of cases, there are places reserved on national executives for local authority members, while at the more local levels councillors have the *ex-officio* right to sit on party local and district committees. All of the parties hold occasional briefing and training sessions for elected members. However, the consistency and strength of such channels of communication fluctuates from year to year and is probably at its most vibrant approaching general elections.

Councillors also engage with the wider process through their representation on the three local authority representative bodies: the Association of Municipal Authorities of Ireland, the General Council of County Councils and the Local Authority Members' Association (see below). Although these bodies are cross party in their membership and objectives, their programmes of frequent meetings facilitate councillors dispersed throughout the country to meet and exchange information within their party groups. This is particularly the case with the major annual conferences organised by these bodies, which, as well as their ostensible educational purpose, manage to take on the character of unofficial party conventions in their social programmes, with members of the various parties working the crowd to seek support for nominations to positions and especially to the Seanad.

And it is this Seanad link that provides a significant channel of representation between the body of councillors and the parliamentary echelon. The members of the county and city councils are the principal electorate for membership of the upper house and as such are courted by senators during the life of the parliament. In 2003 a Seanad sub-committee was formed to review the role, function and composition of the Seanad. It was not thought likely, however, that major changes would be made to the link between local councillors and the Seanad.

Representative Associations

There are three representative associations in Irish local government: the General Council of County Councils (GCCC), the Association of Municipal Authorities of Ireland (AMAI) and the Local Authority Members' Association (LAMA). These representative bodies enjoy an unusual status in the local government sector. They are not public bodies but they do have statutory recognition (most explicitly in the Local Government Act, 2001, sections 225 and 226). Local authorities subscribe to membership on a voluntary basis but in practice all county and city councils and almost all town councils are members of the appropriate association. The associations may therefore be described as voluntary bodies with statutory recognition, although this recognition does not imply mandatory consultation by government.

The GCCC and AMAI are funded by subscription from their member councils. In the case of LAMA, funding comes by way of subscriptions from individual councillors. All three derive income from conference and seminar events, which are essential fixtures in the annual diaries of all councillors.

The functions of the representative associations, as set out in the Local Government Act, 2001, are:

- the undertaking of research and other studies
- the promotion of education and training
- the provision of policy support to constituent authorities
- the making of submissions to the minister or to other public authorities.

However, the capacity of the associations to develop policy and training objectives is limited, given that their structures consist of large plenary bodies working though extensive committee structures of elected members with little or no professional policy staff. In addition, the associations do not have the capacity to engage in detailed policy analysis across the wide range of local authority services and, in practice, they concentrate their policy input on the status, powers and remuneration of elected members.

In real terms the main role of the representative associations is as a two-way channel of communication between the Department of the Environment and Local Government and the body of councillors generally. Draft legislation and policy initiatives are considered by the associations and communicated to the memberships by meetings, seminars and briefing circulars. The feedback gained through this process may generate submissions from the individual associations urging amendment to the department's drafts. On occasion the three associations have combined forces, most notably in parliamentary and ministerial lobbying during the passage of the Local Government Act, 2001. However such consultation by the department is not mandatory and, despite the apparent political leverage of the associations, their proposals are entirely subject to the attitude of the department and the governmental priorities of the day.

An increasing interest of the associations has been that of training and education for councillors. This has taken the form of direct training through engaging specialists to give briefings at meetings and also indirect training by way of proposing topics that might be delivered through other agencies with more experience in training.

An important, if little recognised, contribution of the representative associations is their capacity to provide a degree of cohesion among the various political groupings represented in council chambers across the country. Through working together on association committees and through meeting in the social environs of annual conferences and general meetings, which have become quite large affairs, typically numbering over 400 councillor delegates, a certain camaraderie evolves based on the common experience of local service.

The major events of the three associations are their annual conferences. These events normally feature talks on contemporary local government issues and are a focus of political networking and social activity.

Local Authority Members' Association (LAMA)

LAMA was founded in March 1980 to campaign for recognition of the workload faced by councillors in the context of an increasingly strident public expectation of local government activity. The association prioritised a campaign to seek better expenses for councillors leading eventually to a framework for a salary-type payment and retirement scheme. The association was also active in pioneering links with councillors in Britain and Northern Ireland and established firm co-operation with the British Association of Councillors and particularly its Northern Branch. It has also been active in European affairs, holding meetings in Brussels and a number of European countries.

LAMA membership comprises councillors from county, city, borough and town councils. They meet annually to elect executive and administrative committees. LAMA has representation on a number of national committees, including An Chomhairle Leabharlanna.

Association of Municipal Authorities of Ireland (AMAI)

The AMAI is the representative body for the town and borough councils in Ireland although its membership also embraces the city councils, thus numbering eighty-four member authorities. The association was founded in 1912 and since then it has brought a particular focus to the concerns of town authorities. As might be expected in an urban setting, the provision of housing has been a major theme of the association through the decades.

A core activity of the AMAI is the preparation of an annual deputation to the minister covering an extensive schedule of issues raised at its annual conference. A volume of replies from the minister is prepared and distributed to members at the subsequent annual conference.

The AMAI lobbied the department during the preparation of the Local Government Bill 2000 (later to become the Local Government Act, 2001) to maximise recognition for town local councils and this was granted by way of provisions for the chairs of the town councils to be *ex-officio* members of area committees of the county councils together with changes in terminology which modernised the Victorian descriptions that had been applied to various categories of town authority.

The association is governed by an officer board and executive committee elected on a provincial basis and has an extensive committee structure for specialist purposes. The AMAI has commissioned its own website and organises a well-supported annual conference and seminar. It is a nominating body for Seanad Éireann.

General Council of County Councils (GCCC)

The GCCC was formed in 1899 by the first democratically elected councillors in Ireland. For a number of years it had representatives from all the county and city councils on the island. It adopted an increasingly vociferous Home Rule policy in the early 1900s. For a time it was proposed as the nucleus of an indigenous Irish parliament. On a more pragmatic basis it developed policies symbolising the political aspirations of most of the population: for instance in 1908 it was instrumental in the campaign for the establishment of the National University of Ireland (NUI). The GCCC was again prominent in 1920 and 1921, when its membership acted as a clandestine channel of communications between the local government department of the then subversive Dáil Éireann and the nationalist-minded councils as they seceded from British control.

In modern times the GCCC has been prominent in representing councillors' views ahead of the *Better Local Government* and Local Government Act, 2001 reforms. An intensive schedule of meetings, conferences and publications facilitated debate, information exchange and consultation. It has also been active in briefing and informing councillors nationwide of the detail and implications of the Act as the various provisions were put in place. The GCCC compiles and maintains an extensive database and website on issues relevant to the 883 county and city councillors in the state, which provides a substantial research resource on, for example, the dual mandate and female participation in local government. It also tracks changes in the composition of the national corps of councillors and picks up on changes in party allegiances, co-options and so forth.

The GCCC has statutory membership of the UCD governing body. It nominates a member to An Chomhairle Leabharlanna and participates in the National Economic and Social Forum and numerous departmental working groups. It also has a statutory role in the nomination of the chairperson and members of An Bord Pleanála. It has been a nominating body to Seanad Éireann since 1947.

The GCCC is the Irish secretariat of the Irish councillors' delegation to the Congress of Local and Regional Authorities in Europe (see appendix 10). It also maintains contact as appropriate with the Northern Ireland Local Government Association and colleague associations in the UK and elsewhere in Europe.

The thirty-four county and city councils are each represented by three councillors who make up the 102-strong general council, which in turn elects an executive committee each year.

General

The three representative associations perform a useful role in terms of providing a consultative channel for councillors and for the department in advance of major new policy initiatives. However, a lack of policy and research capacities (only the GCCC has a full-time secretariat) together with the administrative and expense demands of extensive schedules of meetings, conferences and seminars means that their potential as an effective lobbying resource has yet to be realised. There is also a question mark over the efficacy of having three representative associations with overlapping objectives and memberships. Section 225 of the Local Government Act, 2001 provides for the possibility of a unified representative organisation for local government – this would be a logical, but politically unlikely, evolution of local government representation in Ireland.

Councillor Payments and Expenses

Traditionally, the only payment to councillors was the public service mileage and day subsistence rates paid on the basis of claims for attendance at meetings. However, new forms of payment in 1994 and again in 2002 have improved the compensation available to elected members, recognising that their representational duties extend beyond attendance in the council chamber.

Since 1 January 1994, all councillors are entitled to an annual expenses allowance, which is intended to cover mileage and subsistence expenses for attendance at meetings of their parent councils and also costs, such as postage and telephone, arising out of their community representation duties. The actual sum involved varies between councils according to an index figure (specified in SI No. 391 of 1993) of perceived activity levels of councils. There are also different rates for the various categories of town authority.

From 1 January 2002, councillors, except those who were also Oireachtas members, became entitled to a new form of payment known as the representational payment. Its colloquial name – salary-type payment – reflects the view among councillors that council membership approaches the commitment of a full-time occupation. The payment for county and city councillors is based on one-quarter of the annual salary of a member of the Seanad and will rise accordingly as the payments for Seanad members rise through national wage rounds or special increases. A smaller but proportionate amount is payable to town and borough councillors, which varies according to the size of the council. Holders of county and town seats qualify for the higher payment only (SI No. 552 of 2001). In common with salary-type payments generally, representational payments are taxable. The initial payment was backdated to 4 May 2000, the date on which the Local Government Bill 2000 was published.

Councillors generally have access to a budget heading for attending conference-type events throughout Ireland and also abroad, sometimes known as ad hoc expenses payments. In relation to domestic events, travelling expenses are paid at mileage rates equivalent to the highest rates of the public service mileage schedule. The total fund available in each council is set by the councillors themselves at budget time and the sums involved have been growing considerably. Details of the total costs involved and events attended must be included in a public register and also in the council's annual report.

Since 1991, councils have had legal authority to pay an allowance to their cathaoirleach/mayor. In addition, the Local Government Act, 2001 gave approval to pay an allowance to the leas-chathaoirleach and to chairpersons of the strategic policy committees (anomalously there is no similar authority for payment to the chairs of area committees). This means that on a county or city council, six or seven members will be in receipt of extra allowances at any given time.

Thus, in summary, councillors receive payment from their councils through:

- annual expenses allowance
- representational payment or 'salary'
- expenses for attendance at conferences etc.
- allowances for posts of responsibility – cathaoirleach, leas-chathaoirleach and SPC chairs.

It should also be noted that councillors nominated as members of vocational education committees, health boards and so forth are paid expenses by those bodies as an extension of their core local government activities.

Retirement Schemes

There was no retirement scheme for councillors until 1998 when the minister announced an unprecedented gratuity scheme (SI No. 232 of 1998) offering compensation for each year of service up to a total of forty years. A key condition of this scheme was that the applicant-councillor would not contest the 1999 local government elections or any subsequent local election. This scheme was so novel that it generated interest among local authority organisations in the UK and Europe. Some two hundred county and city councillors retired voluntarily in 1999. It was made clear by the minister at the time that this scheme would not be repeated at subsequent elections.

Following the enactment of the Local Government Act, 2001, a gratuity scheme was published in June 2002 to compensate councillors who would cease office at any point in the future whether through voluntary retirement, permanent incapacity or loss of office at election (SI No. 281 of 2002). This scheme is based on a rate of 15 per cent of the representational payment amount at the time of retirement multiplied by the years of service, being not less than three or more than twenty. Unlike the 1998 scheme, there is no restriction on contesting future elections and previous service is only reckonable from 4 May 2000 when the representational payment became legally payable.

Conclusion

The body of councillors forms a reservoir of political representation with many strengths and some weaknesses. Its strengths lie in its closeness to its electorate by which it ensures that local issues are given potent expression in a democratic forum. From time to time, councillors can also succeed through council, party or representative association channels in communicating local concerns to the higher levels of government. Councillors are responsive, communicative and involved. Their main weakness lies in the narrowing range of society from which elected members are drawn and the ever-present pressures to respond to short-term demands rather than concentrating on longer-term potential.

Developments such as new committee structures which provide links between traditional local government and new types of community activism and the belated but welcome constitutional recognition of local government may all help to reinvigorate the place of the councillor as one of the building blocks of Ireland's culture of democracy.

7

City and County Management

Edward Sheehy

This chapter examines the evolution of the local government management system in Ireland and the role and functions of city and county managers. County manager or city manager is the title given to the chief executive of Irish local authorities. He or she is recruited following a publicly advertised competition organised by the Local Appointments Commissioners, an independent national recruitment agency. The commissioners make a recommendation to the county or city council and the successful candidate is then appointed by formal resolution of the elected members. A county manager automatically becomes manager for any borough or town council, and for certain joint bodies, within the county.

Evolution of the Management System

The United States Experience

The evolution of cities necessitated the development of some form of city government to ensure that the affairs of the city were run in a proper and efficient manner. The concept of an appointed administrator for US cities goes back at least as far as President George Washington's suggestion to the secretary of the navy, Benjamin Stoddard, in 1792: 'It has always been my opinion . . . that the administration of the federal city ought to be under the immediate direction of a judicious skilful superintendent appointed and subject to the orders of the commissioner'. However, the suggestion was not acted upon at that time.

During the nineteenth century, various reform movements developed with the goals of ending 'boss rule' and electing honest men to city hall. These reformers also recognised the need for changes in the basic structure of city government in order to make cities less prone to corrupt party influence. This reform movement, together with increased urbanisation, the growing popularity of business and corporate ideals and the development of scientific management and public administration, contributed to the evolution of the city manager system in the US.

The first city manager, a civil engineer, was appointed in Staunton, Virginia in 1908. In 1901, a new form of city government, which became known as the commission plan, had emerged in Galveston, Texas, where, following a hurricane that devastated the town, municipal affairs had been handed over to a five-man group of business executives who were dramatically successful in bringing order out of chaos. In 1909, the two ideas were married by an energetic, pushy young advertising man called Richard S. Childs and city management proper was born. At first it was known as the commission-manager plan, and Childs was pertinacious and dogmatic in insisting that the commission part was just as essential to the success of the plan as the manager. Both elements were necessary to translate business organisation into municipal terms: the commission flanked by the city manager was a close analogue of the board of directors and general manager that characterised the business corporation. The plan was first enacted in 1912 in Sumter, South Carolina.

Local Administration in Ireland Prior to the Management System

The methods of administration in Irish local authorities prior to the introduction of the management system were the traditional British methods embodied in the pre-1922 local government legislation for Ireland. The legislation made the elected body both the deliberative assembly and its own executive working through officers under its control. The more important authorities worked through committees under the general control of the parent body. The outstanding defect of this method of disposing of business was that responsibility for carrying on the executive work was not concentrated on anyone. Instead, it was diffused amongst the whole body which was collectively responsible for its decisions. Local government was tainted by suggestions of nepotism, corruption, administrative abuse and inefficiency. Following independence, these difficulties led to tensions with central government, which responded in many cases by dissolving the recalcitrant local authority and appointing a commissioner (or commissioners) to run its affairs. As O'Halpin (1991, p. 5) notes:

> . . . the Cosgrave governments of 1922–32 were impatient at the defects of the administrative system they inherited from the British . . . Many areas had suffered severely during the war of independence and the subsequent civil war, and after years of disruption local authorities were ill-prepared financially and administratively to carry out the repairs and reconstruction. Some councils and boards were dominated by republicans who declined to carry out statutory functions such as striking a rate.

In other cases, sheer administrative incompetence and inertia meant that urgent problems went unaddressed.

The Irish Reformers

The rapid spread of city management in the US, known as the Progressive Reform Movement, attracted attention and interest abroad. Its first Irish publicist was a Cork solicitor, John J. Horgan, who published an article, 'City Management in America', in *Studies* in 1920. In addition to this and other articles, he founded a civic reform body, called the Cork Progressive Association, which helped to bring about the dissolution of Cork Corporation in 1924 and the appointment of a commissioner in its stead. Horgan followed up this victory with vigorous pressure for the adoption of a commission-manager plan modelled closely on US ideas.

In a small work published in 1929, Horgan staked his claim to be the architect of the Cork scheme – the prototype which gave Irish management its distinctive, even unique, character. He was a convinced adherent of the Childs doctrine and his brief account of the origins of city management starts in 1914 with Dayton, Ohio, the first large town to adopt the commission-manager plan. Horgan struggled hard to keep the commission idea and limit the number of councillors. He was only moderately successful in this, but the sharp division in law between the council's reserved and the manager's administrative or executive functions was first clearly enunciated in the Cork Bill. The reserved functions, then few in number, were carefully spelt out; the manager was in charge of everything else. This arrangement has stamped city and county management ever since.

In the meantime, the reform movement had been proceeding in Dublin under the influence of a body calling itself the Greater Dublin Movement. The Dublin board of guardians was replaced by commissioners in late 1923 and the corporation dissolved in May 1924 after a rather perfunctory inquiry. This unprecedented display of force by government against the most ancient form of local self-rule in Ireland was received with equanimity by the citizens, who seemed to share the accepted view of the corporation as a combination of corruption and inefficiency. But the inquiry, such as it was, discovered little evidence to support the indictment and the suspicion has persisted that the government welcomed the opportunity of denying a platform to their political opponents and critics. In July 1924, the government set up the Greater Dublin Commission, under the chairmanship of Professor William Magennis. The commission was a blend of politicians (both local and national), business representatives, labour representatives and academics.

Witnesses generally favoured a board of management for Dublin with or without a city manager – the US commission system or its variant the commission-manager plan. There were few advocates of the city manager as a one-man show – Professor Alton of Trinity College Dublin thought it 'hopelessly undemocratic'. There was much support for the ideas canvassed by Monsignor Michael Cronin, Professor of Ethics and Politics at University College Dublin, in an article, 'City Administration in Ireland', in *Studies* (September 1923) in which he argued for a large elected council responsible for legislation and financial appropriation and a small commission elected to oversee the whole work of administration, rather than the Dayton system of the small elected commission working on the legislative side with a city manager on the administrative side. The influential Greater Dublin Movement favoured this plan.

The commission's report, when it appeared in 1926, was said to have been written by Magennis, working mainly on a submission put in by the Greater Dublin Movement. It proposed a thorough modernisation of the city government. Lord mayor, swordbearer, macebearer and city marshal were to be swept away and the redundant Mansion House would become a municipal art gallery. The city council would be restricted to matters of civic policy, budget, rating, adoptive legislation and general supervision. Civic administration would be in the hands of a city manager and board of directors.

> The scheme of city management under an elective council accords with the best experience of the United States, Germany, and the more progressive cantons of Switzerland. Civic administration is a business; accordingly the Commission recommends the entrusting of the civic management of Greater Dublin to the business conduct of a body of Directors (Greater Dublin Commission of Inquiry, 1926).

But the scheme was poorly worked out, and the board turned out to be an advisory board of department heads, subordinate to the city manager who had sole executive authority.

The report, according to Seán Lemass who was then an opposition TD, was 'treated by government as a sort of joke'. It was remitted by the Minister for Local Government and Public Health, General Richard Mulcahy (who had replaced Séamus de Burca in June 1927), to a departmental committee for further study. General Mulcahy said later in the Dáil (26 February 1930) that 'the Commission's proposals . . . were not satisfactory and . . . did not provide effectively for the carrying out of the business of the people'.

The departmental committee reported in less than a year, drastically revising the commission's plans for a Greater Dublin Council and recommending that, in lieu of a direct transition to the city management, the new city council should act through a board of management with collective responsibility. This board would consist initially of the three Dublin commissioners, to be appointed by the minister for a period of five years. The council would then take over and make appointments for seven-year terms.

City Management in Cork

The Cork City Management Bill was introduced in the Dáil in June 1928, about the time when the departmental committee finished their examination (in relation to Dublin) and as the Bill had a fully drawn scheme of city management the committee's plan for a management board for Dublin was put into abeyance until the Oireachtas had decided on the Cork scheme. The outcome was that the government's intention to use Dublin as a model was frustrated by the delay and Cork slipped in ahead. Cork's problems were less complex and its proposals better presented and more tenaciously urged. And so Cork, against the odds, carried the banner of city management into Irish local government.

The Cork City Management Act, 1929 was a considerable modification of the original plan imported by Horgan from the National Municipal League of America and owed much to E. P. McCarron, the first Secretary of the Department of Local Government and Public Health. The Bill introduced in the Dáil in June 1928 was cautiously accepted in principle and, despite sustained Labour opposition and criticism by the new Fianna Fáil party, survived the parliamentary process with few changes. The most significant alteration was an increase in the size of the city council from fifteen (in the Bill) to twenty-one. The old Cork City Council had fifty-six members.

The Cork prototype had virtually all the ingredients that continue to characterise Irish city and county management. The reserved powers (an expression said to have been borrowed from the Bombay Corporation Act, 1889 but in fact derived from the Home Rule Bills) of the elected members were precisely set out and included rating, borrowing, legislation, elections and a few others. The city manager had the residual powers, acting by way of signed orders, a register of which was kept for inspection by the members. The manager had the right of attendance at meetings and could take part in discussions but not vote; prepared the city budget; and advised and assisted the council in getting through the reserved business.

The city manager was an officer of the corporation, appointed, although not selected, by the council. The first manager was named in the Act: he was a former secondary school teacher and mayor of Drogheda, Philip Monahan, who had been commissioner in Cork since 1924, and as supremo had developed that autocratic manner characteristic of some early managers. Thereafter, selection was to be made by the Local Appointments Commissioners. The salary of the manager was fixed by the minister.

The office of town clerk was (until 1941) a separate job. In the Dublin and subsequent City Management Acts, the town clerk's position was merged with that of city manager.

City Management in Dublin

Dublin's turn came next. The Local Government (Dublin) Bill was introduced in December 1929. A long, complex Bill covering both the city and Dún Laoghaire, it ran immediately into heavy weather and its progress was not helped by a novel and unpopular proposal to modify the local government franchise in Dublin by instituting a 'commercial register' giving special representation to business on the new city council. The council was to be cut down from an impressive eighty-four to twenty-five members. The triumvirate of commissioners (P. J. Hernon, Dr W. Dwyer and Seamus Murphy) was passed over for nomination as first city manager in favour of the well-liked and respected town clerk, Gerald Sherlock.

The demarcation lines between council and manager followed the Cork model in its main features, but the government conceded a number of enlargements of the council's powers in the course of the debate. The most noteworthy of these was a power – hedged about with discouraging procedural barriers – to direct the manager to do a particular executive act. After a rough passage, the Bill was passed in July 1930. Council size in Dublin had been raised to thirty-five – thirty ordinary and five commercial members. The coastal borough plan attracted much artillery fire, in the course of which the new Dún Laoghaire lost its mayor and had to make do with a chairperson. For some reason the idea of a mayor in rebaptised Kingstown brought out the worst in the opposition. The realities were preserved (the chairperson got a mayor's stipend), but there was a certain loss of colour.

The Other County Boroughs (Cities)

City management was extended to Limerick in 1934 at the request of the city council. During the early part of the 1930s the tide ran strongly in favour of management in urban affairs following the relative success of the Cork and Dublin experiments – although Cork's attitude towards Monahan was always ambivalent: respect for his consummate ability was strongly tempered by resentment at his authoritarian style of action. At the opposite end of the spectrum, in Dublin, Sherlock was reluctant to range outside his old job of town clerk, leaving decisions to the council and its revived committees and never becoming city manager in anything but name.

There appeared to be no local demand for city management in Waterford, but it is probable that central government wished to clear the decks in anticipation of the expected struggle in the counties. The Waterford City Management Act, 1939 completed the county borough coverage. The Limerick and Waterford Acts followed the pattern hammered out in Cork and Dublin – a tribute to the suitability of the system to Irish conditions and a comment also on the durability of departmental policies in spite of political change.

A borough manager was seriously considered by the citizens of Galway on the occasion of their private Bill for restoring borough status to the city in 1937. The idea was rejected because, it is said, of the expense. The Local Government (Reorganisation) Act, 1985 constituted Galway borough as a county borough and appointed Seamus Keating, the existing Galway county manager, as the city manager (in addition to his position as county manager) with effect from 1 January 1986. Following Keating's retirement, a separate city manager was appointed.

Background to County Management

The Poor Law Commission of 1925 to 1927 recommended that county boards of health should be abolished and replaced by paid officers who would take full charge of the poor law services under the general oversight of county councils 'in the same manner as a general manager of a company under the control of a board of directors'. This would have been the equivalent of a county manager for the home assistance, medical, hospital and other institutional services provided by boards of health. The suggestion was not, however, put into operation before the government changed in 1932.

In May 1931, Ernest Blythe, then Minister for Finance, announced a radical reform of county government as a condition of adding £750,000 (€952,304) to the agricultural grant, which reduced the impact of rates on land holdings. Boards of health would be 'drawn into county councils', the councils would be reduced substantially in size and managers would be appointed in the style of those in Cork and Dublin. An acerbic reference to the need to curb council 'windbags' gave great offence. But the plan was stillborn: the government fell a few months later. When Fianna Fáil took over in March 1932, nothing further was heard of county management, at least in public. In 1931, de Valera had announced his party's opposition to the idea of extending management to counties. The Minister for Local Government and Public Health, Seán T. Ó Ceallaigh, favoured reform and it is speculated that the curious developments which followed were an effort to reconcile the public commitment to oppose county management with the minister's determination to reform administration in the counties.

The Department of Local Government and Public Health had, it appears, plans for an even more fundamental reconstruction of county government than was implied in county management. A scheme of county commissioners was prepared in the department in 1933. Local elected councils, it was argued, were a relic of British administration. With independence and the advent of a national government, local bodies had become, according to one Department of Finance memorandum, 'an expensive anachronism'. Moreover, many locally administered services were national in scope: housing, public health, hospitals, roads and so on. Local finances were becoming increasingly dependent on the state. The criticisms of local administration – the intrusion of irrelevant political issues, inefficiency and so on – were aimed less at urban than county government and the scheme visualised the survival of city councils and a number of large urban councils.

The Introduction of County Management

The proposals for the virtual abolition of county councils were submitted by the minister to the Executive Council early in 1934. They met with powerful opposition and after some months were withdrawn from the cabinet agenda.

Later in 1934, the question was remitted to a cabinet sub-committee under P. J. Little, then chief whip, and a scheme of county management was gradually worked out. There was no pressure to hurry things up – the minister's own attitude seemed ambiguous. Eventually, the County Management Bill was introduced in the Dáil in July 1939. The Bill became law in June 1940, but did not come into operation until August 1942 because of the volume of preparatory work (selecting managers and so on) to be done. The abolition of boards of health also gave rise to much consequential reshuffling. The first managers were mainly existing county secretaries or secretaries of boards of health, but they also included four commissioners.

The County Management Act was an expression in county terms of the city management principles worked out since 1929. Council and manager occupied much the same relative positions in the city and county systems, but county management had a number of special characteristics as listed below.

- A manager was selected by the Local Appointments Commissioners at the request, not of the council, but of the Minister for Local Government and Public Health. The person selected automatically became manager. This device forestalled possible recalcitrance on the part of the councils.
- The manager acted not only for the county council, but for all elective local authorities in the county – boroughs, urban councils and towns, and this continues to be the case for borough and town councils under the Local Government Act, 2001. The intention was to assert and advance the paramount position of county councils and at the same time to raise the standard of administration in smaller units by providing well-qualified expert staff to augment the efforts of town clerks. In particular, the department pressed the first cycle of managers to improve financial management in the many urban councils which needed attention.
- Certain counties were grouped for management purposes:
  Kilkenny and Waterford (degrouped 1 April 1965)
  Tipperary North Riding and Tipperary South Riding (degrouped 1 April 1969)
  Carlow and Kildare (degrouped 1 January 1975)
  Leitrim and Sligo (degrouped 1 December 1976)
  Longford and Westmeath (degrouped 1 June 1977)
  Laois and Offaly (degrouped 1 April 1982).
- Dublin city and county were also grouped and the Dublin city manager became county manager. This idea surfaced during the passage of the Bill

through the Oireachtas as a concession to the strong movement of opinion in favour of a Dublin Metropolitan Council which emerged from the Report of the Greater Dublin Tribunal (1938).

- Assistant managers were to be appointed: two in Dublin city and county, two in Cork county, one in the two ridings of Tipperary. Others could be appointed if the minister made orders to that effect. This subsequently occurred, with assistant managers in twelve counties by 2001, when the position was effectively replaced by the post of director of services.

- County rate collectors were to be appointed by county councils, not by managers. This item (it totally traverses the management principle) was so odd, and caused such curious behaviour on the part of local councillors, that it was thought by many people to have been left behind in deliberate error as a cautionary relic of the bad old pre-management days. The explanation is said to have lain in the semi-political nature of the county rate collector's job. The error, if it was an error, was retrieved by the County Management (Amendment) Act, 1972.

'Fine-Tuning' City and County Management

Although the County Management Bill had passed relatively peaceably through the Oireachtas, trouble appeared soon after the Act came into operation in 1942.

A minority of managers, some of them new to local government, took a literal view of their role as set out plainly, it seemed, in the County Management Act, 1940. For example, Denis Hegarty, the Sligo-Leitrim manager, stated:[1]

> It is important to note that the manager is not selected by the council. The manager is, in fact, responsible for practically all the functions of the local authority, and he is entitled to take decisions on nearly all executive matters without reference to the elected council, though he may keep them informed of his activities. For instance, subject only to the Minister, he may appoint, retire, remove or fix the remuneration of the officers of the local authority, and the elected body may not interfere in the matter. The independent control thus given to the manager distinguishes him from the managing director of a commercial concern who would, of course, be subject to the majority control of his co-directors; or from the American city manager, who is appointed by the council who have delegated functions to him which they may withdraw if the council and the people of the area should so decide.

What seemed to be managerial arrogance in the lecture was probably less obvious in the daily conduct of business, but nevertheless uneasiness about their novel condition began to spread among county councillors. The position, moreover, was not helped by the actions of one or two former commissioners who were slow to adjust to their altered situation.

---

[1] In a 1944 lecture to the Civics Institute, see *Public Administration in Ireland*, vol. 1, 1944.

Disharmony between councils and managers showed in a number of places and many local councillors were clearly unhappy under the new system. The minister issued a series of circular letters in the period 1942 to 1946 underlining the importance and extent of councils' powers. These were amplified by a White Paper entitled *The Powers and Functions of Elected Members and Local Bodies* (Government of Ireland, 1945), but councillors remained unconvinced.

When the first inter-party government took over in 1948, the new Minister for Local Government (T. J. Murphy, Labour Party) undertook a radical modification of county management. The object of the 1950 Local Government (County Administration) Bill was to substitute for management a system of administration by small executive committees and county officers, who would exercise employment, house tenancy and individual health functions. The latter were a new breed of officers, representing an amalgam of county manager and county secretary. The Bill lapsed with the dissolution of the Dáil in May 1951 and was never re-introduced. The need for some kind of readjustment nevertheless remained in the air and the 1953 County Management (Amendment) Bill was intended to do the necessary minimum. Its main provision strengthened the financial controls exercisable by councils over managers. It also proposed to degroup counties, giving each county the opportunity of having its own manager. This Bill did not survive the change of government in 1954.

The second inter-party government (1954 to 1957) was less radical than the first in its approach to the problem, and the relevant part of its twelve-point programme read:

> To restore democratic rights in respect of local government by amending the County Management Acts and giving to local authorities greater autonomy and effective power in local affairs.

This item could be read as a statement of intent to assert local power against central government, but that aspect was speedily lost sight of in the re-opening of the debate about county management. The Fine Gael minister of the time, Patrick "Pa" O'Donnell, entered the fray without pre-conceived notions and his first step was to visit every county and hear its views and grievances at first hand – a display of impartiality which may have owed something to Fine Gael pride of paternity as the inventors of Irish city management. The eventual outcome was the City and County Management (Amendment) Act, 1955.

This Act restored the position of councils vis-à-vis managers and brought the two into some sort of equipoise. Its provisions were by no means earthshaking: a power enabling councils to direct their managers to keep them informed of what they were about to do in executive matters (such as house tenancies, contracts, planning decisions and so on), consultation before undertaking new works and the need for council approval of new posts or changes in levels of salaries. The procedure for directing a manager to act in a particular way in doing an executive function (apart from staff matters) was simplified – rather oversimplified as it turned out, at least in some counties. The Act, which in effect brought the long and acrimonious dispute to a peaceful conclusion, illustrates the fact that the sense of helplessness which assailed many councillors in the years after 1942 was due as much to lack of information as to lack of power. There was of course a definite accession of power to councils in 1955, although in many cases the new statutory powers remained unused. However, one must not lose sight of the fact that most managers adjusted to the new situation and did what was needed without waiting to be ordered to do so.

The Act made no difference to the balance of power, if one can call it that, between central and local interests (although a new power under section 4 did become significant; see below). There was formal surrender of ministerial authority in sending requests to the Local Appointments Commissioners and in appointing county managers. The 1972 transfer from councils to county managers of the power to appoint rate collectors met with little opposition (County Management (Amendment) Act, 1972). Many councillors, it was said, were glad to be relieved of what had become a contentious and troublesome chore.

A more recent tendency has been for central government to designate certain responsibilities as executive functions, particularly where these involved locally contentious issues on which elected members can encounter difficulty reaching agreement. The precedent was established by section 14 of the Housing (Traveller Accommodation) Act, 1998, which provides that should the elected members fail to adopt a local Traveller accommodation plan 'the manager shall by order adopt the draft accommodation programme'. Difficulties for elected members in adopting waste management plans in a small number of local authorities resulted in the Waste Management (Amendment) Act, 2001, which states that 'the duties of a local authority under this section with respect to the making of a waste management plan shall be carried out by the manager of the authority and, accordingly, the making of such a plan shall be an executive function'.

City and County Management: Operation

The bodies with which managers are associated are county councils, city councils, borough councils, town councils, any joint board or committee established to execute functions of these authorities, and burial boards. Managers of county councils also serve as managers of borough or town councils in their county area. Managers were never appointed for vocational education committees, county committees of agriculture, old age pension committees, school attendance committees or committees under the Diseases of Animals Acts. Where not less than half the members of a joint board or committee (other than a pier or harbour authority or a vocational education committee) are appointed by two or more rating authorities, the appropriate minister may bring the board or committee within the management system.

Reserved and Executive Functions

The law relating to management recognises two categories of function: reserved and executive. Any function of a local authority that is not specifically designated in law as a reserved function (that is, the responsibility of the elected members) is deemed to be an executive function (that is, the responsibility of the manager). The powers and functions reserved for direct performance by the elected members have grown in number and significance since 1929 and now constitute a formidable armoury. They fall into five main categories: finance, legislation, political affairs, policy decisions and control of the executive branch.

Financial business, the 'power of the purse', was of paramount importance as a lever in the hands of the council in bringing its weight to bear on a manager. In the early years of management, the budgetary function was represented to elected members as, and no doubt actually was, an engine of democratic control and (in relation to the manager at any rate) overriding power. With the expansion of council functions, both in numbers and significance, there has been less emphasis on rates and borrowing as key concerns of elected members, but there was nevertheless considerable opposition to the 1977 Local Government (Financial Provisions) Bill on the grounds that it diminished local responsibility and freedom in financial matters by the abolition of domestic rates. Section 13 of the Local Government (Financial Provisions) Act, 1978 removed 'the making of a rate' from the list of reserved functions, at the head of which it had stood since management was introduced in 1929. The making of the rate was then taken to cover the determination of a rate in the pound and the application of that decision to a multitude of individual rateable properties, the results being detailed in rate books. This ambiguity was clarified over the years and the 'making' of a rate had come to mean assessment subsequent to the 'determination' (Street, 1955, p. 501). As the work of making out assessments was essentially an executive task, it was no longer appropriate to the reserved functions and section 13 of the 1978 Act assigns it to the manager.

Councils are generally precluded from involving themselves in staff matters other than the appointment of managers and, if necessary, their suspension or removal with the minister's consent.

Generally, the reserved functions are those which determine the policy parameters (for example the annual budget, the development plan, the library development programme and bye-laws). A further set of reserved functions allow for a general supervisory role or continuing oversight of the manager's conduct of the council's business – this role is exercised by resolution of the elected council. City and then county managers were required by law to submit to the members at each meeting a register of the orders made since the previous meeting. Later, provision was made in the Management Acts for intervention by the council in the executive area, by passing a special resolution directing the manager to act in a particular way. This power, contained in section 4 of the City and County Management (Amendment) Act, 1955 (subsequently repealed and replaced by the Local Government Act, 2001, section 140)[2], applies to all executive functions with the exception of staff control and management; but it cannot be used to dictate a line of action in all cases of a specified kind.

Neither can the manager be coerced under the so-called 'section 4 procedure' to do anything of an illegal nature. This escape hatch has been used on a number of occasions including in 1979 in one of the later episodes of the Wood Quay affair. The newly elected Dublin Corporation sought to halt progress on the civic offices project at Wood Quay pending clarification of the position vis-à-vis the Viking remains and the archaeological excavation of the site, part of which had been declared by the High Court to be a national monument. The deputy city manager, acting on the law agent's unambiguous advice, said it would be illegal for him to do what the council wanted. The lord mayor followed the deputy manager and ruled the section 4 motion out of order. The council was supplied with the opinions of the law agent and senior counsel.

The practice in certain local authorities of directing managers, by the use of the section 4 procedure, to grant planning applications which were otherwise unlikely to be granted brought the procedure into considerable disrepute. In at least one local authority, because of the number of such motions (and the statutory requirement that they be dealt with before any other business), there were several meetings at which no other council business was reached. Section 44 of the Local Government Act, 1991 amended the procedure in relation to planning decisions by providing that at least three-quarters of the councillors for the particular electoral area must sign the section 4 motion and at least three-quarters of the entire membership of the council must vote in favour of the motion before it has any effect; this special voting procedure in relation to planning matters is now provided for in section 34(6) and (7) of the Planning and Development Act, 2000.

A series of High Court and Supreme Court decisions in relation to planning section 4s – upholding managers' decisions not to comply with directions to grant planning permissions, where the courts accepted that the elected members had not complied with all of their legal obligations to act in a quasi-judicial manner – has

---

[2] Section 140(2) of the Local Government Act, 2001 states that 'Subject to this section, an elected council or joint body may by resolution require any particular act, matter or thing specifically mentioned in the resolution and which the local authority or manager concerned can lawfully do or effect, to be done or effected in the performance of the executive functions of the local authority'.

meant that such motions are a thing of the past in most local authorities. It is likely that many elected members are happy with the demise of the procedure, as inevitably their support for a particular planning section 4 motion led to pressure on them to support many others.

It is the manager's duty to advise and assist the council in the exercise of its reserved powers and in such other matters where it may require his or her help. The manager must attend meetings of the council or a committee of the council if requested to do so by the council. The manager also has the right of attendance at council meetings, where he or she may take part in the discussions but may not vote.

Managers

The city manager is an officer of the city council. The county manager is an officer of the county council, but is also manager of each borough council, town council and every joint body whose functional area is wholly within the county. The manager's salary, fixed by the minister, is paid by the county council, which recovers portions from the other bodies concerned either as a county-at-large charge or in the form of contributions fixed by the minister. A deputy city or county manager must be appointed to function during the manager's absence on vacation, sick leave or otherwise. Deputies may be designated either by the manager or, if circumstances require, by the (lord) mayor or chairperson of the county council. Notification of the appointment must be made to the Minister for the Environment and Local Government (Local Government Act, 2001, section 148).

The manager acts formally by way of written orders, signed and dated. The early requirement that an order should show the time when made was altered by the City and County Management (Amendment) Act, 1955, section 20 (now provided for under the Local Government Act, 2001, section 151), to say that a statement of date was sufficient. A register of orders must be kept and a record of orders made since the previous meeting must be available to the members at each meeting.

There are thirty-four managers in local government – five city and twenty-nine county managers (including North Tipperary and South Tipperary, and the three 'new' counties of South Dublin, Fingal and Dún Laoghaire-Rathdown). Each county and city has its own manager. The City and County Management (Amendment) Act, 1955, responding to local opinion, provided a degrouping procedure for paired counties which were not happy to continue sharing a manager. All six of the paired counties opted to split during the period 1965 to 1982, the last pair being Laois and Offaly. The procedure could also be availed of to separate Dublin county from the city, but it was never so used. However, the Local Government Act, 1991 provided for the establishment of three new counties, each with its own manager, to replace the former Dublin County Council; and ended the Dublin city manager's responsibility for Dublin county. The new county councils were established on 1 January 1994 by the Local Government (Dublin) Act, 1993.

Appointments of city and county managers are made only on the recommendations of the Local Appointments Commissioners. A manager can be suspended by a three-quarters majority of the city or county council (section 146(5), Local Government Act, 2001) and removed from office with the consent of the minister. The manager is the chief executive officer for the local authorities in his or her bailiwick. He or she organises, controls and if necessary disciplines the staff; enters into contracts; gives or withholds planning permissions; allots house tenancies; and makes a host of other decisions as part of the day-to-day business of the local authorities. A major preoccupation is the budgetary process, in which the manager has a central role – preparing the annual budget (formerly known as the estimates) and seeing it through the council. Even where an estimates committee was appointed, the responsibility and the burden of work were often shouldered by the manager. Obviously, it would not be possible for the manager to personally perform all of these functions and in practice many are formally delegated to directors of services and other senior staff.

Assessments of the System

An admirable account of the Irish management system is given by Dr A. H. Marshall in *Local Government Administration Abroad* (1967), a series of reports on American and European systems commissioned by the Maud Committee on Management of Local Government. Marshall commented on: the large measure of acceptance and appreciation of the system he found among the elected members; relations between managers and technical officers, 'the one unsettled problem of the manager system'; the persistent tendency among members to underrate their collective capabilities; and, in general, despite some objections, the obvious merits of the system. He sums up:

> The undeniable fact is that Ireland having sought for an answer to the problem of reconciling ultimate democratic control with prompt discharge of duties, has found a solution which under Irish conditions is working well. The name 'manager' is perhaps unfortunate. There is no doubt that it is responsible for a good deal of the misunderstanding in the country itself, and certainly outside, where the name 'manager' conveys the impression that the Irish manager is like his American counterpart. This is not so. The Irish manager is a manager neither in the commercial sense nor in the American local government sense. He is in fact more akin to the English official, especially in his relations with the elected members.

Marshall's assessment has not been contradicted in its general findings, and may be accepted as reasonably accurate.

A subsequent report, *Strengthening the Local Government Service* (McKinsey, 1971), dealt less with the position and performance of managers than with staff structures, but the recommendations imply a general view that managers were involved too closely in detailed administration – a position forced on them, perhaps, by their experience with councils – and not enough in planning and organisation. The report's recommendations included proposals for:

- management posts under the county manager for each of the major services, thus integrating technical and administrative responsibility
- a planning and development officer in each county both for preparing county plans and for facilitating economic development (in co-operation with IDA)
- a personnel and administration officer in each county for recruitment and training and co-ordination of administrative services
- a county finance officer for all financial and management accounting services.

These proposals were based on a projected integration of town and county staffs and the amalgamation of several pairs of smaller counties under a single manager. In general, the proposed re-organisation of staff structures did not exactly occur as planned. However, it could be said that the restructuring of senior grades in 2000 and 2001 and the appointment of directors of services (directly beneath the position of manager) for various service areas represents a move towards the proposals referred to in the first of the points above. Also, by the start of the twenty-first century most county and city councils had dedicated officers working on personnel, finance and planning issues.

Tenure of City and County Managers

There was no specific age limit for the first managers. They held office subject to their death, resignation or removal from office. The 1946 Local Government (Officers' Age Limit) Order fixed the age limit for all pensionable officers of local authorities at 65 years. The Local Government Act, 1958 repealed the statutory tenure of the office of managers and effectively set a retirement age for them. This disposed of the anomaly which had caused some difficulty with the first generation of managers and which resulted in a successful High Court action by Liam Raftis, the then Waterford city manager, who served until the age of seventy-two.

In 1991, the Barrington Report recommended that managers should be appointed for ten years. Section 47 of the Local Government Act, 1991 enabled the minister to specify by order periods and ages relating to the office of manager. The 1991 Local Government (Tenure of Office) Order provided that persons appointed to an office of manager after 21 May 1991 hold office for seven years or until age sixty, whichever is earlier.

Whilst *Better Local Government* (Department of the Environment, 1996) suggests that the new arrangements are working satisfactorily, there was some concern that the insecurity generated by the seven-year tenure resulted in a number of managers moving within a few years to a different local authority where a new seven-year term would commence. This results in a lack of continuity in the affected counties and in order to discourage this, the 1997 programme for government suggested that the seven-year term would be increased to ten years and that a loyalty bonus would be paid to those managers who stayed for the full term. The Local Government Act, 2000 allows managers in their fifth year of service to opt to extend their seven-year tenure by a further period of three years – subject to not exceeding the overall age limit of 65 years. This provision is restated in section 147 of the Local Government Act, 2001.

Comparison with Local Authority Chief Executives in the UK

Most local authorities appointed chief executives after a 1974 reorganisation of local government in England. The chief executive is the 'head of paid service' and is appointed directly by the council following interview by a small group of members, usually assisted by external consultants or advisers (for example a chief executive of a similar authority). Each council determines the functions that it wishes to delegate to the chief executive and other chief officers. As a result, the duties of chief executives vary considerably. Many of the day-to-day executive decisions, which in an Irish local authority would be carried out by formal order of the manager, are carried out by formal resolution of the council or delegated to committees. The Irish manager, on the other hand, is appointed by the council following a competition conducted by the Local Appointments Commissioners and derives his or her powers, functions and duties from statutory provision rather than from delegation by the council.

Another contrast, pointed out by Asquith and O'Halpin (1997, p. 84) is that the managers in Ireland tend to have worked in various local authorities and in various areas of local authority service before becoming managers. In the UK, it is not uncommon for chief executives to have worked in a number of different local authorities, but equally chief executives have often followed a career plan in specific disciplines such as law, finance or planning.

Strengthening the Management System

Better Local Government (Department of the Environment, 1996) states that the role of manager as envisaged when the system was established is very different from what is needed now. Not alone do local authorities have a significantly wider range of functions with consequent demands on the manager's time, but managers are also expected to play a wider role in the affairs of the community generally and to take on many functions not directly related to the traditional core activities of the local authority. Collins (1987, p. 59) points out that managers have to spend some time contributing to the wider local government system, through for example serving on various national organisations, attending meetings in central government departments, discussing new issues and legislation with their peers and serving on interview boards in other local authorities.

Better Local Government suggests that below the level of manager and assistant manager, the management structure has not evolved with the changing role of local authorities and a proper policy development role has not been built up. In order to strengthen the policy development role of the elected members, each county council and city council was required to establish a number of strategic policy committees (SPCs) made up of councillors and representatives of appropriate sectoral interests (see chapter 3). The establishment of a new tier of management with clear and unambiguous responsibility for the programmes of the local authority was proposed to support these committees and to strengthen the service at management level.

These new directors of services, appointed in 2000 and 2001, are delegated functions by the city or county manager. With this new grade came the demise of the positions of assistant manager, county/city engineer and county secretary. Directors of services constitute a new tier of local authority officials below the level of manager, with a responsibility for providing services in a specific function of the local authority (say, for example, housing and recreation), as well as providing advice and supporting the policy role of the SPC for that functional area. Some local authorities have gone for an area-based approach, where directors have a policy role in relation to a specific function but, on an operational basis, are responsible for delivering all services in a specific electoral area. It is expected that this new structure will enable the manager to devote more of his or her time to strategic issues.

The chairs of the strategic policy committees and the cathaoirleach/mayor of the local authority together form the corporate policy group (CPG), which acts as a sort of cabinet and provides a forum where policy positions affecting the whole council can be agreed for submission to the full council (such as the budget). This group is serviced by the manager and, under the Local Government Act, 2001, must be consulted in the preparation of the draft budget and the authority's corporate plan.

The reserved/executive framework was originally introduced to bring professionalism and efficiency into the administration of the business of local authorities. A working group of councillors, local authority managers and departmental representatives concluded in 1992 that the general allocation of roles in the framework is essentially correct. A similar system was introduced for health boards by the Health (Amendment) (No. 3) Act, 1996 and for vocational education committees by the Vocational Education (Amendment) Act, 2001.

Conclusion

Whilst the Irish local authority management system is praised by many observers and is generally regarded as having made an enormous contribution to local government since its introduction in 1929, some argue that it has resulted in a democratic deficit where many decisions and policies are initiated and implemented by a non-elected manager.

The provision in section 40 of the Local Government Act, 2001 to introduce full-time chairpersons of county and city councils, directly elected by the people, from 2004 could have signalled a further evolution of the role of the manager. The intention was that a full-time chairperson with a five-year mandate would improve the perceived imbalance between the democratic mandate and executive function. The provision was, however, repealed under the Local Government (No. 2) Act, 2003. It must also be remembered that the manager is already fully accountable to the elected council for his or her decisions and reports to them and their committees in public (and invariably with local media present) several times each month. This level of accountability and public scrutiny is unique for managers either in the public or private sectors in Ireland. Indeed, in a contribution to a review of the role of local government chief executives in different European countries, Asquith and O'Halpin (1998, p. 71) point out:

> Managers have always been public figures to some extent. This is due both to their statutory functions, and to the fact that they attend council meetings and speak on the record, sometimes in the face of very vigorous comments from councillors, and so are in the public eye in a way that civil servants are not.

There is a tendency to overestimate the power of the manager. For example, one survey of the attitudes of local politicians ranked county and city managers in second place amongst those they perceived to be the most influential in the region, just behind government ministers and well ahead of the press and interest groups (Coyle and Sinnott, 1992, p. 76 and p. 92). Local councillors, by contrast, were ranked in twelfth place. As Asquith and O'Halpin (1997, p. 86) put it, 'the "popular" view of the generally subservient politician within Irish local government is one which appears to have passed into folklore'. This is despite the development, in their view, of a cadre of some elected members that are willing to look at long-term strategic issues, as well as looking after the representations of individual constituents.

Chubb (1992, p. 278) gives what is probably still the definitive verdict on management in Irish local government. He notes two tendencies that should make for conflict but are in fact complementary. One is the emergence of the manager as 'the main source of initiative in local government'. The other is the gradual accretion of power to the council in both the reserved and executive areas. The result has been that 'the roles of councillor and manager have evolved differently from those that were first envisaged and that the original statutes spelled out'. This is tellingly borne out by a quotation from Matthew Macken, a former Dublin city and county manager, which is worth reproducing here:

> The original intention of the legislators to draw a clear line, both in law and in practice, between the Council's reserved functions and the Manager's executive functions has been lost sight of in some degree in the evolution of the system. Managers find themselves involved in business reserved to the Councils . . . On the other hand Councillors have gained over the years considerable influence in relation to the Manager's functions (Chubb, 1992, p. 285).

In reality, the functions of the local authority are carried out on a partnership basis by the manager and the elected members in consultation with the local community. The establishment of strategic policy committees will allow councillors and sectoral interests a more meaningful role in policy review and development and enhance their partnership with the manager.

The strengthening of the structure through the recent appointment of directors of services and other senior officials will enable the manager to delegate many of his or her operational responsibilities to these new appointees. This, in turn, will enable the managers to concentrate their efforts on the major strategic issues facing their counties and cities such as infrastructural development, economic development, e-government, information and communications technology, tourism, improved quality of life and relationships with other organisations. Thus the role of the county and city manager is continuing to evolve to meet the challenges of the third millennium.

8

Process: How the System Operates

John Tierney

Local authorities carry out the tasks assigned to them in several ways: by the members of the authority acting as a body at meetings, through committees, through the manager and through officers who have been given the necessary authority to act. For instance, only the members at a meeting can decide how much is to be raised by way of commercial rates in any year; they cannot delegate this duty. Vocational education cannot be administered directly by the council; a committee must be appointed for this purpose. The control of officers and the discharge of executive functions are matters for the manager in the case of bodies for which a manager is appointed, and when a particular officer has been assigned a duty by statute the duty must be discharged by that officer.

Meetings and Procedures

Meetings

With the enactment of the Local Government Act, 2001, the provisions relating to the meetings and proceedings of local authorities were consolidated into a uniform code (section 44 and schedule 10). On the basis of these provisions, detailed regulations were introduced in 2001 (Local Government Act, 2001 (Meetings) Regulations 2002 [SI No. 66 of 2002]). Certain meetings must be held at prescribed times; others may be held at the discretion of the local authority. Each year local authorities are required to hold an annual meeting, a budget meeting and other meetings as are necessary (schedule 10, paragraph 1). Where practicable, meetings shall be held in the principal offices of the local authority.

The cathaoirleach/mayor may convene a special meeting at any time or any five members may convene a special meeting if the cathaoirleach/mayor, after requisition by five members to do so, refuses. The business to be transacted at a meeting is that specified in the agenda for the meeting. Notification of the meeting and agenda is sent to the members and public notice must be displayed at the principal offices of the local authority. The names of members present at each meeting are recorded as well as the names of members voting for or against where there is a division. The cathaoirleach/mayor presides or, if he or she is absent, the leas-chathaoirleach/deputy mayor officiates. If both are absent, members choose a member present at the meeting to take the chair. In the case of an equality of votes, the person chairing the meeting has a second or casting vote (schedule 10, paragraph 12). This rule does not apply in the case of the election of the cathaoirleach/mayor by the council.

Local authorities regulate their meetings and proceedings by means of standing orders (schedule 10, paragraph 16). The minister may issue general directions in relation to standing orders and the provisions to be included in them. Guidelines on standing orders were issued in 2002. Decisions are normally taken by the majority of the members present who vote, not necessarily the majority present (schedule 10, paragraph 12).

Special procedures (section 37) apply with regard to the election of the cathaoirleach/mayor. All candidates must be proposed and seconded at the outset. In the case of more than one candidate, a poll must be taken and if a majority of the members present vote for a particular candidate he or she is deemed elected. Where no candidate gets a majority in these circumstances, then the candidate getting the least number of votes is eliminated at each stage until the number is reduced to two. If there is an equality of votes between three or more candidates, a candidate is excluded by lot. If there is an equality of votes between two candidates, a candidate is elected by lot. As already indicated, the casting vote procedure does not apply in relation to the election of the cathaoirleach/mayor.

For every authority a quorum is fixed – one-quarter of membership (always rounded up) plus one (schedule 10, paragraph 11). Decisions cannot be questioned on the grounds that a vacancy existed or a member was disqualified. Minutes of proceedings must be kept by a meetings administrator and authenticated by the signature of the cathaoirleach/mayor (or the person chairing the meeting at which they are confirmed).

Proceedings are usually reported at length in the local and sometimes in the national press. Most local authorities experience little demand from the public for admission unless there is some controversy or a question of uncommon local concern being debated. Meetings of vocational educational committees are also usually open to the press.

Members of local authorities have a qualified privilege in respect of defamatory statements. The basis of this qualified privilege for a local authority public representative is his or her public representative capacity and that the statement is made in this capacity on a matter which is relevant to the public representative's constituents. However, this privilege is lost if the public representative makes a statement with malice, that is with ill will, spite or improper motive. This is in contrast to members of the Oireachtas who have an absolute privilege against defamation in relation to statements made by them in the Houses of the Oireachtas. This absolute privilege is derived from the Constitution and is strictly defined.

Travelling Expenses, Allowances and Representational Payments

Payment of expenses to councillors was introduced by section 63 of the Local Government Act, 1925 and extended by section 80 of the Local Government Act, 1941. Subsistence allowances were added by the Local Government Act, 1946, section 67. A new system of fixed annual expenses was provided for in regulations and directions under section 51 of the Local Government Act, 1991 and these provisions remain in force under the Local Government Act, 2001, section 142(8). The new system came into operation on the 1 January 1994. As a consequence, every local authority member became entitled to a composite annual allowance covering his or her expenses as a local authority member, other than expenses payable separately under other provisions.

In the case of county and city council members, the annual allowance is calculated individually for each member. The annual allowance comprises three elements: travel, subsistence and a fixed annual allowance to cover postage, telephone and miscellaneous representational expenses. The travel and subsistence expenses elements are calculated on an annual basis by reference to each member's distance from the council's headquarters and an index figure applicable to the local authority concerned. The index figure is related to the overall number of meetings considered reasonable for that local authority. Following the introduction of strategic policy committees (SPCs) in 1998, it was decided to increase the annual allowance for all members and introduce an additional allowance for the chairpersons of SPCs. Members of town councils are entitled to expenses at a flat-rate composite annual allowance, at the rate specified for the authority concerned. Members must fulfill certain attendance requirements in order to qualify for the full annual allowance, which covers all meetings of the authority, committees, joint committees and so forth. Expenses for conference attendance are paid separately.

The question of paying an actual salary to local authority members was widely discussed during the 1990s and provision has been made for the remuneration of elected members in section 142 of the Local Government Act, 2001. In 2001, the minister announced details of representational payments for elected members, with the levels for counties and cities linked to one-quarter of the salary of a member of Seanad Éireann (see chapter 6).

Section 143 of the Local Government Act, 2001 provides for the payment of an allowance for reasonable expenses (to cover entertainment duties and so forth) to the cathaoirleach/mayor and leas-chathaoirleach/deputy mayor of a local authority. The decision to pay such an allowance, and the determination of the amount, is a reserved function.

In July 1998, and pursuant to section 12 of the Local Government Act, 1998, the introduction of a local authority members (gratuity) scheme provided for the payment of a once-off gratuity to members of local authorities who are or were serving at any time following the previous local elections and who decided not to go forward for election in 1999. Serving members who would have had at least five years qualifying service at the date of the local elections in 1999, or those who had retired or died since the last local elections with at least five years qualifying service, were eligible provided they made an application in writing by 15 September 1998 (applications were obviously not required in respect of members who had died before that date). The intention of the measure was to encourage some of the longer serving members to stand down and create opportunities for new entrants. A permanent scheme has been provided for under section 142 of the Local Government Act, 2001 (see chapter 6).

Conflict of Interest

Conflict of interest may arise where a councillor or a local authority employee encounters, in the course of local authority business, an issue in which he or she has a personal interest. The position is that the legal safeguards as they affected members were removed with the introduction of the management system. Thus, the disqualifying clause in article 12(4) and the prohibition in article 36(6) of the 1898 Local Government (Application of Enactments) Order, together with section 2 of the Municipal Corporations (Ireland) Act, 1842, were repealed by the Local Government Act, 1941. The reason was that the decisions involved were executive functions in which members could not intervene. However, the position was complicated by the introduction of the City and County Management (Amendment) Act, 1955, section 4 of which gave elected members the power to direct the manager to perform an executive function in a particular manner. The prohibitions against taking part in decision making where councillors have a personal interest were revived by the Housing Act, 1966 (section 115), the Local Government (Planning and Development) Act, 1976 (section 32(4)) and subsequently the Planning and Development Act, 2000 (section 148(2)). The planning provisions applied not only to councillors but to prescribed classes of local authority officials, as well as members and employees of An Bord Pleanála.

The Ethics in Public Office Act, 1995 sets out the requirements for ministers and Oireachtas members in relation to declaration of interests. The provisions of this Act (as strengthened by the Standards in Public Office Act, 2001) were extended to local authorities under the Local Government Act, 2001, section 180, in part due to a number of well-publicised controversies in the 1990s, particularly in the planning process. The ethical framework for the local government system instituted in 2001 builds on the provisions of the planning code and the principles underlying the Ethics in Public Office Act. In general terms:

> . . . in carrying out their functions under this or any other enactment, it is the duty of every member and every employee of a local authority and of every member of every committee to maintain proper standards of integrity, conduct and concern for the public interest (Local Government Act, 2001, section 168).

Under the Local Government Act, 2001, the minister is empowered to issue national codes of conduct as guidance on the standards expected of local authority members and employees in the performance of their duties (section 169). Elected members and certain officials of the local authority must submit an annual declaration of interests (section 171). Penalties are provided for submitting false or misleading information. Each local authority manager must appoint an ethics registrar, who keeps a register of interests that must be made available for public inspection (section 172). The position of ethics registrar may not be held by the same person for more than two consecutive years.

Where an issue is raised at a local authority or committee meeting and an elected member has an interest in the matter, the member must disclose the nature of his or her interest, withdraw from the meeting and not take part in any discussion or voting on the matter. Similarly, should a manager or other employee have an interest in a particular matter they must disclose this fact. If such a matter is normally exercised by the manager (and the manager has declared an interest), it will be delegated to another employee (sections 177 to 179). The Standards in Public Office Commission, established under the Ethics in Public Office Act, 1995, section 21, can also investigate and report on alleged or possible breaches of ethics. In 2002, the Local Government Act, 2001 (Part 15) Regulations (SI No. 582 of 2002) were published on the ethical framework for local government and the new framework applied as and from 1 January 2003.

Public Participation

Local government is the level of government that is most accessible to the average citizen and presents the most opportunities for participating in public affairs. Part of its rationale is that it provides access to decision making in local affairs. However, the number of local authorities in Ireland does not compare favourably with other European countries. The number of inhabitants per county and city council (which are the 'primary units' of local government under the Local Government Act, 2001 and are responsible for most local government functions) is much larger than in other

European countries with the exception of Britain. See chapter 26 for further discussion of this issue. In the Irish context there is a need to reform the structure at sub-county level to make local government less remote and to strengthen the concept of participation. The movement for modifying local government to increase its sensitivity to local opinion has been finding a more ready response in recent years.

There are a number of statutory provisions for public consultation, for example, planning as regards draft development plans, local authority development and individual planning permission, and environment as regards draft waste management plans and environmental impact statements. Where the desired change has not taken place at the statutory level, the pressure to participate in or influence decisions has taken the form of non-statutory community councils, development associations, residents' associations and interest groups of various kinds. A further impulse towards the creation of voluntary groups has come from a combination of factors tending to diminish the discretionary scope of local elected members such as the bureaucracy of local authorities, the growth of professional decision making, the removal of effective powers in most issues to central government and the strength of party politics in local councils.

Attempts to incorporate voluntary effort in some formal way in the official system have encountered difficulties. The machinery in the Local Government Acts, 1941 and 1955 for creating 'approved local councils' was not utilised to any great extent (although the provision has been replaced in an updated format by section 128 of the Local Government Act, 2001, which provides for 'recognised associations'). The suggestion in the White Paper on local government reorganisation (Government of Ireland, 1971, pp. 45–6) for county area committees made up of elected councillors and nominees of community councils ran into strong opposition and was not proceeded with at the time. The proposals contained in the Barrington Report (1991, pp. 33–7) regarding district councils/committees were not acted upon.

It was not until the launch of *Better Local Government* (Department of the Environment, 1996) that the issue of broadening involvement in local government was further considered. Each county and city council was required to establish strategic policy committees (SPCs) mirroring the major functions of the local authority. One-third of the membership of these committees is drawn from sectoral interests such as trade unions, farming organisations, the business/commercial sector and the community/voluntary/disadvantaged sector. These committees have now been set up in all counties and cities. Town councils also have the option of establishing municipal policy committees (MPCs) with a similar composition and policy remit. The new committee structure also provides city and county councils with the option of establishing area committees (see chapter 3).

There are numerous examples of joint citizen action for local improvements, conservation and lobbying activities. The emergence of group water (and occasionally sewerage) schemes in rural districts is a good example. Clubs and local associations have been successful in providing swimming facilities with the aid of official grants and other forms of assistance. Tidy towns committees have been very effective in raising the standard of communal care and maintenance in villages and small towns. Voluntary activists have also been prominent in the area of social housing, environmental campaigns and controversies about development.

A number of national organisations have been based on federations of local voluntary organisations. The National Association of Tenants Organisations (NATO) gave a central focus to agitation by groups of local authority tenants; and the Association of Combined Residents' Associations (ACRA) filled a similar role for private houseowners and tenants. Muintir na Tíre and the Irish Countrywomen's Association (ICA) are concerned in different ways with community development and enhancing the quality of rural life. The National Federation of Group Water Schemes Society Ltd was formed as a response to the abolition of domestic charges for consumers on public schemes. In the urban context, the Chambers of Commerce of Ireland are becoming more influential.

A vote every five years, in terms of real participation, is altogether too blunt an instrument in our rapidly changing society. This problem was exacerbated in the 1990s with the postponement of elections. The citizenry needs to be better engaged in the initiation, execution and evaluation of policy. It remains to be seen whether the new committee structure will prove to be effective in this regard.

Central Government Controls

The principal departments of state concerned with local administration are enumerated in chapter 3. Some thirteen out of the fifteen departments have local involvements. The methods by which control is exercised from central government are laid down in statutes. The most common is to require the sanction, approval or concurrence by the minister to a decision before it can take effect. It is normal practice for the Houses of the Oireachtas, where complete legislation would burden statutes with excessive detail, to authorise the minister concerned to make regulations to fill in these details. Such regulations are usually laid before the Houses of the Oireachtas, which can annul them within a specified time. The minister in making regulations may, therefore, be said to legislate for the local authorities and guide them in implementing law with the tacit approval of the Dáil and Seanad.

Removal of Members from Office

The most drastic of all the numerous forms of control available to the minister is removing the elected members and appointing a commissioner to perform the reserved functions. Although it is provided for in part 21 of the Local Government

Act, 2001, this device is rarely used (at the time of writing it had not been called into play since the case of Naas Urban District Council in 1985). The minister may remove the members of local authorities from office for any of the following reasons:

- if the minister is satisfied after a local inquiry that the local authority is not duly or effectually performing its functions
- if the local authority neglects to comply with a judgment, order or decree of any court
- if the local authority refuses or wilfully neglects to comply with an express requirement imposed on it by any enactment
- if the local authority fails to comply with the requirements concerning the adoption of the budget
- if the number of members are insufficient to form a quorum for meetings.

Control of Officers

Local authorities employ some 36,000 people with an annual payroll cost of over €635 million (2002). Although the appointment of officers still rests with the local authority, it can only exercise this power within certain parameters provided for in national legislation. In the case of vacancies that must be referred in the first instance to the Local Appointments Commissioners for their recommendation, the law makes the act of appointment by the local authority a matter of form. In the case of other appointments, it prescribes either competitive examinations or some other impartial method of selection. Qualifications have been prescribed for almost all offices and where that is the case no further qualifications can be prescribed by local authorities without the sanction of the minister.

Redress

Local administration, in common with central government, operates subject to judicial review. This process comes into play where exception is taken to any local action or decision and redress is sought from a competent court. Some decisions or practices may be open to criticism as conflicting with an article of the Constitution, particularly in the area of fundamental rights.

The doctrine of *ultra vires* applied to local government up to 1991. A local authority had to be able to adduce legal authority for its actions. If a local authority purported to do something in exercise of its powers but was acting beyond the powers, it was said to be acting *ultra vires* and could be restrained by the High Court. In order to get over this restriction, a general competence provision was introduced (Local Government Act, 1991, section 6, subsequently repealed and replaced by Local Government Act, 2001, section 66). If, on the other hand, a local authority fails to carry out a duty imposed by law, the court may direct it to perform the duty. The court may review and, if necessary, quash decisions of a judicial character taken by a minister exceeding his or her statutory powers and therefore acting without jurisdiction. The High Court may act by way of the prerogative orders of prohibition, *mandamus* or *certiorari*. A rare form of order, *quo warranto*, has been invoked in disputed elections or appointment to offices. Charges and surcharges made by the local government auditor may also be brought before the court for review. Local authorities can be sued for acts that caused damage to others and be made amenable for the consequence to others for their neglect or default. The members are not, however, individually liable.

The Ombudsman

The Office of the Ombudsman was established under the Ombudsman Act, 1980 and was originally restricted to investigating complaints regarding the civil service. The role was extended in 1985 to investigate complaints about administrative actions, delays or inaction adversely affecting persons or bodies in their dealings with a local authority.

On the basis of its findings, the Office of the Ombudsman may make recommendations for improvements. The Ombudsman also publishes annual reports which give an account of some of the more noteworthy cases each year, including cases involving local authorities.

Freedom of Information

The Freedom of Information Act, 1997 came into operation in relation to local authorities in October 1998. The Act asserts the right of members of the public to obtain access to official information to the greatest extent possible, consistent with the public interest and the right to privacy. The Act established a legal right for each person to:

- access information held by public bodies
- have official information relating to him/herself amended where it is incomplete, incorrect or misleading
- obtain reasons for decisions affecting oneself.

In addition, the Act provided for the establishment of an independent Office of the Information Commissioner to review decisions relating to freedom of information (FOI) made by public bodies and to make binding decisions. The Information Commissioner publishes an annual report with details of FOI requests made to public bodies, including local authorities.

The FOI Act requires local authorities to publish information about themselves, the information they hold and the internal rules and guidelines used in decision making. This information has been published by each local authority under what are commonly referred to as section 15 and section 16 manuals.

Some changes were made to the 1997 legislation under the Freedom of Information (Amendment) Act, 2003, although many of these changes concerned central government records and cabinet papers in particular.

Loans and Grants

Loans cannot be raised by local authorities without the sanction of central government (Local Government Act, 2001, section 106). This applies even to temporary loans from banks by means of overdrafts. The Oireachtas formerly fixed limits beyond which borrowing for some purposes cannot be effected, but these limits were removed in 1960.

Grants voted by the Oireachtas and other subventions that flow from the exchequer to local authorities all go through the appropriate departments and final payments are not, as a rule, made prior to an examination of the relevant expenditure. The great increase that has taken place in these grants since 1978 has made local authorities very dependent on government for financial assistance (see chapter 18).

Central–Local Relations

The relationship between central and local government has tended to develop on an ad hoc basis rather than according to a general principle. In the period before the reform of parliament in 1832, local authorities were left very much to their own devices. Occasionally there was intervention, as in the attempt to regulate the borough corporations in the seventeenth century, but such intervention was exceptional. In the nineteenth century there was no consistent policy as regards control. Although in 1838 strict supervision was established over the poor law authorities, the borough corporations were in 1840 allowed autonomy except in a few matters such as loans and the disposal of corporate property. It is only since local government has been put on a representative basis, and local services have grown, that the need for a uniform system of regulation has been felt.

The dominant thinking during the nineteenth century, in spite of Bentham and Chadwick and the poor law system they helped to shape, was that of J. S. Mill whose *Representative Government* furnished much of the intellectual basis for English local government. Chapter 15 includes the following assertion:

> The Authority which is most conversant with principles should be supreme over principles, while that which is most competent in details should have the details left to it. The principal business of the central authority should be to give instruction, of the local authority to apply it. Power may be localised, but knowledge, to be more useful, must be centralised.

The Local Government Board (1871) and its Irish equivalent reflected, in part at least, this liberal philosophy and, although the devolutionary ideas inherent in the

Acts of 1888 and 1898 were never fully realised, central intervention in local affairs, even in Ireland, was kept to a decent minimum. Control, however, expanded with the extension of the franchise and the increase of state subsidies. Only in the case of one service, public assistance, was there any express power of general direction and control given to the appropriate minister, but in practice the degree of central supervision exercised was not noticeably less in other services such as roads, health, housing and technical education.

Observers have repeatedly remarked on the unusually subordinate status of our local authorities since independence. The Devlin Report (1969, 5.3.16) noted:

> The striking feature of the Irish system of local government, whether it is compared with local government systems abroad or with other administrative systems within the country, is the degree and extent of the controls exercised over it. The Maud Committee on the Management of Local Government in Britain . . . made a perceptive study of local government in seven countries including Ireland. They concluded that, in Ireland, central control is the most stringent of all.

The 1971 White Paper on local government reorganisation recognised excessive controls as one of the problems of local government reorganisation and devoted a chapter to the subject (Government of Ireland, 1971, pp. 53–5). It dealt with the scope for liberalising law and practice in the three major areas of control: statutory, financial and administrative.

The Barrington Report (1991, p. 14) neatly summarised the problem being caused by central control:

> In sum the restricted functions, lack of autonomous funding and the level of central controls, inhibit local stimulation of social, economic and cultural development. This can result in a combination of frustration at local level and passive dependence on the centre.

The Local Government Act, 1991 (Removal of Control) Regulations 1993 (SI No. 172 of 1993) were regarded as an attempt (albeit a minor one) towards a less restrictive legal framework. These regulations removed certain controls that required local authorities, in performing specified statutory functions, to obtain consent, sanction or the like from the minister. Miscellaneous controls under nineteen separate pieces of legislation were removed as were specific controls in relation to staff/personnel matters and land disposal. The Road Traffic Act, 1994 removed a number of statutory and administrative controls in relation to traffic management and there was further devolution of responsibility for personnel matters in 1996 (Circular LA (P) 4/96).

It should not of course be overlooked that a central department's major claim to authority does not rest solely on its powers of control, however formidable these may be. A department must justify its existence by other means. It must provide a degree of leadership for the system as a whole by introducing new policies or amending the old. It must gather, and as appropriate disseminate, facts, opinions and information. It must conduct research or at least tap research resources elsewhere. And it must, as far as possible, provide guidance and technical assistance for local authorities which lay on the services that are the end product of the system and the inducement to the public to continue, however reluctantly, paying for it.

Some examples are relevant in this regard. The Local Government (Planning and Development) Act, 1963 gave physical planning a much-needed facelift and local government generally a shot in the arm at the time. The 1971 White Paper furnished a volume of information and proposals to the public on local government reorganisation. It may not have reached statutory fulfilment but that is not necessarily the point. The 1972 White Paper on local finance and taxation was the culmination of a series of reports from an interdepartmental committee. It projected a programme of reform. The department commissioned the Economic and Social Research Institute to research this area further and an excellent report (Copeland and Walsh, 1975) on local authority expenditure and finance was submitted in December 1975. But these studies came too late. They were trumped almost immediately by the abolition of rates on domestic and certain other premises. This was a salutary but nevertheless bitter lesson in the dangers of neglecting until the eleventh hour a problem that had been crying out for attention.

Other aspects of the department's concerns received attention, for example roads and road traffic, water pollution, the fire services and housing. In 1991, the Barrington Report proved an informative document with many worthwhile proposals. Some of these proposals, such as the introduction of a general competence for local government and the setting up of regional authorities, were included in the Local Government Act, 1991.

There was an excellent study on local government finance carried out by KPMG at the behest of the department and published in 1996, but when *Better Local Government* was published subsequently the decision to abolish domestic water and sewerage charges was confirmed (Department of the Environment, 1996, p. 47). This decision, allied to the new funding regime, has increased local dependence on central funding. In other areas, there were more positive proposals aimed at widening the role of local government and enhancing democracy.

Central government appears to be muddling through rather than plotting a strategic direction for local government. There have been a number of reports but these have been met by an unwillingness to bring about fundamental reform. The approach has tended to be ad hoc and not always to best effect.

Services

A final departmental function that calls for mention is the provision of services for local authorities. These include the Local Appointments Commissioners, Local

Government Computer Services Board, Local Government Management Services Board and Local Government Audit Service. Certain services of local impact are administered directly by the department, for example housing grants and driver testing. They involve large-scale executive operations and are at variance with the main purposes of the department, which are advisory, supervisory and directive.

Powers and Functions

Local authorities derive their powers, functions and duties from Acts of the Oireachtas and originally, in the case of boroughs, from charters. Statutes that were in force in Ireland in 1922 were continued until repealed or amended and under the Constitution of 1937 the then existing laws were also continued. The law relating to the functions of local authorities is to be found principally in Public Acts but some of it is in Private Acts. It is also to be found in statutory instruments, formerly called statutory rules and orders, made under the authority of the Oireachtas, in provisional orders that with some exceptions have been confirmed by parliament or the Oireachtas, and in bye-laws made by local authorities which may or may not require confirmation by the central authority.

General Competence

Local authorities, as previously pointed out, were bound by the legal rule that prohibited the spending of money other than for objects authorised by statute. This rule of law had emerged in the courts during the nineteenth century; it had never been enacted by parliament in these terms, but the general effect of a series of decisions, combined with the scrutiny by local government auditors, had magnified its importance.

The *ultra vires* rule had been criticised in a number of reports (see, for example, Devlin Report, 1969, 25.3.8; Government of Ireland, 1971, pp. 56–7; Barrington Report, 1991, p. 45). Eventually, under section 6 of the Local Government Act, 1991, local authorities were given a general power (general competence) to take action to promote the interests of the local community in such a manner as they consider appropriate. This power of general competence was re-iterated in section 66 of the Local Government Act, 2001. This provision was intended to relax the outdated *ultra vires* principle and allow for a much freer and more flexible statutory framework. An action or measure is deemed to promote the interests of the community if it promotes social inclusion or the social, economic, environmental, recreational, cultural, community or general development of the local authority area or of the local community. A local authority may:

- carry out and maintain works of any kind
- provide, maintain, preserve or restore land, structures of any kind or facilities

- fit out, furnish or equip any building, structure or facility for any purpose
- provide utilities, equipment or materials for particular purposes
- provide services that are likely to benefit the local community
- provide assistance in money or kind
- enter into contracts or make such other arrangements considered necessary, either alone or jointly with any other person.

This general power cannot be used by a local authority to perform a function which is conferred otherwise by law on the authority and action may not be taken which would prejudice or duplicate activities arising from the performance of a statutory function of another body or involve wasteful or unnecessary expenditure.

Public and Private Acts

In the nineteenth century, boroughs and other towns promoted a large volume of legislation relating to their towns and in this way obtained powers to effect improvements. For instance Cork City promoted fifteen, and Dublin twenty, Acts in the period 1852 to 1899. This legislation dealt with improvements, waterworks, markets, drainage, rates, fire brigades, boundary extensions and other matters. As local government developed and general legislation covered a wider field, the necessity for this type of local legislation diminished. Moreover, some legislation of only local interest has been dealt with in Public Acts. Conspicuous instances of this are the group of Acts beginning with the Cork City Management Act, 1929, followed by the Local Government (Dublin) Act, 1930 relating to Dublin and Dún Laoghaire, and the City Management Acts for Limerick (1934) and Waterford (1939). The Local Government (Galway) Act, 1937, which restored borough status to Galway was, on the other hand, a Private Act.

Provisional Orders

Provisional orders can serve to shorten proceedings in the Oireachtas by allowing matters to be inquired into locally instead of by parliamentary committees. The Public Health Act, 1878, the Local Government Act, 1898 and other statutes give the central authority power to make provisional orders conferring powers in certain matters on local authorities. The local authority, instead of applying to the Oireachtas for the powers it desires to have, applies to the appropriate minister. After holding a local inquiry at which objections are heard, the minister may make a provisional order. When made, the order is normally submitted by the minister with other such orders in a Bill for confirmation by the Oireachtas. Not all provisional orders have, however, to be confirmed by the Oireachtas. Provisional orders for the compulsory acquisition of land, under the Acts of 1878 and 1898 referred to above, were confirmed by the minister or the Circuit Court in accordance with rules prescribed in 1925. The provisional order system has not been utilised in relation to local government matters for some time.

Bye-Laws

Local authorities have broad powers to make laws called bye-laws governing the operation of various facilities, for example parks provided by the local authority, and a general power to control or regulate any matter which, in the interests of the local community, should be regulated or controlled, provided the matter is not subject to existing law. The general requirement that bye-laws be confirmed by the relevant minister was removed in 1994 – although the minister may by regulation designate any matter in relation to which a bye-law would require ministerial confirmation before coming into force (Local Government Act, 2001, section 201).

There are many examples of specific legislation where local authorities may also make bye-laws: the Casual Trading Act, 1991; the Control of Horses Act, 1996; and the Road Traffic Act, 1994. This latter Act empowers local authorities to make bye-laws concerning speed limits. Bye-laws must be reasonable, consistent with and not repugnant to the general law, provide something additional to the general law, be certain and free from ambiguity and be obligatory on everyone in the area without discrimination. It must be within the power of the local authority to make them.

Development Corporations

The developmental role of local government was given statutory recognition by the Local Government (Planning and Development) Act, 1963, under which local authorities were 'invested with wide and flexible powers to engage in economic activity and to further the development of their areas'. The White Paper on local government reorganisation (Government of Ireland, 1971, p. 14) went further: 'Local authorities therefore must now regard themselves and be regarded as development corporations for their areas'. The Planning and Development Act, 2000 provides that, in addition to statutory issues which must be included in development plans, the local authority development plans may also include objectives facilitating the provision of hospitals, recreational, social or cultural centres, or facilities for the elderly and disabled.

The description of local authorities as 'development corporations' may be thought to overstate the case a little. The expression derives from British legislation on the creation of new towns and signifies a state body with extensive powers of land acquisition and development: constructing roads, streets and open spaces, houses, flats, shops, offices, factories and all the components of a town; providing services and (at least for a time) managing the properties so created. The project involves very heavy capital investment supplied by the state. No Irish local authority is in a position to take on and accomplish an undertaking of this magnitude. The Shannon Free Airport Development Company, Dublin Docklands Authority and Temple Bar Properties Ltd are more akin to development corporations.

Despite a shortage of resources, local authorities do play a significant role in facilitating development, for example under the urban renewal programme. Many innovative projects have also been developed in the community, recreational and tourism areas.

Local Government Functions

A comparison with any of the more developed local government systems in Europe demonstrates Ireland's rather meagre range of local services. For example, Swedish municipalities and county councils are responsible for:

+ consumer affairs	* building control
+ tourism	* libraries
* emergency services	+ cultural affairs
* land supply	+ sports and recreation
compulsory schools	* parks
primary and secondary education	* roads and streets
+ higher education (part of)	* street cleaning
adult education	* water supply
hospitals	* environmental protection
outpatient care	+ conservation
psychiatric care	* housing
health education	* planning
+ childcare including pre-schools	* waste management
care of elderly	+ regional development
medical and dental care	+ industrial and economic matters
immigrant matters	public transit.

The services operated through local authorities in Ireland are marked * (twelve out of thirty-two) while those in which there is a limited involvement are marked + (nine out of thirty-two). Local services in Ireland are broken down into eight programme groups as follows:

1.   Housing and Building
Assessment of housing need, the adequacy of housing and the enforcement of minimum standards; management and provision of local authority housing; assistance to persons housing themselves or improving their houses; Traveller accommodation; homelessness; administration of the social housing options.

2. Road Transportation and Safety
Construction, improvement and maintenance of roads; public lighting; traffic management; road safety education; collection of motor taxation; licensing of drivers.

3. Water Supply and Sewerage
Public water supply and sewerage schemes; group schemes; public conveniences.

4. Development Incentives and Controls
Physical planning policy; control of new development and building; development and implementation of a housing strategy; promotion of industrial and other development; urban and village renewal.

5. Environmental Protection
Waste management; burial grounds; safety of structures and places; fire protection; pollution control; Local Agenda 21; litter control.

6. Recreation and Amenity
Swimming pools; libraries; parks; open spaces; recreation centres; art galleries; museums; theatres; preservation and improvement of amenities.

7. Agriculture, Education, Health and Welfare
Appointments to vocational educational committees and regional health boards; administration of higher education grants.

8. Miscellaneous Services
Financial management and rate collection; elections; coroners and inquests; consumer protection measures; abattoirs; corporate estate.

This list demonstrates the heavy emphasis on the provision and maintenance of infrastructure and the physical aspects of the environment. Housing is the only area of social service provision that local authorities are involved in.

Perhaps the best treatment of how the current range of local authority functions could be expanded is to be found in the Barrington Report (1991, p. 19):

> If local government is to develop, rather than be relegated mainly to the provision of a narrow range of utility and regulatory functions, all public services that can be administered locally, should as far as possible be considered as candidates for devolution and this challenge will have to be faced up to.

The report recommended the devolution of functions in the following areas:

- matters administered centrally which would seem more appropriate to administration directly by local government, even within the very

restrictive Irish functional range, for example housing grants, foreshore licences, driver testing, standards and controls for safety at work
- activities, for example health, policing, education, welfare and heritage, in which a substantial local government role should be developed
- services carried out locally by national agencies which need to be linked at suitable crossover points with the reformed local government system as proposed in the report.

In the area of education, for example, a local education committee linked to local government was suggested (p. 21). This committee would cover the education system at pre-school, primary and secondary levels. It could also co-ordinate matters such as youth, adult education, optimum use of school premises, school maintenance and in general have a role in the planning and operation of the education system at local level.

Under health and social welfare, it was proposed that the community care programme should be linked with local government at the district level and integrated with the social welfare system. The aim would be to move to a geographic base in the delivery and planning of personal services, which would draw together the various public support services and voluntary bodies. The potential of transferring responsibility for many of the services that come under the title of community care to local authorities was recommended for examination (pp. 21–2).

An enhanced role for local government in the areas of transport and traffic; heritage and amenity; tourism; police, courts and justice; consumer protection; and general information services was recommended. It was agreed, for example, that local authorities should be given prime responsibility in the general amenity and heritage area; that local tourism offices should be brought within the local authority framework and local authorities given a role in the promotion and development of local tourism.

Since the publication of the report, there has been some progress in relation to the above. Devolution in the traffic area has already been referred to. There has been some advancement in the development of one-stop-shop initiatives, with local authorities having been given the lead role. Local authorities have a greater role in the heritage area. However, in the courts area the limited functions of local authorities relating to courthouses have been transferred to the Courts Service.

Overall the progress in devolving functions and widening the role of local government has been poor. A number of opportunities to develop the role since 1991 were not availed of. This was particularly evident in the area of local development. Partnership groups, LEADER groups, county and city enterprise boards and county tourism committees were established with limited local authority involvement. The reasons for bypassing local government were set out in *Better Local Government*:

The limited financial resources available to local authorities, the demands of traditional services and the lack of buoyancy in their financing system were seen to limit their capacity to take a wider role in community development (Department of the Environment, 1996, p. 28–9).

These reasons would hardly be accepted by those involved in the local government system. All of the local development initiatives have been funded directly by central government with EU assistance. The structures could easily have been set up within the remit of local government without duplicating administrative systems. Indeed, the one local development initiative funded through local government, the urban and village renewal programme, has worked very well and the department did not allow for any administrative costs and only limited technical assistance. There has been an attempt in recent times to address the need to integrate local government and local development systems through the establishment of city and county development boards. It can be argued that this presents an opportunity for local authorities to enhance their role in a reformed process of local governance. However, it could also be seen as further evidence of the unwillingness at the central level to engage in fundamental reform of the local government system in accordance with internationally accepted principles.

Functions

9

Housing

Michelle Norris

In the public mind housing stands in the forefront of local services. There are cogent reasons for this – its strong social and community significance, an economic significance deriving from the heavy capital investment it involves and its prominence in the building industry and as an employer . . . It is hardly surprising then that housing performance has been an abiding issue in local and even national politics (Roche, 1982b, p. 220).

The two decades since the publication of *Local Government in Ireland* in 1982 have been characterised by radical change in the local authority housing function, the extent of which is such that, by the late 1980s, Roche's observations regarding the traditional importance of this service must have appeared completely at variance with the tone of national policy. By this time, the rate of new public house-building had reduced to the extent that some commentators raised doubts as to whether local authorities would continue to be involved directly in housing provision (Lord Mayor's Commission on Housing, 1993).

By the late 1990s, however, the wheel had turned almost full circle and housing regained the position of importance within local authority services attributed to it by Roche. Nevertheless, the focus of the service has changed significantly from its traditional role. Although, in the face of rapid growth in housing waiting lists, new public house-building has increased from the historic low levels of the late 1980s, a more dramatic expansion has occurred in local authorities' housing functions. In addition, they now hold important new responsibilities in relation to enabling the development of housing by other agencies such as housing associations and co-operatives, building affordable houses for sale and planning for the implementation of national housing policy at the local level.

This chapter aims to map the main trends in the development of the local authority housing function from the beginning of local government involvement in this area in the mid-1800s to the start of the twenty-first century. This sweeping review focuses in particular on the contribution that local authorities have made to addressing housing need and on the principal items of legislation, relevant to the local authority housing service, which were introduced in this period. In the second part of the chapter, a more in-depth examination of the development of the housing function since 1980 is presented. This concentrates mainly on the changing focus of the service highlighted above. On the basis of this discussion, the conclusion to the chapter will consider whether local authorities will rise to meet the challenges associated with these new strategic functions.

Local Authority Housing in the Pre-Independence Period: Laying the Foundations

The local authority housing service in Ireland is almost as old as local authorities themselves. Its roots can be traced back to the period of the foundation of the modern local government system in the mid-1800s. At this time, many European countries experienced growing concern about the housing conditions of the low-income population – inspired by a range of interests including: philanthropists and social reformers, the emerging labour movement and a belief that housing conditions in urban slums were creating public health problems and fostering social unrest. This concern led to the creation of systems of state-subsidised housing for rent to low-income and disadvantaged groups known as social housing (Harloe, 1995). Ireland was no different in this regard, with the important caveat that its status as part of the UK until 1922 meant that the early development of its social housing was shaped by UK legislation, which has bequeathed both countries an atypical system of social housing provision in the wider European context. In addition, the distinctive political concerns of Ireland meant that the early development of social housing in Ireland had some unusual features which differentiate it from Britain and have influenced its evolution over the long term.

The foundations of local authority involvement in the provision of urban social housing in both Britain and Ireland lie in two policy developments: the gradual extension of slum clearance legislation throughout the latter half of the nineteenth century, which empowered local authorities to identify, close and clear unfit dwellings; and legislation requiring the licensing and inspection of common lodging houses, beginning with the Common Lodging Houses Act, 1851, which established the principle of state involvement in enforcing minimum housing standards. The advent of state subsidisation of housing provision to ensure higher standards was a logical extension of these provisions.

Subsidies of this type were originally introduced in Ireland under the Labouring Classes (Lodging Houses and Dwellings) Act, 1866, which provided low-cost public loans over forty years to private companies and urban local authorities for up to half the cost of a housing scheme. Although this initial housing legislation produced relatively modest outcomes, social house-building increased significantly under its successor – the Artisans' and Labourers' Dwellings Improvement Act, 1875. This Act provided low-cost public loans to the larger urban local authorities for the clearance of unsanitary sites which could then be used for new house-building.

It is important to note that the majority of output under the early social housing legislation was not by local authorities. In fact, the 1875 Act allowed local authorities to build dwellings only if no alternative provider could be found. Instead, dwellings were provided by philanthropic bodies such as the Guinness Trust (later renamed the Iveagh Trust) founded in 1890 and by semi-philanthropic organisations such as the Dublin Artisans Dwellings Company. The latter was established in 1876 and was run as a business paying a modest dividend of between 4 and 5 per cent to shareholders. With the aid of the low-cost loans provided under the housing legislation, together with grant aid from Dublin Corporation, organisations of this type had built 4,500 dwellings, accounting for approximately 15 per cent of Dublin's housing stock by the outbreak of World War I (Fraser, 1996). These dwellings were generally high density in design, they took the form of either four or five storey flats such as the Iveagh Buildings in Dublin's south inner-city which was built by the Iveagh Trust, or of terraced housing such as the Oxmanstown Road area in Stoneybatter, Dublin which was built by the Dublin Artisans Dwellings Company.

In contrast, local authority provision in towns and cities was slower to get off the ground. Ireland's first urban local authority housing scheme was completed in 1879 by Waterford Corporation in Green Street, Ballybricken, however Fraser (1996) estimates that urban authorities completed only 570 dwellings in the decade that followed.

As figure 9.1 demonstrates, urban local authority building began to increase after the introduction of the Housing of the Working Classes Act, 1890, which provided for central government loans on more attractive terms and for the first time allowed social house-building on greenfield sites (as well as in slum clearance areas) to meet general housing need. However, it expanded significantly subsequent to the Housing Act, 1908, which introduced even better loan terms and established an Irish Housing Fund which financed the first direct exchequer subsidy for urban housing. In contrast to the norm in countries such as Germany, Denmark and Sweden, from this period onwards local authorities took over from non-statutory bodies as the main providers of social housing for rent in Ireland.

Figure 9.1 Local Authority Dwellings Built Under the Housing of the
Working Classes Acts and the Labourers Acts, 1887 to 1918

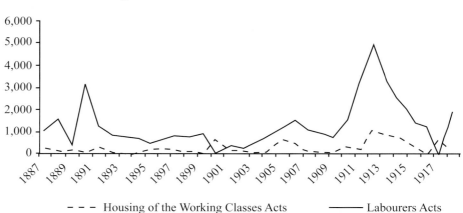

Source: Minister for Local Government (1964)

In the case of the semi-philanthropic companies, the reasons for this turn of
events are straightforward – the main providers including the Dublin Artisans
Dwellings Company were forced out of business by the pre-World War I
economic slump. The story of why a significant philanthropic housing movement
did not emerge in Ireland at this stage is, however, more complex. Power (1993,
p. 321) emphasises that the Dublin Artisans Dwellings Company and the Iveagh
Trust were owned by the Protestant elite and argues: 'it was inevitable therefore
that Dublin Corporation, with its Catholic voters and Nationalist councillors,
would feel forced to do something about the problems of the very poor'. In
contrast, Fraser's (1996) account of the period stresses that these religious
divisions frustrated the development of a philanthropic housing movement large
enough to resolve the chronic housing problems of Ireland's urban poor and that
the voluntary agencies which did emerge concentrated on housing the better-off
sections of the working class such as skilled artisans and tradespeople. Thus, he
argues that the increasingly more generous housing subsidies introduced during
the late 1800s and early 1900s allowed urban local authorities to build dwellings
of increasingly high standard at lower rents, which encouraged them to expand
their housing provision to meet the needs of the poorest sections of society.

An unusual aspect of the early development of local authority housing in
Ireland in comparison with Britain, is the heavy emphasis placed on provision for
low-income workers in rural areas. Initiatives in this regard began with the
Dwellings for the Labouring Classes (Ireland) Act, 1860, which allowed
landlords to borrow from the Public Works Loans Commission for the purpose of

building cottages for their tenants. However, as a result of landlords' disinterest, this initiative was largely unsuccessful. It was followed by a series of increasingly more radical rural housing schemes, which granted subsidies that were significantly more generous than their urban counterparts, starting with the Labourers (Ireland) Act, 1883 (as amended in 1885) which enabled boards of guardians to provide cheap housing for rent to farm labourers, subsidised out of local rates and low-cost loans from central government.

As is detailed in figure 9.1, this initiative, together with the Labourers Act, 1886, which extended housing eligibility to part-time agricultural labourers, resulted in the completion by rural local authorities of 3,191 labourers' cottages in 1890 alone. Output over the following decade averaged at 700 dwellings per year, but it rose dramatically after the introduction of the Labourers (Ireland) Act, 1906. This Act established a dedicated Labourers Cottage Fund to provide low-interest loans for rural local authority house-building and, most significantly, sanctioned that 36 per cent of the loan payments would be met by central government.

Fahey (1998) links the advent and expansion of the labourers' cottage programme with the campaign for the redistribution of land from landlords to tenant farmers, which was one of the main preoccupations of Parnell's Irish Parliamentary Party during the late nineteenth and early twentieth centuries. Fahey characterises the programme as a 'consolation prize' for the farm labourers who were excluded from the process of land reform but were numerous enough to warrant the attention of the Irish Parliamentary Party. His argument in this regard is supported by the fact that each of the Labourers Acts referred to above was introduced immediately following a Land Act that provided subsidised loans to allow tenant farmers to purchase their farms, and subsidies for house-building under the Labourers Acts were strikingly similar to the land purchase subsidies.

The combination of World War I, the 1916 Rising and the War of Independence obstructed any further significant development of local authority housing in the pre-independence period. Even though the Housing (Ireland) Act, 1919 offered more substantial state subsidies for urban local authority house-building it had relatively little impact before 1922. However, by the foundation of the state, the main focus of the housing service to be provided by local authorities for much of the rest of the twentieth century had already been determined. Local authorities, rather than the non-statutory sector, would be the main providers of social housing for rent and, beginning with the Small Dwellings Acquisition Act, 1899, which empowered county councils and urban authorities to provide loans to aid occupants to buy private rented dwellings from their landlords, they would also play a significant role in extending home ownership.

Furthermore, the combination of the various Housing of the Working Classes Acts and the Labourers Acts bequeathed the infant Irish state a very sizeable local authority housing stock, albeit one which would prove inadequate to meet the needs of the urban poor. Before 1914, Irish local authorities had completed approximately 44,701 dwellings, in comparison with only 24,000 council dwellings built in Britain during the same period (Malpass and Murie, 1999). By independence, 50,862 local authority dwellings had been built in Ireland, 41,653 of which were constructed under the terms of the Labourers Acts, and accounted for about 10 per cent of the total rural housing stock, while only 8,861 dwellings had been completed by urban authorities (Fahey, 1998). This geographical pattern of provision was the opposite of that which prevailed in Britain, where Fraser (1996) estimates that 98 per cent of pre-World War I local authority housing was in urban areas.

Housing in Independent Ireland, 1922 to 1960

In the years immediately following independence, housing remained at the top of the agenda of the new administration. Although the labourers' cottage schemes had more or less satisfied housing need in rural areas, housing conditions among the low-income population in towns and cities were still very poor. In order to address this problem an imaginative 'million pound scheme' was launched which, as its name implies, provided one million pounds for local authority house-building – 50 per cent of which came from central government, 12.5 per cent from local authority rates and the remainder from short-term bank loans. The scheme achieved an immediate response and by the time of its completion, at the end of 1924, 959 dwellings had been built, all of which were in urban areas (see figure 9.2). From the architectural and planning perspective, the most significant development built under the auspices of the scheme was at Marino in Dublin, where a housing estate was constructed in an innovative design with streets radiating from two circular greens in the manner of the spokes of a bicycle wheel. This design was influenced by the British 'Garden City' architectural movement, which endeavoured to combine the virtues of urban and rural life by building suburbs with layouts akin to traditional country villages (Fraser, 1996).

However, by the mid-1920s the political agenda shifted away from public housing provision, as the new Cumman na nGaedheal government focused on increasing private output. The result was the Housing (Building Facilities) Act, 1924, which introduced substantial private house-building grants of £100 (€127) for serviced dwellings and £90 (€114) for unserviced dwellings, enough to cover approximately one-sixth of the usual building cost at the time. These grants triggered a dramatic increase in private building and the vast majority of new private dwellings built after 1924 availed of the grants (Minister for Local Government, 1964).

Local authorities were not denied a role in this new policy departure. They could supplement the grants with loans, free or cheap sites and remission of rates.

Figure 9.2 Local Authority Dwellings Built under the Housing of the
Working Classes Acts and the Labourers Acts, and Private
Dwellings Built with State Aid, 1923 to 1960

- - - Housing of the Working Classes Acts   ———— Labourers Acts
······· State-aided private dwellings

Source: Minister for Local Government (1964)

However, their house-building programme was reined in because central
government proved unwilling to continue the programme of long-term
subsidisation of public house-building initiated under the Labourers (Ireland) Act,
1906 and the Housing Act, 1908 or even to treat public housing more favourably
than private construction. Instead, the Housing (Building Facilities)
(Amendment) Act, 1924 offered amounts similar to private grants for urban local
authority house-building, although the Housing Act, 1925 tilted the balance in
favour of local authorities by reducing private grants to a maximum of £75 (€95)
while maintaining the standard grants, of up to £100 (€127) a house, for urban
authorities and extending this subsidy to include labourers' cottage schemes.
However, difficulties in raising bank loans, combined with the high cost of this
source of finance, inhibited local authorities from undertaking large-scale
building programmes. Output only began to increase significantly in 1929, when
the government decided to restore the practice, suspended since 1922, of helping
local authorities with state capital. The local loans fund was revived by the
Minister for Finance and low-interest loans were made available for public house-
building. As a result, output of urban local authority dwellings rose to 1,789 in
1929, although building under the Labourers Acts remained low and only 385
dwellings were completed by rural local authorities between 1923 and 1930.

However, even this expanded level of output proved insufficient to meet
housing need in the towns and cities. Surveys undertaken by urban authorities in

1929 estimated total housing need at 40,000 dwellings. In 1931, central government introduced the Housing (Miscellaneous Provisions) Act which replaced the slum clearance provisions of the Housing of the Working Classes Act, 1890 with new, more effective procedures. The policy of state assistance to public house-building by means of lump sum grants, which had prevailed throughout the 1920s, was replaced with annual subsidies towards loan charges, which Roche (1982b, p. 224) assesses as 'generous for those depression times'. Additionally, the Act sought to enable further expansion of owner occupation by enlarging the scope of the Small Dwellings Acquisition Act. Local authorities were authorised to lend to persons intending to build, as well as to private sector tenants who wished to purchase the dwelling which they rented, and to increase the cost-limit for houses financed under the Act.

Although the 1931 Act laid the foundation for the radical expansion of public house-building during the 1930s, several of its provisions never came into effect. They were superseded by the Housing (Financial and Miscellaneous Provisions) Act, 1932 introduced by the first Fianna Fáil government which took office that year with the support of the Labour Party. The 1932 Act further increased the central government subsidies to loan charges for public house-building introduced by its predecessor. As figure 9.2 demonstrates, these subsidies resulted in a dramatic increase in public house-building. Output under the Housing of the Working Classes Acts rose to a pre-World War II high in 1936 when 4,215 dwellings were completed and building of Labourers Acts' schemes was also revived and peaked in 1939 which saw the completion of 2,867 rural dwellings. A total of 48,875 public rented dwellings were constructed between 1933 and 1943, as compared to the 9,994 units completed in the previous decade. Although public sector output began to slow in the late 1930s and early 1940s, as a result of government concerns about capital expenditure and the impact of World War II, it still remained relatively buoyant in comparison with private sector output during the war years. In fact, 1933 to 1943 was the only decade in the history of the state in which house building by the local authority sector exceeded private sector output.

It is interesting to note that almost one-third of the public rented dwellings built during the 1930s and 1940s were constructed by Dublin Corporation as part of a massive clearance programme which targeted inner-city slums. Between 1932 and 1948 the Dublin Corporation housing architect, Herbert Simms, oversaw the building of 17,000 dwelling units in the inner-city. Since the construction of the Marino estate referred to above, a lively debate had raged in architectural circles in Ireland concerning the propriety of suburban or urban locations for social house-building. Simms was firmly in the latter camp, and as a result the majority of the dwellings constructed during his tenure were located in inner-city areas including: Pearse Street, Cuffe Street, James Street and Marrowbone Lane. These dwellings were constructed as four-storey blocks of flats, the perimeter of which respected the existing street pattern, with communal courtyards at the rear which provided access, play space, clothes drying areas and storage. After Simms's death, the urban design ethos was replaced by stripped down suburban development by Dublin Corporation, which bore little resemblance to the garden suburbs advocated in the 1920s. The result was large, low-density estates of similar design with little or no landscaping such as Crumlin, Drimnagh, Donnycarney, Cabra and Ballyfermot.

From the perspective of the local authority housing service, the 1930s are also notable for the introduction of a universal right of purchase for tenants of labourers' cottages, replacing the previous system whereby local authorities could at their own discretion apply to the Department of Local Government to establish sale schemes. This reform was initiated on the recommendation of a commission of enquiry on the subject, which reported in 1933, and legislated for in the Labourers Act, 1936 which obliged all county councils to prepare sale schemes for their labourers' cottages. The dwellings would be sold by means of fixed-term annuity payments, which were originally set at 75 per cent of the rent but were reduced to 50 per cent in 1951. Like many other distinctive aspects of public housing policy in Ireland, the impetus behind the introduction of rural tenant purchase, three decades before the scheme was extended to include urban tenants and forty-five years before the British government introduced a similar universal right to buy for all council tenants, lay in the land reform movement.

Fahey (1998) argues that the de Valera government was finally forced to concede to the sale of labourers' cottages – after many years of lobbying from tenants – because its 1933 Land Act had made significant reductions in the annuities payable by tenant farmers who purchased their holdings. Furthermore, he contends, the way in which 'land reform continued to influence the substance of housing policy . . . gave Irish public housing a character that in some respects was unique in Europe' (p. 10). As was mentioned above, the influence of land reform during the nineteenth century had conferred the Irish public housing system with a uniquely rural character. In the twentieth century, the land-reform-inspired advent of tenant purchase would contribute in the long run to the reduction of the social rented stock in this country to a level which is low in comparison with most other northern European countries. As this scheme was initially confined to labourers' cottages, the contraction impacted first on rural areas. By 1964, approximately 80 per cent of the 86,931 labourers' cottages built by that date had been tenant purchased, in contrast to only 6,393 urban dwellings (Minister for Local Government, 1964).

Despite this high level of sales, in absolute terms the number of local authority dwellings available for letting did not decline during the next decade, as the rate of new building remained high. The 1948 White Paper on housing estimated that 100,000 new dwellings were needed – 60,000 of which should be provided by local authorities and 40,000 by the private sector (Department of Local Government, 1948). In order to achieve this, the rates of subsidy for local authority house-building fixed in 1932 were not amended. Instead, the Housing (Amendment) Act, 1948 extended the loan repayment and subsidy periods. In addition, direct central government capital grants were introduced in order to compensate local authorities for increased building costs, together with extra grant aid to maintain the effective interest rate on loans for public house-building at 2.5 per cent. As a result, new local authority house completions increased more than tenfold between 1948 and 1954 and, although they declined somewhat towards the end of the 1950s, output for the years 1950 to 1959 totalled 52,767 dwellings – more than double that of the previous decade.

Notwithstanding this impressive level of construction, in relative terms the share of total housing output contributed by local authorities fell in the 1950s. This is because, contrary to the predictions of the 1948 White Paper, private building increased even faster than public sector output. By the time local authorities had reached their target of 60,000 new dwellings in 1963, just over 68,000 private sector dwellings has been completed – significantly more than had been envisaged in 1948. This development, which was largely a consequence of a series of Housing Acts offering ever higher subsidies to private builders, marked the start of a long-term trend which not only has persisted but has accelerated in the decades since the 1950s.

Housing Modern Ireland, 1961 to 1979

Sociologists identify the 1960s as the period in which Irish society and economy modernised. From this time, the number of people employed in agriculture began to fall, the pace of industrial development quickened and widespread social change meant that society became less traditional in terms of religious observance and family structures (Breen et al., 1990). In common with wider Irish society, the local authority housing service also modernised during the 1960s. For instance, housing law was reformed, rationalised and updated and local authorities began to utilise modern building techniques in their housing developments. More significantly, during the 1960s and 1970s the public rented tenure contracted in size for the first time in the history of the state and it became apparent that local authorities would play a more modest role in housing the population of modern Ireland than they had in the past.

The rationalisation of the public housing legislation was achieved at a single stroke by means of the Housing Act, 1966. This Act replaced more than fifty earlier legislative provisions with a simple statement of powers enabling housing authorities to deal with unfit dwellings and districts within their operational areas; requiring them to assess local housing needs at least every five years, to develop a programme of building dwellings for people unable to adequately house themselves on the basis of this assessment, to allocate these dwellings according to a scheme of letting priorities which should give preference to households in greatest need of housing; and enabling them to manage these dwellings and to sell them to tenants. Indeed, such is the extensive scope of the 1966 Act that most aspects of local authority housing administration still fall under its remit. The Act also had an important modernising function, as it encompassed all levels of local government and thus marked the end of the tradition of separate legislation governing urban and rural public housing which had prevailed since the foundation of the service in the 1800s.

However, this aspect of the Act is not as innovative as it ostensibly appears. Rather, it is the culmination of a thirty-year trend whereby new housing laws tended to make identical provisions for urban and rural areas, the extent of which was such that by 1966 only three significant outstanding differences between the two codes remained for the Housing Act to abolish. These were: the lack of a universal right of purchase for urban tenants, minor divergences in land acquisition procedure and procedures for the repossession of dwellings (Minister for Local Government, 1964). As well as rationalising and modernising the public housing legislation, the 1966 Act instituted a number of reforms to the service, the most important of which relate to rent setting. The Act empowered the minister to make state subsidies for public housing conditional on the dwellings being let on rents which vary according to the tenant's family income, and since 1967 rents of all new public housing tenancies have been set using this 'differential rent' system.

Another interesting reform introduced by the 1966 Act is the provision of additional state subsidy to housing authorities constructing blocks of flats of six or more storeys. This subsidy was part of a series of initiatives introduced by the Department of Local Government during the 1960s and 1970s to encourage the use of modern building techniques, which it was envisaged would help to rapidly expand housing output to meet the demand created by the growing population and the economic boom at that time (Minister for Local Government, 1964). Many of the housing schemes that were constructed using these modern methods were built by local authorities. A semi-prefabricated or 'system' building technique was used in the construction of mixed estates of houses and three-storey flats at Mayfield, the Glen and Togher for Cork Corporation, while Dublin Corporation employed a similar system of pre-cast concrete panels to build Ireland's only high-rise estate at Ballymun. They were aided in this work by the National Building Agency, which was established in 1961 with the object of building houses for key state and industrial workers, but soon adopted a broader role of advising local authorities on house construction and building schemes on their behalf.

In comparative terms, Irish local authorities' embrace of modern building methods was belated – these techniques had been in common use in other

European countries since the end of World War II, especially among exponents of the modernist architectural movement. Furthermore, it was short lived – ironically Ballymun was completed in 1969, just seven months before the collapse of the Ronan Point tower block in London signalled the beginning of the end of the high-rise experiment in Europe. However, in the public imagination these system-built public sector dwellings have assumed an importance which is disproportionate to their modest numbers. In Ireland, as in Britain and many other EU countries, the unpopularity of high-rise estates among tenants and the well-publicised structural problems of many system-built dwellings contributed to the 'delegitimation' of the social rented tenure as a whole. In the public mind, local authority housing was no longer seen as the best solution to poor housing conditions and was increasingly seen as the cause of them (Dunleavy, 1981).

The 1960s are also significant in the history of the local authority housing service because from this period local authorities became more involved in providing accommodation for members of the Traveller community. The importance of involvement in this area was heavily promoted by the Commission on Itinerancy. Its 1963 report on the problems faced by Travellers was predicated on the argument that:

> All efforts directed at improving the lot of itinerants and at dealing with the problems
> created by them, and all schemes drawn up for these purposes, must have as their aim
> the eventual absorption of the itinerants into the general community (Commission on
> Itinerancy, 1963, p. 106).

The commission concluded that setting Travellers in conventional housing would be the most effective method of achieving this objective and it envisaged that most of this housing would be provided by local authorities. The argument that providing adequate accommodation is key to improving the living conditions of Travellers was reiterated in the next major government review of this issue, which was produced in 1983 by the Travelling People Review Body. This report also envisaged that local authorities would be the main providers of accommodation for Travellers, but unlike its predecessor it recognised that this section of the population should be offered a number of accommodation options. This differentiates between families who wish to:

- live in standard housing among settled people
- live in a house, but situated among other Travellers (group housing)
- remain living in a caravan in a place on which they are entitled to park but with the benefit of amenities
- continue travelling but who would avail of authorised serviced sites on which they can remain as long as they wish.

Finally, as mentioned above, during the 1960s and 1970s the percentage of the national housing stock rented from local authorities fell from 18.4 per cent in 1961 to 16 per cent in 1971 and to 12.5 per cent in 1981 (Central Statistics Office, various years). As figure 9.3 demonstrates, to some extent this phenomenon is due to the continued fall in the relative contribution of public sector building to total housing output during these decades. As in the 1950s, the number of public rented dwellings completed rose in absolute terms during the 1960s and 1970s, but private sector completions grew at a much faster rate. However, a more significant factor in the decline of the tenure is the steady rise in the level of tenant purchase of dwellings after the introduction of the Housing Act, 1966. As was mentioned above, this Act bestowed a common power of sale of dwellings on both urban and rural local authorities. In addition it streamlined tenant purchase procedures by removing the requirement for specific ministerial consent to individual sales and empowering the minister to lay down minimum terms of sale instead.

Figure 9.3 Local Authority Dwellings and Private Dwellings Completed and Local Authority Dwellings Sold to Tenants, 1960 to 1980*

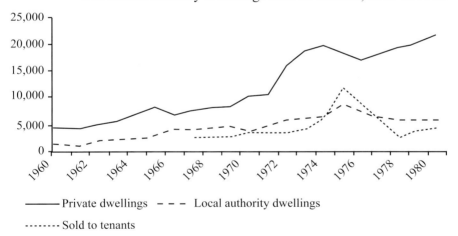

——— Private dwellings – – – Local authority dwellings

----- Sold to tenants

* No figures are available on sales before 1967; figures from 1967 to 1970 include both Labourers Act dwellings sold and all dwellings sold under the 1966 Housing Act; figures from 1970 onwards include dwellings sold under the 1966 Housing Act only. Details of dwellings which were sold in urban areas at the discretion of local authorities after the enactment of the 1966 Housing Act are not included in this graph; therefore it slightly underestimates the true level of sales

Source: Department of Local Government (various years), *Department of Local Government Report,* and Department of the Environment and Local Government (various years), *Annual Housing Statistics Bulletin*

The sale terms initially set by the minister were generous. Purchasers were offered a reduction on the sale price for every year of residency subject to a maximum discount of 30 per cent in urban areas and 45 per cent in rural areas. Not surprisingly sales rose steadily, with this increase being particularly marked in urban areas where the lack of a universal right to buy had created some pent-up demand. Figure 9.3 also points up a sharp rise in sales between 1973 and 1979. During part of this period, tenant purchase of dwellings outstripped new building. This is due to the introduction of a new tenant purchase scheme in 1973, which offered buyers the same maximum discount off the sale price as the previous scheme, but calculated the sale price on the basis of the initial cost of providing the dwelling updated to current monetary values, rather than the market value. As a result, dwellings were sold for approximately 19 per cent less than under the preceding tenant purchase scheme (An Foras Forbartha, 1978).

From Residualisation to Regeneration, 1980 to 2002

The introduction to this chapter suggested that the two decades from 1980, more than any other since the foundation of the state, have been characterised by radical change in the local authority housing function. The title of this section encapsulates this turbulent period as a progression from the residualisation of the tenure during the 1980s and early 1990s to the regeneration of the local authority housing service in later years.

Residualisation refers to the phenomenon whereby 'council housing has increasingly become the tenure of the least well off' (Malpass and Muire, 1999, p. 22). The concept was first used in British housing research in the late 1970s to explain the increasing level of poverty in the public rented tenure in the UK, which until the 1940s had been dominated by skilled manual workers and lower-middle-class families.

In contrast to their British counterparts, Irish local authorities have always tended to charge low rents and to let to disadvantaged groups, and therefore it is reasonable to assume that since its foundation the public rented tenure in Ireland has been more or less residualised (Fraser, 1996). However, in common with the UK, the available evidence indicates that the level of residualisation of public housing in Ireland worsened considerably during the 1980s and 1990s. This evidence is set out in table 9.1, which demonstrates that between 1987 and 1994 the number of public rented households with incomes below 60 per cent of the national average grew from 59.1 per cent to 74.6 per cent.

The reasons for this development are twofold. They are related to the broader socio-economic environment of the period and to housing policy. In relation to the former, there is little doubt that the economic crisis of the 1980s had a strong negative impact on local authority tenants, who tend to have low educational

Table 9.1 Income Poverty among Households in the Republic of Ireland by Tenure, 1987 and 1994

	% of households with incomes below 40 per cent of average		% of households with incomes below 60 per cent of average	
	1987	*1994*	*1987*	*1994*
Owned outright	16.8	18.1	30.0	37.8
Owned with a mortgage	6.7	8.7	2.5	14.6
Local authority tenant purchased	17.8	21.8	27.5	41.6
Local authority rented	37.4	49.8	59.1	74.6
Other rented	14.4	15.1	27.7	34.0
All households	17.0	18.8	29.1	34.6

Source: adapted from Nolan et al. (1998, p. 24)

qualifications and work in unskilled manual jobs and therefore are at high risk of becoming unemployed and falling into poverty (Nolan et al., 1998). The reason why poverty among local authority tenants continued to increase during the 1990s, despite the improved economic environment, is related to housing policy. From the mid-1980s, the number of new local authority dwellings built fell steadily (see figure 9.4), to a post-World War II low in 1989 when only 768 units were completed. Although output increased to between 2,000 and 3,000 dwellings during the 1990s, it has remained well below 10 per cent of total new house construction, which is significantly lower than in the period 1930 to 1980 when public housing comprised an average of 20 to 30 per cent of total output (O'Connell, 1999). Low levels of building reduced the number of dwellings available for letting and, because local authority dwellings are allocated on the basis of need, it is reasonable to assume that only the most disadvantaged households secured tenancies during the 1980s and 1990s.

Figure 9.4 also reveals that the level of tenant purchase of dwellings increased substantially between 1987 and 1991, spurred on by extra discounts for buyers introduced in 1986 and 1988. This trend is important because sales have an acute residualising effect. Sales reduce the number of dwellings available for letting and, because local authority dwellings are allocated on the basis of need, therefore stimulate an influx of disadvantaged people into the tenure. Furthermore, as table 9.1 demonstrates, because tenant purchasers tend to be wealthier than public renting households (although they are still poorer than other owner occupiers) sales also facilitate an exodus of better-off households.

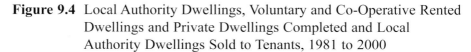

Figure 9.4 Local Authority Dwellings, Voluntary and Co-Operative Rented
                Dwellings and Private Dwellings Completed and Local
                Authority Dwellings Sold to Tenants, 1981 to 2000

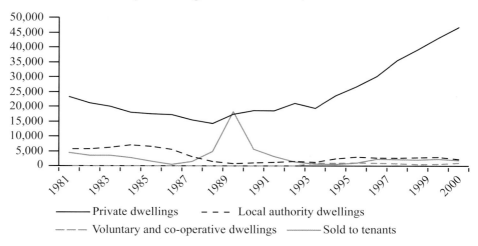

Source: Department of the Environment and Local Government (various years), *Annual
Housing Statistics Bulletin*

In addition, the process of residualisation was exacerbated by the advent of the
'surrender grant scheme' in October 1984. This scheme, which allocated £5,000
(€6,349) to local authority tenants and tenant purchasers who were prepared to
surrender their dwelling and to buy a home in the private sector, was intended to
free-up dwellings for letting without incurring the cost of new building.
Blackwell (1988a) reports that by the time the scheme was abolished in March
1987 a total of 7,700 surrender grants had been paid out – accounting for 6.5 per
cent of the entire public renting population at the time. A study carried out by the
housing advice agency, Threshold (1987), of the effects of the grant in the Dublin
area, confirms that practically all of the families who took advantage of the
scheme were in employment and that the residualising effects associated with the
departure of these households from public sector estates were compounded by the
fact that many of those who moved into the dwellings vacated under the scheme
were lone parents or single unemployed men.

On a more positive note, by the mid-1980s growing central government concern
about social problems and poor living conditions in acutely residualised public
sector estates inspired the instigation of a number of measures intended to
regenerate these areas, mainly by means of refurbishing the built environment. The
first of these estate improvement schemes – the remedial works scheme established
in 1985 – funds improvements to dwellings and to public space in rundown estates.

It targets, in particular, estates built before 1940 and the system-built estates of the 1960s and 1970s. Remedial works funding has been exploited with considerable enthusiasm by local authorities and in the period 1985 to 1999 a total of 16,520 local authority dwellings, accounting for approximately 16.6 per cent of the current national public housing stock, were refurbished under its auspices (Norris, 2001).

In more recent years, efforts have also been made to attract private sector funding for regeneration projects by making investment in designated local authority estates eligible for tax relief under the 1998 Urban Renewal Act. The best-known application of this mechanism in practice is in Ballymun, where Dublin City Council has set up a designated company, Ballymun Regeneration Ltd, tasked with planning for and managing the demolition of all of the tower blocks and their replacement with conventional housing and low-rise apartments organised around a new town centre which will contain private rented dwellings, shops, offices and a hotel (see Ballymun Regeneration Ltd, 1998a and 1998b). The rebuilding of the local authority dwellings in the estate will be funded directly by central government, but it is envisaged that most of the town centre will be developed by the private sector.

By the 1990s, the attention of policy makers shifted from the regeneration of individual local authority estates to the reform and renewal of the entire local authority housing service, and indeed of the social rented tenure in general. The advent of this new policy agenda was first signalled in the 1991 White Paper, *A Plan for Social Housing,* a slim document, whose modest looks belie the fact that it marked a watershed in the development of housing policy in Ireland (Department of the Environment, 1991). Previous policy statements had been mainly concerned with estimating the numbers of people in need of social housing and making provision for this demand to be met, principally by means of local authority building. *A Plan for Social Housing* advanced beyond this and presented a strategic analysis of all potential methods of accommodating low-income households – by the private sector, local authorities and the voluntary and co-operative sector. Furthermore, on the basis of this analysis, it proposed a number of reforms to mechanisms for housing these groups which, it admitted, 'imply significant changes in the traditional role played by local authorities' (p. 30).

The most significant of these changes involved widening the traditional role of the local authority housing service, beyond building dwellings for rent. *A Plan for Social Housing* explained that while 'this wider remit will, of course continue to include the traditional functions, it will also require of local authorities a new facilitating and promotional role aimed at improving and speeding up access to housing' (p. 30). The policy statement emphasises that a key aspect of this new enabling role will be encouraging higher levels of building by voluntary housing associations and co-operatives. As was mentioned above, agencies of this type had built a large number of dwellings in the late 1880s, but for a number of reasons they did not emerge as major social housing providers for most of the twentieth century. However, as figure 9.4 demonstrates, this began to change in the late 1980s when voluntary sector output, particularly of accommodation for special needs groups such as elderly, disabled or homeless people, began to increase from its traditionally low base, stimulated by the establishment of the capital assistance scheme in 1984, which was the first designated funding scheme for housing associations.

A Plan for Social Housing announced the provision of funding under the capital assistance scheme of up to 90 per cent of the cost of dwellings; the introduction of a new scheme to fund the provision of communal facilities in voluntary sector estates; and the establishment of a rental subsidy scheme, later renamed the capital loan and subsidy scheme, which provides capital funding by way of loans to approved housing bodies for the provision of housing and subsidy on the loan charges, as well as an annual allowance for management and maintenance for each unit of accommodation provided. As is outlined in figure 9.4, the result of these reforms was that voluntary sector house-building increased further during the late 1990s. Output of general needs, family-type accommodation grew especially quickly during this period.

In addition to rental housing, *A Plan for Social Housing* announced a series of new measures which local authorities can utilise to enable low to middle income households to buy a home of their own. For instance, the maxima for local authority housing loans were increased, as were the income limits for borrowers; extra incentives were introduced to encourage local authorities to provide low-cost housing sites on which families could construct their own dwellings; a mortgage allowance of €4,190, payable over five years, was made available to local authority tenants or tenant purchasers who bought a private house and a new 'shared ownership' scheme was established which enables low-income aspirant home owners to acquire at least 50 per cent in the equity of a private sector dwelling of their choice, and rent the remainder from their local authority until they can afford to buy out the entire property.

As well as examining alternative social housing providers, *A Plan for Social Housing* also casts a critical eye over the quality of the service provided by local authorities to their tenants and recommended a number of reforms. For instance it highlights 'the need to avoid building large local authority housing estates which have, in the past, reinforced social segregation' and suggests that, as an alternative, local authorities should build smaller schemes and consider purchasing existing houses to add to their stock (p. 11). In more recent years, local authorities have been given extra powers to combat social segregation by the Planning and Development Act, 2000 (as amended by the Planning and Development (Amendment) Act, 2002), which allows them to designate up to 20 per cent of new private sector developments for use as social/affordable housing.

A Plan for Social Housing raises a number of concerns about the management and maintenance of local authority estates, albeit in a rather low-key fashion, as it argues that the quality of these services must be improved if public investment in public house-building and refurbishment is to be protected. However, a more detailed analysis of the standard of public housing management appeared soon after this in a 1993 memorandum from the Department of the Environment to local authorities on the preparation of the statements of policy on housing management which they are obliged to produce under the terms of the Housing (Miscellaneous Provisions) Act, 1992. The introductory section of this memorandum sets out what O'Connell (1999, p. 60) terms a 'devastating catalogue of weaknesses common in local authority housing management', the most significant of which are: lack of long- and medium-term planning, which is compounded by inadequate management information and insufficient monitoring of the information that is available; over-centralised management structures which prioritise administrative issues over communication with tenants; inadequate co-ordination of different housing management functions; prioritisation of cost reduction over value for money and customer service; over-reliance on the remedial works scheme as a solution to the problems of unpopular estates and chronic inefficiencies in the maintenance service.

Central government's concern about the quality of public housing management inspired the introduction of a range of ameliorative measures during the late 1990s. Some of these had an enabling orientation insofar as they aimed to assist local authorities to improve their housing management performance through the provision of guidance, training and targeted grant aid. Others can be categorised as enforcement tools which set benchmarks of required performance and established systems to monitor local authority housing management performance. The housing management initiatives grants scheme, which was established in 1995, was the first of the enabling measures to be introduced. It provides grant aid towards the cost of practical pilot projects intended to improve housing management. Since its establishment, it has funded over 130 projects, most of which are concerned with involving local authority tenants in housing management and decentralising housing management to meet the needs of individual estates and communities more effectively (Brooke and Norris, 2002).

Soon afterwards, three further significant enabling measures were initiated by the Department of the Environment – the Housing Management Group, which produced two reports setting out the broad framework which the reform of public housing management should follow (Housing Management Group, 1996, 1998); the Housing Unit, which was set up in order to provide social housing management guidance, information and training; and the Housing (Miscellaneous Provisions) Act, 1997, which gives local authorities additional powers to deal with tenants and squatters in public sector dwellings who are committing anti-social behaviour.

Examples of the enforcement measures introduced include: the Department of the Environment and Local Government's (2000b) circular LG 9/00, which instructs local authorities to monitor their performance in specified aspects of housing management and to publish this information in their annual reports, and a range of reforms to the remedial works scheme which made funding conditional on detailed monitoring and evaluation of projects.

The process of reform and expansion of the local authority housing service has been further extended as local authorities have gained important new responsibilities in relation to planning for the implementation of national housing policy at the local level. The advent of this new remit is of course linked to the wider programme of local government reform mapped out in *Better Local Government* (Department of the Environment, 1996), which resulted in the establishment of strategic policy committees within each local authority. These are made up of councillors and local business and community representatives who are responsible for initiating and developing policy for the different local government functional areas, including housing.

From the perspective of the housing service, this reform is a logical progression of the local authority's other work in facilitating the provision of housing by other agencies, as the experience on the ground indicates that local planning is vital for the effective operation of this enabling function. For instance, the Housing Act, 1988 requires local authorities to carry out triannual assessments of housing need in their operational areas and empowers them to make necessary arrangements with voluntary bodies to accommodate homeless people, but the available evidence indicates that these provisions have had a limited impact (Harvey, 1995). In order to rectify this problem, all local authorities are now required to establish a homeless forum made up of the statutory and voluntary agencies dealing with homelessness in their operational areas and to draw up an integrated strategy to combat homelessness (Department of the Environment and Local Government, 2000c).

Similarly, despite the recommendations made by the Commission on Itinerancy in 1963 and the Travelling People Review Body in 1983, the latest government analysis of the situation of Irish Travellers – the *Report of the Task Force on the Travelling Community* – concluded that local authorities had largely failed to provide adequate accommodation for this section of the population (Task Force on the Travelling Community, 1995). As a result, under the terms of the Housing (Traveller Accommodation) Act, 1998, all major local authorities are required to produce five-year Traveller accommodation strategies to meet the existing and projected accommodation needs of Travellers in their areas.

Another notable example of local-level planning is the housing strategy that each local authority must prepare under part V of the Planning and Development Act, 2000 (as amended by the Planning and Development (Amendment) Act, 2002). These strategies comprise estimates of the housing need which will arise in their operational areas over a six-year period, together with details of how these needs will be met by the private sector, local authorities and the voluntary and co-operative sector. Although in most cases the production of these plans has been managed by planning rather than housing departments, housing staff would have helped to produce the estimates of future social housing need using information from housing waiting lists. Furthermore, local authorities will also play a key role in implementing the housing strategies. They will construct local authority rented dwellings, enable the provision of social rented housing by the voluntary and co-operative housing sector and enable the provision of affordable housing in order to address spiralling house prices and which allows local authorities to provide dwellings for sale at a reduced cost to low-income households.

Concluding Comments

This chapter has reviewed the development of the local authority housing service from its foundation to the beginning of the twenty-first century. For most of its history the service was mainly concerned with the direct provision of dwellings for rent to low-income households. However, in recent years its focus has broadened. As well as building social rented accommodation, local authorities now devote greater attention to the management and maintenance of their housing stock and have gained important new responsibilities in relation to enabling the provision of social housing by other agencies and planning for the implementation of national housing policy at the local level.

As a result of the high numbers of local authority dwellings sold since the 1930s, the outcome of the house-building programme on which local authorities have concentrated their efforts for most of their history may not appear very impressive to contemporary eyes. The 1991 Census indicates that only 9.7 per cent of all housing in Ireland is rented from local authorities. This is considerably less than the tenure's peak in 1961 when it accounted for 18.4 per cent of the national housing stock. If voluntary and co-operative dwellings are added to the rented and local authority stock, the total number of social rented dwellings in Ireland is 10 per cent of stock. This is far smaller than the norm in other northern European nations such as Denmark, the UK and the Netherlands where 17 per cent, 25 per cent and 38 per cent respectively of all housing is rented from social landlords (European Union, 2001). Furthermore, as was mentioned above, the remaining local authority tenure in Ireland is acutely residualised and it is fair to say that due to a combination of social problems and negative media attention some local authority estates are also stigmatised.

Despite these problems, however, the local authority house-building programme has made an important and largely underestimated contribution to Irish society. A study of seven diverse local authority housing estates in different parts of the country (Fahey, 1999) reaches largely positive findings about the quality of life enjoyed by the residents of these areas. It concludes: 'local authorities have made a fundamental contribution to social progress and social cohesion in Irish society through the expansion of housing provision and the raising of minimum standards of housing among the less well-off', but quantifies the full extent of this contribution as follows:

> Local authorities have been providing housing in Ireland since they came into existence a hundred years ago. Over that time they have built some 330,000 dwellings, which amounts to over 30 per cent of the present housing stock in Ireland. These dwellings provided accommodation of reasonable quality to successive generations of low-income households at a cost those households could afford. Local authority housing has also played a major but little recognised role in promoting home ownership. Of the 330,000 dwellings constructed . . . some 230,000 have been sold to tenants through the longstanding tradition of tenant purchase . . . These privatised local authority dwellings now account for about one-in-four of the owner occupied homes in Ireland, and are a major reason why the overall level of owner occupation in this country (at 80 per cent of total housing) is so high by European standards (Fahey, 1999, pp. 3–4).

As was mentioned above, the focus of the local authority housing service has broadened. Local authorities have taken on a number of new strategic functions, in addition to their traditional role of direct provision of social housing for rent. Figure 9.5 sketches the results of the expansion process and demonstrates that the typical local authority housing department is now responsible for up to fifty separate functions, in addition to its often overlooked obligation to make detailed annual or multi-annual returns to the Department of the Environment and Local Government on its execution of these responsibilities.

There is no doubt that the delegation of these new functions has the potential to regenerate the housing service and restore it to its traditional position of importance within the local government system. However, this regeneration will only be achieved if local authorities can rise to meet the challenges associated with their new strategic role. Shortcomings of the local authority housing management and maintenance service which were highlighted in this chapter would raise some concerns about the prospects of doing so – although the barriers which stand in the way of their effective performance in this area are not insurmountable.

For instance, the recent reforms to the staffing structure of local authorities, which were first proposed in *Better Local Government*, improve local authorities'

Figure 9.5 Typical Structure and Functions of Local Authority Housing Departments, 2002

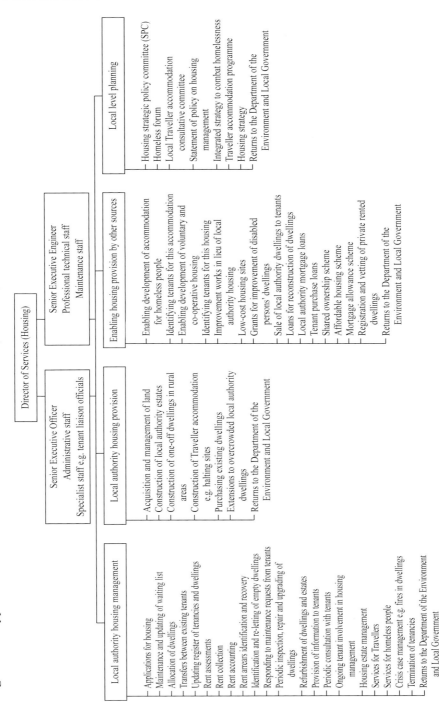

prospects of coping with the challenges associated with their new strategic mandate. This document provided for the appointment of directors of services in all local authorities, who are tasked with the management and strategic development of each of the local government functional areas, including housing, and with the development and implementation of each authority's housing policy in conjunction with the strategic policy committees. The appointment of the directors of housing, together with the establishment of a range of new middle management grades, will not only help to fill the strategic management and policy-making vacuum which has previously existed in the local authority housing service, it will also provide staff who are interested in specialising in housing with a viable career path in this service, while still having the option to transfer to other departments of the authority if they wish.

However, the problems of local authority housing services are not caused solely by factors internal to the local government system and addressing them will also require change on the part of central government. Appropriate reforms include changing the traditional relationship between central and local government, with less emphasis on auditing the activities of local authorities and more emphasis on providing in-depth guidance for housing departments on the operation of their new functions. Extra funding needs to be provided for staff training and education and for research within local authority housing departments to enable them to perform their traditional and new housing functions more effectively.

10

Roads and Road Traffic

P. J. Howell

A road is a passage open to everyone, a part of the surface of the land dedicated to the public in order that they may pass and re-pass along it.

Although most of Ireland's roads may never have been formally dedicated, uninterrupted use by the public over a long period is taken to imply dedication and public acceptance. A road may be created other than by dedication and acceptance. A county council, city council, borough council and certain town councils, each of which is a road authority, has power to acquire land to make new roads where necessary and may declare a road to have a public right of way over it. The purpose of declaring a road a public road is to allow the road authority to maintain it. A public road that ceases to be of any use to the public does not cease to be a public road until it has been legally abandoned (Roads Act, 1993, section 12). A road authority also has powers to extinguish a public right of way (ibid., section 73).

A road authority has the duty of keeping every road under its control fit for the ordinary traffic that passes along it and this duty may be enforced by the courts. If the traffic changes, as it did when mechanically propelled vehicles carrying heavy loads came onto the roads, the road must be made suitable to serve the new traffic passing along it. The road authority may recover from the person responsible any expenses incurred in repairing damage to a road from exceptional traffic (Public Roads (Ireland) Act, 1911). The road authority cannot at present be made liable for injuries due to its not repairing the road, but if injuries are due to some positive act the road authority has done it may be made liable. Section 60 of the Civil Liability Act, 1961, which alters the law of liability for failure to maintain, has not so far been brought into operation.

Early Roads

The oldest roads in Ireland have their origins in prehistoric times. They probably began as tracks followed by people and animals moving from one place to another. Short stretches of ancient paved roads have been found, from which it would appear that in the first centuries of the Christian era, Roman methods of road construction were known in Ireland. The ancient road system (such as it was – there cannot have been a developed national system) fanned out not from Tara but from Dublin. A northern road went through Armagh to the coast. Western roads went through Rath Croghan in Roscommon to Galway and the road to Galway crossed the Shannon at Clonmacnoise. A road along the East Coast was carried over the Liffey by a hurdle bridge and went southwards through Bray. The main highway through Leinster branched from this road and went on to Cashel. Another road went on to Limerick through Naas, Roscrea and Nenagh. Much of the traffic went by river and sea, and stone bridges do not appear to have been built before the twelfth century.

Early Legislation

Early in the seventeenth century an unsuccessful attempt (Highways Act, 1614) was made to introduce a system to statute labour that had been tried in England for maintaining roads. The inhabitants of every parish were required to furnish free labour, tools and materials for road work. This system was abolished in 1765, but more than a century earlier the roads had been placed, by an Act of 1634, under the grand juries who could vote money for them and levy it by means of the county cess.

The number of Acts, many of them of a local character, relating to roads which were passed in the eighteenth century by the Irish parliament showed that the increase in population and traffic was causing greater use of the roads. The canal system relieved the roads of much heavy traffic, but horse and foot passengers, carts, coaches and carriages grew in numbers. Experiments in road making went on in order to raise the standard of the roads and enable them to cope with heavier usage. The first to use a layer of small broken stones to make a foundation for a road was John Metcalf, an eighteenth-century road contractor of Yorkshire. The vehicles on the road forced the broken stones into the soil; before that time round stones had been used, but were easily pushed aside by the passage of wheels. Metcalf's work was carried forward by Telford and McAdam. The necessity for good post roads to carry the mails and the turnpike system were also factors in road improvements.

To improve the post roads, the Commissioners of Public Works were given power to repair these roads if asked to do so by the Post Office. The money for the work came in the first instance from state funds and improvement was carried out under the superintendence of a surveyor appointed by the commissioners. When the repair of the road was completed the expenditure was certified to the grand jury which was bound to refund the sum required to defray the cost. Half the cost of repairing and improving the post roads was levied off the county and half off the relevant barony. It was much better for the grand juries to improve the post roads themselves than allow the commissioners to do it at their expense.

The first of numerous Irish Turnpike Acts was passed in 1729 to improve the road from Dublin to Kildare. The law permitted turnpike trusts to be formed to maintain stretches of road and levy tolls on certain kinds of traffic. The users of the road were thus compelled to pay for their use of it. The name turnpike comes from the bars which revolved on a pillar and were used as toll gates. The coming of the railways made the turnpikes no longer profitable. They were abolished in 1857 and all existing turnpike roads became public roads. Toll bridges and ferries also existed. The owner of a ferry outside a town was given the power by the Grand Jury Act, 1836 to erect a bridge in place of the ferry and charge the same toll as could be charged for the use of the ferry.

Public works including the making or maintenance of roads were carried out up to 1899 in the counties by the grand juries. All road works were put out to tender and done by contract. The grand jury was not a permanent body. It could not purchase the equipment needed for repairing roads that were defective and consequently the contract system became the normal system of road making and repair. If no-one came forward with a tender the county surveyor had to execute the works within whatever amount was allowed.

The cost of road maintenance, improvement and repair incurred by the grand juries was met out of the county cess levied off the occupiers of rateable property. It was not until 1888 that some relief was given to the ratepayers in respect of road expenditure. A proportion of the probate duty, for which part of the estate duty was afterwards substituted, was assigned for that purpose and distributed to councils in proportion to their 1887 road expenditure.

The development of the railways had an effect on the roads. The railways, wherever they extended, put an end to all long-distance passenger traffic by horse, coach, long car or carriage. The flyboats on the canals ceased to run, along with river steamboats to towns to which railways extended. The transfer of much of the road traffic to the railways enabled road authorities to keep road expenditure within bounds but the coming of the railways merely postponed the road crisis. In the twentieth century, the importance of roads as through-traffic routes grew rapidly. The full circle of the revolution away from the road to the railway and back again was completed in less than one hundred years.

Local Government (Ireland) Act, 1898

Although the first motor cars had appeared on the roads a few years before the Local Government Act, 1898 created county and district councils and made them road authorities, the framers of the Act could not have foreseen the effects the motor car, bus and lorry were going to have, not only on road administration but on the whole structure of local government. The Act is characterised by a nineteenth- rather than a twentieth-century outlook. So far as roads were concerned, the Act raised some obstacles to improvement where none had existed before.

The grand jury had a convenient method of taking land for new roads. If they did not propose to go through an enclosed deer park or run the road through a house or its out-offices, all they needed to do was to give notice to the owners before the application for a vote of money for the road was considered. This simple procedure was not made available to the county councils because county councils in England did not happen to have that power at the time and the expensive procedure of the acquisition of land by provisional order was substituted.

The fear that the new councils might be extravagant in regard to roads also found expression in the Act – which prohibited expenditure on roads exceeding by more than one-quarter the average for the three years before the passing of the Act, unless by consent of the Local Government Board. Against these defects must be set the provision which gave the county council power to purchase steamrollers and other machinery and take quarries. The councils were enabled to place both the machinery and materials at the disposal of contractors.

Main Roads

The county councils were given power to declare which roads were to be main roads. The effect of declaring a road a main road was to transfer half the expenses of maintaining it from the county district to the county council. Fourteen councils made no declarations and consequently those counties had no roads of that class. The power to originate and determine expenditure on roads rested primarily with the rural district councils, which were not abolished until 1925. The occupiers of land were strongly represented on these councils. The anomalous position of the county council in regard to the main roads soon became apparent when motorists came onto the roads with their machines raising dust, scattering mud or disintegrating the surface. The county councils were offered grants but they were not free to enter into commitments regarding future maintenance because the district councils had the power in this regard.

Motor Traffic

Bicycles with pneumatic tyres appeared on the roads in great numbers about the mid-1890s and cyclists began to complain about the condition of the surfaces, but their complaints had little effect. The safety of the roads was threatened and the roads themselves were being subjected to unusual wear and tear by the weight and speed of the new motor traffic. The question, not by any means new, then arose as to whether it was the duty of the ratepayers to make roads to suit every new form of traffic. Although motorists were relatively few in number they had considerable influence. The Locomotives Act, 1865, which required every locomotive propelled by other than animal power to have a man with a red flag sixty yards ahead to warn all drivers of horses that the engine was coming, was repealed in 1896. The Motor Car Act, 1903 required motor cars to be registered and licensed, to carry identification marks, to be driven by a licensed driver and to have a horn or alarm and lights. It also fixed a speed limit for them.

The demand that the motorist should pay something towards the maintenance of the roads was conceded to in the budget of 1909. The Finance Act, 1909 put a licence duty on motorcars and a tax on petrol. The government did not adopt the established device of making grants out of the produce of these duties to local authorities. If they had done so the money might have gone merely in relief of rates. Instead of making such grants they set up, under the Development and Road Improvement Funds Act, 1909, a Road Board, which was to devote funds derived from the new taxation to road improvements that might take the form of new roads, or straighter or wider roads, or better surfaces, particularly a dust-free surface. This was not the kind of relief ratepayers were looking for because it left them with all their existing liabilities. The Road Board lasted until 1919 when its functions were merged with those of the Ministry of Transport established in that year. In 1922 the functions of the roads department of the Ministry of Transport passed to the Provisional Government and were, until 2002, the functions of the Minister for the Environment and Local Government. Responsibility for national roads was transferred to the newly established Department of Transport in 2002.

Road Fund

The Roads Act, 1920 made county councils and county borough councils (city councils) the authorities for registering and collecting duties on motor cars and also constituted the Road Fund into which the duties levied by the councils found their way, together with fees for driving licences and petrol pumps and certain other receipts. Neither excise duties on imported motor spirit nor customs duties on imported car parts went to the fund. County and county borough councils were paid their expenses of levying the duties and collecting fees, and the expenses of government departments and the commissioner of An Garda Síochána in administering the Act were met out of the fund. In 1978, the government decided to terminate the arrangement and substitute other forms of finance.

Local Government Act, 1925

The first steps towards implementing a new road policy taken by the new government were embodied in the Local Government Act, 1925. Under that Act, roads were divided into main roads, county roads and urban roads. Main roads were those declared to be such by order of the minister. This removed from the county councils the power to determine which were main roads. All expenses in regard to these roads fell on the whole county including the urban districts. The county roads were constructed and maintained at the cost of the county excluding the urban districts and the cost of urban roads fell on the urban districts.

For the purposes of administration the chief roads were divided into trunk roads, which were the most important arteries, and link roads. It was decided to improve the worst portions of the trunk roads of which there were about 1,500 miles. This was done without waiting for the necessary revenue to accrue to the Road Fund. A scheme was adopted by which the exchequer would advance the money, which would be repaid over a period out of the revenue from motor taxation.

From 1925, the number of motorbuses on the roads outside Dublin began to rise and to compete with the railways. Under the Railways (Road Motor Services) Act, 1927, the railway companies received powers to run passenger and goods services on the public roads along approved routes. The Local Government Act, 1925 contained a number of minor amendments to the law relating to roads, such as the power to have buildings removed that obstructed the view on roads and to have trees and hedges trimmed; as well as the improvement of signposts and control of the erection of petrol pumps on roads.

Road Improvements

The roads in 1922 consisted for the most part of unrolled waterbound macadam, the surface of which was not dressed. With the revenues of the Road Fund increasing, it was possible to provide substantial improvement grants. On the main roads the waterbound macadam was given a waterproof and dustproof surface. Up to 1926/7 all grants were confined to improvement works but from 1927 contributions were given towards the upkeep of main roads. The grant from the Road Fund was used as a lever to induce county councils to provide more money from their resources from rates. In little over a decade the surfaces of the main roads had all been improved and attention could then be given to widening and improving alignment. At this stage money became available for relieving unemployment by putting men to work on roads. Grants out of the employment schemes vote were offered on condition that the road authority made a small contribution and took on men who were in receipt of unemployment assistance.

World War II practically suspended road improvements, as tar and bitumen were no longer available in sufficient quantities. At the same time turf had to be brought to the towns. Many roads deteriorated under these conditions. When the war was over the immediate business was to restore these roads and a new system of grants increasing with the rate of expenditure from local funds was devised. For the first time the county roads became eligible for grants. This system of restoration grants continued for three years. When it came to an end the normal system of improvement and maintenance grants for main roads was restored and an improvement grant for county roads was provided.

The effect of all these measures was a marked improvement in both main and county roads; many dangerous corners were removed and the principal roads were strengthened and made more suitable for the ever-increasing volume of traffic. Grants to urban district councils were instituted to deal with the problem of urban roads.

Bridges

The term 'roads' includes 'bridges' and in general the law on the construction and maintenance of roads applies to bridges. A road authority is not permitted to construct or reconstruct a bridge or viaduct over, or a tunnel under, a railway, unless it has the consent of the Minister for Transport or over any inland waterway within the meaning of the Minister for Arts, Heritage, Gaeltacht and the Islands (Powers and Functions) Act, 1998, or any navigable water, save with the consent of the Minister for Community, Rural and Gaeltacht Affairs. A bridge over navigable water cannot be built without the consent of the Minister for Communications, Marine and Natural Resources. Again, bridgework over any watercourse cannot be undertaken without the consent of the Commissioners of Public Works under the Arterial Drainage Act, 1945. In the case of an important bridgework a substantial exchequer grant is generally made available.

Special provisions, either in general or in local Acts, deal with particular bridges or particular classes of bridge. For example, in the case of road bridges over railways and canals the general position is that the transport company is responsible for maintaining the bridge in its original condition. When such a bridge is being replaced by an improved structure the transport company pays a proportion corresponding to the cost of replacing the original structure and the local authority pays the balance.

Road Traffic Act, 1961

The process of modernisation undergone by virtually all local services in the post-war period began for roads and road traffic with the Road Traffic Act, 1961. This Act substituted a wider and more up-to-date battery of powers for the rather faded provisions of the Road Traffic Act, 1933.

The annual report of the Department of Local Government for 1962/3 contains an excellent account of roads administration, problems and strategies at the time. Road Fund assistance for arterial roads was being doubled and certain limited, department-financed, research projects were in progress in University College Dublin. In 1964, however, with the establishment of An Foras Forbartha (National Institute for Physical Planning and Construction Research) major studies began in road planning, with a special focus on arterial roads. A 1969 report on the administration of the arterial roads programme recommended the transfer of responsibility for arterial roads to the Minister for Local Government. A further study of highway construction and maintenance management pointed towards a reclassification of the roads system, suggesting three grades: national routes, primary and secondary; regional roads, primary and secondary; and county roads.

Local Government (Roads and Motorways) Act, 1974

The above reports, and the discussions which followed them, provided the groundwork for the Local Government (Roads and Motorways) Act, 1974. This, the first important revision of roads law since 1925, gave road authorities power to construct motorways and reinforced local powers to construct dual carriageways, central medians and flyovers and to provide traffic route lighting. The Act diverged somewhat from an earlier government decision (July 1969) that the prospective legislation should transfer the national route system to the Minister for Local Government, the work of construction and so forth to be done by local authorities on an agency basis. Under the Act, local authorities retained responsibility for the entire road system but were subject to strong ministerial direction and control in relation to arterial routes. The Act empowered the minister to declare a public road to be a motorway or national road and, after consultation with the road authorities concerned, to direct the planning and execution of works on national roads and motorways in the interests of efficiency and uniformity of standards.

National primary and secondary roads were also designated and from 1974 their improvement and upkeep became wholly a charge on, first the Road Fund and later the exchequer. At the same time the separate grants to road authorities for main and county roads, tourist roads, county borough and urban roads were replaced by general or block grants for roads purposes. A formal order under the Act identifying the national road system was made in June 1977.

Road Policy and Planning

May 1979 saw the publication of a road development plan for the 1980s, the first major centrally co-ordinated programme for the development of the national road network. The plan was developed in the context of the availability of substantial financial assistance from the EU (then the EEC), and a Council Decision in 1978 that the EU must be notified of plans and programmes for the development of transport infrastructures which would serve as a guide for action by the government of the member states. The principal aims of the plan were:

- the provision of an adequate strategic inter-urban road system connecting the principal towns, seaports and airports
- the adoption of a minimum two-lane standard for the national route network with higher standards for particular sections
- the provision of bypasses of a number of towns on the national routes
- a programme of new river crossings, ring roads and relief routes in the cities and other major urban centres.

The plan included a programme of major improvement schemes on the national primary and secondary routes and in the major urban areas. The plan was reviewed in 1985 by the document *Policy and Planning Framework for Roads* (Department of the Environment, 1985b). The review echoed the main thrust of the 1979 plan and included a requirement to provide €6.35 million per annum for a ten-year period to upgrade short-span masonry bridges to cater for greater vehicle weights resulting from an EU Directive on weights and dimensions adopted in December 1984. A government welcome was expressed for the involvement of private sector investment in the roads infrastructure. The Local Government (Toll Roads) Act, 1979 had empowered local authorities to enter into agreements with private interests for the construction, maintenance and management of toll roads and bridges. Such agreements were subject to public notice, and public inquiry if objections were received, and decisions were reserved to the elected members of local authorities. The toll schemes for the Eastlink and Westlink crossings of the River Liffey in Dublin were made in 1984 and 1990 respectively and toll facilities are operational at these locations. Further toll schemes have been made and adopted by the board of the National Roads Authority: M4 Kinnegad–Enfield–Kilcock (2001), M1 Gormanstown to Monasterboice (2002), N8 Rathcromac/Fermoy bypass and N25 Waterford bypass (2003).

The operational programme for road development prepared within the framework of the national development plan for 1989 to 1993 was designed to prepare the economy to compete successfully in the Internal Market due to be completed in 1992 and to stimulate the domestic growth needed to reduce unemployment and to raise per capita incomes towards average EU levels. The programme was costed at €1,257 million (1989 prices) and included thirty-four major improvement projects involving the provision of dual-carriageway or motorway on 290 kilometres of national primary routes with a further 270 kilometres being upgraded to class II, two-lane road standard (7.3 metre single carriageway with two 3 metre hard shoulders).

The operational programme for transport for 1994 to 1999 took a broader remit than its predecessors, involving an integrated package of investment in roads, public transport, ports and airports. Between 1989 and 1992 road travel (expressed in vehicle kilometres) had grown at an average of 5 per cent per annum with a higher growth level of 6.75 per cent on the national network. The total number of registered vehicles grew by 13 per cent between 1989 and 1993 to 1.151 million vehicles. The operational programme involved a total investment of €3,316 million (1994 prices) of which €1,396 million would be spent on the national primary network with a focus on four key strategic corridors:

- north/south: Belfast – Dublin – Rosslare – Waterford – Cork
- southwest: Dublin – Limerick/Shannon – Cork
- east/west: Dublin – Galway – Sligo
- western: Sligo – Galway – Limerick – Waterford – Rosslare.

The overall target was to complete the development of the national primary road network by 2005 and to provide an inter-urban travel speed on completion of 80 kilometres per hour. At the end of 1993, 35 per cent of the network was adequate or improved and this would be extended to 53 per cent by end of 1999 with the improvement of a further 11 per cent underway. Total time savings of 204 minutes were projected for the four corridors as a result of the improvements in the programme.

The national roads priority for 2000 to 2006, as set out in the national development plan, has the following objectives:

- to improve the reliability of the road transport system by upgrading major interurban routes to motorway/high quality dual carriageway standard, removing bottlenecks, remedying capacity deficiencies and reducing absolute journey times and journey time variance
- to improve internal road transport infrastructure between regions and within regions, contribute to the competitiveness of the productive sector and foster balanced regional development
- to facilitate better access to and from the main ports and airports with the main objective of offsetting the negative effects of peripherality

- to contribute to sustainable transport policies, facilitating continued economic growth and regional development while ensuring a high level of environmental protection
- to help achieve the objectives of the government strategy for road safety in relation to reducing fatalities and serious injuries caused by road accidents.

The total investment envisaged for the national roads priority is €6.75 billion. The focus of the investment will be on:

- development of five major inter-urban routes (Dublin to the border, Dublin to Galway, Dublin to Cork, Dublin to Limerick, Dublin to Waterford) to motorway/high quality dual carriageway standard
- a programme of major improvement works on other national primary routes
- completion of the M50 motorway and Dublin Port Tunnel
- improvement of national secondary routes of particular importance to economic development

Traffic Studies

With the multiplication of motor vehicles, traffic had become a problem in many cities and towns. Symptoms of approaching crisis began to appear in Dublin as early as 1970 and in the *Dublin Transportation Study* (1972) An Foras Forbartha presented 'a co-ordinated transport and planning exercise undertaken jointly by Dublin Corporation, Dublin County Council, Dún Laoghaire Borough Corporation, Wicklow County Council, Bray Urban District Council, the Department of Local Government and An Foras Forbartha' (Hall, 1980). The proposals included some seventy miles of motorway in the Dublin region, which were, however, slow in materialising. In 1978, the minister set up the Transport Consultative Commission to advise on measures necessary to deal with goods and passenger traffic generally, giving priority to urban passenger services. In 1980, the commission's first report recommended the establishment of a new Dublin transportation authority with the main object of securing effective co-ordination and policy integration between local authorities, An Garda Síochána and the Departments of the Environment and Transport. The government accepted this recommendation and the Dublin Transport Authority was established in October 1986. However, following a change of government, the authority was abolished under the Dublin Transport Authority (Dissolution) Act, 1987 before it had become operational.

In 1978, the local authorities for Cork City and County published a comprehensive analysis of the land and transportation requirements of the Cork region as it moved towards the twenty-first century. The Cork Land Use and

Transportation Study (LUTS) contained a number of recommendations for infrastructural development including new city-centre bridges and an improved road network. A key element in the strategy was a proposed new downstream crossing of the River Lee – the Jack Lynch Tunnel, at a cost of some €133 million, was opened to traffic in May 1999.

The situation in Dublin continued to be a cause of concern and in 1988 the minister appointed the Dublin Transportation Review Group, with representatives from the relevant government departments, local authorities and CIÉ to review transportation planning arrangements for the Greater Dublin Area. The review group recommended a new transportation study and the resulting Dublin Transportation Initiative (DTI) final report was published on 1 August 1995. The DTI strategy consisted of an integrated set of infrastructural and transport policy initiatives, a switch of investment towards public transport in the form of light rail, quality bus corridors, DART upgrading and extension, other rail improvements, further examination of a rail link to Dublin Airport, development of park-and-ride facilities, improved access to public transport for people with disabilities and mobility impairment, an integrated fare structure and ticketing and new interchange facilities for public transport services in Dublin city centre.

The government agreed that the DTI strategy should provide the general policy framework for the future development of the transport system in the Greater Dublin Area and established the Dublin Transportation Office in November 1995 to oversee implementation of the strategy. It also agreed to the appointment by Dublin Corporation of a director of traffic who would have overall responsibility for traffic management in Dublin City. The Road Traffic (Immobilisation of Vehicles) Regulations, 1998 enabled the director of traffic, local authority or An Garda Síochána to introduce wheel clamping for illegally parked vehicles, which considerably improved the availability of on-street parking in Dublin. A number of other local authorities have since introduced clamping in urban areas.

Throughout the 1990s, Dublin witnessed extraordinary growth in the demand for travel. Between 1991 and 1999 total peak hour trips grew by 111,000 (65 per cent) from 172,000 in 1991 to 283,000 in 1999. The vast bulk of this growth has been accounted for by private car commuting. It is forecast that, by 2016, total peak hour trips will have increased to 488,000, an increase of 95 per cent on 1997 levels.

In November 2001, *A Platform for Change* – an integrated transportation strategy for the Greater Dublin Area for the period 2000 to 2016, was published (Dublin Transportation Office, 2001). This strategy aims to:

- achieve a city and region which embrace the principles of sustainability
- encompass a leading European city, proud of its heritage and looking to the future

- have at its heart the national capital, seat of government and national centres of excellence
- develop a strong, competitive, dynamic and sustainable region
- achieve a living city and region, on a human scale, accessible to all and providing a good quality of life for its citizens.

The plan has objectives dealing with bus, suburban rail, LUAS (on street light rail) and metro transport; traffic and demand management; as well as roads transport. The total capital cost of implementing the plan is estimated at €22 billion. It is hoped to reduce average peak journey times from 76 to 34 minutes.

Non-National Roads

In 1977, the government decided to abolish road tax on private vehicles up to 16 horsepower and on all motorcycles. With this abolition, the Road Fund lost much of its original purpose and the government decided to terminate it from January 1978. Rates on domestic and other dwellings were abolished at the same time and these measures together with a relatively poor national economic performance resulted in reduced discretionary funding for local authorities. There was a marked deterioration in the condition of non-national roads throughout the country during the 1980s. Considerable political lobbying was undertaken on this issue in a number of areas and in the 1990 local government elections a number of 'pothole' candidates were elected.

In August 1988, the County and City Engineers' Association presented the results of a survey of regional and county roads to the minister. This updated a study originally undertaken in 1985/6 and its main conclusions were that the structural adequacy of 33 per cent and the surface adequacy of 37 per cent of regional roads was either critically deficient or deficient and that the pavement condition of 34 per cent of county roads was either critically deficient or deficient. The cost of remedying accumulated defects was estimated to be €243 million for regional roads and €572 million for county roads. The association suggested that rescue programmes were needed for both regional and county roads and proposed a five-year programme for regional roads involving an annual expenditure of €126 million. Expenditure at the end of the programme would have to be maintained at €77 million, also well in excess of the existing levels. In the case of county roads they proposed a fifteen-year programme, involving annual expenditure of €194 million in the first five years, €133 million annually in the subsequent ten years and €116 million per annum following completion of the programme.

The situation did not improve until 1995 when the minister announced a major ten-year restoration programme for regional and county roads. The bulk of the additional funds have been devoted to surface dressing, surface restoration and road reconstruction works. The restoration programme was facilitated by a non-national road condition study, commissioned by the Department of the Environment in 1996, to determine the extent of the backlog of deficiencies on regional and county roads and to quantify the remedial works required to restore these roads to a satisfactory condition. In addition, the Department of the Taoiseach, in 1997, appointed consultants to examine the efficiency and effectiveness of county councils' operations on non-national roads with the aim of securing the best value for money and maximising outputs from expenditure on public roads by county councils. The report, published in December 1997, recommended, *inter alia*, the introduction of key performance indicators to monitor the performance of local authorities in the non-national roads area (Department of the Taoiseach, 1997).

The national development plan provides for expenditure of €2.03 billion on non-national roads in the 2000 to 2006 period. This expenditure is being channelled through the regional operational programmes of the Border Midlands and Western (BMW) and Southern and Eastern (S&E) Regional Assemblies, who are the managing authorities for the non-national roads programme. The main emphasis of the non-national roads programme is the continuation of the restoration programme. The EU co-financed specific improvement grants scheme is continued in the 2000 to 2006 period. It is expected that EU funding of €192 million will be available under this grant category. The EU aid rate in the BMW region is 75 per cent and in the S&E region it is 50 per cent.

Roads Act, 1993

Legislation relating to the construction and maintenance of public roads was updated by the Roads Act, 1993. The Act introduced a new road classification system comprising national, regional and local roads. The classification of roads as national or regional roads is the function of the Minister for Transport. All other public roads are deemed to be local roads. In 1995 the lengths of roads in the different categories was as follows: national: 5,400 kilometres, regional: 11,500 kilometres and local: 78,900 kilometres.

The 1993 Act provided for the establishment of the National Roads Authority with the primary function of securing the provision of a safe and efficient network of national roads. For this purpose, the authority has overall responsibility for the planning and supervision of construction and maintenance works on national roads. The authority has a statutory obligation to have these functions undertaken on its behalf, as far as possible, by the relevant local authority, but may become directly involved where it considers that this would be more advantageous for convenience, expedience, effectiveness or cost reasons.

The Local Government (Roads and Motorways) Act, 1974 was superseded by the 1993 Act which empowered road authorities to make a motorway scheme, including compulsory purchase of land, which would be submitted to the minister for approval following statutory public notice. However, under the Planning and Development Act, 2000, confirmed by Roads Regulations 2000, the functions of the minister in relation to a motorway scheme were transferred to and vested in An Bord Pleanála, which must hold an oral hearing and thereafter may approve the scheme with or without modifications. A road authority must prepare an environmental impact statement (EIS) for a motorway scheme and, under the 1994 Roads Regulations, for all roads which are being constructed or widened to a width of four lanes or more and which are at least 8 kilometres in length in a rural area or 500 metres in an urban area, and any bridge or road tunnel over 100 metres in length.

The Planning and Development Act, 2000 requires local authorities to apply to An Bord Pleanála for approval regarding developments for which an environmental impact statement has been prepared. Before making an application, the local authority must publish a notice of its intentions in a local newspaper, inviting the public to inspect the environmental impact statement and to make submissions and observations to An Bord Pleanála. The requirement for public consultation with regard to road schemes was further extended by part X of the Local Government (Planning and Development) Regulations, 1994, superseded by part XI of the Planning and Development Act, 2000, which decrees that a road authority, before proceeding with the construction of a new road or the widening of an existing road greater than 100 metres in an urban area or one kilometre in a rural area, or the construction of any bridge or tunnel, must give notice in a newspaper of such proposals and consider any submissions made to it. Finally, the Act provided for the construction of cycleways and the making of bye-laws by local authorities to regulate and control skips on public roads.

The Roads (Amendment) Act, 1998 was introduced to clarify the powers of local authorities to compulsorily acquire a substratum of land for the construction and maintenance of a road tunnel, as part of their powers under the Roads Act, 1993, without acquiring any further land above or below the substratum. This issue arose in the course of the planning of the Dublin Port Tunnel. The Act also amended the Transport (Dublin Light Rail) Act, 1996 to provide similar power in that legislation relating to a tunnel for light rail development, and the Roads Act, 1993 to allow a light rail system access to a motorway, subject to the consent of the National Roads Authority.

Road Traffic Act, 1994

The Road Traffic Act, 1994 has given new powers and greater discretion to local authorities in dealing with speed limits, traffic calming measures and traffic signs. Under the Act, the making of bye-laws specifying the speed limit which shall apply to specified public roads is a reserved function of a road authority. Before making the bye-laws the authority must consult with, and consider any representations made by, the Garda Commissioner. The consent of the National Roads Authority is required in relation to speed limits on all national roads.

Inappropriate speed in urban areas has long been recognised as a problem in Europe and the concept of speed management and traffic calming has developed in response. Traffic calming is a relatively new and continuously evolving process aimed at reducing accidents and improving the living environment, mainly for urban dwellers. The 1994 Act provides road authorities with new general powers to carry out traffic calming measures to encourage drivers to match their speeds to local conditions by self-enforcing traffic engineering measures. While it is not a legal requirement, traffic calming schemes should generally be planned and implemented with full public consultation.

The Act involves a significant transfer of power to road authorities in relation to traffic signs. Authorities now have total control in the provision of information and warning signs. They must consult with the Garda Commissioner regarding regulatory signs but the final say rests with the authorities. However, all traffic signs provided on public roads must comply with regulations made under the Road Traffic Acts or with the Traffic Signs Manual or other directions given by the Minister for Transport. In 2002 the Minister for Transport directed Dublin City Council to remove signs relating to new orbital routes in the city centre as they contained unapproved content and colouring. Local authorities are also responsible for the making of bye-laws governing the type of paid parking controls to be applied in their areas.

Licensing of Taxis and Hackneys

The 1995 Road Traffic (Public Service Vehicles) (Amendment) Regulations introduced a number of changes relating to the licensing of taxis and hackneys. The function of licensing taxis and hackneys was transferred from the Garda Commissioner to local authorities. The Garda Commissioner continued to license large public service vehicles (buses) and to grant licences for the drivers of small public service vehicles. Other features of the regulations were that local authorities can introduce full taxi services to new areas by the creation of taximeter areas and can retain all income collected in relation to licensing fees. An Garda Síochána continues to be responsible for enforcement of the regulations.

Following the High Court decision in Christopher Humphrey and Others *v.* Minister for the Environment and Local Government and Others (High Court Judicial Review Record No. 38JR/2000) in October 2000, the Road Traffic (Public Service Vehicles) (Amendment) (No. 3) Regulations 2000 were brought into effect to provide a revised basis for taxi licensing. They provided, *inter alia*, for the revocation of regulatory provisions involving quantitative restrictions on the licensing of taxis and hackneys.

Road Safety

Concerns regarding the safety of road users over the years have resulted in regulations and campaigns designed to influence the competence and behaviour of road users in general and drivers in particular. Regulations in 1964 made the issue of new driving licences conditional on passing a competency test. The minister became the issuing authority for certificates of competence. This involved the recruitment of a corps of testers and the organisation of some forty test centres around the country. In addition to the practical driving test, applicants for first provisional licences must pass a driver theory test, introduced in June 2001.

Following the 1963 report of a commission on driving while under the influence of drink or a drug, the Road Traffic Act, 1968 introduced a procedure by which driver incapacity would be assessed by reference to blood-alcohol levels. The Medical Bureau of Road Safety was set up for the analysis of blood and urine samples. Enforcement of the Act was hampered by legal difficulties resulting in Road Traffic (Amendment) Acts in 1973 and 1978. The provisions were further strengthened by the 1994 Act, which lowered the maximum alcohol level to 80 milligrams per 100 millilitres of blood and gave the minister powers to lower the limits further by regulation. The Act provoked some controversy and a further Road Traffic Act in 1995 relaxed the circumstances in which an automatic driving disqualification would apply and provided for different periods of disqualification for certain drink-driving offences, to be determined by the level of alcohol found in a person's breath, blood or urine.

Road traffic regulations made in December 1978 made it obligatory for drivers and front-seat passengers of private cars to wear safety belts and for crash helmets to be worn by motorcycle drivers and pillion passengers. The fitting of seat belts in rear seats became mandatory in January 1992 and the wearing of them has been obligatory since January 1993.

Road accident statistics and trends have been published since the early 1970s in the annual *Road Accident Facts Ireland*, which was originally produced by An Foras Forbartha and later by the National Roads Authority. The peak years for fatalities were the early 1970s with over six hundred per annum and this figure dropped to around three hundred and fifty in the mid-1980s. The numbers rose to 472 fatalities in 1997, but the trend in recent years has been downward, reducing to 377 in 2002.

Road safety campaigns were launched by the Department in 1965, with the aid of a Road Safety Propaganda Consultative Committee. In 1973, the minister set up the National Road Safety Association to take over the department's work in publicity and education. Its functions were transferred to the National Safety Council established in 1987 with a remit to promote road, water and fire safety through education, training programmes and publicity campaigns. In 1997, the Garda Commissioner established a dedicated National Traffic Policy Bureau within An Garda Síochána to prioritise and co-ordinate action for road safety. The government published its strategy for the period 1998 to 2002, *The Road to Safety* (Department of the Environment and Local Government, 1998f), which set the primary target of reducing road fatalities in Ireland by 20 per cent over the five years of its term by a concerted effort in three particular areas: speeding, alcohol use and seat belt wearing. It also proposed a system of penalty points for minor driving offences, which was provided for in the Road Traffic Act, 2002, together with provision for preliminary breath testing of a driver involved in a road accident or a breach of road traffic law.

Testing Roadworthiness of Vehicles

Roadworthiness testing of heavy goods vehicles, buses and ambulances was introduced in 1982 and was extended to light goods vehicles in 1993. Testing is carried out by authorised testers appointed by county and city councils.

A national car test was required under an EU Directive (Directive 96/96/EC) and was introduced in 2000. Following an international competitive tendering process, the National Car Testing Service was awarded a ten-year contract by the minister to establish and operate the testing system. The contract was a public private partnership initiative for the department.

Land Use and Transportation

The unprecedented economic growth in Ireland during the 1990s led to significant increases in car ownership and new house building. These factors, combined with low-density housing and decreasing average household size, contributed to traffic congestion problems in cities and towns throughout the country and a growing realisation that traffic and transportation issues could not be resolved without considering the patterns of land use and development.

The *Strategic Planning Guidelines for the Greater Dublin Area*, published in 1999, provide a coherent strategic planning framework for development plans and for the provision of major transportation, sanitary services and other infrastructure. The report predicted that the Greater Dublin Area would continue to grow from a population of 1.4 million in 1996 to 1.65 million by 2011 and the number of households would increase from 450,000 to 660,000 over the same period. The report recommended that this growth be consolidated in the existing built-up 'metropolitan area' and in designated development centres in the surrounding 'hinterland area' which would be linked to the metropolitan area by transportation corridors. This strategy was designed to achieve a reduction in the growth in demand for transport and to increase the emphasis on transportation alternatives to the private car with a particular focus on public transport.

The strategic planning guidelines were given statutory effect by the Planning and Development Act, 2000, which obliges local authorities in the Dublin and Mid-East regions to have regard to them when making and adopting development plans. In March 2001, the Department of the Environment and Local Government and the Department of Public Enterprise introduced a consultation paper considering the institutional arrangements for land use and transport in the Greater Dublin Area and proposing that a strategic land use and transportation body should be established by statute (see chapter 25).

In November 2001, the Dublin Transportation Office published its integrated transportation strategy for the Greater Dublin Area for the period 2000 to 2016 entitled *A Platform for Change*. This strategy is based on the predictions of the strategic planning guidelines and proposes major investment in public transport, including light rail and metro, to increase morning peak trips from 70,000 to 300,000 by 2016. The Dublin Transportation Office also commissioned land use and transportation studies for a number of development centres in the Greater Dublin Area. Meanwhile, similar studies have been undertaken in Cork, Limerick, Galway and Waterford.

The integrated nature of transportation has been recognised by government, which, in 2002, transferred a number of road functions including road policy, safety and traffic, and the National Roads Authority, to a new Department of Transport. Non-national roads continue to be the responsibility of the Department of the Environment and Local Government.

National Roads Needs Study, 1998

The National Roads Authority (NRA) published a *National Roads Needs Study* in 1998. The main objectives of the study were to identify (a) the type of roadway which would be appropriate for each segment of the inter-urban national roads system in order to cater for projected traffic flows over a twenty-year horizon (2000 to 2019) and to achieve an average inter-urban travel speed of 80 kilometres per hour, and (b) the specific road improvements necessary to achieve these objectives and the associated costs.

The NRA study sets out a schedule of road improvement needs on national roads costing €7.75 billion over the twenty-year period to 2019. It provides an assessment of Ireland's infrastructural deficit in terms of national road development and was an important input to the national development plan for 2000 to 2006.

The Road Ahead

Policy and planning for road development in Ireland have been conducted in latter years in the context of EU planning horizons, and the significant funding available through a number of operational programmes since the late 1970s has facilitated major improvements in the road network. Ireland's increasing prosperity in the late 1990s, together with the accession of new poorer member states to the EU, will result in a reduction in EU Structural and Cohesion Funds for infrastructural development in the years ahead. However, further major investment in infrastructural development, including road improvements, is essential to maintaining continuity and the sustainability of Ireland's economic performance. The shortfall in funding from the EU will require greater input from the national exchequer and from the private sector.

There is a strong government commitment to the greater involvement of the private sector in the provision of Ireland's infrastructural requirements, including road projects. The vehicle for this involvement will be public private partnerships (PPPs). These are essentially partnerships between public sector organisations and private sector investors and businesses for the purposes of designing, planning, financing, constructing and/or operating infrastructure projects normally provided through traditional procurement mechanisms by the state. The government in 1999 established a number of discrete PPP units in relevant government departments and agencies, including the Department of the Environment and Local Government and the National Roads Authority, for the purpose of developing the PPP approach and to oversee the implementation of a number of pilot projects, including road projects. These units will lead the way in developing the principles and ground rules under which the PPP approach can operate.

As noted above, *National Development Plan 2000–2006* envisages expenditure of €5.97 billion on national roads, €2.03 billion on non-national roads and €2.84 billion on public transport, of which €2.01 billion will be spent in the Greater Dublin Area. This represents an unprecedented level of expenditure on the state's roads and transportation infrastructure and it provides a unique opportunity to upgrade that infrastructure so that it will appropriately reflect a modern and thriving economy.

11

Water Services

Liam Gleeson[1]

Adequate water services are essential for economic development, the protection of the environment and public health. Ireland requires continued major investment to sustain its water services and to maintain and develop the infrastructure necessary for a modern and expanding economy. The provision of water services includes the treatment and distribution of drinking water and the collection and treatment of waste water.

Sanitary/local authorities are responsible for the day-to-day operation of water services along with ongoing refurbishment, upgrading and replacement of facilities and the planning, development and construction of new water services facilities. The Department of the Environment and Local Government develops and implements national water services policy; prioritises schemes for investment; secures exchequer and European funding for the capital investment programme; allocates water services funding to sanitary authorities and administers and monitors the financial and physical progress of schemes in the water services programme. The department also underpins national water services strategy through national studies, reviews and provision of guidance, technical expertise and advice to sanitary authorities.

Sanitary Authorities

Responsibility for sanitation is one of local government's oldest functions. Ireland's ninety sanitary authorities (county, city and town councils) have responsibility

---

[1] This chapter was prepared by the Water Services and Water Services Policy Units of the Department of the Environment and Local Government and co-ordinated by Liam Gleeson, Water Services Policy Unit.

under Irish law for the provision of water services. From January 2004 town councils will cease to be sanitary authorities and the water services function will be consolidated to county and city level. As can be seen from figure 11.1, the cost of operating water services is escalating. In this regard the cost to sanitary authorities for the operation and maintenance of the water services infrastructure was €304 million in 2001. This figure is expected to continue to increase as new state-of-the-art water services facilities are introduced and operating contracts for these facilities are entered into with the private sector. In 2003, around 2,500 local authority staff are employed on a full-time basis in the water services sector.

Figure 11.1 Local Authority Maintenance Costs, 1990 to 2001

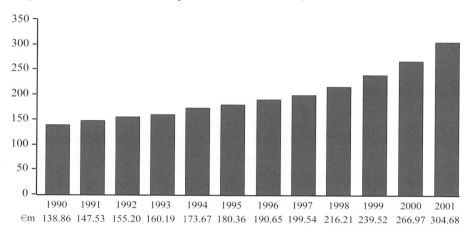

	1990	1991	1992	1993	1994	1995	1996	1997	1998	1999	2000	2001
€m	138.86	147.53	155.20	160.19	173.67	180.36	190.65	199.54	216.21	239.52	266.97	304.68

Sanitary authorities have primary responsibility under national law for the provision of water services. Authorities are required to produce and deliver high-quality drinking water, to collect and treat sewage effluent and to dispose safely of residual sludges. This requires a range of resources and expertise from project planning, to design and development, to administration and operation. The principal activities of sanitary authorities include the following areas.

- The assessment of needs and ranking of capital works: sanitary authorities are required to prepare an assessment of needs in relation to their water and sewerage systems. These assessments are used to prioritise improvement works and to make proposals for central funding.[2]

---

[2] The compilation of these assessments is assisted by national water and waste water studies that include separate catchment/county reports. The *National Water Study* was completed in 2000 (Department of the Environment and Local Government, 2000g) and the National Urban Waste Water Study is to conclude in 2003. A separate water study was carried out in the Greater Dublin Area, while an examination of Dublin's waste water system is advanced.

- The implementation of capital projects: the sanitary authority is responsible for the carrying out of capital works and for associated contractual commitments. Exchequer funding of up to 100 per cent, subject to the application of the polluter pays principle, is provided for water services capital works. Operational costs are directly recovered from the non-domestic sector along with the marginal capital costs (the additional, non-domestic, capital requirement above the cost of providing for the domestic capacity on a scheme) on new schemes. Figure 11.2 demonstrates a sustained and incremental increase in water services capital investment.

Figure 11.2 Water Services Capital Investment, 1990 to 2002

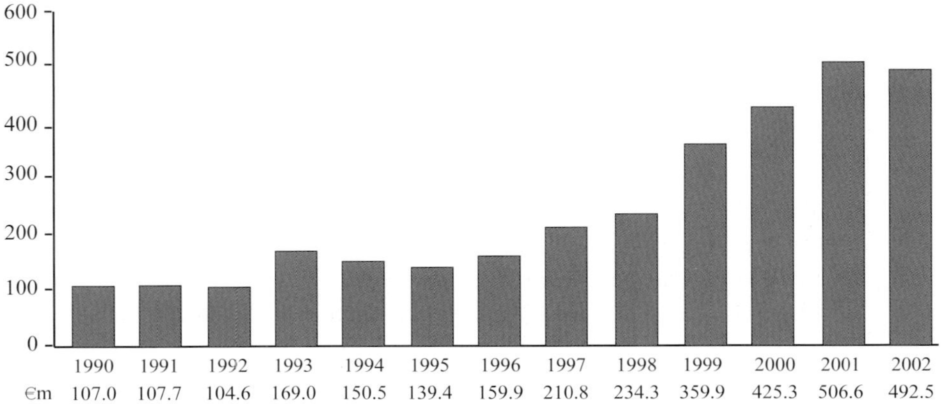

	1990	1991	1992	1993	1994	1995	1996	1997	1998	1999	2000	2001	2002
€m	107.0	107.7	104.6	169.0	150.5	139.4	159.9	210.8	234.3	359.9	425.3	506.6	492.5

- The operation and management of water services: once a scheme is completed, the functions of operating, maintaining and repairing the scheme rest with the sanitary authority. More recently, sanitary authorities have contracted the private sector to operate and maintain newly commissioned water treatment facilities. Average operational costs are recovered in respect of the provision of water services to all users other than to domestic households. National policy requires that the associated costs of providing water services to domestic households will be progressively met in a transparent way from the Local Government Fund.
- The implementation of national and EU legislation: the sanitary authority is responsible for the implementation of relevant European environmental legislation, particularly drinking water regulations and the Urban Waste Water Treatment Directive. In addition, EU investment in water services infrastructure means that the EU has a significant regulatory and financial impact on the activities of sanitary authorities.

The Urban Waste Water Treatment Directive requires that the larger towns and cities provide treatment to set standards before discharging to rivers, lakes and the sea. In this regard all waste water discharges from systems with a population equivalent greater than 2,000 must be treated by 31 December 2005. A deadline of end 2000 applied to the treatment of discharges for a 15,000 population equivalent, which covers all major cities and towns including Dublin, Cork, Limerick, Waterford, Galway, Clonmel, Dundalk and Drogheda. The installation of higher standards of sewage treatment is also required at every municipal sewage treatment plant discharging into waters sensitive to pollution.

• The implementation of national water services pricing policy: in 1998 the government adopted a water services pricing policy framework. This requires the recovery of average operational and marginal capital costs of water services provision from all non-domestic users; the completion of the metering of all such users by 2006; and the maintenance of the status quo with regard to not charging for domestic water services provision and the meeting of these costs through the Local Government Fund in the case of operational costs and through the department's capital programme in the case of infrastructural costs. Exchequer funding of up to 100 per cent, subject to the application of the polluter pays principle, is provided for water services capital works. Average operational costs are recovered from the non-domestic sector along with marginal capital costs (on new schemes).

The government's water services pricing policy was rolled out with effect from March 2000 with regard to the application of marginal capital costs for infrastructure provided under Ireland's water services investment programme. This programme makes up an integral component of the EU co-financed Community Support Framework, operating under the national development plan. On the operational side, the policy is being introduced on a phased basis in the context of a commitment to achieve universal metering of all non-domestic customers (other than households) by 2006. This policy framework also meets Ireland's obligations in respect of water services cost recovery under article 9 of the Water Framework Directive. The Minister for Finance and the Committee of 'Wise Men' (set up to review public expenditure) suggested the reintroduction of water charges for domestic users. A major review of local authority finances is also planned.

Historical Development of Water Services

The 1946 Census shows that almost 92 per cent of dwellings in urban districts and towns with over 1,500 inhabitants were provided with piped water. At the same time a relatively small number of dwellings in rural areas, fewer than 10 per cent, had piped water supply and only 5 per cent of farm buildings had piped water.

In 1959, the government launched a major drive with the twin objectives of spreading the benefits of piped water and sanitation to rural Ireland and improving the facilities already available in urban areas, which were unable to cope with rising population, higher living standards and growing industrial demand. The programme involved the provision and upgrading of water treatment works for cities and towns, the extension of public schemes to rural areas and the promotion, through individual grants, of private group water schemes.

The provision of community-based water services schemes assisted by central and local government has benefited rural communities across Ireland. The development of a private water sector was recognition that given the dispersed nature of the Irish population it was not possible for the public authorities to provide water and sanitation facilities for all areas on demand. The development of the rural programme was greatly assisted by publicity in the form of films, literature and stands at national and local agriculture shows and mobilising rural organisations. The campaign was very successful and by 2000 over 5,500 group water schemes, of all sizes, had been formed. These provide an essential part of the water services infrastructure in rural areas.

Consistent investment in water services brought about a steady improvement in facilities, as seen in the national Census figures for 1946 to 2002 (see table 11.1).

Table 11.1 Percentage of Dwellings with Piped Water Supply, 1946 to 1991

Year	Urban areas (%)	Rural areas (%)	Total (%)
1946	92	8.6	38.6
1961	97	25	57
1971	99	58	78
1981	100	89	95
1991	100	97.1	98.8

Water Services Investment Programme, Influences and Progress

The aims of the water services investment programme include:

- provision of a sufficient quantity of good quality water to meet the needs of an expanding economy and to provide for serviced land for housing development

- delivering compliance with the Urban Waste Water Treatment Directive
- improving the quality of drinking water to meet higher standards and, in particular, to provide support for the private group scheme sector
- maintaining and improving river and lake water quality
- upgrading the ageing water distribution networks in the major urban centres and resolving high levels of leakage and a poor quality water delivery.

National Development Plan 2000–2006 (NDP)

The protection of the environment is a key national and EU priority. Following the successful completion of the 1994 to 1999 national development plan Ireland's water services infrastructure is progressing. It has, however, a substantial way to go before matching water services in comparative EU member states. Delivery of this requirement is being met through an unprecedented level of investment in water services under the NDP (Government of Ireland, 2000a), which, in the period to 2006, envisages an almost threefold increase in water services capital investment over the previous national plan.

The NDP contains provision for water services investment of €4.4 billion (€3.8 billion for major schemes and €0.6 billion for rural water) over the seven years to 2006. This is divided into the following environmental services operational programme measures:

• waste water	€1,657 million
• water supply	€579 million
• rehabilitation and management of infrastructure	€862 million
• infrastructural support for economic activity	€702 million.

An amount of €644 million has been provided for the rural water programme through the regional operational programmes.

European Union Co-Funding

Water services capital projects have been carried out with European Structural Fund support since the 1980s and through the Cohesion Fund since the 1990s. Investment was organised into operational programmes, approved by the European Commission and implemented by the national and local authorities.

Since 1993 the bulk of investment has come from the Cohesion Fund, which funds individual, major water and waste water projects. A total of €990 million has been committed to water services infrastructure under the fund. At its peak in the late 1990s, over 75 per cent of total water services investment was co-financed by the EU at aid rates of up to 85 per cent. In 2001, water services capital investment of €507 million benefited from €213 million in EU assistance.

Support for Housing

One of the fundamental requirements for an adequate supply of affordable housing is the availability of serviced residential land. The Serviced Land Initiative and other key water and sewerage programmes have underpinned delivery of housing policy by reducing constraints on new house building in areas approved for development. Based on an analysis carried out by local authorities for the department's housing division in 2002, it is clear that the position in relation to the current stock of serviced building land is encouraging.

By the end of 2001, a total of 272 schemes representing more than 200,000 sites had been approved with €90 million in exchequer funding allocated for approved projects. This requires 60 per cent local authority co-financing and total investment in the region of €227 million.

Water Conservation Programme

A crucial support that has underpinned economic growth is the availability of reliable supplies of potable water. The unprecedented investment in water conservation of €276 million underway in 2003 demonstrates a commitment to maximising efficiency in the way Ireland's water resources are managed and utilised. The national campaign to identify unaccounted for water and to eliminate wastage is, however, going to take many years to complete.

The *National Water Study* (NWS) published by the department in 2000 estimates that up to 47 per cent of all water produced is unaccounted for and that in some areas this level of unaccounted for water is much higher. The results of the NWS and the Greater Dublin Water Supply Strategy Study confirm that a very significant amount of water is lost into the ground every day. This represents an unsustainable and unacceptable cost and drain on the resources of local authorities and the state and on the environment.

Over €63 million was invested between 1996 and 2003 on fifteen water conservation schemes located throughout the country. Significant reductions in leakage have been achieved with, for example, water loss (in the water conservation area) reduced in Dublin from 42.5 to 28.7 per cent, in Meath from 47 to 34 per cent and in Kilkenny from 45 to 29 per cent. In addition to the environmental benefits, the water conservation schemes are a practical, realistic and economic way of meeting much of the extra demand for water and a viable alternative to the provision of new water supply infrastructure. This is clearly demonstrated in Dublin, where the requirements of exceptional growth rates have been met through a combination of modest increases in supply and a comprehensive leakage control campaign.

The 2003 (first round) allocation for a nationwide water conservation programme, designed to identify and substantially reduce the levels of unaccounted for water in Ireland's water supply network, was rolled out in May 2003. This investment builds on the fifteen fact-finding water conservation schemes carried out by selected local authorities since 1996. The trend in water conservation investment is that 15 per cent of investment has been in respect of fees for consultant engineers, metering, mapping and so forth; 10 per cent for pilot repair and rehabilitation projects including rehabilitation studies; and the remaining 75 per cent for rehabilitation work. The investment package provides for:

- €194 million to allow those authorities that have already completed the study phase to carry out the necessary major network rehabilitation, water conservation and leakage reduction schemes identified by those studies
- €82.5 million to allow the remaining authorities to commence studies to map out their water supply networks and to establish the level and sources of unaccounted for water. As part of the study phase, authorities will also undertake pilot water conservation and leakage reduction projects and identify measures to be incorporated in longer-term strategies.

Additional funding will be made available for further investment in water conservation.

Water Supply for the Greater Dublin Area

A study of short-term water supply sources for the Greater Dublin Area, underway in 2003, will identify additional water supplies that can be mobilised in the short term to cater for increasing demands, particularly in the period until the Ballymore Eustace water treatment plant is expanded to full capacity. A further study is also planned to examine options and identify the optimum project to deliver a major new water supply for the Dublin region which will cater for long-term strategic growth (that is twelve years or more).

Rural Water Programme

The rural water programme is composed of a number of targeted initiatives to address deficiencies in:

- group water schemes serving some 150,000 rural households
- small public water supply and sewerage systems in rural villages
- private individual supplies to some 130,000 rural households where an alternative group or public supply is not available.

Responsibility for the administration of the rural water programme is devolved to county councils. The main focus of the programme is on the improvement of water quality in group water schemes dependent on private sources, many of which are subject to organic pollution from agricultural and domestic sources. The programme is being implemented in a spirit of partnership and co-operation between the main stakeholders including the National Federation of Group Water

Schemes, rural organisations (Irish Farmers Association, Irish Creamery Milk Suppliers Association, Irish Countrywomen's Association), local authorities and the Department of the Environment and Local Government.

The National Rural Water Monitoring Committee was set up to advise the minister on rural water supply policy and to monitor the local authority implementation of the devolved programme. The fact that some 40 per cent of all group water schemes have no water disinfection or treatment equipment in place is central to the problem of poor quality group scheme supplies. It is anticipated that water treatment facilities will be required on as many as 500 individual group schemes, which are dependent on private sources such as rivers, lakes and boreholes. The committee investigated and pilot-tested new technologies and new approaches for treating small-scale rural supplies. This in turn resulted in a strategic response at national level in favour of design, build, operate (DBO) procurement of water treatment plants coupled with the bundling of schemes under a single contract. This strategy will ensure a maximum return on the investment and will result in essential infrastructure being provided in the shortest possible timescale.

The department will provide a 100 per cent capital grant for the provision of essential water disinfection and treatment equipment on schemes. An annual subsidy towards the operational cost of group water schemes, amounting to as much as €197 per house, is also payable where essential disinfection and treatment equipment has been provided by way of DBO procurement. There is the threat of legal action by the European Commission to ensure that group water schemes comply with relevant EU standards.

Water Pricing

Ireland is moving towards making the full cost of water and waste water services to all sectors transparent and securing full cost recovery from non-domestic customers (commercial and industrial users). In 1998, the government adopted a water services pricing policy framework which provides, *inter alia*, for full cost recovery from the non-domestic sector and metering (by 2006) along with the continued prohibition of water services charges for the domestic sector.

The framework represents significant progress towards the development of a more sustainable approach to water services management in respect of the non-domestic sector by fully internalising the costs of water usage and waste water generation. It is also in keeping with the application of the polluter pays principle and the requirements of the EU Water Framework Directive in so far as it applies to non-domestic users. This is not the case when it comes to domestic users, although the Department of Finance wants water charges to domestic users to be reconsidered.

The implementation of the water services pricing policy is being advanced incrementally. Measures include: issuing circulars and information sheets on pricing policy; preparing comprehensive model agreements and guidance on policy implementation that was rolled-out to local authorities early in 2002 and supported by a series of regional workshops; and advancing a major pilot metering demonstration project.

Future Influences and Challenges

Major changes in water services practices and national and EU legislation will influence future water services programmes.

Water Services Bill

The general scheme of a Water Services Bill received government approval in July 2001. The Bill focuses on management of water 'in the pipe' as distinct from broader issues such as river water quality. The preparation of the Bill represents a major legislative exercise involving:

- consolidation and modernisation of the existing diverse body of water services legislation (extending over some eighteen Acts and as far back as the nineteenth century)
- a licensing system for the group water sector
- improvement of national water services infrastructure management generally.

EU Water Framework Directive

Ireland, along with other EU member states, will take a co-ordinated approach in achieving the objectives of the Water Framework Directive (WFD) and the implementation of programmes of measures for this purpose. The WFD sets a framework for the comprehensive management of water resources in the EU, within a common approach and with common objectives, principles and basic measures. It addresses inland surface waters, estuarine and coastal waters and ground water. The objectives of the WFD are to:

- protect and enhance the status of aquatic ecosystems (and terrestrial ecosystems and wetlands directly dependent on aquatic ecosystems)
- promote sustainable water use based on long-term protection of available water resources
- provide for sufficient supply of good quality surface water and ground water as needed for sustainable, balanced and equitable water use
- provide for enhanced protection and improvement of the aquatic environment by reducing/phasing out discharges, emissions and losses of priority substances
- achieve 'good status' (as defined) in surface waters and ground waters within a fifteen-year timeframe

- mitigate the effects of floods and droughts
- protect territorial and marine waters
- establish a register of 'protected areas', for example areas designated for protection of habitats or species.

The Directive requires the co-ordination of measures for water management in relation to river basins. River basin districts (RBDs) must be identified and established to form the 'administrative areas' for a co-ordinated approach. A particular requirement is the preparation of a river basin management plan in relation to each RBD. The WFD requires that river basins which cross national frontiers must be assigned to an international RBD. This will involve joint action with authorities in Northern Ireland in relation to cross-border catchments.

The development of a management plan for each RBD will require the participation and co-operation of a wide range of government departments, local authorities and other public agencies that have statutory functions in relation to water management and other matters encompassed by the Directive. High priority must be given to public consultation.

Ireland is generally in a good position to implement the Directive. Irish legislation provides (since 1977) for water quality planning on an integrated basis (to include surface and ground waters, including estuarine and tidal waters) and for inter-authority planning. Since 1997 Ireland has promoted a catchment-based national strategy to combat eutrophication in rivers and lakes. Major catchment-based initiatives have been developed in respect of Loughs Derg, Ree and Leane and the Rivers Suir, Boyne and Liffey, linked to a major programme of investment in sewage infrastructure in these catchments.

National Water Quality

Water quality in Ireland is generally good and compares very favourably with other EU member states. The main challenge is to deal with eutrophication arising from excess inputs of phosphorous from all sources. The extent of eutrophication in the river system has been increasing persistently since the 1970s and has been identified by the Environmental Protection Agency (EPA) as probably the most serious environmental pollution problem in Ireland. The principal challenge for Ireland is to maintain the trend in unpolluted waters as described in the 2002 EPA *Report on Water Quality in Ireland 1998–2000*.

The report confirms an increase in the length of unpolluted river channel for the first time since national surveys commenced in the 1970s: an increase from 67 per cent in the 1995 to 1997 period to 70 per cent in the 1998 to 2000 period. The pollution levels affecting the remaining 30 per cent of river channel are slight (17 per cent), moderate (12.4 per cent) and serious (0.8 per cent). The improvement is attributed to the wide range of catchment-management measures applied, particularly in the large projects delivered by local authorities, including investment in the upgrading of sewage treatment works.

Phosphorus from diffuse agriculture sources, waste water treatment plants and rural septic tanks continues to be the main cause of water pollution in Ireland. Nitrate is also an important pollutant – particularly in ground water. Another major problem is the contamination of individual well water by nitrate and bacteria.

There has been a steady improvement in the quality of drinking water supplied. The latest EPA reports on the quality of drinking water in Ireland show that public supplies are of a good quality with over 94 per cent compliance across a broad range of parameters. However, water quality problems persist in the group water sector, particularly in those privately sourced schemes which serve some 50,000 rural households nationally. These are being addressed through a range of measures, with up to 100 per cent capital grant assistance for the accelerated provision of water disinfection and treatment facilities on schemes dependent on quality deficient sources.

Conclusion

Water services are going through an ambitious period of development and change. From the outsourcing of the operation and management of water services facilities to the systematic improvement of rural water quality, local authorities continue to deliver innovative responses to the requirements of the water services sector. The construction of state-of-the-art water and waste water treatment facilities is being advanced around the country including the provision of sophisticated waste water treatment for the major population centres of Dublin, Cork, Limerick, Galway, and Waterford. Ireland can look forward to a continued upgrading of drinking water quality and waste water treatment, which will assist improved water quality in its rivers and lakes and the sustainable development of water services to meet economic and social demands.

12

Planning

Berna Grist

Background

With the commencement on 1 October 1964 of the Local Government (Planning and Development) Act, 1963, physical planning became a mandatory function of local government, whereas under the earlier Town and Regional Planning Acts, it had been discretionary (Grist, 1999, p. 1). Eight subsequent planning acts were introduced between 1976 and 1999 to remedy various deficiencies which became evident in the course of operating the system, while a small number of other pieces of legislation also amended the Planning Acts, mostly in order to implement European Directives.

All local authorities, except town commissioners, were entrusted with the full range of planning responsibilities in 1964, giving eighty-seven planning authorities for a population of 2.8 million. Under the Local Government (Dublin) Act, 1993 this number increased to eighty-eight with the creation of Fingal, South Dublin and Dún Laoghaire-Rathdown county councils. The preliminary report of the 2002 Census indicates that the total population stands at 3.9 million, while planning authorities, all of whom have the same variety of functions, range in size from 1,460 (Trim Town Council) to 495,101 (Dublin City Council).

The general election of 1997 brought a new minister to the Custom House, Noel Dempsey TD, who lost no time in starting the comprehensive review of planning legislation signalled in the programme for government, *An Action Programme for the Millennium* (Fianna Fáil and Progressive Democrats, 1997). A widespread process of consultation with interest groups and the general public took place over a three-month period from August 1997 – an innovative and inclusive approach to legislative reform and essential in the circumstances. Over its thirty-five years, the planning system had become more and more central to the economic and social development of the country, just as environmental concerns had grown to occupy a significant place in the lives of individual citizens.[1] Planning is probably the part of local government with which people are most likely to have contact and, in the commencing public phase of his review, the minister recognised this when he gave an opportunity to everyone – social partners, community groups, conservationists, developers and individuals – to make observations on the operation of the system and suggestions for its improvement.

The Core Principles

From the beginning, three core principles underpinned the minister's vision of a planning system for the twenty-first century. It was to have an ethos of sustainable development, be strategic in approach and deliver a performance of the highest quality. When the minister presented the 1999 Planning and Development Bill to the Seanad some two years later, he was able to point out where these principles had been incorporated into the new legislative code.

The long title of the Bill, which became the Planning and Development Act, 2000, amended the second legislative purpose of the 1963 Act to read: 'to provide, in the interests of the common good, for proper planning and *sustainable* development' (author's italics). The adjective sustainable qualifies development wherever this key phrase is used in the 2000 Act. However, what is meant by 'sustainable development' is specifically not defined because, as the minister noted, the concept is dynamic and all embracing and will evolve over time, so a legal definition would tend to restrict and stifle it.[2] Whether this lack of a statutory definition will result in merely a change of image rather than one of substance remains to be seen in the operation of the new system, but it has to be recognised that, at its best, sustainability is a nebulous concept which can mean very different things to different people.

The stated objective of having a strategic approach was dealt with in a more concrete way. Instead of each of the eighty-eight planning authorities adopting their own development plans, as previously, and relying on the co-ordinating role of the manager and co-operation between adjoining authorities, the 2000 Act introduced a hierarchy of plans, all to be placed within the context of a national spatial strategy (NSS). The hierarchy of guidelines, development plans and local area plans is discussed below. Although the NSS was declared to have been completed at the end of 2001, it still had not seen the light of day when Minister

---

[1] Introduction, *Proceedings of the Convention on the Review of Planning Legislation*, Department of the Environment and Local Government, 27 November 1997, p. 1.

[2] *Seanad Debates*, 14 October 1999, col. 803.

Dempsey moved to the Department of Education and Science on 6 June 2002 (on the formation of the new government following the May 2002 general election).

Political pragmatism may well have dictated that the run-up to a general election would be a most inappropriate time to unveil a policy document with such far-reaching consequences for the future development of communities at all levels of the planning hierarchy. However, the level of strategic planning possible for those planning authorities which started to prepare their development plans before 28 November 2002, when the NSS was finally published, was limited by the delays. A further complication arises in that there are very few opportunities for planning authorities with partly made development plans to amend them in the context of the NSS because the plan-making process must follow an inflexible statutory timeframe, an issue which is discussed later in this chapter. The national spatial strategy is described and analysed in Chapter 20.

The delivery of a quality planning service, the minister told the Seanad, would be provided for by changes in the legislation to ensure quality and timely decisions, an accessible planning service and proper enforcement. New time limits were introduced for each stage of the plan-making process, with tighter and more specific time limits being set for the processing of planning applications. Accessibility to the planning process was stated to be improved by giving third parties a statutory right to make submissions to the planning authority on planning applications and by the provision of statutory recognition for pre-planning discussions. One of the widespread concerns identified in the public consultation phase related to enforcement and the minister responded by simplifying and strengthening this part of the legislation, in particular by eliminating the 'do nothing' option for planning authorities which receive a complaint regarding compliance.

Commencement of the 2000 Planning Act

The Planning and Development Act, 2000 was brought into force in five phases between 1 November 2000 and 11 March 2002. In certain respects, it could be described as framework legislation because it required extensive regulations for its implementation. Any planning system has to achieve balance between the aspirations of individuals (developers or third parties) and the needs of the community as a whole, so its procedures have to be open, clearly understood and fair to all participants in the process. The details of how these procedures operate have always been set out in regulations. The new legislative provisions relating to housing strategies, strategic development zones, the hierarchy of development plans and the licensing of outdoor events, together with the changed development control and enforcement provisions, necessitated a complete review of the existing 1994 Planning Regulations and their enlargement.

This final part of the reform of the planning code was completed with the publication on 19 December 2001 of the consolidated 2001 Planning and

Development Regulations (SI No. 600 of 2001). In order to give planning authorities, An Bord Pleanála and private sector consultants an opportunity to familiarise themselves with the changes and to make provisions for the transition from the old to the new procedures, only planning applications made on or after 11 March 2002 were to be dealt with under the new regulations. To date, therefore, there has been only limited experience of the operation of the 2000 Act in its entirety but some strengths and weaknesses have already become apparent.

Most readers will already be aware of the principal features and elements of the planning system as it was prior to the enactment of the 2000 Act and there is a range of publications on the pre-2000 system to which reference can be made where more detail is needed – for example Galligan (1997), Grist (1999 and 2001), Nowlan (1999), O'Donnell (1998), O'Sullivan and Sheppard (annual) and Scannell (1995). Consequently, this chapter focuses on the main changes brought about by the 2000 Act and the impact these may be expected to have or indeed are already having where the relevant sections have been in force for a sufficient period to allow for informed comment.

Housing Strategies

One of the two most serious planning issues in Ireland in 1999 was housing supply – the other being transportation. The cost of housing, particularly in the Dublin area, had put the goal of home ownership completely beyond the reach of most first-time buyers and economic prosperity had brought investors into the market who were competing strongly and successfully with prospective owner-occupiers. In November 1997, the Department of the Environment commissioned the first of three studies from economic consultant Peter Bacon, who recommended fiscal and planning changes to improve the supply and affordability of housing.

When the 1999 Planning and Development Bill was published, by far the most controversial element was the new requirement imposed on planning authorities to prepare housing strategies for incorporation into their development plans and, subsequently, to implement them through the development control system. In itself, the identification of total housing demand in the authority's functional area did not present problems. This demand was to include private housing, the traditional category of persons on the housing list (social housing) and the new category of persons whose relevant income was inadequate to obtain a sufficient mortgage to buy a newly built house in the functional area of the planning authority on the open market (affordable housing). There would have been general recognition that many development plans could be criticised for zoning too little or too much land for housing and that the estimates of housing demand over the five-year period of development plans all too often lacked sufficient methodology and rigour. The systematic, open forecasting of demand in a housing strategy and the provision of sufficient zoned and serviced land to meet this demand in the development plan would both eliminate controversies over zoning and, by matching supply of land to demand, would moderate land prices.

Constitutionality

It was the implementation of housing strategies that gave rise to serious problems. As published, the Bill provided that a planning authority could attach a condition to planning permission requiring a developer to enter into an agreement under which up to 20 per cent of the land comprising the development would be ceded for social and affordable housing, at existing use value rather than market value. During its passage through the Oireachtas, this was modified to also allow a developer to meet this obligation by providing serviced sites or houses actually built for such purposes but on the same basis regarding the cost of the land involved. Whichever of the three methods would be proposed by the developer, a constitutional issue resulted relating to the property rights of the developer as landowner.

The rights to private property are contained in Article 40.3 and Article 43 of *Bunreacht na hÉireann*. In Article 40, the state guarantees in its laws to respect and defend the personal rights of citizens, among which are property rights. In Article 43, the state acknowledges 'that man . . . has the natural right . . . to the private ownership of external goods'. This Article goes on to recognise that the exercise of such right 'ought, in civil society, to be regulated by the principles of social justice'. Accordingly, the state 'may as occasion requires delimit by law' the exercise of the rights to private property 'with a view to reconciling their exercise with the exigencies of the common good'. The most important function given to the President in the Constitution is the power under Article 26 to decide to refer a Bill to the Supreme Court before signing it into law. The Supreme Court, consisting of at least five judges, must then consider whether the Bill or any specific provisions of it are repugnant to the Constitution.

After its rapid passage through both Houses of the Oireachtas, the 1999 Planning and Development Bill was presented to the President for signing on 26 June 2000. Having consulted the Council of State, as the Constitution requires, the President referred part V of the Bill to the Supreme Court on 30 June for a decision as to whether any provision of this part was repugnant to the Constitution. The full housing strategy mechanism is contained in part V, from preparation through incorporation into the development plan to implementation by development control. This conveniently allowed the Article 26 reference to relate only to sections 93 to 101. The matter was heard before the Supreme Court on 24 and 25 July, with the Attorney General arguing in favour of the Bill and counsel assigned by the court arguing against it. The judgment upholding the constitutionality of part V was delivered on 28 August, in accordance with the very tight timeframe laid down in Article 26.

The judgment of the Supreme Court runs to some seventy-five pages and, insofar as it is possible to do so, the position may be summarised as follows. The court accepted that the serious social problems created by the housing crisis warranted interfering with constitutionally protected property rights and that the housing strategy mechanism constituted a delimitation of those rights proportionate to the desirable social objective of providing both affordable and public housing in an integrated manner. The significance of this Article 26 reference was that no litigant could subsequently question the validity of the housing strategy mechanism although, of course, the rest of the 2000 Act could be subjected to scrutiny.

The President signed the Bill into law on the day the Supreme Court delivered its judgment and the first provisions of the Act to come into force were those relating to housing strategies and strategic development zones, a new and related concept discussed below. These became operative on 1 November 2000 together with the simplified procedure for making a variation of a development plan, an adjunct to the adoption of housing strategies.

Amendment

However, in December 2002, the Minister for the Environment and Local Government, Martin Cullen TD, introduced a Bill to the Oireachtas, the primary purpose of which was to amend part V of the 2000 Act in order to give developers additional choices of methods for complying with their obligations to provide social and affordable housing. This Bill was the result of a review of the operation of the new housing strategy mechanism carried out by the department and it was swiftly enacted as the Planning and Development (Amendment) Act, 2002.

Instead of having to provide lands, sites or houses within the boundaries of a proposed housing development for social and affordable housing, the developer can now propose to provide land, sites or houses at a completely different location within the functional area of the planning authority (no maximum acceptable separation distance is stipulated) or simply to pay a specified sum of money in discharge of this obligation. Although the 2002 Act requires planning authorities, in reaching an agreement regarding such alternatives, to take a number of factors into account, including the need to counteract undue segregation, the two additional methods obviously must result in a lesser degree of social integration than the provision of a mix of private and social or affordable dwellings in each new housing development. Furthermore, the fact that part V as approved by the Supreme Court has been amended means that the constitutional integrity of part V has been interfered with and the validity of the housing strategy mechanism has been re-opened to possible constitutional challenge.

Content and Procedure

Each planning authority had to prepare its first housing strategy by 1 July 2001. To assist them, the department published guidelines covering content, assessment of housing need, estimating social and affordable housing need, agreements with developers and the role of the housing strategy in the development plan process (Department of the Environment and Local Government, 2000h). A model housing strategy was also prepared for County Louth, to provide planning authorities with a step-by-step pathway through this unknown new process.

Housing strategies must include measures to provide for the housing needs of the existing and the anticipated future population within the functional area of the planning authority, broken down into the various relevant categories, including:

- persons requiring social or affordable housing
- persons with both small and large incomes
- households having varying requirements with regard to type and size of dwelling unit, such as students, the elderly and the disabled.

Housing strategies also have to counter undue social segregation in residential communities. The housing needs for the overall area over the period of the development plan must be estimated and the housing strategy has to provide that a specified percentage (not exceeding 20 per cent) of land zoned for residential use, or for a mixture of residential and other uses, shall be reserved for social and affordable housing.

There is no prescribed role for either elected members or the public in the preparation of the housing strategy. Once completed, the housing strategy is to be incorporated into the development plan by means of a variation of the plan, and the procedure to adopt such a variation had to be commenced by 1 July 2001 in order to give effect to the first housing strategies. Thereafter, the housing strategy forms part of the development plan and will have to be reviewed in the process of plan preparation. Any future development plans must include a housing strategy. In conjunction with the inclusion of the housing strategy in the development plan, a planning authority has to ensure that sufficient suitable land is zoned for residential uses to meet the requirements of the strategy over the plan period and that no undue shortage of zoned and serviced land occurs during the currency of the plan. Planning authorities are required to include objectives in the plan to secure the implementation of the strategy and, in particular, are required to include objectives relating to the ceding of up to 20 per cent of land zoned residential for social and affordable housing.

Under the 2000 Act, a clear distinction is drawn between making a development plan and making a variation of a development plan. The procedure for making a variation to an existing plan has been simplified and made shorter. A four-week period of public display, during which submissions may be made, is followed after a further four weeks by the manager presenting a report on the submissions to the councillors. The councillors must consider the proposed variation, together with this report, which includes the manager's response to the issues raised, within the next six weeks. The councillors then make the variation, with or without modification, or refuse to make it. If they decide to modify the proposed variation, no further period of public display is required, which means the entire variation procedure has been reduced to fourteen weeks.

A Hierarchy of Land Use Plans

The development plan has always been and continues to be the basic policy document of the planning authority in which the planning objectives for the area are set out. Each planning authority was obliged to make a development plan within three years of the commencement of the 1963 Planning Act (that is, by 1967) and thereafter to review the development plan at no greater than five-yearly intervals and either vary it or replace it by a new development plan. The minister could and frequently did extend the period for reviewing the development plan because planning authorities had great difficulty keeping to the five-yearly scheduled reviews. In 1999, some 43 per cent of planning authorities were relying on a development plan more than five years old and concerns had been expressed by a variety of persons and organisations about the difficulties arising from out-of-date plans. Making or varying a development plan has always been a reserved function. Indeed it was indicated by the department that the new procedures were intended to give the elected members greater scope in exercising their policy-making functions.[3]

Development Plans

The new provisions relating to development plans came into force on 1 January 2001. The life of a development plan has been extended from five to six years. More significantly, there is now a strict statutory timeframe to plan making, whereas planning authorities formerly had discretion as to how long they would take at the various stages of the process. As previously, a general duty is imposed on each planning authority to take the steps necessary to secure the objectives contained in its development plan. In order to ensure this obligation is not overlooked, the manager is now required to give a report to the councillors on the progress being made towards achieving the objectives two years after the plan is adopted.

Four years after the development plan is made, the process of review must commence. The first stage consists of widespread consultation, commencing with notice to a variety of statutory authorities and advertisements in newspapers circulating in the area, inviting submissions. Public meetings and oral hearings may form part of this process which informs the preparation of the draft plan. A

---

[3] Ken Mawhinney, 'Development Plans, Local Area Plans and Regional Planning Guidelines', at the Department of the Environment and Local Government seminar on the 1999 Planning and Development Bill, Galway, 1 October 1999.

period of at least eight weeks has to be allowed for consultation, following which the manager submits a report to the elected members on the issues raised, setting out recommendations on the policies to be included in the draft plan. Having considered this report, the members can give directions to the manager regarding the content of the draft plan, which is then prepared by the officials and submitted to the members before being put on public display. Formerly, pre-plan-making consultations may have taken place in some areas but only on an ad hoc basis. Making them a formal requirement constitutes a significant improvement in providing for public participation. People now have the opportunity to be proactive by making positive contributions to the preparation of the plan instead of being confined to the reactive submission of objections to the draft plan when published.

The draft plan is put on public display for a period of ten weeks. As formerly, there is a procedure of public notification. Copies are sent to the prescribed bodies and written submissions can be made. The manager now prepares a further report on these submissions, including his response to the issues raised in the context of any directions given earlier by the councillors on the content of the plan. The councillors have twelve weeks to consider the draft plan and the manager's report. If they decide the draft needs to be amended, and if the amendment would amount to a material alteration of the draft plan, the amendment must be put on display for four weeks, during which time objections relating only to the amendments can be submitted.

The plan-making process must now be finalised. The councillors, having received the manager's further report together with the amendment, may adopt the plan with or without the proposed amendment or, in the light of the objections and the manager's report, they can modify the amendment as they consider appropriate. No further public display is required nor, because of the week-by-week timeframe set out in the legislation, would it be possible. If the councillors fail to adopt the plan within two years of commencing the pre-plan-making consultation phase, the manager has the duty of completing the process, subject to the limitation that so much as has been agreed by the elected members cannot be altered.

This major change to the development plan procedure was necessitated by the leisurely approach taken by some planning authorities and is intended to focus the councillors' attention on bringing plan making to a conclusion. However, it must be questioned whether the same inflexible timeframe is appropriate to both large and small development plans. The six-yearly plan-making schedule could still be achieved while giving any planning authority, which considers it needs additional weeks at a particular stage in the process, the opportunity to take more time over that part of their plan. Because of the way section 12 is worded, early commencement of the first stage – the review – does not give additional weeks at the later stages, in particular for the executive and reserved functions relating to the consideration of public submissions. Planning authorities could be specifically empowered to commence the review phase between three and four years after the adoption of a development plan in order to secure an enlarged period later in the plan-making process, subject to the overall requirement of compliance with the six-yearly review schedule. Such an amendment would afford an additional element of local autonomy and flexibility in the very rigid new plan-making procedure.

The content and role of development plans were also altered by the Planning and Development Act, 2000. As part of the strategic approach to planning for the twenty-first century, development plans are now required to set out the overall strategy for the proper planning and sustainable development of the entire functional area of the planning authority. Plans must also contain information on the likely significant effects on the environment of their implementation. It will no longer be possible to take an incremental approach to plan making because the 2000 Act removed the option of making a development plan for part of the area or in respect of only some matters. While development plans still consist of maps and a written statement, the list of objectives which must be included has been enlarged from eight to thirteen and there is no longer any distinction between the objectives in plans for urban and rural areas.[4] The additional mandatory objectives include the provision of infrastructure, the preservation of the character of the landscape and the protection of the linguistic and cultural heritage of Gaeltacht areas. County development plans formerly had to incorporate plans for towns listed in the first schedule to the 1963 Act, predictably known as scheduled towns. These plans are now replaced by a new concept, the local area plan.

A further aspect of the strategic approach is that development plans are required to be consistent with national plans, policies and strategies and, while the decision to adopt the development plan rests with the councillors, the minister has important powers to require two or more authorities to co-ordinate their plans and to direct a planning authority to take specific measures to ensure its plan is in compliance with the Act.

Local Area Plans

In the 2000 Act, planning authorities were given the option of making a new type of plan, a local area plan, for any part of their functional area where they consider it would be suitable. The level of detail is not specified but it would be envisaged that a local area plan would set out objectives in far greater detail than a city or county development plan and might well include development control standards. Areas needing renewal, Gaeltacht areas and newly zoned lands on which large-scale development is likely to take place within the plan period are particularly suited to a local area plan. The local area plan replaces the scheduled town plan

---

[4] Section 10(2) of the Planning and Development Act, 2000. For the mandatory objectives under the 1963 Act, as amended, see Grist (1999) p. 6.

and is mandatory in the case of towns with a population of more than 2,000 which are located in the functional area of the county council and are designated as a town in the census. This is a more flexible definition than that used in the 1963 Act, where towns were permanently listed on the basis of their population in the 1961 Census. Where a local area plan is mandatory, it must be made within two years of the adoption of the county development plan.

Local area plans must be consistent with the objectives of the development plan. While a planning authority can decide at any time to make a local area plan and has complete freedom to set a plan period which extends beyond the life of the six-year county development plan, any provisions of the local plan which conflict with a new county plan cease to have effect. Local area plans can be amended or revoked at any time. The procedure is far simpler than that for making a development plan. The planning authority is given discretion regarding pre-plan-making consultations but must consult Údarás na Gaeltachta if a Gaeltacht area is involved. The draft local area plan is put on public display for at least six weeks and the manager prepares a report for the councillors on the issues raised. In a reversal of the position relating to the making of a development plan, unless the councillors by resolution vote otherwise, the local area plan is deemed to be made, amended or revoked in accordance with the manager's report.

Regional Planning Guidelines

The third element in the strategic approach to plan making is the new power given to regional authorities to make regional planning guidelines for the whole or part of their region in order to provide the context of a long-term framework for individual development plans.

Neither regionalisation nor regional planning were mentioned in the 1963 Planning Act and, despite various attempts to incorporate a regional dimension into the planning system, it was not until 1991 that the minister was empowered by the Local Government Act to establish regional authorities 'for the purpose of promoting the co-ordination in different areas of the State of the provision of public services'. In January 1994, eight such authorities were established covering the entire country (see appendix 4). Membership is composed of city and county councillors selected by the constituent authorities. In a press release on their establishment, the minister carefully reassured councillors that these regional bodies would not diminish or restrict their powers. The regional authorities were given two functions: promoting the co-ordination of the work of public authorities on a regional basis and monitoring/advising on the implementation at regional level of the various operational programmes for delivery of EU Structural and Cohesion Funds.

Regional planning was given a new impetus in mid-1998, with the discovery that recently achieved national prosperity in the east of the country would exclude the entire Republic of Ireland from the highly desirable Objective 1 status under the 2000 to 2006 round of EU structural funding. The response was to subdivide the country into two regions, with two assemblies established, in Ballaghadereen, County Roscommon and Waterford City, to ensure the poorer counties could continue to benefit from maximum EU funding levels.

In 1998, the Dublin and the Mid-East Regional Authorities, together with the department, commissioned the preparation of a non-statutory document of immense planning significance, the *Strategic Planning Guidelines for the Greater Dublin Area* (1999). This was done because the unprecedented rate of growth in Dublin, Meath, Kildare and Wicklow was such as to overwhelm the planning process. The objective of these guidelines was to put in place a broad planning framework for the entire Greater Dublin Area to provide an overall strategic context for the development plans of each planning authority. The guidelines were launched to widespread acclaim as representing the best way of ensuring comprehensive and co-ordinated planning. Subsequently, the principle of regional authorities having the power to prepare strategic guidelines was incorporated into the Planning and Development Act, 2000.

Statutory regional planning guidelines can only be made by the regional authority after consultation with its constituent planning authorities. The procedure also involves public consultation. Regional planning guidelines have a time horizon of twelve to twenty years and address strategic matters such as population projections, economic and employment trends and transportation. Once made, regional planning guidelines must be reviewed at minimum every six years, which ensures they will be revoked or updated as necessary. Planning authorities must have regard to any regional planning guidelines in force for their area when making a development plan.

The Strategic Planning Guidelines for the Greater Dublin Area were specifically given the status of statutory regional planning guidelines in the 2000 Act. These guidelines have been reviewed and updated annually since their publication.

Ministerial Guidelines and Directives

While the minister cannot become involved in any individual planning application or appeal,[5] he or she has been given a statutory power under the 2000 Act to issue guidelines to planning authorities regarding any of their functions.

---

[5] Section 30 of the Planning and Development Act, 2000. With the transfer of Dúchas, the Heritage Service, to the Department of the Environment and Local Government in June 2002, following the general election, amending legislation was required to resolve potential conflict between the general legislative prohibition on the minister becoming involved in individual planning applications and the consultative role of Dúchas in individual cases which involve significant heritage issues. The relevant Act is the Minister for the Environment and Local Government (Performance of Certain Functions) Act, 2002.

This replaces the ministerial power contained in the 1982 Planning Act of issuing general policy directives. Planning authorities and An Bord Pleanála must have regard to such guidelines just as they were required to have regard to directives. The department also published a number of non-statutory guidelines, mainly from 1996 onwards, relating to new and controversial types of development such as windfarms and telecommunications antennae. These documents now have the status of statutory ministerial guidelines.

The minister has been given a new power to issue policy directives to planning authorities regarding any of their functions. Unlike the ministerial guidelines and the 1982 Act general policy directives, this new type of instrument will be binding on the planning authorities and, where applicable, on An Bord Pleanála.

Ministerial guidelines and directives are not limited to plan making but could address enforcement, the preparation of planning schemes, the operation of development control in strategic development zones or any other aspect of the planning system. They are intended to ensure a reasonably standardised approach to planning on a national basis, while allowing for variations to suit local circumstances, and to provide a mechanism for offering guidance and support to planning authorities in the performance of their functions.

Development Control

The basic concept underpinning the planning code is that permission must be obtained from the planning authority before commencing development. Development is defined in section 3(1) of the Planning and Development Act, 2000 as 'the carrying out of any works on, in, over or under land or the making of any material change in the use of any structures or other land'. An exemption from the obligation to obtain permission is given in respect of certain categories of development.

Role of Elected Members

Since the introduction of the management system in 1940, powers of local government have been divided between the elected members (reserved functions) and the manager (executive functions). In broad terms, powers reserved to the elected representatives concern policy and financial matters, while the manager is responsible for those decisions which involve the execution of settled policy and which, in particular, might be open to political or personal influence. Thus, within the planning system, the councillors adopt the development plan and the manager makes the decision whether to grant or refuse individual planning applications.

Despite the significant efficiencies secured by the management system, which has been described by Ronan Keane (1982, p. 18) as 'the most important single development in the history of Irish local government' in the twentieth century, the councillors did not accept it easily. The City and County Management (Amendment) Act, 1955 went some way towards redressing what councillors perceived to be an imbalance in the democratic process. Section 4 of this Act gave the elected members the power to direct the manager as to how to perform any of his or her executive functions. It provided that a local authority could 'by resolution require any particular act, matter or thing specifically mentioned in the resolution and which the local authority or the manager can lawfully do or effect to be done or effected in performance of the executive functions of the local authority'.

This reserved power of the elected members was used (some would say misused) over the years to require managers to decide planning applications in a particular way. Usually section 4 'planning' resolutions, as they came to be known, required the manager to grant the permission sought. The frequency and ease with which such resolutions were passed, the spuriousness of some of the grounds advanced by members proposing such resolutions and allegations of payments to political parties and to individual councillors had, by the late 1980s, brought the planning process into disrepute. Most section 4 resolutions were viewed with disfavour by all the local residents except the potential beneficiaries. Consequently, controversial section 4 resolutions were usually proposed by councillors from outside the electoral area in question, who might thus expect to escape subsequent retribution at the polls.

The Local Government Act, 1991 set more stringent procedures for section 4 resolutions in respect of planning permission than in respect of any other function, requiring such resolutions to be signed by at least three-quarters of the members for the electoral area where the site is located (rather than by any three members) and to be passed by three-quarters of the total members of the authority (instead of one-third). These provisions have now been incorporated into the 2000 Planning Act and, with the repeal of the Management Acts attendant upon the enactment of the Local Government Act, 2001, section 4 has been replaced by section 140 of the 2001 Act. The management system and the respective roles of councillors and managers are described and analysed in detail in chapter 7.

In a significant number of cases, section 4 resolutions have been used to direct the manager to grant permission for single houses in the countryside, against the advice of the professional staff of the planning authority. The pressure for one-off rural housing has, if anything, increased in recent years, while simultaneously there is general agreement that unrestrained urban sprawl has adverse economic, social and visual consequences. This issue is discussed further in the chapters 20 and 21.

Overview of the Main Issues

Part 4 of the 2001 Planning Regulations deals with the procedural aspects of getting an initial planning permission or extending the duration of an existing planning permission. For over twenty years, complaints have been made about the delays and uncertainties caused to the planning process by third-party appeals. In the 1982, 1983 and 1992 Planning Acts, changes were made to the appeals system to answer these complaints. The most significant changes were made in 1992 when strict time limits were introduced for every stage of the appeal procedure and An Bord Pleanála was given the objective of deciding appeals within four months. The power to dismiss an appeal on the grounds that it is vexatious or without substance was introduced in 1982 and fees for appeals were provided for in 1983. However, as environmental concerns became more of an issue for the public, awareness of the general third-party right of appeal became widespread. Rumours circulated of individuals, interest groups and community organisations who lodged an appeal on stateable planning grounds, only to withdraw their objections on receipt of payment from the developer. Developers also expressed extreme frustration when, having secured permission from the planning authority, a hitherto undeclared objector lodged an appeal. With the growth in construction activity between 1993 and 1999, the number of appeals doubled and the percentage of cases determined within the four months objective dropped from 78 per cent to 47 per cent.[6]

This exacerbated the problem for developers. Meanwhile, genuine third parties could have difficulty keeping themselves informed of the up-to-date position regarding planning applications about which they had concerns. Complaints were frequently made about illegible and inadequately positioned site notices. The two-month period within which a planning authority had to give its decision could be extended through any or all of the following procedures: a request for additional information, clarification of the submitted additional information or consent of the applicant.

As pressures on private consultancies to prepare and lodge planning applications increased during the 1990s, some agents acting for large developments responded by what can best be described as submitting major planning applications on an incremental basis according as they completed sections of the proposal, which caused considerable problems of comprehension for both third parties and planning authorities. Incomplete and poorly prepared applications were identified by the minister's review of the 1963 system as a cause of delays. While planning authorities had the power to reject such applications as invalid, custom and practice meant they were reluctant to do so, instead using the additional information mechanism in an attempt to put right the deficiencies in the application as originally submitted.

To address these issues, the development control process has been changed by a rebalancing of rights, which was presented as streamlining the system to make it more efficient in delivering the planning service. These changes were strenuously opposed when the Bill was published.

---

[6] *Source:* Annual Reports of An Bord Pleanála.

Third-Party Rights

In respect of applications lodged on or after 11 March 2002, a third-party appeal cannot be made unless the appellant made submissions in writing to the planning authority. The only exception to this restriction on the former general third-party right of appeal is where an adjoining landowner can show An Bord Pleanála that, by reason of conditions attached to the planning authority's grant of permission, the development would differ materially from that proposed and would materially affect his enjoyment of the land. Third parties have five weeks from the date an application is received by the planning authority to make their submission and must pay a fee of €20. Understandably, this restriction was very badly received by interest groups and community associations, who pointed out that, in an area subject to widespread development pressures, they would be prevented from contributing to the planning process because the multiplicity of relatively small fees would exceed the voluntary contributions they could collect from their members.

In both the Dáil and the Seanad, and through department officials at the regional seminars held to explain and get responses to the Bill, the minister laid considerable emphasis on the fact that he was strengthening the role of the local authority as key decision-maker in the planning process by giving statutory recognition to submissions or observations made to it on an application. While third parties had not been given any express statutory right to make submissions on planning applications at local level in the 1963 Act, the manager was not prohibited from considering such representations either. The position, therefore, was open to interpretation and with the passage of time, an informal local objection procedure came to be developed. This was given recognition in the 1994 Planning Regulations, which established a general right to make submissions to a planning authority. Groups representing third parties were consequently unimpressed with the minister's assertions regarding what he described as an 'important new right' in relation to planning at local level. However, with the publication of the 2001 Regulations, what the minister meant by this statutory recognition has become clearer.[7]

All submissions on planning applications must be acknowledged in writing, the planning authority is precluded from making any decision within the five-week period allowed for submissions, anyone who makes a submission is entitled to be notified of subsequent changes in the status of the application (such as the receipt of additional information or modified plans) and is entitled to comment thereon and, most importantly, must be notified of the decision of the planning authority within the same three-day timeframe as the applicant. It may well be that the third party is satisfied with this decision and has no wish to appeal, but, in the event of an appeal being made, would want to bring his or her concerns or

7 See 2001 Planning and Development Regulations, articles 29(2), 30, 31, 35 and 69.

opinions to the attention of An Bord Pleanála. The legislation governing appeals always made provision for submissions by such persons, known as observers because they are not a party to the appeal. Partly because of the difficulties in keeping track of applications at local level (as outlined above) and partly because of the absence of any formal publication of appeals in an easily accessible format, persons in this position often found out about an appeal too late to participate in the process. Planning authorities are now required to notify any person who made a submission on the application that an appeal has been lodged when they themselves receive a copy of the appeal from An Bord Pleanála.

Access to Documents

Under the 1994 Planning Regulations, a planning authority was required only to make documents on a planning file available for inspection during office hours at the offices of the authority. This created significant difficulties for persons in employment, living at a distance from the planning authority's offices or suffering from impaired mobility. With regard to major and complex applications, days might be required to study the proposal. Some planning authorities made photocopies of certain documents, others found themselves unable to supply such a service and all were subject to the copyright legislation which did not allow plans, maps or drawings to be copied. These restrictions put third parties at a considerable disadvantage. The 2000 Copyright and Related Rights Act removed the prohibition on copying drawings while the 2000 Planning Act requires planning authorities to make copies of all documents submitted as part of a planning application available for inspection and purchase. These legislative provisions have improved the possibility of meaningful participation by third parties and may be anticipated to act as a counterbalance to the limitations imposed on the third party right of appeal.

Validity of Applications

The reluctance of planning authorities to return applications on grounds of invalidity has been referred to above. This created problems not only for third parties but also for planning authorities themselves in subsequently trying to unravel the conflicting documents on file. Since 11 March 2002, it is a requirement of the 2001 Regulations that, if an application fails to satisfy any of the extremely detailed particulars set out in part 4, the planning authority must declare it invalid and return it to the applicant. This is a necessary corollary to the streamlined new procedures which have reduced the basic period for decision making to eight weeks (from two months), reduced the time for assessing additional information from two months to four weeks, and removed the possibility of following a request for additional information with an agreed extension of the two month decision-making period. It is also hoped that formalising pre-application consultations will result in an improved standard of application.

The first three months of the new procedure were problematic, with a 100 per cent rejection rate in some planning authorities and a considerable variation in approach between authorities. The success rate has improved as all participants became familiar with the system and it can be anticipated that a convergence of approach will develop based on planning authorities exchanging information on best practice. After one year in operation, it was estimated that around 50 per cent of submitted applications satisfied the regulations.

An as yet unaddressed problem at validation and at assessment stage is the uniform procedure set by the legislation for both major and routine domestic proposals. In a very complex application, it could take nearer to five than the guideline two weeks to scrutinise all the documents, which can amount to boxfuls, and declare the application valid. The option of an agreed extension of time after submission of additional information is no longer available, nor are serial agreed extensions. However, the hoped for improved standard of applications, which is necessitated by the invalidity rule, should obviate the need to request further information in almost all cases and developers are likely to continue to respond positively to suggestions for an extension of the decision-making period because such requests usually signal a positive approach to their proposal on the part of the planning authority.

An unforeseen and very serious consequence of the complicated validation requirements is the delay in registering the lodgement of applications. There have been a number of cases where interested third parties, alerted by the public notice of a proposed development, have visited their local planning office only to be told that no application had been made, when, in fact, the application had been submitted but not yet validated and, consequently, was not traceable. This meant that the five weeks for submission of third party observations had been running yet third parties were unable to have sight of the proposal. In effect, the timeframe for third party participation is less than the five weeks given in the 2001 Regulations because of the interconnected operation of the strict validation requirements.

Strategic Development Zones

The concept of a strategic development zone (SDZ) is new to the Irish planning system. The purpose for which this designation was originally intended, when the 1999 Planning and Development Bill was published, was to allow a streamlined planning process to operate on specific sites, selected by the government for reasons of strategic importance to the national economy, in order to facilitate inward investment by internationally mobile companies. However, during the passage of the Bill through the Dáil, part IX was amended to include designation of

SDZs for residential development and the first three sites designated in June 2001 were all for housing purposes in the Greater Dublin Area. This gives an interesting indication of the shift, over a three-year period, in the official perception as to which planning issues were of national economic and social importance.

Before proposing any site to the government for designation, the minister must consult the relevant development agencies and the local planning authority. The state-sponsored bodies that are development agencies are listed in section 165 of the 2000 Act and, apart from the National Building Agency, all have a basic economic remit. If the government accepts the minister's proposal, it makes an order designating the site for the establishment of a strategic development zone and specifying the relevant agencies and types of development appropriate. The agencies concerned, together with the landowner, have two years from the date of the order to prepare a draft planning scheme for the site and submit it to the planning authority.

A planning scheme consists of a written statement and a plan, indicating the overall framework as to how the site will be developed and giving information on any likely significant impacts on the environment. If the draft scheme relates to residential development, it must be consistent with the housing strategy and must include a specific objective reserving land for social and affordable housing. When the scheme has been prepared, it is submitted to the planning authority which sends copies to the minister, An Bord Pleanála and a number of prescribed authorities. The planning authority also places the draft on exhibition for at least six weeks, during which time the views of the public are invited by an advertisement placed in a newspaper circulating in the area. The manager then presents a report on the submissions to the councillors, covering the issues raised, his or her response to them and any relevant government or ministerial policies or objectives. The councillors must consider the draft scheme and the manager's report and, unless they decide to modify or reject the planning scheme within six weeks of receiving the manager's report, the scheme is deemed to be made.

The development agency and any person who made a submission on the draft scheme may appeal the adoption of the scheme to An Bord Pleanála within four weeks of the date on which it is deemed to have been made. The final decision is then made by An Bord Pleanála, which can approve the scheme with or without modifications or refuse to approve it.

Once made, a planning scheme automatically forms part of the development plan and supersedes any contrary provisions in the plan. Applications for planning permission in an SDZ are made in the same way as everywhere else. However, the planning authority is required to grant permission for any proposed development that is consistent with the planning scheme and is prohibited from granting permission for development that would be inconsistent with it. There is no appeal against the planning authority's decision, which can be subject to conditions. A planning scheme can be amended or revoked, with the consent of the relevant development agency. Revoking or amending a scheme is a reserved function.

The procedure for making a planning scheme is an interesting hybrid of plan making and development control. The elected members and An Bord Pleanála both have statutory functions in its adoption and, once made, the manager has the exclusive decision-making role in relation to specific proposals. The government designated three sites as SDZs – Adamstown, Lucan (South Dublin County Council); Hansfield, Blanchardstown (Fingal County Council); and Clonmagadden Valley, Navan (Meath County Council) – with effect from 1 July 2001. It was anticipated that, together, they would be able to supply some 12,000 housing units.

South Dublin County Council, as the specified development agency for the Adamstown site, gave public notice of the preparation of the first draft planning scheme on 6 January 2003 and the Adamstown Planning Scheme, incorporating sixty-two modifications to the original draft scheme, was made on 7 May 2003.

Exempted Development

As identified above, the central principle of the planning system is that permission is required in respect of the development of land. There are two basic categories of development: carrying out works and making a material change of use. The statutory definition of works is wide, including any act or operation of construction, excavation, demolition, extension, alteration, repair or renewal. Taken literally, it would mean that, for example, a householder replacing gutters would have to go through the full planning permission procedure. Obviously, such a requirement would be unwarranted and certain types of minor development by private individuals have been given an exemption from the obligation to obtain planning permission.

The planning code identifies a second and very different category of exempted development on the basis of the identity of the person or body carrying it out. The underlying presumption here is that development by state and local authorities is undertaken in the interests of the common good and, therefore, need not be subject to the same level of public scrutiny as development proposed for private benefit.

Exempted development rights arise from three different parts of the 2000 Planning Act.

- Section 4(1) grants specific exemptions, for example to a planning authority carrying out development within its own functional area and, in certain circumstances, to any person carrying out maintenance works on a building. In the case of a protected structure, the exemptions do not apply if the works would materially affect the character of the structure or any significant element thereof, whether internal or external.

- Section 4(2) enables the minister to make regulations adding classes of exempted development to those contained in section 4(1) and, in particular, to exempt changes of use within certain broad use classes. The Exempted Development Regulations are contained in part 2 of the 2001 Planning Regulations.

- Section 181 enables the minister to make regulations excluding from planning control particular classes of development by state authorities which, in the minister's opinion, are related to national security, defence, the administration of justice and public safety. These exemptions are contained in part 9 of the 2000 Planning Regulations and are generally similar to those under the previous regulations.

Declarations

The concept of exempted development involves mixed issues of fact and law. The 2000 Act makes improved provision for clarifying what constitutes exempted development in the circumstances of a specific case. Any person, not just the landowner, may request the planning authority to give a declaration as to whether the development in question is or is not exempted development. If the planning authority fails to issue the requested declaration within four weeks, the person who raised the matter may refer the question on to An Bord Pleanála within the next four-week period. The planning authority also has the option of referring the question forward to An Bord Pleanála for decision. If the planning authority issues a declaration in response to a request by a third party, a copy must be sent to the owner and occupier of the land or premises and any of these persons can refer the declaration for review by An Bord Pleanála.

Under the 1963 Act, planning authorities had no statutory role in deciding questions relating to exempted development, which were addressed directly to An Bord Pleanála, with provision for an appeal to the High Court. While the staff of many planning offices were prepared to offer guidance if a query was raised, in others there was a policy of not responding because of the absence of any statutory function for planning authorities in the matter of exempted development. The new provisions hopefully will ensure that persons everywhere will be able to get an opinion within a specified timeframe when an issue as to the need for planning permission arises. A planning application involves the assessment of a proposal to ascertain if it is in accordance with the proper planning and sustainable development of the area and, if the planning authority fails to issue a decision within eight weeks, permission is granted by default. However, questions concerning exempted development encompass both facts (the details of the works or use) and law (whether the works/use fall within one of the exempted categories). For this reason, the planning authority's failure to issue a declaration cannot metamorphose development which requires permission into exempted development or vice versa. This means there cannot be a default provision regarding the issue of declarations.

Protected Structures

The Planning and Development Act, 1999 made provision for enhanced protection of the built environment (consolidated in part IV of the Planning and Development Act, 2000). Under the 1963 Act, a planning authority had the option of including objectives in the development plan for the preservation of buildings of artistic, architectural or historical interest. Some development plans contained extensive lists of buildings, some had none, and there were vastly different standards in different plans as to what merited inclusion. Under the 1999 Act, planning authorities were now obliged to prepare a record of protected structures and to include objectives for the protection of structures in their development plans. Any buildings listed for preservation when the 1999 Act came into force on 1 January 2000 became protected structures and immediately enjoyed the benefit of the new legislative provisions. However, as these imposed greater obligations on the owners and occupiers of such structures, planning authorities had to re-notify owners and give them an opportunity to object to the inclusion of their property on the record of protected structures.

Under the 1963 Planning Act, the interiors of listed buildings had to be separately designated for protection and very few interiors were actually listed. Protection meant that works which hitherto had been exempt because they were internal (such as plastering, painting, removing walls, installing en-suite bathrooms in listed houses and so on) lost their exempted status if they materially affected the character of the structure or any element that contributed to its special interest. In order to clarify the position, the 1999 Planning Act introduced a new procedure whereby the owner or occupier of a protected structure could ask the planning authority for a declaration as to the type of works which it considered would not materially affect the character of the structure and which, therefore, would not need permission.

Alterations to the interiors of churches and other places of public worship, which are protected structures, present very difficult issues. As with any other protected structure, the status of protection means that an application to carry out works that would materially alter the internal character of a church has to be considered in the context of the development plan objective of protection. The statutory definition of protection includes, where appropriate, the preservation and conservation of all fixtures and features that form part of the interior. The interiors of many formerly listed churches are of sufficient importance to require a high level of preservation yet, if they are to continue to serve the function for which they were intended, churches must adapt to changing liturgical requirements.

These obviously include the rearrangement of spaces and removal or alteration of fixtures that are no longer needed by the congregation. The legislation and the guidelines (see following paragraph) acknowledge the need for balance where permission is sought for alterations to the interior of a protected structure that is regularly used as a place of public worship. In such cases, in addition to other statutory considerations, planning authorities and An Bord Pleanála must respect liturgical requirements. The legislation provides that permission should only be granted for the demolition of a protected structure in exceptional circumstances.

Draft guidelines on *Architectural Heritage Protection* were issued to planning authorities in December 2001 to assist them with the implementation of the 1999 Act, now incorporated into part IV of the 2000 Act (Department of Arts, Heritage, Gaeltacht and the Islands, Dúchas and Department of the Environment and Local Government, 2001). These guidelines cover criteria for including structures on the record of protected structures, identifying architectural conservation areas, the preparation and content of declarations and related development control issues. They were made jointly by the Minister for the Environment and Local Government and the Minister for Arts, Heritage, Gaeltacht and the Islands, who was responsible for the National Inventory of Architectural Heritage and had an obligation to issue guidelines to planning authorities concerning development objectives for protecting structures. When finalised, they will have the status of ministerial guidelines under part II of the 2000 Planning Act and planning authorities will have to have regard to them in the performance of their functions.

Enforcement

The requirement to obtain planning permission before commencing development is supported by a range of statutory sanctions. In addition to imposing the obligation to obtain planning permission, the 1963 Planning Act provided that any person carrying out unauthorised development would be guilty of an offence, a provision repeated in the 2000 Act. As prosecution and conviction secures the punishment of wrongdoers but does not secure the proper planning and development of the area, planning authorities were also given power to implement planning controls by means of enforcement notices which require developers to conform to the planning code.

Initially, control of unauthorised development was solely a matter for planning authorities, which were not required to take action in all cases but were given the power to serve an enforcement notice if they decided it was 'expedient to do so'. Proceedings on foot of such a notice were a District Court matter. District judges were reluctant to convict landowners who pleaded that they had been unaware of the new requirement to obtain permission and explained that they had applied for permission to retain the development as constructed since receiving the enforcement notice and were confident of obtaining such a permission. A series of adjournments might be granted if the proposal was appealed and, as set out above, the appeal timeframe was open-ended until the 1992 Planning Act brought in the four-month objective. The delays and the small fines that could be imposed by the court meant that the enforcement notice procedure was ineffective in controlling unauthorised development of a serious nature.

The Planning Injunction

The 1976 Planning Act created a new and important form of enforcement action, which came to be known as a section 27 or planning injunction. The most significant aspect of this type of action is that it makes enforcement available not only to the planning authority but also to any member of the public, irrespective of having an interest in land or being able to claim to be suffering particular damage from the development in question. Injunctions of their nature are obtainable quickly. The jurisdiction was originally vested in the High Court, which took a much stricter approach towards breaches of the planning code than the District Court had done. Failure to obey an injunction constitutes contempt, an offence punishable by imprisonment. These four features of the planning injunction make it an extremely significant addition to the mechanisms for planning control. The 1992 Planning Act provided that a planning injunction could also be obtained in the Circuit Court, thus opening the remedy to a section of the general public who might have been hesitant to approach the High Court because of the costs involved.

Despite these provisions, when the consultative review of the planning system took place in 1997, the lack of enforcement was one of the major issues raised. This reflects the significant place environmental concerns have come to occupy in the public mind. It was decided to simplify and improve the enforcement mechanism, while introducing tougher penalties for persons who deliberately break the law. The enforcement code is contained in part VIII of the 2000 Act.

The scope of the planning injunction has been enlarged in that it can now apply to anticipated future unauthorised development as well as to unauthorised development which is being or has been carried out. The 1980s and 1990s saw the growth in popularity of outdoor pop concerts, usually in football grounds, but occasionally on other sites considered suitable by the promoters, such as Slane Castle. These events caused major disruption to the surrounding community, particularly in terms of traffic restrictions, noise and litter. Different provisions of the planning code were used on different occasions to prevent outdoor pop concerts, as a consequence of which many planning authorities came to the conclusion that such events constituted development (Flynn, 1997). An attempt made by three residents of the Lansdowne Road area in Dublin to get a planning injunction preventing anticipated advertised concerts in August 1997 was unsuccessful. The Supreme Court held that section 27 of the 1976 Act was limited to ensuring the discontinuation of unauthorised development or use of land and that it did not give the court power to make an order in relation to an anticipated breach. This limitation on the planning injunction was removed in the 2000 Act, where the provisions relating to the planning injunction are contained in section 160.

Towards a Culture of Enforcement

The other two principal amendments relate to the abuse of retention permission as a defence in enforcement actions and the discretion given to planning authorities as to whether in any given case they would institute proceedings for breach of the planning code. The 2000 Act specifically provides that it is no longer a defence to apply for or be granted permission after the initiation of proceedings. The option to regularise the position regarding unauthorised development by obtaining permission for retention is still available, because such breaches of the planning code can be unintentional, but the exclusion of this defence is intended to eliminate wilful and persistent disregard of the obligation to obtain permission before carrying out development.

The variety of enforcement and warning notices have been consolidated into a single procedure whereby, if a complaint of unauthorised development is made to a planning authority and it appears to be well founded, the planning authority must issue a warning letter to the owner and occupier within six weeks. The planning authority must then carry out an investigation and has a duty to decide as expeditiously as possible whether to take the matter further. While the planning authority continues to have discretion in reaching its decision, the matter cannot be under consideration for an indefinite period because the planning authority has a statutory objective to make the decision within twelve weeks. This is not an absolute time limit but it is intended to put a timeframe on dealing with complaints and to introduce a culture of enforcement into local planning. The decision as to whether to take action or not, together with the reasons on which it is based, must be entered in the planning register, which makes the process transparent and open to the general public. The complainant must be directly notified. If the planning authority decides to take action, it serves an enforcement notice on the person carrying out the development, specifying the breach of planning law and the steps to be taken to regularise the position. Failure to comply constitutes an offence.

Outdoor Events

The vexed question as to whether outdoor concerts need planning permission has been resolved by the provision that the holding of what is described as an event does not constitute development within the meaning of the 2000 Act. It was generally recognised that the planning system is not suited to controlling this type of public performance, which has instead been made subject to licence by the relevant county council or city council.

Related Legislation

A number of other legislative codes, some derived from Europe but most originating in the Oireachtas, are relevant to the operation of the planning system. These are outlined below.

Environmental Impact Assessment

Environmental impact assessment (EIA) is the term applied to the systematic examination of the likely impacts of development proposals on the environment prior to the initiation of any development works. It does not pre-determine whether or not development takes place but ensures that any unacceptable effects identified are avoided or reduced.

The European Directive on the assessment of the effects of certain public and private projects on the environment was implemented in Ireland by the 1989 European Communities (Environmental Impact Assessment) Regulations, which were made under the 1972 European Communities Act. Being necessitated by Ireland's obligation to comply with community law, as a member state of the EU, these regulations were able to amend existing legislation, including the Planning Acts of 1963 to 1999. Similarly, the second Directive on environmental impact assessment was also transposed into Irish law by regulations. The 2000 Act took the opportunity of consolidating all five existing sets of EIA regulations into primary legislation, insofar as they affect the planning code.

The original 1989 EIA Regulations grafted EIA in respect of private projects onto the planning application procedure and this position remains unchanged. Planning applications for developments specified in schedule 5 of the 2001 Planning Regulations must be accompanied by an environmental impact statement (EIS). In principle, these are the same types of developments as those prescribed previously and the content of environmental impact statements remained unchanged. An important provision contained in the 2001 Planning Regulations reflects the streamlined application procedures discussed in the section on development control above. Formerly, if a planning application was submitted without an accompanying EIS where one was mandatory, the regulations merely require the planning authority to notify the applicant. Since 11 March 2002, however, the entire application is invalidated by the absence of the EIS and must be so declared and returned to the applicant in line with the new, rigorous approach to development control. To enable planning authorities to deal efficiently with an application, if an EIS is required ten copies must be submitted.

Criticism has been voiced over the years that project-based EIA, which is what is required by the two Directives, fails to provide a strategic perspective of the impact which development proposals will have on the environment. This has been addressed in the 2000 Act, which requires both development plans and regional planning guidelines to include an assessment of the likely significant effects of their implementation on the environment.

Since the enactment of the 2000 Act, further regulations have been introduced relating to initial afforestation and peat extraction. The purpose of these regulations was to comply with a ruling of the European Court of Justice that the EIA thresholds adopted by Ireland for these types of projects failed to take account of the nature, location or cumulative impact of sub-threshold projects. The 2001 European Communities (Environmental Impact Assessment) (Amendment) Regulations and related Planning Regulations removed initial afforestation from the planning control system to coincide with the introduction of a new statutory consent system and reduced the planning threshold for the peat extraction to 10 hectares. Readers who require background information on planning controls of afforestation and peat extraction are referred to Grist (1999), chapter 5.

The Environmental Protection Agency

The Environmental Protection Agency (EPA) was established in 1993 with wide-ranging responsibilities for environmental matters. Its most important planning-related function is the regulation and control of industrial activities, which have the potential to cause environmental pollution, by means of integrated pollution control (IPC) licences. Prior to the enactment of the 2000 Act, if a proposed development was subject to IPC licensing, neither the planning authority nor An Bord Pleanála could take the risk of environmental pollution into account in assessing the proposal. In general terms, the planning assessment was confined to issues relating to design, traffic and visual impact.

The situation was less than satisfactory, particularly for third-party appellants who wanted to set out their objections in a comprehensive and holistic framework. While planning authorities are still prohibited from subjecting any permissions for licensable activities to conditions for the purpose of controlling pollution, they may decide to refuse permission altogether if they consider that a development is unacceptable on environmental grounds. Before making such decisions, the planning authority or An Bord Pleanála has the option of requesting the EPA for observations and, if such are received, they must be taken into account. Making observations does not fetter the EPA in any future performance of its functions. It remains to be seen how this somewhat complex relationship will resolve itself in practice.

Nature Conservation

Two European Directives have been specifically aimed at nature conservation, the Habitats Directive and the Birds Directive. The former is one of the most ambitious pieces of European legislation. It provides for the establishment of a network of protected sites, known as special areas of conservation, across all member states in accordance with specified scientific criteria. Incorporation of the Habitats Directive into Irish domestic law was particularly problematic because of the restrictions designation would inevitably impose on landowners. The 1997 European Communities (Natural Habitats) Regulations implemented the Directive and the process of designating sites has been underway since then.

Planning authorities must ensure that an appropriate assessment is made of any application that is likely to have a significant effect on a special area of conservation or a special protection area designated under the Birds Directive and permission may only be granted after having ascertained that the proposed development would not adversely affect the integrity of the sites in question. Development plans must contain objectives for the conservation and protection of these European sites.

Noise Control

Noise can be controlled by conditions attached to a planning permission or to an integrated pollution control (IPC) licence issued by the Environmental Protection Agency (EPA). However, provision is also made under the Environmental Protection Agency Act, 1992 for the general control of noise which is a nuisance or would endanger human health, damage property or harm the environment, all of which are included in the statutory definition of environmental pollution.

The EPA, if the activity in question is subject to IPC licensing, or the local authority, in other cases, can serve a noise prevention notice on the person in charge of the premises from which the noise is emanating. The notice sets out the measures required. The person served with the notice has a stated timeframe in which to respond and failure to make a response constitutes acceptance of the terms and restrictions contained in the notice. Thereafter, it is an offence not to comply with the terms of the notice and the offender can be prosecuted summarily by the EPA or, under the Environmental Protection Agency Act, 1992 (Noise) Regulations 1994 (SI No. 179 of 1994), by the local authority.

While members of the public can, of course, report a noise nuisance to the local authority or the EPA and ask that a noise prevention notice be served, there is also a noise complaint procedure directly available to the individual under section 108 of the 1992 EPA Act. Where noise constitutes a nuisance, any person may complain to the District Court, which has the power to issue an order to the person responsible for the noise, requiring them to take specified abatement measures. Whereas the noise prevention notice mechanism is only applicable to cases concerning commercial or trade premises, the complaint mechanism can be used to deal with noise coming from domestic property. Both these procedures are of significance as residential densities increase, more people work irregular or anti-social hours and noise levels in urban areas from a variety of sources continue to rise.

Renewal Schemes and Planning

By the mid-1980s, urban dereliction had reached crisis level and the country was in recession. Department plans had made various attempts to secure the renewal of obsolete areas, including allowing a much more financially attractive proportion of commercial to residential land uses in areas identified as in need of rejuvenation, but these policies had had little impact on the property market. The Urban Renewal Act, 1986 and the Finance Act, 1986 introduced a package of financial incentives to bring about investment by the private sector and, thereby, to generate a self-sustaining process of urban renewal. Under these two pieces of legislation and the Temple Bar Area Renewal and Development Act, 1991, three models for urban renewal were established. The most radical was that applied to the Custom House Docks in Dublin, where development over a sizeable geographic area was exempted from normal planning control. For discussion of the structure and operation of the three original urban renewal schemes, the reader is referred to Grist (1999, chapter 10).

In 1996, the Department of the Environment commissioned the carrying out of a study on the impact and effectiveness of these schemes. The consultants recognised that urban renewal in Ireland had become inextricably linked to tax incentives and identified two principal difficulties with the schemes to date. Firstly, the existing statutory development plans were prepared on too large a scale to provide the type of framework necessary for targeted urban renewal to be achieved and, secondly, the process for selection for designation had lacked sufficient rigour and focus.

To address these defects, the fourth generation of urban renewal schemes, under the Urban Renewal Act, 1998, provided that allocation of designated status would henceforth be underpinned by an integrated area plan (IAP), which would be prepared by the relevant local authority. Some seventy-eight IAPs were drawn up identifying carefully targeted sub-areas of towns on the basis of criteria supplied by the department. This new type of plan addressed not only physical development (which had been dealt with successfully under the earlier urban renewal schemes) but also the wider issues of local socio-economic benefits and environmental regeneration. IAPs provided much closer linkage between urban renewal and the planning system because IAPs were prepared by local planning authorities. Furthermore, qualification for tax incentives was made subject to certification by the relevant local authority that the development in question complied with the objectives of the integrated area plan.

Renewal of smaller towns, that is towns of a population of between 500 and 6,000, was addressed by the 1999 town renewal scheme. Guidelines for preparation of town renewal plans (TRPs), which showed clear similarities to the fine-grained formula of the IAPs but adapted to take account of differences of scale and socio-economic function, were circulated to all the planning authorities in July 1999 and areas in one hundred towns received designated status a year later. The central aim of the scheme was to increase the attractiveness of small towns as places to live in, with the intention of countering the trend of people moving to the outskirts and the surrounding countryside.

Despite the well-recognised and documented problem of urban sprawl, rural depopulation in the north-west (especially County Leitrim) in the late 1980s, coupled with the below-average rates of economic growth in the 1990s in the Border Regional Authority area, led to demands for regeneration of these rural areas through the mechanism of tax incentives. In June 1998, the Minister for Finance designated the Upper Shannon Basin for a pilot tax incentive scheme under which relief was given for both residential and commercial developments. However, unlike the later models of urban renewal schemes, the rural renewal scheme returned to the broad approach of designating large geographical areas without any specific planning framework to guide and focus development. While the scheme has been successful in reversing the trend of rural depopulation, especially in Counties Longford and Leitrim, concerns have been expressed by An Taisce among others that it is contributing to the suburbanisation of the rural landscape. The duration of the rural renewal scheme has been extended to December 2004, while its geographical area and broad framework have remained unaltered.

In approach, the rural renewal scheme is closer to the seaside resort renewal scheme model than to the later generations of urban renewal schemes. During the early 1990s, Bord Fáilte and the Department of Trade and Tourism promoted the idea of using tax incentives to halt the downward spiral of decline affecting traditional seaside resort towns since the inception of the package holidays in the 1960s. Fifteen seaside resorts were designated in the Finance Act, 1995 but, rather than devising criteria for establishing the extent of designation, the geographic boundaries of the resort areas were decided by means of a consultation process between the relevant central and local government stakeholders. The element of this scheme that proved most popular with investors in the boom years at the end of the 1990s was the provision of self-catering holiday accommodation. Many of the developments of holiday homes built in the designated resorts in the period 1995 to 1999 have been criticised for their extent and suburban appearance. Again in this case, the existing statutory development plans had not been prepared on a sufficiently detailed scale to provide adequate guidance when planning applications for individual holiday home developments came to be assessed.

The living-over-the-shop scheme was introduced in September 2000 and aims to promote the conversion of vacant space over commercial premises into residential accommodation. It has its origins in a 1994 pilot scheme which had somewhat mixed results. Criteria were identified by the department on the basis of which the local authorities were invited to make proposals for the selection of streets or part of streets of at least 25 metres in length for designation. The focus on streets rather than individual buildings is intended to secure restoration of streetscapes. In April 2001, a combined total of almost 13,000 linear metres of street length was designated in Dublin, Cork, Galway, Limerick and Waterford. It is generally accepted that the local authorities will have to devote considerable efforts to promoting the scheme, which will be operative until December 2004.

The Flood Tribunal

In October 1997, the Oireachtas decided to establish a tribunal of inquiry to investigate certain planning matters following the making of allegations that payments of money had been made to politicians and/or officials in the north County Dublin area in order to procure favourable planning decisions. In the following month, Mr Justice Feargus M. Flood, who had been a High Court judge since 1991, was appointed as the sole member of the tribunal. Assisted by a team of lawyers and administrators, Mr Justice Flood began his work in December 1997. Apart from preliminary sessions in 1998 to hear applications for legal representation by various interested parties, the tribunal carried on its work in private for the first year.

Public sessions began in Dublin Castle in January 1999. Between then and December 2001, some 170 witnesses gave evidence, with considerable media attention being focused on Mr James Gogarty, a retired engineer whose allegations were central to the establishment of the tribunal. In September 2002, Mr Justice Flood published his second interim report, which ran to 400 pages. Public interest was intense and the first printrun of 25,000 copies sold out in a few days, with people queuing outside Government Publications to buy the report.

The report covers what Mr Justice Flood described as three separate modules. The first details former minister Mr Ray Burke's involvement with builders Mr Tom Brennan and Mr Joseph McGowan and their related companies (the Brennan and McGowan module), the second deals with Mr Burke's relationships and dealings with Century Radio during the period when he held the position of Minister for Communications (the Century module) and the third covers the allegation that caused the tribunal to be established, the payment of money to Mr Burke at his home at Briargate, Swords, in June 1989, and related matters (the Gogarty module). Writing in a clear and unambiguous style, Mr Justice Flood also reported his interim conclusions, when he found it possible and appropriate to do so, setting out where, when and by whom corrupt acts took place.

In July 2001, Mr Justice Flood requested the Dáil to appoint additional members to the tribunal, in effect two to sit with him and a reserve member. Three Circuit Court judges were appointed to the tribunal in 2002, Mrs Justice Mary Faherty, Mr Justice Alan Mahon and Mr Justice Gerard Keys, under the continued chairmanship of Mr Justice Flood. It is anticipated that the work of the tribunal will continue well into the first decade of the twenty-first century.

Observations on the Future

Despite anticipation to the contrary, Mr Justice Flood did not make any recommendations in relation to legislative amendments in his second interim report. However, as he stated in the preface that this was because the report was only of an interim nature, it may confidently be expected that a future Flood report will make proposals for changes to planning, local government and ethics in public office legislation, proposals which it will be very hard for the Oireachtas to ignore.

At the time of writing, the planning legislative code is also under scrutiny from another perspective. The All-Party Oireachtas Committee on the Constitution is examining the constitutional protection of property rights, including the interaction of these rights with the planning process. By public notice placed in the national newspapers in April 2003, the committee invited submissions from individuals and groups on issues including the zoning of land, the price of development land and house prices. Following publication of the committee's findings, it may be necessary to amend the Constitution if any of the proposed changes to the planning acts have constitutional implications, such as very severe restrictions on the development rights of landowners.

At the end of his Second Reading statement in the Seanad, Minister Dempsey acknowledged that the new functions given to planning authorities and the greater demands to be placed on them by the streamlined planning system would require extra resources. He elaborated on this issue to the Dáil on 2 February 2000, when he indicated that he had been in contact with University College Dublin, the location of the only planning school in the country,[8] about the increased need for professional planners. He gave a commitment to provide the necessary resources. The enlarged volume of applications and appeals was recognised by many Oireachtas members to be a major factor in existing delays. The professional planning institutes, while strongly supporting the main direction and components of the Bill, expressed very serious reservations about the ability of already over-stretched planning offices to deliver the reframed planning service with its more rigorous structures and warned that, unless this issue was resolved, the enactment of the Bill with its many eagerly anticipated features would 'rapidly be consumed by public frustration'.[9] In the event, the intake of students to the planning school in UCD was doubled in autumn 2000, from 25 to 50, and this cohort of professional planners graduated in autumn 2002, just in time to make a significant contribution to the establishment of the operation of the new planning system.

---

[8] Subsequently, a planning degree programme was also established by the Dublin Institute of Technology.

[9] Irish Planning Institute and the Royal Town Planning Institute (1999), *Joint Submission to the Minister for the Environment and Local Government on the Planning Bill*, p. 14.

13

The Environment:
Protection and Services

Seán O'Riordain

In essence, the range of responsibilities in environmental services comprises: waste management, burial grounds provision, safety of structures and places, fire prevention and protection, and pollution prevention and control.

This chapter covers those local government responsibilities grouped together under programme group 5 (see chapter 8), which includes a number of functions that may not be traditionally associated with the title 'environment', including burial grounds and the fire service. Other areas of local government activity impacting on the environment are addressed elsewhere in this book. For example, the area of water supply and water treatment infrastructure and services is dealt with in chapter 11. Environmental responsibilities in the drafting of development plans and the issue of environmental impact assessment are addressed in chapter 12, while chapter 21 deals with sustainable development and Local Agenda 21.

The renaming of the Department of the Environment as the Department of the Environment and Local Government in 1997 marked, in some respects, a return to a recognition of the critical role which local government plays in sustaining the health and vigour of Ireland's natural environment. Since its establishment in 1924 as the Department of Local Government and Public Health, this department has overseen the protection of the environment, supported the operation of the local government system and facilitated the move towards an advanced European economy based on the principles of the free market and democracy. Its renaming marks the standing which both local government and the environment now have within general government policy. It recognises the increasing importance of a vibrant local government system in a state that seeks to maintain a high-quality

253

environment. Local government now plays the most significant role of all public institutions in delivering on national and EU environmental policy. It does so against the background of constant economic, social and environmental change.

The remarkable economic transformation that Ireland experienced in the 1990s has resulted in the state seeking to protect an environment which is under pressure from population growth, home ownership expansion, agricultural intensification, service industry expansion, and the internationalisation of institutions, capital and human resources. Therefore, it is not surprising that local authorities find their legislative framework to be much changed since the publication of Roche's *Local Government in Ireland* in 1982. These changes, in many respects driven by Ireland's membership of the EU, have political, budgetary and personnel implications on a scale not witnessed since the establishment of the department in 1924. Significantly for local authorities, it is now recognised that the environment underlies economic and social development and that an inadequate application of environmental legislation has a negative impact on standards of living and quality of life. Local authorities are thus increasingly required to ensure the creation of a process of sustainable development.

The legislative and organisational responses to these changes in economic dynamics and political imperatives, and their effect upon the core functions of local government, are reviewed in the subsections that follow. Thereafter, the role and functions of the Environmental Protection Agency are examined and the interfaces between local government and the agency are explored.

Waste Management

The National Economic and Social Council (2002, p. 487) has described the effective management of waste as 'one of the highest priorities in Ireland'. This assessment is reiterated in *Sustaining Progress*, the partnership agreement adopted by the government and social partners in 2003 (Government of Ireland, 2003, p. 31).

The adoption of the Waste Management Act, 1996 consolidated and updated what had been a poorly structured legislative framework for dealing with one of the key services of local authorities. The Act has enabled a more integrated approach. It clearly defines the meaning of waste, its various streams and the degrees of responsibility for its management. A key provision in the Act is that it enables local authorities to enter onto property with a view to dealing with a risk of pollution. It enables a risk reduction or preventive approach rather than a need to react to pollution from solid and other wastes.

Part II of the Act deals with the issue of waste management planning. It places a general duty of care on holders of waste and gives statutory effect to the adoption of a waste management plan by each local authority. Provision is also made for the making and adoption of a national hazardous waste management plan. This is the responsibility of the Environmental Protection Agency (EPA), and such a plan was adopted by the agency in 2001. In addition, each local authority waste management plan provides for the 'prevention, minimisation, collection, recovery and disposal of non-hazardous waste within its functional area'. Local authorities are empowered to prepare joint plans, which are increasingly seen as the way forward given the economies of scale associated with waste. The plans recognise the polluter pays principle and reflect modern thinking which increasingly views waste as a potential economic resource rather than something simply needing burial.

Part III of the Act enables the government and a local authority to support waste reduction through the separation and recycling of waste. Section 33 imposes a qualified obligation on county and city councils to collect or arrange for the collection of waste within their functional areas. The same section goes on to enable borough and town councils to do likewise, but they do not have a statutory obligation for collection. Under section 35, local authorities are able to issue bye-laws concerning the presentation of waste for collection.

Part V of the Act covers the duty to provide any facilities necessary to enable the collection and disposal of the waste stream, as well as the licensing of waste management facilities by the EPA. In this case the authorities can provide civic waste facilities and other facilities that provide for the segregation, mixing and baling of waste and its treatment and storage (section 38). Such facilities do require a waste licence provided by the EPA. The EPA can attach conditions which must be complied with by the local authorities and other operators, and generally cover the full operation and aftercare of such facilities as it deems appropriate. There is provision for full public consultation – oral hearings, giving of evidence and receiving of objections – by the EPA prior to its decision to grant or refuse a licence.

Part VI of the Act includes a series of provisions concerning general environmental protection. It enables the serving of notices which may require actions to be undertaken to prevent or limit pollution arising from a waste management process. Where these are ignored, the local authorities are empowered to seek redress through the judicial system. A specific power to deal with abandoned vehicles rests in section 71 of the Act.

The impact of the new legislative framework set out in the 1996 Act was further expanded upon in a policy document on waste management, *Changing Our Ways* (Department of the Environment and Local Government, 1998b), which adopted the EU's broad objective of introducing a waste management hierarchy. This policy sets out to establish the following in the period to 2010:

- the diversion of 50 per cent of overall household waste away from landfill
- a minimum reduction of 65 per cent in biodegradable municipal wastes going to landfill sites

- the establishment and development of facilities capable of treating, through composting and other biological treatments, 300,000 tonnes of organic waste each year
- the recovery of up to 85 per cent of construction and demolition waste
- the recycling of materials from municipal waste to reach 35 per cent
- the rationalisation of landfill sites across the state.

In seeking to achieve these targets, local authorities must make considerable effort to develop a regional approach to waste. Waste has become an increasingly controversial topic and a number of local authorities have experienced difficulty in agreeing a waste management strategy for their area. Opposition to the location of landfill sites and incinerators on grounds such as health and traffic volumes in certain localities created difficulties in the political process. In some areas, there was also opposition to the location of civic amenity facilities and recycling centres.

Further developments in the legislative base were introduced in the form of the Waste Management (Amendment) Act, 2001 and the Protection of the Environment Bill 2003. These changes enable the county/city manager to adopt, vary or replace waste management plans in circumstances where the council has failed to do so properly. The 2001 Act also enabled the imposition of a national levy on plastic bags, the establishment of an environment fund and the introduction of a landfill levy. The 2003 Bill will also allow local authorities explicit powers to discontinue the collection of domestic waste where householders have not paid their waste charges and includes a number of provisions strengthening the enforcement regime in the waste area.

Litter

The issue of litter remains a constant concern for Irish residents and visitors to the state. Local authorities have provided street-cleaning services since their establishment. A concerted effort to tackle the problem is covered under the Litter Pollution Act, 1997. The Act replaced what was seen as a largely ineffective Litter Act, 1982. Part II of the 1997 Act provides for the offence of littering. Section 3(1) states unambiguously that 'no person shall deposit any substance or object so as to create litter in a public place or in any place that is visible to any extent from a public place'. It is equally an offence to interfere with or move a litter receptacle that has been provided by a local authority or any other person without their prior authorisation. Littering from vehicles and skips is also prohibited, while the occupiers of land that is in a public place or adjoining it are required to keep the area free of litter.

Part III of the Act covers the role of local authorities and their duties. Section 7 requires them to keep public roads in their functional area free of litter as far as practicable. They may also, under section 8, take measures to prevent litter and promote awareness and public participation in anti-litter campaigns. Where they provide litter receptacles, arrangements must be made for regular emptying. A further important power is provided through section 9, which enables a local authority to issue a notice requiring a person to remedy a littering problem on land or grounds occupied by that person. Section 10 provides for the preparation of litter management plans by local authorities. They may be jointly prepared by more than one local authority and have to be reviewed every three years. The plan should contain details on appropriate objectives to prevent and control litter, encourage public awareness and education, develop ways of appraising the litter programme and enable the enforcement and attainment of the plan's objectives. An annual report to the elected members is also required.

Part IV places a responsibility on owners of mobile outlets to prevent litter. It empowers local authorities to deal with potential 'hot spots' of litter, for example cinemas, schools, events involving large crowds such as rock concerts, and bus and rail stations. The concern with litter does not just apply to papers on the ground or in hedgerows. Increasingly the problem of defacement of public structures through graffiti, illegal advertisement, fly posting and so forth needs to be addressed. Section 19 enables an authority to take action to prevent this arising. This does not apply to election posters in presidential, general, local or European elections and referenda. There is a period of exemption for such posters during an electoral period and up to seven days following an election. The provision of bye-laws to prohibit or regulate the distribution of advertising material to the public is covered under section 21 of the Act. The powers available to local authorities to adopt litter bye-laws will be enhanced under the Protection of the Environment Bill 2003. Section 22 provides for the offence of failure to clean up dog faeces by the person in charge of the animal.

Part V, as amended by the Waste Management (Amendment) Act, 2001, provides for enforcement, traditionally the weakest element of the earlier litter legislation. On-the-spot fines may be issued by a litter warden or a garda, with higher fines available to the courts. In this regard, section 26 has the important provision of recognising that the contents of litter that give rise to a 'reasonable suspicion' concerning the identity of the person making a litter deposit can be used in court as evidence unless otherwise proven. Section 27 provides that the owner, hirer or user of a vehicle involved in the commission of a litter offence will each be guilty of an offence. It is a defence for the registered owner or hirer to show that another person was using the vehicle when the offence was committed and that the use was unauthorised.

A large number of city and county councils employ environmental education/awareness officers to heighten awareness among local communities on issues such as environmental protection, litter prevention and recycling.

A national tidy towns competition is organised each year by the Department of the Environment and Local Government. A similar event takes place in Northern Ireland. The winners from both compete in an island-wide competition for Ireland's best-kept towns. Most local authorities work closely with the committees that have become a mainstay in the battle against the ever-rising tide of litter. Other initiatives are underway involving the National Rehabilitation Board (recycling, particularly of bottle glass) and the various farm organisations in an attempt to deal with plastic and other wastes associated with agriculture. A national business-driven campaign is also active and reflects an increasing concern about litter on the part of employers and traditional environmental organisations such as An Taisce, who recognise the need for a clean environment and its role in creating an ongoing sustainable economy.

Pollution Control – Water

Ireland is extraordinarily well endowed with water resources. This, for the foreseeable future, will provide the country with a competitive advantage given the levels of water abstractions in the rest of Europe. Nonetheless, there are continuing pollution issues associated with agricultural and industrial activity, plus newer risks associated with tourism which, if not properly managed, could have severe implications for these very sectors and their continued development. The Local Government (Water Pollution) Act, 1977 could be considered to be the first in what was to become a huge body of environmental legislation in recent times. It provided for the licensing of effluent discharges into water courses (section 4) and sewers (section 16). The Act was updated and extended by the Local Government (Water Pollution) (Amendment) Act, 1990 following a large spate of agriculture-based fish kills.

Section 3 of the 1977 Act prohibits the entry of polluting matter to waters subject to the licensing of such discharges by a local authority and other defined authorities in the Foreshore Act, 1933 and the Harbours Act, 1946. County and city councils are empowered under section 4 to license discharges to waters and drainage facilities. Sections 4 and 16 are, however, only applicable to industries and others not covered by the licensing regime of the Environmental Protection Agency Act, 1992. A local authority or indeed any person is further empowered to seek remedy in court under sections 10 and 11 of the Act where pollution of water is at issue. Section 15 provides for the adoption of a water quality management plan by a local authority either in its own right or, as is normally the case given the nature of water catchment areas, on a joint basis with other local authorities adjoining a river/lake catchment area.

Vis-à-vis the power to discharge to waters, a distinguishing factor of the power to license discharges to sewers under section 16 is that the licence is issuable, where not covered by the EPA Act, by a sanitary authority. Sanitary authorities are defined under the Local Government (Sanitary Services) Acts 1878 to 1964 (note that, under the Local Government Act, 2001, such functions are to be consolidated at county and city level by 2004). Only county and city councils may license discharges to waters. Licence reviews must be undertaken at intervals of not less than three years following their issue.

The 1977 Act also provides for the establishment of water quality control authorities that could take on the functions of a local authority under the Act. To date, this option has not been exercised, although calls for such have been made, generally following a series of pollution incidents.

The Local Government (Water Pollution) (Amendment) Act, 1990 considerably increased the powers of the original Act by increasing levels of fines and other penalties and creating a civil liability on damages caused by polluters. It also provides for the making of bye-laws regulating agricultural activities in its functional area to prevent/eliminate pollution of water. This provision under section 21 of the Act was considerably strengthened with the adoption of section 66(3) of the Waste Management Act, 1996, which provides for the adoption of nutrient management plans by the owners of land engaged in agriculture or related activities.

Pollution Control – Air

The second Act of importance in the updating of environmental legislation covers the issue of air pollution. The Air Pollution Act, 1987 consolidated controls originating in early twentieth-century legislation such as the Alkali etc. Works Regulation Act, 1906. This was necessary given technological and industrial changes and the levels of stress on air quality in the cities in the 1980s. It also built on an extensive range of EU laws. Section 53 of the 1987 Act provides for the prohibition by ministerial regulation of fuels that could create polluted air. The Act places an obligation on the occupiers of premises, other than private dwellings, to use the best practicable means to limit air emissions. In addition, occupiers of all premises, including households, shall not cause or permit emissions that would become a nuisance. Emissions of smoke are also covered in section 25 of the Act and local authorities can require an occupier to carry out measures to limit or prevent air pollution.

Part III of the Act empowers local authorities to license industrial plants (not covered by the EPA) making emissions into the surrounding air. Appeals are provided for to An Bord Pleanála. Part IV provides for the adoption of special control areas by local authorities. These are put into place by special control area orders (section 40) that may prohibit emissions of specified pollutants and may prohibit use of unauthorised fuels among other powers. They were used to give effect to targeted controls in Dublin and have generally been subsumed into regulations covering urban areas adopted by successive ministers. A local authority, under section 46, may adopt an air quality management plan. There is also provision under section 102 of the Environmental Agency Protection Act, 1992 for the EPA to do so under order of the minister.

Pollution Control – Noise

Section 107 of the Environmental Protection Agency Act, 1992 enables local authorities to serve notices on persons in charge of premises, processes or works not covered by the EPA itself, to prevent or limit noise. A failure to address the notice on the part of the recipient could result in the authority seeking redress in the District Court.

Individuals may request a local authority, or where appropriate the EPA, to exercise its powers with regard to the control of noise. Under section 108 of the 1992 EPA Act, any person may take an action in the District Court to seek a court order to deal with the noise.

Derelict Sites

The extent of dereliction in Ireland's urban areas has been tackled to a large degree through tax-incentive programmes provided for under various Finance Acts. Nonetheless, dereliction does still arise and, in dealing with it, local authorities may have recourse to the Derelict Sites Act, 1990, which completely repealed an earlier Act of 1961. Section 3 of the Act defines a derelict site as that 'which detracts, or is likely to detract, to a material degree from the amenity, character or appearance of land'. This may be because of:

- structures in a ruinous, derelict or dangerous condition
- its neglected, unsightly or objectionable condition
- the presence of litter, rubbish, debris or waste not covered by an exercise of a statutory right or common law right.

Section 9 places a general duty on all owners and occupiers of land to take reasonable steps to prevent dereliction. Section 10 requires local authorities to take steps to prevent dereliction in their functional area. Where dereliction does arise, a local authority may either require the owner/occupier to correct the dereliction or it may choose to do so itself. The power of a compulsory acquisition of a derelict site rests with an authority under section 14. Part III of the Act provides for a derelict sites levy. This is based on the market value of the land and can be set by a local authority subject to appeal to the Valuation Tribunal established under the Valuation Act, 1988. A further right of appeal to the High Court exists.

Burial Grounds

The Public Health (Ireland) Act, 1878 provides for burial grounds. It was supplemented by the Local Government (Sanitary Services) Act, 1948. Most graveyards in Ireland are provided by local parishes and are generally controlled by the local clergy. There is a duty on local authorities, as sanitary authorities, to provide graveyards where an existing burial ground is closed.

Cremation is covered under the 1948 Act and is licensed under the 1992 EPA Act, while exhumation licences must be issued in all cases by a local authority under the provisions of the 1948 Act, as amended by the Local Government Act, 1994.

Dangerous Structures/Places

The Local Government (Sanitary Services) Act, 1964 was adopted on 28 July 1964 following an accident where a building in Dublin collapsed causing several deaths.

Section 1 of the Act defines both a dangerous place and a dangerous structure. A dangerous place includes excavation sites, quarries, pits, wells, reservoirs, ponds, streams, dams, banks, dumps, shafts or land which the local authority as sanitary authority for the area considers as dangerous. A dangerous structure covers any type of building or structure or anything attached to them that the local authority considers to be dangerous to any person or property. Sanitary authorities, under sections 2 and 3, can carry out preventive works by the giving of notice to owners and occupiers of either a dangerous place or structure. This could include the demolition of the structure.

An alternative to the authorities carrying out the work directly is to have it completed by the owner/occupier. Again this is enabled through the serving of the appropriate notice. There is an appeal mechanism to the District Court if the work is not carried out. In some cases it may be necessary to acquire land that is, or was, a dangerous place. This may be carried out by means of normal land purchasing. Provision is made, however, under section 6 for a compulsory purchase. Section 12 requires a sanitary authority to act with 'all convenient speed' to ensure the prevention of injury to health or the amenities of a neighbourhood.

An additional feature in the area of public roads and the safety of traffic is that section 10 of the Roads Act, 1993 places an obligation on owners and occupiers of land to ensure that roadside structures do not act as a danger to road users. In this instance a local authority, as the roads authority, may serve a notice requiring the removal or modification of the roadside structure. Where work of this nature is not carried out by the owner/occupier, the road authority may carry it out and recover its costs through the courts.

Fire Prevention and Protection

The tragic fire at the Stardust disco on 14 February 1981, in which forty-seven
people lost their lives, resulted in the adoption of the Fire Services Act, 1981. The
Act repealed in full the Cinematograph Act, 1909 and the Fire Brigades Act, 1940.
It also resulted in the amendment of several other pieces of legislation in order to
bring Irish legislation up to an acceptable level. The Act established fire authorities
in county councils, city councils, Drogheda Borough Council and Dundalk and
Athlone Town Councils. The Dublin City Fire Service provides, on an agency basis,
emergency services for the counties of Fingal, South Dublin and Dún Laoghaire-
Rathdown. In addition, Galway City Council's fire department provides services to
Galway County Council, and Westmeath County Council's fire department
provides services to Athlone Town Council. Section 10 covers the functions of a
fire authority: it is required to provide for the prompt and efficient extinguishing of
fires in buildings and other places of all kinds and for the 'protection and rescue of
person and property from injury by fire'. Provision is made for training, which has
resulted in a considerable upgrading of the training in the fire service nationally.

The Fire Services Council is provided for under section 16 of the 1981 Act and
appointed by the minister. Its functions include the preparation of guidelines,
codes of practice, standards and regulations relating to fire safety. They may also
undertake research and carry out fire investigations.

Part III of the Act provides for a comprehensive system of fire safety control
in potentially dangerous buildings. Section 18 places a duty on every person on a
premises covered by the section to 'conduct himself in such a way as to ensure
that as far as is reasonably practical any person on the premises is not exposed to
danger from fire'. The power to issue a fire safety notice on the owner/occupier
of any building that appears to the fire authority as potentially dangerous is
covered in section 20. This can prohibit the use of a building or a part of a
building for activities described in the notice. It can also impose requirements to
upgrade a building to the satisfaction of the fire authority. A power of inspection
is provided under section 22 where an authorised person of the authority may
enter, at all reasonable times, any land or building other than a dwelling house to
inspect it for the purposes of the 1981 Act. An appeal to the High Court to prohibit
use of land and/or buildings is covered under section 23. Section 24 requires
applicants for licences under the Licensing Acts, 1933 to 1981, the Registration
of Clubs Acts, 1904 to 1981 and the Public Dance Halls Act, 1935 to notify the
authority of the applications. The fire authority may then inspect the premises and
give evidence in court prior to the granting of the licence. Section 26 provides for
the adoption by the elected members of the local authority of the fire and
emergency operations plans. These must include the organisation and equipping
of the authority's fire brigade.

In 2001, the department commissioned a wholesale review of the fire service. The review was generally positive on the operation of the service as a whole, but proposed a number of changes in how it operates at local, regional and national level, which may herald a number of future changes to the system (Farrell Grant Sparks, 2002).

The report noted that in the past there has been an emphasis on fighting fires and responding to emergencies. However, international best practice and evidence would support an enhanced emphasis on a risk-based approach and prevention and mitigation programmes to ensure that the public is aware of risks and can minimise them. The report recommended the establishment of a new fire and civil protection/emergency services authority at national level, which would involve expanding the role of the existing Fire Services Council to cover a number of functions currently administered by the department and other bodies. Legislative changes were proposed, including the introduction of a statutory obligation on fire authorities to carry out fire safety programmes. The report also recommended examining whether the use of on-the-spot fines could be extended.

The report stated that '37 fire authorities, ranging from 25,000 to over 1,000,000 in population, each being staffed and resourced to independently discharge the full range of fire and civil protection/emergency services functions is too many for a country of our size' (Farrell Grant Sparks, 2002, p. 105).

The report argued that the use of 'section 85 agreements' should be further examined (section 85 of the Local Government Act, 2001 allows a local authority to decide that a function be performed by another local authority on its behalf).[1] These were already used in a number of areas (see above). While 'strongly urging' other local authorities to give consideration to the use of this model, the review stopped short of recommending that this be made a mandatory requirement, instead believing it to be a matter for local government management and elected members. The review also stopped short of proposing the establishment of new formal regional structures to co-ordinate fire services on a regional basis – but argued that the option should not be excluded indefinitely.

Another proposal was that local fire authorities be redesignated as fire and civil protection/emergency services authorities, and that their role could be expanded in certain areas. Local fire authorities could develop their role in implementing fire prevention regimes, community fire safety programmes, local promotion, and awareness and education safety programmes in schools, workplaces, multiple occupancy buildings and private dwellings. Local fire and civil protection/ emergency services authorities should also produce three-year rolling plans, to be reviewed and approved by relevant strategic policy committees and the elected council, which would then be submitted to the new national authority.

---

[1] Prior to the enactment of the Local Government Act, 2001, these were known as 'section 59 agreements', provided for under section 59 of the Local Government Act, 1955.

The report recommended changes to structures at local level. In particular, it identified a need to integrate existing local authority fire services and building control functions into a unified structure.

The review decided against mandatory national standards for local fire authorities and instead concluded that local authorities should continue to have statutory responsibility for determining cover and response requirements. Nevertheless, it believed that local authorities could be guided by and conform to a nationwide process for determining such standards.

Civil Defence

The provision of civil defence services comes under the remit of the Minister for Defence. The Department of Defence has overall policy responsibility for planning and organisation under the provisions of the Civil Defence Acts of 1939 to 2002. The actual promotion and development of civil defence planning is undertaken by a Civil Defence Board, established under section 8 of the Civil Defence Act, 2002. The Act empowers county and city councils to provide for civil defence. Each prepares a civil defence plan that is reviewed at least once every three years. National training is carried out via the Civil Defence School in Dublin. The local training remains within the ambit of a civil defence officer (CDO), a number of whom are part-time. The CDO is responsible for local planning, the recruitment of voluntary personnel and the provision of appropriate equipment.

Other Environmental Services Responsibilities

Temporary Dwellings

Part IV of the Local Government (Sanitary Services) Act, 1948 provides for the regulation of temporary dwellings and the use of land for camping. Section 34 provides for the licensing of land for use for camping and caravanning. Licensing in this instance is generally applied in local authority areas that have a significant tourist sector. Section 30 enables the making of bye-laws, while section 31, as amended by section 113 of the Environmental Protection Agency Act, 1992, provides for the prohibition of temporary dwellings and the unauthorised parking of temporary dwellings. Interestingly, the order for the making of a prohibition is a reserved rather than an executive function. Prior to the making of an order the council must consider whether the erection or retaining of temporary dwellings would be prejudicial to public health or the area's amenities and whether there would be unreasonable interference with road traffic. A further provision for dealing with temporary dwellings on national roads exists under section 69 of the Roads Act, 1993.

Casual Trading

The Casual Trading Act, 1995 requires persons wishing to trade to hold a casual trading licence issued under section 4 by local authorities. Casual trading areas are designated by local authorities under section 6 of the Act through the adoption of bye-laws by the authority.

Dogs Homes

Local authorities are empowered to issue dog licences under the Control of Dogs Act, 1986. In general, the provision of facilities under the Act occurs through organisations such as the ISPCA or persons associated with animal welfare such as a veterinary surgeon. Bye-laws relating to dog control may also be adopted.

Flood Relief

The Local Authorities (Works) Act, 1949 provides for works by local authorities where the need is identified. Arterial drainage is generally carried out by the Office of Public Works. Serious concern is arising from coastal erosion and a number of local authorities are undertaking work under the Coast Protection Act, 1963.

Swimming Safety

Irish Water Safety oversees the promotion of water safety. It was established under the Local Government Services (Corporate Bodies) Act, 1971 (and for a time formed part of the National Safety Council). It receives funding from a variety of sources including the Department of the Environment and Local Government and local authorities. Local authorities have a role in the promotion of water safety in their areas through the provision of safety equipment, lifeguards and so forth. County councils appoint a water safety development officer to work with local Irish Water Safety volunteer committees who organise local water safety events and courses.

Nuisances

Nuisances in the legal sense have been defined in ten categories by the Public Health Acts. In general they are all those conditions that are injurious to health, but they also include such things that diminish the comfort of life although not actually damaging health. It is the duty of the sanitary authority to detect nuisances and see that they are abated, if necessary getting an order of court for the purpose and abating the nuisance itself if the order is disobeyed.

The Environmental Protection Agency (EPA)

The importance of environmental protection and the furtherance of national environmental policy objectives are underpinned by the role of the EPA and the overriding influence of the Environmental Protection Agency Act, 1992. The critical relationship between the EPA and local authorities stems from the circumstances surrounding the agency's establishment and the passing of the EPA Act. Prior to 1992, there was increasing public concern with regard to the responses to specific pollution instances and an increasing perception that local authorities either were unable or unwilling to address the issue of pollution prevention and control.

The 1992 Act provides a framework to 'make further and better provision for the protection of the environment and the control of pollution, to establish an Environmental Protection Agency . . .'. The EPA was formally established by order of the minister on 26 July 1993. Section 19 of the Act covers its establishment. The agency, which consists of a director general and four other directors, is a body corporate. Its headquarters are in Wexford, in addition to which it has five regional offices in Cork, Dublin, Kilkenny, Mayo and Monaghan. A number of its staff worked for local authorities prior to joining the agency.

EPA Functions

Part III of the EPA Act covers the extensive functions of the agency. The EPA covers the licensing, regulation and control of activities concerned with environmental protection. It carries out the monitoring of the quality of the environment in co-operation with local authorities, provides support and advice to local and other public authorities, engages and promotes environmental research, liaises with the European Environment Agency in Copenhagen, and may carry out any other function assigned to it by the minister. Of particular relevance to local authorities is its role in monitoring local authorities' water and sanitary services and supervising the general statutory performance of local government in aspects of environmental protection. As noted above, the EPA has a particular role in licensing landfill and waste facilities operated by local authorities under the Waste Management Act, 1996.

The agency is required to publish, on a five-yearly basis, a state of the environment report for Ireland. It has prepared guidelines on environmental impact assessment and other various codes of practice. Part IV of the Act provides for the adoption of an integrated approach to pollution control (IPC) licensing. These provisions are to be updated under the Protection of the Environment Bill 2003, which introduces more stringent requirements and places a greater emphasis on pollution prevention. The licensing regime is to be retitled 'integrated pollution prevention and control' (IPPC) to reflect these changes.

Such licensing applies to activities including:

•   minerals and other materials extraction
•   energy production and use greater than or equal to fifty megawatts

- metal production and processing
- mineral, fibre and glass production
- chemical production
- intensive agriculture
- food and drink production
- wood, paper, textiles and leather production
- extraction/use of fossil fuels
- cement production
- waste incineration and heat use
- surface coating processes.

The Protection of the Environment Bill 2003 proposes to add the following to this list:

- intensive agriculture
- food production
- production of paper, pulp or board.

In all, the IPPC licensing process administered by the EPA now covers much of what would have been dealt with under the Water and Air Pollution Acts by local authorities.

Conclusion

Considerable progress in the field of environmental legislation has been made following Ireland's entry into the EU. Ireland now has a legislative and policy framework similar to other advanced economies. This, however, is not to be seen as the conclusion to the environmental debate in Ireland. National policy does recognise the continuing significance of integrating environmental policy into other national and local policy agendas. In addition, although the legislative framework is well established, resourcing issues with regard to enforcement remain to be fully resolved, and changing public attitudes and levels of understanding on environmental issues is required by both local and national authorities in regard to waste management, water usage and other controversial issues in the state.

14

Recreation and Amenity Services

Joe MacGrath

A local authority's areas of responsibility in programme group 6 include swimming pools, parks, libraries, archives, the arts, heritage and the Irish language. Traditionally, this aspect of local government services has been overshadowed by other programme groups (see chapter 8), particularly in the construction area. However, there has been a considerable expansion of local authority activities in recreation and amenity services. For example, revenue expenditure of county councils under this heading increased by over 100 per cent between 1991 and 2001. The revenue expenditure increase for city councils amounted to 98 per cent in the same period, from some €40.2 million to €80 million. The application of the general competence rule under the Local Government Act, 1991, together with a series of national funding schemes, has encouraged the active involvement of local authorities in the provision of museums, arts centres and heritage centres. In addition, the traditional role of local authorities in the library services expanded considerably throughout the 1990s and into the early years of the new millennium.

The legislative position in relation to the provision of recreation and amenities services was amended several times in the 1990s and afterwards. The Local Government Act, 1991 provided a general competence to a local authority to take such measures, engage in activities or do such things in accordance with the law as it considers necessary or desirable to promote the interests of the local community. This could include the social, economic, environmental, recreational, cultural, community or general development of the functional area of the local authority. The Local Government Act, 1994 expanded on and clarified the general competence provision in its application to amenity, recreation, library and other functions. The Act identified the types of facility that could be provided by local authorities including:

- artistic and cultural activities
- sports, games and similar activities
- general recreational and leisure activities
- civic improvements
- environment and heritage protection and improvement
- the public use of amenities.

Part 9 of the Local Government Act, 2001 re-enacts much of the previous law in a consolidated and updated format insofar as it applies to recreation and amenities services (section 67). For the first time in local government law, the 2001 Act contains a general statement of local authority functions: to provide a democratic forum and civic leadership, to carry out functions conferred by the Act and other enactments (for example relating to housing, fire, roads, sanitary services), to carry out any ancillary functions and to take action to promote the community interest. In carrying out these statutory functions, local authorities are required to have regard to the availability and effective use of resources, the need to maintain essential services, co-operate and consult with other relevant authorities and organisations, adhere to government policy, promote social inclusion and work towards sustainable development.

Swimming Pools and Parks

Traditionally, some sanitary authorities provided indoor and outdoor swimming pools and other bathing facilities. Under the Local Government Act, 1955 (much of which has been repealed), a sanitary authority could either undertake the work itself or contribute towards the provision of a swimming pool by swimming clubs, local authorities or other such bodies. The procedure was that the sanitary authority raised the loan through the local loans fund and sought state assistance in the form of a contribution to the loan charges. The usual subsidy was at the rate of 50 per cent. This gave rise to an ambitious programme, launched by the minister in the late 1960s, for the provision of swimming pools throughout the country. By 1977, work on some sixty-six new pools had been completed. The financial provision in relation to subsidies for swimming pools was subsequently discontinued. This, coupled with the financial cost of maintaining public swimming pools, gave rise to more private sector involvement particularly within the context of leisure centres. Some local authorities developed joint ventures with other public and private organisations to deliver the service on a more commercial basis.

The provision and refurbishment of swimming pools is co-ordinated by the Department of Arts, Sport and Tourism, under the local authority swimming pools programme. Under the programme running from 2000 to 2003, grants of up to €3.81 million were available towards the provision of a new pool or for the refurbishment of an existing pool, subject to a maximum limit of 80 per cent of the eligible cost of the project. While other organisations can apply, they must obtain the support of the local authority.

Local authorities can generally acquire land by agreement or compulsorily for recreation facilities. Local authorities may also undertake subsequent and subsidiary activities including maintenance and the making of bye-laws to govern the use of the facility.

Local authorities, over the years, have had various powers conferred on them for the provision and operation of parks, pleasure grounds and recreation areas zoned by them. Playing fields and open spaces are frequently incorporated into the designs for new local authority housing schemes. The parks function of a local authority is not just confined to large public parks but is also concerned with the development and maintenance of small open spaces in housing estates when taken in charge. Throughout the 1980s and 1990s, local authorities worked jointly with FÁS under the social employment scheme and subsequently the community employment scheme in the provision of amenity areas. The provision of parks and open spaces is particularly relevant in urban areas. Dublin City has, for example, 750 public green spaces comprising 2,000 hectares with an annual budget of over €13.5 million for their maintenance and development.

Libraries

There are thirty-two library authorities in the state. Twenty-six of the twenty-nine county councils and four of the five city councils are library authorities for their own areas. The two Tipperary County Councils have a joint library committee between them, while Galway County Council operates a library service for itself and on behalf of Galway City Council.

In 2001, the combined expenditure of the library authorities exceeded €69 million, following growth in library funding over a number of years. For many years, local authorities concentrated their expenditure on infrastructural investment. However, the improving economy in the 1990s provided an opportunity for the expansion of the library service. Local authorities recognised during this time that the social and cultural dimensions of local development must be addressed. Public libraries are now recognised as one key element to the social and cultural development of local areas. In 2001, there were some 321 public libraries in Ireland employing over 1,300 people. The average rate of library membership nationally is 24 per cent and this implies a total library membership of approximately 850,000 people. However, many non-members also use the library service and a survey carried out in November 1997 indicated that 32 per cent of the adult population use public libraries, when usage by non-members is taken into account.

In addition to the library authorities, An Chomhairle Leabharlanna (The Library Council) is a corporate body established under the Public Libraries Act, 1947. It has a council of thirteen members, ten of whom are drawn from the Higher Education Authority, Trinity College Dublin, National Library of Ireland, General Council of County Councils, Association of Municipal Authorities of Ireland, Local Authority Members Association and the Library Association of Ireland. Two local authority members are directly appointed by the Minister for the Environment and Local Government. The chairperson is appointed by the Minister for the Environment and Local Government in consultation with the Minister for Education and Science. An Chomhairle Leabharlanna's role is to make recommendations to the Minister for the Environment and Local Government and to advise library authorities on public library matters. It also promotes and facilitates library co-operation.

The historical development of the public library service can be traced to legislation in 1855 that allowed town councils to levy a rate, not exceeding one penny, for library purposes, which could also be used for the expenses of museums or schools of arts and science. In 1902, rural district councils were empowered to adopt the Act. Initially, town councils were slow to do so. In the late nineteenth century, a few municipal libraries came into existence. However, there was no public library provision at that time over the greater part of the country. Andrew Carnegie encouraged the library movement by presenting buildings and shelving if a free site was made available and a full rate levied, but the absence of trained librarians and the limited rate levied made satisfactory development difficult. In 1920, the limit on the rate was raised to three pence with power to raise a further three pence in county boroughs subject to the consent of the central authority. In 1946, the rate limit was removed.

When the rural district councils were dissolved in 1925, county councils were given power to adopt the Library Acts for the rural areas. Urban district councils were enabled to hand over their powers to county councils. The Carnegie United Kingdom Trust, created in 1913, abandoned the policy of presenting library buildings but gave financial assistance to the county councils in establishing libraries. In 1923, the Irish Central Library for Students was established by the trust in order to supply books other than fiction that may not be available locally; it was transferred to An Chomhairle Leabharlanna in 1948.

An Chomhairle Leabharlanna carried out a survey of the public library service between 1951 and 1953, the results of which were published in two separate reports in 1955 and 1958. A scheme of grants to library authorities by way of subsidy on loan charges was introduced in 1961.

The report of the Public Library Service Review Group (1987, p. 14) noted in a review of the service between 1961 and 1986:

> There have undoubtedly been improvements in the public library service. These improvements are, however, from a very low base . . . issues increased by only 38.68 per cent from 10.55 million to 14.63 million between 1960-61 and 1985 . . . registered membership increased from 13 per cent to only 19 per cent of the population in the same period. A most serious fact is that in terms of issues and membership, the library service remained virtually static between 1980 and 1985.

The difficulties experienced by the public library service during the 1980s were reflected in most services provided by local authorities. By contrast, the 1990s witnessed substantial expansion in both library services and capital investment. By 2002 local authorities spent €75 million per annum on library services, with over eleven million visits to public libraries annually.

The Local Government Act, 1994 repealed the provisions of the Public Libraries Act, 1947 but retained the establishment of An Chomhairle Leabharlanna as a body corporate with perpetual succession. The 1994 Act empowers library authorities to take such measures, engage in such activities or do such things in accordance with the law for the provision of library services as are considered necessary or desirable. These include the provision of premises or facilities including mobile facilities; the engagement in activities and events of educational, cultural, recreational or similar interests; and the provision of such information services in conjunction with the functions of the library. Such provisions were subsequently re-enacted as part of the Local Government Act, 2001.

Library authorities are required to prepare and adopt a programme for the development of library services. The library programme contains:

> . . . an outline of the existing library services, the development objectives and priorities for the library service, the measures taken and proposed to be taken to secure those development objectives, the financial or other implications of the library development programme and other matters which are considered necessary by the library authority or as the Minister may specify in writing (section 78(6), Local Government Act, 2001).

The 1994 Act also removed some doubt that existed in relation to the power of library authorities to acquire land. This provision repealed the Public Libraries (Ireland) Act, 1955 and specifically identified the power of the library authority to acquire land by agreement or compulsorily. Part 9 (chapter 3) of the Local Government Act, 2001 repeals and restates much of the reference in the 1994 Act but takes account of the expanded library facilities in areas such as the provision of audiovisual and IT services.

A blueprint for the future development of the library services was published in 1998, entitled *Branching Out – A New Public Library Service* (Department of the Environment and Local Government, 1998a). This report recognised the importance of public libraries. It sought to ensure that Ireland would move rapidly to embrace the opportunities of the information society so as to support economic and social progress and its contribution to the establishment of an inclusive society in which all citizens can participate fully in the social and economic life of the country. The public library service was therefore viewed within a broader social policy context, where it provides a resource for information, learning, culture and imagination, especially among children and young people and can also play a role in supporting social inclusion (see, for example, An Chomhairle Leabharlanna, 1999, pp. 58–70).

The recommendations in *Branching Out* for the future development of the public library service were made under three headings: strategic, financial and service delivery. In a strategic context, the report recommended that investment in library infrastructure and services should enhance equity of access to information and that it should form part of the government's national anti-poverty strategy. In a financial context, the report highlighted the need for a revised programme of investment in library infrastructure. It recommended specifically that a sum of not less than €69.8 million should be provided directly by the exchequer in the period 1999 to 2006 for a revised programme of investment in library infrastructure. This recommendation included a cap on funding of individual projects to be set at 75 per cent, which was subsequently applied by the minister. The service delivery recommendations placed considerable emphasis on the need to extend opening hours, the need for investment in human resources and a specific requirement that library authorities carry out a fundamental review of how they serve isolated communities, whether in rural or urban areas.

In 1999, the Library Association of Ireland published a report entitled *Public Libraries 2000: National Network – Local Service*. In the context of the development of the library service as a resource for learning information, the report emphasised the important role within an information and communications technology sphere. Interestingly, the report reflects on writings by Michael Davitt in the 1880s, which called for libraries to be 'the centre of light and learning in the locality'. While Ireland has changed dramatically since that time, the fundamental view is that:

> . . . the purpose of the public library is to meet the public's needs for general education, information and recreation, to support study and the independent quest for knowledge, and to meet the public's interest in books and reading and the arts and by so doing to recognise and increase the social and cultural opportunities of every member of society.

Modern libraries provide core services including the lending of books and other materials, as well as access to reference and information services. In the context of the information society, they also facilitate access to the Internet. In addition, each library authority provides a local studies section that focuses on material produced within the authority's area or outside that area. Individual local studies sections contain material of high historical, literary and commercial value. Effectively, they comprise a resource of great national and indeed international importance. Most library authorities are also involved in activities such as lectures, exhibitions or educational courses in a wide range of topics.

Archives

The Local Government Act, 1994 requires local authorities to make arrangements for the proper management, custody, care and conservation of local records and local archives and for inspection by the public of local archives. The provisions of the 1994 Act were re-enacted and updated in the Local Government Act, 2001 (section 80). This particular function is extended to allow the local authority to acquire, by purchase, donation, bequest or loan, archival material of local interest that is in the possession of another person or body.

While, traditionally, the maintenance of archives has been a function of many library authorities, the effects of the 1994 Act, combined with the requirements of freedom of information legislation, expedited the role of local authorities in this particular area. The Department of the Environment launched an initiative providing for the co-financing of archivists in local authorities on a regional basis. Given the extent of the archival function, many local authorities proceeded, in their own right, to employ archivists and establish archives sections within their library headquarters. The archives hold records of local authority origin including minute books of council meetings. However, the service also acts as a repository for archives of relevance to the social, cultural and economic history of an area.

The combined statutory requirements on local authorities under freedom of information legislation and the local government Acts highlighted the need for local authorities to adopt best practice in records management, which was addressed in the 2002 national retention policy for local authority records.

Arts and Culture

The Arts Act, 1973 gives to local councils the reserved function of assisting the Arts Council or any person:

> . . . with money or in kind or by the provision of services or facilities (including the services of staff) . . . organising an exhibition or other event the effect of which . . . would . . . stimulate the public interest in the arts, promote the knowledge, appreciation and the practice of the arts or assist in improving the standards of the arts (section 12).

This Act opened up an entirely new range of activities and patronage to local government and a number of councils responded to this opportunity. Most local authorities make grants available to local festivals, cultural activities, artistic events and artists. Many city and county councils also employ arts officers on a co-financing basis with the Arts Council.

The provisions of section 31 of the Local Government Act, 1994 gave local authorities powers to provide amenities and associated facilities and services. These include artistic and cultural activities, sports, games, general recreational and leisure activities, civic improvements, environmental and heritage protection and improvement, public use of amenities, allotments, fairs and promotions of public safety. Section 67 of the Local Government Act, 2001 repeals and extends this provision. Examples of activities under each of these headings were further expanded upon in schedule 13 of the Local Government Act, 2001.

The development of the arts and culture function within the local government system can be traced back to the Museums and Gymnasiums Act, 1891, which gave an independent power to borough corporations and urban councils (borough and town councils) to provide museums and gymnasiums. The Local Government Act, 1955 authorised county councils and county borough councils (city councils) to contribute towards local museums. The Local Government Act, 1960 enabled city councils to provide, or assist in providing, concert halls, theatres and opera houses. These provisions were used by the city councils in both Dublin and Cork to provide financial assistance to the Olympia Theatre and Cork Opera House respectively.

Traditionally, therefore, the role of local authorities has been in the facilitation of the arts. However, this role changed significantly in the 1980s and 1990s when local government became a direct provider of museums and arts and other cultural facilities. Examples include the Geraldine Museum in the Ashe Memorial Hall, Tralee, financed by Tralee Town Council; the Waterford Treasures provided by Waterford City Council; the Cavan County Museum in Ballyjamesduff provided by Cavan County Council; and the Clare County Museum in Ennis provided by Clare County Council and Ennis Town Council. This shift in policy direction was made possible through national and EU co-financing schemes, coupled with the National Heritage Council's policy of promoting the development of local-authority-provided county museums. By 2001, ten county museums had been provided by local authorities in Cavan, Clare, Cork, Donegal, Kerry, Limerick, Louth, Monaghan, South Tipperary and Waterford.

The emphasis of local authority arts policy is now concentrated in four areas:

- support and development of individual arts practice
- enhancement of arts provision for artists and the public
- development of a vibrant public arts programme
- increase in access to and participation in the arts.

The Arts Plan 2002–2006 observes that 'new structures in local government offer considerable potential for local arts planning to be better integrated' (The Arts Council, 2002, p. 22). The five-year plan proposed a number of activities designed to bring the arts closer to local communities including agreeing with local authorities and others the responsibility for local delivery of grants, schemes and development supports. The Arts Bill, which was also published in 2002, specified that local authorities would prepare and implement plans for the development of the arts within their functional areas – a practice which was already effected within the policy framework of the local authority. The Bill also provided that local authorities can supply financial assistance for the purposes of stimulating public interest in the arts; promoting knowledge, appreciation and practice of the arts; or improving standards in the arts.

As well as running grant schemes, many local authorities provide workspace for artists, local communities and schools at arts centres and other venues, encouraging community participation and promoting the cultural traditions of the area.

One of the most visible roles of local authorities in the arts has been in the 'per cent for art scheme', which enables local authorities to dedicate a percentage of the approved cost of construction projects to a specific arts project. The overall maximum budget for this scheme is €63,500. While initially the scheme concentrated on public monuments by sculptors, local authorities have broadened its scope to include other forms of artistic expression.

Heritage

While the Local Government Act, 1994 envisaged the provision of heritage protection services by local authorities, this function did not begin in earnest until 1999, when a heritage officers programme was initiated in a partnership arrangement between local authorities and the Heritage Council. The initial purpose of the programme was to create a comprehensive network of heritage officers and a forum for the exchange of expertise and knowledge between local authorities, the Heritage Council and the general public.

The creation of a heritage function within the local authority is consistent with other services including the arts, planning and environmental services. A number of local authorities have appointed heritage officers. The priority developmental actions within a heritage context include the preparation of local heritage plans, the provision of support and advice on heritage issues to local authority officials and the preparation of heritage appraisals (a requirement which is now mandatory as part of the planning process).

The Heritage Council, established in 1995, continues to support the work of local authorities in this area. The *National Heritage Plan* (Department of Arts, Heritage, Gaeltacht and the Islands, 2002b, p. 54) envisaged 'an increasingly important role for local authorities, which are considered to be ideally placed to promote heritage conservation generally in local plans and programmes'.

The Planning and Development Act, 2000 requires a local authority to include a record of protected structures in its development plan. In this context, protected structures includes those structures which form part of the architectural heritage and which are of special architectural, historical, archaeological, artistic, cultural, scientific, social or technical interest (see also chapter 22).

The Irish Language

Section 68 of the Local Government Act, 2001 enables a local authority to take steps to encourage the use of the Irish language in the performance of its functions. This is a new statutory provision reflecting initiatives taken by individual local authorities, particularly those with Gaeltacht areas, to promote the everyday use of the Irish language. The Act provides for the issue of guidelines by the minister relating to codes of practice or other guidance as regards the use of Irish language in local government. Such codes of practice can relate to correspondence with members of the public, the provision of services in the Gaeltacht, the provision of training for employees and the promotion generally of the Irish language. The minister is further empowered to appoint an advisory group to assist in this function.

The development of a partnership arrangement between local authorities and Foras na Gaeilge (previously Bord na Gaeilge) during the 1990s, through the employment of an oifigeach Gaeilge – Irish officer – within the local authority has highlighted the key role which local authorities can play in promotion of the language. The emphasis is primarily on the development and provision of local authority services bilingually and secondly on the visible usage of Irish within the local authority area and the encouragement of other public bodies to do likewise.

Amenity and Community Services and Promoting Tourism

The provision of amenity services as defined in its traditional format within local government has been expanding since the mid-1980s when local authorities began to develop partnerships with other public and voluntary organisations to promote local amenity schemes and provide employment. The social employment scheme that operated under the umbrella of FÁS is an example of such an initiative. This scheme and its successor, the community employment scheme, carried out much needed and highly visible enhancement work within local communities.

The urban and village renewal scheme was introduced in 1995 with the objective of adopting a targeted approach to towns and villages throughout the country. The scheme was initiated under the operational programme for local urban and rural development in the period 1994 to 1999 (Government of Ireland, 1995) and is equally provided for under the national development plan for 2000 to 2006 (Government of Ireland, 2000a). It is a separate scheme from the tax-incentive-based urban renewal scheme launched in 1999, which is based on integrated area plans (see chapter 12). Under the urban and village renewal scheme, grant-aid is provided to local authorities and other bodies to finance a range of measures that would rejuvenate the social, cultural and economic life of cities, towns and villages, rehabilitate the built environment and restore and conserve important elements of Irish architecture and heritage.

Many local authorities make direct financial contributions to community and voluntary organisations for amenity and local services. This direct assistance is often applied through the housing programme, with the aim of rejuvenating local authority housing estates. Local authorities also play an active role in the annual tidy towns, *entente florale* and blue flag for beaches and marinas competitions.

Mention should also be made of the Gaming and Lotteries Act, 1956, which provides that a local authority may by resolution adopt part III of that Act, which covers the licensing of amusement halls and funfairs. The local authority may adopt the provisions of part III of the Act for the whole, or a specified part, of its administrative area, and can also decide to rescind such an adoption. Subsequent to a local authority adopting part III of the Act, applicants can apply to the District Court for a licence to run a gaming hall, amusement hall, slot machines, funfair and so forth.

In 2002, the Community Warden Service was launched in five local authorities: Galway county and city, Leitrim, Wexford and Naas. The objective of the service is to build better communities by developing contacts with the neighbourhood watch and community alert schemes and to act as a conduit on community issues.

Many local authorities have played a very proactive role in attracting tourism to their area through the provision of walkways, heritage trails, public parks and marketing activities, as well as through the protection of the natural environment, the improvement of the built environment and the provision of infrastructure.

Conclusion

The Barrington Report (1991) recommended that local authorities should be given prime responsibility in the general amenity and heritage area. While devolution of the form envisaged by the report has not occurred, a number of independent factors have combined to enhance the role of the local authority in recreation and amenity services. In particular, the public library service faced new challenges presented by the information age society in order to support economic and social progress as well as a more participative democracy.

15

Agriculture, Education, Health and Welfare

Joe MacGrath

This chapter outlines some of the functions of local authorities in the programme group 7 areas of agriculture, education, health and welfare. In comparison to other European countries, where typically local authorities would have a prominent role in these areas, for example in the provision of primary and secondary education or daycare health centres, local government responsibilities are relatively limited in Ireland (see chapters 8 and 24).

In the main, the functions of Irish local authorities in these areas could be regarded as residual functions that have remained with local government after the bulk of the responsibility for these services was transferred elsewhere. For example, county and city councils were responsible for healthcare provision until this responsibility was transferred to the health boards under the Health Act, 1970. Local authorities had extensive responsibilities in the field of agriculture until the adoption of the Agricultural Advisory Education and Research Authority Act, 1977 (see chapter 2).

The main headings within this programme group include certain functions in agriculture, land drainage, piers and harbours, coastal development works, higher education grants and contributions to the vocational education committees. The *de facto* position is that the activities covered by this programme group represent those that are generally outside the immediate control of the Irish local authorities. In many instances they merely represent a financial contribution on the part of the local authority to other agencies or the provision of a service on an agency basis.

Agriculture

Historically, county and city councils had certain functions under the Diseases of Animals Acts since 1898 (see also chapter 3 for information on the county committees of agriculture). The functions of local authorities in this area have gradually diminished, particularly since the adoption of the Agricultural Advisory Education and Research Authority Act, 1977. However, local authorities are still required to employ a veterinary inspector for certain functions. For example, under the Sheep Dipping Orders 1966 to 1977, the local authority was responsible for ensuring compliance with sheep dipping requirements. The compulsory dipping of sheep was subsequently removed although sheep scab remains a notifiable disease. Where a sheep scab outbreak occurs, flocks must be treated in the presence of a local authority inspector for which charges are levied.

The Abattoirs Act, 1988 and regulations made under that Act govern the standard of veterinary control and hygiene at domestic slaughterhouses (slaughterhouses dealing with produce for export are dealt with under separate arrangements). The main purpose of the legislation is to provide standards of veterinary control and hygiene at local slaughtering premises and to regulate the handling of animal carcasses. County and city councils are responsible for the supervision of domestic slaughterhouses in which both ante- and post-mortem meat inspections are carried out. Local authorities also carry out inspections of liquid milk to ensure quality under the Milk and Dairies Act, 1935 and regulations on the hygienic production of milk products adopted in 1996.

In 1999, local authorities entered into service contracts with the Food Safety Authority of Ireland. Under these contracts, local authorities agreed to inspect, approve and license premises and equipment used in connection with the manufacture, processing, disposal, transport and storage of food (for example butcher's shops). The contracts were made under the Food Safety Authority of Ireland Act, 1998.

In addition to these services, local authorities also operate dog control, horse control and pound services. Under the Control of Dogs Acts, 1986 to 1992, to which some amendments were made by the Local Government Act, 2001, dog control involves the employment of dog wardens and the provision of premises for impounding stray dogs. Local authorities may make bye-laws relating to the control and licensing of horses in specified urban areas and may provide for impounding facilities for stray horses under the Control of Horses Act, 1996.

During the outbreak of foot and mouth disease in 2001, the veterinary service of local authorities was deployed in a number of preventive measures in rural areas throughout the country. Although only one case of foot and mouth disease was confirmed within the Republic of Ireland, the impact on everyday life within the country generally was substantial, leading to the cancellation of sporting and other events and a significant reduction in tourism. The role played by local veterinary services during this national crisis ranged from intensification of inspection on herds in suspected foot and mouth cases to the distribution of advice on dis-infection in accordance with guidelines issued by the then Department of Agriculture, Food and Rural Development.

Drainage, Piers and Harbours and Coastal Development Works

Local authorities are also responsible for land drainage, piers and harbours and coastal development works.

Drainage districts were constituted under the Drainage Acts, 1843 to 1866. The Local Government Act, 1898 provided for the transfer of drainage districts to county councils and a number of districts were transferred under this Act. In the early 1900s, very little drainage work was done and districts fell into disrepair. In 1924, the Commissioners of Public Works were empowered to carry out repair work. Loans raised for this work were charged on the lands and the county funds. When the works were completed, they were transferred to the county councils concerned, which could levy a drainage rate on the benefited occupiers. At the time of writing, there were twenty joint drainage committees, which group together two or more county councils. The local authorities concerned make a contribution towards the costs incurred by these bodies, which are responsible for the maintenance of drainage works along specific river basins or water canals.

Perhaps of more significance for coastal local authorities is coastal protection and coastal development works. While substantial grants for harbours/piers development and coastal protection works have been made to local authorities, most of these also require a contribution from the local authority's own resources. In many cases, the aggregate size of local contributions impacts significantly on the revenue estimate. Coastal protection works are carried out under the Coast Protection Act, 1963, with grant aid from the Department of Communications, Marine and Natural Resources.

Education

The Barrington Report (1991, p. 21) recommended that:

> The functions now discharged by the Department of Education, which are essentially outside of broad planning and policy and relate to local matters, should be devolved . . . what is required is something to oversee the educational system generally at a local level which will allow for necessary local input and decision. Education is without doubt a service in which local people have a genuine and direct interest.

No progress has been made on this recommendation although regional education officers are to be established by the Department of Education and Science. There are, however, two functions relevant to the operation of local authorities within the education area in connection with contributions to vocational education committees and the higher education grants scheme.

In addition, the city councils of Dublin, Cork, Waterford and the former borough area of Dún Laoghaire until 2002 had school attendance committees responsible for ensuring that children aged from six to fifteen attend school (see chapter 3). In 2002 these responsibilities were transferred to the National Education Welfare Board, provided for under the Education Welfare Act, 2000. Also, borough and town councils may make a contribution towards the cost of providing school meals for children attending national schools in their area.

Vocational Education Committees

Local authorities appoint members to the vocational education committees (VECs), which are statutory committees under the Vocational Education Act, 1930 (see chapter 3). There are thirty-three VECs operating in respect of county council areas, the city areas of Cork, Galway, Limerick and Waterford and the former borough of Dún Laoghaire. These committees have their own corporate status and do not come within the system of city and county management. They provide and manage vocational schools and community colleges, employ administrative and teaching staff and provide vocational and lifelong education for their administrative areas. These activities are financed mainly from state funds, with a small contribution from local rates. The relevant local authorities make financial contributions to the VECs by way of statutory demand based on valuation of commercial property and also towards the total superannuation contribution and pensions of retired VEC staff. In the latter case, this is recouped in full from the Department of Education and Science.

Higher Education Grants Scheme

County and city councils administer the higher education grants scheme. Prior to 1968, county and city councils awarded grants to students pursuing courses at second and third level. The Local Authorities (Higher Education Grants) Act, 1968 abolished the making of grants for second-level education and revised the system of grants for third-level education. While the adoption of a higher education grants scheme is a reserved function of each local authority, the practice is that the scheme is a national scheme whereby grants are awarded for higher education to eligible candidates in accordance with the provision of Local Authorities (Higher Education Grants) Acts, 1968 to 1992. The schemes prescribe eligibility of candidates, residence requirements and means testing. For the award of a grant to be made, the reckonable income of the parents of the third-level student is required to conform to specific income limits. Issues such as number of dependent children are also taken into account in determining the amount of the grant. The amount paid out in grants by local authorities is recoupable from the Department of Education and Science with the exclusion of a small fixed contribution, which applies annually.

A review of the higher education grants system was underway in 2003. One of the possible changes being considered was the transfer of responsibility for administering higher education grants from local authorities to the Department of Social and Family Affairs.

Health and Welfare

County and city councils before 1971 had responsibility for providing healthcare and hospital services in their area and this represented a major area of local government activity at the time. These functions were transferred to regional health boards under the Health Act, 1970 (see chapters 2 and 3).

Local authorities continue to be responsible for the payment in respect of officers employed in their former public assistance sections prior to the health boards taking over that particular function. Local authorities are also liable for the maintenance costs of children committed to special schools by the courts.

The health functions of local authorities diminished considerably following the division of the local authority and health systems in the early 1970s. However, county and city councils continue, under the Health Act, 1970, to appoint members to the health board in whose region they are located. A significant proportion of the membership of the board is made up of representatives of county and city councils, with the remainder being elected by the medical professions and health interests or nominated by the Minister for Health and Children. At the time of writing, the health system was under review.

Coroner Service

County and city councils employ coroners to carry out post-mortems and inquiries into sudden and unexplained deaths. Under the Coroners Act, 1962, coroners are appointed by local authorities for a particular coroner district within their area, on the basis of a recommendation of the Local Appointments Commissioners. There is one coroner and one deputy coroner (who can be called upon when the coroner is unavailable due to absence or illness) for each district. In most cases, coroner districts are roughly equivalent to local authority areas. In the cases of medium-sized and larger counties, there are two or more districts within the county area.

A review of the coroner service, published in 2000, argued that 'appointment by the local authority is a matter of historical precedent' (Working Group on the Review of the Coroner Service, 2000, p. 44) and recommended that in future coroners be appointed by the Minister for Justice, Equality and Law Reform and that coroner districts be based on regions rather than local authority areas. At the time of writing, legislation was expected to be introduced to give effect to these proposals.

Conclusion

The functions of local authorities in the areas of agriculture, education, health and welfare are limited, typically involving the making of contributions or the operation of schemes under an agency basis for other services. Total expenditure represents some 6 per cent of annual revenue expenditure, most of which is accounted for by the higher education grants scheme. The reserved functions of the local authority include the appointment of persons to serve as members of health boards, vocational education committees and certain other bodies. The local authority is also empowered to examine and consider a drainage scheme sent to it by the Commissioner of Public Works. While the preparation and submission of a scheme for higher education grants is also a reserved function, in practice a nationally determined set of criteria are adopted by each of the county and city councils.

In the context of the local government reform proposals with specific reference to devolution of functions, it is perhaps in this area that the greatest scope for change exists. The 1991 Barrington Report advocated a range of functions that could be administered by the Irish local government system. Specifically, the expert committee recommended the devolution of functions in areas including health, policing, education and welfare.

In 1997, the Devolution Commission proposed a grouping of services under three headings: local social services; local economic and development services; and local environmental, infrastructure and transport services. It recommended that 'the focus of devolution should be on grouping services so that they are delivered at the appropriate level (regional, county or area) under local political direction and managed in an integrated way in order to achieve the synergy that such an approach can deliver' (p. 15). The local social services grouping advocated by the commission included social welfare services, community health services and education services. The local economic and development services grouping included agriculture and rural development services, with a wide range of other enterprise, marine-based and tourism services. The commission concluded that all of these services are capable of being provided under local political direction.

16

Community and Enterprise

Jack Keyes

Through the development of ideas in policy discourses, systems of meaning can be changed. Through changing ways of thinking governance, authority may be exercised in different ways and material resources allocated by many parties in different patterns (Healey, 1997, p. 61).

Local government's role in the area of enterprise, economic and community development may be summarised as significant. It has been partially limited in its effect locally because of the centralisation of decision making and poor funding availability. In recent years, however, new thinking, expressed in an institutional context by structures such as city/county development boards, has led to an expansion of interest and activity.

This chapter examines the theoretical and practical developments in the areas of local development, governance and partnership/collaborative planning. It focuses on other actors in the local development scene – for example ADM (Area Development Management) Ltd, area partnerships, LEADER groups, county enterprise boards (CEBs) – and examines their current and future contribution. Local government's traditionally strong role in physical planning and economic development is acknowledged. However, new challenges are posed by globalisation, the knowledge-based economy, social cohesion, entrepreneurship and the participation and development of community. Areas where local government, working in a leadership role and in collaboration with many diverse actors, can expand its effectiveness and deal with these challenges include: enterprise development, local social partnership, strategic thinking and planning, cultural activity, active citizenship, co-ordination of service delivery, increased value for money and integration of social, cultural and economic development.

Definitions of development vary. The philosopher Denis Goulet (1995) named life sustenance, esteem and freedom as the essential elements. The UNDP (1994) lists the following forms of security as essential to development: economic, food, health, environmental, personal, community and political. These definitions illustrate the complex challenge to future local governance.

A Brief History

Perhaps the wonder of local government in relation to local development is how it achieved so much with so little. It could be argued that development would have been almost non-existent without the energy and commitment of elected representatives and administrative and technical staff. Local authorities have been active in the attraction of industry, the enhancement of infrastructure and the consolidation of a strong local representative democracy. This role has been expanding since the early 1990s. The creation of infrastructure has been central to local government's contribution. Excellence in engineering and administration, reinforced in recent decades by architects, planners and other professions, developed many of the physical components of Irish society.

Consider the case of a typical traditional water supply, so essential to underpin many of the securities listed above. A project is mooted, based on local need identified by technical and political strands. Local feasibility studies follow. The project progresses by working in partnership with officials from the Department of the Environment and Local Government. The proposal is examined on a regional basis, very often through formal contact between local authorities. Private sector involvement often begins with the engagement of a consultant. The search for funding from central government continues. Eventually, detailed design and tender processes are followed by further private sector involvement such as civil engineering and mechanical/electrical plant contracting. After completion and commissioning, the maintenance of the project becomes the job of the local authority. Underpinning the above is an effective administrative system. The areas served by the project are now in a position to develop their local economy.

The local authority has played a proactive role for the community at all stages of the process by networking with local government, contracting and working in partnership with the private sector and managing the project from inception to delivery. This traditional role is evolving with the introduction of public private partnerships and other alternative delivery mechanisms. Enhanced consultation mechanisms are being used to inform and facilitate the input of the community into the process. Social partners and communities now input into the decision-making process through the strategic policy committee and community development board structures.

Local government's role in educational and cultural development is significant. Recent improvements in the arts and heritage areas build on the notable work of the library service (see chapters 14 and 22). The move towards more direct involvement with the community has gathered momentum and is likely to expand.

While the pragmatic and energetic role of local government in local development must be fully acknowledged it has often restricted itself to:

- economic planning without a full consideration of social, environmental and cultural development
- physical development which managed rather than facilitated the interdependence between the economy, the environment and society
- maximising efficiency and increasing value for money without focusing fully on quality of life outcomes
- rational policy making and incrementalism, relying on the formal mechanisms of governance as opposed to facilitating a balanced interaction between formal and informal structures, the latter giving voice to many who have been excluded from the decision-making processes of society.

New Initiatives

In the 1980s, high unemployment, a lack of opportunities for young people and the long-term unwaged and the existence of marginalised groups led to a range of new initiatives. A proverbial jigsaw of structures, policies and procedures emerged. Partnership processes, which helped to provide the basis for national economic growth, were equally linked with developments locally. The persistence of problems in certain areas shaped a policy response that emphasised: social partnership, local development initiatives to create employment, local co-ordination of services and an enhanced role for the community sector. This response marked a move towards a new localism in Irish public policy, developed with EU support, but largely outside of local government (see chapter 24).

There have been a number of attempts to reform local institutions (see chapter 4). The Barrington Report (1991, pp. 14–15) identified the following deficiencies:

- little integration of public services at the different levels of government, particularly local and regional
- the lack of a coherent and comprehensive delivery mechanism below city/county level and the relatively narrow range of functions assigned to local government
- the poor relationship between local government and the community sector.

The reports of the Devolution Commission (1996 and 1997) and the Task Force on the Integration of Local Government and Local Development Systems (Department of the Environment and Local Government, 1998e) and *Better Local Government* (Department of the Environment, 1996) advanced the thinking on these issues and instituted the process of reform. These changes are addressed below. At this stage it is appropriate to examine the role of agencies, other than the local authority, which have been involved in the delivery of local services and in some cases the development of partnership approaches in the local arena.

Area-based partnerships between state funders and local development groups had for some time formed the basis of Gaeltacht development co-operatives. This concept was applied during the late 1980s in initiatives such as integrated rural development companies. Strong informal networking at local level had been a cornerstone of local development for many decades and existing skills were harnessed into emerging formalised arrangements.

Local partnership programmes can be divided into two categories: those which promote greater co-ordination in service provision and those which encourage local economic and social development. Examples of the former include the third EU poverty programme (1989 to 1994), community development programmes, early area-based responses to long-term unemployment, local employment services and the integrated services initiative. A feature of these was the targeting of resources at a defined geographical area or on occasion towards a particular marginalised group.

Turning to local socio-economic development initiatives, seven programmes were established to promote local development during the 1990s. This novel movement recognised the general role which local actions can play as a catalyst for economic, social and environmental action. The programmes differed slightly as some emphasised local job creation while others concentrated on targeting areas or groups experiencing social exclusion. Partnership structures are the principal delivery mechanism. While organisational forms vary, most share common features including:

- local groups drawing up their own local development plans
- funding decisions taken locally
- involvement of local communities and individuals within a locally co-ordinated framework
- establishment of links between local development initiatives and local authorities, the latter being recognised as the main 'engines of development and the providers of support infrastructure and services for local communities' (*Operational Programme for Local Urban and Rural Development 1994–1999*).

The seven programmes and their important characteristics are summarised in table 16.1.

Table 16.1 Local Development Programmes, 1990s

	Area Programme for Integrated Rural Development (1988 to 1990)	Global Grant for Local Development (1992 to 1995)	LEADER I and II (1991 to 1994 and 1995 to 1999)	Local Enterprise Programme (1993 to 1999)	Urban Community Initiatives (1995 to 1999)	Programme of Integrated Development in Disadvantaged Areas (1995 to 1999)	Territorial Employment Pacts (1997 to 1999)
Support agency	Department of Agriculture	ADM Ltd	Department of Agriculture and Food	Department of Enterprise and Employment	Department of Tourism, Sport and Recreation	ADM Ltd	Department of the Taoiseach
Resources	€1.9m	€10.2m	€98.2m	€77.8m	€19.7m	€99.7m	€0.97m
Aim	Promotion of small businesses and other activities	Promotion of community, enterprise and other initiatives	Promotion of small businesses and other development activities	Promotion of small enterprise and an enterprise culture	Promotion of community, employment and minor infrastructural initiatives	Promotion of community, enterprise, education and employment initiatives	Co-ordination of local employment creation initiatives
Target area	Rural communities	Targeted communities	Rural communities	Unemployed and entrepreneurs	Disadvantaged urban communities	Disadvantaged and other local communities	High unemployment areas
Structure	Local support groups	Local partnership companies and groups (40)	Local development groups (37)	Local enterprise boards (35)	Steering committees (3)	Local partnership companies (38), community groups and sectoral bodies	Local and regional partnership structures
Description	To improve employment, earnings, quality of life and a sense of community in rural areas	To promote local socio-economic development in twelve areas	To develop a partner-ship dynamism, local animation etc. Also to provide financial assistance to enterprise and employment projects mainly in rural tourism	To support micro-enterprises at local level	To develop innovative management structures in three urban areas with an enhanced role for local authorities	To promote local socio-economic development through a variety of measures and to focus on the unemployed and community development	To maximise the job creation potential of the structural funds through local initiative, partnership, innovation and integration

Source: substantially based on table 3.2 in Walsh et al., (1998, pp. 40–1)

Up to 1999, funding for these various programmes relied heavily on EU structural monies. This situation has been largely reversed under the national development plan (NDP) for 2000 to 2006 where funding for these programmes is more dependent upon the exchequer (Government of Ireland, 2000a). Under the NDP for 1994 to 1999, the local development programme broke down into three sub-groups: local enterprise, integrated development of designated disadvantaged and other areas, and urban and village renewal (local authority based) (Government of Ireland, 1993). These accounted for just 3.7 per cent of Structural Funds during the 1994 to 1999 period. Funding for community initiatives (for example NOW, Horizon, LEADER) amounted to €300 million. The important distinction for practitioners in local government is the apparent discretion with which this money could be allocated and spent in contrast to the tight central control over, albeit far greater, blocks of finance administered by local authorities.

County/City Enterprise Boards

Enterprise boards promote local development through the provision of grant aid and advisory/management ('soft') supports to micro enterprises (ten employees or fewer) in manufacturing, services and tourism. Their grant aid role has decreased under the NDP for 2000 to 2006. There are thirty-five enterprise boards, of which there are four each in Dublin and Cork, two each in Limerick, Waterford and Tipperary and one in each of the remaining counties. They dispose of an annual budget of some €25.4 million, of which €20.3 million is allocated to enterprise development (1999 figures).

The enterprise boards are relatively staff intensive (an average of four or five employees disbursing an annual budget of €762,000. The provision of training and grant assistance to the emerging enterprises and non-traded services sector with a minimum of dead-weight or displacement has contributed to fostering local entrepreneurship and wealth creation. More importantly, the enterprise boards have been a significant force for employment growth in their areas, having assisted in the creation of 11,000 jobs (all year 2000 figures). They have had a traditionally close relationship with local government.

ADM-Funded Partnerships and Community Groups

Partnerships are independent companies with a board of directors drawn at local level from representatives of the social partners, the state agencies and community and voluntary organisations active in economic and social development. The structure of each board both encourages and enables it to work in partnership and within an ethos of participation and consultation. The first partnerships were established in 1991 and the majority in 1995 and 1996. The NDP for 2000 to 2006 and the *Programme for Prosperity and Fairness* for 2000 to 2003 (Government of Ireland, 2000c) continued their role with no change of administrative boundary.

Their work is important because they focus exclusively on issues of combating disadvantage and on target groups such as the long-term unemployed. In addition, there are a number of ADM-supported community groups outside designated areas of disadvantage which operate to a similar agenda. An OECD review (Sabel, 1996) described them as 'extraordinarily innovative but they have been better at creating new things than at building stable institutions that embody and extend their innovations'. Their mandate was to improve co-ordination and evaluation at local level of mainstream programmes and policies to ensure their effective delivery to the long-term unemployed and the socially excluded and from this experience to contribute to the national policy-making process.

The first partnerships were established under the *Programme for Economic and Social Progress* (Government of Ireland, 1991). The social partnership at local level was, up to 2000, applied through the process, procedures and actions of partnerships. Partnerships were sometimes perceived to work alongside other existing systems without the traditional democratic controls. This perception was exacerbated by the fact that councillors were not, as a result of a decision made at central level on the establishment of the original partnerships, represented on the boards of area partnership companies. This decision has subsequently been reversed.

ADM is responsible for managing the programme of integrated development in disadvantaged areas, evaluating progress, providing support and encouraging new initiatives. This private company is also responsible for facilitating the dissemination of know-how and good practice within the programme.

LEADER Groups

LEADER is an EU community initiative which is based on the bottom-up principle and provides the opportunity for the rural community, through local action groups, to involve itself directly in its own development. Thirty-seven groups – thirty-four area-based groups covering all rural parts of the country and three with a sectoral remit – have been approved to implement local development plans which they themselves have drawn up. Total funding under LEADER II was about €110.5 million (2000 figures). The LEADER+ initiative, approved in 2001, continues this work for the period from 2000 to 2006, alongside a parallel national rural development programme. This is funded through the exchequer and during the 2000 to 2006 period funds some of the groups that received LEADER funding during 1994 to 1999.

LEADER has been effective in mobilising community and voluntary effort for local development. As an area-based approach, the programme identified and responded to local needs and opportunities and local knowledge is brought to bear on investment decisions. In general, the groups' boards have a tripartite structure comprising representatives of the community and voluntary sector, state agencies and local authorities and the private sector (farming, local business and so forth). This structure has been an effective means of co-ordinating activities at local level, particularly from the point of view of the participation of state agencies.

Further details on county/city enterprise boards, area partnerships and LEADER groups are contained in chapter 3.

County/City Development Boards

The relative success of the above three groups/initiatives illustrates the positive outcomes of the decentralisation of decision making, based on a bottom-up, multi-agency approach. Different local needs require different local actions. Reform is instituted without the influence of a highly directive centre and citizens become, to some degree, the co-producers of services as well as consumers of them. The response to the ambiguity and complexity of the modern world involves pragmatic institutions addressing difficult issues whose solutions change in time.

In spite of the success of these initiatives, a number of reports highlight a degree of overlap, inefficiency and occasional poor service delivery. As outlined below, the government's response to such reports was to establish county/city development boards (CDBs). CDBs led by local government were established in 2000 in each county and city to bring about the more coherent delivery of services by state agencies at local level. Central to their work is a commitment to combat social exclusion and promote local development. The CDBs were also set up against the background of the need to bring local authorities and local development bodies (area partnerships, LEADER groups and county/city enterprise boards) closer together and to avoid inter-agency duplication and turf wars.

The CDBs are composed of representatives of state agencies (for example FÁS, Garda Síochána, health board, vocational education committee), the social partners, local authorities and local development bodies. Thus representatives from farming, trade unions, business, local government, the community/voluntary sector and the larger state-funded agencies work together to produce a county/city vision to guide local development over a ten-year period. The CDBs adopted their county/city strategies for economic, social and cultural development in 2002. The process was overseen by an interdepartmental task force chaired by the Minister for the Environment and Local Government. Each CDB includes the chairpersons of each local authority SPC (strategic policy committee) and the county/city cathaoirleach/mayor and manager. Its strategies propose inter-agency actions as a response to local complex issues, thus building on social partnership principles.

The central aim of the CDBs is to ensure gaps are filled and co-ordination is achieved. This represents an institutional approach that recognises the valuable work being done by a variety of organisations and the value of:

- increased local participation/partnership
- community development based upon a process of collaborative planning
- democratic legitimacy based upon an integrated framework of elective and participative forms of governance.

In this way the achievements resulting from allowing local development initiatives to thrive without the imposition of a common spatial framework or organisational structure can continue. This successful and uniquely Irish approach to local development may gain fresh momentum within a flexible local spatial framework.

Local Government's Changing Role in Local Development

The Department of the Environment and Local Government published the *Report of the Task Force on the Integration of Local Government and Local Development Systems* in 1998, *Preparing the Ground: Guidelines for the Progress from Strategy Groups to County/City Development Boards* in 1999 and *A Shared Vision for County/City Development Boards: Guidelines on the CDB Strategies for Economic, Social and Cultural Development* in 2000. These reports attempted to address many existing weaknesses particularly in relation to local government's role in responding to factors in its operational environment. A key feature of this process is the existence at central level of a cross-departmental team of senior officials to plan and oversee implementation of the local reform process. The increased level of administrative buy-in at national level has helped the local social partnership process to advance. The key features of the above reports are:

- a focus on the implementation of a model of good governance at local level
- an emphasis on multi-sectoral co-ordination
- a broad socio-economic planning model
- linkages with all connected subsequent policies issued by the government.

A key feature in terms of institutional reform is the county/city development board structure and, in particular, the primary responsibility to set out a strategy to include:

- a ten-year vision
- associated three to five-year manageable targets
- the encompassing of all local public services
- democratic endorsement by the local elected members
- wide cross-sectoral representation
- a role in proofing organisational plans and programmes.

As part of this process, all public sector policies corresponded with this approach; in particular, the statutory development plans were also required to take account of this economic and social strategy. See figure 16.1 for an illustration of the institutional framework for the CDB process.

Figure 16.1 Institutional Framework

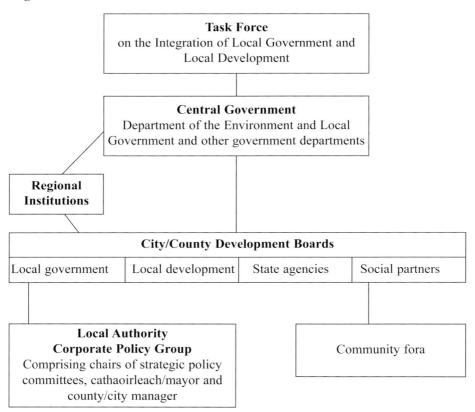

There is now a clear recognition in the policy-making process of the link between spatial considerations and socio-economic planning. This is particularly relevant in the context of the NDP for 2000 to 2006, wherein there is a clear focus on the local role of the CDBs particularly in terms of the co-ordination of local service delivery including all social inclusion measures. CDBs will play a pivotal role in developing the relationship between public service planning at county/city and regional authority levels. This aspect is also highlighted in the *Programme for Prosperity and Fairness*, while statutory recognition is provided in sections 10(1), 11(2) and 12(1) of the Planning and Development Act, 2000. The theme is further developed in section 129 of the Local Government Act, 2001, which gives specific statutory provision to the CDB process.

In policy terms, this reflects the emergence of a local process charged with strategic development and with the necessary statutory backing to make things happen. In addition, CDBs are composed of agencies primarily concerned with operational delivery of public services at a local level. Again, from an institutional perspective, this structure is reciprocated in the regional authority/ assembly structures mainly by way of the various monitoring and evaluation committees.

The CDB process is a serious attempt to address the deficiencies associated with the four models of developed governance: representative democracy, pluralist democracy, corporation and clientelism, all of which, it is argued, are no longer capable of playing the role of facilitator. The new model arising is based on collaborative planning from the process of sustainable development. Healey (1997) identifies three approaches associated with the drive to reform, which seek to achieve processes of inclusion, collaboration and consensus building by respecting the widening network of the public management stakeholder. These approaches are:

- criterion driven – devolving public service delivery to the most appropriate level (subsidiarity)
- entrepreneurial consensus – a form of local corporatism concerned with the management and facilitation of horizontal networks associated with local development
- inclusionary augmentation – providing specific inclusionary and collaborative processes to avoid the exclusion of stakeholders.

These three processes reflect changes in public management, but are also key to that change.

Social Inclusion/Cohesion

National policy documents have increasingly focused on progressing the concept of a more socially inclusive society. At a local level, one of the key principles in the preparation of county/city strategies is recognition of the needs of the socially excluded. The development of community and the enhancement of enterprise will increasingly take cognisance of social inclusion implications. Local government's role in this area has been significant largely through the delivery of its many services. This role is now being enhanced through its leadership of the CDB process, the development of a local government anti-poverty network of officials and councillors and an increasing recognition of the need to proof actions against the effect on the socially excluded and poverty.

In addition to contributing to a rising economic tide cognisance is increasingly taken of the need for targeted local responses and for increased levels of community development. At the time of writing, a number of pilot social inclusion units have been established in nine local authorities. Social inclusion is likely to become a priority strategic issue for local government over the coming decades and the issue is dealt with in further detail in chapter 23.

Active Citizenship, Participation and Representative Democracy

The concept of European citizenship is becoming more dynamic as the EU strives to construct a sense of common purpose. The then European Commission President, Jacques Santer, speaking at the first European Social Policy Forum in March 1996, stated that 'Dialogue is essential and nothing can be done without grassroots involvement. We must set out on the road towards a more active participatory society'.

> Active citizenship, taken broadly, can mean any form of productive contribution to society . . . people's capacity to take an active role in public affairs whether through formal democratic structures, through the press, through public debate, through associations, political parties, trade unions, local clubs and societies or simply through informal networks and mutual aid amongst neighbours, friends and family (Chanan, 1997, p. 5).

Enhancing the importance of representative democracy and increasing the importance of the role of the elected representative is a central aim of the reform process in which the CDB sits. This recognises the centrality of the representative system to Ireland's democratic and value systems and to human freedom.

The local government system, while seriously under-resourced, has delivered an outcome which reflects well on the work of the local elected representatives over many decades. It is now embracing the new challenge of local social partnership through structured active co-operation with local development bodies, state agencies and social partners. Central to this is the fostering of participation of people in their communities, the development of ideas and the raising of awareness. Citizens have both responsibilities and rights. They are entitled to govern and be governed by the local governance system. They have the right to be an active participant, to know and understand the policies and decisions of public agencies, to have their interests and concerns taken on board and to participate in the decision-making process. Active citizenship is a means of strengthening democracy.

The community/voluntary sector's involvement at local institutional level follows on from the increasing voice of the sector in national social partnership. SPC and CDB structures are designed to develop a meaningful voice for the sector in the decision-making process. Central to this has been the establishment and growth of the community fora within the CDB framework. The fora have contributed significantly to the process of strategic thinking that is central to the CDB strategies.

Thus a local governance system that recognises the public as citizens will seek to build active citizenship. The development of activity is the antidote to apathy. Citizens do not speak with one voice and a necessary part of democracy is the balancing of the views of one group against those of another. A leadership role must be provided by the institutions of governance and in particular by a reformed local government system. This leadership is informed by its active citizenry.

The question of local governance and participation is further discussed in chapter 28.

Local Enterprise Development

Local government's role in local economic development has been pivotal for many decades. This has been achieved by:

- prudent management of service delivery mechanisms
- physical development planning
- local regulation (for example planning control)
- use of informal networks to bring key local players together
- a particularly strong role in infrastructural development.

The role is now expanding into areas such as:
- leadership of local development and the development of multi-sectoral responses
- enhanced role of ICT in dealing with enterprise
- increased use of discretionary funding to facilitate local entrepreneurship and economic development.

Thus local government's contribution to enterprise development is likely to increase in significance as regional responses to the challenges of the global economy grow in importance. The CDB process brings together enterprise entities that contribute to local strategic planning and implementation in a spirit of innovation and partnership.

Conclusion

Local government has played a central role in the areas of enterprise/broad community development for many decades but particularly since the early 1990s. New challenges, posed by a rapidly changing macro-environment, require responses in areas such as social cohesion, entrepreneurship, participation of citizens, development of community and creation of a knowledge-based economy. Local social partnership has been part of a unique response to the new challenges. County/city enterprise boards, ADM-funded area partnerships and groups and LEADER initiatives are examples of a local response developed outside of the local government system. The creation of county/city development boards has established a new framework for local governance based on the successes of existing initiatives but embedded in an institutional framework that pays particular attention to co-ordination of services, collaborative actions and strategic planning. Local government is taking the leadership role in this new institutional environment.

Horizontal Themes

17

Human Resources

Gerard O'Beirne

The human resource function is concerned with the management of an organisation's work force. Given the diverse and dynamic nature of human beings and the rate of change in the modern work environment, this is indeed a considerable task. Local authorities employ in excess of 35,000 people at an annual cost of over €600 million (on average, 30 to 40 per cent of annual revenue expenditure). Local government services are labour intensive in nature and therefore the effectiveness of staff management policies and practices is a key determinant of the effectiveness of the overall system.

The local authority staff function is often viewed as a small internal support service solely associated with the human resource department. In practice, however, the staff function is discharged at a national level in order to ensure consistency and co-ordination and at a local level through line managers and the staff of the human resource department. This chapter details some of the principal human resource features of the local government system as well as current practices and trends.

Role of Central Government

Under the Local Government Act, 2001, local authorities are provided with the general power to employ 'such and so many persons' as they may from time to time think proper and to determine and alter their remuneration and conditions of employment. This broad power is tempered by the financial constraints that exist within a system which allows for limited local discretion on the generation of additional revenue. More significantly, the Department of the Environment and Local Government exercises overall control in relation to issues such as staff numbers, grading structures, recruitment practices and employment conditions. General pay negotiations are conducted centrally via the Local Government Management Services Board and with the Department of Finance in the background exercising a regulatory role on behalf of the state within an overall context of public expenditure restraint.

This centralised framework has significantly advanced the creation of an integrated and cohesive local government system, within which both common practices and values have been established across the 114 local authorities. The establishment of common conditions of employment has enabled local authority employees to view their careers in the context of a broad local government service rather than an individual authority. Local authorities, as employers, can readily tap into a broad local government labour market and benefit from the transfer of experience and the creation of functional networks. For human resource practitioners, it avoids duplication of effort in relation to many industrial relations issues and prevents both comparative pay claims and migration of the most talented staff to the best-resourced authorities.

It is, however, generally accepted that the controls exercised by central government were historically of such a degree as to inhibit local authorities in the execution of their plans and in the development of responsive customer-focused services. The capacity of an individual local authority to respond quickly to specific local opportunities and demand variations may be reduced by the need to secure central government approval for matters such as the creation of additional posts or the making of variations to employment terms and conditions. Rigid central control can also have a negative impact on the level of accountability within the system and the acceptance of local responsibility or ownership for staffing decisions.

In response to these difficulties, some flexibility has been introduced through the devolution of responsibility for aspects of specific staff matters to local authorities (for example staff suspensions and dismissals, superannuation and creation of new posts). Under *Better Local Government*, the department has expressed a commitment to further extend this process. The extent of future devolution may be limited by the need for local authorities to adhere to government policies on public sector pay and employment levels and the need for collective action to ensure consistency and avoidance of comparative claims.

Dual Structure

Administrative and technical grades have traditionally been organised in two separate hierarchical systems. Staff in both streams report upward through relatively long lines of command, which only formally link at the highest levels. This parallel system or dual structure has been the subject of much criticism. Technical/professional staff with extensive qualifications and experience often feel that relative to their administrative colleagues, they are on the periphery of the decision-making process. The matter is further compounded by limited opportunities for cross-disciplinary mobility whereby technical/professional grades can only formally secure a more central position in the decision-making process by seeking promotion to the most senior positions within the organisation. To achieve this end, such staff would have to abandon their chosen profession in favour of a management role. Although not critical to the same extent, administrative staff have expressed frustration at being responsible or seen to be responsible for specific work areas but without any control or influence over the technical input.

Overall, the dual structure is seen as increasing the potential for demarcation disputes and rivalries. It facilitates responsibility avoidance and can lead to delays arising from the duplication of approvals both within and between each of the parallel streams. *Better Local Government* recognised the need to address this issue in its attempts to advance the creation of a more customer-focused and democratic system. Below the level of county/city manager, it saw the abolition of the senior administrative and technical positions and the introduction of a new grade of director of services. Based on the programme manager concept, each director has responsibility for one or more of the local authority service areas and competitions for vacancies arising at this level are open to all staff within both streams. *Better Local Government* has also resulted in the creation of new senior administrative and senior technical posts below the level of director. Consequently, while not seeking to underestimate the positive benefits of these restructuring reforms, the dual structure remains in the system, albeit not at the same level as previously. It is equally important not to overstate the problem or perhaps more accurately not to understate the common sense and flexible approach adopted by local authority workers and management in the operation of the system to the best effect.

There has been an increasing acceptance and recognition of a broader concept of professionalism within the service as a result of the recruitment of skilled staff in generalist areas, for example finance, social services and information technology, as well as a greater acknowledgement of the skilled nature of existing generalist posts. At a practical level, technical and administrative staff, particularly in the small to medium-sized authorities, work in close proximity to each other, thereby giving rise to significant formal and informal communications at all levels. Improvements have also been supported by the increased delegation of responsibility to all staff, but particularly the delegation of responsibility for operational matters to front-line staff, for example area engineers. In addition greater use has been made of cross-disciplinary and sometimes cross-departmental project teams, often leading to informal cross-disciplinary reporting relationships.

It is suggested that future developments in relation to the dual structure could productively concentrate on attempts to match the pay and conditions of posts in one stream with the other. By having at least some administrative and technical staff on the same pay and conditions, work could be assigned to the postholder from whichever stream had the most appropriate competencies and abilities. This approach would preserve professional roles and jobs and allow flexibility in work allocation. It would create the potential for more formal cross-disciplinary reporting relationships and facilitate the development and better utilisation of the best talent from both streams.

Grading

The local authority grading system is structured on the basis of relatively steep hierarchies. Clerical/administrative grades start at clerical officer (grade III) and rise through assistant staff officer (grade IV), staff officer (grade V), senior staff officer (grade VI), administrative officer (grade VII), senior executive officer (grade VIII) and onto the senior management grades of director of services and county/city manager.

On the core technical/professional side, the structure begins at graduate level moving to assistant, executive, senior executive and senior, before advancement to the director of services and management positions.

The most numerous groups of workers within the local authority service comprise manual workers and tradespeople, often referred to as outdoor workers. In addition to a general services supervisory post there are a number of sub-structures including up to five grades in the craftworkers' structure, eight grades in the general operative (and related grades) structure and five grades in the water and sewerage caretakers' structure.

Long bureaucratic structures can inhibit efficient service delivery and prompt decision making. They can also result in demotivation and feelings of resentment amongst employees. In theory, grades have relative worth by virtue of their associated work complexity or by virtue of the contribution the post makes to the achievement of organisational objectives. Over the years, incremental adjustments have been made as a result of pressures arising from the need to retain skills, the need to limit/resolve industrial relations disputes or the need to control costs. At the same time, the nature of individual jobs and their complexities have changed dramatically due to the introduction of new work practices, information technology and the need for additional or new skills in order to respond to changing work demands. For these reasons, the grading system can sometimes appear to be somewhat illogical.

However, grading is the key determinant of the level of an individual's financial reward and while many employees excel in their performances they do not avail of or secure promotions to higher grades. This may be due to the fact that opportunities (which are limited relative to the number of aspiring candidates) can be scarce for long periods of time or the fact that an employee may be particularly successful and satisfied in his or her existing post. The individual local authority does not have the freedom to match excellent performances with additional financial reward whether by way of accelerated incremental progression or otherwise. The matter is further compounded by the fact that despite grading purporting to provide some expression of relative work complexity and anticipated performance value it is becoming increasingly difficult to discern real distinctions between some grades within and across local authorities.

Attempts to reform hierarchical structures generally concentrate on grade flattening or the introduction of broadbands of grades with variable incremental progression linked to performance. Within the local government system some progress has been made through the amalgamation of grades up to grade III and further progress could be made within the grade IV to VII posts. As with the practical operation of the dual structure, local authority staff have adopted a very flexible approach to the grading system, both in terms of acceptance of responsibility and the flexibility of reporting/working practices. Given the need for the issue to be considered in a broader public service context, and the potential for significant cost increases or industrial relations difficulties, it may take some time for further rationalisation to be secured.

Recruitment

Local authorities are multi-functional organisations that operate in an environment that is characterised by varied and somewhat competing demands and expectations, which always exceed the financial and other material resources available. As such, their capacity to attract and retain creative and energetic people is a key determinant of the extent to which they can exploit, to maximum effect, the opportunities available and deliver services of the highest quality. Recruitment in the local authority sector is particularly important given the labour-intensive nature of the system and the 'job for life' culture whereby terminations (whether related to outward mobility or disciplinary proceedings) are relatively rare. Historically the local government system has been very successful in attracting able recruits, partly because of the lack of alternative opportunities and partly because of the selection processes employed to secure the best possible candidates.

Selection on the basis of ability, with objective criteria being used in the assessment process, is an essential requirement for an effective and transparent recruitment system. One of the most crucial developments for local authorities in this regard was the establishment of the Office of the Local Appointments Commissioners in 1926. Mirrored on the Civil Service Commissioners, its purpose has been to select and recommend to local authorities persons for appointment to senior managerial and professional grades. For the remainder of positions, selection is effected by the local authorities themselves within the boundaries of well-established practices common to all local authorities. Under the proposed Public Service Management (Recruitment and Appointments) Bill (to be introduced in the summer of 2003), a new public appointments service will be established as the centralised recruitment and selection body for senior management positions in a variety of public sector bodies including local authorities. It is envisaged that commissioners of public service appointments will be responsible for the probity of the recruitment process in the local authority sector through the use of codes of practice and a licensing regime.

On the clerical/administrative side, entry to the local service can be gained at grade III or IV. Appointments to grades V to VII are made by promotional competitions held at local level with access confined to those with the specified work experience in organisations in a common recruitment pool including any local authority, health board, vocational education committee, institute of technology, the General Medical Services (Payments) Board, St James's Hospital Board, Beaumont Hospital Board, An Bord Altranais, the Local Government Computer Services Board, and the Border, Midlands and Western and South and Eastern Regional Assemblies. An exception to the foregoing relates to appointments within Dublin City Council and Dún Laoghaire-Rathdown, Fingal and South Dublin county councils where, because of the large numbers employed, competitions are restricted to eligible staff members from within the authorities themselves. In the main, the bulk of appointments at grades IV to VII are awarded to people who have spent some years in the local government service.

Appointments to the posts of senior executive officer, director of services and city/county manager are filled by the Local Appointments Commissioners through external competitions open to all persons who fulfil the established qualification criteria. While past local government service is not part of the qualification criteria, the majority of successful candidates are sourced from within the broad local government system.

For technical/professional grades, selection competitions are generally open but many of the middle grade positions also require past local authority experience (particularly non-engineering posts). Consequently there is limited potential for people outside the service to join above the entry grades. Senior technical/professional posts are also filled following selection by the Local Appointments Commissioners, with the majority of appointees once again coming from within the system.

Vacancies arising within the outdoor grading structure are filled by a mixture of internal competitions (confined to staff members within the authority) and open competitions (usually filled by people within the general locality).

Over the years, there have been a number of important functional or organisational reform packages agreed at national level between representatives of the local authorities and staff unions. These agreements have given rise to promotional opportunities confined to staff members within the local authorities under each county/city manager's control. Local authorities can restrict some competitions at grade IV level to existing staff and many local authorities also confine some of their outdoor grade vacancies as promotional opportunities for existing staff. In addition, the county/city manager can create new posts, up to the level of grade VII in the administrative structure and technician grade I in the technical structure, with an option to fill such posts for the first time by means of confined competitions. This power is subject to a number of requirements including the necessity to stay within budgetary and approved staffing levels.

In deciding the most appropriate recruitment practice, human resource practitioners will be conscious of the competing arguments relating to the confinement of competitions to local staff, the confinement of competitions to those with any local authority experience and the extension of competitions to an unrestricted pool of candidates. Issues arising include the need to maintain and enhance existing staff morale, the need to develop and implement effective career development policies, the need to secure industrial peace and the need to limit induction costs and uncertainty in the recruitment process. Also of relevance will be the need to attract new ideas, skills and knowledge and secure a broader experience base.

While the mixture of mechanisms employed in the local government system for the filling of posts may appear to provide a reasonable balance between these competing demands, there are a number of difficulties particularly in the clerical/administrative and some technical grades. Qualification requirements relating to past local government or similar experience effectively convert middle grade vacancies into promotional opportunities either for staff within the individual authority or within the service itself. Past arguments relating to the extensive pool of candidates available within the local government system are becoming increasingly questionable. Societal changes relating to workforce participation by both partners/spouses as well as high transfer costs may limit the degree of mobility within the overall system. At the same time the increasing range of local government activity and other changes in the work environment can give rise to a need for new or additional skills and experiences.

Although not unknown, it is unreasonable to expect highly qualified and experienced people to be attracted to local government service if they are required to enter the system at the lowest grades in the hope that they will avail of rapid promotion from within. As a result, local authorities have no option sometimes but to create special temporary or contract positions in order to secure the skills or experiences required. Given the potential for industrial relations problems and the fact that some positions will continue to require experience-based knowledge (due to the specialised nature of local government) it is possible that change in this area will be relatively slow. However, the need for continued promotion of open recruitment procedures is specifically detailed in the national agreement, *Sustaining Progress* (Government of Ireland, 2003). It includes a commitment to a cross-sectoral review of recruitment issues pertinent to the grades to which the common recruitment pool applies including greater accessibility and the introduction of a graduate entry level.

Job descriptions and personal specifications are contained, albeit in very general terms, in the particulars and qualifications relating to the particular post. The minister (which for the majority of posts is the Minister for the Environment and Local Government) may declare qualifications for employment within any particular class or grade. The minister will consult with the Local Appointments Commissioners if the employment in question is one that falls to be recruited through the commission. The minister can also provide, by transfer order, for the setting of qualifications by the Local Government Management Services Board. If the minister or the board have specified qualifications for a particular employment, an individual local authority cannot amend same without approval. Particulars and qualifications have been set by the minister for clerical/administrative, technical/professional and managerial posts. Under the Local Government Act, 2001, a local authority may fix qualifications for any employment provided that qualifications for such employment have not previously been declared by the minister. This flexibility enables local authorities to respond quickly and effectively to atypical employment needs.

Selection from amongst eligible candidates is effected by means of competitive panel-based interviews. Interview boards comprising three members is the norm. This process is supplemented by past employment reference checks and medical assessment. Interview board members are generally sourced from within the local government system, within which a considerable body of expertise has been established in the interviewing process. Local authorities rarely engage the services of recruitment companies. While limited use is made of proficiency tests – for example typing skill tests – aptitude tests, personality tests, projection tests and other assessment forms are unknown in the system. Panels established as a result of the interview process are normally retained for a period of twelve months so that further vacancies arising in that period can be filled promptly. The interview boards for competitions conducted by the Local Appointments Commissioners in respect of senior administrative and technical posts usually include a member from the private sector, for example a management consultant or other professional/technical person as appropriate.

The system of staff recruitment and selection within local authorities is sometimes criticised as being slow, particularly by internal line managers. The problem has become more acute due to increased demands arising from staff restructuring agreements and the need to recruit additional staff to implement local government's very significant portion of the national development plan. The introduction of freedom of information and equality legislation in an increasingly litigious society has also generated the need for additional reports and records to support decisions taken. Despite its shortcomings it is generally accepted that the local government recruitment system is fair, objective and increasingly transparent and overall has been to the satisfaction of local authorities and employees.

The recruitment challenges faced by local authorities have increased considerably in recent years. In past decades, the focus of attention centred on the selection process, as there always appeared to be a ready pool of talented candidates available. With a much more competitive labour market, local authorities are being challenged to develop more imaginative approaches in order that they may continue to attract high calibre recruits. A number of innovations have been introduced particularly through the Local Government Management Services Board. These include the establishment of a local authority recruitment website, participation in recruitment fairs, international advertisements for skilled positions and nationally co-ordinated media campaigns.

Improvements have also been made to remuneration levels and career paths through organisational restructuring agreements and the granting of improved incremental credit for certain past work experience outside the local government system. While the security and remuneration benefits available no longer offer a competitive advantage, local authorities have unique selling points including: a special public service ethos, challenging and satisfying positions, the capacity to change the environment within which the worker lives, close relationships with the public and communities served, variety of work, career development opportunities and flexible work arrangements. The effective articulation of these benefits to a broader audience will become a key feature of recruitment practice for the future.

Equality

The Equality Act, 1998 prohibits discrimination on grounds of marital status, family status, gender, age, religion, race, disability, sexual orientation and membership of the Traveller community. In recent years local authorities have developed policies that seek to avoid discrimination in accordance with these legislative provisions and, more importantly, promote the concept of equality within the workplace. Selection boards generally reflect gender balance and all boards are provided with detailed guidance on appropriate and inappropriate interview techniques. Codes of practice have been developed, and are regularly reviewed, in the areas of bullying, harassment, sexual harassment, diversity and the promotion of equal opportunities. Significant flexibility has been introduced to work practices so as to enable employees to better balance their home and work demands (for example work sharing, flexitime, career breaks, special leave as well as improved statutory entitlements for parental, adoptive, maternity and *force majeur* leave). Equality officers and equality action teams have been appointed at local level to promote equality issues and devise measures to achieve improvements.

In relation to the employment of people with disabilities, progress has been made in achieving the government target for the numbers of disabled persons employed, which is 3 per cent of staff. There are also improved opportunities for mobility (by means of confined competitions) from outdoor manual and trade grades to indoor clerical grades.

Notwithstanding the achievements made to date there are areas of concern, particularly in the matter of gender equality. Progress towards increasing female participation in senior management grades has been particularly slow and while there has been some improvement in the level of female participation in professional grades there appears to be a marked reduction in the level of male recruitment at the clerical entry grades. Much of the attention in relation to gender equality has focused on the fairness of recruitment practice and the flexibility of working conditions. The more complex challenge for the future will centre on how each authority markets the attractions of all posts to all potential candidates and how its training and development function operates so as to more adequately link personal development opportunities with the cycle of external non-work-related demands.

Training and Development

One of the basic elements of the local authority human resource function is the establishment and ongoing development of systems that stimulate, assist and support staff towards the achievement of their full potential. Training refers to systematic efforts to enhance employee skills, knowledge and attitudes through learning experiences with a view to improving workplace performance. Development on the other hand is a broader concept and it focuses on the enhancement of employee capacity to take on future tasks and responsibilities.

From an employee's perspective, training and development leads to better promotional prospects and improved job satisfaction. For the local authority, investment in training and development can improve motivation, increase organisational loyalty, develop shared values, enhance creativity, improve long-term effectiveness and in general create better public servants.

In past decades training and development in the local government service was often approached as though it were an isolated task. Its costs were rarely included in the planning of new work programmes or organisational changes and in the annual budgetary allocation process it tended to lose out to what appeared to be more urgent demands. However, it has received considerably greater attention in recent years for a number of reasons, not least of which is the active pursuit of maximum value for money from all expenditure. With benefits accruing to local authority performance from ongoing reviews of financial and fixed assets it is inevitable that payroll as the largest revenue expenditure item should be identified as the area where the most significant long-term gains are to be made.

In addition, the nature and pace of change in the external and internal environments demand the adoption of effective training and development policies. Issues of relevance include advances in information technology; legislative developments; changing public demand, expectations and expertise; system restructuring; alternative work practices; the expanding role of local government; and the ever-reducing lifespan of existing qualifications as scientific and business theory and practice evolve. There are also higher expectations from all staff who reasonably expect opportunities to develop their potential in existing or new fields. The importance of effective training and development is emphasised in a variety of policy documents on public sector reform and it is generally accepted that investment in this area should be at least 3 per cent of payroll costs.

If local authorities are to be effective in their approach, it is essential that training and development be treated as a shared responsibility between the human resource department, the individual employee and his or her line or departmental manager. Over-reliance on employee input may result in an imbalance in training provision between upwardly mobile employees and others, with little connection between training/development benefits and current job performance or organisational goals. Equally, over-reliance on line management input may result in a deferment of provision in favour of fulfilling other commitments or the adoption of a relatively short-term focus centring on operational issues. In general the staff development responsibilities of line managers are not very well developed within the local government system. This is perhaps a reflection of limited appraisal of line managers on the issue.

Over-reliance on the human resource department is equally problematic, as local authority business plans and departmental action plans are often insufficiently developed to enable decisions on training priorities without the input of line managers. The current grading structure is based on generalist administrative or technical/professional grades and in the absence of individual job skills specifications, detailed performance appraisal and adequate current competence data there is a risk of inappropriate training selections or selections that are influenced by political correctness as much as any other issue.

Good training practice begins with the development of a policy that has regard to the authority's strategic objectives and plans as well as to the internal and external work environment. This is followed by the identification of training and development needs, the making of decisions as to how these needs should be fulfilled, the implementation of training mechanisms and finally detailed assessment of the actual benefit derived by the employee and the local authority.

Most authorities periodically undertake training needs analysis and in many cases common areas of need have been highlighted. These include induction training for recruits; information technology skills training; communications and customer service training; health and safety related training; freedom of information training; training for contact persons, mediators and so forth in relation to issues such as bullying and sexual harassment; equality (including disability) awareness training; management skills development; and training relating to legal issues, procedural matters and best-practice techniques.

Each local authority has a designated training officer to support the training and development function. However, with the exception of a few of the larger authorities, this function is the responsibility of a staff member from within the human resource department who quite often deals with a range of other staff-related and sometimes non-staff-related matters. As such, he or she is not particularly specialised in terms of functional responsibility.

A variety of training and development mechanisms are used to respond to the needs identified. The most common include formal induction training, group coaching, the provision of opportunities to attend training courses and generous financial and leave benefits to support staff who wish to obtain additional qualifications from educational institutions. Amongst the latter, the Institute of Public Administration, whose aim is the furtherance of public sector management development, is particularly important.

In all but the largest local authorities there has been a tendency to rely exclusively on external training providers. This is to be expected given the scale required for employment of specialist trainers on a full-time basis. However, in recent years a number of specialised training programmes have been designed (often with the assistance of FÁS) for delivery at local level by local authority employees. Such employees would be drawn from the related work area and receive induction in the delivery of training. In addition, a number of local authority training centres have been provided at regional level for the provision of training by authorities on a collective basis.

Most local authorities have achieved or exceeded the training spend target of 3 per cent of payroll and, as with many other organisations, can produce positive data detailing the number and range of training courses, numbers of training days and expenditure per employee. However, there has been a tendency in staff training and development programmes to concentrate on courses that provide detailed knowledge of the law and procedural matters to the exclusion of other aspects, particularly in the area of management skills development and ongoing personal development. There appears to be rather limited assessment of the benefits derived by either the employee or the local authority.

The statistical data do not adequately reflect the less formal training mechanisms that are or could be availed of. For example, placement and mobility practices, that is, putting the individual employees in a work area that corresponds with their interests, abilities and qualifications and subsequent appropriately timed transfers throughout their career so as to maximise learning potential. Such career transfers are viewed as important in the context of promotion for employees who are characterised by reference to generalist grades rather than functional specialisation. Other long-term development techniques include mentoring, project work secondments, coaching, and shadowing. Despite their potential, these techniques are rarely applied and when they are used it tends to be on an ad hoc and unstructured basis.

Training and development is a demanding and complex area of work. Future local authority attention will continue to focus on a broadening of training subject matter, the introduction of more personal development policies, greater linkages between the service provided and the long-term needs of the organisation and the individual employees, and more detailed assessment of the actual benefits derived by both.

Remuneration

While the local government service tends to be a good employer, it is not the market leader in terms of remuneration. For lower grades, pay levels tend to be similar to those obtainable in the private sector. At the more senior levels, the financial rewards do not correspond with those obtainable in the top levels of business or the professions. Similar characteristics are to be found in other public service agencies both nationally and internationally.

Multi-annual national agreements have become the key determinants of pay improvements for local authority employees. Over the years this corporatist approach has become comprehensive both in terms of the variety of partners involved in the negotiations (employers, trade unions, farmers, community and voluntary groups) and the subject matter of the final agreements. The national agreement for the 2003 to 2005 period, *Sustaining Progress* (Government of Ireland, 2003), includes a broad range of provisions such as:

- special initiatives relating to: housing and accommodation, cost and availability of insurance, migration and interculturalism, long-term unemployed, vulnerable workers and those who have been made redundant, tackling educational disadvantage, literacy, numeracy and early school leaving, waste management, care – children, people with disabilities and older people, alcohol/drug misuse, including everyone in the information society, ending child poverty
- building, maintaining and sharing economic development and prosperity – policies relating to infrastructure, the environment, adaptation to continuing change

- delivering a fair and inclusive society – poverty and social inclusion, health and addressing health inequalities, equality, access to quality public services
- pay and the workplace conditions – private and private sector pay and related issues, statutory minimum pay, redundancy payments, partnership at the workplace, worker participation (state enterprises), workplace relations and environment, gender pay gap, work/life balance programmes, workplace childcare
- quality public services – commitments to modernisation and flexibility.

There are important distinctions between the public and private sectors in the implementation of agreed national income policies. It is not unusual for enterprises in the private sector to adapt pay provisions in line with local circumstances. If market conditions are favourable, additional benefits are provided, whereas if they are poor, employees have to wait until better times. In this way, blunt national pay policies are adjusted to meet the needs of different enterprises across all sectors. In contrast, local authorities, as with other public bodies, are required to strictly adhere to the commitments made on their behalf including the pay increases agreed. In times of rapid economic growth or economic decline, local authorities may find themselves significantly out-of-step in relation to normal labour market pay rates.

On occasion, public sector discontent with growing imbalances in pay levels has been alleviated with clear breaches of agreed national pay policy. The additional increases secured may be linked to restructuring/reform agreements or what are often thinly disguised as productivity agreements following industrial unrest. Such agreements, of course, can present their own difficulties at local level, where for example the costs, particularly for poorly resourced local authorities, are seen as significant relative to the productivity/flexibility benefits secured. In addition, they can give rise to increased expectations or new pay demands from other groups of workers throughout the service.

The benchmarking provisions of the national agreement for 2000 to 2003, *Programme for Prosperity and Fairness* (Government of Ireland, 2000c), represent a bolder approach to the issue. However, notwithstanding the general acceptance of this more scientific approach, it may take some time for employees to adapt to the principle of award variations and the abandonment of traditional pay relativities. Similarly, it may be difficult for assessment bodies at national level to withstand pressure for the award of generous increases in order to maintain industrial peace. It is interesting to note that some local authority grades, for example craftworkers, have participated in well-established benchmarking exercises for many years.

The 2002 benchmarking awards for local authority grades will give rise to significant difficulties for the sector. Apart from achieving the required changes that the pay increases are contingent upon, local authorities have to meet the benchmarking costs from their own resources. This is not the case throughout the broad public sector, where provision has been made by the exchequer for the additional costs. This will compound the local authorities' problems of meeting additional costs in difficult financial times when, for example, they also have to make councillor payments from their own resources.

The setting of pay levels for senior positions within the service presents its own difficulties. Remuneration must be sufficiently high, relative to that available in the private sector, in order to attract and retain the best possible leaders but also sufficiently low so as to limit pay expectations within the general public service. Since the late 1960s, the government has been advised by a number of reports of the Review Body on Higher Remuneration in the Public Sector. Recommendations relate to pay levels for a broad range of senior posts within the public service, including county/city managers and directors of services in the local government system.

Local authority employees are paid in accordance with the grade to which they belong without any analysis of the value to the organisation of the work undertaken or to the performance of the individual relative to the organisation's expectations. This approach is based on the assumption that people of the same grade do work of a similar nature and perform to a similar standard or at least to the minimum accepted standard. While greatly simplifying pay determination and pay administration, it becomes a questionable practice if the aforementioned assumptions do not hold to be true in all cases. There are increasing variations in work demands within each grade across all local authorities due to information technology advances and other internal and external adjustments. The extent to which greater local flexibility may be introduced without the knock-on effects of comparative claims and pay-related migration is dependent on a number of issues. These include local capacity to implement effective job evaluation techniques and the sophistication of local performance management systems.

The only significant area where local authorities have flexibility in determining financial benefits, within nationally established bands, is in relation to site supervision staff employed on capital projects. A review of the application of this flexibility and its impact might provide some useful guidance for future developments.

Superannuation

Retirement from the service is normally between the ages of 60 and 65 years. The vast majority of local authority employees are members of pension schemes that are designed to ensure that following retirement with full service they have a total income of half their retiring remuneration together with a tax-free lump sum.

Most employees are also members of a separate scheme that provides for pension payments to widows and orphans in the event of death.

Staff who joined the service after April 1995 contribute to their pensions at a rate of 1.5 per cent of full pay and 3.5 per cent of co-ordinated pay (that is, full pay less twice the rate of old age pension – as their council pension entitlements are co-ordinated with their contributory old age pension entitlements). Staff within the former officer grades who joined the service before that date pay lower rates of PRSI and have no additional contributory pension entitlements. Accordingly their combined contribution of 5 per cent is not co-ordinated. Contributions for the widows and orphans pension scheme is set at 1.5 per cent co-ordinated or unco-ordinated as appropriate. Pension contributions form part of the local authority's general receipts and unlike normal pension arrangements are not lodged in a separate fund for future investment growth. This can give rise to significant financial pressures particularly if there are age distribution imbalances within the workforce.

Despite their technical complexity the local government pension schemes are considered to have operated satisfactorily with a range of benefits designed to deal with the uncertainties of life. The operation of the same schemes by all authorities has also facilitated significant mobility within the service.

Performance Appraisal

Performance appraisal is concerned with the measurement of employment performance against predetermined job requirements or standards. In theory, appraisal has two basic functions: to assess how well an employee has performed relative to the standards or targets set (including output and behavioural processes) and to inform development decisions. Performance appraisal systems vary considerably in how they are effected (for example who is appraised, how often, who carries out the appraisal, what stakeholders are involved, whether it is treated as confidential) and what they are used to achieve (for example organisational development, legal/procedural requirement, job satisfaction, employee development, pay and benefits, behavioural conformity, training needs, promotion potential).

Within local government, formal appraisal of employees is of a very limited or basic nature. All new employees to the local government service are recruited on probationary periods of six to twelve months and permanent appointment is dependent on satisfactory performance in that period. It is extremely rare for employees not to be appointed at the end of their probationary period. Occasionally probationary periods are further extended, but this action is usually in response to breaches of conduct or other behavioural problems rather than inadequate quantity or quality of work output as measured against predetermined targets. A similar position exists in relation to the award of annual pay increments, which are so seldom withheld that many employees assume them to be automatic entitlements. In the majority of authorities staff are appointed following probation and annual increments awarded without face-to-face discussion between line managers and employees.

It would however be wrong to conclude that performance is not an issue for local government. The plans, actions and performance of all local authorities and their staff are open to scrutiny and comment to an extent not paralleled elsewhere in the public service. Local authority staff, particularly at middle and senior management levels, are far from anonymous bureaucrats and tend to be closer to their service consumers than other public officials. This contact together with the scrutiny of regular meetings and extensive coverage in the local media ensures that performance is always to the forefront of their thoughts. Local authorities have adopted corporate and service action plans with detailed measurable targets and in many cases linkages between these targets and the responsibilities of all staff in the organisation. The availability of such written targets will be an important step in the introduction of formal individual performance assessments within each council. Given the difficulties associated with performance appraisal it is likely that formal individual assessment by line managers or human resource specialists will only emerge following full development of the formal organisational and team performance assessments associated with corporate planning.

Notwithstanding the limitations of pay as a motivating influence, a degree of local flexibility could greatly assist an individual local authority in responding effectively to its employment needs and performance expectations. Concepts such as organisation/team/individual results or performance-related payments are unknown within the service. Proposals have been made for the introduction of a performance bonus system for senior managers. Such proposals inevitably raise complex questions in relation to the implications for other staff members and their expectations as well as the actual means for assessment. Equally problematic are the variations in local authority resources and demands and the potential public perception in relation to the motivations associated with unpopular projects such as waste management facilities. The practical experience of other performance-related systems, such as those introduced for senior managers within the civil service, Defence Forces and An Garda Síochána, together with the development of local authority corporate and service action plans, may provide useful guidance for the resolution of some of these issues.

Staff Welfare

It is inevitable that individual local authority employees, at some time in their careers, would encounter personal difficulties. Examples include the trauma of bereavement, accidental injury or illness, family difficulties or addiction. The human resource function is expected to be knowledgeable in relation to these issues and to have the capacity to offer support where appropriate subject to the individual's right to privacy. Many local authorities have established staff welfare programmes, which provide both internal and independent external counselling and other professional assistance. In addition many authorities, as part of an extending safety, health and welfare brief, provide lifestyle improvement programmes including health screening, dietary and exercise advice and stress management training. Progress has also been made in the provision of improved working conditions for indoor and outdoor workers including mobile facilities, canteens and crèches.

Ethics

For both staff and elected members a considerable degree of regulation is in operation in order to ensure public confidence in the integrity of the local government system. Local authority staff members are prohibited from engaging in any gainful occupation, other than as employees of the authority, to such an extent as to impair the performance of their duties. They are also prohibited from engaging in any occupation that might conflict with the interests of the local authority or be inconsistent with the performance of their duties. An employee whose conditions are wholly or in part professional is not permitted to engage in private practice in the profession in which he she is employed by the local authority or in any cognate profession. Local authorities are required to determine appropriate disciplinary action including suspension with or without pay and termination of employment where relevant breaches occur.

Provision is made within existing regulations for declarations of interests, by designated grades of staff, which are available for public examination (part 15 of the Local Government Act, 2001 and associated regulations). Provision is also made under the Act for the appointment of an ethics registrar within each authority and the issuing of codes of conduct by the minister.

The elected members have virtually no direct role in the human resource function. This is the only area of local authority activity where there is such an extensive exclusion and perhaps it owes something to claims of subjective and inappropriate influences in the years following independence. The powers of elected members in this area are limited to the following:

- appointment of the county/city manager following receipt of a recommendation from the Local Appointments Commissioners and the suspension and removal of the county/city manager. One should note that if approval to the manager's appointment is not forthcoming the appointment becomes effective automatically after a period of three months

- the county/city manager consults with the cathaoirleach/mayor of the county/city council before appointing an employee to be deputy manager and, if the manager is temporarily unable to act and there is no such arrangement in place, the cathaoirleach/mayor may make the necessary appointment.

The Irish local government system provides limited potential for mobility between the positions of elected member and staff member. The Local Government Act, 2001 restricts a local authority from employing persons who themselves are members of any local authority. The provision will become effective from 2004 and the minister may by order designate grades to which the exclusion will not apply. Traditionally a restriction applied to all but junior grades and in relation to the neighbouring and home authorities.

Industrial Relations

Industrial relations is concerned with the establishment and operation of employment relationship rules. For most local authorities it constitutes a significant element of the human resource department's workload. With remuneration being determined centrally, conditions of employment (including ancillary benefits), changes to work practices and occasional disciplinary issues have become the most common matters for local negotiation and discussion. The system of industrial relations practised in Ireland was traditionally largely voluntary in nature. Employers' and employees' representatives were free to regulate their own relationships and the outcomes of their discussions. The state to a significant degree limited its role to one of providing mechanisms for assisting dispute resolution and promoting good industrial relations practice.

Since the 1980s, through the transposition of EU legislation and the expansion in the subject matter of national agreements, the state has increasingly set down minimum standards and rights to be enjoyed by workers. Examples of such legislative instruments include:

- Safety, Health and Welfare at Work Act, 1989
- Worker Protection (Regular Part-Time Employees) Act, 1991
- Redundancy Payments Acts, 1967 to 1991
- Unfair Dismissals Acts, 1977 to 1993
- Minimum Notice and Terms of Employment Acts, 1973 to 1991
- Payment of Wages Act, 1991
- Terms of Employment (Information) Act, 1994
- Maternity Protection Act, 1994
- Organisation of Working Time Act, 1997
- Employment Equality Act, 1998

- Adoptive Leave Act, 1995
- Parental Leave Act, 1998
- National Minimum Wage Act, 2000
- Protection of Employees (Part-Time Work) Act, 2001
- Terms of Employment (Information) Act, 2001.

As a consequence, staff in the human resource department must have a high degree of expertise in all matters of employment law.

In discharging the industrial relations function, local authorities are provided with extensive support by the Local Government Management Services Board. The board is comprised of local authority managers with representation from the department. It employs a range of human resource specialists and, in addition to general management services, provides support and advice to local authorities on all aspects of the human resource function. It negotiates on behalf of local authorities on industrial relations issues of common interest and consequently many issues which would normally be dealt with by a human resource department are actually handled elsewhere.

Local authority staff members are one of the most strongly unionised groups of workers in Ireland. Over the years there has been considerable consolidation within the trade union movement and the principal unions representing local authority workers now are:

- IMPACT (Irish Municipal, Public and Civil Trade Union), which in the main represents workers in clerical, administrative, managerial and some professional grades
- SIPTU (Services, Industrial, Professional and Technical Union) and ATGWU (Amalgamated Transport and General Workers Union), which largely represent manual workers, tradespeople and some professional grades.

In addition, there are a number of specialised unions particularly in the craft area such as the TEEU (Technical Engineering and Electrical Union), the AEEU (Amalgamated Engineering and Electrical Union) and the UCATT (Union of Construction Allied Trades and Technicians).

All local authority staff members, other than the county/city manager, can seek access to the industrial relations support institutions. These include the Labour Relations Commission, Rights Commissioner, Employment Appeals Tribunal, Equality Officers and the Labour Court.

Worker Participation

The traditional relationship between management and unions in the local government system appears to have been based on conflicting interests of management and staff. This conflict was addressed through negotiations within which management representatives sought to secure a balance between various competing interests and demands. These interests included the various requirements of central government, elected members, service consumers and employees. This pluralist tradition is characterised by high union membership and well-established adversarial negotiation mechanisms, which form a significant element of the human resource department's activity.

In the 1990s, a somewhat different approach began to emerge, with management in some local authorities seeking to emphasise and promote the mutuality of interest between local authorities as employers and their employees. Examples of this change include radically improved communication systems between management and employees, encouragement and acceptance of employee suggestions, increased delegation of responsibility, increased use of cross-functional departmental teams together with increased concern for employee motivation, satisfaction and development.

This new approach was significantly advanced under *Partnership 2000, for Inclusion, Employment and Competitiveness* (Government of Ireland, 1996):

> . . . it is recognised that successful change must be based on a partnership approach both at the overall public service level and within individual organisations. The objective is to achieve joint ownership by management, unions and staff of the entire process. To this end an adversarial approach to change must be replaced by an open co-operative process based on effective consultation and participation by all concerned.

A central component of the Partnership 2000 agreement was a commitment to modernise the public service. In order to further this objective, a two-tier structure has been created to support the establishment and development of partnership throughout the service. A national partnership advisory group (LANPAG) was formed to co-ordinate, advise and support local authorities in the development of the partnership process. At local level, partnership committees have been set up within each city/county authority with representatives of management, trade unions and staff. Partnership committees, normally comprising eight to twelve members, meet on a regular basis and are supported by full-time facilitators.

Following detailed examination, often with assistance from sub-committees drawn from the general workforce, the partnership group agree and put forward proposals for change within the local authority. The partnership process presents a challenge to union representatives who have acquired significant experience in traditional negotiation mechanisms. It also challenges management to adopt a truly consultative approach in determining the direction of organisational change and service improvement. To date many of the issues examined by partnership committees have been in the softer staff welfare arena and it is anticipated that as the process develops organisational change and service delivery issues will come more centre stage. In this context, the strategic plan for 2003 to 2005, *Deepening Partnership in Local Government*, published by LANPAG provided a blueprint for the implementation and further development of workplace partnership in local authorities, moving to what can be described as second generation partnership.

Strategic Human Resource Management

In recent years many organisations in the public and private sectors have begun to use the term human resources rather than personnel when referring to their staff. This change is by no means cosmetic, and implies a radically different approach within which there are different roles for and expectations of the staff management function. Personnel management suggests a service to the organisation that is focused on immediate or short-term issues. Its objectives, policies and plans are not integrated into the overall objectives, policies and plans of the organisation. It tends to be reactive rather than proactive and, in terms of workload, it is heavily focused on detailed operational issues such as recruitment, pay administration and industrial relations with limited delegation of staff management functions to line managers.

Human resource management, on the other hand, seeks to link staffing issues with overall organisational goals. It seeks to establish objective strategies and policies in relation to matters such as staff recruitment, deployment, development and reward that are effected through long-term plans that complement, inform and support the organisation's long-term strategic plan. It extends greater responsibility to line managers for much of the day-to-day implementation of staff policies and emphasises the need for staff policies that support individual employee development and satisfaction.

This more strategic approach to human resource management requires regular and ongoing analysis of the organisation's long-term objectives and strategies as well as its external and internal environment. In doing so it seeks to develop the capacity to measure such things as current employee skills levels, productivity standards, management competence, advancement potential, satisfaction levels, age distribution, acceptance of and understanding of organisational goals, absenteeism trends, turnover rates, organisational structure, culture dynamics and values, communication and decision-making mechanisms and the overall effectiveness of current staff policies. It examines the impact of these conditions on the achievement of organisational goals, with anticipation of external changes (for example technological advancements, legislative changes and labour market trends), and develops staff policies that inform and assist the effective achievement of organisational goals.

This approach to staff management requires the human resource department to concentrate on strategic rather than operational issues. So, for example, in the area of recruitment it would seek to identify the types of staff required well into the future and devise recruitment and development policies rather than solely concentrating on the filling of individual vacancies. In the area of appraisal it would decide what the council should value in the long term and establish appraisal and potential identification systems rather than concentrating on the operation of increment approval or time attendance controls. In the area of rewards it would determine how staff should be rewarded and put in place appropriate financial and non-financial systems rather than concentrating on the correct administration of pay and pension systems. In the area of training it would plan development experiences and develop long-term systems to manage individual and council needs for flexibility and stability.

The local authority human resource function was historically, and continues to be, largely concerned with operational matters. Some limited progress has been made in the adoption of a more strategic approach especially in the areas of recruitment and staff development/training. Further changes in focus will be facilitated by the increased delegation of responsibility for operational issues (including staff issues within established policies) to line managers. Of more importance to any possible transition is the availability of written corporate and service action plans which detail the organisation's objectives and targets in all areas in the years ahead. The reorientation of the human resource department with a view to concentration on issues of strategic importance to the organisation inevitably takes a number of years. Factors that may need to be addressed in order to further the process include:

- human resource capacity and management support: the staff of the human resource department, due to their generalist nature, may not possess the skills necessary to advance strategic human resource planning. In the competitive internal resource allocation arena the staff function may not be awarded a sufficiently high priority and it is often required to take responsibility for a variety of miscellaneous services
- staff support: existing human resource staff have acquired a great deal of operational expertise and may be reluctant to transfer operational responsibilities to line managers and have their own roles significantly altered. Conflicts may also arise in relation to senior management grades in other departments particularly under the new system of directorates. Such senior managers may view an elevated role for the human resource department as an encroachment on their territory
- prevailing assumptions: such inappropriate assumptions include the view that local authorities will always be able to recruit high calibre and appropriately qualified staff at short notice or that the human resource element of strategic planning should be treated as a short-term

implementation issue rather than as one of a number of driving forces. This leads to, at best, human resource planning being addressed with little knowledge or understanding of the internal capacity of the organisation and its future objectives

- poor quality of strategic planning within the organisation itself: all local authorities have produced corporate and customer service action plans supplemented by detailed departmental action plans. The development of complementary human resource plans will be very difficult if these are insufficiently specific, have limited environmental analysis or do not have a balanced focus on organisational inputs, processes, outputs and outcomes.

Conclusion

This chapter has sought to review the practices and current issues relating to the basic elements of human resource management in the local government system. These elements include recruitment, remuneration, industrial relations, worker participation, training and development, performance appraisal, ethics, equality and welfare. In reviewing these areas, it is apparent that, despite the complexity of the staff management function, the local government system has devised effective practices with many positive attributes.

The question for the future relates to how the human resource function should be further developed so as to maximise its contribution to the bottom-line performance of each local authority. It is suggested that the introduction and ongoing development of strategic management principles within all areas of local government could play a significant part in determining the role of the human resource function in the future. Any transition to more strategic human resource activity will be supported by the ever-increasing expectations of a well-educated, if not over-qualified, workforce, challenges arising from a rapidly changing operational environment and the increasingly complex management demands within a multi-functional system.

The human resource function deals with the local authority's most important resource in terms of cost, potential impact and length of investment timeframe. It cannot be left adrift from overall organisational planning, responding to each new pressure as it arises.

18

Local Government Finance:
The Policy Context

Gerard Dollard

Local authorities spend a sizeable portion of the national income on the various services they provide. Expenditure by local authorities in 2001 was €5,872 million (approximately six per cent of GNP) and comprised €2,665 million for day-to-day revenue/current expenditure and €3,207 million for capital expenditure.

Trends in local expenditure can be seen from an examination of the *Returns of Local Taxation/Local Authority Estimates,* which are the official statistics compiled to reflect the expenditure of local authorities. Substantial changes occurred in current expenditure during the period from 1981 to 2002. Overall revenue expenditure increased by 372 per cent. See table 18.1 for a breakdown of expenditure by programme group.

Day-to-day expenditure on the housing and building programme has seen a substantial change since the early 1980s. The impact of various tenant purchase schemes, the curtailment of the national house-building programme in the late 1980s and the involvement of financial institutions in the local authority housing loans market have changed the composition of housing expenditure. Roads and sanitary services programmes have maintained their share of total expenditure but in monetary terms have shown very substantial increases. An increasing regulatory framework, coupled with the economic boom of the 1990s, has resulted in a major emphasis on development control and forward-planning activity under the development, incentives and controls programme. There is a marked increase in the proportion of the budget allocated to the area of environmental protection, related primarily to the maintenance of landfill sites to a much higher standard and the increased resources being applied to the area of environmental management. Expenditure on fire services has also shown substantial increases, particularly

Table 18.1 Local Authorities' Revenue Expenditure, 1981 and 2002

Programme	1981		2002	
	€m	%	€m	%
Housing and building	236	28	499	16
Road transportation and safety	241	29	920	30
Water supply and sewerage	112	13	350	11
Development incentives and controls	19	2	149	5
Environmental protection	77	9	557	18
Recreation and amenity	46	6	272	9
Agriculture, education, health and welfare	55	7	180	6
Miscellaneous services	47	6	172	5
Total	833	100	3,099	100

Source: Department of the Environment and Local Government (annual), *Returns of Local Taxation* and *Local Authority Estimates*

following the enactment of the Fire Services Act, 1981. The growing proportion of the budget allocated to recreational facilities demonstrates the increasing importance of these types of activities in the local authority context. Swimming pools, libraries, recreation centres and, particularly, the development of the arts now constitute a sizeable element of the overall budget of a local authority.

The period 1981 to 2002 also saw the ending of the supplementary welfare allowance demand (1986) on local authorities, as well as the end of various other statutory demands and a reduction in the local authority liability to the local loans fund by the elimination of certain loan repayments (1988). These changes were accompanied by appropriate adjustments to government grants received.

Capital Expenditure

A local authority's capital expenditure is heavily dependent on the public capital programme determined by central government. Each year, allocations for housing construction, road improvement and other capital schemes are notified by the Department of the Environment and Local Government to local authorities. Expenditure on the capital programme has increased significantly over the period 1981 to 2002 (see table 18.2).

The local authority and social housing allocation reflects the expansion of the national house-building programme and an increasing emphasis on voluntary housing schemes. The introduction of new social/affordable housing measures

Table 18.2 Local Authorities' Share of the Public Capital Programme, 1981 and 2002 (€m)

	1981	*2002*
Local authority and social housing	187	1,125
House purchase loans	121	416
Roads	80	1,357
Water supply and sewerage	85	569
Environmental services	17	145
Other	–	89
Total	490	3,701

Source: Department of the Environment and Local Government (annual), *Returns of Local Taxation* and *Local Authority Estimates*

and funding for the provision of Traveller accommodation has contributed to the increased allocation in this area. The launch of a new type of loan scheme in 1991, the shared ownership loan scheme, arising from an effort to make housing available to lower income groups, created a new demand for housing loans from local authorities. The practice had been to encourage would-be borrowers to seek funds from other financial institutions, with the local authority being the lender of last resort. The new scheme – together with other schemes introduced under *A Plan for Social Housing* (Department of the Environment, 1991), for example the rental subsidy scheme – required provision of additional capital funding.

Improvements in roads and sanitary services infrastructure have arisen from the necessity to upgrade these facilities to comply with EU Directives. The European Regional Development Fund (ERDF) and the Cohesion Fund have been the main source of financial assistance for such improvement works (see chapter 24). The balance of the funding comes from the exchequer. As national wealth increases and as the enlargement of the EU progresses, the level of EU funding for infrastructural projects in Ireland steadily decreases. This places an increasing financial burden on the national exchequer in providing funding for capital projects.

Public private partnerships (PPPs) have been introduced to address this and other issues and form a key part of the national development plan for 2000 to 2006 (Government of Ireland, 2000a). While the capital cost of these schemes does not fall on the local authority, the annual maintenance costs of new, more complex and improved infrastructure must be borne at local level. This is, and continues to be, an increasing financial concern for local authorities.

Sources of Revenue

The current expenditure of local authorities is met from rates, government grants, charges for services and other less important sources. Expenditure on works of a capital nature, so far as it is not met out of either exchequer grants or EU funds, is as a rule met by borrowing (see chapter 19). A substantial proportion of current income is met by rates (see table 18.3). Following the abolition of domestic rates in 1977 and the subsequent introduction of service charges in 1983, the proportion of current income funded by rates reduced. The trend was reversed, however, when the rate support grant (introduced to compensate local authorities for the loss of rates on domestic properties) failed to keep pace with the yield from domestic rates. This, coupled with stiff resistance to the payment of the new service charges in many local authorities, resulted in the burden for local funding falling again on the commercial ratepayer.

Table 18.3 Rates Proportion of Local Authorities' Income Receipts, 1977 to 2002 (%)*

	1977	*1983*	*1991*	*2002*
Rates	34	12	21	24
Government grants	46	65	61	47
Other	20	23	18	29
	100	100	100	100

* The figures in this table are indicative and not directly comparable due to changes in accounting practice over the years

Source: Department of the Environment and Local Government (annual), *Returns of Local Taxation* and *Local Authority Estimates*

Local charges, other than service charges, also began to form an important source of local income from 1993 arising from, *inter alia*, the introduction of planning application fees, building control fees and significant increases in waste disposal charges. The overall position again changed in 1997 with a decision by government to abolish local water service charges on domestic properties and effectively transfer the burden to state funding.

Early Local Finance

In the nineteenth century, expenditure on the basic services then locally administered – highways, poor relief, sanitation and certain aspects of law and order – were met almost wholly from local resources. Problems began to emerge when social legislation imposed heavier burdens on local authorities than unaided local taxation could bear.

The practice of augmenting local revenues from central taxation became an accepted feature of public finance from 1850 onwards. State grants continued to grow in number and amount and the setting up of a local taxation (Ireland) account in the late nineteenth century was an effort to preserve the separation of local from central liabilities. The opposite proved to be the case when, in 1898, the replacing of the grand juries by the county councils was accompanied by a major subsidy in aid of rural ratepayers as part of the reform package.

The period from 1922 to 1939 witnessed a steady growth in local services with a corresponding rise in state subvention. Agricultural grants were augmented, the Road Fund expanded with the growing use of motor cars, housing subsidies enlarged to encourage slum clearance and house building and public health improvements were secured with the aid of state money. Despite the greatly enlarged state assistance to local authorities, rate levels continued to rise in the period following World War II. There was much criticism of both the rating system and the general structure of local finance.

1960s

An investigation into the economics of local authority finances by Professor David Walker of the Economic Research Institute resulted in the publication of *Local Government Finance in Ireland: A Preliminary Survey* (Walker, 1962). Walker's general conclusion regarding rates was that while a formidable case could be built up against them – particularly where the foundation of the system, valuation, was completely out of date – it would be unrealistic to think of the abolition of local rates or even of drastic changes in their scope. He also concluded that it was probably best that local authorities should be financed both from resources under their own control and by state grants which may be (a) specific, (b) equalising or redistributive and (c) general or neutral. Walker also noted that the state grant system was not designed to help poorer counties more than their better-off counterparts.

Following Walker's paper, an informal committee was established by the government to examine and report on the system of financing the operations of local authorities. The Interdepartmental Committee on Local Finance and Taxation published three reports, dealing with: *Valuation for Rating Purposes* (1965), *Exemptions from and Remissions of Rates* (1967) and *Rates and Other Sources of Revenue for Local Authorities* (1968).

The report on valuation rehearsed the case for a general revaluation of rateable property. In the matter of land, a distortion of relativities had emerged shortly after the completion of Griffith's valuation in the mid-1850s and valuation of buildings was also open to question, besides being grossly out of date. The recommendation of the committee in favour of a general revaluation excluded from its scope all agricultural land outside the four county boroughs.

The report on rates exemptions and remissions recommended that concessions should be on the grounds of principle, temporary remissions should be at the discretion of rating authorities and the rating of half rents should be abolished. The government's response was to phase out rates relief on buildings other than new and reconstructed houses – Local Government (Temporary Reduction of Valuation) Act, 1970 – and to abolish the rating of half rents – Local Government (Rateability of Rents) (Abolition) Act, 1970. The committee's recommendations on rates relief in cases of hardship and on payment of rates by instalments were given statutory recognition in the Local Government (Rates) Act, 1970, but were shortly superseded, as far as domestic rates were concerned, by the de-rating of dwellings in 1977.

The report on rates and other sources of revenue recommended retention of the rating system as an independent source of revenue for local authorities. The report rejected the concept of site value rating, decided that a local income tax would not be practicable and recommended the introduction of a limited local turnover tax and local entertainment taxes.

1970s

In December 1972, the government issued a White Paper on local finance and taxation. The principal proposals were:

- valuation to be modernised as a matter of urgency
- rates remissions and exemptions to be drastically curtailed
- local authorities to be given a general power to make charges for their services and to undertake trading services ancillary to their normal functions.

The report also makes reference to the substantial increase in current expenditure that would result from the increased capital investment in housing, sanitary services and so on. It pointed to the need for improved budgeting, audit and accounting arrangements. The White Paper (Government of Ireland, 1972, 4.1.2) concluded that:

> . . . the Government consider it essential that local authorities should have power to levy local taxes. Moreover, they believe that these taxes should be capable of financing a significant proportion of local expenditure, if local democracy and a sound local government system is to survive . . . Any major local tax must . . . be capable of being fixed independently, at different levels in the different local authority areas and . . . it must also be capable of being administered efficiently, even by relatively small local authorities.

The government concluded that only local rates would satisfy these criteria. Site value rating, local income taxes, poll tax and so on were dismissed as possible alternatives.

The steep rise in local rate levels at that time was mostly attributable to health expenditure, which was the largest and fastest growing item in the rates bill. The White Paper rejected the view that health expenditure should be a wholly state charge. Fine Gael and the Labour Party had, however, developed the principle that large-scale social expenditure should be a national charge and when the national coalition took office in 1973, it set about putting this principle into practice by phasing out the rates contribution to the cost of health services and public assistance. This was completed in 1977.

During the same period, the Minister for Local Government referred the rates problem to the Economic and Social Research Institute. Its report, *Economic Aspects of Local Authority Expenditure and Finance* (Copeland and Walsh, 1975), confirmed the international use and general acceptability of rates as a form of local taxation. On the general issue of local finance, it concluded that most countries had a greater variety of local taxes and that general or block grants, rather than grants for specific services, were common features of most local support systems. Despite the favourable verdict of the Copeland and Walsh report, the coalition government decided towards the end of 1976 to phase out domestic rates and, in 1977, announced a 25 per cent cut, with a hint of more to follow.

In the meantime, Fianna Fáil had developed their own plans – immediate abolition of domestic rates and, in addition, removal of rates from secondary schools, community halls and such farm buildings as were still subject to rating. With the Fianna Fáil victory in the 1977 election, these plans were put into operation with effect from January 1978. The opposition could not attack the main aims of the bill, on which all parties were agreed, and confined their criticisms to the methods proposed – particularly the new financial controls. For the first time local discretion in fixing rate levels was to be fettered. Under the Local Government (Financial Provisions) Act, 1978, the Minister for the Environment, with the consent of the Minister for Finance, was given power to issue directions to rating authorities setting limits in rate increases each year.

The abolition of domestic rates in 1977 had the single largest negative effect on the finances of local authorities. It interfered with the local democratic process, curtailed local accountability, weakened local discretion, reduced the amount of money available to local authorities (in later years the rate support grant did not keep pace with inflation) and made local government more dependent on central government. As Roche (1982b, p. 157) put it, 'the nagging irritation of domestic rates had been finally cured – by amputation'. However, the result of laying the rates problems to rest was a fundamental alteration of the character of local government.

1980s

The period from 1978 to 1984 was a dramatic time for local authority finances. Apart from the abolition of domestic rates in 1978, the actual financial position of local authorities deteriorated steadily from that time. The grant in relief of domestic rates provided by the government (known as the rate support grant) was intended to compensate local authorities in full for the loss of domestic rate income. This commitment was fulfilled up to 1982, but was accompanied by rate limits on local authorities during that period. The capped rate increases did not keep up with inflation, so local authority income from the rate support grant fell in real terms over the period.

To reduce the burden of paying the full level of grant in relief of domestic rates, the government introduced two major changes to the funding of local authorities in the Local Government (Financial Provisions) (No. 2) Act, 1983. First, the Minister for the Environment was relieved of the responsibility for meeting the full amount of income lost from the abolition of domestic rates. And second, to make up for any shortfall in income that might arise, all local authorities were empowered to charge for services such as domestic water, sewerage and refuse charges. While consumers in rural areas had been paying water charges for some time, the 1983 Act allowed county councils to charge for all domestic services and it extended these powers of charging to the urban authorities.

The grant in relief of domestic rates paid to local authorities from 1983 onwards fell far short of the income that authorities would have received from domestic rates. In some authorities the amount of grant actually fell from one year to the next. The hoped-for increase in local authority income through service charges, to meet the shortfall in grant, never really materialised. From the start there was strong public resistance to paying these charges, particularly in urban areas. There was a perception that the charges were a further tax on an already overtaxed public. It was argued that income tax had already been increased when domestic rates were abolished and the levying of charges to fund services, previously funded by domestic rates, was, in effect, double taxation.

Another critical factor that led to the decline in local authority finances was the termination of rates on agricultural land. A 1982 High Court decision found that the basis for agricultural rates was unconstitutional. This decision was upheld by the Supreme Court in 1984. The government decided that the rate support grant would be increased to make up for losses arising from the Supreme Court ruling, but again this grant failed to keep pace with inflation.

The impact of all these changes reduced the income available to local authorities and resulted in a greater reliance on commercial rates and charges for services to pay for day-to-day expenditure. Such was the resistance to domestic service charges that Naas Urban District Council was removed from office in

1985 for failure to adopt its local authority budget (then known as its estimate of expenses), which included revenue from domestic service charges. The council was replaced by a commissioner.

In 1984, the government announced its intention to introduce a new farm tax, with those with smallholdings of less than twenty acres to be treated as exempt. The rate of the tax was determined by central government, and there was no power for local authorities to vary the rate. Some €6.6 million was levied by local authorities for 1986, with some €5.5 million being collected (Coughlan and de Buitleir, 1996, p. 68). However, a new government came into power in 1987 and abolished the tax.

The National Economic and Social Council (NESC) published a report entitled *The Financing of Local Authorities* in May 1985. While a centrally financed system for local government was not ruled out, the NESC expressed the view that local authorities should have greater discretion to determine their own overall spending levels; in effect they should have an independent source of revenue. While accepting that charges for services were a desirable link between consumption and payments, the NESC pointed out that the scope for such charges was limited in practice. The report was of the view that charges should bear some relationship to usage. It recommended the introduction of a property tax based on capital values, initially based on self-assessment. The NESC failed to agree on the extent to which a property tax should be applied to farmland. In relation to grants, it was concluded that specific government grants should be available to finance national services, with a block grant to support other needs. Grants should attempt to compensate for a low tax base or high spending needs. The NESC report warned that 'the financing of local government stands at a watershed' and that without some change 'there is likely to be further escalation of what are already serious financing difficulties for local government as a whole' (NESC, 1985b, p. 21).

The fourth report of the Commission on Taxation, also published in May 1985, covered similar ground to the NESC report and reached broadly similar conclusions in recommending that local authorities should have a significant independent source of locally raised revenue, which should be levied as a broadly based property tax. This was seen as the only practical method of raising significant sums through local taxation. A valuation system based on self-assessed, open market capital values for residential property was suggested. Values would be classified into broad brands, remain valid for five years and be administered and audited by local authorities. Industrial and commercial properties would be taxed on the basis of rental valuations.

The report classified local authority services into two categories, local and national, and concluded that national services should be financed from central taxation by way of government grants. It recommended that central government grants be consolidated into a single 'local taxation support' grant, which should be distributed on a needs and resources basis.

Taken together, the NESC and Commission on Taxation reports made a very powerful case for a return to local property taxation, albeit on the basis of market valuations rather than rateable valuations. In recommending a local property tax, both reports clearly stated that the objective was not to generate additional taxation, but rather to substitute one form of central taxation for another form of local taxation. The general thrust of the report, in so far as local taxation was concerned, was generally supported in a government policy statement, *Reform of Local Government*, also issued in May 1985. This included 'the aim that local authorities should have opportunities of raising a reasonable proportion of the resources required to meet local needs from local sources' (Government of Ireland, 1985a, p. 26). Despite these three publications, a proposal to reform the local government system did not emerge.

1990s

In April 1990, the Fianna Fáil/Progressive Democrat coalition put forward their strategy for local government reorganisation and reform. An advisory expert committee was set up to review the structures, function and organisation of local authorities. The terms of reference were fairly general, except with regard to finance, where the committee was required 'to make recommendations on the criteria on which the contribution from central funds to local authorities should be made on a statutory basis'. The committee's report (known as the Barrington Report) was produced in 1991.

In relation to finance, the Barrington Report concluded that there must be a link between spending and raising money in order to promote responsibility and accountability. The view was expressed that local authorities should raise a significant proportion of revenue from non-central sources, with the liability dispersed widely among the electorate and not confined to any one sector. On the distribution of central funds and local authority funding generally, the report recommended that government grants should be consolidated into a single general equalisation grant distributed on the basis of needs and resources. The introduction of an equalisation system was likely to result in gainers and losers and, accordingly, the report recommended that the transition to such a system would be phased in over a period of years. It also recommended that maximum discretion be given to local authorities where local spending priorities were concerned.

As part of the review, the committee commissioned a study, carried out by the Institute for Fiscal Studies in the UK, to consider the basis on which the contribution from central funds to local authorities should be made. The study found that about two-thirds of government grants were in the form of specific grants. The most substantial change proposed was that the distribution of the rate support grant would include an element of equalisation. A follow-up study in

1992 outlined a proposed system for redistribution of the rate support grant on an objective scientific basis. Implementation of the recommendations in the report would have resulted in about half the local authorities gaining extra rate support grant, while the other half lost out. The report was not universally accepted and its methodology was questioned by many. The report's recommendations were never implemented.

The government generally accepted many of the committee's recommendations. Statutory effect was given to a number of recommendations with the enactment of the Local Government Act, 1991. However, the question of funding was not addressed.

At the end of 1994, the rainbow coalition of Fine Gael, Labour and Democratic Left took office. Their policy agreement, *A Government of Renewal*, recognised the need to provide for the satisfactory funding of local government. To this end, the government committed itself to commission a professional study to see how a fair, equitable and reasonable system of funding could be introduced with a view to publishing a White Paper on the subject and seeking to develop the maximum degree of consensus on the issue. Recognising the fact that local service charges were seen by some as double taxation, the government, as a short-term measure, introduced a tax allowance for service charges to remove this argument. Legislation was also enacted to delimit the power of local authorities to disconnect domestic water supply for non-payment of service charges. This legislation proved exceptionally cumbersome to implement and was challenged in the courts. Local authorities consequently found it more difficult to collect service charges in the new environment.

The government commissioned three separate reports on different aspects of local government. The Local Government Reorganisation Commission (1996) delivered a report on town local government. The Devolution Commission was established in July 1995 to make recommendations on the additional functions to be devolved to local authorities and published its interim report in June 1996 and a further report in April 1997. In relation to local government finance, the minister commissioned a study to assess the future expenditure requirements of local authorities and consider a comprehensive range of options for developing a fair, equitable and reasonable system of local government funding. The funding options identified that would most likely yield positive results were to be subject to further study. The report, entitled *The Financing of Local Government in Ireland*, was prepared by KPMG and published in June 1996.

The KPMG report reviewed likely future expenditure needs and concluded that if projected investment programmes were implemented, local government current expenditure would be of the order of €1.84 billion in 2000, at 1995 prices. Current expenditure in 1995 was €1.55 billion. The major sources of likely future expenditure increases were on the roads programme and the cost of operating and maintaining infrastructure which was under development, particularly in the areas of sewage treatment, waste disposal and environment protection. The report also systematically examined the various strands of existing and potential sources of funding for local authorities. It concluded that the addition of a local property tax or a local income tax to the then existing funding system would bring about the necessary buoyancy which it felt was lacking. It also recommended that any future funding system should contain an equalisation element, which would provide support for those authorities with a weak funding base.

On the issue of service charges, the view was expressed that the linking of charges to the level of consumption would help remove the perception that charges were a form of taxation. In relation to water charges, it was pointed out that extensive metering of households to measure water consumption was not considered a viable alternative having regard to the capital costs and ongoing maintenance costs involved. The report concluded: 'therefore the system of weekly or annual charges per household should remain pending the advent of cost-effective metering/weighing [refuse] systems' (KPMG, 1996, p. 42).

Better Local Government – A Programme for Change

Following on the publication of the various government-commissioned studies, the minister promised a comprehensive strategy statement on local government before the end of 1996. The publication of *Better Local Government – A Programme for Change* in December 1996 represented the most radical reform programme for the local government system since the early part of the century. The report itself stated: 'Reform of local government has been on the political agenda for 25 years, although real progress and meaningful change has been limited to date. It is now time for action' (Department of the Environment, 1996, foreword).

The reform programme was based on four principles: enhancing local democracy, serving the customer better, developing efficiency and providing proper resources. As part of the programme, the minister proposed to revise and modernise the existing accounting system for local authorities, broadly in line with commercial accounting practices. The intention was to shift the emphasis from that of an accounting system to a financial management system – a first priority in establishing an 'efficiency approach' to local government finances.

In terms of funding, the arrangements put forward, which were introduced in 1997, marked the most fundamental change to the local government funding system in the twenty years since rates had been abolished. The main features of the new system involved the termination of the rate support grant, the abolition of domestic water and sewerage charges and the assigning of motor taxation proceeds to local authorities. In general, local authorities were entitled to retain 80 per cent of motor tax income from private cars and motorcycles, the balance being paid into a new local government equalisation fund. Local authorities were also empowered to increase motor tax rates in their areas by up to 6 per cent. The equalisation fund was designed to ensure that local authorities did not lose out as a result of the new scheme and to help weaker authorities to provide an acceptable level of service. A provision was included in the relevant legislation for the establishment of an equalisation council to manage the equalisation fund and decide on allocations to local authorities.

Better Local Government (Department of the Environment, 1996, p. 46) states:

> A locally available, independent and buoyant source of finance is vital in the renewal process for local authorities . . . new sources of funding are urgently required by the local authority system but there is general political and community agreement that the provision of new funding should not involve an increase in the overall burden of taxation.

Motor taxation revenue was thus seen as being the solution. The total of motor tax proceeds exceeded the combination of domestic water/sewerage charges and rate support grant, which were being abolished. Buoyancy in motor tax in future years, together with the potential income on the local variation element, would ensure a margin of comfort for local authorities into the future.

There were mixed views about the new scheme. On the positive side it was seen that the new system would immediately inject extra funding to local government. Car sales were particularly buoyant in the 1990s, with income from motor tax proceeds delivering an extra €48 million for local government in 1997 compared to 1996. Buoyancy in motor tax, together with the potential revenue from the local variation element, would guarantee continued growth in funding into the future. The new system also recognised the need for equalisation. On the negative side, the abolition of local charges was seen as a retrograde step. Local accountability, decision making and discretion were reduced by the abolition of the charges. The prospect of different rates of motor taxation applying in different local authority areas did not seem practicable. The abolition of domestic water and sewerage charges could threaten the availability of EU monies on the basis that it was counter to the polluter pays principle.

The revised proposals were enacted in the Local Government (Financial Provisions) Act, 1997. The system was being put into operation when a general election in June 1997 brought about a change of government. The programme of the new Fianna Fáil and Progressive Democrat coalition government, *An Action Programme for the Millennium,* accepted the general thrust of the overall programme for reform in *Better Local Government*, but with some changes to the proposals for local government financing.

A New Deal for Local Government

Pending the finalisation of the new proposals, local authorities were requested not to invoke their recently acquired powers to introduce a local variation of motor tax. The new financing system under *Better Local Government* was short lived and terminated on 31 December 1998. A new funding system for local government was launched in January 1999 and introduced under the Local Government Act, 1998. The central feature was the replacement of the local government equalisation fund with a new Local Government Fund. The new fund was to be financed from two sources: an exchequer contribution (€420 million in 2002) and the full proceeds of motor taxation. The initial exchequer contribution was specified in legislation and was ring fenced and future proofed. Under the Act, the contribution was to be increased each year, at least in line with inflation, and annual adjustments to the fund were to have regard to changes in the functions and cost base of local authorities. The full proceeds of motor taxation were to be paid into the fund. The fund was to be used to meet the general purposes needs of local authorities and provide all government grants for non-national roads.

Motor taxation rates would continue to be set nationally with rates being increased by 3 per cent from August 1998 and a further 3 per cent from January 1999. These were the first increases to motor tax rates since 1992. The new system had positive features in that the Local Government Fund was ring fenced in legislation, belonged in law to local authorities and had guaranteed income sources.

Equalisation was to be a critical element of the new system and a pilot study began in Galway County Council in an attempt to devise an acceptable needs and resources model. The approach was founded on the principle that 'an equalisation process that does not reduce the amount of funds currently available to any authority is more likely to be implemented than a process which radically changes the amount of funds available' (Department of the Environment and Local Government, 1998d, p. 7). This was a fundamental difference in approach from the 1992 Institute of Fiscal Studies report, *Rate Support Grant Distribution in Ireland*, which was prepared as a follow-on to the Barrington Report but never implemented.

A complex distribution model was developed which attempted to measure the needs and resources of each local authority. The model was first utilised in July 2000 to distribute a supplementary grant from the Local Government Fund. County councils, with the exception of Monaghan County Council, all received additional allocations from this initial distribution. Notably, urban authorities did not fare well under the model, with no city council receiving additional funds under the initial distribution. This prompted the view that the model was biased in favour of rural authorities. A review body comprising departmental and local authority personnel was established in 2001 to accept submissions and make recommendations for change to the model. The resulting distribution model has become an important element in determining annual allocations from the Local Government Fund to local authorities.

As part of the new package of funding measures, the minister announced his intention to limit commercial rate increases. For 1998, local authorities were requested to keep within a guideline maximum increase of 4 per cent. For 1999, the minister made an order setting a maximum ceiling on rate increases at 5 per cent more than 1998. Ministerial orders were also made setting a rate cap for 2000 and 2001, although no cap on rates was set for budgets adopted in 2002.

Other elements of the reform package were advanced, including the introduction of a new financial management system for local authorities; the enactment of the Valuation Act, 2001, which provided for a review of the law in relation to the valuation of property; and proposals were developed for a comprehensive review of rating law (see chapter 19).

Local Finance . . . The Debate Continues

In recent decades local government financing has evolved from a system where a substantial portion of local income was generated locally – the domestic rates era – to an attempt to generate substantial income from local service charges (1983) and finally a return to a centralised funding system with the abolition of domestic charges and the introduction of the Local Government Fund in 1997/8. The fundamental issue of whether some powers of local taxation are essential to local government – a necessary item in the degree of local autonomy – still remains unresolved. There are strongly divergent views on the topic. The Barrington Report (1991, p. 38) was of the view that:

> . . . there must be some link between spending and raising money in order to promote responsibility and accountability . . . democracy and responsibility can be looked on in this context as two sides of the one coin. This implies that local authorities should raise a significant proportion of the revenue from non-central sources such as charges or local taxation.

The KPMG study (1996, p. 6) concluded:

> . . . there has been a consensus in previous reports that substantial levels of local funding should be available to local authorities. However, none of the literature indicates what the ideal mix of local/central funding should be.

These views contrast with those expressed earlier by de Buitleir (1974, p. 72), who dismissed the link between local discretion and local sources of revenue and stated that 'the belief that local authorities must finance from their own resources a significant amount of their expenditure, if they are to have a reasonably free hand in the administration of services, is crippling local government'. However, the Netherlands is an example of a viable system of local government based almost entirely on grant finance, with local taxes representing less than 10 per cent of income. General grants are funded from a municipalities fund on the basis of an equalisation formula, which takes account of size, population, number of houses and other factors.

Clearly the debate over local government financing has not run its full course. An independent estimates review committee in 2002 stated that reintroducing water charges on domestic properties could be considered if the exchequer position worsened, as a 'charging regime could contribute to more efficient use of what is becoming an extremely expensive resource', and observed that 'Ireland is unique amongst OECD and EU Member States in not charging domestic consumers' (Bonner et al., 2002, p. 49). This call was publicly supported by the Minister for Finance in 2003. An NESC report also commented that there was scope for increased use of environmental taxes, charges and incentives in a range of areas (NESC, 2002, p. 334). It noted the possibility of a development land value tax where land values are increased through new public investment in infrastructure, arguing that 'it is appropriate that those whose assets gain in value from wider economic and social development should return some portion of their gain back to society' (NESC, 2002, p. 336). Meanwhile, yet another review of the system of local government financing was announced in 2002.

While the debate on the issue will no doubt continue, the approach to local government financing at the start of the twenty-first century is based firmly on central government funding, limited local discretion and a developing equalisation system. It is generally conceded, however, that under a system based mainly on central funding, a grant system can be designed which gives considerable local autonomy.

19

Local Government Finance: The Financial Process

Tony Davis

This chapter deals with many of the financial issues that arise in local authorities including the budgetary process, rates and valuation, central government grants, local authority charges, audit and financial control, value for money and the local authority financial management system.

Budget Preparation and Making of Rate

Local authorities are required to prepare a local authority budget each year under section 102 of the Local Government Act, 2001. This Act uses the words 'local authority budget' in place of the phrase 'estimate of expenses' that had been traditionally used to refer to local authority budgets before 2001. The classification of receipts and expenditure in the budget is by programme group, of which there are eight (see chapter 8). Funding of local authority current expenditure is met from rates on commercial properties, government grants, charges for services and other sources. Funding of capital expenditure is met from exchequer or EU grants or by borrowing.

On the basis of the budget adopted by the council, an annual rate on valuation (known as the rate in the pound before the 2001 Act) is determined, which will finance the deficiency in the funds of the authority. This deficiency is the element of the estimated expenditure not met from either state grants or the local authority's own resources from goods and services (see below).

County, city, borough and most town councils are empowered to levy rates. However, some town councils (ex-town commissioners) do not levy rates but levy a demand on the county council, which in turn levies an additional rate on the town (Local Government Act, 2001, section 101). Non-rating bodies such as regional authorities are funded by local authorities by way of estimate and demand.

In 1974, the local authorities' financial year changed to the calendar year (Exchequer and Local Financial Years Act, 1974). The change was determined by EU Standards. The 1974 financial year was a nine-month period (1 April to 31 December). Thereafter, the financial year coincided with the calendar year. All bodies now prepare their budgets towards the end of each financial year for the forthcoming financial year. The Minister for the Environment and Local Government prescribes the period for the preparation of the budget. In 2002, the dates for the 2003 budgets were prescribed as:

Non-rating bodies:	15 November 2002 to 16 December 2002
County councils:	25 November 2002 to 13 January 2003
City and (rating) town councils:	25 November 2002 to 13 January 2003.

In accordance with the provisions of the Local Government Act, 2001, the county or city manager, in consultation with the corporate policy group (CPG), prepares the local authority budget showing the monies required for each service for the forthcoming financial year. The draft budget is considered by the full council at the local authority budget meeting (formerly known as the estimates meeting). Under the provisions of the Local Government (Financial Provisions) Act, 1978, the minister has the power to limit rate increases. Such limitations were applied in 1983, 1984, 1985, 2000, 2001 and 2002. No cap was applied for 2003.

A small number of local authorities had estimates committees to assist the manager in the preparation of the budget. This task has now been taken over by the CPG, and the draft budget must be prepared by the manager in consultation with the CPG in the case of county and city councils. When the draft budget is prepared, a copy, together with formal notice of the local authority budget meeting, is sent to each elected member seven days before the date agreed. Public notice is also given in a newspaper circulating in the local authority area.

The council has twenty-one days to adopt the budget either as presented or as amended. Failure to adopt the budget within the statutory times results in the matter being reported to the minister. The minister can remove the council and appoint a commissioner to carry out its functions in such an eventuality, although this is rare and, at the time of writing, has not happened since 1985. On adoption of the budget the cathaoirleach/mayor and meetings administrator/town clerk sign the statutory certificate confirming that the budget and rateable valuation multiplier were adopted at the meeting. A copy of the budget is then sent to the minister.

Under the Local Government Act, 2001, a number of powers are conferred on elected members in relation to financial issues. These include the adoption of the annual budget; authorisation of excess expenditure, borrowing and lending; the consideration of the annual financial statement and of the auditor's report; and the adoption of a community initiative scheme to raise funds. The elected members may also establish a special audit committee and may require the submission to the council of financial reports of such detail and frequency as they may specify. Councillors also determine the level of the local rate and, through the budgetary process, the amount of local service charges.

Rating System

In 1977, the government decided to exempt domestic property from rates with effect from 1978 and to compensate local authorities for the loss of this revenue by way of a rate support grant. At first, this grant represented the full loss of domestic rate monies. However, over the years, the compensation began to reduce and by 1983 the shortfall was significant.

In 1984, the Supreme Court upheld a challenge to agricultural rates on land and these too were abolished – in particular the court held that the levying of rates on land by reference to the poor law valuation system was inconsistent with the Constitution. As a result, local authorities were paid a grant in lieu of rates on agricultural land that was in addition to the rate support grant.

These events had a severe impact on local authority finances and as a result legislation was introduced in 1983 to allow local authorities to charge for services such as domestic water and domestic refuse collection in urban areas. Such charges were already levied in county council areas. In addition, to lessen the impact of large rate increases, the minister imposed a percentage rate increase limit on local authorities. Few changes were made to the rate support grant until 1997 when a new system allowed local authorities to retain 80 per cent of motor tax receipts, with the surplus being paid into a Local Government (Equalisation) Fund, which would be used to pay a state grant to local authorities. This system, which also gave local authorities the power to vary rates of motor tax by up to 6 per cent, operated for a period of eighteen months and came to an end in December 1998.

In 1999, a new Local Government Fund was established. It is funded from the following sources: an exchequer contribution (€420 million in 2002) and the full proceeds from motor taxation (€540 million in 2002). These sources amounted to a total fund of €960 million in 2002, ring fenced solely for local government purposes. The power to vary rates of motor tax in different local authority areas was abolished. The Local Government Act, 1998, which established the new funding system, provided that the exchequer contribution would be index-linked in line with inflation and would take account of the additional funding needs of local authorities. The fund is used to finance the general-purpose needs of local authorities and the non-national roads programme.

In 1999, a major study of local authority financial needs and resources was undertaken, with a view to designing a model for the equitable distribution of monies from the Local Government Fund in accordance with local authority needs. The initial studies were based on 1999 local authority budgets with further studies based on the actual outturns of 1999 from the annual financial statements. This expenditure, receipt and statistical analysis resulted in a redistribution of the Local Government Fund monies in 2000. A review of the needs and resources model was underway in 2003.

Valuation

Certain kinds of fixed or immovable property (although not domestic dwellings) are liable for rates. This property consists principally of land and buildings and includes mines, commons and rights of commonage, profits out of land, rights of fishery, canals, navigation and rights of navigation, railways, rights of way and other rights, tolls levied in respect of those rights and all other tolls. The valuing of property for rating is carried out by the Commissioner of Valuation. There is right of appeal to the Valuation Tribunal against valuations determined by the commissioner. Rating authorities do not have valuing powers.

Rating legislation is spread across numerous Acts, many of which date from the nineteenth century. The primary legislation relating to rates is the Poor Relief (Ireland) Act, 1838 and the Valuation (Ireland) Act, 1852. With the exception of the Local Government (Financial Provisions) Act, 1978, which removed domestic dwellings from rates liability, and the Supreme Court decision in 1984 relating to agricultural rates, only minor changes and adjustments have been made to the rating system – although the Valuation Act, 1988 did provide for revision of valuation and for appeal to the Valuation Tribunal.

An interdepartmental review of the valuation system was undertaken in 1994 by the Department of Finance, the Department of the Environment and the Valuation Office. The Valuation Act, 2001 followed, which provided for:

- updating of the valuation system
- revaluation of all rateable property on a regular basis every five to ten years
- the removal of identified deficiencies in the valuation system
- making the system more transparent to both ratepayers and local authorities.

Exemptions/Remissions

The present situation is that rates are levied only on immovable property in industrial and commercial use, including factories, shops, offices, power stations and mines. There are circumstances where, either for an unlimited period or for a number of years, certain properties get full exemption from rates or remission of part of the rates which would otherwise be payable. These circumstances include:

- mines for seven years after they open
- oil wells for twenty years from the time oil is first extracted
- buildings and properties used exclusively for public or charitable purposes or for the purpose of science, literature and the fine arts
- turf banks when no rent or valuable consideration is payable
- fishery rights (though they are liable for rates struck by the regional fisheries boards)
- lighthouses, beacons, buoys and hereditaments used or occupied solely to afford air raid protection
- new buildings in designated areas or in respect of any increase in the rates attributable to enlargement or improvement of existing buildings in designated areas for ten years.

Remission of part of the liability to pay rates may be applied to premises provided for an industrial undertaking in a designated area. The remission, which is at the discretion of the rating authority, is two-thirds for ten years.

Rate Book

Preparation of the rate book is based on the latest valuation list available from the Commissioner of Valuation at the time of adoption of the local authority budget. It shows the valuation of properties for rating purposes. When the rate book has been prepared, public notice is given in a newspaper circulating in the local authority area, advising that the book is available for inspection for fourteen days.

Once this procedure has been completed, the manager makes an order making the rate – an executive function under the Local Government (Financial Provisions) Act, 1978. The signing of this order by the manager is a formal endorsement of the budget as adopted by the council. Public notice to this effect is again given in a newspaper circulating in the area, indicating rights of appeal and appeal periods should a ratepayer feel aggrieved. Warrants are prepared for the council's collector authorising the collection of rates. Rate demands now issue and collection of rates commences.

Collection of Rates

Rates are payable in two moieties or halves. The first moiety together with any arrears is payable on demand. The second moiety is usually payable on 1 July. County and city council areas are generally divided into collection districts with a number of revenue collectors. Town council areas, depending on their size, may or may not be divided into collection districts. Collectors, who also collect money due for services and under loans, have extensive powers for collecting rates including the seizing of goods (known as levy by distress). Collectors can also issue a six-day notice demanding payment and summoning the defaulter before the courts.

Under sections 11 and 23 of the Local Government Act, 1946, a ratepayer, subject to certain criteria, can obtain a refund of rates provided that the property is vacant on the day the rate was made for the purpose of undergoing repairs, renovations or alterations, or seeking a suitable tenant at a reasonable rent.

All monies collected by the collector(s) must be lodged forthwith. At the close of the financial year the collector(s) must prepare a schedule of uncollected rates. This schedule is then considered by the manager, who must decide on sums to be written off, disallowed or considered temporarily uncollectable. The manager can direct the collectors to lodge any monies deemed disallowed. The monies regarded as temporarily uncollectable are carried forward as arrears and included for collection with the next year's rates.

Reform of the Rates System

In 1999, a working group, comprising representatives from central and local government, was established to carry out a review of rating legislation with a view to the introduction of a consolidated modern rating code. The review had the following objectives:

- update, codify, simplify and reform rating law
- standardise rating law across all rating authorities
- modernise collection and recovery procedures
- make the system more transparent to ratepayers
- secure rates as an important source of local finance.

The main recommendations of the review (Working Group on the Review of Rating Law, 2001) can be summarised as follows:

- all previous legislation should be repealed
- rating law and practice should be standardised across all rating authorities
- liability for rates should remain with the occupier of property or the owner of vacant property
- ratepayers should be given a statutory right to pay rates by instalments
- interest should be payable on outstanding rates
- rates on vacant property should be charged at 50 per cent of the full rate in respect of the period of vacancy
- a rate should only be questioned by an application for judicial review of the making of the rate procedures
- a comprehensive standard power of recovery should be provided in the new legislation

- rates should be included in the list of taxes for which a tax clearance certificate is required prior to the obtaining or renewal of specified licences.

At the time of writing it is understood that legislation is being prepared to give effect to the review group's recommendations.

Other Local Authority Income

State Grants and Subsidies

Prior to 1990, the local loans fund provided loan facilities to local authorities to finance major works such as housing construction, water and sewerage schemes, land acquisition and other capital projects. Local authorities made half-yearly repayments to the fund on the monies borrowed. The department subsidised these repayments at various rates of between 50 and 100 per cent, depending on the type of works. Since the abolition of the fund in 1990, changes have taken place in relation to state grants and subsidies paid to local authorities.

A scheme of capital grants was introduced in the 1990s to enable local authorities to finance capital works. This eliminated the need for borrowing for works such as housing construction and sanitary services schemes. State grants embrace many aspects of local authority operations. These grants are payable by a number of different government departments and include the following:

- capital: housing construction, remedial works, voluntary housing, Traveller accommodation, water supply schemes, sewerage schemes, fire stations, major roadworks
- revenue: roadworks, motor taxation, higher education grants, vocational education, Local Government Fund.

Local authorities continue to have a general power to borrow money (under section 106 of the Local Government Act, 2001) either from financial institutions or from bodies such as the Housing Finance Agency or the National Treasury Management Agency. The decision to borrow money is a reserved function.

Goods and Services

The following are the main sources of income under goods and services:

- housing rents and annuities
- housing loan repayments
- commercial water charges
- refuse charges
- planning application and building control fees
- landfill charges

- fire charges
- library fees.

In addition, there are a number of miscellaneous receipts such as dog licence fees, caravan licence fees and loan application fees.

Contributions from Other Local Authorities

This relates generally to 'county at large' services and is recovered from the town councils in a county through the levying of a county charge (known as the county demand before 2001). This charge is levied for services that the county council provides on behalf of the town council (Local Government Act, 2001, section 100). Calculation of the charge tends to be complex but is based on county at large services provided by county councils divided in proportion to the produce of one penny in the pound. Under the Local Government Act, 2001, the county council can charge for the actual or estimated cost of service having regard to any guidelines or directions of the minister. The town council must provide for the amount demanded in its own budget.

Audit and Financial Management Issues

All local authorities are accountable for public funds under their control and management and are required to maintain proper books and accounts for the control of such funds. As part of this process, local authority accounts are audited annually by the Local Government Audit Service. Public notices prior to commencement and on completion of audit are given in papers circulating in the local authority area. Audited accounts are also circulated to the local authority members and are available to the general public.

Annual financial statements for the financial year 1 January to 31 December must be prepared and submitted to the Department of the Environment and Local Government within twelve weeks of the close of the financial year. Because of the legal formalities involved in the commencement of audits and the finalisation of annual accounts, the audit cycle usually commences from the following April. It is open to a local authority to establish an audit committee to consider the audited financial statement (Local Government Act, 2001, section 122).

The Local Government Audit Service, being an external service, provides independent scrutiny of the financial and regularity stewardship of local authorities. Its purpose is to provide an independent appraisal of the discharge by management of that function and to inform the public of the results of such a review. The outputs from audits are the formal audit opinions incorporated in the local authority's annual financial statement and the issue of audit reports on general matters for the information of the relevant controlling department of state, council members and management, as well as the public. The principles underlying external audit of local authorities are:

- local government auditors are independent in the exercise of their professional functions from both controlling departments and the bodies being audited
- local government auditors have a wide remit covering the audit of authorities' annual financial statements including regularity, probity and value-for-money work
- the issuing of audit reports makes the results of local government audit available to the public.

Local government auditors are empowered to invoke where necessary the statutory powers to:

- hear and adjudicate on objections from the public on matters contained in or omitted from the accounts of a local authority
- take evidence on oath
- require attendance of witnesses
- require production of books and other documents relevant to the audit
- impose a charge or surcharge on officials, managers (and in certain cases elected members) where illegal or unfounded payments are made or where a loss has occurred to the funds of a local authority due to negligence or misconduct.

Staff and members are required to co-operate with an auditor and to supply such information as may be requested – failure to do so is an offence under section 119 of the Local Government Act, 2001.

Value for Money, Efficiency and Performance Indicators

Local authorities are expected to continue improvements in areas such as customer service, efficiency and value for money (VFM). The Department of the Environment and Local Government has carried out a number of VFM studies, including: photocopying, revenue collection, stores, water production and distribution, housing maintenance, debt collection, waste collection, purchasing, advertising, public lighting, energy efficiency, machinery yards, parking charges, differential rents, motor tax, insurance, property management, performance management, treasury management and internal audit. These studies make a number of recommendations with regard to good practice. Many local authorities have VFM sections, which add to and complement these studies and help introduce good practice in individual local authority sections.

Service or performance indicators have also been developed at national level to help local authorities to determine how well they are doing in the delivery of services. The list of service indicators includes the cost of providing specific services (for example the cost per square metre for surface dressing), measures of a local authority's efficiency (for example the time taken to fill housing vacancies) and measures of a local authority's financial performance (for example the percentage of debts collected). Local authorities are also expected to draw up their own local indicators to monitor their performance.

Local Authority Financial Management System (LAFMS)

A new financial management system was introduced to all local authorities during 2000 and 2001. The new system resulted in a move by local authorities to an accrual accounting system, which measures income and expenditure arising in the year in question. Thus, income includes actual receipts taken in as a result of activities during the year as well as debts that become owed in respect of activities during the year – that is income earned during the year. Equally, expenditure includes actual payments made by the organisation in respect to purchases, but also commitments to pay for purchases entered into during the year. The traditional public sector system of cash accounting is based only on payments (as opposed to expenditure, which includes commitments) and receipts (which, unlike income, does not include debts earned).

Under the 1946 Public Bodies Order (since replaced with a more modern financial regulatory regime), local authorities operated a cross between the accrual and the cash system based on expenditure and receipts. This, it was felt, did not accurately reflect the liability that existed for goods delivered for which payment had not been made. Given the ever more complex demands on local authorities, the existing financial reporting system proved deficient as it could not provide a true and full picture of financial performance, the true worth of the authority or information on the cost of service provision. The first steps to address this deficiency came with the amendment to the abstract of accounts, which was renamed the annual financial statement from 1999. This statement, as well as containing details on actual figures concerning a local authority's revenue (current) account and capital account at year end, also includes a statement of accounting policies, a comparison of performance against budget and notes to the accounts. The statement is due within twelve weeks of the end of the year. After consideration by the elected members, it is forwarded to the department.

An accounting code of practice (ACOP) was issued in 1998. It sets out the accounting policies that should be applied consistently in order to present fairly the financial position and transactions of the local authority, and also the minimum disclosure and presentation requirements. One of the main aims of the ACOP is to reduce the differences in accounting treatment and enhance the usefulness of the annual financial statements.

Local Government Act, 2001 and Community Fund

By the end of 2002, the commencement of part 12 of the Local Government Act, 2001 had provided an updated framework for local authority financial procedures and audit, including modern financial management systems with a new format of accounts.

Local authorities are also empowered under the Act to set up a separate 'community fund' to support specific community initiatives such as amenity, recreational, cultural or community development projects. Contributions to the fund may be made by local voluntary, business or community groups, by the local authority itself or raised by way of a community initiative scheme or any combination of these. Such a scheme may be adopted at the discretion of the local authority, following public consultation. A community initiative scheme enables a local authority to collect an annual contribution from each household towards a specific community initiative undertaken by itself or in partnership with local community or other interests. The scheme must describe the particular initiative, specify the amount of the annual contribution, the period of years for which it will apply and the area within which it will be collected.

20

Urbanisation

Pauline Byrne

It is predicted that by 2015, 65 per cent of the world's population will live in cities, with the highest rates of urbanisation occurring in the world's least developed countries. In China, 50,000 peasants arrive every hour looking for work and accommodation in the country's capital, Beijing (Verdú, 1999). Urbanisation refers to the proportion of the total population concentrated in urban settlements, or to a rise in this proportion (Davis, 1967).

Over 60 per cent of the Irish population lives in urban areas (towns greater than 1,500 population, as defined in the 1996 Census) and a much higher figure depend on towns for work and for social facilities. This figure is increasing, having risen from 42 per cent in 1951 to 52 per cent in 1971 and it is expected that the 2002 Census will indicate a slightly higher figure when published. While significant, the rate of increase in urbanisation has not fulfilled past forecasts, for example in 1982 it was predicted that the urban population would grow by upwards of one million in the twenty-year period from 1971 to 1991 (Roche, 1982b, p. 211). Instead, the increase in the thirty-year period to 2001 falls somewhat short of the one million mark. Urbanisation in Ireland remains low in comparison to the rest of Europe. Between 70 and 80 per cent of the populations of most EU countries are urbanised and urbanisation in England is at more than 90 per cent.

This trend towards urban living counters the anti-urban, or at least anti-high-density, bias in Ireland. This bias worked against the growth and development of cities, and stifled their need for continuous reinforcement in order to prosper and compete internationally, in favour of the pursuit of the rural idyll endorsed in the Constitution (Article 45).

Many of the issues currently provoked by increasing levels of urbanisation in Ireland were forecast more than twenty years ago by, among others, An Foras

Forbatha (National Institute for Physical Planning and Construction Research) in their conference series *Ireland in the Year 2000* (1980 to 1985), and the 1968 Buchanan Report. Issues such as congestion, air and water pollution, urban-generated development of rural areas, decline of the rural economy, waste management and environmental degradation all emerged as real and potential problems. Conflicting objectives of state agencies, it was recognised, had to be brought together into an overall planning framework which would become 'an essential prerequisite of Ireland's development strategy' at both an urban and rural level (An Foras Forbatha, 1980). Intricately linked to urbanisation is rural development. The National Economic and Social Council (NESC) study of spatial change in the Irish rural economy confirms the increasing interdependence between agricultural and non-agricultural activities within rural areas and between rural and urban areas (NESC, 1994, p. 62). The national spatial strategy sees urban and rural areas as intrinsically interdependent due to complex flows of people and services (Department of the Environment and Local Government, 2003).

Many counties have experienced sharp population growth, but without any co-ordination on a regional or national level with regards to infrastructure or services provision. Until recently, no co-ordinating frameworks existed within which local authorities could develop their statutory plans. In 1985, An Foras Forbatha lamented the absence of a national physical planning strategy, a situation which was perceived to give rise to regional and lower scale plans devoid of context. More recently, plans such as the LUTS (land use and transportation study) plan for Cork or the *Strategic Planning Guidelines for the Greater Dublin Area* (1999) have attempted to marry land use with transport and infrastructure objectives beyond city and county boundaries. The level of buy-in to these plans has often been unco-ordinated and random, and begs the question as to the potential effectiveness of the national spatial strategy.

Urban Growth

The varied rate of growth experienced by the principal cities in the state in the period from 1946 to 1996 is significant, with Dublin increasing its population by 75 per cent, Cork by 94 per cent, Limerick by 91 per cent, Galway by 207 per cent and Waterford by 63 per cent. Additionally, Leinster's share of the national population has risen considerably from 43 per cent in 1946 to reach 54 per cent in 2002; each of the three other provinces experienced a decline in their share of population over the same 57-year period (Central Statistics Office, 2002).

In 1996, 44 per cent of the population lived in the state's twenty-one largest cities and towns and 36.2 per cent lived in its five principal cities: Dublin, Cork, Limerick, Galway and Waterford (see table 20.1). The percentage of the population residing in urban areas has almost certainly increased since that period, when one considers the extensive residential development that has occurred in all of these towns over the 1996 to 2001 period. For example, Carlow has seen the number of house completions grow year-on-year (with the exception of 1998) by between 11 per cent and 16.3 per cent in the 1996 to 1999 period. This compares to a national average growth of between 10 per cent and 11.5 per cent during the same period.

Table 20.1 Population of Ireland's Largest Cities and Towns, 1996

City/town	Population (000s)
Dublin*	953
Cork	180
Limerick	79
Galway	57
Waterford	44
Dundalk	30
Bray	28
Drogheda	25
Swords	22
Tralee	20
Kilkenny	19
Sligo	19
Ennis	18
Clonmel	16
Wexford	16
Athlone	16
Carlow	15
Naas	14
Malahide	14
Leixlip	13
Newbridge	13
Total	**1,611**
National population	3,626

* Dublin here refers to the Census-enumerated area of Dublin city council and Dún Laoghaire-Rathdown, Fingal and South Dublin county councils including Tallaght, Lucan and Clondalkin but excluding the rural areas and the separate population centres of Swords, Portmarnock and Bray environs (1997)

Source: Central Statistics Office (1997)

The Greater Dublin Area, which comprises large parts of the surrounding counties of Kildare, Meath and Wicklow, dominates the urban structure of the state with a population of 1.4 million inhabitants in 2003. The preliminary report of the 2002 Census (Central Statistics Office, 2003) shows that the combined population of the cities of Cork, Limerick, Galway and Waterford amounted to only 58 per cent of the population of Dublin City and only 25.6 per cent of the combined areas of Dublin City and South Dublin, Fingal and Dún Laoghaire-Rathdown counties.

The rate of growth of the country's urban areas can be partly explained by the following significant demographic and economic developments.

- Population growth. The population of the state was in excess of 3.9 million in 2002, the highest figure since 1881 (Central Statistics Office, 2003). The population of the state could grow by over one million by the year 2020, with the potential for over 80 per cent of this growth to take place in the only major urban centre in Ireland, the Greater Dublin Area (Department of the Environment and Local Government, 2001b, p. 5). Over the period from 1996 to 1998, 65 per cent of population increase took place in the Dublin and Mid-East regions, leaving a 35 per cent population increase to be divided among the remaining six planning regions (Border, Midlands, West, Mid-West, South-West and South-East).

- Household formation. Changing household size and formation, in addition to a rise in the number of households formed due to demographic and societal factors, demands an increase in housing provision – principally in urban areas since this is where the highest rates of population increase are experienced. It is estimated that average household size will fall to 2.5 or lower in the early 2000s (just as it fell from 3.4 to 3.0 during the 1990s) causing increased numbers of dwellings of more varied make-ups to be provided for a similar population size. Related to household formation is the fertility rate, which is extremely low by historic standards, standing at 1.89 in 2002, below the replacement level of 2.1.

- Increased car ownership. Increased private transport opportunities allow people the flexibility of living far from their workplace. As people in cities live further from their place of employment, the footprint of cities widens, resulting in increased urbanisation of the countryside and rural villages. Between 1990 and 2000, the number of cars on Ireland's roads increased by 50 per cent. Predictions indicate that the number of cars is likely to double over the period 1996 to 2016 (Department of the Environment and Local Government, 2003, p. 24). Current car ownership rates are steadily moving from approximately 400 per 1,000 population (McDonald, 2000) towards the European average of 450 per 1,000 population.

- National economic growth. The Irish economy experienced significant growth rates over much of the 1990s, with a GDP growth rate of 9 per cent annually since 1994 and its GDP per capita now surpasses the EU average. While growth rates are not expected to be as high for the foreseeable future, it is thought that expected growth rates will nevertheless contribute to further urbanisation in Ireland.

Phenomenon of Urbanisation in Ireland

No longer a rural society, Ireland is experiencing rapid urbanisation of its countryside due to the environs of towns growing at a disproportionate rate to the town centres (see table 20.2) and a significant rise in the demand for one-off rural housing.

Table 20.2 Examples of Town v. Environs Population Growth

	1981	1986	1991	1996	% change (1981 to 1996)
Carlow	11,722	11,509	11,271	11,728	0.05
Environs	1,053	1,581	1,962	2,388	126.78
Dundalk	–	26,669	25,843	25,762	-3.40*
Environs	–	4,026	4,218	4,433	10.11*
Killarney	7,678	7,837	7,275	8,809	14.73
Environs	1,967	2,358	2,675	3,202	62.79
Letterkenny	6,440	6,690	7,186	7,606	18.11
Environs	1,552	3,174	3,540	4,390	182.86
Tuam	–	4,109	3,448	–	-16.09**
Environs	–	1,992	2,092	–	5.02**

* % change is for the period 1986 to 1996   ** % change is for the period 1986 to 1991

In 2000, of the record 50,000 new homes built in Ireland, 36 per cent were one-off houses in the countryside. A significant proportion of these single dwellings were urban generated, although this figure is more difficult to assess. County Galway, for instance, sees 78 per cent of residential planning applications pertaining to one-off housing in the open countryside. The ability to sustain this way of living must be debated when it is considered that:

- it is entirely car dependent
- it is inefficient to provide public transport to a dispersed and low-density population
- the cost of infrastructure provision (such as sewerage, water supply, telephone and roads) to a dispersed population is far greater than to a clustered population
- the risk to ground water quality due to septic tank usage, which is largely the only option available, is increased
- it places pressure on Ireland's landscape heritage
- it leads to the loss of agricultural and amenity land.

It should be stressed that the problems which Ireland's cities are currently facing are not new and do not result solely from the rapid expansion of the 1990s. Previous national and local policies have ensured that the spatial manifestation of an increase in urban populations has resulted in urban areas expanding beyond their previously accepted boundaries, and in town councils finding their rates base being absorbed into the county area, as town expansions become town extensions.

The lack of affordable housing in town and city centres is currently leading to urban sprawl, increased travel-to-work times, congestion and reduced urban competitiveness. These problems are manifest and are a direct result of the patterns of urban and residential development which have been actively pursued as policy since the 1970s:

- low-density housing development in comparison with other European countries
- facilitation of the development of greenfield over brownfield sites
- tax policy which favours the purchase of newly built housing over refurbishment or regeneration of second-hand housing
- depopulation of city centres
- development of 'new towns' to absorb the relocated populations, which lack essential services and infrastructure provision
- unchecked residential development in rural areas
- inadequate public transport policy.

However, it was not the case that there was a total absence of foresight or recognition of the issues. Stewart, among many others, alluded to the problem in 1980 when he stated: 'We have no policy with regard to urban development for the next twenty years. There is no co-ordinating framework for local authorities to relate to in their statutory Development Plans' (An Foras Forbatha, 1980).

The role of local government in intensifying many of these problems relates as much to the economic climate through much of the 1970s and 1980s as to the ill-prepared state of local government to deal with development pressure. Until recently, many local authorities did not have the specialist planning capability or capacity to regulate development and thus were largely reactive to pressures. Understandably, officials were at times loath to refuse planning permission for housing developments or other applications for fear of losing out altogether following the inactivity of the 1980s during which the population of many local authority areas declined. Under such circumstances, the development of brownfield over greenfield sites was not seen as a priority to encourage repopulation of urban settlements. Nor was the environmental agenda fully considered. Forms of development such as low-density housing were seen as desirable, as was development in rural areas, where it was, and often still is, widely interpreted as a boost for the rural economy. Additionally, since local government has no role in transportation policy, many local authorities did not concern themselves with it in the development of their areas.

Government policy at all levels requires a re-balancing of past objectives, while acknowledging the spatial pattern of development created, with a proactive response to limiting further outward expansion of towns towards a consolidation of their inner areas.

The Greater Dublin Area – Its Ever-Expanding Web

> As urbanized areas expand and collide, it seems probable that life in low-density surroundings will become too dear for the great majority (Davis, 1965).

The impact of the Greater Dublin Area on urbanisation in Ireland is considerable as it envelops close to 40 per cent of the population of the state within four counties. Its population increased from 1.35 million in 1991 to over 1.5 million in 2002, with a forecast to grow to 1.75 million by 2016 (Dublin Transportation Office, 2000). If the 2016 population figure is realised, this would represent an almost 30 per cent increase in population over a 25-year period, with major land use and other environmental implications related to transport, energy consumption, infrastructure provision and waste management.

Dublin City's share of the population of the Greater Dublin Area, which corresponds essentially to that of the *Strategic Planning Guidelines* area, is declining. Contrasting with this decline, the rise in population of the city's environs is spectacular. The commuting distance for employment in Dublin City has reached a 90-kilometre radius, extending to Dundalk, Mullingar, Portlaoise, Carlow and Gorey. This is significantly beyond the 1980s commuter belt which stretched only to Drogheda, Naas and Wicklow Town (see figure 20.1). Significant road infrastructure improvements have facilitated much of the growth in housing in these towns, however this has not been matched by mainline or commuter rail improvements.

Figure 20.1 Dublin's Commuter Belt

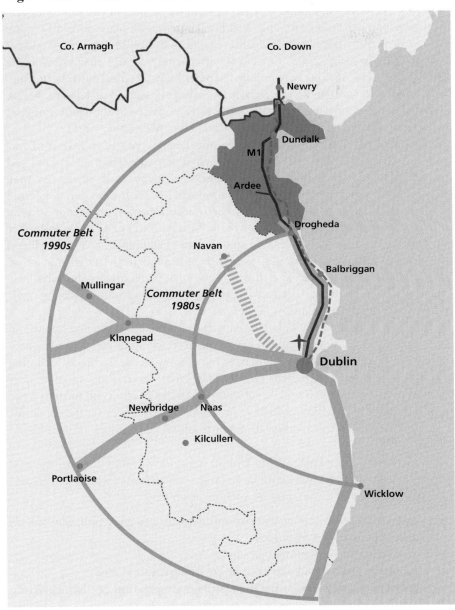

Dublin Commuter Belt

Greater Dublin Area

Transportation Corridor

In its 1996 study, the Dublin Regional Authority calculated that most towns within fifty kilometres of Dublin City have expanded as a result of commuting and ribbon development. In Kildare and Wicklow, growth took place generally in the existing towns and villages but in Meath it manifested itself in the form of one-off housing in rural areas. In 2000, 9.6 per cent of housing built in Leinster took place in Dublin City, with 36.7 per cent built in the outer Leinster counties of Westmeath, Offaly, Laois and Carlow; 25 per cent in the adjacent counties of Kildare, Meath and Wicklow; and 29 per cent in the other three counties of the Dublin region: Fingal, South Dublin and Dún Laoghaire-Rathdown (McCarthy, 2001).

Sustainable development patterns have thus been eschewed in favour of car-based, low-density 'affordable' housing which serves to expand the sprawl and zone of influence of Dublin City, eroding the identity of towns as they increasingly become Dublin-dependent commuter towns. It has been suggested that the spatial dispersal of Dublin has been more infrastructure-supply driven than consumer-demand driven (Williams and Shiels, 2002, p. 17), which further highlights the need for a co-ordinated approach to development at a regional and national level. Social and economic issues arise from this form of dependence on a distant major urban centre as, critically, new inhabitants often contribute little to their place of residence because shopping, socialising and educating their children frequently takes place in the service hub.

It has been suggested that changing household formation rates and household size, as previously outlined, could generate the need for up to 200,000 additional dwellings in the Dublin region alone over the coming decade, without counting the impact of immigration. Eugene Gribbin states that, 'even if the actual number falls short of this estimate, it will be substantial and the location and form of these tens of thousands of dwellings will have profound consequences for the economy, the environment and the quality of life of future generations of Dubliners' (Gribbin, 1998).

The increasing dominance of the Dublin region over large areas of the east coast regions and beyond will continue to raise societal issues which will impact on the development of the country as a whole, such as:

- congestion on the country's road infrastructure causing pollution and an uneconomic use of resources
- unsustainable commuting patterns
- decline in the amount and availability of agricultural land
- pressure for new house building at increasingly further distances from Dublin aimed at lower-income and first-time buyers, resulting in Dublin-induced growth in adjacent regions.

These issues have resulted from the substantial role that Dublin's expansion has had in driving a 'great deal of the economic success of the past number of years, thereby delivering vital national benefits' (Department of the Environment and Local Government, 2001b, p. 5). They pose a significant challenge for the competitive management of the Dublin and adjacent regions and the economic development of the state.

What Current Policies Mean for Urbanisation

> . . . the Government has been focussed excessively on the promotion of housing demand and of home ownership, and has paid too little attention to the locational patterns of residential development and to the undesirable trends in urban form (McCarthy, 2001).

Predominantly guided by the objective of sustainable development, recent government policy looks towards the reinforcement of towns, use-maximisation of existing infrastructure, a broader spectrum of housing provision and integrated land use planning and transportation policy.

The Bacon Report (1998) and *Sustainable Development – A Strategy for Ireland* (Government of Ireland, 1997b), among other documents, call for an increase in housing densities and an intensification of the existing urban area in redeveloping brownfield sites and infill developments to use existing infrastructure more efficiently and to promote a more sustainable 'compact city' approach to the development of Ireland's settlements.

The continued incorporation by local authorities of key policies into their development plans, and the enforcement of these policies, is vital to ensure a coherent and holistic approach across the country in accordance with the national spatial strategy (Department of the Environment and Local Government, 2003) and in the absence of a network of co-ordinated regional authorities with real physical planning responsibilities.

The following key policy documents have had, and will continue to have, significant impact on the shape of urbanisation in Ireland.

Strategic Policy

Sustainable Development – A Strategy for Ireland (1997): sustainable development has been defined as development that meets the needs of the present generation without compromising the ability of future generations to meet their own needs. This strategy (Government of Ireland, 1997b) provides a focus for the concept of sustainable development and a plan for its integration into significant land use and economic sectors. Key to the strategy in relation to urbanisation is the focus on local authorities to take a more strategic view of settlement patterns, development needs and major infrastructural services, combining the statutory five-yearly review of the development plan with a coherent longer-term rolling plan.

Ensuring the Future – A Strategy for Rural Development in Ireland, A White Paper on Rural Development (1999): this commits to 'the maintenance of the rural population, not just in terms of aggregate numbers but also in a balanced spatial distribution' (Department of Agriculture, Food and Rural Development, 1999, section 6.1). It advocates that planning policy should 'facilitate people willing to settle in rural areas, especially those wishing to remain in their own areas of origin' (section 6.4). Government policy, as advocated in this White Paper, could be interpreted as endorsing the trend of increasing urbanisation of the countryside, despite concerns expressed therein relating to conservation of the rural environment and policy favouring the provision of local authority and social housing within villages and small towns. Not all local authorities pursue the objectives of settlement consolidation over rural development, with some experiencing public political censure for their strategy, while in 2002 Mayo County Council proposed the removal of An Taisce from their list of consultees on planning applications because of that organisation's overt resistance to one-off housing in the countryside.

National Development Plan 2000–2006 (NDP) (2000): under the NDP (Government of Ireland, 2000a), over €52 billion will be invested in the key areas of economic and social infrastructure, employment and human resources, the productive sector and regional development, including social inclusion. Rapid economic development throughout the 1990s in Ireland has highlighted the lack of essential physical infrastructure, which the NDP attempts to redress. The less buoyant exchequer of the early twenty-first century may limit vast portions of the NDP.

National Spatial Strategy (NSS) (2003): the NSS (Department of the Environment and Local Government, 2003) makes provision for the realisation of the 2000 to 2006 NDP at a spatial level throughout Ireland. It aims to achieve a balanced, sustainable form of development for the future of the state by setting a national context for spatial planning at regional and local level through regional planning guidelines and local development plans. It suggests how, where and when transport infrastructure, housing, industrial development, waste management, energy generation and telecommunications infrastructure will take place in Ireland over the period to 2020. In essence it should underpin the balanced growth and development potential of the country in the short to medium term. Of most importance, politically, socially and economically, it defines and designates the growth of urban settlements and their role in the urban hierarchy of the state, while building on the current dynamics of the Irish urban network.

At the centre of the NSS is the identification of nine 'gateways' and eleven 'hubs' (see figure 20.2). The gateways are large urban centres whose scale and location will be used in supporting a more geographically balanced growth and development in the regions away from the Greater Dublin Area. The hubs are significant urban centres that should link the gateways to wider areas of the regions. The idea behind the gateways and hubs is that they should be used to direct growth potential to the broader regions and optimise urban to urban and urban to rural linkages.

Figure 20.2 Gateways and Hubs for the National Spatial Strategy

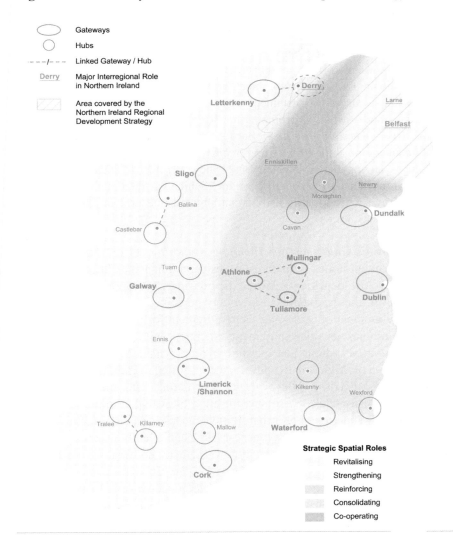

Source: Department of the Environment and Local Government (2003)

However, 'the real challenge of the National Spatial Strategy is not the translation of the NDP in spatial terms . . . but rather to see how we would like to organise our country in a spatial sense' (van der Kamp, 2001, p. 41). Thus, the question is asked whether, in preceding the NSS by the NDP, Ireland put the cart before the horse in investment terms. Ireland may yet pay a high price for not having a spatial framework in place before the NDP.

Shaping our Future 2025 Northern Ireland Regional Development Strategy (2001): this strategy (Department for Regional Development, 2001) is designed to reinforce and strengthen the urban hubs and clusters, corridors and gateways, making best use of key regional assets to accommodate growth. With regards to urban centres, it promotes the ideas of a 'sustained urban renaissance based on maintaining compact cities and towns'. It promotes trans-regional development, particularly with the Irish Republic at key border connections: Derry/Letterkenny, Newry/Dundalk, Enniskillen/Sligo and recognises Belfast, Derry, Newry and Enniskillen as having major inter-regional gateway roles. It equally values the importance of the 'Eastern Seaboard Corridor', which has the potential to provide quality links between Belfast and Dublin, and onwards to Larne or Rosslare.

Planning Policy

Residential Density, Guidelines for Planning Authorities (1999): in September 1999, the department issued guidelines on residential densities in recognition of the traditionally low densities achieved in housing developments around the country. However, these guidelines are widely perceived as being applicable to the Dublin environment only, despite the requirement for planning authorities to adjust their minimum density requirements to concur with the guidelines. Their applicability has been brought into question in areas outside Dublin.

The perception of 'high density' development is often negative and incorrectly associated with 'high-rise'. However, in accordance with the sustainability agenda, higher density leads to use maximisation of available infrastructure and land, and should be applied in all urban settlements as far as is feasible. Quality design and open space standards will necessarily need to enforce a quality of life associated, but not always achieved, with lower density housing.

Strategic Planning Guidelines for the Greater Dublin Area (1999): the strategic planning guidelines (SPG) were developed in the knowledge that Dublin was expanding far beyond its county boundary in an ad hoc manner, causing pressure on infrastructure, blurring of the urban/rural boundary and loss of valuable agricultural land to urban-generated housing. The key strategy for the SPG area to 2011 is to establish a polycentric urban system, where population growth and employment functions are contained within existing urban areas which are capable of absorbing the growth and providing the necessary range of services and facilities and which are located on transportation corridors. It is acknowledged in the strategy that the designated development centres will be dependent in the first instance on the metropolitan area of Dublin and the strategy advocates accommodating the significant commuting envisaged on the evolving public transport network. The guidelines are statutory and the local authorities in the Dublin and Mid-East Regions must have regard to them in the preparation of development plans for their areas.

However, two important considerations in assessing these guidelines centre on the role of Dublin City within the SPG area. It is recognised that Dublin-generated housing has sprawled beyond the range of the guidelines, such that they may no longer represent effective planning tools for the region. Additionally, the population of Dublin City under these guidelines to 2011 will continue to fall to just about 30 per cent of the Greater Dublin Area population, from a high of 53.5 per cent in 1971, while that of Meath, Kildare and Wicklow will continue to rise. 'It is a policy of continued sprawl, with all that sprawl implies by way of hidden cost' (McCarthy, 2001).

Planning and Development Act, 2000: under the 2000 Act, each local authority was obliged to prepare a housing strategy for its functional area before August 2001 to determine the quantity of housing needed, both social and private, to sustain population growth over a ten-year period, the objective being to achieve a more regulated and balanced supply of housing and help suppress spiralling house prices. In assessing the demands of the housing market, the local authorities will designate land to meet that demand. In so doing, they are formulating strategies defining the housing typologies, the resultant social mix and therefore the future and potential urban fabric of their areas.

'A combination of market, societal, demographic and environmental factors has combined together to create a serious mis-match between the supply and demand of residential accommodation servicing the various market sectors in the Dublin Region' (Dublin Corporation, 1999). Part V of the 2000 Act acknowledges the housing shortage. It recognises that neither local authorities nor the market alone can satisfy housing demand and thus gives increased powers to local authorities to address the issue of affordable housing by decreeing that up to 20 per cent of a development of four or more houses should be given over to social or affordable housing. The local authority has the power to specify the percentage required and whether social or affordable housing should be provided. Targets for the provision of social housing set by the current partnership agreement will not be met, according to the government. In order to address this, the minister, Martin Cullen TD, introduced the Planning and Development (Amendment) Act, 2002. The main changes occur in part V of the Act, which provides more flexibility to local authorities and developers to agree land, houses or sites to be provided at alternative locations, land exchanges between developers and authorities or for the developers to make a payment to a local authority fund to provide social and affordable housing. All arrangements agreed must be fully in compliance with local housing strategies and development plans and must ensure social integration. It also provides for extensions to planning permissions that were due to wither under the previous Act.

Under the 2000 Act, local area plans must be prepared for towns with populations in excess of 2,000 or can be made, at the discretion of the local authority, 'for those areas which require economic, physical and social renewal and for areas likely to be subject to large scale development within the lifetime of the plan' (part II, sections 18 and 19(1)(a)). Prior to this provision, the development of all but the major towns in a local authority's functional area was under the remit of the county development plan. While county development plans give broad guidance to the development of towns and rural areas, more specific guidelines have been lacking on how the network of smaller towns and villages should develop. Many smaller towns throughout the country have been experiencing strong residential development pressure due to the lower house prices that can be achieved in comparison to the larger towns. Some have seen the potential for their population to increase two-fold with a single housing development, often in a greenfield site on the edge of the town. The introduction of local area plans establishes a planning framework within which the sustainable growth of smaller towns can be achieved and development pressures can be more easily managed, directed and planned for on a broader county level.

Strategic development zones (SDZs) were introduced under part IX of the 2000 Act. They effectively represent an attempt to develop large infrastructural projects strategically, on sites designated by government and identified as being of economic or social importance to the state. The Act confers wide powers of compulsory purchase for the purpose of implementing SDZs. Their significance is not yet evident, although it does represent an attempt to bypass what has increasingly become an onerous and lengthy public consultation process with regard to major infrastructure projects and a removal of certain powers from the local authority concerned.

The Local Authority Role and Beyond

> . . . it was suggested that our ability to exercise more control over the physical environment depended on more effective planning and in order to achieve this our local government structures would have to become more efficient and democratic (An Foras Forbatha, 1985).

The role of local authorities in Ireland has been evolving in recent years to one of wider co-operation with local community groups, partnerships and other such organisations and networks, towards a more consensual approach to planning through the *Better Local Government* reforms. The impact of such co-operation on the urbanisation process is as yet unclear.

The process of urban development has been too often reactive through the formulation of development plans – reacting to population increases, developer-consumer demand, locational investment demand, employment creation needs and so forth, rather than proactively addressing needs in advance. Certainly, improvements in efficiency in micro-policy issues such as service delivery are recognised. However, macro-policy issues pertaining to waste, water, planning and so forth remain contentious. The department's response has tended towards a centralised management of these issues, such as the proposed establishment of national agencies, for example a national water services authority, thus removing control from local government.

It is evident that clear tensions exist between policy goals and the ability or will of local authorities and their councils to implement them. If this cannot be guaranteed, should established and accepted policy be implemented from central government? Should the removal of the planning agenda from the remit of the locally elected representatives be considered? Whether the critical process of urban development can be regulated by local or national government, or indeed should be regulated at all, is the subject of political ideology concerning the level of state involvement in controlling or directing development.

The waste management strategy, implemented on a regional basis, is perhaps an example of a contentious issue that may face significant 'nimby-ism' (not in my back yard). The pursuit by local authorities of increased rate bases and the attempts of elected representatives to be all things to all people necessarily work against more sustainable development plans being adopted and council decisions being made which look beyond their own borders. Indeed, the inherent conflict between local interests and national objectives has been repeatedly highlighted, not least in the debate on one-off housing in the countryside that is occupying centre stage for local politicians and the public in the formulation of many development plans countrywide.

While acknowledging the essential role local authorities have to play in directing urbanisation, it has long been conceded that 'development plans prepared by individual planning authorities are hardly sufficient per se to cater for the complex environmental issues which must be confronted in the next two decades' (An Foras Forbatha, 1980). Indeed, in hindsight, it may be acknowledged that more was needed to regulate and plan for the rapid pace of development which occurred nationally since the 1980s.

The NDP is directing infrastructural and social investment, and the NSS provides the national context for spatial planning at regional and local level. It is in this respect that the NSS, in conjunction with some of the provisions of the Planning and Development Act, 2000 previously outlined, may lead to the evolution of a more proactive planning system. If coherently developed and fully enforced, it will contribute to balanced development at a rural, urban, regional and national level which maximises infrastructure investment and protects the natural heritage. However, cognisant of the fact that local or indeed central government did not respond to the criticisms and concerns outlined in the 1968 Buchanan and subsequent reports, it is questionable whether they will respond to national policy under the NSS. The provisions for implementation of the NSS appear somewhat fragmented with a monitoring committee comprising representatives of key interest groups to be put in place and charged with overlooking the structures, mechanisms, processes, programmes, guidelines, frameworks and policies to be produced for the strategy's implementation. One cannot but help recognise the potential for the strategy to be subject to opportunistic political will. A truly independent 'auditor' would have been preferable.

With a national population equal to many medium-sized European cities, is Ireland small enough both geographically and in population terms to be managed by one national system of infrastructure provision? Should Ireland be moving towards this one national power instead of regional and local interpretations of same? In the absence of such a national structure evolving, or likely to evolve, the move is instead towards reinforcing and empowering Ireland's regional authorities. In contrast to the high level of regional autonomy in the EU, Ireland displays a low level of regional governance (see chapter 25). The eight regional authorities in Ireland, established in January 1994 under the Local Government Act, 1991 (Regional Authorities) (Establishment) Order, 1993, were given the responsibility of promoting the co-ordination of public services in each region. Problems have essentially arisen because different administrative agencies and public service providers define their own regions with little uniformity of area boundary. In addition, the physical planning powers of the regional authorities are limited.

The NSS places a significant emphasis on the regional authorities' role in the implementation of the strategy. Regional planning guidelines are to be produced to link local development plans to the NSS. The strategy outlines, in somewhat indistinct terms, how the plan will role out in each region. It would further help if regional authorities had the power to co-ordinate solutions to the problems currently experienced at a local level where county boundaries have, at times, become solely statutory and political in nature, and have been over-ridden by the physical reality of urban expansion; for example Limerick City is in effect serviced by Limerick City Council, Limerick County Council and Clare County Council.

The following are suggested measures aimed at achieving a sustainable pattern of urbanisation in Ireland:

- establishment of an all-island spatial strategy so that local authorities in the border regions can co-operate to maximise the potential of their areas
- empowerment of the regional authorities to implement the NSS on key infrastructure projects with national significance
- harmonisation of the area boundaries of key service providers
- increased co-operation by local authorities with regard to housing strategies, waste management, public transport provision and environmental and landscape protection
- centralisation of macro-policy issues such as energy production and the management of natural resources.

Conclusion

It has been suggested that, in order for Ireland to remain competitive through the first years of the twenty-first century, a major commitment to improving the planning process, particularly in relation to physical planning for major urban areas, must be realised (ESRI, 1999).

The process of urbanisation presents a multi-faceted challenge for local government. The interpretation and implementation of new national policy and a new Planning and Development Act, increased levels of development, changing expectations with regards to community participation, the process of educating elected representatives and the public with regard to changing policy, and corresponding pressures on local authority resources of a physical and human nature, all require a new and proactive response from local authorities if urbanisation is to contribute positively to the development of Irish society.

A more proactive role for local authorities should centre on an expansion of their role with a corresponding increase in funding and resources. Recent policy changes and the new requirements of the Planning and Development Act, 2000 are already placing enormous pressure on the resources of local authorities. The Local Government Act, 1998 provides that new functions or changes in the local authority cost base are reflected in the amount of funding allocated to local government and, as such, an expansion of roles should lead to an increase in resourcing.

The promotion of sustainable settlement patterns that exploit existing and underused infrastructure in towns is an essential component of government policy and one on which recently formulated development plans should centre. As facilitators of development and guardians of the public interest, local authorities play a key role as environment protection authorities and agents of sustainable development (Government of Ireland, 1997b). Their commitment to Local Agenda 21, which is seen as the local interpretation of promoting sustainable development, is being pushed forward (see chapter 21).

The objectives of part V of the Planning and Development Act, 2000 to encourage a wider range of affordable housing throughout the urban area will help to balance the trend of providing 'starter-homes' at increasing distances from the urban service centre on greenfield sites.

Increasing densities in existing urban areas would have the effect of consolidating settlements and reducing housing and other pressures on the environs. Additionally, intensifying densities at public transport hubs, to maximise the efficiency of the public transport network, while reducing dependence on the private car will contribute to a less congested and less polluted environment. Correspondingly, the provision of a wider range of quality services in close proximity to populated areas – such as crèche facilities, local recycling facilities and a co-ordinated range of local public transport options – can help to encourage people to appreciate the benefits of living in urban areas and serve to achieve government policy at a local level.

Increased densities warrant higher standards of design than previously required. The establishment of development standards and best-practice design guidelines would serve to improve the standard of housing in Ireland. Quality improvements in the use of private open space, in apartment/house sizes, in security arrangements and so on, would counter the perceived disadvantages of urban living. An emphasis on improved standards of design may warrant training for local government planners to deal with development proposals which go beyond compliance criteria and minimum standards of design. Low-density urban environments elsewhere, for example Melbourne, Australia, have put good design centre stage in an effort to increase the density and diversity of housing stock and yet not adversely impact on their surroundings.

The successful implementation of a future urbanisation policy in Ireland is intrinsically linked to the creation of a more dynamic and proactive local government, which would direct a sustainable management approach to comprehensive national planning. This would result in a framework for the protection of Ireland's natural and built environment and guarantee a balanced quality of life nationwide. Creating a more proactive system means a more flexible system – a system that can facilitate essential and responsive development and establish structures that allow for objective long-term planning. This approach will only work if the system is not subject to the vagaries of short-term political agendas and operates in a regulated and transparent environment that prioritises the protection of the public interest.

21

Sustainable Development
and Local Government

Maureen Doyle

Sustainable development is a broad-based concept, encompassing economic, environmental and social aspects. It aims to improve the quality of life both in the present and for the future. As such, it affects all areas of life and must inform and underpin public policy.

The key role of local authorities in contributing to sustainable development is increasingly recognised. Agenda 21, which is discussed below, states that 'as the level of governance closest to the people, they play a vital role in educating, mobilising and responding to the public to promote sustainable development' (UNCED, 1993, 28.1).

Local authorities in Ireland have wide-ranging responsibilities and functions in relation to the environment, planning, development, housing and the provision of various services. They may also influence other issues such as transport and traffic management, urban renewal and local economic development. Their policies and programmes in these areas have a major impact, not only on the environment and on general quality of life, but also on the overall achievement of sustainable development. Put simply, sustainable development requires a balance between environmental protection and socio-economic development. Planning and administering local authority activities and services with sustainable development criteria in mind can help secure this balance.

This chapter looks at the evolving concept of sustainable development at international and national level and examines developments and implications at regional and local level in Ireland.

Sustainable Development

The change in focus from purely environmental issues to a broader concern for sustainable development perhaps began with the UN Conference on the Human Environment, held in Stockholm in 1972. This was one of the first global attempts to focus on the question of a 'right' to a healthy environment and its recommendations included monitoring air and water quality and addressing the risks to health from environmentally contaminated food. Further conferences dealt with related topics such as adequate food, sound housing, safe water and population issues. In parallel, growing scientific knowledge and public awareness of the serious implications of environmental degradation – notably in relation to such complex global problems as climate change, ozone layer depletion and loss of biodiversity – gave a further impetus to the subject.

The global focus was intensified in 1983 with the establishment of the UN's World Commission on Environment and Development. The commission's brief was to examine the state of environment and development issues and 'to propose long-term environmental strategies for achieving sustainable development by the year 2000 and beyond'. The terms of reference set out by the UN General Assembly also included finding means by which the global community could co-operate in these matters, taking particular account of the differing stages of economic and social development across the developed and developing countries. Following a lengthy period of deliberations, including public hearings held around the world, the commission's report, *Our Common Future*, was published in 1987 (World Commission on Environment and Development, 1987).

The key call of the report was the need to reconcile the twin imperatives of environmental protection and economic and social development. It highlighted existing trends threatening the global environment and common challenges regarding poverty and human resources, food security, the preservation of biological diversity as the resource base for development and the growing urban crisis. It recognised the need for concerted global action to transform the management of society in order to meet these challenges, and for political will to ensure the move towards sustainable development, which it defined as development that 'meets the needs of the present without compromising the ability of future generations to meet their own needs'.

While this is perhaps the most widely used definition of sustainable development, some would question whose needs are considered and by whom they are determined. Alternative definitions have been proposed which focus on the planet's capacity to support human life and society while also protecting natural ecosystems (for example, carrying capacity, living within the bounds of nature, and the ecological footprint concept). Others emphasise the rights of future generations, based on the idea that 'we have not inherited the earth from our parents but borrowed it from our children'.[1] However, if there is still some lack of agreement on what exactly sustainable development means, there is nevertheless a growing consensus that current trends in much of the world's economy and society are not sustainable and must be changed.

International Action

The UN Conference on Environment and Development (UNCED), also known as the Earth Summit, held in Rio de Janeiro in 1992 was the first formal recognition by the international community of the unsustainable development pressures being placed on the carrying capacity of the earth. Attended by delegations from over 178 governments, as well as non-governmental representatives, its main product – Agenda 21, a programme of action for sustainable development into the twenty-first century – reflected a global consensus on environment and development co-operation (UNCED, 1993). Other outcomes of the conference included the Rio Declaration on Environment and Development, new global conventions on biological diversity and climate change and a statement of principles for the sustainable management of forests. The agreements reached at the conference emphasised that successful implementation was in the first place the responsibility of national governments; that national strategies were crucial in achieving this; and that international co-operation should supplement national efforts. Arising out of UNCED, the UN General Assembly established a Commission on Sustainable Development, comprising government representatives, as an ongoing monitoring body to globally examine progress in implementing Agenda 21.

In parallel with the Rio process, the EU's 1993 Fifth Environmental Action Programme, *Towards Sustainability*, took a more holistic view of environmental matters and moved towards a focus on sustainable development (Commission of the European Communities, 1993). It sought to integrate environment, economy and society at various levels and recognised that a broad range of actors, not solely governments, have a role to play in this regard. Focusing on five specific economic sectors – agriculture, energy, industry, transport and tourism – it set objectives and targets to increasingly bring them into line with the principles of sustainable development and identified a range of instruments to achieve this.

The position of sustainable development in EU policy was strengthened by the Treaty of Amsterdam, signed in October 1997, which made a number of important improvements to the environmental provisions of the Maastricht Treaty. Most notably, the goal of 'balanced and sustainable development' was given equal

---

[1] Quoted in the *World Conservation Strategy*, published jointly in 1980 by the World Conservation Union, the United Nations Environment Programme and the World Wide Fund for Nature, emphasised that humanity exists as a part of nature and depends for its future on the conservation of nature and natural resources. The strategy stressed the interdependence of conservation and development and the need to preserve the Earth's capacity to support life.

status with 'economic and social progress' in the statement of the EU's objectives. 'A high level of protection and improvement of the quality of the environment' was also added as an explicit, self-contained requirement in article 2 of the treaty, rather than as a constraint under 'sustainable growth'. The principle of integrating environmental policy into other policy areas was given greater prominence in the principles of the treaty, where it was specifically noted that the integration must be carried out 'with a view to promoting sustainable development'.

Following on from this, the EU developed a sustainable development strategy, which was adopted at the Gothenburg European Council in June 2001 (European Commission, 2001e). The sixth EU environment action programme, *Environment 2010: Our Future, Our Choice*, being developed in tandem, sets environmental objectives and priorities as an integral part of the EU sustainable development strategy and identifies the environmental issues which must be addressed if sustainable development is to be achieved (European Commission, 2001b).

In 2002, a World Summit on Sustainable Development was held in Johannesburg, South Africa. Its objectives were to reinvigorate, at the highest political level, the global commitment to the accelerated implementation of Agenda 21 and the promotion of sustainable development, and to further develop north/south partnership and international solidarity to this end. The political leaders of the participating countries at the summit, including the Taoiseach, declared that they assumed 'a collective responsibility to advance and strengthen the interdependent and mutually reinforcing pillars of sustainable development – economic development, social development and environmental protection – at local, national, regional and global levels' (United Nations, 2002, p. 1).

Developments in Ireland

The programme for government of December 1994 included a commitment to prepare a national sustainable development strategy addressing all areas of government policy which impact on the environment (*Government of Renewal*, 1994). This was supported by a commitment to develop a new set of indicators of sustainable development, taking account of environmental and social factors, which would both demonstrate the scale of the problem and measure progress towards sustainability. Work on the strategy, which was developed over two years, was co-ordinated by the Department of the Environment and included input from, *inter alia*, a public consultation process, the Green Network of Government Departments and a cabinet committee established under the government programme. The resulting document, *Sustainable Development: A Strategy for Ireland*, is a national strategy endorsed by government (Government of Ireland, 1997b). The overall objective of the strategy is:

. . . to ensure that economy and society in Ireland can develop to their full potential within a well protected environment, without compromising the quality of that environment, and with responsibility towards present and future generations and the wider international community (p. 25).

In common with international developments, the strategy focuses particularly on economic sectors whose activities have important implications for achieving sustainability. To the five sectors identified in the EU's Fifth Programme, it adds forestry, marine resources and trade. It also emphasises important supporting policy areas, including planning and land use, the built environment and public action and awareness, and proposes the establishment of new structures and mechanisms for implementing and monitoring the strategy, both at national and local levels.

The growing global trend, originating in Agenda 21, for the development of national bodies to co-ordinate and pursue sustainable development is recognised in the strategy, which notes that 'effective environmental policies require the active participation of society, so that lifestyle changes compatible with sustainable living can become established' (Government of Ireland, 1997b, p. 27). The strategy proposes the establishment of a national sustainable development council; this is complemented by the commitment in the programme for government to 'develop and implement an integrated environmental policy in partnership and consultation with local communities' (Fianna Fáil and Progressive Democrats, 1997, p. 8).

Following a period of public consultation, terms of reference for Comhar – the National Sustainable Development Partnership were agreed by government in autumn 1998 and the partnership was established in February 1999. Comhar's broad terms of reference are to: advance the national agenda for sustainable development, evaluate progress in this regard, assist in devising suitable mechanisms and advise on their implementation and contribute to the formation of a national consensus in these regards. Its twenty-five members are drawn from five major pillars across society – government/public sector, economic sectors, environmental interests, social and community groups, and professional and academic expertise.

In relation to monitoring and measuring national progress, an Inter-Departmental Steering Group on Sustainable Development Indicators, chaired by the Department of the Environment and Local Government, was established in 1998. Its objectives were to:

- produce priority or headline national sustainability indicators
- assess what information is generally produced, by whom, what the gaps are, where there is duplication, how information could be streamlined
- assess information needs as a result of the foregoing
- examine options for thematic publications based on available information.

Following considerable work, including the incorporation of comments from Comhar on the overall content and structure of the proposal, a set of headline indicators was published in 2002.

In a further development at national level, the concept of sustainable development was incorporated into the Planning and Development Act, 2000, with the intention of introducing a sustainable development ethos into the Irish planning system (see chapter 12). The phrase 'proper planning and development' was replaced by 'proper planning and sustainable development' throughout the Act. Section 10 of the Act states that the development plan of a local authority 'shall set out an overall strategy for the proper planning and sustainable development of the area'. While sustainable development is not defined in the Act, it can be argued that this has the benefit of not legally constraining or limiting the process of sustainability, but allowing it to develop at the heart of the planning and development system.

In 2002, the Department of the Environment and Local Government published a review of activities (including those mentioned above) undertaken at national and local levels in Ireland since the 1992 Earth Summit in Rio de Janeiro (Department of the Environment and Local Government, 2002a). The document was also part of Ireland's preparations for the 2002 Johannesburg summit. In addition, Comhar published *Principles for Sustainable Development*, which includes the principles that decision making should be devolved to the appropriate level and that stakeholder participation should be promoted at all levels (Comhar, 2002, pp. 27 and 29).

The Regional Dimension

Sustainable Development: A Strategy for Ireland emphasises the regional dimension of sustainable development and in particular the role of the regional authorities (Government of Ireland, 1997b, pp. 186–7). Important regional measures and actions, either ongoing or planned, specified in this regard include the regional co-ordination of land use policy and development planning, catchment-based approaches to water quality and protection, and assessing the regional impacts of tourism and forestry development.

The strategy noted that *Better Local Government* had identified structural measures to provide better support to the work of the regional authorities (Department of the Environment, 1996, pp. 67–8), which would underpin their roles in areas relevant to sustainable development, including:

- providing a regional perspective on environmental issues
- promoting co-ordination among organisational/institutional structures and providing fora for achieving regional balance between development and sustainability

- promoting partnership towards a unified vision of regional sustainability
- reviewing and monitoring Local Agenda 21 initiatives to ensure regional consistency.

Three specific new tasks were given to regional authorities within the framework of the strategy, to:

- identify and define sustainability priorities for their regions
- recommend appropriate implementation mechanisms based on the involvement of bodies at regional level
- assist in developing relevant regional sustainability indicators.

Local Agenda 21

Agenda 21 recognises that sustainable development is an issue which must be tackled at all levels and in all sectors of society. Local government was one of the nine major groups singled out for specific action, with a chapter dedicated to it. 'Because so many of the problems and solutions being addressed by Agenda 21 have their roots in local activities, the participation and co-operation of local authorities will be a determining factor in fulfilling its objectives' (UNCED, 1993, 28.1). It has been estimated that almost two-thirds of the actions in Agenda 21 require the involvement of local governments (Mehra, 1997, p. 33). In addition to urging national governments to adopt national strategies for sustainable development, Agenda 21 called on local authorities, through consultation with their local populations, to achieve consensus on a Local Agenda 21 by 1996.

Local Agenda 21 is a worldwide challenge. A survey carried out by the International Council for Local Environmental Initiatives (ICLEI) found that, by late 1996, more than 1,800 local governments in sixty-four countries were involved in Local Agenda 21 activities.[2] The survey noted that while developed countries were more likely to focus, at least initially, on environmental protection, they seemed to be better positioned to address one of the key challenges of sustainable development planning: consideration of the long-term impacts of development and the ability to sustain healthy social, environmental and economic conditions over long periods of time. Obstacles to progress were identified, including lack of financial support, information and expertise, at both national and local levels, together with a lack of local community consensus to

---

[2] ICLEI is an international association of local governments dedicated to the prevention and solution of local, regional and global environmental problems through local action. It is formally associated with the International Union of Local Authorities (IULA) (see appendix 10). ICLEI defines sustainable development as 'development that delivers basic environmental, social and economic services to all residents of a community without threatening the viability of the natural, built and social systems upon which the delivery of those services depends' (quoted in Mehra, 1997).

set priorities. By late 2001, following a further survey by ICLEI, the number of local authorities working with Local Agenda 21 was in the region of 5,000.[3]

Local Agenda 21 in Ireland

The nature of Local Agenda 21 means that there is no single, off-the-shelf model applicable to all circumstances. Rather, while there will be common principles and general guidelines which can be followed, a truly local Agenda 21 must be based on local circumstances and needs. This was the rationale behind the department's guidelines on Local Agenda 21 (Department of the Environment, 1995a), which were intended to give impetus and background assistance rather than to impose a unified approach. The guidelines were descriptive rather than prescriptive; they focused on the main concerns of Local Agenda 21 and suggested some ideas for local initiatives, but left the decisions on the process to be followed to individual local authorities, in consultation with their communities.

The guidelines suggested that the pivotal role for the purposes of Local Agenda 21 should be at county/city level, where there is a major concentration of functions and responsibilities central to implementing sustainable development. However, it was recognised that borough councils and town councils might usefully add their own focus and local dimension to a county initiative. A regional overview was considered important, as environment and development concerns often cannot be confined within county boundaries.

Sustainable Development: A Strategy for Ireland required county councils and county boroughs to complete their Local Agenda 21 processes by 1998 (Government of Ireland, 1997b, p. 188). Following a review in early 1998, however, it was clear that progress throughout the country was uneven. In order to give a new impetus to Local Agenda 21 and to emphasise its links with the ongoing local government reform process, a short series of regional seminars for local and regional authorities was organised by the Institute of Public Administration, in association with the Department of the Environment and Local Government, in mid-1998.

Following an official request from the department, each county and city council designated a Local Agenda 21 officer, and these officers have formed networks to enhance the efforts of individual local authorities and bring forward the development of Local Agenda 21 in Ireland. Regional networks comprise the nominated local authority officers and the directors of the relevant regional authorities. In turn, each region has nominated representatives to a national-level network, which is chaired by the department. Training has been provided at both national and regional network levels, with the main focus on practical examples.

---

[3] Quoted by Gino Van Begin, Deputy European Director, ICLEI, in his presentation to the Comhar seminar, 'Setting the Ground for Local Agenda 21 – 10 years on from Rio', in the Institute of Technology, Sligo on 10 November 2001.

A specific task given to the network was the updating of the 1995 Local Agenda 21 guidelines. This work was carried out in conjunction with the Institute of Public Administration and with input from Comhar, which commented in late 2000 on an early draft of the new guidelines. The guidelines were published in October 2001 under the title *Towards Sustainable Local Communities*. Developments in the area of local government reform are recognised in the guidelines, which specifically refer to the establishment of the county/city development boards as providing 'a clearly defined institutional framework for Agenda 21 at county/city level over the coming decade' (Department of the Environment and Local Government, 2001c, p. 8). The guidelines also require local authorities to consider Local Agenda 21 as 'part and parcel' of the process of local government reform.

The enhancement of local democracy is one of the core principles underlying local government reform in Ireland. This includes, *inter alia*, facilitating new forms of participation by local communities in the decision-making processes of their local councils – which is very much in the spirit of Local Agenda 21. *Better Local Government* specifically mentions Local Agenda 21, notably in the context of the strategic policy committees (SPCs) (Department of the Environment, 1996, p. 19). Given that part of the purpose of SPCs is to foster a higher degree of community relevance and local participation, the links with Local Agenda 21 are clear. Both intend that greater involvement of the local community should become a more intrinsic part of the operation of local government, across a broad range of functional areas.

The guidelines for establishing SPCs (Department of the Environment and Local Government, 1997) stressed that SPCs should be set in the wider context across the full range of local authority functions, treating them in an integrated fashion rather than as stand-alone areas. This is in line with the concepts of sustainable development and environmental integration. An important point is that Local Agenda 21 should not be seen solely as an issue for the environmental policy SPC, where such exists. All SPCs must take account of sustainable development, given that it affects all areas of a local authority's operations and functions, and must maintain a connection to municipal strategic decision making.

County/City Development Boards and Sustainable Development

As part of the ongoing process of local government reform, county/city development boards were established in 2000 to bring together the key players at local level to engage in a process of long-term planning for their respective areas. A key role for these boards is to develop and oversee the implementation of an agreed strategy for the economic, social and cultural development of the county or city, encompassing all public services delivered locally and involving the participation of all key local players. While the boards were not specifically identified as players in promoting sustainable development, the concept underpins much of their activities. Indeed, acceptance of sustainable development principles is one of the key overall principles guiding the process of preparing city and county strategies. The integrated nature of the strategies and the emphasis on extensive consultation and participation in their preparation are also closely linked to sustainable development concepts and practices.

More explicitly, boards must 'proof' their strategies against, *inter alia*, the national sustainable development strategy (Department of the Environment and Local Government, 2000a, 3.17 and 3.18). The boards are also required to integrate sustainability issues into all parts of the eight-step approach to preparing their strategies. To avoid becoming aspirational, the department's guidelines proposed a series of specific actions dovetailing with the steps for developing the strategies and stressed that these should be integrated with the process rather than considered as 'bolt-on' extras. First among these was the requirement to include sustainability as a core philosophy of all county/city development boards. Similarities between the eight-step approach and the Local Agenda 21 model under the Aalborg Charter[4] were noted in the 2001 Local Agenda 21 guidelines.

Conclusion

So where does sustainable development stand? The emerging view seems to be that Agenda 21 has been insufficiently implemented and a renewed focus and commitment from the international community is now imperative. At national level, five years after the publication of Ireland's national sustainable development strategy, a review and assessment of progress was carried out as part of the preparations for the World Summit in Johannesburg (Department of the Environment and Local Government, 2002a). This review reflects international experience generally and acknowledges the need to continue and intensify implementation of the strategy. The review also acknowledges the need to take further action in a number of areas, both to tackle growing environmental pressures and to meet increasingly stringent international obligations in areas such as climate change. At the local level, the generally late start in activating Local Agenda 21 means that there is still some way to go to achieve a broad acceptance and implementation of sustainable development (Department of the Environment and Local Government, 2002a, p. 58). At the Johannesburg summit itself, the plan of implementation agreed by national governments also emphasises the need to 'enhance the role and capacity of local authorities as well as stakeholders in implementing Agenda 21' (United Nations, 2002, p. 72).

---

[4] Aalborg Charter (Charter of the European Cities and Towns Towards Sustainability) developed from the Sustainable Cities and Towns Conference held in Aalborg in May 1994.

22

Heritage and Conservation in Local Government

Donncha Ó Dúlaing and Nicki Matthews

Ireland's heritage incorporates both the physical and the intangible, from historical houses to folk memory. As citizens we each have our own perceptions of heritage and its value, equally we all have our own ideas as to how best to conserve, protect, enhance and present these various elements. While at times we might take these resources for granted, our social, economic and cultural standings would suffer greatly without them.

Each generation is entitled to know where it comes from. We, as guardians, have a duty to protect and pass on what has been handed down to us by our ancestors. Our heritage provides us with a sense of identity and continuity, enriching our lives by providing us with a connection to past human experiences. It is our responsibility to ensure that this heritage is passed on, intact, to future generations. Pearson (2000) captures this important message with regard to the built heritage: 'The protection of our heritage is not some kind of zealous, religious adherence to a rigid set of rules that everything old must be retained. It is simply about keeping the best of our past, so we can make the best of the present. It is about preserving our identity and maintaining a link with our roots'.

Heritage and conservation are more recent arrivals to the remit of local government in Ireland. Heritage has a broader scope and this is reflected in the Heritage Act, 1995 where heritage is defined as including monuments, archaeological objects, heritage objects, architectural heritage, flora, fauna, wildlife habitats, landscapes, seascapes, wrecks, geology, heritage gardens and parks and inland waterways. Conservation has a more focused remit underpinned by changes within the legislative framework under the Local Government

(Planning and Development) Act, 1999 and further consolidated by the Planning and Development Act, 2000. It is generally associated with the built environment and understood to signify 'Action to secure the survival or the preservation for the future of buildings, cultural artefacts, natural resources, energy or any other thing of acknowledged value' (British Standards Institute, 1998).

Legislative Changes and Context

Unprecedented development has taken place in Ireland since the late 1980s. This development has affected Ireland's heritage in a number of ways. Most significantly, there has been greater pressure brought to bear on non-renewable resources, from built heritage to natural habitats and native fauna. Greater prosperity has also allowed people more time to consider and to respond to their heritage. It has allowed them to consider the various elements that have conspired to create the environment in which they live. Heritage, and its conservation, is fundamentally important to people's quality of life – to their education, cultural health and wellbeing, enjoyment and amenity – and to the economy and special identity.

While most of society's actions are aimed at addressing present needs, we should be aware that we are also responsible for the heritage of the future. We should be able to take pride in the physical environment that we will leave behind for future generations to inhabit, work in and enjoy. We cannot predict what will be valued in the future; we can only move forward and ensure that decisions taken faithfully reflect our values and are informed by a comprehensive understanding of our heritage.

As Ireland experiences a period of economic growth and a level of hitherto unknown development pressure, legislative change concerning the extant architectural heritage has been timely. The reformation of the planning system in the late 1990s was the most extensive legislative change in planning made since 1963.

This response has a European context encapsulated in the 1996 *Strengthening the Protection of the Architectural Heritage* (SPAH) report to government (Department of Arts, Culture and the Gaeltacht, 1996). Ireland became a signatory to the Granada Convention in 1985 for the protection of the architectural heritage of Europe. Many international charters and conventions have greatly influenced and informed government policy for the protection of the national architectural heritage. Worthy of particular mention amongst these is Agenda 21, which embraces built heritage just as much as natural heritage. Whilst the SPAH report identified many serious limitations regarding the level of protection of Ireland's built heritage, it also progressed a framework that facilitated Ireland meeting its commitment at European level to the conservation and protection of the built architectural heritage. However, even though extensive legislative changes were heralded from the SPAH report in 1996, minimal resources were put in place to assist the implementation of this legislation from the outset. This has proven to be detrimental to the whole process.

Heritage Management

At national level, improved legislation has been introduced to preserve and protect Ireland's heritage; there is also greater emphasis on expertise and models of best practice. There is, however, an ever-present dilemma when attempting to balance the needs of contemporary living, such as better roads, housing and so forth, with the heritage of our past and the obligation of passing on intact to our children what has been handed down to us. It is not possible, of course, to conserve everything. It is more a question of balancing the need for legitimate change with the desire for reasonable conservation.

Much of the direction for the sustainability and conservation of Ireland's heritage has been carried out on a national level through various government departments and non-government bodies. However, it should be recognised that heritage is communal and that everyone has a role to play in its protection. For this reason, the emphasis on identification and understanding of heritage has come to the fore as a prerequisite for development and planning control.

National Heritage Plan

Providing for heritage at a local level was identified as a fundamental action in the *National Heritage Plan* (Department of Arts, Heritage, Gaeltacht and the Islands, 2002b). This is to be achieved, in part, by the production of a local heritage plan in each local authority area. The national plan has seven key areas of action:

- local heritage plans, supported by enhanced levels of heritage expertise within local authorities
- increased levels of assistance for the protection of the archaeological and architectural heritage
- implementation of the national biodiversity plan and addressing the conservation of habitats, species, genetic diversity and the natural heritage
- initiation of a heritage inventory programme and establishment of a central heritage archive and library
- establishment of new structures within Dúchas, the Heritage Service of the Department of the Environment and Local Government, to provide a more efficient, integrated and regionalised service
- provision of total additional financial allocations of €123.16 million on a phased basis over the life of the plan, 2002 to 2006
- deployment of 102 additional staff to enhance existing heritage programmes and to operate the new structures proposed in the plan.

Heritage Officers

In 1999, the Heritage Council established a pilot programme in partnership with local authorities and involving the appointment of three heritage officers. This programme has developed and by April 2003 there were twenty-three heritage officers covering twenty-six local authority areas, with further appointments imminent. The Heritage Council supports the heritage officers, financially and professionally, including an extensive training and development programme. Heritage officers aim to promote enhanced levels of understanding, conservation and preservation by improving the status and perception of heritage in their local area. Heritage officers promote the policies of the Heritage Council, in tandem with addressing the needs of their local authority.

The duties of each heritage officer differ to reflect the preferences and needs of individual local authorities. However, there are a number of common actions undertaken by all. These include the preparation of local heritage plans, advising local authority staff, carrying out heritage appraisals, taking part in public consultation, data collection, liaison with relevant individuals and agencies, public relations and work on specific projects. Local heritage plans and heritage appraisals are described in detail below.

Local Heritage Plans

It is envisaged that a large proportion of a heritage officer's duties will be devoted to the production of a local heritage plan. The formulation of local plans are essential in the context of the national heritage plan, which aims to establish a clear and coherent strategy for the protection of Ireland's heritage while promoting it as a resource to be enjoyed by all. The national plan recognises the importance of local government in heritage matters and places great emphasis on enhancing its role. This role will become increasingly important, as local authorities are the best and proper medium to promote heritage conservation. The preparation of local heritage plans, supported by enhanced levels of heritage expertise within local authorities, will be vital in this process. Heritage officers will facilitate the preparation of plans through co-ordinating a local heritage forum involving local authorities, state agencies, community and voluntary groups and heritage organisations.

Local heritage plans are intended to be agreed, realistic and costed plans, which establish how a local authority, in association with its partners, will identify, preserve, conserve and manage the heritage of a county or city. They will generally cover a five-year period, identifying priority actions that will:

- improve the heritage information base
- enhance communication between all stakeholders
- raise heritage awareness
- put in place best practice
- implement key projects.

A mechanism for review and evaluation will form an important element of the process. Funding, reflecting the commitment to deal with heritage at a local level, will have to be provided in order to allow the implementation of the plan. All such funding would be channelled through local authorities and provided only in the context of approved local plans. The national plan advocates the allocation of €12.7 million for the implementation of local plans over the period from 2002 to 2006. By April 2003, local heritage plans had been produced in Clare, Dublin City, Laois, Offaly, Sligo and Westmeath; with production underway in other local authority areas.

Heritage Appraisal

The Heritage Council has developed a methodology for heritage appraisal of development plans, policies and programmes. Heritage appraisals are used to systematically, comprehensively and impartially assess the effects of plans, programmes or policies on the heritage.

A heritage appraisal helps to ensure that the full scope of heritage considerations is dealt with comprehensively and consistently throughout the preparation of any plan or programme. The appraisal is simple and cost effective and the methodology is flexible enough to allow easy integration into whatever form of plan preparation is adopted by the planning authority. The information generated by carrying out the heritage appraisal contributes to better-informed decision making in the formulation of land use planning policies.

The statutory planning system has a major contribution to make to the conservation of Ireland's national heritage and to a more sustainable environment. Decisions made through the planning process that incorporate heritage appraisal will be an ever-increasing determining factor in the future of that heritage.

Proposed Redistribution of Heritage Roles

In 2003, the Minister for the Environment and Local Government announced a redistribution of heritage responsibilities within the public service system. This would involve:

- the abolition of Dúchas, the Heritage Service
- the minister retaining responsibility for policy and operational matters relating to natural heritage
- the minister retaining responsibility for built heritage policy, while the operational and management functions in relation to the built heritage transfer to the Office of Public Works
- the Department of the Environment and Local Government being renamed the Department of the Environment, Heritage and Local Government
- the retention of the Heritage Council, although its role would be reviewed
- an expansion of the remit of local authorities in relation to heritage matters.

The abolition of Dúchas and the redistribution of heritage responsibilities will result in the fragmentation of heritage services and many commentators have expressed concerns at this move. However, the expanded role in heritage for the local authorities is welcomed providing that sufficient resources, including expertise and finance, are available to carry out the new responsibilities.

Conservation and Planning

The Local Government (Planning and Development) Act, 2000 addressed a number of issues relating to heritage and conservation including the following key areas in relation to strengthening the protection of national built heritage:

- provision of a more effective and immediate response for adding or deleting structures from the Local Authorities Registrar of Protection (Record of Protected Structures)
- extension of the mechanism for preservation of individual buildings to include the context of historic buildings or settings for protection as intrinsic to the character of the historic fabric
- provision of a statutory basis for designating architectural conservation areas of special character and interest
- extension of protection to all elements and features of the historic fabric including its interior and curtilage. The previous system of 'listing' typically referred to the exterior of historic buildings only, unless the interiors were specifically noted for protection. Exempted development for internal alterations under section 4(1)(g) of the 1963 Planning Act permitted significant alterations to historic fabric without planning control intervention
- focus on the endangerment of Ireland's architectural heritage. Responsibility for the care and upkeep has been made the responsibility of the owners of protected structures. Specific measures have been provided to local authorities to enable them to intercede where structures are endangered from persistent neglect
- introduction of penalties that are an adequate disincentive to carrying out acts of endangerment or demolition of a protected structure
- provision of financial assistance to owners of listed buildings
- provision of in-house specialist architectural/conservation expertise within local authorities, part-funded by government (conservation officers).

Conservation Officers

The role of the conservation officer follows on from the provisions of part IV of the Planning and Development Act, 2000. Officers were appointed to provide advice to local authorities and carry out numerous associated tasks such as:

- inspecting and surveying buildings, areas and sites
- assessing the historical and architectural importance of buildings and areas for conservation
- producing advisory designs and specifications for the repair or alteration of buildings
- negotiating with and advising owners, architects, amenity groups, local authorities and government agencies
- managing grant schemes and conservation initiatives.

Whilst partly financed by the Department of the Environment and Local Government, a structure for supporting and organising conservation officers was not envisaged (unlike that for heritage officers). Also, where heritage officers were provided with a clearly defined strategic role, conservation officers were likely to impact throughout the departments of the local authority so wide was their remit and the implication of legislative changes. The main provisions of the Planning and Development Act, 2000, identified above, have far-reaching implications for operational changes throughout the local authority system. The technical and administrative resources necessary to meet the commitment of this legislation have not been fully provided for to date. However, in order to support and give local authorities direction and guidance on the Act's implementation several key publications have been produced.

- Conservation guidelines have been published by the Department of the Environment and Local Government.[1]
- Draft *Architectural Heritage Protection: Guidelines for Planning Authorities* (Department of Arts, Heritage, Gaelteacht and the Islands, Dúchas and Department of the Environment and Local Government, 2001) have been issued and the publication of a final version is pending.
- *Action on Architecture,* a publication by the then Department of Arts, Heritage, Gaeltacht and the Islands (2002a), recognises the European context to which the Irish government has responded by setting out key strategies for the period 2002 to 2005. The principal resolution adopted by the EU Council of Ministers in November 2000 focused on the architectural quality of urban and rural environments. *Action on Architecture* notes that the state, as the 'custodian of architectural heritage', is to ensure the conservation and maintenance of the architectural heritage of Ireland. This provision has been implemented through the consolidation of legal protection of architectural heritage in the Planning and Development Act, 2000. This publication also establishes conservation as a mainstream architectural activity.
- Supporting these measures and objectives regarding Ireland's architectural heritage is the publication of the already discussed *National*

---

[1] Available from the department's website, www.environ.ie.

Heritage Plan (Department of Arts, Heritage, Gaeltacht and the Islands, 2002b). The policy statement on heritage notes the government's objective, 'to ensure the protection of Ireland's heritage and to promote its enjoyment by all', and states that every action in the national plan 'is founded on the principle of sustainable development which states that the needs of the present generation must be met without compromising the ability of future generations to meet their own needs'.

Practical Implementation of the Planning and Development Act, 2000

The provisions regarding Ireland's built heritage contained in the Local Government (Planning and Development) Act, 1999 were consolidated into part IV of the Planning and Development Act, 2000 and implemented from 11 March 2002. It has taken considerable time to comprehend the far-reaching implications of the legislative changes. The following are the key areas to which this legislation has given rise:

• notification of owners and occupiers of protected structures
• requests for declarations under section 57 of the 1999 Act
• development control – pre-planning applications
• development control – processing planning applications
• architectural conservation areas
• enforcement, including buildings at risk, dangerous buildings and derelict sites
• the administration of the conservation grant scheme.

One of the first vital tasks instituted to implement the Act was to serve notice on the owners and occupiers of all protected structures that were formerly listed for protection in the case of each respective development plan. The notices issued informed the owner/occupier that each respective building had a greater status of protection. The protection of the fabric of a protected structure was extended to include its interior and curtilage. General information about the provisions of the Act and the opportunity for the owner/occupier to apply for grant assistance for a structure included in the Record of Protected Structures were also provided. In order to remove the burden of re-notification from the local authority and to provide clarity in the case of purchasers buying historic buildings, building stock needs to be registered under the Registration of Title Act, 1964 to indicate the burden of protected structure status.

Another significant resource implication for the local authority is the provision of a declaration on request for a protected structure, under section 57, which normally has to be produced within three months of receipt of the request. This section provides that a declaration/assessment is carried out, by a suitably qualified/expert person, of the internal and external fabric to give an opinion on whether proposed works can be determined as not affecting the character and therefore as not requiring planning permission for the structure in question.

In response to the numbers of historic structures subjected to extreme levels of neglect, leading in some cases to collapse, sections 59 and 60 ensures that the owner of a protected structure maintains it in good condition to prevent endangerment. The responsibility and remit of the local authority under the 2000 Act is to ensure the security and maintenance of protected structures and, where necessary, to adopt measures to respond to such acts of wilful endangerment. The compulsory purchase of protected structures can be evoked where it is necessary to preserve the protected structure, however, the financial constraints on local authorities could prevent this option being taken.

Each local authority is obliged to have a Record of Protected Structures (RPS), or part of structures, which are of special architectural, historical, archaeological, artistic, cultural, scientific, social or technical interest. In conjunction with the drawing up of the RPS, each planning authority is obliged to include policy objectives to afford protection of the architectural heritage in its development plan. These objectives apply equally to architectural conservation areas, to the settings of protected structures and to individual buildings. The Local Government Computer Services Board has pioneered a software package designed specifically for storing and retrieving this information.

Conclusion

The challenge of protecting and conserving Ireland's heritage continues to grow. Essential tools in the process of consideration and evaluation include local heritage plans, heritage appraisals and the conservation provisions of the Planning and Development Act, 2000, which enable the minimisation or mitigation of adverse impacts to historic fabric and natural assets where possible. Continued financial and professional development support for heritage officers has ensured the success of this new post. In contrast, the parallel role of conservation officer has been badly undermined by the lack of significant funding, resource co-ordination and management at national and local levels.

At the time of writing, the management of Ireland's heritage continues to evolve following the announcement of a redistribution of roles and responsibilities. Operational procedures are awaiting clarification and, with regard to the conservation officers network, strategic co-ordination has yet to be confirmed. Concerns have been expressed as to whether the proposed reorganisation of heritage responsibilities within the state services will result in heritage being subjugated to the pressures of development. Only time will tell whether the present generation can be proud of the heritage it leaves behind for future generations to enjoy.

23

Social Inclusion and Local Government

Mrs Terry Madden

Origins

Traditionally, local authorities concentrated their efforts on roads, waste management, housing delivery and management and the whole array of municipal functions and duties. Issues of health, poverty and education were deemed to be largely the responsibility of other state agencies. However, the following brief overview of the history of local government in Ireland shows that local authorities, since their foundation, have been involved in addressing poverty and the needs of the most vulnerable in society. For further information on the history of local government, see chapter 2.

The origins of what we recognise as local government in Ireland can be traced back to the passing of the Poor Relief Act in 1838; this created the first government agency with responsibility for local affairs in Ireland. The 1838 Act covered the whole country with a network of poor law boards called 'guardians of the poor', made up partly of justices and partly of members elected by the ratepayers. The poor law guardians were essentially set up to deal with the poverty of the years before the Famine. These boards operated under the control of poor law commissioners sitting in London, with the Irish branch based in the Custom House. In 1872, the Poor Law Commission was transformed into the Local Government Board for Ireland, reflecting an increased range of duties that extended far beyond the basic care of the poor and into areas such as hospitals, disease eradication, medical services, sanitary services and housing.

The Local Government (Ireland) Act, 1898 was an extension of similar reforms that had taken place in England ten years earlier. In England, in the nineteenth century, central and local government did not overlap. Central government's focus of attention was defending the country and instigating and legislating laws and acts of national policy. The focus of local government was the relief of poverty, a continuation of the seventeenth-century poor laws, and government at a county level. The passing of the 1898 Act had a profound and long-reaching effect on Irish society and contributed to its development towards a modern independent state. Along with the Wyndham Act of 1903, this democratisation of Irish local government ranks as one of the main British acts that had a positive impact on the Irish nation and the way it emerged after 1921 (see Gailey, 1987, for further information). With one stroke the grand juries were abolished. They, along with the legislation relating to land, were the last great bastions of the Anglo-Irish ascendancy. The franchise was extended to women and the landless classes; thus restrictions of wealth and gender were swept away. In place of the grand juries, a local self-government structure was instituted comprising urban, rural and county councils, all elected with a franchise that exceeded the parliamentary franchise. The £50 (€63.49) property qualification was abolished and the vote was extended to every occupier, irrespective of wealth, sex or religion.

The next significant development occurred in 1924 when the Department of Local Government and Public Health was established. This new department took over the task of supervising the local government system from the Local Government Board. In the 1920s and 1930s, the department's focus was on reform of the operation of the local government system, expansion of the housing programme, development of other infrastructure services, introduction of town planning and growth in health and welfare services. Local government had an extremely important social role in the community. This social connection was originally seen in the concern of the local representatives, particularly in the large cities and towns of the new Free State, with the housing conditions that the vast majority of those who elected them lived in. This concern found active expression in a policy 'to clear' the tenements and slums of the cities.

The Housing Act, 1919 was the first to make special provision for the housing of the elderly and homeless people made by local authority planning and development operations. The Housing Act, 1966 also made provision for a central government subsidy to local authorities for the construction of housing, including high-rise flat complexes.

The welfare role of the local authorities began in the late 1930s, finally becoming a public service policy in 1948 when Dublin Corporation employed welfare officers who served two roles for the local authority. First, they provided a social work intervention service to tenants. Second, they helped to keep the councillors in touch with their electors, facilitating positive and negative feedback concerning policy developed and instituted at city council level.

Local Authorities in Transition

Stemming from the change in how local authorities were funded, the period from 1970 to the mid-1980s saw a few key developments that had implications for social inclusion as a function of local government. The transfer of responsibility for health to the new health boards in 1971 removed a large part of the public health function from the local authorities and in effect severed the final connection between poor law administration and the local authority.

The Housing Act, 1988 was a benchmark in housing legislation. It differed from the 1919 Act as it covered all homeless people not just persons made homeless by local authority actions. It empowered the local authority to provide for the homeless and the Traveller community. It extended the powers of the local authority to assist the non-profit housing associations and voluntary organisations involved in the provision of housing.

The Local Government Acts of 1991 and 1994 and the Local Government (Dublin) Act, 1993 introduced significant change to the local government environment and structures. There was an increase in the number of agencies and community groups that were operating at county level, although not necessarily under direct local authority control. With the impact of EU funding support or directives, citizens were becoming more demanding and expected a quality service from the local authorities. The County and City Managers' Association commissioned a study to document some of the major changes that had taken place and to outline the implications of these changes for the local government management system. Boyle (1986, p. 2), in a report on local government management, noted that 'change has been impacting on the local government system in different ways and from various sources'. The main sources for change were identified as: legislative, EU, environmental, political, the citizen and managerial.

In 1996, the government published *Better Local Government* (Department of the Environment, 1996). This sets out the framework and strategy for significant reforms within local government. One of the main objectives of these reforms was to develop more effective involvement of local councillors and other interests in the development of local government and policy, leading to a co-ordination of local development initiatives. The reform process aims to establish new forms of governance and participative decision-making processes, embracing the concept of social partnership that has increasingly played a key role in policy development and service delivery. This entails the establishment of local multi-agency institutions that provide a local policy framework based on local consensus. It is intended that this new form of local governance implies:

- a new proactive relationship with the community at large
- collaborative consensus planning and implementation
- the involvement of people below multi-agency level

- acknowledging the community as a source of learning
- fostering local debate
- an innovative approach to service delivery
- drawing people into a political process which enhances participatory democracy.

It is widely recognised that a local governance framework of this type is a prerequisite for a successful social inclusion outcome. Central to this outcome is partnership.

Partnership

Partnership is the term used to describe the social dialogue process in Ireland. It is an increasingly important principle in the development and implementation of policy throughout Ireland (Rigney, 2001, p. 1).

Local government is the level of politics closest to the day-to-day life of citizens and may therefore have the greatest potential in terms of realising representative participatory democracy and partnership. The first local area partnerships were established in 1991 as a result of a national wage agreement between the main social partners – private business organisations, trade unions and the government. Until 1999, all area partnerships were part-funded by the EU. However, under the national development plan for 2000 to 2006, partnerships are wholly financed by the exchequer.

The concept of partnership is to achieve and develop an understanding of the needs of targeted areas, both physically and sociologically. Policies of the 1970s and 1980s of depopulating inner-city areas have caused a certain dilapidation to occur. In many inner-city scenarios, the residents are socially excluded, usually as a result of neglect, multi-social problems and chronic long-term unemployment. Opportunities for education beyond primary level are often limited. Partnerships in such areas focus on the development of family living in conjunction with industry. The persons targeted in social partnership programmes are the most excluded: the long-term unemployed, lone parents, members of the Traveller community, marginalised young people, asylum-seekers and persons with alternative lifestyles.

The process of consultation and planning with the people in an area is extremely vital to the concept of partnership. This is the forum where the actual reality of the groups who form the partnership is so important, it is where they are listened to, can talk and have a meaningful dialogue. Habermas (1984 and 1987) advances that it is because human beings communicate with each other that they are capable of reaching partnership and consensus.

The late 1970s and 1980s witnessed the emergence of community development. Communities were gelling together and realising the power and force that a cohesive group can have. Apart from, but parallel to, developments in the social area, local authorities were becoming environmentally aware. Effective means of addressing the ever-growing problem of waste disposal and waste management had to be undertaken; issues such as traffic control and public transport had to be faced; interventions in the area of crime had to be addressed. Politically, local representatives became more aware of the local communities and the problems encountered therein. Resident/tenant associations were formed and were active in their communities. Problems were being tackled at a very 'local' level.

Partnerships are perceived as a more equitable way of distributing power and funding, especially in the context of disadvantaged areas and communities. Partnership is 'community driven, government funded, supported by business and involves each of the sectors' (Dublin Inner City Partnership, 1996).

Social Inclusion

People depend on 'systems' in their immediate environment for a satisfactory lifestyle; these are part of institutional set-ups and organisations such as the local authorities. Three particular systems can be identified (Pincus, 1973):

- informal, such as family and fellow workers
- formal, such as community groups and trade unions
- societal, such as hospitals and schools.

Within these systems people perform their life tasks. One of the aims of local authorities is to get involved in the issues that affect people living in their housing estates.

Social exclusion is multifaceted and can be caused or exacerbated by a number of factors (Government of Ireland, 1997a): homelessness, long-term unemployment, single-parent families, family breakdown and violence, drug dependency, anti-social behaviour and membership of ethnic minorities or the Traveller community. The bottom line is that social exclusion stems from structures and processes which exclude certain people from full participation in the mainstream of Irish society. The excluded experience poverty or are marginalised because they are different (for example gays and lesbians, single-parent families and persons with disabilities).

Dublin City Council set up the first dedicated social inclusion unit within the local government system in April 2000 as one of a series of measures to respond to the needs of communities in areas of serious deprivation and disadvantage. The primary focus of the unit is on flat complexes and housing estates. The unit is working with local communities and voluntary and statutory agencies to ensure that childcare facilities are provided and are accessible to the tenants. Other social inclusion measures include equality, countering involvement in crime and drugs, increases in social welfare payments, a social economy programme, education initiatives and increased local authority housing. As part of an ongoing plan, it is the aim of the unit to actively promote 'poverty proofing' of all services provided by the local authority.

In December 2001, eight pilot social inclusion units were established in the city councils of Waterford, Cork, and Limerick and the county councils of Louth, Wicklow, Fingal, South Dublin and Dún Laoghaire-Rathdown. This brings the total number of social inclusion units to nine. On a phased basis, all local authorities are to develop social inclusion strategies at local level.

Efforts to tackle the problems of social exclusion nationwide resulted in the establishment of county and city development boards (CDBs). Their specific task is to devise strategies for social, cultural and economic development within their county/city and to oversee implementation of these strategies (see chapter 16). In drawing up such strategies, the CDBs are expected to take account of the principles, targets and objectives of the national anti-poverty strategy. The membership of CDBs is drawn from local government, local development bodies, state agencies and the social partners.

Social exclusion is the result of individuals and/or communities suffering from material, cultural or social poverty. Dealing effectively with social exclusion and creating strategies of social inclusion is a challenge facing local authorities. One of the ways local authorities become involved in the issues that affect the lives of people is through estate management. Local authorities can play a proactive role in the social issues affecting tenants – bearing in mind that many of the local authority areas experience serious deprivation. However, one can at times detect in the current local government reform process a genuine desire to move to a more locally autonomous approach. Local residents are becoming involved in decision-making processes concerning their areas and local authorities are improving their relationships with local communities.

Strategic Policy Committees

As well as the CDBs, strategic policy committees (SPCs) have been established in each local authority to develop policy in key local government functional areas (see chapters 3 and 4). One-third of the membership of each SPC is drawn from the sectoral representatives; the council decides which sectors should be represented on each SPC. The community/voluntary/disadvantaged sector is one of the six sectors from which representation is drawn. Representatives are nominated by the community/voluntary sector itself, with facilitation by the local authority. Technical support and resourcing in terms of travel and childcare are provided for in the SPC guidelines (Department of the Environment and Local Government, 1997) to ensure that the most disadvantaged can adequately participate.

The issues that will be addressed by the CDBs and the SPCs will have direct bearing on local communities. The people living in an area can contribute a wealth of information and ideas about what needs to happen in relation to these issues. In addition, interest groups such as Travellers and lone parents have particular needs in relation to issues such as housing. Therefore, to ensure that social exclusion is addressed, it is vital that consultation with, and the participation of, those actually experiencing marginalisation and poverty takes place.

In recent years, considerable developments have taken place in the local context, for example local development partnerships, community development projects and urban initiatives. The national, regional and local structures have increased the opportunities for meaningful participation and consultation with local communities. There is a growing recognition of the need for greater involvement of people in decision making about their own areas. Local government provides a very good starting point for the development of participative democracy. The key challenge for local authorities will be to ensure that those groups in society that are most excluded and have the least opportunity to have an input are represented on the CDB and SPC structures.

The National Anti-Poverty Strategy

The national anti-poverty strategy (NAPS) is a cross-departmental initiative. It provides a framework for action to help achieve the objective of eliminating poverty in Ireland and highlights the national priorities for Ireland in this regard. Part of the work of the CDBs is to ensure that the objectives of the NAPS are reflected in their strategies.

One major area where local authorities have a key role is the provision of housing (see chapter 9). In the past, many local authorities tended to focus on the bricks and mortar aspect of housing. This meant that issues surrounding estate management, the environment and community development were neglected, or at the very least scant attention was paid to them. Now local authorities are seeking to address these issues as part of an integrated housing service.

Local authorities also have a valuable role in enhancing local participation. The CDBs and the SPCs have an extremely important role in ensuring that the principles underpinning the NAPS inform the processes by which policy and strategy are developed within local government. Under the *Programme for Prosperity and Fairness* (Government of Ireland, 2000c), local authorities are obligated to poverty proof their policies against the principles of the NAPS, which are:

- ensuring equal access and encouraging participation for all
- guaranteeing the rights of minorities, especially through anti-discrimination measures

- reducing inequalities and in particular addressing the gender dimensions of poverty
- developing the partnership approach, building on local and national partnership processes
- actively involving the community and voluntary sector
- encouraging self-reliance through respecting individual dignity and promoting empowerment
- engaging in appropriate consultative processes, especially with users of services (Government of Ireland, 1997a, p. 7).

A new social partnership agreement was adopted in 2003, *Sustaining Progress*, which reiterates the importance of the NAPS by including measures dealing with, *inter alia*, the long-term unemployed, educational disadvantage and consistent child poverty. As part of the revised NAPS, the Office for Social Inclusion was established in 2002. This new institutional structure reports to the minister and has taken over the functions of the NAPS Unit in the Department of Social and Family Affairs. The work of the national office is overseen by a management group of assistant secretaries drawn from relevant government departments. The office has a number of key functions in relation to the NAPS; these include: supporting and monitoring the implementation of the strategy, developing a more effective poverty-proofing process and developing a formal data strategy and research programme.

The engagement of the community and the voluntary sector in the new structures of local government is of major importance. Their involvement in policy making and other activities promotes empowerment, advocacy and self-determination/self-help. Local government must reflect the interests of the community and this includes the previously marginalised such as Travellers, members of ethnic minorities, the elderly, disabled, refugees, lone parents and women. However, the potential for local government to contribute to the aims of the NAPS is restricted by the relatively underdeveloped remit of Irish local authorities in social services. The principal potential contributions can be made in the areas of housing, urban regeneration and the provision of decentralised services in one-stop-shops. Compare this to the toolkit of other European countries and Irish local government looks decidedly unequipped (see chapters 8 and 26).

Local Agenda 21

Agenda 21 is the UN agenda for sustainable development in the twenty-first century, to which the Irish government became a signatory in 1992. The Department of the Environment requested all local authorities to prepare a Local Agenda 21 process, which involves local partnerships carrying out local improvements for sustainable development (see chapter 21). Community organisation is required to enable consultation to take place. Such consultation is important insofar as it focuses on the collective rather than individual responses to problems and issues. Therefore Local Agenda 21 encourages and enables local groups and organisations to develop some sense of ownership of their area. It also recognises the existence of marginalised groups, many of which are unable to access existing support structures, and the need to facilitate them to develop skills, knowledge, confidence and influence.

RAPID and CLÁR Programmes

Two local authority-based social inclusion programmes were established in 2001: RAPID (Revitalising Areas by Planning, Investment and Development) and CLÁR (Ceantair Laga Ard-Riachtanais – Programme for Revitalising Rural Areas). These programmes have the objective of targeting statutory investment and integrating service delivery in areas of high disadvantage. The RAPID programme, which is urban based, will include programmes that meet criteria under the headings of unemployment, income levels, family and social structures, educational disadvantage and the concentration of local authority housing. The CLÁR programme, which is rural based, is designed to tackle the problem of depopulation, decline and lack of services in rural areas.

The process involves agreement with local communities of an action/implementation plan over a three-year timescale and the consequent drawdown of funds allocated to social inclusion measures under the national development plan. The structure of the programmes includes:

- a national monitoring group – an interdepartmental group under a chairperson
- area implementation teams – bringing together the local state agency personnel (that is, health board, local authority, vocational education committee, Department of Social and Family Affairs, FÁS, local partnership companies, residents of local communities, and local drugs task forces)
- RAPID and CLÁR co-ordinators for each designated area, appointed through open competition and employed by the local authority
- SIM (social inclusion measures) monitoring group with the county and city development boards
- a national co-ordinator.

Local Government Anti-Poverty Network

The Local Government Anti-Poverty Network was established by the Combat Poverty Agency in 2000. The network was set up to support local authorities in dealing with their expanding role in social inclusion and has the support of the Department of the Environment and Local Government and the Office for Social Inclusion. The aim of the network is to:

- promote and support the development of a strong anti-poverty focus within local government
- provide a forum in which local authorities can consider and develop policies to tackle poverty and social exclusion
- enable local authorities to share information about developing projects and initiatives
- exchange different local experience and best practice.

The work of the network is carried out through seminars, training, research and the disbursement of funds to support these activities.

Promoting Racial Equality

Dublin City Council and the Eastern Regional Health Authority, as major service providers and in the context of their strategic management initiatives and customer care plans, recognised that racial equality needed to be confronted and brought into the public domain. To this end the two institutions jointly devised and adopted a policy aimed at maximising understanding of the needs of ethnic minority groups and promoting their integration in Irish society by recognising the distinct culture of each group. Racism, whether overt, covert or unintentional, is recognised as one of the barriers to this process.

The joint effort, entitled *Many Peoples – One City*, resulted in the publication of an information booklet on health, housing and welfare issues for asylum-seekers and refugees, which was translated into nine different languages (Dublin Corporation and Eastern Health Board, 2000). It also involved a publicity/awareness campaign incorporating newspaper, radio and television coverage of racial equality issues. Community development staff in both agencies were encouraged to implement a structured programme of education and awareness in targeted communities. Both organisations adopted a policy for promoting racial equality, which is intended to enhance the delivery of local authority services and health board services. It was envisaged that staff would be supported in the provision of these services in an increasingly multicultural environment. To facilitate this aim, a joint training programme was developed for relevant staff on the implementation of the policy on racial equality. The aim of the training programme was to promote an understanding of the policy for promoting racial equality. The training programme endeavoured to enhance racial awareness and anti-racist practice.

Traveller Accommodation

The publication in 1995 of a report by the Task Force on the Travelling Community and the subsequent adoption of the Housing (Traveller) Accommodation Act, 1998 marked a change in emphasis in how the state regards the Traveller community. From the establishment of the Commission for Itinerancy (1960), the 'Itinerants' as they were referred to then were defined as a 'problem' and the intention was 'to promote their absorption into the general community' (Commission on Itinerancy, 1963, p. 11). This thinking continued to influence policy with regard to Travellers until the 1983 report of the Travelling People's Review Body. In this report, Travellers were no longer referred to as 'Itinerants' and, as Madden et al. (1996) note, social work and policy in general in relation to Travellers became based on principles of full citizenship which recognised the distinctiveness of Traveller culture, implied minimum legal requirements and emphasised that rights implied obligations.

The Housing Act, 1988 urged local authorities to take responsibility for providing accommodation to Travellers. The 1995 task force report furthered this aim and made several recommendations with regard to accommodation, health, education and gender as well as improving relationships between the Traveller and settled communities. This developed the move from a charity approach to a rights-based/self-determination approach culminating in the Housing (Traveller Accommodation) Act, 1998.

The 1998 Act obliges local authorities to meet the current and projected needs of the Traveller community, taking distinct needs and family circumstances of Travellers into account. The Act requires the local authority to prepare an accommodation programme to meet projected needs over a five-year period. The Act resulted in the establishment of national and local consultative committees to monitor and contribute to these five-year programmes. The Act also specifies the introduction of loans for the purchase of caravans and sites by local authorities. The introduction of a caravan loan scheme has provided Travellers with access to credit – previously they were discriminated against in this area.

The Act empowers local authorities to evict people on anti-social grounds and provides that secondary evidence will be accepted in such cases. In conjunction with the 1998 Act, the Employment Equality Act, 1999 and the equal status legislation have also impacted positively on the Traveller community.

While the 1998 Act has many positive aspects in its endeavour to address the needs of the Traveller community, it has not changed everything and there are many issues that remain to be resolved. One has to query the potential long-term marginalisation effects of some of the works undertaken such as the building of group housing schemes. In the wider context of social policy, there is a desire to end social segregation through the introduction of integrated housing plans.

However, in effect, the Traveller community is almost always accommodated in a segregated fashion. While it is important that Traveller culture be respected, smaller, more spatially diverse accommodation could reduce conflict on sites and in turn improve Traveller and settled relations. Another important feature is the age profile of the Traveller community. Many dwellings are made available for senior citizens in the settled community, as people grow older and their household size diminishes. No such profile is taken into account for the Traveller community. Regarding the caravan loan scheme, while this is a positive advance, there are large numbers of Travellers who do not qualify or cannot afford a loan.

As noted above, local authorities play a major role in counteracting disadvantage through the provision of housing and accommodation. The majority of local authorities that provide a social work service employ social workers. As a general rule, social workers are employed to work exclusively with Travellers, while housing welfare officers are engaged to work with tenants and housing applicants within the settled community. Some local authorities, such as Dublin and Waterford City Councils, use an integrated approach and housing welfare officers work with both settled and Travelling people.

Social Care, Social Inclusion and the Role of the Local Authority Social Worker/Housing Welfare Officer

Following a White Paper entitled *Housing: A Review of Past Operations and Immediate Requirements* (Department of Local Government, 1948) it was recognised that 'One hundred thousand new dwellings were needed, sixty thousand of those to be built by the local authorities and forty thousand by the private sector' (Roche, 1982b, p. 226). The government was determined to clean up the cities and this meant doing something about the slums and tenements. Dublin Corporation responded by appointing a housing welfare officer in 1948 to work with families who were to be housed by the corporation, and was to the forefront in rehousing families from the slums to new suburban estates in Crumlin, Ballyfermot and Cabra.

A 1943 report entitled *Enquiry into the Housing of the Working Classes of the City of Dublin 1939/1943* stated: 'Most families require guidance, encouragement and assistance to enable them to settle down to their new environment and to maintain the highest standard of comfort and happiness' (quoted in Housing Welfare Section, 1988, p. 6). It was suggested by the Civic Institute that female housing managers be appointed to work with such families. The authors of the aforementioned report did not think it feasible for women to be appointed as managers and instead recommended the creation of a role to be known as welfare worker or welfare officer; the holder of which would be the 'tenant's friend'.

However, it was felt that this 'welfare worker' would need an official status and it was recommended that administrative functions be added to the role, including:

- inspection of the domestic apparatus of the dwellings such as cooking stoves and heating ranges
- listening to complaints
- helping in the administration of a system of differential rent rebates
- preventing growth of rent arrears
- keeping the housing department informed of any existing conditions of overcrowding.

Another proposal was that the welfare worker:

> . . . be placed in direct contact with the tenants to be housed, no matter what class, for a suitable period before transference so as to prepare the tenants for the due fulfilment of their obligations and to assist the Allocations Officer in making suitable allocations (quoted in Housing Welfare Section, 1988, p. 7).

The code of ethics for social work issued in 2001 by the British Association of Social Workers states that:

> Social work is the purposeful and ethical application of personal skills in interpersonal relationships directed towards enhancing the personal and social functioning of an individual, family, group or neighbourhood, which necessarily involves using evidence obtained from practice to help create a social environment conducive to the well-being of all.

The social work profession promotes social change, problem solving in human relationships and the empowerment and liberation of people to enhance wellbeing. Utilising theories of human behaviour and social systems, social work intervenes at the points where people interact with their environment. Principles of human rights and social justice are fundamental to social work.

The majority of local authorities provide a social work service – employ social workers – to work exclusively with the Traveller community (see above) and do not employ housing welfare officers. Some of the larger local authorities, such as Dublin, Cork, Limerick and Waterford, employ both social workers and housing welfare officers. Housing welfare officers are engaged to work with tenants and housing applicants within the settled community. In some local authorities housing welfare officers work with both settled and Travelling people; Dublin and Waterford City Councils are two authorities where this practice occurs. This integrated approach may be an optimum development in terms of future welfare initiatives in local authorities.

The social work agency of Dublin City Council is its Housing Welfare Section, which provides a preventive social work service to Dublin City Council's tenants, prospective tenants, members of the Travelling community, ethnic minorities, the elderly, reclusive and eccentric individuals. The social workers in this unique section address the complex problems of families and individuals.

Social work in the welfare section involves, amongst other things, assessment/reporting, advocacy, and counselling and other related therapeutic services. Social workers attempt to relieve and prevent hardship and suffering. They have a responsibility to help individuals, families and groups and communities through the provision and operation of appropriate services and by contributing to social planning. They work with or in the interests of people to enable them to deal with personal and social difficulties and obtain essential resources and services. Their work may include, but is not limited to, interpersonal practice, groupwork, community work, social development, social action, policy development, research, social work education and supervisory and managerial functions in these fields.

The Future of Social Inclusion in Local Government

The state apparatus for dealing with social inclusion in Ireland is complex in its extent but also in its structure. While restructuring and reforms have attempted to provide for greater co-ordination of services, the myriad of agencies, both public and voluntary, that serve the socially excluded is daunting to the citizen and even between agencies there can be confusion as to where responsibility rests. Recent attempts to provide for the integration of the local government and local development systems have recognised the importance of social inclusion as a focus of local development work and local services (Interdepartmental Task Force on the Integration of Local Government and Local Development Systems, 1998, p. 5).

Whether the reorganised structure, with the city/county development board at its centre, will address the shortcomings of the present system in terms of social inclusion, manifested largely in a disjointed administration, still awaits a conclusion. In Ireland, three levels of government administer directly to the public in this area: the Department of Social and Family Affairs at a central level, the health boards at regional level and the local authorities at local level. The potential for confusion among the public, let alone the potential for duplication and service gaps, begs the questions as to the suitability of the structure of services aimed, at least in part, at addressing social inclusion.

One could argue that a more progressive philosophy towards local government would rationalise the relevant services to local government level where the responsiveness and flexibility needed to address social inclusion could be more meaningfully exercised. However, this argument has implications beyond that of social inclusion. The pace and desire (where power rests) of expressions for devolution does not engender any great sense of expectation that areas such as social inclusion will be better served in the foreseeable future.

24

Local Government and the European Union

Mark Callanan

This chapter will focus on the various ways that the European Union has impacted on Irish local authorities since Ireland became a member state in 1973. It has become something of a truism to say that membership of the EU has had a profound effect on Irish society, politics and economics. Indeed, it is also true to say that EU membership has impacted significantly on public administration (see, for example, Laffan, 1991 and 2000; Cromien, 2000).[1] However, such accounts focus either exclusively or largely on the effect EU membership has had on central government with no more than a brief acknowledging reference to local government, usually in the context of EU Structural Funds.

Similarly, most texts on Irish local government tend to concentrate almost exclusively on the interaction between local and central levels of government. For example, Roche (1982b, appendix VI) makes only brief reference to local government's international activities, including some effects of EU membership. The omission of EU issues in many accounts on Irish local government effectively ignores the fact that, apart from the central government and local government levels, there is another layer of policy and law making in operation – policies and laws decided upon by the EU institutions. Legislation and policies agreed in Brussels will often contain significant implications for local authorities.

Overview of EU Law and Decision Making

It is not the intention of this chapter to give a detailed or fully comprehensive account of EU law and institutional arrangements. Numerous textbooks exist on these

---

[1] Laffan (1991, p. 190) goes so far as to argue that EC membership may have been more demanding on the Irish public service than the foundation of the state.

subjects (see, for example, Nugent, 1999; Dinan, 1999). Rather, the following is a brief summary of the main features of EU law, the types of legislation adopted and the main players involved in the policy process, so as to allow for a better understanding of how local government in Ireland has been affected by this system.

Types of Legislation

As Chubb (1992, p. 305) observes, there have been two constitutions in Ireland since 1973: the domestic constitution, *Bunreacht na hÉireann*, and the EU treaties and EU primary legislation. On the basis of the EU treaties, legislation of varying types can be adopted by the EU institutions.

Regulations, once adopted, are immediately binding and become law in all EU member states. Once they are published they must be complied with.

Directives have become a preferred way of enacting law as they can allow some degree of flexibility. Directives will set a goal to be achieved. This goal is legally binding and must be transposed into national law by the member states, thus requiring changes in domestic legislation. Normally, a Directive will contain a specific deadline for it to be transposed into national law. In Ireland's case, Directives are transposed through an Act of the Oireachtas or through ministerial regulations under the European Communities Act. Once adopted, the national legislation has to be notified to the European Commission. Member states can be taken to court by individuals, or more commonly by the European Commission, for not transposing Directives into national law.

Infringements of EU law can range from non-notification (where national measures to transpose Directives have not been notified to the European Commission on time) to incomplete transposition (when the transposing legislation is judged to be faulty or incomplete) and incorrect application (where a member state is alleged to have failed to apply EU law properly – which, amongst other things, can apply to environmental or planning decisions taken by the relevant authorities in Ireland). Information on such infringements arises from a number of sources including complaints made by individuals or groups directly to the European Commission, reports published by statutory agencies and press and media stories. A state can be held liable for loss of earnings caused by a failure to implement a Directive. This was established by the European Court of Justice in the Francovich case in 1990 (case C-6/90, as well as C-9/90).

Decisions are addressed to individual member states, companies (in competition cases) or individuals. They are legally binding on those to whom they are addressed.

Other texts can be adopted by the EU institutions, such as recommendations and opinions. While these instruments can carry political weight, they are not legally binding.

In a number of important rulings in the 1960s and 1970s, the European Court of Justice established the principle of primacy of EU law over national laws. This means that where there is a conflict between EU legislation and national (or indeed local) legislation, EU law prevails. This principle has been consistently upheld by both the European and Irish courts.

Role of EU Institutions

A number of different institutions are involved in preparing and deciding on EU legislation. Some also have a role in implementation, although the task of implementation is most often delegated to national governments and in many cases to sub-national government. The EU institutions largely confine themselves to a 'watchdog' role in investigating whether legislation is being properly observed and enforced by the relevant authorities and, where necessary, taking appropriate action to ensure this takes place.

The *European Commission* drafts and proposes legislation to the other EU institutions in most policy areas. It also carries out a number of specific tasks entrusted to it by the member states, such as management of the EU Structural Funds, and is furthermore charged with a role – often described as 'guardian of the treaties' – which involves ensuring that member states and others abide by the rules and legislation that have been adopted. However, contrary to popular belief, the European Commission has limited administrative resources and therefore has to rely on national and sub-national authorities in the member states to implement much of the legislation adopted at EU level.

The *Council of Ministers* comprises ministers from the respective member states and is one of the key decision makers on legislation. It meets in various formations, depending on the issues under discussion. For example, it will comprise environment ministers from each EU country when meeting to discuss proposals on environmental legislation. The detailed work of ministers is prepared by numerous committees made up of national civil servants from ministries and government departments in each EU country.

While the Council of Ministers was initially regarded as the main decision-maker on legislation proposed by the European Commission, it is increasingly sharing this role with the *European Parliament*. The parliament consists of politicians from each member state directly elected every five years. This body increasingly wields a veto over many areas of legislation. It also possesses budgetary powers regarding a number of areas of EU expenditure and supervisory powers over the other EU institutions.

The *European Court of Justice* interprets EU law and ensures the application of EU law. It is also the responsibility of national courts to ensure the application of EU law.

The *Committee of the Regions* and the *Economic and Social Committee* are two separate advisory bodies, the former representing the interests of local and regional authorities (see appendix 10), the latter representing the interests of the social partners. Despite its rather misleading name, the *European Court of Auditors* is not a judicial body, but is concerned with the auditing of expenditure under the EU budget.

Subsidiarity, the EU and Local Government

Article 1 of the Maastricht Treaty on European Union states that:

> This Treaty marks a new stage in the process of creating an ever-closer union among the peoples of Europe, in which decisions are taken as openly as possible and as closely as possible to the citizen.

The Maastricht Treaty, agreed in 1991, specifically embedded the principle of subsidiarity as a basis for deciding when the EU should and should not act on a particular issue. Under Article 5 of the Treaty:

> In areas which do not fall within its exclusive competence, the Community shall take action, in accordance with the principle of subsidiarity, only if and insofar as the objectives of the proposed action cannot be sufficiently achieved by the Member States and can therefore, by reason of the scale or effects of the proposed action, be better achieved by the Community.

The principle of subsidiarity can be traced to a 1931 papal encyclical letter, *Quadragesimo Anno*, which stated that functions should be delivered and decisions should be made as close to the individual as possible. The document asserted that 'it is an injustice, a grave evil and a disturbance of the right order for a larger and higher association to arrogate to itself functions which can be performed more efficiently by smaller and lower societies' (quoted in Peterson, 1994, p. 117).

From a legal point of view, insofar as it applies to the EU, subsidiarity is restricted to relations between the EU and the member states. It does not, strictly speaking, extend to relations between EU, national and local levels, despite frequent claims to the contrary. That said, the exhortation in the Treaty that decisions should be taken at the level closest to the citizen does have ramifications for local government, at least from a political perspective. It means that the governments of all member states have accepted the principle.

As the level of government closest to the citizen, the principle of subsidiarity is patently of relevance in the context of local/national government competences, as well as national/EU competences. In those countries with a strong regional government, a fourth dimension is added to the hierarchy. In fact, such is the interdependency between local, regional, national and EU levels of decision making that the relations between the various levels have evolved to a system that some have characterised as multi-level governance (see below).

There have been continuing pressures for greater local authority involvement in the EU policy process. This is not just because of the increasing impact the EU has had on local authorities in different member states, but is also due to a commitment to the principle of subsidiarity, decentralisation and local discretion prevalent in many EU countries.

The Influence of EU Policy Priorities and Legislation on Local Government

The increasing volume and complexity of legislation in general can be a frequent source of anxiety for local authorities. However, it is often more appropriate to attribute new legislation to Brussels rather than Dublin. To some extent, the EU influence on local government can be subtle. Many ministerial regulations, statutory instruments, and sometimes Acts of the Oireachtas, are often drawn up to transpose EU Directives into Irish law – their EU origin may not be immediately apparent to all involved. For example, a large body of environmental legislation emanating from the Department of the Environment and Local Government is initiated within the EU institutions rather than the Custom House.

While many in local government initially saw the EU only as a potential source of funding, the situation gradually matured into a more rounded picture of how the EU impacts on local government. While the money accruing to a local authority under the EU Structural and Cohesion Funds is relatively easy to calculate, it is infinitely more difficult to estimate the costs associated with implementing a wide range of EU legislation. As Ireland moves from being a net beneficiary to being a net contributor to the EU's budget, it is likely that the implications (in many cases very costly implications) of EU legislation for local authorities will receive greater scrutiny.

The impact of EU legislation can be felt in various local government activities, and affects local authorities in their role as employers, service providers and property owners; as monitoring, enforcing and licensing bodies; and as agents for the development of their area. It is not possible within the confines of this chapter to give an exhaustive account of all EU legislation impacting on local government. However, the following examples of EU legislative texts should serve to illustrate the diverse range of implications for local authorities:

- Urban Waste Water Directive (91/271/EC). This Directive has had, and will continue to have, large-scale financial implications for local authorities, including major investment in waste water collection and treatment infrastructure in towns and cities above a certain size. While the capital costs for construction of such facilities are provided for by way of EU and central government grants, the costs associated with management and maintenance largely fall to local authorities. There are also administrative implications with regard to sampling requirements.

- Landfill Directive (99/31/EC). This Directive sets out targets for the reduction of biodegradable waste going to landfill sites, obliges member states to draw up national strategies which identify how they plan to achieve these reductions and contains requirements regarding the pre-treatment of municipal waste, collection of gases and procedures concerning controlling and opening, management, closure and monitoring of a site. The Directive and the strict standards associated with it will increase the charges levied on users of landfill and result in a greater emphasis on recycling and waste management strategies.
- Public Procurement Directives (93/37/EEC, 93/36/EEC, 92/50/EEC and 93/38/EEC). There are a number of Directives governing the allocation of contracts by local authorities and other public bodies for public works, supplies and services. Specific provisions, entailing considerable administrative implications, apply to the advertising and publication of notices in the *Official Journal of the European Communities*, tendering procedures (open or restricted procedure), contract award procedures (lowest price or most economically advantageous tender), time limits and specification of standards.
- Working Time Directive (93/104/EC). Local authorities are employers of large numbers of people and consequently employment legislation will have implications for human resource management. For example, this Directive regulates the maximum number of working hours employees can be obliged to work each week.
- Environmental Impact Assessment Directive (85/337/EEC and 97/11/EC). This Directive obliges local authorities to assess at planning stage the environmental impact of projects where certain thresholds are met or where an infrastructure project is likely to have a significant impact on the environment.
- Water Framework Directive (2000/60/EC). This provides for river basin management by catchment area and requires that local authorities co-operate with each other within river basin districts to achieve 'good water status' by 2015.

These examples all concern legislation with direct financial and/or administrative implications for local government. In many cases, however, EU legislation will have indirect financial implications for local authorities. For example, Directive 92/21/EEC on the masses of certain motor vehicles governs the weight of a number of categories of motor vehicle, including heavy goods vehicles, with consequences for the road maintenance and restoration programmes of local authorities.

Other examples might include health and safety legislation, recycling targets, water quality, protection of sites under the Habitats and Birds Directives and the

European Spatial Development Perspective. Many of these carry administrative consequences for local authorities, some of which are very worthy and should be done regardless. Other legislative measures can, on occasion, impose disproportionate burdens on local government. Even in environmentally conscious Sweden, many local authorities view the requirement to check bathing water every two weeks under the Bathing Water Directive as excessive (SALA/SFCC, 2001, p. 60). The effects of the EU's environmental legislation are not confined solely to local authorities' environmental services sections, but are also felt in areas such as roads, water services and planning. Employment legislation will have an important influence on local authority personnel practices with regard to issues such as working conditions, equal treatment, recruitment policy, part-time working, parental leave and health and safety in the workplace. EU initiatives on local employment actions and social inclusion are relevant to the community and enterprise function.

Even where the EU's competence to act is more limited, such as in housing, an EU dimension can be discerned. While there is no EU policy on housing as such, various initiatives have consequences for housing management. For example, Article 9 of Regulation 1612/68 on the free movement of workers, adopted in 1968 and amended in 1976 and 1992, provides that workers from another member state residing in Ireland enjoy the same rights to housing as Irish citizens, including insertion on the housing waiting list. Legislation on minimum standards for the reception of asylum-seekers impacts on the housing function. Article 34 of the Charter of Fundamental Rights of the European Union, signed in 2000, provides for a general right to social and housing assistance to combat social exclusion and poverty and 'to ensure a decent existence for all those who lack sufficient resources'. At the time of writing, the charter was not legally binding, although it was expected that it would be given some legal status during 2003 or 2004. EU co-ordination of policies on social inclusion identifies 'ensuring good accommodation for all' as a core challenge in addressing social exclusion (Council of the European Union, 2001, p. 26). Thus, despite the lack of an EU housing policy per se, a number of EU activities impact on the housing function. National housing ministers from each EU country meet on an informal basis, usually once a year.

Other EU policy parameters could well have 'trickle-down' implications for local government. The EMU restrictions on public debt, and in particular the Stability Pact agreed in 1997 providing for fines on countries running a budget deficit above 3 per cent of GDP, may force governments to limit and in many cases cut back public expenditure, including central government grants to local authorities. The introduction of the euro itself necessitated changes in everything from accounting systems to parking meters. Part of the timing of the introduction of a new local authority financial management system in 2000 and 2001 was to ensure that a euro-compliant system would be in place before euro notes and coins were introduced in 2002.

The European Commission is investing in extra resources to ensure proper enforcement of binding rules. In fact, in the current political climate the European Commission is laying more emphasis on the full implementation and enforcement of existing laws than on proceeding with extensive new legislative programmes. The European Commission launches infraction proceedings against recalcitrant member states when legislation is not transposed and/or enforced to its satisfaction. Recently, it has been keen to publicise such cases in a policy of 'naming and shaming' laggards, and national and local media regularly report cases of infringements being pursued in the European Court of Justice. However, the Maastricht Treaty on European Union gave the EU institutions an additional power to impose fines for continued infractions of EU legislation. The first imposition of a fine by the European Court of Justice under Article 228 of the EC Treaty for non-implementation of EU legislation took place in 2000, when the Greek government was fined €20,000 per day for ignoring a 1992 ruling on toxic and dangerous waste, and in particular over the failure of local authorities in Crete to stop the discharging of toxic and dangerous waste from a tip into a local river (Case C-387/97). In practice, it often falls to local government to implement and administer EU legislation, however, it should be noted that it is always the member state that is held responsible for infringements, even if those infringements occur at local or regional level. Implementation of EU law can be a source of tension between local/regional levels and central government, particularly in the environmental field.

In addition, the European Commission is often seen as a court of appeal for those objecting to construction projects. Any individual can make a complaint to the European Commission, alleging a breach of EU law. On a per capita basis, Ireland is the source of a relatively high number of such complaints. In 2001, for example, 97 complaints were received from Ireland (European Commission, 2002, annex I). Complaints from Ireland made up over 7 per cent of the total number of complaints from across Europe, whereas the population of Ireland is just over one per cent of the total EU population. Problems often arise because of the time needed to investigate allegations. While the investigation may reveal no breach of the legislation, the project under scrutiny will often be delayed significantly until this is verified. The investigations themselves will often become the subject of intense media commentary and often create a negative impression for the project.

When genuine cases are found, where local authorities have failed to fully implement or enforce EU law, media reports are often written in such a way as to leave the reader with the impression that Ireland is the only country to encounter such difficulties. In fact this is by no means the case. Just because the Irish authorities receive negative publicity for a high number of complaints does not mean that Ireland is the worst offender when it comes to applying EU law. Figure

24.1 illustrates the number of infringement cases opened against the different member states.

Figure 24.1 Number of Cases in Motion, by Member State, December 2001

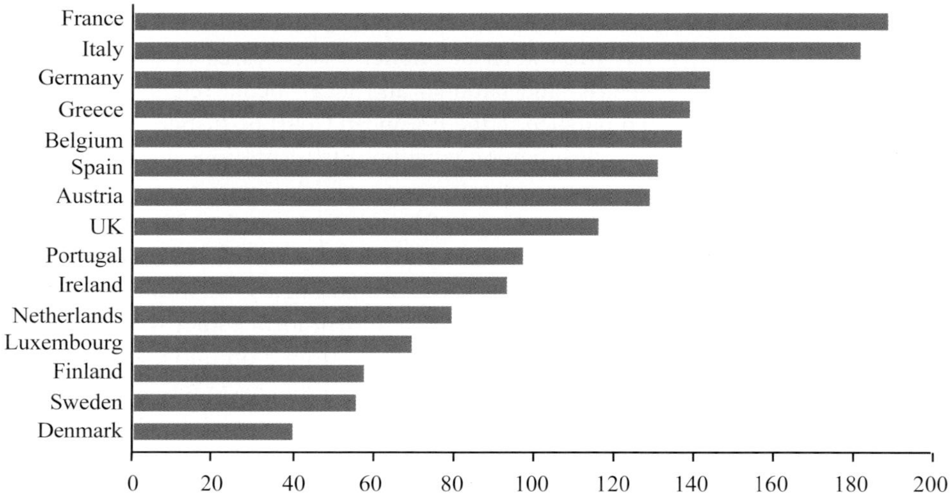

Source: European Commission (2002, p. 12)

All member states have an equivalent number of legislative acts to implement. Indeed, it could be argued that smaller member states, with smaller public services and administrative resources at their disposal, are at a disadvantage vis-à-vis the larger member states in having to implement and enforce the same amount of legislation. Coyle (1994, pp. 66–7) states that 'many EU directives are time-consuming and costly to implement and often require sophisticated monitoring equipment and procedures which place a heavy burden on a small public sector already under strain'.

Most complaints to the European Commission concern alleged infringements of environmental legislation. In this area, there are no unblemished records among any of the member states:

> Practically all Member States should increase their resources for inspection, training, checking for compliance, assisting enterprises as regards compliance, building infrastructure, etc. because everywhere there is chronic underenforcement and chronic understaffing. Resources specifically intended for enforcement and compliance are particularly important . . . As local authorities are much closer to the issues concerned, their administrative, technical and personal capacities need to be strengthened (Demmke and Unfried, 2001, p. 279).

EU Funding

The Structural and Cohesion Funds are always given a prominent place in any discussion on Ireland's relationship with the EU, to the extent that there has occasionally been a tendency in some quarters to exaggerate their importance. Most would argue that the EU's Single Market project has been a more important factor in Irish growth than the Structural Funds. For example, the ESRI has estimated that the two community support frameworks[2] covering the 1989 to 1993 and 1994 to 1999 periods will, in the long run, raise GNP by a modest 2 per cent over the level it would have reached without Structural Funds (Honohan, 1997, p. 55). This compares with an ESRI estimate that GNP in Ireland by 2000 would be just over 5 per cent higher than it would have been without the Single Market (Bradley, 1992, p. 108). The point remains, however, that the Structural Funds have been an important contributory factor (albeit not the only factor) behind Ireland's economic success in the 1990s.

Ireland's receipt of Structural Funds increased through the 1980s and, in particular, the 1990s (see figure 24.2) and local authorities ultimately received a large proportion of this share. For local authorities, EU Structural and Cohesion Funds represented a major source of revenue in the 1980s, a time when scant resources were available elsewhere. EU funding has contributed to local authority activities from large-scale road building and water treatment plants to smaller-scale urban and village renewal plans and arts and cultural facilities.

Figure 24.2 Structural Funds Receipts, 1975 to 1999

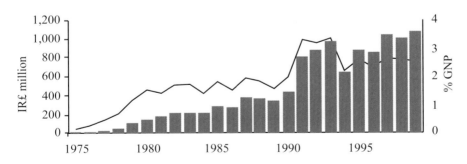

Note: bar is IR£million (IR£ = €1.27), line is the percentage of GNP
Source: Honohan (1997, p. 29)

---

[2] The community support framework represents those elements of the national development plan that are co-financed by the EU Structural Funds. It is a document agreed between the government and the European Commission containing priorities for investment through which Structural Funds are paid.

At the same time, the point is often made that while local authorities were heavily involved in the actual spending of EU Structural and Cohesion Funds, the designation of the whole of Ireland as a single 'Objective 1' region until 1999 restricted the involvement of local authorities in deciding on priorities for EU spending, and led to a highly centralised system of management (Laffan, 1996, pp. 326–7 and 1991, p. 195; Coyle, 1997, p. 91).

The national development plan (NDP) for 2000 to 2006 and the accompanying community support framework for the same period represent an unprecedented investment package of some €51.5 billion, spanning areas such as infrastructure, education and training, aid to the private sector, and local and community development. A large proportion of the commitments in the NDP will be delivered at local level. Ultimately, local authorities are responsible for spending some 40 per cent of the expenditure committed under the NDP, while the figure rises to 74 per cent when spending channelled through the various bodies represented on the county/city development boards is taken into consideration (Government of Ireland, 2000a).

Local authorities thus play a major role in implementing this NDP, as they have done with previous national development plans. They face the difficulties associated with implementation on the ground and have to play their part in meeting the ambitious targets that have been set. EU Structural and Cohesion Funds continue to make up an important (albeit reduced) proportion of the investment under the NDP, and many local authority schemes, projects and programmes continue to be co-financed under these funds.

The impact of the Structural Funds on local government has not been restricted to the actual financial transfers and local authority investment in their area. EU requirements for spending Structural Funds have helped embed a culture of evaluation, monitoring and value for money in the Irish public service, including local government. Drawdown of the Structural Funds also implied moving to a multi-annual programme approach of public sector management, as opposed to an emphasis on annual budgets. 'The role of the European Commission in influencing the approach to the planning and evaluation of expenditure programmes deserves more than a footnote in Irish economic history' (Gray, 1997, p. 52). Local authorities must also work within these new 'rules of the game', and increasingly work on the basis of multi-annual programmes.

EU funding has taken on an added dimension for local government in the context of cross-border co-operation, particularly with programmes such as INTERREG and PEACE. For example, in the case of INTERREG, the programme has financed a number of cross-border networks between local authorities in the Republic and in Northern Ireland, and various EU initiatives have facilitated the development of links at local level between the two parts of Ireland (see, for example, Birrell, 1999, pp. 109–18; Greer, 2000, pp. 52–68; Laffan and Payne, 2001, pp. 96–9).

As well as the 'mainstream' programmes and projects under the Structural and Cohesion Funds, local authorities have been able to benefit from programmes such as *LIFE*, which is geared towards innovative environmental projects, and exchange of experience programmes such as *Pacte, Recite* and *Ecos-Ouverture*. Other initiatives have included the *Urban Pilot Projects*, which supported innovative projects in urban rejuvenation and regeneration in city centre areas, and *Terra*, which was directed at experimental approaches to land-use planning.

In addition to regular programmes, the European Commission frequently invites calls for proposals on issues such as local actions to promote employment, tackle social exclusion and protect the environment. The overall amounts available for projects under this bewildering array of schemes are considerably less than those available under the mainstream Structural and Cohesion Funds. However, funding under these schemes is in most cases transferred directly from European level and thus removes central government from its traditional 'gatekeeper' role between the EU institutions and local government. As Rees (1997, p. 38) observes, central government departments play little or no part in the process – in many cases they are unaware of which local authorities have received funding.

There are differing views on the worthiness of local authorities participating in such programmes. Many local authorities in both Ireland and elsewhere have found that a considerable level of bureaucracy and paperwork accompanies funding under such schemes, with many expressing frustration at late payments, the time involved and the lack of concrete outcomes (see, for example, SALA/SFCC, 2001, pp. 36, 39; Rees, 1997, pp. 40–1; Coyle, 1997, p. 92; Audit Commission, 1991, p. 14). On the other hand, many see these schemes as offering opportunities to exchange experience and broaden horizons on how others tackle problems and challenges – learning how, for example, information technology has been used to improve public services elsewhere – or on building partnerships with locally based statutory and voluntary organisations to promote economic development (see, for example, Pycroft, 1995, p. 25). Such initiatives provide funding for projects that often involve partnerships and networks of local authorities and other local bodies from various EU countries. In many cases they have exposed both elected members and local authority officials to different local government systems and structures.

The EU and the Local Economy

Local authorities have long taken an active interest in the development of their areas, despite their limited range of functions and the fact that a 'general competence' was only provided for local government in 1991 (see chapter 8). Local authorities have contributed to local development, in particular through the provision of the necessary infrastructure (roads, water, waste, housing and recreational amenities). Local authorities are also key players in trying to attract industry to their area in terms of supplying the necessary services for businesses, and local authority representatives often meet with potential investors to discuss the facilities available to companies in the area.

However, increasingly, local authorities have moved beyond the exclusive scope of physical development and started to see themselves as facilitators for the development of their local community and local economy. In recent years, local authorities have been to the forefront in the creation of inter-agency task forces and enterprise initiatives aimed at developing the local economy and job creation. The county/city development boards (see chapter 16) are to some extent an attempt to institutionalise such projects and to develop the role of the local authority as an 'enabling authority' (see chapter 28) for the improvement of the economic, social and cultural wellbeing of the area.

There are a number of different studies examining the impact of the EU's Single Market project on the Irish economy (see, for example, National Economic and Social Council, 1989). The 1992 deadline for the removal of barriers to the movement of goods, services, capital and people meant both increased competition and increased opportunities for Irish companies. The widely held expectation amongst economists was that the removal of barriers, which was at the heart of the Single Market project, would have a number of inter-related effects:

- the generation of greater competition
- increased economies of scale
- greater specialisation in production
- increased productivity and growth.

However, it was clear that certain areas, even within individual countries, were in a good position to take advantage of the opportunities, while other areas might be more exposed to greater competition. Less-developed and particularly peripheral and remote areas had to overcome problems associated with geographical position, which included increased transport costs and delivery periods and less scope for achieving economies of scale. The potential scenario was that disparities would be reinforced, as certain areas gained and others lost out. Goldsmith (1993, p. 684) points out that, in real terms, the effects of the Single European Market, and globalisation in general, impact most heavily at local level through jobs and economic wellbeing. As well as there being winners and losers between localities and regions, there would be winners and losers within localities – in particular a number of economic sectors were identified as being vulnerable (see, for example, Barry et al., 2001, pp. 539–42).

Undoubtedly, access to the rest of the European market helped employment in certain sectors in Ireland to grow. However, it is also argued that the 'cold shower' effect of increased competition exposed inefficiencies and was at least one contributory factor in the gradual decline of traditional manufacturing in Ireland – with economic and social consequences for the localities concerned. In essence, while jobs were becoming available in sectors such as information technology, financial services and pharmaceuticals, factories in more labour-intensive industries were closing down.

The Single Market project opened up the European marketplace to inward investment. Local economies in Ireland, in the context of a Single European Market, increasingly have to compete to secure employment and investment, which is attracted to localities by varying factors such as a well-skilled workforce and educational facilities, the quality of transport infrastructure, housing supply, a good environment, advanced information and communication technologies and so on. Local authorities obviously have a key role to play here and increasingly seek to generate and engineer local conditions that are conducive to investment (Pycroft, 1995, p. 21). Equally, they play a role in working with others to ensure that the local economy can compete in an enlarged market. The EU has also recently recognised the important role that local authorities can play in creating jobs in local areas (European Commission, 2000).

Other areas of EU activity are important for local economies. The Common Agricultural Policy (CAP) is particularly important for rural communities. One would have to regard the CAP as something of a double-edged sword for local authorities. On the one hand, it has tried to secure the future of rural communities through supporting farm incomes and, increasingly in recent years, supporting off-farm investment in rural enterprises to create alternative sources of income for those previously engaged in agriculture. On the other hand, particularly in the 1980s and early 1990s, through providing incentives to produce and through supporting intensive agricultural practices, the CAP often contributed to a deteriorating environment. Farmers were prone to over-fertilisation of their lands causing particularly negative environmental consequences for lakes and rivers.

EU rules on state aid also have an impact on the development of local economies. These can have drastic consequences for localities when the future of a large employer based in the area is at stake (one need only note the long-running debate between the European Commission and the Irish government over the Shannon stopover flights). As a general rule, financial aid from the state and public bodies to private enterprises is banned as it distorts competition in the EU's Single Market. However, a number of exceptions are provided for, within specified limits, for example with regard to regional aid. The government is allowed grant state aid (such as IDA grants) to companies establishing in particular parts of the country. Figure 24.3 depicts the ceilings on state aid that apply to new industrial developments in the eight regional authority areas from 2003 until 2006. As can be seen, higher levels of aid are allowed in those areas of greatest need and the EU co-ordinates its state-aid limits with the identification of Objective 1 areas across

the EU. The intention is therefore to favour towns, cities and counties in regions
where growth levels are lower. In this way, EU rules on state aid influence the level
of state intervention in the development of the local economy.

Figure 24.3 Grant Aid Intensities as a Percentage of New Industrial Investment

Regional Authority	%	
Border	40	
Midlands	40	plus 15% for SMEs
West	40	
South-West	20	
South-East	20	
Mid-West	20	plus 10% for SMEs
Mid-East	18	
Dublin	17.5	

Impact of the EU on Sub-National Structures in Ireland

Drawdown of EU Structural Funds and EU legislation has implied a number of
changes to the sub-national system of governance in Ireland. This has been
primarily felt through the creation of regional structures, local development
groups and new national agencies, all of which have affected the institutional
environment within which local authorities operate.

The European Commission is always keen to emphasise the importance of
local and regional authorities as partners in the decision-making process on
Structural Funds and in the preparation and implementation of programmes.
Since 1988, the EU has insisted that Structural Fund programmes be determined
on the basis of a partnership between the European Commission and national,
regional and local authorities. The European Commission has successively
reinforced this principle and sought to strengthen it during the 1989 to 1993, 1994
to 1999 and 2000 to 2006 rounds of Structural Funds. An examination of the
regulations governing the use of Structural Funds reveals a requirement for
consultation and involvement of local and regional authorities in the preparation,
monitoring and evaluation of plans and strategies (see Council Regulation (EC)
No. 1260/1999, in particular article 8).

Hopes were high in the early days of Ireland's membership of the then
European Economic Community that decisions on EU spending would involve
local government:

Prior to the establishment of the European Regional Development Fund (ERDF) in 1975 there were great expectations among Irish local authorities concerning possible financial flows from the fund. In the event, the ERDF has been managed and administered in a highly centralised manner in Ireland with the Department of Finance using the fund as reimbursement for expenditure through the public capital programme (Laffan, 1991, p. 195).

True to form, the government designated the entire state as one region for the purposes of Structural Funds, maintaining central government's gatekeeper role between sub-national government and the European institutions (Barrington, 1987b, p. 144; National Economic and Social Council, 1989, p. 474; Holmes and Rees, 1995, p. 243; Loughlin, 2001, p. 73). The reasoning behind the government's decision is summed up by Rees and Farrows (1999, p. 6):

> . . . the Government argued that it was concerned with the overall level of economic growth and development which was its main priority and that what was good for the state at a national level was also good for everyone in the state. This view reflected the national goals of the Government, as well as being consistent with the views of officials in the Department of Finance, which was the most powerful department. It was also consistent with the political view that Ireland was too small to have regions and that local government was not to be completely trusted, especially at a political level, where it was seen as being ineffective.

In the run-up to the first national development plan (NDP), which would cover the years 1989 to 1993 (Government of Ireland, 1989), the government hastily established sub-regional structures to advise on the preparation of the plan. This structure was based on seven regions and was composed of one tier of working groups, comprising central government officials, state agencies and county and city managers, and a second tier of advisory groups comprising local authority chairpersons, the social partners and interest groups. The two tiers were later merged to form regional review committees. However:

> . . . there was much local and regional criticism of these arrangements, particularly as the shape and content of the national plan that was submitted to the Commission bore little resemblance to the regional submissions. It was generally felt that the arrangements represented something of a 'cosmetic' exercise to satisfy the desire of the Commission for regional consultation and involvement in the process (Carroll and Byrne, 1999, p. 174).

The European Commission too expressed its disappointment at what it saw as a rather limited and superficial level of involvement on the part of local and regional interests (Laffan, 1991, p. 196, 1996, p. 331 and 1999, p. 101; Rees and Farrows, 1999, p. 8; Coyle and Sinnott, 1992, p. 82).

Eight regional authorities were established in 1994 (for more details on the role and structure of regional authorities, see chapter 25, and on their composition, see appendix 4). With regard to their EU-related functions, regional authorities were to be consulted on development priorities and were to provide the secretariat for regional monitoring committees, to oversee and review spending of EU Structural and Cohesion Funds in their area. They were not given executive functions. One international commentary on the Irish experience of managing EU Structural Funds makes the observation that:

> . . . though the regional authorities remain to some extent rather artificial creations merely to satisfy the European Commission, they have nevertheless led to a greater involvement of regional and local interest groups in the policy process. Despite the fact that the centre of power remains largely at central (and local) government level, and that the regional review process was largely considered unsatisfactory, it is clear that the sub-central interests have to be taken more into account (Bollen et al., 2000, p. 113).

As the Celtic Tiger economy began to pick up, there was a growing acknowledgement that some parts of the country were benefiting far more than others and that a greater regional perspective was needed on development, with a focus on those areas of greatest need. This debate began in the run-up to the 2000 to 2006 funding period, in the context of reduced transfers of EU Structural Funds to Ireland. Until 1999, the whole country had been classified as a single region for the purpose of drawing down EU Structural Funds. With the country as a whole above the eligibility threshold for priority status for receipt of EU monies (so-called Objective 1), a decision had to be taken as to whether part of the country could still benefit from Objective 1 status. A debate began on the issue of regional structures and regional development. A movement emerged which questioned the centralised system of identifying development needs for Ireland as a whole. According to one report on the issue:

> . . . there is a very clear signal from Brussels that any new administrative structures should embody the principle of subsidiarity and involve a significant devolution of power to the regions. This desire in Europe for a strong regional dimension cannot be ignored when administrative restructuring is being considered (Quinn and Foley, 1999, p. 28).

Two new regional assemblies were established in 1999, one for the Border, Midland and Western Region and one for the Southern and Eastern Region. However, the remit of the new regional assemblies did not involve a significant devolution of powers and was largely restricted to administrative duties connected to the management of EU Structural Funds. They were also given a role of advising the government on the regional dimension of the NDP and representation on the various monitoring committees overseeing expenditure under the NDP (for more details on the role and structure of regional assemblies, see chapter 25, and on their composition, see appendix 4). The regional assemblies were also charged with approving the regional operational programmes under the NDP for 2000 to 2006.[3]

Thus, while EU Structural Funds may not have revolutionised central–regional–local structures in Ireland, they have disturbed the relationship between the actors at these levels with regard to the preparation of development plans (see Laffan, 1996, pp. 320, 336; Bollen et al., 2000, p. 116). The Structural Funds and the obligation to draw up a national development plan have also sparked a far more critical debate about regionalism and balanced regional development within Ireland, and to some extent have acted as a focus for those seeking to promote regional and local interests.

EU Structural Funds from the late 1980s and early 1990s assisted a range of local development organisations from LEADER groups to area partnership companies to county/city enterprise boards. The EU financed these organisations at local level in Ireland, which focused on supporting rural development business plans, capacity building and training, and support to micro-enterprises (further information on the activities of these bodies can be found in chapters 3 and 16). In many areas, a co-operative approach between local authorities and these local development groups was adopted at the outset. However, in some quarters the evolution of well-financed groups outside of the local government system was seen as a threat to local government and meant that a defensive approach was pursued by both sides, leading to little interaction and often a lack of synergy. Different local development organisations ultimately reported to different government departments and, on some occasions, there was considerable overlap in terms of activities on the ground. There was sometimes a feeling of resentment on the part of local government that it was being bypassed in terms of access to central government and EU funding (see, for example, Walsh, 1998, pp. 336–7). According to *Better Local Government*:

> . . . local development initiatives have developed flexible, targeted and integrated responses to local needs, and have achieved considerable success in their individual fields of endeavour. However, there is criticism of the numbers as well as the complexity of the structures which have been established; there can sometimes seem to be a confusing multiplicity of organisations, with overlapping functions, giving rise to duplication of services and of administration, and some confusion for potential clients (Department of the Environment, 1996, p. 29).

These problems in part led to the establishment of the county/city development board structures, in an attempt to avoid duplication of effort and to co-ordinate the

---

[3] The national development plan is divided into what are known as operational programmes (OPs). The OPs for the 2000 to 2006 period are: economic and social infrastructure OP; employment and human resources development OP; productive sector OP; border, midland and western regional OP; southern and eastern regional OP; PEACE programme; and an OP for technical assistance.

range of activities pursued at local level by various organisations to promote economic, social, cultural and physical development.

The EU regulatory framework has also contributed to agency building within the public sector in Ireland, again impacting on the institutional environment in which local authorities operate. The establishment of the Environmental Protection Agency (EPA) under the Environmental Protection Agency Act, 1992 was in part due to obligations arising from EU legislation. EU activity in the field of environmental regulation had greatly increased during the 1970s and 1980s and the establishment of the EPA to some extent represented an attempt to improve implementation of EU environmental Directives. Similarly, it could be argued that the establishment of the National Roads Authority in 1993 had much to do with increased EU funding coming on-stream for national road projects in the early 1990s.

Given the EU's influence and role in Ireland in the establishment of new regional structures, local development groups and statutory agencies, it can be viewed as an important contributor to the institutional environment within which local authorities operate.

The Local Authority Response to the EU

By the early 1990s, local authorities in Ireland had recognised the impact 'Europe' was having on a wide range of local government activities – and not just on funding. This had also occurred in the case of local authorities in other European countries, which began to move from a concentration on obtaining EU funds to a more strategic approach to European integration, which encompassed different EU implications for local government, such as funding, legislation and the economic and social development of the locality (Roberts and Hart, 1991, pp. 45–6).

With an increasing realisation on the part of local authorities of the impact the EU was having during the 1990s, the County and City Managers' Association asked the Institute of Public Administration (IPA) to provide a tailored consultancy service on EU developments of interest to local government (Coyle, 1997, p. 83 and 2001, p. 160; Laffan, 1996, p. 337). The service is designed to alert local authorities to new developments at EU level with implications for local government. This initiative was followed up with the provision by the IPA, with the support of FÁS, of a training programme in European affairs, a full-time course for local authorities, designed to establish a cadre of local authority officials with a detailed understanding of how the EU works and affects local government.

Increasingly, some local authorities have come to view the lobbying of EU institutions, in particular the European Commission, as a necessary exercise. In a 1992 survey of local and regional politicians, interest groups and administrative elites, Coyle and Sinnott (1992, p. 100) found that a majority regarded the lobbying of the European Commission as 'necessary' and one-third deemed it to be 'indispensable'.

A number of Irish local authorities in the 1990s took the decision to establish a representative office in Brussels to promote direct contacts with the EU institutions. In 1993, six local authorities (Galway City Council and Donegal, Mayo, Galway, Kerry and Cork county councils), along with Údarás na Gaeltachta and University College Galway, established the West Ireland Liaison Office in Brussels, often known as *Nasc*. Similarly, the four Dublin local authorities established a joint office in Brussels in 1994, although this project was discontinued in 2000. The cost of maintaining a full-time office in Brussels is high and while many local authorities across Europe have established Brussels offices, due to the costs involved they often do so in partnership with others, while some local authorities find the costs prohibitive (Ercole at al., 1997, pp. 231–2; Goldsmith, 1993, p. 695; Audit Commission, 1991, p. 36). Such offices serve as the 'eyes and ears' of the authorities they represent. They are often involved in preparing bids for funding, searching for suitable partners, collecting and disseminating information and formally and informally lobbying EU officials on areas of concern. Figure 24.4 illustrates the number of offices representing local and regional authorities from different member states.

Figure 24.4 Regional Offices in Brussels, 1999

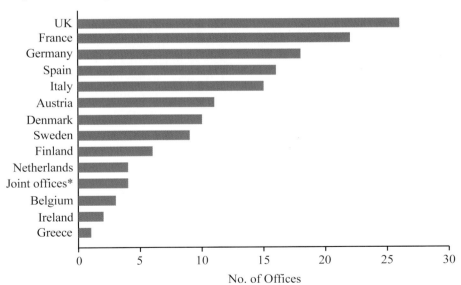

* joint offices between regional/local authorities from two or more member states
Source: adapted from Heichlinger (1999, pp. 27–32)

The Influence of Local Government in EU Policy Making

In most EU countries, local authorities largely respond to EU developments and initiatives rather than seek to influence them (Goldsmith, 1993, p. 693). However, there is increasing evidence that local authorities across Europe are looking to play a more proactive role in shaping EU developments.

In Ireland's case, the early days of EU membership were marked by a reluctance on the part of central government to relinquish its gatekeeper role. In fact central government actively sought to prevent the type of direct contacts between Irish local authorities and the European institutions referred to above (Coyle, 1997, p. 90 and 2001, p. 160; Laffan, 1996, p. 327; Barrington, 1991a, p. 161). A circular was sent from the Department of the Environment in 1988 to county and city managers requiring them to 'notify the Committee on the European Community Internal Market and Structural Funds of all contacts with the European Communities' (quoted in both Laffan, 1996, p. 327 and Holmes and Rees, 1995, p. 243). Holmes and Rees (1995, p. 245) believe that central government in Ireland has resisted attempts by the European Commission to form closer working arrangements with sub-national government and 'guarded its policy prerogative in the face of pressure from the Commission and from local and regional interests'.

However, this cautious and restrictive approach on the part of central government gradually gave way to a more relaxed attitude. With an increasing amount of EU legislation impinging on local authority activity, contacts began to develop between local government and the European institutions. These were fostered through a variety of means, including training programmes and study visits for local authority members and officials in Brussels, seminars involving officials from the EU institutions, and contacts facilitated by the IPA and by local authority offices in Brussels. Local and regional authority involvement in implementation and monitoring of Structural Funds expenditure also contributed to establishing direct links, particularly with the European Commission (Bollen et al., 2000, pp. 18, 73).

One channel of influencing EU policy for local authorities is through the Committee of the Regions (CoR), an advisory body set up under the Maastricht Treaty to represent local and regional authorities in the EU policy process. The first meeting of the CoR was held in 1994.[4] The CoR consists of representatives of local and regional authorities. The nine members from Ireland are all local councillors proposed for appointment to the CoR by the government on the advice of the Minister for the Environment and Local Government, who is

---

[4] In 1988 the European Commission had established a Consultative Council of Regions and Local Authorities, made up of members appointed by the European Commission and jointly nominated by the International Union of Local Authorities (IULA), the Council of European Municipalities and Regions (CEMR) and the Assembly of European Regions (AER). This consultative body was replaced by the CoR.

obliged to have regard to the objective that the delegation as a whole should manifest an appropriate measure of gender and territorial balance.[5] The Irish delegation therefore includes at least one member from each regional authority, who is expected to keep his/her respective regional authority informed of CoR activities (for example by preparing an annual report for his/her authority). Administration and technical support is provided to the Irish members of the CoR by personnel based in the Dublin Regional Authority and by a full-time officer based in Brussels.

Given that it is a relatively young institution, it is too early to make a conclusive assessment of the impact or influence the CoR has had on EU decision making thus far, although the European Commission regularly publishes reports assessing the effect CoR opinions have had on individual proposals. On the one hand, as an advisory body and with relatively narrow legal powers, its influence could be regarded as limited. On the other, the CoR contains a number of high-profile politicians (in particular mayors of large cities or regional ministers from federal countries), who enjoy a national as well as a local profile in their respective countries. This lends potential political clout to the CoR's work and status. The ambition of many of the CoR's members is that it should move beyond its advisory function and be given a stronger role in the EU policy process. For further details on the role of the CoR, see appendix 10.

Another channel for local government is to influence policy via networks built up with local authorities in other countries, in particular Europe-wide local government associations such as the Council of European Municipalities and Regions (CEMR). CEMR brings together national associations of local authorities from the various member states and applicant countries and seeks to lobby the EU institutions on behalf of local interests. It provides the EU institutions with a pan-European interlocutor on local government issues. In fact, the CEMR campaign to have a formal local and regional input into EU decision making contributed in part to the establishment of the Committee of the Regions (Ercole et al., 1997, p. 230). For a brief summary of some of the different pan-European local government bodies, see appendix 10.

Local authorities increasingly began to seek out direct contacts at European level of the type referred to above, drawn by the possibility of EU financing or of influencing EU legislation. Local government sometimes looks to the EU for influence over central government – EU support for a particular policy initiative can often be a useful bargaining tool in negotiation with government departments. At the same time, when seeking to influence EU decisions, care should be taken not to overlook the national dimension, which will always remain important

---

[5] This contrasts with the position in most other member states, where members of the CoR are chosen by national associations of local authorities rather than central government (Council of European Municipalities and Regions, 1999; SALA/SFCC, 2001, p. 138).

(Goldsmith, 1993, p. 698; Coyle and Sinnott, 1992, p. 104). Central government officials can bring the experience of local authorities in their country to the Council of Ministers, when decisions on EU issues are being taken.

In many EU member states, formal consultation mechanisms exist between local/regional level and national level with regard to policy making and drafting of legislation. Such consultation often takes place via strong national associations of local government charged with representing the voice of local authorities on legislative initiatives. This means that local authorities in such countries can seek to ensure that national officials take on board the concerns of local government when formulating the 'national line' at EU level. In Ireland, such formal consultation mechanisms between local and central government are far more limited (see Callanan, 2002b; Council of European Municipalities and Regions, 1999). That said, central government is often made aware of the difficulties in say implementing EU legislation on an informal basis, through, for example, seminars, written communication or a telephone call to the official responsible. In some cases central government departments will organise awareness sessions for local authority representatives on new initiatives. Such informal interaction between local and national government in Ireland fits with Ireland's informal administrative tradition in a relatively small public service, where interaction is based on personal contact rather than setting up rigid administrative structures (see, for example, Laffan, 2001, p. 96 or Coyle, 1994, p. 66).

Within the European Commission, there is an increasing acknowledgement that local authorities across the EU possess an expertise in terms of the realities and practical difficulties in implementing EU legislation that cannot be found elsewhere. For example, in the controversial area of waste management, where local government is in the frontline, local authorities can give feedback on their experience of implementation to the European institutions when such legislation is being amended or when new legislation is being drafted:

> As it is often the local authorities who bear the burden of implementing the requirements of Community waste legislation, the Commission also intends to improve their involvement in the preparation of legislation and the support given for the exchange of experience and best practices amongst them (European Commission, 2001b, p. 54).

This theme was further built on in the European Commission's 2001 White Paper on governance, which contains a number of proposals to strengthen interaction between European, national and local systems of government. It acknowledges that local authorities are increasingly bearing the financial and administrative consequences of EU legislation and that, 'in spite of their increased responsibility for implementing EU policies, their role as an elected and representative channel interacting with the public on EU policy is not exploited'

(European Commission, 2001d, p. 12). In the White Paper, the European Commission promises that, when the time comes for drafting new legislation, it will systematically consult both national associations of local and regional authorities (in each member state) and European associations of local and regional authorities. However, the White Paper also states that:

> . . . the principal responsibility for involving the regional and local level in EU policy remains and should remain with national administrations. But national governments are often perceived as not adequately involving regional and local actors in preparing their positions on EU policies. Each Member State should foresee adequate mechanisms for wide consultation when discussing EU decisions and implementing EU policies with a territorial dimension. The process of EU policy-making, in particular its timing, should allow Member States to listen to and learn from regional and local experiences (p. 12).

The challenge therefore is for central government to put in place arrangements to ensure that local authorities can raise issues of concern on draft EU legislation. There is also a challenge for local government to ensure that it can collectively represent its interests and negotiate with central government on detailed issues (Callanan, 2002b, pp. 76–83).

The White Paper also promised to allow for greater flexibility in how future EU legislation can be implemented, to take account of regional and local conditions – for example through making more use of framework directives, which are less detailed and prescriptive. As another possibility, the European Commission mentioned drawing up target-based contracts between local, national and EU levels.

At the time of writing, the Convention on the Future of Europe, charged with drafting a new constitutional treaty for Europe, was discussing incorporating a number of these principles into the new EU treaty. Many considered it appropriate to recognise local government as part of the democratic structures of the EU in a constitutional-type text.

Conclusion

It is clear from the above that membership of the EU has had numerous implications for local government in Ireland, even if sometimes these implications have been subtle and difficult to discern as they are often channelled through central government and handed down in the form of statutory instruments or ministerial regulations.

From originally seeing the EU almost exclusively in terms of a source of financing, local authorities are developing a broader view on the different ways in which Ireland's membership of the EU has impacted on local government, from funding to legislation to the local authority's role in ensuring that the locality can compete in the European marketplace. In this context, local government is increasingly likely to seek to influence future developments at EU level.

A situation is evolving of complex structures of multi-layered governance, with European, national and local actors all playing a part (see, for example, Marks et al., 1996a). Increasingly, networks are evolving to solidify relationships between these different layers. Links between the local and EU levels look certain to expand. During the early years of Ireland's membership of the then European Economic Community, European–local links were almost exclusively channelled through central government, with government departments playing a gatekeeper role. More recently, however, local authorities have begun to develop direct links with the European institutions.

Contact between the EU and local levels has not been without controversy in Ireland, particularly concerning disputes over alleged infringements of EU legislation. For their part, however, the European institutions seem to have acknowledged the key role that local authorities in Ireland and other member states play in implementing legislation. Utilising that expertise when new EU legislation is being formulated is now seen by the European Commission as one of the keys to better law making.

The EU is in a seemingly endless state of flux. For the foreseeable future there will be a need for local authorities not merely to be informed about pending changes but to be proactive in responding and contributing to new developments.

25

Regional Authorities and Regional Assemblies

Mark Callanan

Various reasons have been suggested for the development of regional[1] government in different countries. John (2001, pp. 110–21) identifies a number of factors related to the evolution of an intermediate tier between local government and central institutions in Western Europe, including:

- the need to promote integration between the various organisations operating at local and regional level
- the need for a level of government to carry out services which cannot be effectively performed by smaller local authorities, but which for reasons of economies of scale and efficiency would be better performed by regional government – typically these services might include strategic or regional planning, transport and economic development
- in the context of growing restrictions on public spending, a desire by central government to offload problematic areas can lead them to transfer responsibility for service provision to regional structures, but at the same time giving them limited budgets and tax-raising powers; for example,

---

[1] Some commentators (such as Sharpe, 1993) prefer to avoid the word region and instead refer to a middle or *meso* level of government between central government and local government. They point out that region is a rather ambiguous term which can be used to describe a wide variety of very different areas. In the Irish context, for example, one could consider the county as a region, in that it groups together urban, suburban and rural areas. Above the county level, two separate regional tiers, described in this chapter, have evolved that group together whole counties and cities. Above these structures, the Republic of Ireland was considered as a single region for the purposes of EU Structural Funds until 1999. Thus the word region can be used in a variety of contexts. For the purposes of this chapter, regions are used to refer to intermediate structures between central government and local authorities.

> regional governments now administer health services in Italy, Sweden, France and Germany
> * the encouragement by the EU of regional mobilisation and the establishment of regional structures, in particular through the arrangements for allocating Structural Funds
> * the pre-empting or acceding to demands from 'historic' regions for greater political autonomy and self-government and the recognition of regional identities; these might include former nations that were absorbed into larger nation-states, for example Scotland or Catalonia
> * the evolution of certain regions as a method of asserting that they are at a different stage of economic development than elsewhere in their particular nation-state.

Some of these factors are present in Ireland, others are largely absent. There is little affinity with regional structures in Ireland, and most Irish people would not profess to holding as strong a sense of belonging to a region as they would do to a county or city (Holmes and Rees, 1995, p. 236). The first manifestation of regions in Ireland might be considered the historic provinces of Connaught, Leinster, Munster and Ulster, essentially areas that were for a time grouped together under kingdoms. Nowadays, however, these provinces are largely of sporting significance only and have little administrative meaning – although they do group together administrative counties, are still used in the compilation of Census statistics and have been used as the basis for electoral constituencies for European Parliament elections.

Various reports and proposals on local government and public service reform have commented on the prospects for a regional tier of government in Ireland. Of course there have been different views in Ireland as to what exactly regional bodies should be responsible for, although most commentaries have highlighted the need for strategic planning and co-ordination of public services at regional level.

The Devlin Report (1969, p. 160) recommended that, 'if there are any new proposals for regional bodies, they should not form an extra layer of government duplicating the activities of existing authorities'. It also pointed out the need for some standardisation of regional boundaries used in the provision of public services, a point emphasised by later reports.

The 1971 White Paper on local government reorganisation supported the concept of regional bodies as instruments for co-ordination of public services and regional planning, but 'in the absence of clear evidence of their desirability and acceptability', did not support the creation of regional authorities with executive powers (Government of Ireland, 1971, p. 24).

More Local Government (Institute of Public Administration, 1971) argued that regional bodies should be responsible for strategic planning, economic development and co-ordination of public services. However, it also believed that regional bodies should have responsibility for providing some services such as large water supply and drainage schemes, control of water and air pollution, certain elements of the fire service, specialist and reference libraries, arterial roads and the valuation of property for rating purposes (pp. 29–32).

This chapter looks briefly at the development of regional bodies in Ireland before examining the structure and role of both the regional authorities and regional assemblies. It considers the proposals for a new regional body for the Greater Dublin Area and concludes with a few observations on regional structures in Ireland. For details on single-purpose bodies operating at regional level (such as health boards and regional tourism authorities) see chapter 3.

Development of Regional Structures in Ireland

In 1969 the government established nine regional development organisations (RDOs), which were based on nine planning regions identified following a number of studies on regional planning (notably Buchanan, 1968) commissioned after the adoption of the Planning and Development Act, 1963. The RDOs were charged with drawing up co-ordinated regional development programmes for each region, and were made up of representatives of planning authorities, state-sponsored bodies responsible for industrial and tourism development, and harbour authorities. The RDOs essentially had an advisory role in regional planning and could carry out research or surveys on regional development. Although ultimately abolished in 1987 as part of a general programme of government cutbacks, the RDOs constituted a recognition of the importance of a regional dimension in economic development.

Preparations for the first national development plan, for the 1989 to 1993 period (Government of Ireland, 1989), saw the establishment of sub-regional structures based on seven regions. Within each region there was a working group made up of officials from central government departments, state agencies, county/city managers and a representative of the European Commission, as well as an advisory group representing local authority chairpersons, the social partners and interest groups. The working group was responsible for drafting a programme for the region in consultation with the advisory group. The working group and advisory group were later merged to form sub-regional review committees, which monitored EU spending in each of the seven regions. However, it was generally felt by both local and regional interests and by the European Commission that the arrangements did not represent a meaningful attempt by central government to engage with regional interests in drawing up the development plans, but was rather the minimum required to satisfy EU rules (see, for example, Carroll and Byrne, 1999, p. 174; Rees and Farrows, 1999, p. 8; Laffan, 1996, p. 331; Coyle and Sinnott, 1992, p. 82).

A number of public services and agencies are operated along regional structures, although they do not conform to a standard pattern. For example, as of 2003, there are two regional assemblies, eight regional authorities, six regional tourism authorities, seven regional fisheries boards and seven regional health boards (in addition to which there is the Eastern Regional Health Authority, and within it, three area health boards). This results in a number of anomalies. For example, Cavan forms part of the North Eastern Health Board, the North West Regional Tourism Authority and the Border Regional Authority. In addition, bodies such as Shannon Development and Údarás na Gaeltachta operate in specific geographic areas. Other public services and organisations, for example An Garda Síochána, FÁS and Enterprise Ireland, operate according to regional structures and have regional offices.

The Barrington Report, published in 1991, again recommended that all public sector agencies use standard regions and that departure from this should not be allowed unless there are real and compelling reasons for doing so. It made the point that common boundaries are needed for collecting data and planning purposes and argued that 'there must be standard regions if regions are to make sense to people, and if regional loyalties are to develop' (p. 26). The report advocated the establishment of eight regional authorities, which would have a role in broad strategic planning and co-ordination between public services. It also stated that 'certain specialised services which need large operational areas, or are only justifiable on such basis, could be provided directly by the regional authority' (p. 28). The report suggested that the possibility of regional authorities being directly elected be further examined.

Section 3 of the Local Government Act, 1991 gave the minister the power to establish regional structures. On the basis of this legislation, eight regional authorities were established from 1 January 1994 (see below). The functions of the sub-regional review committees were transferred to the regional authorities.

Subsequently, in the run-up to the preparation of the national development plan for 2000 to 2006 (Government of Ireland, 2000a), a debate over regional development began. A campaign evolved that highlighted the very different patterns of development that were taking place in different parts of the country and essentially advocated a renewed focus on favouring the western part of the country to ensure balanced regional development (see chapter 24). The campaign in particular focused on the need to create new regional structures involving 'a significant devolution of power to the regions' (Quinn and Foley, 1999, p. 28) to ensure that part of the country could retain Objective 1 status.[2] Because of the need to create new structures for the region that would continue to benefit from

[2] Objective 1 is the designation given by the European Commission to those regions most in need and which therefore enjoy priority status for receipt of EU Structural Funds. An Objective 1 region is a region whose GDP is less than 75 per cent of the EU average GDP over a certain set of years.

full Objective 1 status, as well as structures for the rest of the country, two regional assemblies were established (see below).

Regional Authorities

The eight regional authorities were established under the Local Government Act, 1991 (Regional Authorities) (Establishment) Order, 1993 (SI No. 394 of 1993). The area of each regional authority consists of a number of administrative counties and cities as described in appendix 4.

Membership of regional authorities is confined to county/city councillors appointed by the constituent local authorities in the region after each local election. The cathaoirleach of a regional authority is elected by the members of the authority for a fixed term (generally one year).

The general function of a regional authority is to promote co-ordination of the provision of public services in the authority's region. This may involve the promotion of co-operation, joint action, joint arrangements, agreements, communication or consultation between local authorities or other public authorities in the region or between such authorities and other persons. It may also promote consideration by public authorities of the implications for, or effects of, their decisions, activities or services on the region as a whole.

The authority is required to periodically review the overall needs and development requirements of the region. For example, in 1998 the regional authorities prepared submissions on the investment priorities for their region. They also participated in the preparation of development strategies for the two new regional assembly areas in 1999.

Each regional authority must periodically review the development plans of local authorities in its region and, insofar as this may be relevant, the development plans of local authorities in adjoining regions, with particular regard to the consistency of such plans with the overall needs and development requirements of the region. The authority must prepare a regional report at least once in every five years covering these matters and also publish an annual report on the performance of its functions during the preceding year.

This role of the regional authorities was enhanced considerably through the enactment of sections 21 to 27 of the Planning and Development Act, 2000. This allows regional authorities to adopt regional planning guidelines to provide a long-term strategic planning framework for the development of the region, following consultation with local authorities that are planning authorities in its area, as well as providing public notice and inviting submissions on the topic. Planning authorities must assist and co-operate with regional authorities in the making of such guidelines. Once regional planning guidelines are made, planning authorities must review their existing development plan and consider whether any review or amendment of their plan is necessary in order to achieve the objectives of the guidelines. Planning authorities must have regard to any regional planning guidelines applying to their area when adopting a new development plan and the minister may, by order, determine that planning authorities comply with any regional planning guidelines (or specific elements of those guidelines) when making a development plan. Regional authorities must review regional planning guidelines every six years and may make new guidelines (see also chapter 12). The national spatial strategy (Department of the Environment and Local Government, 2002b) also provides that regional authorities prepare regional planning guidelines during 2003.

At the request of the Minister for Finance, the regional authority is required to provide all such information, proposals, recommendations or advice that the minister requires in connection with the preparation of any plan or programme supporting an application to the EU for Structural Funds. Regional authorities also have powers to review the implementation of measures financed under the EU Structural and Cohesion Funds in their region. To advise and assist it in the discharge of these EU-related functions, the authority is required to establish an EU operational committee consisting of the:

- cathaoirleach of the regional authority
- manager for each constituent local authority
- chairperson and one other representative of each constituent county and city council
- chairperson and one other representative of any borough council and certain town councils in the area
- chief officers of FÁS, Enterprise Ireland and any regional tourism organisations (the functional area of which is situated wholly or partly in the authority's functional area)
- representatives nominated by a number of different organisations including employer and employee bodies, chambers of commerce, county/city enterprise boards, farming organisations, the community and voluntary sector, the construction industry and numerous government departments.

The European Commission is also entitled to be represented at a meeting of the EU operational committee.

For purposes other than EU-related matters, the regional authority is assisted by an operational committee, which consists of the cathaoirleach of the regional authority; the manager of each constituent local authority; the chief officers of FÁS, Enterprise Ireland and any regional tourism organisation the functional area of which is situated wholly or partly in the functional area of the regional authority; plus representatives of health boards, regional fisheries boards, harbour authorities, Shannon Development, Údarás na Gaeltachta, An Post, ESB, Teagasc and CIÉ. The cathaoirleach of the regional authority acts as cathaoirleach of both the operational committee and the EU operational committee.

Some regional authorities have sub-committees. For example, the Midlands Regional Authority has four joint sub-committees dealing with economic and social development, infrastructure, public services, and public policy and EU matters. The South-West Regional Authority has four sub-committees addressing the following themes: rural and marine development; tourism and culture; settlement, communications, energy and environmental protection; and human resources, industry and services.

Sustainable Development: A Strategy for Ireland (Government of Ireland, 1997b, pp. 186–7) highlighted the roles that regional authorities could play in providing a regional dimension to sustainable development, including:

- providing a regional perspective on environmental issues and resources (including strategic waste management, regional water quality and co-ordination of water services, and coastal zone protection)
- acting as a possible forum for achieving the best balance regionally between development and sustainability, where development pressures threaten the sustainability of environmental resources
- securing a unified vision regarding sustainability targets at regional level between the various agencies and interests on the regional authority's operational committee, as well as recommending implementation mechanisms
- reviewing Local Agenda 21 initiatives to ensure consistency across the region (see also chapter 21).

Some regional authorities have been involved in the preparation of regional waste management strategies on behalf of their constituent local authorities. Regional authorities have also been involved in a number of EU-financed pilot projects, in diverse areas such as developing a regional information society strategy, teleworking and supporting the development of SMEs and the craft industry.

The recommendation of the Barrington Report (1991) that regional authorities be responsible for providing certain executive services (see above) was not, however, implemented. Regional authorities in Ireland do not have any executive responsibilities, unlike their counterparts in many other European countries, which are often responsible for providing services such as healthcare or public transport.

Each regional authority has a director and a small permanent staff. The regional authorities are funded by the constituent local authorities in proportion to the population of their area. Additional financial support is provided under the national development plan for a regional authority's EU-related functions.

Better Local Government, in accepting the principle of co-ordinating public service planning at the regional level, felt that there was a lack of commitment from some public bodies to the work of regional authorities. The document set out a number of measures to improve the capacity of the regional authorities to fulfil their mandate and strengthen their strategic planning role (Department of the Environment, 1996, pp. 66–8). Amongst other things, it provided for the designation of a city or county manager in each regional authority area to be responsible for relations with the regional authority and to improve co-ordination with local authorities. The designated manager is required to submit periodic reports on measures being taken by local authorities in the region to ensure co-ordination. *Better Local Government* also stated that there was a case for the review of some regional boundaries, although at the time of writing this had not occurred.

Regional Assemblies

The government decided in November 1998 to apply to the European Statistical Agency, Eurostat, for approval to divide the country into two regions at NUTS II[3] level for the 2000 to 2006 round of EU Structural Funds. Under this proposal, the counties and cities making up the Border, the Midlands and the Western regional authorities, plus the counties of Clare and Kerry, would form a new Objective 1 region. The remainder of the country would form a separate 'Objective 1 in Transition' region.[4] Kerry and Clare were included in the proposed Objective 1 region by the government largely because of well-publicised lobbying by local politicians (Rees and Farrows, 1999, p. 13).

However, the proposed structures proved unacceptable to the EU, in particular since some counties were taken out of their existing regional authority areas to form the proposed regional assemblies. If Ireland wanted to create new regional structures at NUTS II level, the EU was going to insist that they at least be based on existing regional authority areas rather than picking and choosing which counties would be included for reasons of political convenience. In the end, the EU accepted a modified version of the proposed structures. New regional assemblies were established in 1999 for the Border, Midland and Western region (not including Clare and Kerry) and the Southern and Eastern region.

---

[3] NUTS stands for *Nomenclature des Unités Territoriales Statistiques* or Nomenclature of Territorial Statistical Units. The NUTS system is used by Eurostat and the European Commission to classify different regions across the EU for the purposes of Structural Funds. Objective 1 funding is allocated to NUTS II regions. Until 1999, Ireland was designated as a NUTS II region. Since then, the two regional assemblies make up two separate NUTS II regions, while the eight regional authorities are classified by the EU as NUTS III regions (for a comparison of NUTS regions across different EU countries, see appendix 11).

[4] For the 2000 to 2006 period, those regions that were Objective 1 before 1999 benefit from 'Objective 1 in Transition' status, which is a phasing out arrangement for those regions no longer eligible, whereby regions receive a gradually reducing level of EU support up to 2006.

The regional assemblies were established under the Local Government Act, 1991 (Regional Authorities) (Establishment) Order, 1999 (SI No. 226 of 1999). The assemblies were established under the same parent legislation as the regional authorities, and are strictly speaking considered regional authorities under the Local Government Act, 1991. This route was taken, rather than the adoption of primary legislation, due to the necessity to have regional assemblies in place at short notice.

The two regional assemblies are the Border, Midlands and Western (BMW) Regional Assembly and the Southern and Eastern (S&E) Regional Assembly. The constituent counties and cities of each regional assembly area are detailed in appendix 4. The BMW Regional Assembly has its offices in Ballaghaderreen, County Roscommon, while the S&E Assembly is located in Waterford City.

Each constituent local authority may appoint a certain number of their members to the regional assembly. Members appointed to a regional assembly must also be members of the relevant regional authority for the area. The members elect a cathaoirleach for the regional assembly to serve a specified term.

The general function of a regional assembly, according to the 1999 Establishment Order, is to promote co-ordination of the provision of public services in the assembly's region (and is thus very similar to the general function of a regional authority). Promoting the co-ordination of public services may include the promotion of co-operation between local authorities, regional authorities or other public authorities in the region. It may also promote consideration by public authorities of the implications and effects of their decisions, activities or services on the region as a whole.

The assembly is required to periodically review the overall needs and development requirements of the region and to consider the reviews of local authority development plans carried out by regional authorities (see above). The assembly must prepare a regional report at regular intervals addressing the development needs of the region, the reviews of local authority development plans and the co-ordination of public services in the region. Regional assemblies also publish an annual report outlining their activities for the preceding year.

At the request of the Minister for Finance, a regional assembly is required to make proposals/recommendations or to give advice which may be required by that minister in connection with the preparation of any plan or programme supporting an application to the EU for Structural Funds.

The regional assemblies also have important administrative duties as 'managing authorities' for the two regional operational programmes under the *National Development Plan 2000–2006* (Government of Ireland, 2000a). They are responsible for overseeing the spending of monies under a range of measures and schemes, some of which are financed wholly by the exchequer and some of which are part-financed by EU Structural Funds. The BMW Regional Assembly is the managing authority for the Border, Midlands and Western Regional Operational Programme (2000) and the S&E Regional Assembly is the managing authority for the Southern and Eastern Regional Operational Programme (2000). Under Council Regulation (EC) No. 1260/1999, which establishes general provisions regarding the use of EU Structural Funds, the responsibilities of a managing authority include:

- drafting of the operational programme and the programme complement (which contains details on the type of activities to be financed under individual measures)
- chairing and providing a secretariat for the monitoring committee (which reviews the implementation of the operational programme)
- assembling statistical and financial information required for monitoring and evaluation of the operational programme
- preparing documents for the monitoring committee and, where necessary, making proposals for financial reallocations
- compiling an annual implementation report on progress on its operational programme, which must then be submitted to the European Commission
- organising the mid-term evaluation of the operational programme
- submitting payment claims to draw down financing for the operational programme and arranging payments for those bodies administering different schemes and measures
- ensuring that proper financial management and accounting systems are in place and that EU co-financed expenditure is accounted for
- ensuring the correctness of operations by implementing internal controls
- ensuring compliance with EU and national policies on the environment, equal opportunity, poverty, rural development, competition and state aids, as well as compliance with EU rules on publicity and the award of public contracts.

It is these tasks that take up the bulk of the work of the staff of the regional assemblies.

To advise and assist the regional assemblies in the discharge of their functions, each assembly is required to establish an operational committee consisting of the:

- cathaoirleach and director of the regional assembly
- cathaoirleach and director of each respective regional authority within the regional assembly area
- manager for the local authority in which the assembly is situated, as well as the designated manager for each respective regional authority
- chief officers of FÁS, Enterprise Ireland and any regional tourism authority (the functional area of which is situated wholly or partly in the assembly's functional area)

- chief officers or representatives of health boards, regional fisheries boards, harbour authorities, Údarás na Gaeltachta, Shannon Development, An Post, ESB, Teagasc and CIÉ.

The cathaoirleach of the regional assembly acts as cathaoirleach of the operational committee.

The regional assemblies may also set up other committees as appropriate. For example, the BMW Regional Assembly has five joint sub-committees, most of which review the implementation of other operational programmes in the area, as well as sub-programmes of the BMW regional operational programme. For example, the infrastructure sub-committee reviews the implementation of the economic and social infrastructure operational programme in the BMW area and reviews the implementation of the local infrastructure sub-programme under the BMW regional operational programme. There are also sub-committees on: productive investment and enterprise; employment, human resources and social inclusion; agriculture; and the national spatial strategy. The S&E Regional Assembly has put in place a similar sub-committee structure. These sub-committees are composed of both members of the assembly and public officials.

The two regional assemblies each have a director and a number of staff. The assemblies' EU-related duties are jointly financed by the EU Structural Funds and the Department of Finance, while other activities are financed collectively by the constituent local authorities in proportion to their respective populations.

Some see the creation of the regional assemblies as a commitment by government to further regionalisation. Certainly, the aim of achieving balanced regional development within the national development plan for 2000 to 2006 can be seen as an acknowledgement that regional considerations are being given greater priority. The work of the regional assemblies also involves a rather unusual working relationship between the regional assemblies and central government departments, whereby the departments must report to a regional body on their stewardship and management of a measure, and submit payment claims to the regional level. A rather unusual set of circumstances has developed, where, for example, local authorities report on their activities in the field of non-national roads to a central government department, which in turn reports to the regional assemblies. This level of reporting, from the local to the central and then to the regional, applies for all measures funded under the two regional operation programmes during the 2000 to 2006 period. This reporting arrangement to the regional level could be said to have forced a limited change in the mindset of those working in central government departments and agencies.

However, it is equally important not to overstate the powers of the regional assemblies. Rees and Farrows (1999), while noting that, 'to some extent, the assignment of the management of regional programmes represents a devolution of responsibility' (p. 16), conclude that 'it is difficult to conceive of these structures having much political or regional significance, beyond being administrative entities for the national government' (p. 17).

The Greater Dublin Area

The growth of urban areas has been a phenomenon in various parts of the country. A number of plans and strategies have been adopted to try to manage future growth in different urban agglomerations, such as the land use and transport strategy (LUTS), which serves as the basis for local planning in the Greater Cork Area.

However, the Greater Dublin Area, home to one-third of the population of the state, faces particular problems associated with rapid growth and development that has extended far beyond the boundaries of the Dublin local authorities. There has been extensive debate over what would be the most appropriate institutional structures to co-ordinate and manage the development and infrastructure needs of the area surrounding the capital. In its 1971 White Paper, the government proposed establishing a single authority for Dublin City and County to provide local government services throughout the area (Government of Ireland, 1971, p. 33). Another report recommended the maintenance of county and city structures, with the addition of a separate regional body for Dublin, Meath, Kildare and Wicklow with responsibility for strategic planning and some executive functions (Institute of Public Administration, 1971, p. 33). These proposals were not followed up.

At the time of writing, the Dublin and Mid-East Regional Authorities, established since 1994, have responsibility for co-ordinating public services and reviewing development plans of local authorities to ensure consistency with the overall development needs of the region (see above). In 1995, the Dublin Transportation Office (DTO) was established to oversee the implementation of the Dublin Transportation Initiative, a framework for the development of transport in the Greater Dublin Area (see chapter 10).

However, in April 2001, plans were unveiled to establish a new regional body dealing with land use and transport for Greater Dublin. A consultation paper was published (Department of the Environment and Local Government and the Department of Public Enterprise, 2001) which advocated establishing a strategic land use and transportation body to improve co-ordination and integration of delivery of key transport projects under the national development plan. The new body will also review and update the strategic planning guidelines for the Greater Dublin Area at least once every six years and will oversee their implementation in accordance with the Planning and Development Act, 2000.

The new regional structure will cover Dublin City and Dún Laoghaire-Rathdown, Fingal, South Dublin, Kildare, Meath and Wicklow Counties. The consultation paper proposes that a number of functions will transfer from the

Dublin and Mid-East Regional Authorities to the new strategic land use and transport body and makes the comment that the future of these two regional authorities will require further consideration (pp. 13–14).

The proposed structure of the regional body would consist of a council representing local authority elected members and managers, social partners and government nominees, which would be responsible for policy matters. An executive board of three to five persons would be responsible for implementing policy decisions.

The Planning and Development Act, 2000 also allows the minister to determine, by order, that a local authority must comply with any regional planning guidelines or part thereof when making a development plan and the minister can also issue a direction that an existing development plan be amended to comply with such guidelines. The consultation paper proposes that these powers be vested in the new land use and transport body.

The strategic land use and transport body will review and update the integrated long-term (15 to 20 year) transportation strategy at least once every six years and ensure its implementation. It will also adopt medium-term (5 to 7 year) implementation programmes and short-term (2 to 3 year) action plans setting out priorities, detailed arrangements and key performance indicators. The Dublin Transportation Office would be subsumed into the new body. Once established, the strategic body would develop and co-ordinate an area-wide approach to traffic management, control and enforcement and ensure that the activities of the various agencies involved in transport are consistent with the long-term strategy.

A review of all traffic management and enforcement activities of local authorities is planned to identify if these functions might be best performed at regional rather than local level. Measures which need to be addressed on a regional basis, because of their strategic importance and because it is more efficient to do so since they transcend local authority boundaries, will be assigned to a director of traffic, acting for the Greater Dublin Area as a whole or for Dublin City and County, as appropriate. Local authorities would retain responsibility for local traffic management functions and would be expected to review their arrangements for the implementation of these functions with a view to strengthening them where necessary.

It is also proposed that the strategic body be responsible for setting detailed service requirements and standards for various modes of public transport (bus, light rail, metro, Dublin suburban rail, although not mainline rail), the management of an integrated fares and ticketing system, the regulation of fares and promoting increased use of public transport.

The proposed body would have the power to allocate state expenditure for transport (public transport, non-national roads and traffic management) in the Greater Dublin Area. This power will be similar to that given to the National

Roads Authority (NRA) under the Roads Act, 1993, where the NRA receives annual block grants (capital and current) from the exchequer and allocates them to individual projects and programmes. The financing powers of the new Greater Dublin strategic body will not extend to national roads expenditure, although it is intended that the NRA will be obliged to consult the new body before making grant allocations to local authorities.

Conclusion

The development of regional authorities and assemblies in Ireland has been on an ad hoc basis, largely as a response to EU requirements for regional monitoring and management of the spending of Structural Funds. Some thought, but relatively little effort, has gone into aligning the different regional structures across functional areas such as health, tourism, fisheries, enterprise development and inward investment. The proliferation of regional entities, largely acting independently of each other, has continued apace with the establishment of regional authorities, regional health boards, regional tourism authorities and regional assemblies. While there may be reasonable grounds for the selection of the different areas, the different administrative regional areas prevents the emergence of any regional consciousness amongst citizens. It also makes co-ordination of public services at regional level, one of the roles of both regional authorities and regional assemblies, more difficult. If anything, the patchwork of regional structures is set to be further complicated with the likely creation of a new body dealing with transport and land-use planning issues for the Greater Dublin Area.

The regional authorities are not, in the main, decision-making bodies. They are largely confined to reviewing the decisions of others. In what might be considered a rather prophetic statement, *More Local Government* argued that 'representational or consultative bodies without powers of decision tend to lose effectiveness and responsibility and to become merely centres of demand' (Institute of Public Administration, 1971, p. 12). One report on the operation of regional authorities noted that many members on the operational committee expressed dissatisfaction with the fact that the bodies are not decision-making entities (Fitzpatrick Associates, 1997, pp. 107–8).

It is rather precarious to try to compare regional structures in different countries, given the wide variety of regional government systems that exist (see, for example, Keating, 1998). Even within Europe, the powers of regions range from those that could be termed maximalist (directly elected regions in federal states exercising powers entirely autonomously from central government) to minimalist (regional structures with nominated representatives restricted to a limited set of functions or a co-ordinating role). Marks et al. (1996b, p. 176–7) have developed a regional autonomy index as a composite measure of regional autonomy, based on scores given for the constitutional scope of regions (that is a highly unitary state or a federal state), the competencies exercised by regions and the role regions have in central government decision making. Each country is scored between 0 and 8 depending on the factors above. Marks et al. gave Irish regional authorities a regional autonomy index of 0 (regions in Denmark, Greece, Luxembourg, Netherlands, England and most of Portugal also scored 0). Of the twelve countries surveyed, only Belgium, Germany and Spain received an index of 4 or more. Irish regional structures could be fairly described as minimalist. They are not directly elected, they do not have executive powers or provide any services directly to citizens and there is little sense of public identity with them.

While there have been examples of regional or territorial mobilisation in recent years, with the campaign to retain Objective 1 status in 1998 and 1999 being a notable example, there is little in the way of a regional consciousness in Ireland. Most Irish citizens, if asked, could not identify regional authority or regional assembly boundaries. Instead, they would have a much stronger affinity with their nation and/or their county/city. In this respect, regional structures in Ireland could be regarded as rather artificial creations. Their titles, which generally refer to points of the compass, illustrate that, for the most part, they are not based on historic or traditional areas with distinctive names, but rather are functional groupings of counties and cities. That said, many regions in other countries are largely artificial. Keating (1998, p. 21) points out that most of the German regions (the *Länder*) were artificial creations after World War II and that the feeling of identity with these areas was created by political institutions.

One can, however, raise an obvious question: does a country the size of Ireland really need regions? According to this train of thought (see, for example, Government of Ireland, 1971, p. 23), strong regions may well be appropriate as an intermediate tier of government in large countries such as Germany or even where there are ethnic, linguistic or cultural differences that require representation in a regional form of government (for example, in countries such as Belgium or Switzerland). But does a relatively homogeneous country of just under four million people like Ireland need strong regions? There is no conclusive answer to this question. Again, looking elsewhere, it is clear that some countries of a similar size to Ireland have more extensive regional structures – although there is by no means any consistency across different countries as to what responsibilities regions have.

In many countries, regional governments are responsible for a number of executive functions which may include one or more of the following: healthcare, secondary schools, energy, social work, economic development and business support, public transport, regional and strategic planning, and environmental inspection. Regions in Europe are often also responsible for co-ordinating the activities of local authorities in their area. On the other hand, when compared to either local or central levels of government, it has to be acknowledged that regional bodies for the most part remain relatively weak, even if they do play a role in managing welfare services (Le Galès, 1998). The strong regions that are often referred to as case studies (such as Catalonia, Bavaria, Flanders or Scotland) tend to be the exception rather than the rule.

The Council of Europe has drawn up a draft charter of regional self-government, setting out the principles of regional government, following the model established by the European Charter of Local Self-Government (Council of Europe, 1985a; see chapter 1 and appendix 1). Article 3 of the draft charter provides a definition of regional self-government as:

> . . . the right and the ability of the largest territorial authorities within each State, having elected bodies, being administratively placed between central government and local authorities and enjoying prerogatives either of self-organisation or of a type normally associated with the central authority, to manage, on their own responsibility and in the interests of their populations, a substantial share of public affairs, in accordance with the principle of subsidiarity (Council of Europe, 1997).

It is doubtful whether Irish regions could be considered as conforming to even this rather broad definition of regional self-government.

When compared to most other European countries, the regional tier of government in Ireland is weak. Regional authorities and regional assemblies have been established largely as a result of EU necessities rather than as part of a government commitment to regionalisation:

> An unfortunate failure in the Irish approach has been the obsession with accessing EU funds to the neglect of developing and implementing regional policies to address the reduction of inter-regional disparities within Ireland and the promotion of balanced regional development in the country. That this approach still persists is exemplified by the decision to regionalise the country for the purpose of maximising the amount of EU assistance for the state under the next round of structural and cohesion funds rather than because of any new conversion to the merits of regionalism (Carroll and Byrne, 1999, p. 185).

Certainly regional structures in Ireland have scope to evolve. However, the prospects of regional authorities or regional assemblies evolving beyond their strategic planning and co-ordination role, and being given executive responsibilities, would appear to be remote. Given that Ireland is likely to receive a relatively small amount in EU Structural Funds during the 2007 to 2013 programming period, the temptation may exist among policy makers for another redrawing of regional boundaries in the run up to 2006 with a view to maximising EU transfers.

A Comparative Perspective

26

Irish Local Government in a Comparative Context

Bríd Quinn

Forms of local government have been recorded since the glories of Ancient Greece, Rome, Israel and Egypt. Local government systems have continually evolved and reflect contextual factors such as history, topography, demography and the political, economic and social structures that have influenced their development. Just as the observation and analysis of local government systems has continued since earliest times, so too has the practice of comparison. Plato compared the various city-states in his quest for the set of circumstances which would bring forth the 'just' state. Much later, Montesquieu compared the different European political systems in an attempt to identify the institutional arrangements most conducive to true liberty. More recently, there has been a focus on the analysis and comparison of systems of self-government, administration and citizen involvement. This chapter focuses on comparative local government and sets the Irish system in a comparative context with particular emphasis on the Anglo-Saxon and various European models.

While parliamentary democracy is strong in Ireland, local democracy has not flourished. The power and autonomy of local government in Ireland is far more restricted than is the case in most other jurisdictions. The Irish political system is strongly centralised with functions such as health, education and policing (functions which are the responsibility of local government in most other jurisdictions) being carried out by central government departments. The share of public employment at local government level in Ireland (12.7 per cent) is the lowest of the fourteen countries cited in John's comparison (2001, p. 38), thus indicating the relative insignificance of the local public sector in Ireland and contrasting with the situation in the US where 61.1 per cent of public employment is within the local government sector (Pollitt and Bouckaert, 2000, p. 44).

Although the clientelist political culture supports easy access to Irish politicians, the ratio of voters to elected local politicians is quite high. The average population of the 114 local authorities in Ireland is 36,100 (second only to the UK which has untypically large local authorities), while in Switzerland it is 2,352 and in France 1,491. The population scale of local government units has implications for effectiveness and community identification as well as the role of the elected politician. Ireland, with its single tier of directly elected local government (for the 85 per cent of the population that do not elect a town council), low levels of local public sector employment and its high ratio of voters to representatives, would seem less well served than many of its continental counterparts.

Parameters for Comparison

According to Eckstein and Apter (1963) the factors promoting effective government include the nature and origin of the regime, the sense of community, the legitimacy of the political system and the degree of pragmatism in the political culture. This chapter examines how the Irish system, described as 'one of the most centrally controlled of local government systems' (Barrington, 1987a, p. 143), scores on these factors. Various approaches can be used to compare systems of government. Loughlin and Peters (1997) distinguish between four state traditions: the Anglo-Saxon, the Germanic, the Napoleonic and the Scandinavian. They argue that the dominant logic of the socio-political system influences all parts of the system. Using this model, Ireland would fit under the Anglo-Saxon classification although it displays some distinctive features such as the county and city manager system and, more recently, innovative efforts at increased participation. Norton (1994) outlines nine current systems of sub-national government, which he classifies according to five groups (South European, North European, British, North American and Japanese) and thirteen characteristics ranging from powers to party systems. Ireland would be classified within the British group but with its own unique variation.

Another effective approach to explaining the different forms of sub-national government is to base the classification on the chronology and methodology of democratic development or as Rose (1996) terms it 'the tempo and pressures to change'. Some states such as the Scandinavian countries, Belgium and the UK embody the gradual, linear development of a democratic system since the early nineteenth century. A second wave of democratisation can be traced in the aftermath of World War I, but few of the countries granted independence at that time have maintained their democratic systems. Ireland, however, is one example of a democracy established in that epoch which has flourished. In other countries, such as Spain, the process of democratisation emerged as the antithesis of the authoritarian or totalitarian rule to which they had been subject. Ireland's system of local government still incorporates many aspects of the effective model introduced by Britain but these aspects have been augmented by innovations appropriate to the evolving Irish political and social systems. However, the innovations have frequently contributed to increased centralisation and bureaucracy.

State Form

Another useful general comparator is the state form within which the system of local government is nested. Thus, systems are classified by their underlying structural logic. In comparing government systems a major distinction can be made between federal and unitary states.

In a federal system authority is shared between the centre and the constituent states and political, legal and economic powers are clearly designated to the different layers of government with some powers being exclusive to a particular level, some powers being concurrent and the residual powers automatically coming within the competence of the lowest level. Elazar (1996, p. 426) counts twenty-two federations in existence today, accounting for 40 per cent of the world's population, among them the US, India and Switzerland. Within most federal systems there is a further tier of local government, which varies within the different sub-national units. In Germany, for example, the constitutional framework of local authorities is determined by the laws of the individual *Länder*, resulting in considerable structural variation. In Austria, despite the federal structure, the centre determines the powers of local authorities; while in Switzerland the cantons determine their own local government systems. Similarly, the US's federal system allows the individual states to create and determine the functions and structures of local government.

By contrast, in unitary states sovereignty resides exclusively with central government. Some unitary states such as Japan and France have evolved from strong monarchies or empires and others, particularly the smaller South America countries, reinforce a centralised presidential system. Ireland falls into the unitary state category with a highly centralised system of local government. Luxembourg is also an example of a centralised unitary state but reforms in 1988 have made central control over municipalities less extensive.

Political scientists also differentiate between fused and dual systems of local government. In a fused system central government is represented at each level. In France, for example, the *préfet*, appointed by central government, performs a supervisory role over local authorities. The *préfet* is charged with promoting government policy and monitoring the budgetary, administrative and electoral actions of sub-national government to ensure compliance with national policies. Similarly, in Bulgaria the role of the regional governor is part of the central executive's power. The extent of central government control over local government activities varies widely within the countries that employ a fused system and local units, although enjoying a degree of autonomy, operate a uniform system of administration.

Ireland is a frequently cited example of the dual system. In a dual system there is a formal separation of central and local government and the lower level must operate within the strict parameters laid down by the centre. Although local government within a dual system enjoys autonomy, it is, as John (2001, p. 32) states, 'the creature of statute and has little protection from re-organization and centralization'. This is the case in Ireland, where formal relations between local authorities and central government are regulated through a single department – the Department of the Environment and Local Government – which has administrative, financial and technical control over the lower units (Coyle, 1996; Daemen and Schaap, 2000). Consequently, the Irish system is highly centralised. In Ireland there are only two tiers of elected government, the central level and the local level. Although eight regional authorities were created in 1994 and two regional assemblies were established in 1999, both structures comprise elected members of the constituent local authorities and their remit is limited (see chapter 25 and appendix 4). In countries such as Germany, Spain and Denmark the intermediate tier of government plays a more significant role.

Within many other political systems the municipality serves as the basic unit of local government with the town/city and its hinterland forming a distinctive unit. In Ireland the system of local government focuses on counties, with only the five largest cities having equal status with the counties. The county structure is paramount and where municipal structures such as town councils do exist, they frequently, for reasons of finance and efficiency, delegate some of their limited functions to the county authority. The eighty municipalities cover not much more than 15 per cent of the Irish population and have such a limited role that they have been described as 'not so much a tier as a ledge' (Barrington, 1991a, p. 152).

In Sweden the directly elected county councils are responsible for administering designated health and education services because county units are perceived as having the most appropriate size of population for delivering these services effectively. However, the municipalities are the units with responsibility for most functions of local government including planning and social welfare. There is no hierarchical relationship between the municipalities and the county councils. Denmark, with a geographic size similar to that of Munster, has an intermediate tier with fourteen directly elected councils. Functions such as responsibility for hospitals are delegated upwards by the municipalities to the regions when those functions could be carried out more effectively at that level. In most countries, municipalities and communes cover the entire territory of the state, which allows municipalities to work with their neighbouring municipalities in the provision of certain services. This is not an option in Ireland where town and borough councils are geographically isolated from each other and instead have county councils as their neighbours.

The Scale of Local Government

As illustrated above, systems of local government vary enormously. A numerical comparison of the average population represented by the basic tier of local government reinforces this image of diversity (see table 26.1). Ireland has quite a high ratio of population per unit of local government. This has the effect of making local government remote from the people and is among the factors reducing the likelihood of participation.

Table 26.1 Average Population of Lowest Tier of Sub-National Government

Country	Average population of lowest tier	No. of authorities (includes all tiers)
France	1,491	36,880
Portugal	2,342	4,526
Switzerland	2,352	3,021
Netherlands	2,723	584
Italy	7,182	8,215
Belgium	11,000	601
Finland	11,206	455
Denmark	18,000	289
Sweden	33,000	333
Ireland	**36,100**	**114**
United Kingdom	137,000	472

Source: adapted from John (2001, p. 35)

Coyle (1996) uses a different approach when placing the Irish system in a comparative context. Starting with an earlier comparison made by Barrington and allowing for factors such as size and population, she ranks eighteen European countries in terms of the number of local authorities they boast. France tops the list with 36,757, Turkey comes almost midway with 1,867, while Ireland is bottom of the league with 114. Of these, eighty are municipal authorities with even less power and significance than the county/city units. As Coyle asserts, 'the municipalities cover only 15% of the population, represent only about half the small towns of comparable size in the country and collectively only account for around 6% of the total expenditure of Irish local authorities' (1996, p. 280). The high ratio of population per unit of local government, the limited remit of the municipal authorities and the asymmetric arrangement of sub-county units means that Irish citizens are less well served than the citizens of most other countries.

Functions, Powers and Philosophy

Earlier chapters have outlined the origins and organisation of Irish local government and have delineated the structures, range of functions and financial resources assigned to the sub-national level. This section sets the Irish model of local government in opposition to other systems.

In Germany, for example, local authorities may fulfil any functions that have not been allocated to another level of government, so their responsibilities include social affairs, education, local economic development and business development. Similarly, local authorities in Denmark may deal with all domestic issues for which the public sector is responsible and indeed many of their functions are mandatory. Among the functions for which Danish local government is responsible are primary and adult education, social security assistance and public utilities.

Only in recent years has the power and status of local government in Ireland been somewhat enhanced. Until 1991, Irish local authorities were constrained by the doctrine of *ultra vires* and were considered to be acting outside their powers if they performed any functions not specified in law. The Local Government Act, 1991 abolished this restriction, thus giving local authorities general powers of competence and encouraging a more proactive style of management. Yet, the exercise of this power by local authorities must not conflict with national policy. Critics such as Coyle (1996) suggest that local authorities have not exploited their new general powers of competence. Meanwhile other political scientists such as Blair (1991) assert that in many countries the significance of general competence is symbolic rather than substantive. Therefore, the reaction of Irish local authorities to their extended competence is not atypical, particularly when cognisance is taken of their financial and resource dependencies on central government.

For many years the lack of constitutional recognition was a feature which differentiated Irish local government from other systems. It was only in June 1999 (following a referendum) that Article 28A was added to *Bunreacht na hÉireann*, finally bestowing constitutional recognition on directly elected local government in Ireland (see appendix 2). Previously, local authorities had been regulated by statute, with central government having the power to defer local elections and limit the functioning and financing of local authorities by an Act of the Oireachtas. Thus, although Irish local authorities had legal autonomy, their actions were circumscribed by central edict.

The Local Government Act, 2001 consolidated much of the discrete legislation that pertained to local government and introduced some innovations such as the direct election of the cathaoirleach/mayor of county and city councils (this was later repealed by the Local Government (No. 2) Act, 2003). The 2001 Act fell short of prior expectations in that it recognised but did not increase (and in cases failed to define) the powers of local authorities and it failed to include a provision preventing politicians from holding a dual mandate at both national and local levels of government. However, the dual mandate was eventually abolished with the passing of the Local Government (No. 2) Act, 2003.

Ireland was later than most other European countries in ratifying and signing the European Charter of Local Self-Government in 1998. The charter embodies a framework for local government which emphasises devolution of functions and autonomy to local authorities (see appendix 1). The Irish system has also been influenced by developments within the EU, particularly the enshrinement of subsidiarity and the insistence of involvement of sub-national authorities in the various regional and local development processes funded by the EU. The combination of domestic and externally induced changes has served to cumulatively reinforce the position of local government within the Irish system without breaking the hold of the centre.

The accepted functions of local government can be summarised as providing services, implementing national policies, fostering the public good and representing the community within and outside the territory. A 1988 Council of Europe survey found that there was a certain homogeneity between the functions performed at the basic level of local government whether the local authorities operated with a list of specified tasks or enjoyed general competence (Norton, 1994). However, contrasting approaches exist to the designation of local government functions. In systems such as the Scandinavian or German models local authorities are responsible for most public services and responsibility is only passed upwards when implementation of these functions can be more effectively carried out at a higher level. For example, in Denmark, responsibility for basic healthcare lies at local level but responsibility for hospitals is entrusted to the regional level.

The Irish system reflects a more top-down approach, with specific functions being allocated to local authorities by central government, which exercises strict control. The functions assigned to local authorities in Ireland generally fall into one of eight programme groups: housing and building; road transportation and safety; water supply and sewerage; development incentives and controls; environmental protection; recreation and amenity; minor aspects of agriculture, education and welfare; and miscellaneous services (see chapter 8 for a brief description of each). This is a more limited range of functions than is the norm in other EU states. For example, Irish local authorities do not have responsibility for health, education, policing or social welfare. Instead, these functions are carried out by central government departments or state agencies.

It is also noteworthy that Irish local authorities have not traditionally been motors of local economic development. It is only since the 1980s that they were formally included as partners with various local development bodies. Recent local government reforms include a focus on formal integration of local government and local development agencies. This is strengthening the economic development role of local authorities, which previously would have focused only on providing infrastructural support for industry. The Irish situation contrasts with Germany and Scandinavia where local authorities have played a more proactive role in local economic development.

Furthermore, as a result of their restricted functions, the role of Irish local authorities in national policy making is also limited. This contrasts with the greater involvement of sub-national government in the national policy-making process in countries like Austria and Belgium (where the involvement of the regions is constitutionally specified) or Italy and the Netherlands where formal consultative mechanisms are widely used. In Denmark the representative body for local authorities, known as LGDK (Local Government Denmark), is a key player in the national policy-making process and frequently participates in working groups established by central government. Ireland lacks such a body. However, some changes can be noted in the Irish system. Elements of governmental reform have combined with the growth of local development bodies to bring about a greater localism in Irish public policy (Coyle, 2001). This reflects the patterns evident elsewhere in Europe.

The limited range of functions carried out by Irish local authorities is mirrored in low levels of spending and low levels of public employment in the authorities. OECD research showed that only 12.7 per cent of public employment is at local government level in Ireland. This contrasts sharply with the rates of 75 per cent in Finland, 70.8 per cent in Denmark and 52.3 per cent in the UK; while only 17.3 per cent of Swedish public employees work for central government (OECD, 1997). Spending by Irish local authorities is, again, low by comparison with other systems as the lack of autonomous funding sources restricts their discretionary powers. In Scandinavia local income tax is the most important source of local government income. In Finland 17.5 per cent of income is paid to local government, yielding half the budget of local government (Daemen and Schaap, 2000, p. 2). In the UK, property tax provides a significant proportion of local authority income.

Irish local authorities are far more dependent on central government for funding. Approximately one-third of local authority income comes from specific grants from central government. In administration of these grants local authorities are agents of central government rather than governors with discretion. Less than one-quarter of local authority income comes from goods and services and on average 25 per cent from rates on commercial buildings. However, a new Local Government Fund was established in 1998 (see chapter 18) and this has ameliorated the situation somewhat by guaranteeing that the exchequer contribution will be index-linked each year and will also take account of the additional expenditure needs of local authorities. Nevertheless, Irish local authorities, in comparison to their counterparts elsewhere, continue to be restricted by their limited sources of revenue.

Identity and Culture

Many systems of local government have a territorial base. Territorial systems initially emerged through personal and kinship links. The affective dimension of community was gradually replaced by structured patterns of co-operation, exchange and social and political interaction taking place within defined territorial units. Despite the growth of the nation-state and the growing impact of globalisation, territorial identity remains an important feature of local government (Keating, 1999). This is particularly evident in Spain, France and Italy. In Ireland the territorial dimension is also significant and has been so since the dominance of the *tuath* in pre-Christian times. Whelan (1996) refers to 'the territorial imperative in the Irish experience', while poets like Kavanagh, Yeats and Heaney have celebrated the Irish fixation with place and space. Despite some vicissitudes, since the Middle Ages the county has become the chief administrative unit as well as the 'reference point of identity' and evokes political and sporting allegiance among citizens (see Daly, 2001).

Reference has been made above to the dominance of the county in the Irish system. Yet, significant differences exist between counties in terms of area, population and resources. County Leitrim has a population of 25,032, while South Dublin County Council has a population of 218,401. The area of County Cork is 749,995 hectares, while County Louth has an area of 82,613 hectares.[1] These differences reflect diverse demographic and geographic endowments and varying organisational factors, yet all Irish local authorities operate within the same centralised framework.

Such differences in size, population and local government resources are not unique to Ireland. France, for example, has units of local government varying in size from less than 200 to more than 100,000 inhabitants, while the population base of Finland's municipalities ranges from 130 to 520,000. Financial equalisation mechanisms have been put in place in several countries in order to address the uneven income of local authorities, with the systems in place in Germany and Sweden being particularly effective. The new local government

---

[1] Central Statistics Office (2002), www.cso.ie.

funding system referred to earlier is Ireland's first attempt at equalising the resource base of local government but the system is as yet underdeveloped.

Political culture is a dimension of local government that makes for interesting comparison. Countries with highly developed welfare systems and a social democratic approach to governance tend to have an associative political culture. Thus, Sweden, Germany and the Netherlands, for example, have systems predicated on and facilitative of active involvement in local affairs and the acceptance of local responsibility. Other countries, particularly those in southern Europe, tend to take a more clientelist approach, with the politician in the role of benevolent patron. In Italy and Greece this clientelism is an integral element of party politics. Loughlin (2001, p. 281) asserts that the Greek political parties function with 'ideological considerations coming behind personal patronage in their priorities'. Belgium is another country with a clientelist tradition. Political votes are frequently given in return for services rendered by politicians. Hendriks (2001) suggests that four out of ten Belgian voters who have used the services of a politician actually give a vote to that politician.

Ireland also falls into the clientelist category with patronage as a dominant paradigm. The tradition of the dual mandate, where politicians hold office at both local and national levels, reinforced clientelism as politicians sought to ensure their election to national office by 'looking after' their local voters. Of the 166 members elected to the Dáil in the general election of 2002, the number also holding seats on county and city councils was 101.[2] A large part of the reluctance in accepting the abolition of the dual mandate in the Local Government (No. 2) Act, 2003 was the loss of the patronage factor.

The strong sense of community that has always been evident in Ireland and the high levels of voluntary activism have also reinforced the personal approach by placing the politician in the role of local promoter. Both politicians and the electorate have been socialised into norms of patronage and brokerage so change will probably come slowly and the country has shown that it is not yet ready for change. Therefore local and national politics will continue to be interwoven. The question may well be posed whether this reduces local politics to a 'vehicle of clientelistic access to the centre', as Batley (1991) described the Irish system, or whether it serves to ensure that local values and priorities influence the centre. The strong, locally focused role played by independent TDs in the 1997 to 2002 Dáil would seem to indicate the latter.

Ireland also contrasts with its European counterparts in its leadership system and in the fact that the vast majority of elected members of Irish local government are part-time politicians. The leader of the local council is elected by the members for a one-year term, according to a rota agreed by the dominant political parties in the council. The leadership role is ceremonial rather than substantive with the

---

[2] *The Irish Times*, 23 May 2002.

professional city/county manager playing the key role in the day-to-day running of the local authority. Of the 883 city and county councillors elected in the 1999 local elections only 196 described themselves as 'public representatives' – of the 196 in this category, 118 were also members of the Oireachtas (Kenny, 1999, p. 20). The Local Government (No. 2) Act, 2003 repealed the provisions for the direct election of mayors contained in the Local Government Act, 2001. However, the door has not been completely closed on the idea of directly elected mayors and it is thought that it may be back on the agenda by the time of the 2009 local elections.

Leadership practices in other countries vary. In France and Italy mayors (who are also the representatives of the state in the municipality) are elected by local councils but play a significant brokerage role between local and central governments. In Sweden and Finland councils elect an executive body which designates a leader who is appointed for the full term of the local government. Germany operates a number of leadership systems within its local government. In the south of Germany, for example in Bavaria and Baden-Württemberg, the directly elected mayor heads the administration as well as the council. In the northern states it was customary for the elected council to vest power in the *magistrat*, the municipal executive consisting of elected councillors and paid officials. However, during the 1990s there was a move towards directly elected mayors with states such as Lower Saxony and North-Rhine-Westphalia adopting such systems.

Direct elections and the full-time professional role assigned to the mayor in other countries have led to the emergence of strong local leadership and are perceived as enhancing local identity and the salience of local government. The party political nature of the selection process and the short term of office held by local authority leaders in Ireland have not facilitated their emergence as significant political actors vis-à-vis their counterparts in Europe.

Conclusion

Irish society has undergone tremendous social and economic change, but the system of local government for long remained unchanged – limited in scope, function and finance – yet fulfilling the basic needs of its citizenry. The system contrasts in scale with most of its European neighbours, in function with all but some southern countries and in scope with its northern counterparts. However, change is underway – change which will lead towards local governance, but a local governance still subject to the centre.

The Local Government Act, 2001 rationalised the local government structures and introduced a code of conduct for elected members. Previously, the Planning Act, 2000 had consolidated and reformed Irish planning laws and systems (see chapter 12), while the gradual implementation of *Better Local Government* (see chapter 4) has modernised and, to an extent, energised local administrative structures. The various steps to integrate local development bodies with the local government system have served to strengthen the participatory dimension, while facilitating local authorities to take a leading role in the economic, social and cultural development of their areas. Involvement in the EU's regional policy process, collaboration with local authorities in other member states, participation in transnational networks and involvement in the Committee of the Regions have broadened the horizons of Ireland's local authorities.

Despite these positive developments, many challenges remain for Irish local government – the challenge of responding to increasing social obligations; the challenge of new roles such as those implied in national initiatives like the national childcare, anti-poverty and rural development strategies; the challenge posed by the creation of single-purpose national agencies, such as the Environmental Protection Agency, whose roles impinge on the workings of local authorities; the many practical challenges such as co-ordination of public services, waste management, environmental protection and technological adaptation as well as the need to balance sustainable development with economic and social progress; the challenge of increasing citizen involvement in an era of voter apathy and changing political culture; the challenge of adapting to the public-private-partnership approach; and the challenge of managing the change from local government to local governance.

In meeting these challenges there is much to be gained by using a comparative lens – some practical examples are outlined below. The well-developed social welfare elements of Scandinavian local government offer insights as to how to discharge the ever-increasing social obligations confronting Irish local government. The financial equalisation system in Germany could influence any future expansion of Ireland's nascent system. Should Ireland ever proceed with the direct election of mayors, the diverse experiences of Germany, France, Italy and the Netherlands will provide useful models. In the quest to increase citizen participation the mechanisms adopted or discarded by other countries suggest possible solutions such as the introduction of local referenda (Switzerland, Germany), the establishment of user boards (used effectively in Swedish geriatric centres and kindergartens), the holding of 'future' workshops (Netherlands) and the establishment of citizen panels (UK).

Enlightenment is also to be gained from an awareness of the difficulties encountered in other systems, for example the complexity caused by the multiple roles of French politicians, the difficulties experienced in facilitating autonomy while ensuring equality in federal systems, the problems resulting from unquestioning adoption of the tenets of new public management in the UK and the devastating impact of economic recession on the welfare systems that were a cornerstone of Scandinavian local government systems.

The Irish system of local government reflects the course of Irish history and its evolution derives much from external influences – the local focus of the Celts, the municipal organisation of the Normans, the county basis of the Westminster system, the manager models of India and the US and the regional focus advocated by the EU. The system that emerged was, as stated earlier, one that ensured a controlling role for the centre, with limited functions, restricted finances and a rather ineffective structure for units of local government. This chapter has highlighted some of the contrasts that exist between the Irish system and other important local government systems. The comparative approach helps us to understand the different politico-institutional practices across Europe and the ways in which they shape and reflect specific political and social norms.

Despite its limitations, the local government system worked in the homogeneous society that was Ireland of the twentieth century. The economic, social and politico-administrative changes of recent decades have impacted on local government, which is currently undergoing change and facing severe challenges. Meeting these challenges and managing that change can be made easier by observing developments in other local democracies.

27

Northern Ireland Local Government

Colin Knox

Historical Context and Background

Local government in Northern Ireland is a product of the Local Government (Ireland) Act, 1898, which, in turn, was derived from 1888 and 1894 legislation for England and Wales. The 1898 Act established a two-tier system of local government in which county boroughs and county councils formed the upper tier and urban and rural districts formed the lower tier. The Act also extended the franchise to include all adult male ratepayers, a provision which made the new county councils a focus of growing nationalist agitation for the separation of Ireland from the United Kingdom. The 1898 Act, therefore, established the structure of the local government system that obtained in Ireland at the time of the establishment of the Irish Free State and the devolved government in Northern Ireland (Alexander, 1979).

The devolved government of Northern Ireland comprised six Irish counties which formed the administrative state. Within the six counties, the local government framework comprised two corporations, six county councils, ten boroughs, twenty-four urban districts and thirty-one rural districts – a total of seventy-three local authorities serving a population (by 1966) of about 1.4 million. This ranged from Tandragee Urban District with 1,300 people to the City of Belfast with 407,000 (Birrell and Murie, 1980). Councils were responsible for the key functional services (for example education, health, housing, planning, roads, water, refuse collection) with the exception of protective services such as police and civil defence. Elections were held every three years and all councils except rural districts had rating functions.

In the post-1920 period, a number of controversial changes occurred which were designed to create and maintain a unionist local government system. The Local Government (Northern Ireland) Act, 1922 replaced proportional representation by the simple majority method of election. This in turn created the opportunity to redraw electoral divisions and ward boundaries. The 1922 Act also altered the franchise by incorporating ownership of property as a qualification for the vote. Britain abandoned the property vote and reverted to universal suffrage in 1945, and the Republic of Ireland introduced adult suffrage for local elections in 1935. Unionist politicians considered that to be a dangerous strategy since some local authorities would be lost to them. Tomlinson (1980, p. 100) described it bluntly: 'while Britain and the Irish Republic had been democratising local government, the Unionist government was consolidating its grip on local politics by fixing ward boundaries, distributing votes to the propertied and by disenfranchising the propertyless'.

From the 1940s onwards there was an acceptance of the inadequacy of local government to provide services efficiently. This precipitated the growth of ad hoc statutory bodies and the removal and centralisation of council functions. These changes subsequently created pressure on the Stormont government to reform and modernise local government. Simply, there were too many councils, inadequately resourced through a limited rate base and dependent on central government grants as a source of income. Hayes (1967, p. 82) provides an overview: 'our present local government structure was erected to meet a set of problems in Victorian times . . . the whole edifice is now lop-sided and unable to support the more sophisticated organisation needed to cope with the problems of a complex modern society'. The Northern Ireland government responded with two White Papers advocating a simplified two-tier system and the suggestion of a boundary review to reflect the proposed administrative structures.[1]

Reactions centred almost entirely upon the likely political complexion of the suggested area councils. Both documents failed to address the sectarian politics of local government. There were, for example, twelve local government areas with a Catholic majority in the population and yet a Protestant/unionist majority on the council, leading to allegations of discrimination against Catholics. Buckland (1981, p. 116) argued that unionist majorities in local government were 'bolstered by discriminatory housing policies, carefully drawn electoral areas and the persistent refusal to adopt the British practice of one man [sic], one vote. Protestants continued to receive preferential treatment in the allocation of local housing and a disproportionate share of local government jobs'. Unionists argued in response that charges of discrimination were greatly exaggerated, that the same charge could be levelled at nationalist councils and that such discrimination as did take place was justified by the disloyalty of the Catholic community to the state.

---

[1] White Papers: *The Reshaping of Local Government,* Cmd 517, 1967; *The Reshaping of Local Government: Further Proposals,* Cmd 530, 1969.

The Stormont government's moves to reform local government were overtaken by the political events of 1968 when the first civil rights march took place, central to which were demands for changes in council practices: universal voting rights, removal of gerrymandered boundaries, laws against discrimination by local authorities and allocation of public housing on a points system. By 1969, Northern Ireland had witnessed the breakdown of law and order and the deployment of British troops. Local government was stripped of its responsibility for housing, its most controversial function. The then permanent secretary in the Ministry of Development remarked: 'everyone saw that whatever the merits of this decision it would tear the heart out of local government as we knew it and render it impossible to create a new system with anything approaching a full range of functions in the British or Irish tradition' (Oliver, 1978, p. 90).

In December 1969, Brian Faulkner (Minister of Development, with overall responsibility for local government) appointed a high-powered review body under the independent chairmanship of Patrick Macrory, a prominent businessman, to review local government. The resulting report recommended that services be divided into two categories – regional services requiring large administrative units and district services suitable for smaller areas. The Stormont parliament would take responsibility for the former and district councils would administer local services. The report listed seventeen functions, in addition to housing, which were currently provided wholly or partly by local authorities that would pass to regional control. These included services such as education, personal health, welfare and childcare, planning, roads and water. This allocation left local authorities with matters of a purely local nature to administer.

Macrory recommended the establishment of twenty-six borough or district councils, the abolition of existing county councils and boroughs, and the setting up of appointed area boards to decentralise the administration of health and education services. The recommendations were subsequently passed into law under the Local Government (Northern Ireland) Act, 1972. New boundaries were established, adult suffrage introduced and the voting system changed by the British government to proportional representation (PR), which was used for the first district council elections in May 1973.

Principal Features

Functions

The new single-tier councils became executive on 1 October 1973 and the functions of former local authorities that were regional in character were transferred to central government departments (as Northern Ireland ministries became known) after the Northern Ireland Constitution Act was passed. The Act provided for a Northern Ireland assembly and an executive instead of a parliament and government. District councils were given four key responsibilities:

- ceremonial functions: such as hosting civic events, recognising the achievements of famous citizens and presenting a positive public profile of the area
- executive functions: limited to regulatory services –licensing of street trading and entertainment venues, building control and environmental health protection – and direct service provision principally in the areas of street cleaning, refuse collection and disposal, leisure and tourism provision, community development and community relations and a limited input on economic development
- representative role: local councillors are nominated to serve on area boards (for example education and library boards) in recognition that elected representatives should be represented on relevant bodies to express views on the provision and operation of major public services not under their charge
- consultative role: district councils have to be consulted on matters of general national interest and on central government functions which affect their area. In most cases central government departments engage in consultation with councils on their strategic plans for council areas, for example planning, roads, water and housing.

Finance

In 2001/2, total net spending by the twenty-six district councils amounted to £276 million out of an overall public expenditure budget for Northern Ireland of £5.8 billion (Northern Ireland Executive, 2001). The latter was the budget available to the devolved government of Northern Ireland and excludes spending by the Northern Ireland Office on policing, security policy, prisons and criminal justice. Councils therefore account for less than 5 per cent of public spending in Northern Ireland.

Local government services are financed through a property tax system or rates. The tax base is the rentable value of the property (residential and business) or its net annual value. Two rates are levied, the district rate set by each local authority for services provided by them and the regional rate fixed by central government. The regional rate represents a payment towards the provision of education, housing, personal social services, roads, water and sewerage, referred to as 'local authority type services' – a comparison with similar services operated by councils in Britain. The regional rate is set at a uniform level throughout Northern Ireland and is effectively a central government tax. Both rates are collected by central government and the product of the district rate repaid to local authorities.

Councils have three main sources of funding – the district rate, a general grant and specific government grants (approximately 78 per cent, 18 per cent and 4 per cent respectively in the 2001/2 council budgets). The specific grants are a proportion of approved expenditure for certain functions (for example community services) and are relatively small in nature. The general grant is the principal grant towards the relief of rate income which takes account of (a) loss of rate income arising from industrial derating and (b) a resources element to help poorer councils afford a standard of service without the need to levy excessive rate poundage (Chartered Institute of Public Finance and Accountancy, 1997; Local Government Staff Commission, 1993).

Political Control

In spite of the dramatically reduced powers available to councils since 1973, local government elections have been the foci of revitalised electoral competition. In 1973, for example, there were 1,222 candidates for 526 seats compared to the previous local government elections (1967) in which a majority of the seats had been uncontested. Election turnout rates remain consistently high. There was a 68 per cent turnout in the local government elections held in June 2001 compared to 25 to 30 per cent rates for council polling in Britain.

The political composition of councils also reflects the PR electoral system in that, for the period 2001 to 2005, there is no council where one party has an overall majority and there is a greater representation of minority parties and independents. Unionists (mainly a combined Ulster Unionist Party (UUP) and Democratic Unionist Party (DUP) grouping) control Antrim, Ards, Ballymena, Ballymoney, Banbridge, Carrickfergus, Castlereagh, Coleraine, Craigavon, Larne, Lisburn, Newtownabbey and North Down councils. Nationalists/republicans (mainly a Social Democratic and Labour Party (SDLP) and Sinn Féin grouping) control Cookstown, Derry, Down, Dungannon and South Tyrone, Fermanagh, Limavady, Magherafelt, Newry and Mourne, Omagh and Strabane councils. There is one hung council – Armagh, and no overall party control in Belfast or Moyle.

The most recent trends in political representation in local council elections chart the rise in the fortunes of the DUP and Sinn Féin – a swing away from the moderate parties of unionism and nationalism (see table 27.1). This hardening of public opinion at the council level replicated the 2001 Westminster elections (held on the same day), which witnessed the political map of Northern Ireland redrawn into a re-partitioned green/orange state. As Carmichael (2002) argues, 'the trends established over successive local government elections serve as a consistent barometer of opinion, giving a fairly reliable indication of the balance between "extremism" and "moderation" in the public psyche'.

Table 27.1 Party Shares of Local Government Poll, 1973 to 2001 (%)

Year	UUP	DUP	Alliance	SDLP	Sinn Féin	Indep. unionist	Others
1973	41.4	4.3	13.7	13.4	–	10.9	16.3
1977	29.6	12.7	14.4	20.6	–	8.5	14.2
1981	26.5	26.6	8.9	17.5	–	4.2	16.3
1985	29.5	24.3	7.1	13.4	11.8	3.1	10.8
1989	31.4	17.7	6.8	21.2	11.2	3.9	7.8
1993	29.3	17.2	7.7	21.9	12.5	2.7	8.7
1997	27.8	15.6	6.6	20.7	16.9	2.5	9.9
2001	23.0	21.5	5.0	20.7	19.4	–	10.4

Significant Developments

The first significant development in the present system of local government was the election of Sinn Féin councillors in 1985 when the party secured 59 out of a total 566 seats (11.8 per cent of the vote) in accordance with their adopted 'ballot box and armalite' strategy. Although Sinn Féin had contested the Assembly, Westminster and European elections of October 1982, June 1983 and June 1984 respectively, their presence in council chambers was anathema to unionists. Both unionist parties (DUP and UUP) pledged in the 1985 local election campaigns to 'smash Sinn Féin' and subsequently employed tactics to isolate Sinn Féin councillors by excluding them from committees and preventing them from speaking at meetings, where possible. These tactics were legally challenged and found to be unlawful by the High Court. Further attempts to exclude Sinn Féin by demanding that councillors sign a declaration against violence were also challenged by a judicial review and again unionists were defeated (Knox, 1990). Despite continuous disruptions in council chambers, with occasional fist fights breaking out, the government refused to proscribe Sinn Féin in response to unionist pressure.

The 1985 Anglo-Irish Agreement ushered in a new wave of protest and became the second significant development in local government. Despite government assurances to the contrary, unionists viewed the Anglo-Irish Agreement as thinly veiled joint sovereignty over the province by Dublin and London. Their burgeoning local government protest against Sinn Féin was superseded by a campaign of unionist opposition against a 'sell-out' to Dublin. Eighteen unionist-controlled councils adopted a policy of adjourning all council meetings and refusing to strike a district rate. They argued that to administer local government was to give tacit support to the London–Dublin partnership. The decision to suspend meetings and delegate business to council officials was tested in court and declared unlawful.

Faced with unionist recalcitrance over the affair, the minister took new powers to appoint a commissioner and empower council officials to carry out council functions. Belfast and Castlereagh, at the forefront of the protest campaign, remained defiant despite legal contempt proceedings against them on the policy of adjournment. Eventually the government stepped in to maintain essential services. Yet cracks began to appear in the protest campaign. Proposals for a mass resignation of all UUP and DUP councillors were rejected, some local authorities met to strike a rate for the financial year (1987/8) and accusations abounded of surreptitious business taking place in some unionist councils. The protest campaign against the Anglo-Irish Agreement at local government level was proving counterproductive. Services continued to be provided amidst fears that nationalist councils were gaining more resources through regular ministerial contacts. The protest eventually withered away to an inauspicious end (Connolly and Knox, 1988).

The local government elections of 1989 marked a turning point in council chambers with a degree of moderation not unrelated to the decline in representation from the political extremes (see table 27.1). From this more stable political context, an experiment in 'responsibility sharing' developed (this term was used in deference to unionist sensitivities over the words 'power sharing') (Knox, 1996). Dungannon and South Tyrone is credited with leading the way in rotating the council chair between the two main political parties, the SDLP and UUP (although some councils – Down, Omagh and Newry and Mourne – claim to have been doing this for years in a low-profile manner). In addition, the Enniskillen bombing of November 1987 appears to have had a profound impact upon local politicians. One observer noted that 'councillors felt the need to bring an end to sterile adversarial politics . . . and found in their opposition to political violence more in common than they had previously recognised' (Beirne, 1993, p. 7).

In the wake of the 1989 elections, eleven local authorities appointed mayors/chairpersons and deputies from both political traditions. This trend has continued. Following the 2001 elections fourteen councils were operating some form of power-sharing arrangement.[2] Inter-community working at the local government level heralded similar provisions contained in the Belfast Agreement of 1998. A power-sharing executive and ten statutory assembly committees, constituted on the basis of d'Hondt, were to formalise what had been happening at the local government level for some years (but without the fanfare).

The final significant development was the growing confidence that councils acquired through innovative service delivery within the confines of a narrowly defined functional remit. In economic development, for example, councils had

---

[2] Armagh, Coleraine, Cookstown, Derry, Down, Dungannon and South Tyrone, Fermanagh, Limavady, Lisburn, Magherafelt, Moyle, Newry and Mourne, Omagh and Strabane.

been seen as small-part players working in the shadows of the Local Enterprise Development Unit and the Industrial Development Board (both replaced in 2002 by Invest Northern Ireland). Since 1992, however, councils have been permitted to spend up to five pence in the pound from rates for the specific purpose of economic development. Councils have embraced this opportunity enthusiastically, putting aside party differences and committing to the welfare and prosperity of their council areas. The more innovative have established extensive networks with private companies, set up arms-length enterprise development facilities and used their limited resources as seed-corn finance or matching grants to tap into larger EU funding sources.

The increasing prominence of councils in delivering economic development has been paralleled by their involvement in the field of community development and community relations. In 1989 the Central Community Relations Unit (a dedicated unit established within central government charged with formulating, reviewing and challenging policy throughout the government system with the aim of improving community relations) invited councils to participate in a grant-aided community relations programme. After some initial faltering, councils have participated fully in this work.

The community relations remit put consensus firmly on the policy agenda of councils, which was symbolically important in making progress on the wider political front. Moreover, given the chequered history of discrimination and sectarianism, an active involvement in this area has added to the emerging climate of cross-party co-operation and stability within which local authorities have demonstrated a more responsible approach to an incremental increase in their powers. This includes a significant role played by councils in district partnerships set up to disburse monies (PEACE I) under the Special Programme for Peace and Reconciliation and their successors, local strategy partnerships, to administer a further tranche of European assistance (PEACE II) aimed at reinforcing progress towards a peaceful and stable society (Knox, 1998a).

Local authorities have also been given a pivotal role in the area of community safety as a result of a review of the criminal justice system (Criminal Justice Review Group, 2000). The district policing partnerships, established under the Police (Northern Ireland) Act, 2000, are premised on local authority structures and inputs from elected members. The centrality of local government to 'a new beginning' in policing (see Patten Report, 1999), in particular monitoring the performance of police in implementing local policing plans, is key to the recent legislation.

Future Challenges and Proposals for Change

During the 1990s, local authorities in Northern Ireland began to emerge from an era characterised by discrimination and sectarianism (Knox, 1998b). As a result, various suggestions were made to enhance the role of councils and to allow for greater devolution of power to local government. When making such recommendations, the need for effective safeguards to guard against abuses of power and to allay the fears of nationalists is also acknowledged. For example, Archbishop Eames, Church of Ireland Primate, in his submission to the Opsahl Commission (a non-governmental forum established in February 1993 to elicit community views on the way forward), argued for more powers to be given to local councils where there is evidence of a sharing of responsibility. This, in his view, should be part of a 'slow, steady progress in building up inter-community confidence and trust' (Eames, 1993, p. 3).

The return of powers to the Northern Ireland Assembly in December 1999, with full legislative and executive authority over the functions of 'direct rule' civil service departments, precipitated a rethink of governance arrangements in the province. The executive's *Programme for Government* pledges 'to lead the most effective and accountable form of government in Northern Ireland' (Northern Ireland Executive, 2001, 7.1). It stresses the need for change, outlines the internal and external pressures driving the change process and emphasises 'the need to consider the rationalisation of public administration so that resources can be used best to serve the public rather than maintaining bureaucratic structures'. The programme reflects on the system of public service administration under direct rule:

> We have inherited from the last 30 years a wide range of public bodies. Their organisation and structure reflected the needs of those times. They helped maintain services at a time of very limited public accountability. But now that devolution has been achieved, there is a need for change that will provide not only greater accountability, but should ensure that organisations that deliver many key services throughout Northern Ireland are more coherently organised. It is therefore important that we set about a major process of reform in central government (Northern Ireland Executive, 2001, 7.1.1).

The central theme in this proposed review of public administration is effective and accountable service provision.

Northern Ireland has moved from a position of 'democratic deficit' to surfeit mode with 18 Westminster MPs, 108 members of the legislative assembly, 582 local councillors and 3 MEPs, all for a population of 1.7 million. In short, the province is over-governed. Aside from considerations of political representation, the focus is now on ways to rationalise public service provision as the assembly struggles (without the benefit of tax-raising powers) to meet the ever-increasing demands of public service provision. It has inherited a system of non-departmental public bodies (quangos) responsible for major functions such as health, education and housing, which consume half of the devolved budget. In addition, to satisfy the exigencies of a power-sharing executive, it has itself superimposed a cumbersome system of eleven government departments (to replace six). This complex mosaic now represents the structure of public administration in Northern Ireland.

The role of local government has acquired prominence as a target for radical reform. This may have more to do with public profile than any administrative logic, given the councils' self-evident democratic credentials, relatively small share of public sector spending and limited scope to achieve further value-for-money savings. When questioned about the centrality of local government to the review, then deputy first minister, Seamus Mallon, stated:

> Much of the thought and many of the utterances on this issue have centred inexplicably on the question of local government. It is clear from the expenditure that it is a crucial part of this. However, it is only a part. The general administration is crucially important.[3]

The pressure for local government reorganisation may well be a classic example of 'bureau-shaping' behaviour by civil servants and politicians, whereby they use changes to organisational structures as a way of enhancing their own welfare (Dunleavy, 1991). Civil servants argue that the eleven government departments were created as part of the political compromise necessary to secure the implementation of the Belfast Agreement and should remain sacrosanct. Politicians, starved of executive authority for over twenty-five years, eschew any notion of subsidiarity. Therefore, attention turns to local government and a prosaic debate ensues around reducing the number of councils from twenty-six to five or six.

This debate is fuelled by the 'super-councillor', who, as both a local government elected representative and a member of the legislative assembly, is a career politician with the associated perks of office (full-time salary, lavish surroundings of Stormont, administrative and secretarial support) and status well beyond the often thankless (and sometimes dangerous – a number have been victims of sectarian attacks) role of a councillor. There appears little allegiance to local government. Moreover, in the absence of tax-raising powers, the only room for flexibility by the assembly in raising local funds comes through varying the regional rates. Greater control of local government would facilitate this.

The first and deputy first ministers launched the terms of a review of public administration on 12 February 2002 and suggested that the review 'has the potential to recommend changes which would transform the operation of the public sector in Northern Ireland'.[4] The ministers pointed out that among the most important issues to be addressed by the review are the structure, accountability and responsibilities of local government, non-departmental public bodies and

---

[3] Northern Ireland Assembly Oral Questions, 11 December 2000.
[4] News release issued by the Office of the First and Deputy First Minister on 12 February 2002 entitled 'Preparation for the Review of Public Administration'.

government agencies. The eleven departments established by the Belfast Agreement were not included in the review's remit. The review of public administration should be an independent, open and transparent, 'root and branch' review of all key public services. The parameters established for the review have already constrained its outcomes.

In the evolving political and administrative situation in Northern Ireland, it is a mistake to underestimate the importance of elected local authorities. The focus on the number of councils eclipses the more important debate on what precisely the role of local government should be in a new devolved structure. The council elections held in June 2001 produced an average turnout of 68 per cent, with some areas reaching 80 per cent (Magherafelt, Cookstown and Dungannon and South Tyrone). This testifies to the importance of local decision making, even accepting that every election in Northern Ireland is fought along ethno-national cleavages and that local service provision features little.

People feel an affinity with their local district council areas and principal towns in Northern Ireland. Changing boundaries should be avoided if possible. Evidence from Britain suggests that a patchwork quilt of local government structures seriously underestimated residents' sense of place.

The UK Labour government's modernising agenda has bypassed Northern Ireland at central and local government levels, with the notable exception of 'best value'.[5] Yet there is a real opportunity for local councils to promote the economic, social and environmental wellbeing of their areas and to work with other bodies to prepare community strategies, similar to the discretionary 'wellbeing' powers applicable under the Local Government Act, 2000 in Great Britain. Alongside this, the functions of a large number of the smaller executive quangos could be integrated within local authorities. There is also an opportunity to democratise the larger executive quangos with elected members as the majority participants on decision-making boards in the key areas of health, education, housing and social services.

The role of local authorities has been increasing since the 1970s and councils could further expand their functions both as a direct provider (for example minor roads, street lighting, town centre management, car parking, the youth service and libraries) and as a co-ordinating body for public services provided by other government bodies in their areas. There is no desire in local government to deliver the major public services such as housing, education, social services and so on (Carmichael and Knox, 1999). That said, there may be opportunities for

---

[5] The 'best value' initiative is part of a wider series of reform introduced by the Labour government 'to modernise Britain and build a fairer, more decent society'. Central to this programme is an agenda to modernise local government set out in a White Paper in July 1998 entitled *Modern Local Government: In Touch with the People*. Best value is a concept designed to promote local accountability and continuous improvement in service performance.

local government input to larger services. The overriding consideration here is that councils want the opportunity for more influence over other public sector providers in their area; they want the elected forum to be a focus of accountability without necessarily having to take on the role of service deliverer.

With the establishment of the Northern Ireland Executive and Assembly, there is a need for a formal mechanism to regulate the relationship between local and central government. Local government's advocacy role at the centre is poorly served through the existing arrangements of the local government division within the Department of the Environment (NI). Effective intergovernmental models now exist in both Wales and Scotland that could inform this relationship in the future.

Conclusion

In any review of public administration in Northern Ireland some thought needs to be given to the respective roles of councillors and members of the legislative assembly. Experience thus far is that people continue to go to councillors to seek help with public service matters that are well beyond the brief of local government. The democratic deficit under direct rule and the accessibility and willingness of councillors to deal with a wide range of public service issues during that period has placed local authority members at the heart of their communities. This should not be overlooked in the race to review the way in which functions are organised and delivered. Local authorities are only one part of a complex mosaic of agencies operating at the local level, but they remain a uniquely pivotal, multifunctional, directly elected part of the mosaic and should not be sidelined in the review of public administration in Northern Ireland.

The role of local authorities has changed, particularly in Britain, but that should not be allowed to obscure their continuing importance. As British Prime Minister, Tony Blair, has argued:

> Where councils embrace this agenda of change and show that they can adapt to play a part in modernising their locality, then they will find their status and powers enhanced. If you are unwilling or unable to work to the modern agenda then the government will have to look to other partners to take on your role (Blair, 1998, p. 20).

District councils have a record of accountable service provision to the public despite at times their tumultuous history under direct rule. As one political initiative after another foundered, local government remained the bedrock of democracy in a society that appeared on occasions to be close to collapse. Local authorities want to see their role strengthened, not emasculated, in any future reconfiguration of public services.

Conclusions

28

Where Stands Local Government?

Mark Callanan

Writing in 1991, Tom Barrington described the history of local government in the Irish administrative system as:

> . . . the steady working out of a logic of a set of values, implicit and explicit, in what is largely an intellectual vacuum, in conditions not of dialectic but of drift. These values are the acceptance of a substantial role for government in a highly centralised parliamentary democracy, the tolerance of considerable incompetence in the consequential structures and performance, the growth of bureaucracy, and indifference to the place of local democracy in the modern nation state (Barrington, 1991a, p. 155).

While there is evidence of a shift in this mindset since 1991, it applies to some values more than others. There has also been a change in the environment in which local government operates. This chapter will review and assess these developments and the challenges that they present.

Some Limitations in Irish Local Government

> To date, local government in Ireland has rarely been accorded a status commensurate with its democratic mandate or been accepted fully as a valid partner in the process of government. Historically, Irish local government developed largely from a judicial system introduced under a colonial regime and from town corporations with limited community involvement. It tends therefore to lack the deep community roots that go to form the basis of continental local government – which evolved over time and predated national governments as widely accepted representative institutions (Department of the Environment, 1996, p. 14).

This explanation cannot wholly account for a lesser status of local government in Ireland compared to elsewhere. The view of many Irish citizens that government is something exercised by 'them' on 'us' applies to central as well as local government. Present-day continental European systems of local government did not spring, as the quote suggests, from fully formed democratic local institutions in the nineteenth century. Rather there was a gradual process of evolution into democratic and legitimate forms of local government. Also, if local government in Ireland has not had strong community roots, this must be partly due to the fact that since 1970, with the exception of housing, Irish local authorities have until recently had little involvement in the social services. Instead, many local government functions were focused on the physical environment. This is in contrast to most European systems, which see local government as ideally suited to deliver services such as education, social welfare or health, and which facilitate the development of links between community and local government.

For Irish citizens, local government is most often associated with 'bad news'. An individual's dealings with a council usually concern issues such as the levying and collection of charges, development and other regulatory controls or the payment of motor tax. Many of local government's positive contributions to society are either of general benefit (such as urban renewal) or are taken for granted (such as the supply of water). In contrast, many local development groups in receipt of public money are exclusively concerned with 'good news' such as training and development and the allocation of grants to individuals. Loughlin (2001, p. 75) points out:

> . . . that traditional local governments operate in a regulatory environment. For example, local authorities have to manage or monitor traffic, construction and land use, and industrial discharges to the environment; and thus they are obliged to constrain the activities of some groups in the community. This of course, contrasts with the relatively unconstrained activities of the partnership groups.

Ultimately, however, the limitations of local government are related to its mandate and responsibilities, financial resources and structures – all of which have been the subject of successive reports. The general theme running through many of local government's limitations (and throughout this book) is the centralisation of government in Ireland. A convincing case has yet to be made for the extent of centralisation in Ireland's political system. Centralisation reflects an undervaluing of the importance of local circumstances and the role of local government, as well as an unswerving faith in the virtue and omnipotence of the centre.

Centralism Versus Localism

An Irish Tradition?

The different roles of local government, as outlined in chapter 1, and the relative importance attached to each role, are important in the debates over how local government operates, its range of functions and its relationship with central government. For some commentators (for example, Jones and Stewart, 1985), the rationale behind local government lies in the notion of local authorities giving expression to local diversity and responding to the different needs and priorities of an area with appropriate action. They argue that a reliance on a purely functional perspective of service delivery offers little to justify local authorities as services can also be delivered by unelected agencies.

A crucial determinant of the role played by local authorities is the relationship between local and central government. As noted above, some of the limitations of Irish local government are due to central control, as expressed through local government's narrow range of functions and its limited autonomous sources of revenue and dependency on central government grants. On the spectrum of centralised to decentralised nations, Ireland is generally regarded as a highly centralised state.

Centralisation is strongly imbued within Irish administrative culture. Barrington (1991c, pp. 143–5) points out that nationalist leaders at the beginning of the twentieth century focused on achieving independence, but had not worked out a value system for what should follow. Once independence was achieved, the drive for efficiency and uniformity resulted in small units of administration being regarded as extravagant. Garvin (2001, pp. 33–4) observes that the turbulence which marked the transition to independence influenced the political system that emerged:

> Local government was a British invention, expensive and anti-national. The virtuous felt themselves obliged to take away from the local councils powers that might be wielded by unsuitable people. Irish democracy was to be heavily shaped by the idea of embattled heroes in power struggling against a perceived collective moral mediocrity ultimately originating in a popular slave culture. Consequently, they created the most centralised democratic state in Europe. Centralisation of this kind is a characteristic outcome of revolution; successful revolutionaries like to keep the reins of power in their own hands.

In essence, local discretion took second place to central diktat. This was reflected in an infamous 1934 Department of Local Government and Public Health memorandum, which proposed the gradual merging of national and local administration and the phasing out of locally elected representatives. This vignette of centralism argued that the local government system was 'defective and unsatisfactory' and that local authorities were 'a relic of British administration' and 'an expensive anachronism' (quoted in O'Halpin, 1991, pp. 14–15). Undoubtedly the system was in need of reform in the 1930s. However, the prospect of abolishing local government altogether reflected central government preoccupations with efficiency over local diversity and decision making. One former civil servant, while acknowledging that much central government intervention was well meant, believes that 'there is a certain grandmotherly or nursemaid attitude in Irish government: the children, for their own good of course, are not really to be trusted' (Barrington, 1991c, p. 148). Certainly, such attitudes epitomise the latent centralist culture that still pervades today. More recently, Haslam (2001, p. 103) has remarked that the relationship between central government departments and local authorities 'evolved as one of principal and agent rather than partnership' and that 'while some relaxation has taken place in recent years, local authorities have a long way to go before they are treated as inclusively as similar institutions in other countries'.

Many European countries embarked on a process of decentralisation in the 1970s and 1980s. Ireland, however, pursued further centralisation through, for example, the abolition of domestic rates in 1978. Centralisation in Ireland came about not so much through an ideological and concerted assault on local government, but rather through a haphazard and often unconnected series of policy decisions and piecemeal legislation at central level, often motivated by a simple assumption that the centre 'knows best' and with little regard for their collective effect. 'Irish local government is faced not with positive change or remodelling but a steady process of decay. Occasionally hastened by acts of omission and commission by a central government largely inspired by expediency' (Barrington, 1991a, p. 165).

In an Irish context, where centripetal tendencies are so prevalent in political culture, it is important to challenge some of the assumptions that support centralism.[1] Simple statements, accepted at face value and regularly repeated, become the accepted truth, despite a lack of evidence to prove their veracity. For example, it is common to hear those involved in central government, and indeed the national media, refer to local government as unpopular. Yet, while it is true that most people's faith in government in general has lessened, there is no evidence to show that local government is any less popular than central government.

Uniformity and Diversity

An assumption closely linked with centralisation is that there is a need for uniformity across the country. However, while citizens do have a right to a minimum level of service wherever they live, central government may allow for discretion rather than adopting a prescriptive approach. As Jones and Stewart (1985, p. 13) point out:

> If the public were asked whether they wished to have a common standard of services, they would probably say Yes. They would also say Yes if they were asked whether services should vary according to the wishes of local people and the needs of local

---

[1] For example, two prominent defenders of local government in the UK, Jones and Stewart (1985, 1997) set out to expose some of the myths surrounding centralism – this section draws on some, though not all, of their arguments.

areas . . . Common standards for services have emerged more from the decisions of different local authorities than from the interventions of central government. Local authorities are themselves elected bodies, subject to the popular pressures of society. When there are pressures for common standards, local authorities will reflect them.

Another common assumption is that in times of trouble, or when a crisis unfolds, the correct response is to re-assert central control. However, centralising reduces flexibility. The 'one size fits all' approach is problematic. Local areas differ in population, in their urban/suburban/rural profile (or combination of each), in topography and crucially in the needs and demands of the local population. What works in Dublin may not work in Leitrim, and vice versa. As society becomes increasingly complex, uniform solutions applied from the centre, which take no account of diversity, are more and more likely to fail.

Many observers (for example Stewart, 1995, pp. 250–1; Hesse and Sharpe, 1991, pp. 611–2) note that, in an ever more complex society, central governments in continental European countries have come to realise that the centre's capacity to meet challenges is limited, and that central government needs to focus on those issues it can deal with, while strengthening local government to respond to issues that can be met locally.

> In short, the force of events supersedes old centre-local attitudes of stand-off, rivalry and mutual contempt. There is now a mutual acceptance of the necessity not only of pulling together but of active partnership. This poses an awareness of the need to reallocate tasks according to a general acceptance of what each can do best (Barrington, 1991b, p. 53).

One of the strengths of local government is that it can promote efficiency by identifying solutions to fit local conditions and specificities. This is not to say that every local initiative will succeed – undoubtedly some will fail. But surely it makes sense to have some local initiatives succeed and some local initiatives fail than to have one failed central solution applying right across the country. Local authorities can learn from the strengths and weaknesses of diverse approaches to tackling problems and can refine and improve initiatives as required.

One need only look at issues such as social inclusion or environmental protection to see that problems are becoming more cross-functional and increasingly transcend traditional sectoral boundaries. As Clarke (1998, p. 6) points out, while issues such as poverty and the environment undoubtedly have national and international dimensions, they unquestionably require local action. In a report on social inclusion and poverty, governments from all EU countries outlined ten key principles for inclusive services and policies, the first of which is subsidiarity – noting that 'policies and services become more inclusive when designed and delivered as close to people as possible' (Council of the European Union, 2001, p. 81). Small, multi-purpose local authorities, in many cases working with others, are in a better position to manage crosscutting issues than central government departments or single-purpose agencies organised along sectoral lines. However, developing local solutions assumes some degree of flexibility to allow local authorities to adapt solutions to fit local problems.

Political Centralism

The focus in Irish politics and political contests is on control of the Dáil, and ultimately on national government, where decision-making power resides. The political commitment to local government is weak. In the 2002 general election, only one political party (Labour Party) articulated a dedicated vision for local government in its election manifesto. Other manifestos referred to local authorities in passing (in the context of service areas such as housing, waste management and so forth). It could be that parties are just reflecting the fact that local government is not an issue that excites the minds of a large number of people. The emphasis in the Irish consciousness would seem to be very much on the role of local government as a service provider, rather than as an expression of local democracy.[2] However, it may also be argued that people will only take a real interest in local government when it is given a comprehensive range of responsibilities and discretion in raising revenue.

Administrative Centralism

Centralisation not only weakens local democracy, but also overburdens a central government operating with limited resources. Central government is facing strains with the volume of work involved in supervising national policy making and administration, and in engaging in the EU policy process at supranational level. Detailed supervision of local government activity adds to these burdens.

Central government of course has an important role to play in terms of determining a framework, according to national policies, within which local authorities work. However, it is often the case that central government sets down overly prescriptive details rather than broad policy parameters. It is ironic that at a time when central government preaches the virtues of deregulation for the private sector, the same principles are not applied to local government. This point was emphasised in a 2001 recommendation from the Council of Europe's Congress of Local and Regional Authorities of Europe, which stated that the prolific use of regulations by central government in Ireland is contrary to the spirit of local self-government (Council of Europe, 2001, point i).

Manifestations of central control include the everyday circulars emanating from government departments and the regular obligation on local authorities to

---

[2] This may also have been reflected in the lack of public protest or concern when central government has threatened to remove elected members from office or when, in the past, local elections were postponed.

seek ministerial approval or sanction before undertaking a series of activities or procedural measures. Local government is subjected to detailed supervision of its activities, more often than not through ministerial regulation rather than through framework legislation (Barrington, 1991c, pp. 147–8). While each individual circular or statutory instrument may appear relatively innocent and well intentioned, the cumulative effect is often to chip away at local discretion. *Better Local Government* (Department of the Environment, 1996, p. 7) recognises this problem, but promises little in the way of specific change aside from a relaxation of central government controls on human resources.

Centralisation and overly prescriptive regulation makes it more difficult for members of the public to make complaints or to have their voices heard. There is little point in an individual making a complaint to a local authority about actions which, although carried out by that authority, were centrally determined and carried out on instruction. Referring the individual to central government where the decision was made simply adds to the frustration.

Detailed regulation by central government is justified by some on the basis of the necessity to implement EU legislation according to requirements. However, the European Commission (2001d, p. 20) has given a commitment that it intends to allow for greater flexibility in how Directives are implemented, to take account of regional and local conditions. Central government in Ireland needs to give a similar commitment to local authorities when national legislation is being drawn up. Local authorities, as separately elected bodies, must have the potential to determine local priorities. If local government is not about expressing local priorities, and if local authorities have little discretion in decision making, why bother with local elections in the first place?

A particularly alarming phenomenon is an appetite on the part of some at local level to be instructed by central government to do something, and to be told precisely how to do it, rather than being held responsible for taking action. This trend of pragmatic acquiescence to administrative centralism, which one hopes is not too widespread, reflects an abdication of the responsibility local government has to reflect local priorities.

Financial Centralism

It is perhaps in the area of local financing that the extent of centralisation and of local government limitations becomes most apparent. Local government in Ireland has few tax-raising powers. In 1997, local taxes (in the form of commercial rates) made up just 2.1 per cent of the total share of government taxation. This compares with an average 12.7 per cent across the OECD industrialised countries, and particularly high rates of 31.2 per cent in Denmark and 30.5 per cent in Sweden (OECD, 1999, p. 21).

The figures reflect Irish local government's reliance on central government grants, and in many cases on specific grants where local authorities have little or no discretion on expenditure. While central government grants are used in many other countries, particularly for equalisation purposes, most systems of local government typically have a greater share of discretionary local sources of revenue, often through local property, income or sales taxes. As pointed out in chapter 18, the 1972 White Paper recognised this by stating that it is essential that local taxes finance a significant proportion of local expenditure for local democracy and a vibrant local government system.

Thus, local government in Ireland is largely dependent on central government grants and annual allocations. Local accountability is diluted when local government does not receive most of its income from its own taxpayers – the link between taxation and services is blurred. In local elections in many countries, tax is a key issue. If the local population want better services, they have to be prepared to pay through local taxes. If the local population want to pay less tax, hard choices have to be made about local services.

The issue of an adequate source of local income has been raised in so many reports and commentaries on local government in Ireland that one senses exasperation whenever the topic is broached. But the point needs re-emphasising that the decision to abolish domestic rates had a profound impact, not just on local government's financial resources, but on its autonomy. It could also be argued that dependency on central government grants reduces the responsibility, as well as the accountability, of local government. O'Halpin (2001, p. 38) argues that the abolition of domestic rates in 1978 provided local politicians with 'the ultimate free lunch, because responsibility for any financial shortfalls and consequent inadequacies in services could now be blamed on niggardly central government'. At a broader level, Lee (1993, p. 44) argues that centralisation:

> . . . helps foster among us the familiar 'rights without responsibilities' mentality. The state has connived – with our willing, not to say eager, collusion – at turning us all into suppliants on its centralised largesse, providing sinister but seductive support for the debilitating effect on national character of the 'something for nothing' syndrome.

Rather than being determined by levels of local taxation, choices about the level of local services in Ireland are effectively made at the centre through annual allocations and the frequent tendency to cap increases in commercial rates. This encourages local authorities to spend as close to their maximum allocation as possible, because the choice about whether to spend more or less money has little consequence for elected members. Jones and Stewart (1997, p. 14) argue that with capping, there is an 'inevitable tendency to assume the authority should spend at the cap. After all, if you do not do it this year, who knows what the cap may be next year'. Without the accountability that comes from local government raising a large proportion of its expenditure from local voters, local authorities are likely to continue pushing for higher levels of grant support from the centre. Recent research in the UK has raised serious doubts about many of the suppositions and arguments in favour of central control of local government expenditure, and questioned whether capping is a suitable instrument for such control (Fender and Watt, 2002).

The existing local government financing system in Ireland means that taxes levied at local level fall on one sector – local businesses. Arguably, any new emphasis on local government discretion needs to be accompanied by other sources of revenue, such as a local property tax or a local income tax, as proposed by KPMG (1996, p. 79), and a reduction in central grants (in particular, specific grants). Central government decided not to take up this critical recommendation of the KPMG report. Instead, it cherry-picked those recommendations it considered most appealing and used the report to justify the abolition of water charges.

While acknowledging that confining rates to commercial property has led to 'a serious problem of accountability', de Buitleir (2001, pp. 149–50) concludes that the political problems associated with reintroducing rates or a local property tax are insurmountable, no matter how good the arguments look on paper. One cannot ignore such political problems. If the history of local government finance teaches us anything, it is that Irish people appear to have a particular antipathy to property taxes or local charges. The introduction of the residential property tax in 1983 and its abolition in 1997, as well as the more short-lived farm tax (introduced in 1984 and abolished in 1987), show the difficulty in getting Irish citizens to accept taxes on property. The same can be said about charges for water or refuse services (although this would appear to be a problem particular to urban areas). And yet, if the introduction of a local tax was complemented by a parallel and explicitly linked reduction in central government taxation, its chances of being accepted should improve (Callan, 1991, p. 27). Also, local authorities in many other countries levy local taxes without negative implications for national borrowing requirements, and where there is a stronger relationship between the services being demanded by the local electorate and the local electorate who pay for those services.

To a greater or lesser extent, central government grants make up an element of virtually all systems of local government financing. Specific grants earmarked for specific projects are often favoured by central governments as they fit neatly into the system of public expenditure planning. They are, however, instruments of central control. As well as favouring a proportion of local government revenue being raised through local sources, there is a clear preference for general or block grants over specific grants in the European Charter of Local Self-Government, signed by the Irish government in 1997 (Council of Europe, 1985a, article 9; see appendix 1). The government has made a welcome move in this direction through the establishment of the Local Government Fund. Specific grants could in future be confined to areas where local government acts on an agency basis on behalf of central government.

Functional Centralism

Many services provided by local authorities in other European countries are provided by either central government or state agencies in Ireland. This point is made by several commentators on local government in Ireland (see, for example, Roche, 1982b, p. 7; Barrington, 1991a, p. 158; McManus, 1993, p. 37), and it is a theme raised by a number of the contributors to this book.

The extensive range of local government functions in many countries reflects the priority attached to the principle of subsidiarity. In the context of services being provided and decisions being made as close to the citizen as possible, the assumption made under the subsidiarity principle is that functions are delivered locally. If a function is not suited to the local level, the case must be made for it to be devolved upwards to regional or central levels. In Ireland, by comparison and despite a number of calls for change and recommendations for devolution (Barrington Report, 1991; Devolution Commission, 1996 and 1997), the assumption is that the centre should deliver and that the case needs to be made to devolve down.

A Devolution Commission was established to consider functional responsibilities (see chapter 4), however, one must ask why its work has not been linked to the reforms implemented under *Better Local Government*. This has been a key omission of the local government reform process that began in the late 1990s. Thus far, there has been remarkably little change in the balance of functions between central and local government levels in Ireland. That said, what change there has been is welcome. For example, the *Programme for Prosperity and Fairness* states that 'local authorities will continue to expand their role in social inclusion' (Government of Ireland, 2000c, section 3.5) and a number of social inclusion units have been established in local authorities on a pilot basis on the foot of this commitment. Local authorities have also been given new responsibilities in the fields of heritage and conservation.

However, it appears that many politicians, even committed advocates of local government reform, have given up the ghost of a major devolution of functions to local authorities. When introducing the Local Government Bill (later to become the Local Government Act, 2001) to the Dáil in 2000, the then Minister for the Environment and Local Government, Noel Dempsey TD, commented:

> Local government in any country derives from the particular tradition, history, culture and circumstances of that country and prospects for change must bear this in mind. The delivery of functions such as policing, public transport, health and social welfare, comes within the local government system in some other countries.

However, if we are realistic, given current Irish circumstances, it is unlikely that in the short-term these will be subsumed within our local government system or that there is a demand for such, much as we might wish it so. In short, if local government is to progress in this country, it demands that we approach change in a realistic way taking account of how functional responsibilities have evolved and how they are currently organised.[3]

It is interesting to note that some of the areas that central government has devolved to local government, such as group water schemes or taxi licensing, could be regarded as controversial or 'problem' areas.

At a time when the phrase 'decentralisation' is most often used in Ireland to refer to a potential relocation of civil servants from Dublin, rather than a genuine devolution of functions from central to sub-national levels of government, one can only be pessimistic about the prospects for central government entrusting local government with a new range of responsibilities. Decentralisation (in its particularly Irish context) is ironically likely to prevent future devolution of functions from central to local government. If and when large numbers of central government officials are relocated to various towns and cities around Ireland, what politician is going to suggest that a particular function be transferred to local government, when the transfer of that function would result in the closure of a large office of civil servants working on the issue in a specific town? The transfer would have the same effect as the closure of a local factory.

The question remains, however, as to why Ireland has locally based offices of government departments to deliver services that could, with the proper resources, be delivered by local government on an agency basis (as is the case in many other countries). A simple question that has been met, on the surface at least, by a resounding silence.

The essential difference between a local authority and other agencies and bodies is that a local authority is elected to identify local priorities. An intermediate alternative is for local government to be consulted by other public bodies and agencies delivering local services, or that local government be given a formal right of inquiry into the activities of other organisations. Another suggestion might be to give local authorities, as the elected representatives of the community, a legal power to insist on a higher level of service than is currently provided by agreeing to supply the required funding from its own resources to the relevant public body.

One should also note that local authorities are looking at new ways of delivering services, a point elaborated on below. Increasingly, they are working with others in service delivery. A local authority can therefore be legally responsible for a service

---

[3] *Dáil Debates*, vol. 532, col. 831. Such sentiments were echoed in the Seanad by the former minister of state at the department, Dan Wallace TD (*Seanad Debates*, vol. 167, col. 1336).

without necessarily having to deliver it itself. Local authorities are now working with local stakeholders on strategic policy committees, through formal consultation procedures and also through more informal contacts.

Local government has a prominent role in the county/city development board (CDB) process. Local councils must approve the county/city strategies for economic, social and cultural development, which will act as a framework for the operations of all public bodies and groups in the area. This should be welcomed as an improvement on previous arrangements. But it does not in itself address the fundamental issue of the transfer of new executive functions from central to local level. It would appear that central government has embraced the thinking of the National Economic and Social Council, which in the mid-1990s argued that there is 'uncertainty as to whether economies of scale would permit the full devolution of many policy functions to local authorities' and that local authorities should instead be a focus for co-ordination and linkage at local level (1996, pp. 260–1). Clearly, the seeds of the CDB process were in this train of thought.

An alternative viewpoint on devolution was expressed by the Congress of Local and Regional Authorities of Europe in a recommendation on local democracy in Ireland, which raised concerns that 'limiting local authorities to matters which do not have wide implications for the local community would risk relegating them to a marginal role in the long run' (Council of Europe, 2001, point a). Equally, the task force report that first proposed the CDB structures acknowledges that local government functions do not cover an adequate range of responsibilities and that the Irish system is out of line with the European norm (Department of the Environment and Local Government, 1998e, 5.2). However, rather than proposing devolution to local government, its recommendations leave all the various agencies delivering local services intact, with each reporting to separate government departments and with co-ordination at local level through the CDB structure. This is not a criticism of the task force report, which is a welcome attempt to address the problems encountered by a plethora of agencies and offices at local level; it is rather a lament that a more in-depth programme of devolution proved politically and administratively impossible. One cannot avoid the conclusion that powerful interests in different government departments do not wish to see duties carried out by 'their' local offices or agencies being assigned to local authorities, which are perceived by many civil servants as 'belonging' to the Department of the Environment and Local Government.

One can at times detect reluctance among some within local government to take on new functions. Part of this hesitancy relates to the experience, particularly during the 1980s, when new functions and obligations were foisted upon local authorities without an accompanying increase in financing or personnel. If anything, financial and staffing resources were further restricted at that time. This negative experience appears to have left a residual doubt in some quarters about whether local government should seek new functions or simply protect the status quo. However, there is an onus on local government to respond positively to the few areas where local authorities are being encouraged to take up a greater role, for example in the area of social inclusion or providing broadband infrastructure in rural areas. The opportunity to show what local government can deliver needs to be seized.

'The Nuclear Option'

One of central government's most draconian powers over local government is its ability to suspend local authorities, a faculty first introduced by Irish legislators under section 12 of the Local Government (Temporary Provisions) Act, 1923 (although there was provision for dissolution under the Poor Relief (Ireland) Act, 1838). Section 216 of the Local Government Act, 2001 still allows the minister to suspend a local authority on a number of grounds, including the failure to adopt a budget, the refusal to comply with statutory requirements or a court order, or where, after the holding of a public enquiry, a local authority is found to have not 'duly or effectually' performed its functions. The minister may appoint a commissioner to exercise reserved functions until a newly elected council is in place. While the number of actual suspensions has been small, the threat of suspension has been used on a number of occasions. Such a power is inconsistent with the principles of local democracy, where it is up to the local population, and not central government, to hold irresponsible councils to account.

Local government can provide a political counterpoint to central government. The diffusion of power, through a vibrant local government system where local authorities can exercise some influence at national level, can be regarded as a healthy safeguard in democratic societies. However, in a situation where individual local authorities can simply be suspended by central government, it is doubtful whether local government in Ireland is in a position to play this role. The ability of central government to overturn the results of a local election is a serious and some might say a dangerous power. The assumption that this is an acceptable state of affairs has yet to be coherently justified.

Proximity to the Citizen

One of the criticisms of national politicians is that they often focus on local issues and neglect their responsibilities as national policy makers.[4] This can be partly attributed to the fact that many local issues are determined at central government level. A case could be made that, because of its proximity to the communities it serves, local government is better equipped and better informed to tackle and decide on a broader range of issues.

---

[4] 'All Politics is Local', a speech to the Humbert School by the then Minister for the Environment and Local Government, Noel Dempsey TD, in 2001.

National governments in other countries know from their contacts with local government that a complex and changing society cannot be governed from the centre alone. It does not possess all knowledge and wisdom. Rather, understanding and information at the local level have to be used and its capacity for initiative released (Jones and Stewart, 1997, p. 23).

The value of locality, as Frazer (1996) argues, is often neglected or overlooked, particularly by the advocates of centralism. The fact that local government is closer to the individual than central government means that it is more sensitive to local needs. Both elected members and local officials live close to the people they serve. Local councillors in many cases are more accessible than national politicians. A simple glance at the figures shows that while there are 166 TDs and 60 senators at national level, there are 1,627 locally elected councillors. At official level, local authority officials are regularly in the public eye in a way that civil servants rarely, if ever, experience (see, for example, Asquith and O'Halpin, 1998, p. 71; Jones and Stewart, 1985, p. 21).

The value of 'closeness' to the local population has been realised by local authorities themselves, many of which have embarked on a process of internal devolution in the form of area-based management. Under these arrangements, elected members and officials run much of their operational business at the sub-county or sub-city level, on the basis of individual electoral areas or wards, making elected members and officials ever closer to the public they serve.

In many of the functions exercised by local government, the public has the legal right of consultation, from waste management planning to compulsory purchase orders to the drafting of the development plan. Apart from these statutory obligations, local authorities have developed more proactive forms of public participation. The capacity for active public participation is more limited at central government level and can effectively be restricted to well-mobilised and well-financed groups.

The visibility of local government, and the fact that it operates on a scale that makes it more accessible to the local community, naturally opens it to greater pressures to ensure that local considerations are taken into account, and ultimately to ensure local democratic control in a way that is more easily achieved than through larger national departments or unelected bodies. This explains why local authorities are sensitive to local situations and problems.

The contention here is not that local authorities are perfect. Local communities will often criticise the decisions of a local authority. Local government, and indeed local communities, can be insular or parochial. To give one example from outside of Ireland: in the late 1980s and early 1990s, the London Borough of Tower Hamlets devolved a number of service areas, including decisions over housing allocations, to local neighbourhood committees. However, some committees were exploited and hijacked by unrepresentative groups, which resulted in poor housing being allocated to ethnic minorities and further ghettoisation. The local authority attracted widespread media criticism because it had allowed racist groups to take control of local committees.

However, Jones and Stewart (1985) argue that because of the visibility and accessibility of local government, it is more open to scrutiny and it is easier to highlight problems and expose inefficiencies. They further believe that 'the public locally should make use of the many channels that exist to constrain local councils to be responsive to their wishes' (p. 24). Where local authorities show themselves to be responsive to local demands, they can, where criticisms are justified, act appropriately.

In the Irish context, mistakes made by local authorities are sometimes used as the basis for intervention, and occasionally for appropriation of a responsibility, by the centre. The reverse does not seem to apply – mistakes made by central government are not held to justify devolution to local government.

Prospects for Change in the Central/Local Balance

In essence, excessive central power leads to:

- remote, rigid and uniform solutions that are inflexible to complex, local circumstances
- a reduction in the accessibility of government and decision making
- an overburdening of central government and administration
- a potentially dangerous concentration of power in a democratic society.

The benefits of allowing discretion to local authorities to adapt solutions to local problems need highlighting. Local government is well placed to promote diversity in solutions based on local knowledge and proximity to the citizen. Local government is in a position to offer:

- diversity in approach enabling resources to be better matched to needs
- greater localness, visibility, accessibility and transparency
- a greater capacity, than central structures, to manage crosscutting issues
- diffusion of political power.

Local government will always have to work within a national framework and a constitutional setting. One should not confuse greater local government autonomy with local isolationism, where local authorities would become more inward looking and unconcerned about national policy. Rather, what is needed is a greater balance to reflect the interdependency that exists between central and local levels of government. Devolution must encompass different levels of government in the shaping, implementation and monitoring of policy. This needs to be reflected in a more developed interaction and dialogue between central and local government. In particular, this interaction must be two-way – with local government feeding into national policy as well as national policy providing the framework for local action (Callanan, 2002b, pp. 72–5; Clarke, 1998, pp. 13–16).

In the context of an ever-increasing proportion of legislation and policy being determined at European level, the EU institutions have undertaken to provide for a greater input from local government into EU decision making (Callanan, 2002b, pp. 68–70) and have acknowledged the value of involving local government as a separately elected, democratic level of government. Central government in Ireland should follow this example.

Although change has long been discussed, there has been little action. One explanation offered for this is as follows:

> Governments may propose but self-defending public institutions dispose, and one is left wondering whether there is a fully responsible centre to this intensely centralised society . . . Functional and institutional forces recruit ministerial voices to fight their cause around the Cabinet table itself. When these forces are powerful and self-cancelling the casualty is coherence, consistency and overall responsibility of government . . . Irish society is moving rapidly . . . Its public institutions are locked into ideas deep frozen since early in this century. They are apparently incapable of learning from the experience (Barrington, 1987b, p. 146).

In truth, if devolution of functions to local authorities was to occur, it would probably have to be part of a major overhaul of all public and state structures and a thorough re-examination of what functions are appropriate to different levels of government.

Similarly, the introduction of local taxes would appear unlikely in isolation from changes elsewhere in the tax system, particularly given government policy in recent years to reduce taxes on income and on business. However, in contrast to most other European countries, the lack of a strong voice at national level representing the interests of local government makes fundamental change less likely. There seems to be an inertia about fundamental change in government. The culture of centralisation may be changing, but such deeply entrenched attitudes do not change quickly.

Changing Trends in the Role of the State and Local Government

Developments in public management and the role of the state have influenced how local government in Ireland operates. Internationally, one of the more influential reassessments of the role of government has been Osborne and Gaebler's *Reinventing Government*, written in the context of the US system of government. Osborne and Gaebler (1992), who call for an 'American *perestroika*', identify the various ways in which entrepreneurial public bodies work as:

- focusing not simply on providing public services but on acting as a catalyst for the public, private and voluntary sectors; they steer as much as they row – catalytic government
- empowering communities rather than simply delivering services – community-owned government
- encouraging competition between service providers rather than monopolies of service provision – competitive government
- enabling the actions of an organisation to be driven by its missions and goals, not by its rules and regulations – mission-driven government
- defining and measuring outcomes rather than inputs – results-oriented government
- meeting the needs of the customer rather than the needs of the bureaucracy; turning clients into customers through offering them choices – customer-driven government
- earning money, as well as spending it – enterprising government
- investing in prevention rather than cure and taking a proactive approach to prevent problems before they emerge rather than offering services to deal with them afterwards – anticipatory government
- decentralising authority within organisations, participatory management and market mechanisms over bureaucratic mechanisms – decentralised government
- solving problems by levering the marketplace rather than creating public programmes – market-oriented government.

It is noteworthy that many of the examples offered by Osborne and Gaebler of the entrepreneurial spirit in the public sector are taken from programmes and institutions at the level of sub-national and local government. Much of this thinking can be associated to new paradigms that emerged in the 1970s and 1980s including public choice theory and new public management.

Boyle (1995) illustrates some of the tensions between new public management and more traditional public administration (see table 28.1). He argues for a balance to be maintained between the two models, and states that the challenge for all public bodies will be 'to ensure that the values driving the shift to new public management, such as efficiency and professionalism, be incorporated in such a way that they do not drive out the traditional values such as probity and due process' (pp. 39–41).[5] International experience suggests that decentralising decision-making powers to regional and local levels and relaxing the traditional rules and control focus have created a more responsive and community-driven ethos.

---

[5] Prior et al. (1995, pp. 48–62) offer a critical appraisal of some of the traits of new public management.

Table 28.1   Managing the Tensions between Traditional and New Public
Management

Traditional		New Public Management
Focus on probity and due process	←•→	Focus on performance
Highly planned	←•→	Responsive
Hierarchical	←•→	Contractual
Tight central control	←•→	Delegation
Cost control	←•→	Quality control
Monopolistic	←•→	Competitive

Source: Boyle (1995, p. 40)

Closely related to new public management is the concept of public choice theory, which is essentially based on introducing market-type mechanisms for service provision to generate competition. Developed in the 1970s, it found strong support in the UK in the 1980s and some of its basic premises are finding expression in Ireland as well. According to public choice theory, there is a clear preference for services being provided by private companies because public sector providers have an inherent tendency to overspend. Mobilised sectoral interests push for higher levels of expenditure to favour their needs. Bureaucrats seek to maximise their own budgets and resources. Politicians are often only too happy to oblige with extra spending since it will enhance their prospects of being re-elected. The disorganised and those without a voice lose out through having to pay increased levels of taxation. Thus, according to the advocates of public choice theory, there should be limits to the services provided by the public sector. Those services where there is a case for public sector provision should be financed through service charges or special taxes rather than through general taxation.

The public choice approach favours the supply of services by a number of small-scale organisations rather than by one large public service provider. This fragmentation of service provision generates competition and citizen choice. A preference is also expressed for contracting and measuring performance rather than employing direct labour. Instead of asking whether local government should do more, public choice theory questions direct service provision and challenges local government with a new motto: do less, but better.

Increasingly local government does work with and through others. It contracts out some services to private contractors and levers the private sector to promote investment in its area. Local authorities work with the voluntary sector in areas such as provision of housing for those in need, as well as providing housing services themselves (see chapter 9). Apart from the non-state sector, local authorities also have to work with state agencies and organisations established by central government. These include semi-state bodies, specialised agencies at national level such as the Environmental Protection Agency and the National Roads Authority, and specialised bodies at local level including the various organisations involved in local development (see chapter 3).

A wave of institution building began in the 1980s and established a number of specialised single-purpose bodies at both national and local level.[6] As new demands arose, some resulting from EU developments and others from national policy initiatives, a pattern formed whereby central government would establish new bodies rather than increase the capacity of local government to undertake new tasks. This has profoundly affected the environment in which local authorities operate and has to some extent fragmented the system of local government. Nevertheless, local authorities are devising new ways of working with other organisations to promote the common good. This trend too has raised questions over a new role for local government.

A much-quoted term used in the new models of local government is the concept of the 'enabling authority'. This view of local government sees local authorities playing a role in the mobilisation, guidance and stimulation of activities undertaken by various organisations in the locality towards improving the area, whether they be public, private or voluntary bodies (see, for example, Brooke, 1989; Stewart, 1990). Under such arrangements, the fact that a local authority is responsible for a service does not automatically imply that the local authority is involved directly in service provision, employing all the necessary personnel to undertake that service. Some use the term enabling authority in a relatively restricted manner to describe the trend of contracting out services to private enterprises. Others give it a broader meaning:

> The enabling authority can deliver services directly but can operate in many different ways. Services can also be delivered on behalf of the local authority through private contractors, co-operatives, companies formed through management buy-outs, voluntary bodies, or through a joint agency formed with other local authorities or public bodies . . . The enabling authority will regulate, inspect and license activities. It will use its statutory powers to assist initiatives by other organisations. The enabling authority will act as advocate or lobbyist, influencing other organisations.

---

[6] In the nineteenth century, local politicians were elected to replace the 'old magistrates', and Stewart and Davis (1994, p. 27) believe that there is now a danger that elected members are being replaced by 'new magistrates'. Referring to the growth of non-elected quangos (both state-appointed and voluntary) setting local priorities in the UK, they argue that a system of 'new magistrates' has developed and express concerns about a lack of accountability to local people, the method of selection of boards and an absence of proper rules on public standards.

It will advise and guide, providing information and insights into opportunities. A local authority can be a forum for raising issues or can be a stimulus to other organisations to come together (Stewart, 1990, pp. 362–3).

Clearly, local government in Ireland has not been immune to such trends. In fact, the concept of the enabling authority actually describes a phenomenon that is already apparent in local government in Ireland – a fact illustrated by the title of a recent publication on Irish local government, *Local Authorities: More Than Service Providers* (Carroll, 2000). One can argue that, rather than being consciously pursued, the enabling role is a practice that has been labelled retrospectively. Local authorities have increasingly shown themselves to be eager to work in new ways with other organisations in the provision of services. They have also shown themselves to be willing to enable local communities to participate in the management of their own affairs through, for example, tenant participation schemes – providing a far more sophisticated degree of participation than catered for by many of the social services run by central government.

Of course, service delivery will remain a key remit of local government and indeed it will often be the fundamental role on which local government is judged. However, local authorities are willing to engage in partnerships with various other bodies operating at local level. The local authority's prominent position in the county/city development board process is an example of its enabling role – bringing together various stakeholders in the community to reach agreement on the best way forward, to identify local needs and to set out the role of the various partners in meeting those needs and achieving established goals. In order to fulfil this role, the local authority needs to develop its ability to network, influence, negotiate, listen and persuade. It must also look outwards to other organisations and encourage greater consensus in decision making.

From Local Government to Local Governance

Amongst the general public, there is an increasingly widespread feeling of distance from representative bodies at all levels of government. Commentators point to declining turnouts at elections as evidence of the growing malaise that many citizens feel with the democratic process. This phenomenon is by no means unique to Ireland (see, for example, Council of Europe, 2000, p. 10). While it is to some extent understandable that the individual might view the EU or even national government as distant, such a feeling is more serious for local government given that it is the forum where the individual and the community have the greatest scope to influence decisions. The less involvement civil society has with government, the more likely it is that the public will distrust, and become further estranged from, government (see, for example, Boyle and Humphreys, 2001, p. 80).

The demand at community level for active involvement in local affairs is not new (see, for example, Institute of Public Administration, 1971, p. 16) and local authorities have long been engaged in public participation of one sort or another – with extensive experience of say tenant participation in housing and widespread consultation in many service areas. Leach and Wingfield (1999, pp. 49–50) identify four broad types of public participation used by local authorities in the UK:

- traditional: public meetings, question and answer sessions, issuing of consultation documents
- customer oriented: customer satisfaction surveys and opinion polls, complaints procedures, suggestion schemes
- innovative methods to consult citizens: interactive websites, citizens' panels, focus groups and referenda
- innovative methods to encourage citizen deliberation: planning cells, citizens' juries, environmental fora, visioning exercises.

They note that, while the first two categories have been around for some time, the second two are relatively recent phenomena. Local authorities in Ireland and elsewhere in the 1990s established civic and community fora to provide a mechanism for local groups to have an opportunity to contribute to local decision making (some of these participation methods are reviewed from an Irish perspective by Iredale, 1999). Other methods are also being used or considered in other countries, for example the more frequent use of the consultative referendum or provisions allowing a certain number of the electorate to call for a new local election.

In countries such as Germany, the US, Canada and Spain more radical mechanisms have been established to obtain the views of local people to new initiatives. These include planning cells and citizens' juries. Essentially, a cross-section of the local population is chosen from the electoral register to examine and make recommendations on what the best approach to a particular issue might be. The jury, which meets for a specific period, can call witnesses and is supported by experts and officials from the local authority (see, for example, Smith and Wales, 2000). Such an approach is often used to source ideas at the early stages of important planning decisions. The process is designed to supplement other participatory and consultative mechanisms. Thus the jury feeds its recommendations to inform those preparing the project before the statutory consultation process begins.

Such initiatives were inspired by concern over declining turnouts at election time and demands by citizens for a voice between elections. The point is sometimes made that representative democracy needs to be, and to some extent already has been, supplemented by greater participation on the part of citizens or community groups – what some call participative democracy. Democracy is no longer simply about casting a vote at a polling station every five years.

Some have questioned whether there is necessarily a link between local democracy and elected local authorities (National Economic and Social Council, 1996, p. 262). And yet the electoral process and elected representatives will always be the cornerstone of democracy. The fact that local authorities are directly elected marks them out from other local bodies, whether they be organs of the state, sectoral interests, community groups or voluntary associations. *Better Local Government* (Department of the Environment, 1996, p. 14) acknowledges this important distinction. No other body at local level can claim such direct public accountability to the entire local population. This mandate is all too often glossed over (see, for example, National Economic and Social Council, 1994, pp. 131–9) both by other local actors who choose to ignore it and by central government which frequently relegates the local authority to the simple status of an agency delivering services and administering national laws.

Local government, as well as delivering important services to the community, is also supposed to be, as Blair (1991, p. 51) puts it, 'the corporate manifestation of the local community'. While its elected status marks it apart from other local agencies and groups, local government has to involve the community in decision making if it is to fulfil this role. There is a growing acknowledgement that democracy, in addition to direct elections and the important role played by elected members, also means greater involvement for stakeholders in the political process in between elections.

This is a common trend in many countries, and is being applied at various levels of government. At national level in Ireland, employers, trade unions, farmers and the community and voluntary sector have been involved since 1987 in setting priorities in a wide range of public policy areas under the social partnership process. The EU, under proposals contained in the White Paper on European Governance (European Commission, 2001d), is seeking to generate greater involvement on the part of local and regional authorities, and civil society, as well as national governments, in the EU policy process. At local government level in Ireland, a trend has been to involve local stakeholders in policy making and setting priorities through vehicles such as the strategic policy committees and county/city development boards. The need to encourage greater ownership of, and participation in, local decision making is also reflected in a number of documents emanating from the Department of the Environment and Local Government, including:

- *Better Local Government* (1996)
- *Report of the Task Force on the Integration of Local Government and Local Development Systems* (1998e)
- *Preparing the Ground: Guidelines for the Progress from Strategy Groups to County/City Development Boards* (1999a)

- *A Shared Vision for County/City Development Boards: Guidelines on the CDB Strategies for Economic, Social and Cultural Development* (2000a)
- *Towards Sustainable Local Communities: Guidelines on Local Agenda 21* (2001c).

The Local Government Act, 2001 states that local authorities may take such steps as they consider appropriate 'to consult with and promote effective participation by the local community in local government' (section 127) and suggests a number of ways of doing this (see chapter 16 for a discussion of the question of active citizenship and its relationship with local government).

Government policy clearly sees a role for models of both representative and participative democracy:

> Moves towards a more integrated framework at local level need to recognise the democratic legitimacy of local government while building on the opportunity for more effective participation by local communities based on the partnership model. This would recognise the reality that local government is the only institution outside of the Dáil and Presidency elected fully by universal suffrage . . . Local Government must become participative as well as representative (Department of the Environment and Local Government, 1998e, 3.1).

At the heart of initiatives to increase participation and involve others is an acknowledgement that government does not always 'know best'. The benefits of participation mechanisms in local government, according to Lowndes et al. (2001a, p. 211), are: better-informed decision making, improved services, empowering citizens to take part in public life and increasing awareness of the problems facing local government.

The word 'governance' has evolved to describe the trend of governments working with other organisations to achieve common goals. Under the new system of governance, government operates in an environment with increasingly hazy distinctions between public and private, where it often works through voluntary organisations, where some services are contracted out to private companies and where local government acts as a regulator of activities. Increasingly, government and service delivery will rely on networks of organisations and the management of effective relationships and interaction between these organisations.

The word 'governance' has become so fashionable and is so often employed in literature that it can be used in a number of contexts. However, for our purposes, the OECD (1995, p. 158) supplies a helpful definition: 'the term covers public administration and the institutions, methods and instruments of governing. It further incorporates relationships between government and citizen (including business and other citizen groupings) and the role of the state'. Rhodes (1996, p. 666) defines governance as 'self-organizing interorganizational networks' and believes that the trend may 'blur, even dissolve, the distinction between state and civil society'.

Many commentators associate recent changes in local government in the developed world with a movement towards local governance. Andrew and Goldsmith (1998) associate governance with globalisation, EU membership and the Europeanisation of public policy, liberalised flows of capital, as well as with a number of themes touched upon in the preceding section such as contracting out, a focus on customers and the growth of special-purpose agencies at national, regional and local levels. John (2001, pp. 14–17), while broadly accepting these features of local governance, adds a number of others including new ways of involving people in decision making, greater networking between organisations at local level (and at EU and international levels), decentralised bureaucratic structures and a stronger political executive (such as directly elected mayors).

It is clear that local government in Ireland has been affected by these trends. For example, as noted above, local authorities are working with organisations such as voluntary housing bodies or tidy towns committees for the improvement of the local community. Stewart (1995, p. 254) sees working with others as part of the broader reform of local government:

> The authority seeks to provide services not *to* the public, but *for* the public and *with* the public . . . The responsive local authority looks outward to the community it serves rather than looking inward to the organisation. It works not merely through traditional departments, but in decentralised offices and with user organisations, community groups and tenants' cooperatives.

It is often argued that the involvement of voluntary associations and citizens carries advantages: 'participation of citizens in the management of local public services often represents a valuable resource in kind, and serves to develop community spirit and to strengthen solidarity between various groups of citizens' (Council of Europe, 2000, p. 34). In some countries, local authorities are turning over some entire service areas either to private companies or voluntary non-profit organisations. Such a widening of participation in decision making must be accompanied by an agreement on the part of stakeholders to take responsibility for decisions. Power without responsibility – for example a body blaming the local authority for a decision that it approved of – should not be an option.

There are of course problems with public participation. Different interests will not always agree. There are definite tensions between elected members and community groups as to who speaks for the locality. Other difficult areas, as described by Walsh (1998), include access to central government and EU funding, accountability, representation, lack of co-ordination and weak linkages both within local development and between local development and local government. However, the strategic policy committees and county/city development board structures, as well as trying to remedy some of these difficulties, carry an implicit acknowledgement that both representative and participative models have a meaningful role to play in identifying local needs and aspirations and in local policy making.

There can also be a difficulty in ensuring that public participation is balanced. Invitations by local government to engage in participation can lead to a low level of response. While well-organised and well-financed interests can be mobilised to participate, others (typically those in poverty, the young and minority groups) may not be able or inclined to give up time to take part, partly because they believe that they have 'heard it all before'. Some of the barriers to public participation identified in a survey of local authorities and citizens' groupings in England in 1998 include a lack of resources and time and, in many instances, a lack of public interest. Some of the negative effects encountered were the possibility of raising unrealistic expectations, adding to the time and costs of decision making and allowing issues to be captured by groups that are not representative of the wider community (Lowndes et al., 2001a, pp. 212–13; Lowndes et al., 2001b, pp. 447–8).

A mechanism needs to be found to secure balanced participation. Without it, the danger is that the local authority will be listening only to those with the loudest voice (see numerous accounts such as Leach and Wingfield, 1999, p. 56; Davis, 1997, pp. 39–40; Jeffrey, 1997, p. 25; Beetham, 1996, p. 43; Cochrane, 1996, pp. 206–8; or, writing from a community development perspective, Henderson and Salmon, 1999, p. 84). The most vocal may not necessarily be the most representative. It is necessary to ensure that participation provides a mechanism, not just for involving the well organised, but also to prevent further marginalisation of the excluded, as the Tower Hamlets experience referred to above shows. Local authorities, and particularly elected members, need to provide leadership on issues and should ensure that they do not blindly follow the arguments of the loudest protest group in an area. Where appropriate, it is necessary to challenge any misleading assumptions or statements that are made. The job of government is to balance the differing views and pressures in the interests of the whole community.[7]

The other tensions in providing for greater public participation receive much less attention. Enhancing public participation can add to costs, complicate decision making or service provision and takes time – which may be at odds with other goals such as providing an efficient and effective service. When a local authority is embarking on a new urban/village renewal scheme, should it not provide for a relatively lengthy consultation process to allow all local residents to

---

[7] Wilson (1999, p. 256) questions whether more participation really means more democracy, given the very small numbers of people that take an active part in participation mechanisms and interest groups: 'Far more people would prefer to watch sporting events or go to the cinema than attend public meetings about community based issues . . . Permanent mobilisation is not only utopian, it also rules out the possibility that people might be inactive because they have better things to do and are reasonably satisfied. The widespread lack of interest often enables small cliques to dominate public meetings and other forums'.

express their views and to facilitate the local authority in assessing the best way forward? In principle, the answer will be yes. But long periods of consultation/ participation may not be viewed very positively from an effectiveness perspective.

The emergence of performance indicators could add to these tensions. As Leach and Wingfield (1999, p. 55) put it, 'the issue is perhaps best illustrated by the league table of local authority speed of response to planning applications. Quicker response rates may involve inadequate consultation in the interests of speed'. Similarly, Alcock et al. (1996, p. 46) argue that the pressure to show results can lead to short-termism in policy planning. Therefore, marrying the aims of public participation and providing a quality and efficient service will not always be easy.

Thus, problems remain over greater participation in local decision making. One should also note that patterns of civic engagement are not constant. Recent studies on the decline in social and civic engagement in different US states suggest that people's happiness increases with both their own and their state's measure of social capital[8] (Putnam, 2001, p. 50). The OECD finds that there is evidence of declining participation in traditional forms of civic organisations (such as trade unions, churches and women's groups), but that new social movements (including environmental and single issue groups) have grown. It also finds

> . . . some evidence of shifting engagement towards more informal forms of social connection, which tend to be more individualistic and transient but not necessarily more materialistic or selfish. Newer forms of civic participation appear to be narrower and more individualistic, and may be less focused on collective or group interest or purpose (OECD, 2001, pp. 48–9).

Clearly, local government will have to respond to such developments in civic engagement as they may apply in Ireland.

The problems and challenges associated with greater public participation should not be seen as insurmountable. It is necessary to acknowledge them as realities and potential pitfalls, so that they can be apparent to all from the beginning and tackled appropriately. For example, acknowledging that greater public participation is likely to make decision making a more time-consuming

---

[8] The OECD (2001, p. 41) defines social capital as 'networks together with shared norms, values and understandings that facilitate co-operation within or among groups'. Putnam has developed measurements of social capital based on a composite index of factors such as intensity of involvement in community life (for example number of local public meetings attended), public engagement (for example turnout at elections), community volunteering, informal sociability (for example visiting friends) and reported levels of interpersonal trust. Thus, operationally, Putnam (2001, p. 48) views social capital as the degree to which an area is 'either high or low in the number of meetings citizens go to, the level of social trust its citizens have, the degree to which they spend time visiting one another at home, the frequency with which they vote, the frequency with which they do volunteering, and so on'.

process and that it could generate conflict is important. However, part of government's role is to seek out the views of its citizens and to balance different arguments and points of view. Public participation is a means of fulfilling this requirement. As Norton (1991, p. 39) observes:

> . . . perhaps there should be less fear of complicating the process of decision-making by wider involvement with the community and bargaining. Levels of government should be active in seeking closer relationships and a wider basis of support outside themselves if they are to emulate some of the best characteristics of developments on the West European mainland.

Conclusion

The environment in which local government operates is always going to affect and condition what local authorities do on a day-to-day basis. This environment is constantly evolving. While a number of important reforms have been undertaken in local government, particularly during the 1990s, many issues remain to be addressed. The reform process has not made any radical changes to the distribution of functions between central and local government and it would appear that there is to be little movement in this direction in the foreseeable future. The element of financial discretion enjoyed by local government remains limited. Central supervision and controls, for the most part, remain intact. Neither devolution nor local finance appear as priorities on the political, administrative or public agenda.

Local government has had to respond to the challenge of developing working relationships with private sector, community and voluntary organisations and of playing a facilitating or enabling role to promote improvements in different localities. This has necessitated changes in the way local authorities operate and deliver services. Local government is also being challenged to engage in newer, as well as traditional, forms of public participation, whilst acknowledging the mandate of its elected members and retaining its fundamental responsibility to listen to and consider all points of view.

29

The Future

Justin F. Keogan and Mark Callanan

A number of recent developments have affected the nature of local government and are likely to continue to do so in the foreseeable future. Many have been touched on in this publication. There are question marks over the future role of the state and what services the state should provide, which pose questions for local as well as central government.

Central government will continue to play a key role in shaping the way that local government develops. In addition, a wide variety of non-state actors, the private sector, voluntary bodies, as well as single-purpose agencies, are increasingly involved in service delivery and policy making at local level.

Further European integration, and at a broader level globalisation, will pose significant challenges for local government. Indeed, such challenges may question the whole concept of a locality governing itself in an increasingly interdependent world.

The recent reform programme experienced by local government improved its ability to confront such challenges. However, to ensure that the investment in an endeavour such as *Better Local Government* is justified by results, some internal issues remain to be addressed. While the changes brought about should make local government more effective in what it does, remaining challenges include embedding a customer service ethos, developing management capacity and improving approaches to staff recruitment and development.

However, one can detect the beginnings of a phenomenon in Irish local government that the OECD (2000, pp. 65–6) titles 'reform fatigue' – whereby successive reform efforts can make even the most committed to reform overwhelmed and cynical. There can be a restlessness about the change process that gives it a momentum of its own. Central government needs to be selective as to where reform is genuinely needed, rather than pursuing reform for the sake of appearing to be active. When new reforms are proposed, serious consideration must be given to whether enough time has been allocated to past initiatives to determine and evaluate their level of success.

Experience from other countries suggests that the cost of change and the reasoning behind change must be scrutinised before new initiatives are undertaken. Further attempts at reform should avoid the mistakes made in Britain, for example, and place less emphasis on auditing or supervising local government and more on expanding functions, powers, guidance and learning. There is a need to ensure a greater role for local government in feeding into the decisions and policies that affect it. This carries through to both national and European policy and decision making.

One has to ask whether local government is in a position to confront the challenges facing it. If it cannot, future generations may suffer; as the present generation does from challenges that were poorly tackled in the past. To use an example from the area of planning and urbanisation: many people now experience a longer working week than was the case twenty years ago, despite the statutory reduction in the working week, because commuting time adds hours to their working day. The need for leadership at local government level is required in order to avoid short-term planning pressure and to provide for education to broaden the public's understanding of higher urban densities and better quality urban design. It is vital to address these issues to ensure the sustainability of future services at a reasonable cost both economically and socially. The difficulty of this challenge should not be underestimated and yet it is only one of a list of many that includes waste management, social inclusion, service charges and heritage protection.

The public perception of local government in Ireland is not as positive as it might be. To many it is an invisible layer of government. In recent times, the image of local government has been 'badly compromised by allegations of corruption and ongoing tribunals of inquiry' (Fitzgerald, 2003). The perceived relevance of local government to people's daily lives is very poor in comparison to national government or even to the European Union. This manifests itself in a lack of interest and also in a lack of trust.

The perceived lack of relevance comes from two sources. The first is the cultural domination of national politics and government in Irish society and the second is the limited involvement of local government in services such as health, education and policing. The first source partly originates in the importance of the national question of state independence achieved in the early part of the twentieth century. This is despite the fact that for a brief period prior to independence, local government was run by nationalists who endeavoured, with some success, to confine the British establishment's presence in Ireland to Dublin Castle.

The fact that local government is not involved in such vital services as health, education and policing reduces the stake that people feel they have in local government. Therefore, people look to national rather than local government to address their concerns. This situation presents a significant challenge to local government if it is to achieve satisfactory autonomy in providing for the substantive needs of its citizens.

In order that the relationship between central and local government be addressed, a willingness must exist on the part of central government, and a positive perception on the part of the public, with regard to the development of local government's role. Until these are present, local government in Ireland cannot hope to develop as a self-governing organ or to achieve a position at the heart of the civic state. And, in order for any of these changes to occur, local government needs a voice to champion its cause.

To improve how central government relates to local government, clarity needs to be brought to the agency role that local authorities play for central government and the extent to which they respond to a local mandate. More decisions need to be made more rapidly at a local level instead of doing the grand tour of central government departments. The issue is not just one for central government, as the Dublin City Manager, John Fitzgerald, points out, there is 'little sense of responsibility for taking on local issues and running local affairs', there is a 'tendency right through the system to look to someone else to solve problems, particularly where finance is required' (Fitzgerald, 2003).

Two of the central aims of the Strategic Management Initiative (SMI) are to make government departments more strategically rather than operationally focused and to achieve a greater customer or citizen focus in service delivery. These have not yet been realised to the extent that it was hoped. Local government offers a considerable opportunity for central government if it really wishes to deliver on the promise of the SMI. Decision making at local level without deference to central departments would permit central government to disengage from operations and concentrate on policy and strategy. Devolving service groups would achieve greater effectiveness through a synergy of service design and provision, as was recognised by the Devolution Commission (1997). Having the design and delivery of public services closer to the citizen would avoid confusion and achieve more responsive services.

The distribution of service provision across national, regional and local layers of government causes disorder, duplication and ineffectiveness. Many functions of national and regional agencies that operate at a local level in a parallel administration to local government, such as enterprise development, vocational training, tourism, health administration and agricultural services, could be delivered by local government.

For decision making to be made locally, the balances of power between central and local government and between the elected members and the city or county manager need to be examined to ensure proper accountability. Ireland is one of the few European countries where the powers and functions of a local authority manager are decided at national rather than local level. However, it is by no means clear that elected members would welcome extra powers, as extra power brings extra responsibility. In order to address these balance of power issues, a mechanism, such as a performance agreement, needs to be found whereby power can be delegated with accountability to the manager while limiting political interference in operational matters by councillors.

As already stated in previous chapters, finance is the litmus test for any improvement in local government. There may be a lack of political appetite for service charges, but this should not be used as an excuse for avoiding the issue. Imaginative solutions could be found, as they have been in other jurisdictions. Indeed, Ireland could learn from its European counterparts with regard to many of the challenges it faces in everything from service design and delivery to political structures and from financing to citizen involvement.

Boyle and Humphreys (2001) paint the following picture of the expectations citizens will have of Irish public bodies, including local government, in the future and the challenges that these expectations imply.

- Society will continue to become more complex and diverse and people will require an efficient and technologically advanced public service.
- Accountability is already important (as manifested in such issues as value for money, transparency and freedom of information) and it will remain so. The 'tribunal effect' not only impinges on elected politicians, but also affects those working in organisations that spend taxpayers' money. From a broader perspective, accountability also means promoting the involvement of individuals and stakeholders in decision making, both through elections and other means.
- Delivering a quality customer service will be central to citizens' expectations. Principles such as equality, access, timeliness, complaints, appeals, consultation of users, evaluation and better co-ordination must be imbued in all practices and activities.
- The use of information technology (e-government, e-services) will continue to expand, particularly as IT in schools and IT training raise levels of IT literacy.
- The management of cross-cutting issues is another challenge for all public bodies. This will be particularly challenging for issues such as social inclusion (tackling drugs, homelessness, needs of children), protecting the environment and providing for transport infrastructure. These issues are typically not the responsibility of one local organisation, let alone one government department. Their management requires the development of new systems and procedures – which takes time and involves a learning process on the part of all involved. It also requires a focus on working together rather than identifying institutional boundaries.

Stewart (1995, p. 261) suggests a number of ways in which local authorities could act to meet community needs. While some may involve direct service provision, other methods at the disposal of local government include regulation and enforcement, provision of financing, using its influence in the local area as a major employer and purchaser of goods, helping others through the knowledge it possesses, bringing together different organisations/groups and individuals, contracting with organisations for the provision of services, involving users in the running of services and voicing the concerns of its area.

Local government has one attribute that no other local body can have: its members are directly elected by the public (the Dáil and Presidency are the only other offices in the country that can claim the same legitimacy). Therefore, local government must be the focus for direct public accountability at local level, and an active and strengthened local government system should provide the basis for representing local interests and responding to local needs. However, it is also vital that local authorities remain outward looking and continue to work with others. Two prominent defenders of local government have argued that representative democracy is strengthened by participative democracy:

> Representative democracy should be based on the involvement of citizens. Participation does not reduce the need for representative democracy. It makes it more important. The public does not speak with one voice. A local community contains many communities with differing demands, tastes and interests. The role of the elected representative is to seek to reconcile, or if that is impossible, to balance and to judge. This task requires they be informed by citizen participation (Jones and Stewart, 1997, pp. 26–7).

The key role for representative democracy will remain, but can be supplemented by other forms of participation, given the sometimes hard reality that increasingly people no longer see the ballot box as the only source of legitimacy. Accountability comes from an active citizenship as well as from elections.

The challenges for local government for the future will be: first, to remain close to their communities to listen, learn, inform and respond; second, to work in new ways (influencing, enabling and working through others, as well as providing services); and finally to retain a concern for the welfare of its citizens beyond its statutory functions. In all of these respects, Irish local government is far from dealing with a blank sheet.

Appendices

Appendix 1

Text of the European Charter of Local Self-Government

Preamble

The member States of the Council of Europe, signatory hereto,

considering that the aim of the Council of Europe is to achieve a greater unity between its members for the purpose of safeguarding and realising the ideals and principles which are their common heritage

considering that one of the methods by which this aim is to be achieved is through agreements in the administrative field

considering that the local authorities are one of the main foundations of any democratic regime

considering that the right of citizens to participate in the conduct of public affairs is one of the democratic principles that are shared by all member States of the Council of Europe

considering that it is at local level that this right can be most directly exercised

convinced that the existence of local authorities with real responsibilities can provide an administration which is both effective and close to the citizen

aware that the safeguarding and reinforcement of local self-government in the different European countries is an important contribution to the construction of a Europe based on the principles of democracy and the decentralisation of power

asserting that this entails the existence of local authorities endowed with democratically constituted decision-making bodies and possessing a wide degree of autonomy with regard to their responsibilities, the ways and means by which those responsibilities are exercised and the resources required for their fulfilment

have agreed as follows:

Article 1

The Parties undertake to consider themselves bound by the following articles in the manner and to the extent prescribed in Article 12 of this Charter.

Part I

Article 2   Constitutional and legal foundation for local self-government

The principle of local self-government shall be recognised in domestic legislation, and where practicable in the constitution.

Article 3   Concept of local self-government

1. Local self-government denotes the right and the ability of local authorities, within the limits of the law, to regulate and manage a substantial share of public affairs under their own responsibility and in the interests of the local population.

2. This right shall be exercised by councils or assemblies composed of members freely elected by secret ballot on the basis of direct, equal, universal suffrage, and which may possess executive organs responsible to them. This provision shall in no way affect recourse to assemblies of citizens, referendums or any other form of direct citizen participation where it is permitted by statute.

Article 4   Scope of local self-government

1. The basic powers and responsibilities of local authorities shall be prescribed by the constitution or by statute. However, this provision shall not prevent the attribution to local authorities of powers and responsibilities for specific purposes in accordance with the law.

2. Local authorities shall, within the limits of the law, have full discretion to exercise their initiative with regard to any matter which is not excluded from their competence nor assigned to any other authority.

3. Public responsibilities shall generally be exercised, in preference, by those authorities which are closest to the citizen. Allocation of responsibility to another authority should weigh up the extent and nature of the task and requirements of efficiency and economy.

4. Powers given to local authorities shall normally be full and exclusive. They may not be undermined or limited by another, central or regional, authority except as provided for by the law.

5. Where powers are delegated to them by a central or regional authority, local authorities shall, insofar as possible, be allowed discretion in adapting their exercise to local conditions.

6. Local authorities shall be consulted, insofar as possible, in due time and in an appropriate way in the planning and decision-making processes for all matters which concern them directly.

Article 5   Protection of local authority boundaries

Changes in local authority boundaries shall not be made without prior consultation of the local communities concerned, possibly by means of a referendum where this is permitted by statute.

Article 6   Appropriate administrative structures and resources for the tasks of local authorities

1. Without prejudice to more general statutory provisions, local authorities shall be able to determine their own internal administrative structures in order to adapt them to local needs and ensure effective management.

2. The conditions of service of local government employees shall be such as to permit the recruitment of high-quality staff on the basis of merit and competence; to this end adequate training opportunities, remuneration and career prospects shall be provided.

Article 7   Conditions under which responsibilities at local level are exercised

1. The conditions of office of local elected representatives shall provide for free exercise of their functions.

2. They shall allow for appropriate financial compensation for expenses incurred in the exercise of the office in question as well as, where appropriate, compensation for loss of earnings or remuneration for work done and corresponding social welfare protection.

3. Any functions and activities which are deemed incompatible with the holding of local elective office shall be determined by statute or fundamental legal principles.

Article 8   Administrative supervision of local authorities' activities

1. Any administrative supervision of local authorities may only be exercised according to such procedures and in such cases as are provided for by the constitution or by statute.

2. Any administrative supervision of the activities of the local authorities shall normally aim only at ensuring compliance with the law and with constitutional principles. Administrative supervision may however be exercised with regard to expediency by higher-level authorities in respect of tasks the execution of which is delegated to local authorities.

3. Administrative supervision of local authorities shall be exercised in such a way as to ensure that the intervention of the controlling authority is kept in proportion to the importance of the interests which it is intended to protect.

Article 9   Financial resources of local authorities

1. Local authorities shall be entitled, within national economic policy, to adequate financial resources of their own, of which they may dispose freely within the framework of their powers.

2. Local authorities' financial resources shall be commensurate with the responsibilities provided for by the constitution and the law.

3. Part at least of the financial resources of local authorities shall derive from local taxes and charges of which, within the limits of statute, they have the power to determine the rate.

4. The financial systems on which resources available to local authorities are based shall be of a sufficiently diversified and buoyant nature to enable them to keep pace as far as practically possible with the real evolution of the cost of carrying out their tasks.

5. The protection of financially weaker local authorities calls for the institution of financial equalisation procedures or equivalent measures which are designed to correct the effects of the unequal distribution of potential sources of finance and of the financial burden they must support. Such procedures or measures shall not diminish the discretion local authorities may exercise within their own sphere of responsibility.

6. Local authorities shall be consulted, in an appropriate manner, on the way in which redistributed resources are to be allocated to them.

7. As far as possible, grants to local authorities shall not be earmarked for the financing of specific projects. The provision of grants shall not remove the basic freedom of local authorities to exercise policy discretion within their own jurisdiction.

8. For the purpose of borrowing for capital investment, local authorities shall have access to the national capital market within the limits of the law.

Article 10   Local authorities' right to associate

1. Local authorities shall be entitled, in exercising their powers, to co-operate and, within the framework of the law, to form consortia with other local authorities in order to carry out tasks of common interest.

2. The entitlement of local authorities to belong to an association for the protection and promotion of their common interests and to belong to an international association of local authorities shall be recognised in each State.

3. Local authorities shall be entitled, under such conditions as may be provided for by the law, to co-operate with their counterparts in other States.

Article 11 Legal protection of local self-government

Local authorities shall have the right of recourse to a judicial remedy in order to secure free exercise of their powers and respect for such principles of local self-government as are enshrined in the constitution or domestic legislation.

Part II Miscellaneous provisions

Article 12 Undertakings

1. Each Party undertakes to consider itself bound by at least twenty paragraphs of Part I of the Charter, at least ten of which shall be selected from among the following paragraphs:

   - Article 2
   - Article 3, paragraphs 1 and 2
   - Article 4, paragraphs 1, 2 and 4
   - Article 5
   - Article 7, paragraph 1
   - Article 8, paragraph 2
   - Article 9, paragraphs 1, 2 and 3
   - Article 10, paragraph 1
   - Article 11.

2. Each Contracting State, when depositing its instrument of ratification, acceptance or approval, shall notify the Secretary General of the Council of Europe of the paragraphs selected in accordance with the provisions of paragraph 1 of this article.

3. Any Party may, at any later time, notify the Secretary General that it considers itself bound by any paragraphs of this Charter which it has not already accepted under the terms of paragraph 1 of this article. Such undertakings subsequently given shall be deemed to be an integral part of the ratification, acceptance or approval of the Party so notifying, and shall have the same effect as from the first day of the month following the expiration of a period of three months after the date of the receipt of the notification by the Secretary General.

Article 13 Authorities to which the Charter applies

The principles of local self-government contained in the present Charter apply to all the categories of local authorities existing within the territory of the Party. However, each Party may, when depositing its instrument of ratification, acceptance or approval, specify the categories of local or regional authorities to which it intends to confine the scope of the Charter or which it intends to exclude from its scope. It may also include further categories of local or regional authorities within the scope of the Charter by subsequent notification to the Secretary General of the Council of Europe.

Article 14 Provision of information

Each Party shall forward to the Secretary General of the Council of Europe all relevant information concerning legislative provisions and other measures taken by it for the purposes of complying with the terms of this Charter.

Part III

Article 15 Signature, ratification and entry into force

1. This Charter shall be open for signature by the member States of the Council of Europe. It is subject to ratification, acceptance or approval. Instruments of ratification, acceptance or approval shall be deposited with the Secretary General of the Council of Europe.

2. This Charter shall enter into force on the first day of the month following the expiration of a period of three months after the date on which four member States of the Council of Europe have expressed their consent to be bound by the Charter in accordance with the provisions of the preceding paragraph.

3. In respect of any member State which subsequently expresses its consent to be bound by it, the Charter shall enter into force on the first day of the month following the expiration of a period of three months after the date of the deposit of the instrument of ratification, acceptance or approval.

Article 16 Territorial clause

1. Any State may, at the time of signature or when depositing its instrument of ratification, acceptance, approval or accession, specify the territory or territories to which this Charter shall apply.

2. Any State may at any later date, by a declaration addressed to the Secretary General of the Council of Europe, extend the application of this Charter to any other territory specified in the declaration. In respect of such territory the Charter shall enter into force on the first day of the month following the

expiration of a period of three months after the date of receipt of such declaration by the Secretary General.

3.   Any declaration made under the two preceding paragraphs may, in respect of any territory specified in such declaration, be withdrawn by a notification addressed to the Secretary General. The withdrawal shall become effective on the first day of the month following the expiration of a period of six months after the date of receipt of such notification by the Secretary General.

Article 17 Denunciation

1.   Any Party may denounce this Charter at any time after the expiration of a period of five years from the date on which the Charter entered into force for it. Six months' notice shall be given to the Secretary General of the Council of Europe. Such denunciation shall not affect the validity of the Charter in respect of the other Parties provided that at all times there are not less than four such Parties.

2.   Any Party may, in accordance with the provisions set out in the preceding paragraph, denounce any paragraph of Part I of the Charter accepted by it provided that the Party remains bound by the number and type of paragraphs stipulated in Article 12, paragraph 1. Any Party which, upon denouncing a paragraph, no longer meets the requirements of Article 12, paragraph 1, shall be considered as also having denounced the Charter itself.

Article 18 Notifications

The Secretary General of the Council of Europe shall notify the member States of the Council of Europe of:

a.   any signature
b.   the deposit of any instrument of ratification, acceptance or approval
c.   any date of entry into force of this Charter in accordance with Article 15
d.   any notification received in application of the provisions of Article 12, paragraphs 2 and 3
e.   any notification received in application of the provisions of Article 13
f.   any other act, notification or communication relating to this Charter.

In witness whereof the undersigned, being duly authorised thereto, have signed this Charter.

Done at Strasbourg, this 15th day of October 1985, in English and French, both texts being equally authentic, in a single copy which shall be deposited in the archives of the Council of Europe. The Secretary General of the Council of Europe shall transmit certified copies to each member State of the Council of Europe.

Appendix 2

Text of Article 28A of
Bunreacht na hÉireann

Local Government

1   The State recognises the role of local government in providing a forum for the democratic representation of local communities, in exercising and performing at local level powers and functions conferred by law and in promoting by its initiatives the interests of such communities.

2   There shall be such directly elected local authorities as may be determined by law and their powers and functions shall, subject to the provisions of this Constitution, be so determined and shall be exercised and performed in accordance with law.

3   Elections for members of such local authorities shall be held in accordance with law not later than the end of the fifth year after the year in which they were last held.

4   Every citizen who has the right to vote at an election for members of Dáil Éireann and such other persons as may be determined by law shall have the right to vote at an election for members of such of the local authorities referred to in section 2 of this Article as shall be determined by law.

5   Casual vacancies in the membership of local authorities referred to in section 2 of this Article shall be filled in accordance with law.

Appendix 3

County, City, Borough and Town Councils in 2003

Local authority	No. of members
County councils	
Carlow	21
Cavan	25
Clare	32
Cork	48
Donegal	29
Dún Laoghaire-Rathdown	28
Fingal	24
Galway	30
Kerry	27
Kildare	25
Kilkenny	26
Laois	25
Leitrim	22
Limerick	28
Longford	21
Louth	26
Mayo	31
Meath	29
Monaghan	20
North Tipperary	21
Offaly	21
Roscommon	26

Local authority	No. of members
County councils contd.	
Sligo	25
South Dublin	26
South Tipperary	26
Waterford	23
Westmeath	23
Wexford	21
Wicklow	24
City councils	
Cork	31
Dublin	52
Galway	15
Limerick	17
Waterford	15
Borough councils	
Clonmel	12
Drogheda	12
Kilkenny	12
Sligo	12
Wexford	12
Town councils (former urban district councils)	
Arklow	9
Athlone	9
Athy	9
Ballina	9
Ballinasloe	9
Birr	9
Bray	12
Buncrana	9
Bundoran	9
Carlow	9
Carrickmacross	9
Carrick-on-Suir	9
Cashel	9
Castlebar	9
Castleblayney	9
Cavan	9

Local authority	No. of members

Town councils (former urban district councils) contd.

Clonakilty	9
Clones	9
Cobh	9
Dundalk	12
Dungarvan	9
Ennis	9
Enniscorthy	9
Fermoy	9
Kells	9
Killarney	9
Kilrush	9
Kinsale	9
Letterkenny	9
Listowel	9
Longford	9
Macroom	9
Mallow	9
Midleton	9
Monaghan	9
Naas	9
Navan	9
Nenagh	9
New Ross	9
Skibbereen	9
Templemore	9
Thurles	9
Tipperary	9
Tralee	12
Trim	9
Tullamore	9
Westport	9
Wicklow	9
Youghal	9

Town councils (former town commissioners)

Ardee	9
Balbriggan	9
Ballybay	9

Local authority	No. of members
Town councils (former town commissioners) contd.	
Ballyshannon	9
Bandon	9
Bantry	9
Belturbet	9
Boyle	9
Cootehill	9
Droichead Nua	9
Edenderry	9
Gorey	9
Granard	9
Greystones	9
Kilkee	9
Leixlip	9
Lismore	9
Loughrea	9
Mountmellick	9
Muinebheag	9
Mullingar	9
Passage West	9
Portlaoise	9
Shannon	9
Tramore	9
Tuam	9

Appendix 4

Regional Authorities and Regional Assemblies

Regional Authorities

Regional authority	Constituent city/county councils	No. of members*
Border	Cavan, Donegal, Leitrim, Louth, Monaghan and Sligo	37
Dublin	Dublin City, Dún Laoghaire-Rathdown, Fingal and South Dublin	29
Mid-East	Kildare, Meath and Wicklow	21
Midlands	Laois, Longford, Offaly and Westmeath	23
Mid-West	Clare, Limerick City, Limerick County and North Tipperary	26
South-East	Carlow, Kilkenny, South Tipperary, Waterford City, Waterford County and Wexford	35
South-West	Cork City, Cork County and Kerry	23
West	Galway City, Galway County, Mayo and Roscommon	26

* The figures in this column relate to the number of members of each regional authority, as provided for in the relevant Establishment Order (SI No. 394 of 1993). However, in the event of a member of a local authority being appointed to serve on the EU Committee of the Regions (see appendix 10), who is not already a member of the relevant regional authority, he or she is deemed to be a member of the regional authority and its number of members is temporarily increased by one as long as that person remains a member of the EU Committee of the Regions. Thus, at certain times, the number of members of a regional authority may be slightly higher than indicated in this column.

Regional Assemblies

Regional assembly	Constituent city/county councils	No. of members[*]
Border, Midland and Western (BMW)	Cavan, Donegal, Galway City, Galway County, Laois, Leitrim, Longford, Louth, Mayo, Monaghan, Offaly, Roscommon, Sligo and Westmeath	29
Southern and Eastern (S&E)	Carlow, Clare, Cork City, Cork County, Dublin City, Dún Laoghaire-Rathdown, Fingal, Kerry, Kildare, Kilkenny, Limerick City, Limerick County, Meath, North Tipperary, South Dublin, South Tipperary, Waterford City, Waterford County, Wexford and Wicklow	41

Appendix 5

Central Authorities and Ministers Responsible for Local Government, 1838 to 2003

Central authorities	
Poor Law Commissioners (English)	1838–1847
Poor Law Commissioners (Ireland)	1847–1872
Local Government Board for Ireland	1872–1922

Ministers for Local Government	
W. T. Cosgrave	1919–1922
Earnán de Blaghd	1922–1923

Ministers for Local Government and Public Health	
Seamus de Búrca	1923–1927
Richard Mulcahy	1927–1932
Seán T. Ó Ceallaigh	1932–1939
Patrick Ruttledge	1939–1941
Eamon de Valera	1941
Seán McEntee	1941–1948

Ministers for Local Government

Timothy J. Murphy	1948–1949
William Norton	1949
Michael Keyes	1949–1951
Patrick Smith	1951–1954
Patrick O'Donnell	1954–1957
Patrick Smith	1957
Neil T. Blaney	1957–1966
Caoimhghín Ó Beoláin	1966–1970
Robert Molloy	1970–1973
James Tully	1973–1977

Ministers for the Environment

Sylvester Barrett	1977–1980
Ray Burke	1980–1981
Peter Barry	1981–1982
Ray Burke	1982
Dick Spring	1982–1983
Liam Kavanagh	1983–1986
John Boland	1986–1987
Pádraig Flynn	1987–1991
John Wilson	1991
Rory O'Hanlon	1991–1992
Michael Smith	1992–1994
Brendan Howlin	1994–1997

Minister for the Environment and Local Government

Noel Dempsey	1997–2002
Martin Cullen*	2002–

* At the time of writing it was expected that the minister's portfolio would be re-titled 'Minister for the Environment, Heritage and Local Government' during 2003.

Appendix 6

Population of Counties, Cities and Regions, 1996 and 2002

Counties and Cities

	1996	*2002*	*% change in population 1996–2002*
Carlow	41,616	45,845	10.2
Cavan	52,944	56,416	6.6
Clare	94,006	103,333	9.9
Cork City	127,187	123,338	-3.0
Cork County	293,323	324,843	10.7
Donegal	129,994	137,383	5.7
Dublin City	481,854	495,101	2.7
Dún Laoghaire-Rathdown	189,999	191,389	0.7
Fingal	167,683	196,223	17.0
Galway City	57,241	65,774	14.9
Galway County	131,613	143,052	8.7
Kerry	126,130	132,424	5.0
Kildare	134,992	163,995	21.5
Kilkenny	75,336	80,421	6.7
Laois	52,945	58,732	10.9
Leitrim	25,057	25,815	3.0
Limerick City	52,039	54,058	3.9
Limerick County	113,003	121,471	7.5

Counties and Cities contd.

	1996	*2002*	*% change in population 1996–2002*
Longford	30,166	31,127	3.2
Louth	92,166	101,802	10.5
Mayo	111,524	117,428	5.3
Meath	109,732	133,936	22.1
Monaghan	51,313	52,772	2.8
Offaly	59,117	63,702	7.8
Roscommon	51,975	53,803	3.5
Sligo	55,821	58,178	4.2
South Dublin	218,728	239,887	9.7
Tipperary North	58,021	61,068	5.3
Tipperary South	75,514	79,213	4.9
Waterford City	42,540	44,564	4.8
Waterford County	52,140	56,954	9.2
Westmeath	63,314	72,027	13.8
Wexford	104,371	116,543	11.7
Wicklow	102,683	114,719	11.7
State	**3,626,087**	**3,917,336**	**8.0**

Regions

	1996	*2002*	*% change in population 1996–2002*
Border	407,295	432,366	6.2
Dublin	1,058,264	1,122,600	6.1
Mid-East	347,407	412,650	18.8
Midland	205,542	225,588	9.8
Mid-West	317,069	339,930	7.2
South-East	391,517	423,540	8.2
South-West	546,640	580,605	6.2
West	352,353	380,057	7.9
State	**3,626,087**	**3,917,336**	**8.0**

Source: Central Statistics Office

Appendix 7

Turnout in Local Elections by County, City and Town, 1999

Counties and Cities

	Number of seats	Electorate	Total poll	% poll
County councils				
Carlow	21	35,010	17,867	51.03
Cavan	25	44,325	27,818	62.76
Clare	32	9,166	46,311	58.50
Cork	48	239,530	134,869	56.31
Donegal	29	107,697	66,271	61.53
Dún Laoghaire-Rathdown	28	150,679	58,103	38.56
Fingal	24	124,610	48,201	38.68
Galway	30	106,848	61,370	57.44
Kerry	27	103,926	65,078	62.62
Kildare	25	103,868	46,410	43.66
Kilkenny	26	58,582	32,467	55.42
Laois	25	42,417	25,423	59.94
Leitrim	22	22,307	16,419	73.60
Limerick	28	88,941	49,046	55.14
Longford	21	25,143	17,552	69.81
Louth	26	74,947	35,866	47.86
Mayo	31	91,561	57,360	62.65

Counties and Cities contd.

	Number of seats	*Electorate*	*Total poll*	*% poll*
County councils contd.				
Meath	29	96,471	44,384	46.01
Monaghan	20	41,793	27,387	65.53
Offaly	21	47,365	26,686	56.34
Roscommon	26	42,448	28,874	68.02
Sligo	25	44,944	30,753	68.43
South Dublin	26	162,822	54,990	33.77
Tipperary NR	21	48,859	31,555	64.58
Tipperary SR	26	60,319	37,690	62.48
Waterford	23	43,517	25,168	57.83
Westmeath	23	52,609	23,725	54.58
Wexford	21	87,016	43,977	50.54
Wicklow	24	82,276	41,570	50.53
Total	**753**	**2,309,992**	**1,223,190**	**52.95**
City councils				
Cork	31	93,357	43,073	46.14
Dublin	52	360,640	125,892	34.91
Galway	15	39,995	17,681	44.21
Limerick	17	38,279	18,211	47.57
Waterford	15	30,042	13,451	44.77
Total	**130**	**562,313**	**218,308**	**38.75**
Overall total	**883**	**2,872,305**	**1,441,498**	**50.19**

Source: Department of the Environment and Local Government

Borough and Town Councils

	Number of seats	Electorate	Total poll	% poll
Borough councils				
Clonmel	12	11,085	6,586	59.41
Drogheda	12	20,834	9,002	43.21
Kilkenny	12	13,617	6,998	51.39
Sligo	12	14,770	8,857	59.97
Wexford	12	13,360	6,582	49.27
Total	**60**	**73,666**	**38,025**	**51.62**
Town councils (former urban district councils)				
Arklow	9	6,859	4,436	64.67
Athlone	9	10,833	5,557	51.30
Athy	9	4,409	2,481	56.27
Ballina	9	7,215	4,116	57.05
Ballinasloe	9	4,341	2,726	62.80
Birr	9	2,790	1,605	57.53
Bray	12	20,410	8,677	42.51
Buncranna	9	3,790	2,521	66.52
Bundoran	9	1,361	1,095	80.46
Carlow	9	11,355	4,926	43.38
Carrickmacross	9	2,891	2,005	69.35
Carrick-on-Suir	9	4,344	2,637	60.70
Cashel	9	2,214	1,645	74.30
Castlebar	9	7,892	4,007	50.77
Castleblaney	9	2,758	1,849	67.04
Cavan	9	4,693	2,421	51.59
Clonakilty	9	2,667	1,777	66.63
Clones	9	1,787	1,247	69.78
Cobh	9	6,438	4,009	62.27
Dundalk	12	20,138	9,194	45.65
Dungarvan	9	5,766	3,589	62.24
Ennis	9	13,291	5,826	43.83

Borough and Town Councils contd.

	Number of seats	*Electorate*	*Total poll*	*% poll*
Town councils (former urban district councils) contd.				
Enniscorthy	9	5,930	3,439	57.99
Fermoy	9	3,989	2,255	56.53
Kells	9	3,158	1,964	62.19
Killarney	9	7,255	4,737	65.29
Kilrush	9	2,528	1,690	66.85
Kinsale	9	2,363	1,527	64.62
Letterkenny	9	10,005	5,692	56.89
Listowel	9	3,628	2,215	61.05
Longford	9	5,180	3,496	67.49
Macroom	9	2,252	1,608	71.40
Mallow	9	6,332	3,731	58.92
Midleton	9	5,071	2,904	57.27
Monaghan	9	5,194	3,234	62.26
Naas	9	11,877	4,722	39.76
Navan	9	10,465	4,675	44.67
Nenagh	9	5,138	3,402	66.21
New Ross	9	4,992	2,540	50.88
Skibbereen	9	1,865	1,314	70.46
Templemore	9	1,821	1,295	71.11
Thurles	9	6,102	3,513	57.57
Tipperary	9	4,147	2,369	57.13
Tralee	12	16,217	8,737	53.88
Trim	9	4,531	2,150	47.45
Tullamore	9	8,358	4,291	51.34
Westport	9	3,606	2,348	65.11
Wicklow	9	5,944	3,033	51.03
Youghal	9	4,886	3,292	67.38
Total	**450**	**301,076**	**164,519**	**54.64**

Borough and Town Councils contd.

	Number of seats	Electorate	Total poll	% poll
Town councils (former town commissioners)				
Ardee	9	2,651	1,394	52.58
Ballbriggan	9	5,854	2,584	44.14
Ballybay	9	967	741	76.63
Ballyshannon	9	2,344	1,799	76.75
Bandon	9	3,560	2,271	63.79
Bantry	9	2,602	1,782	68.49
Belturbet	9	1,070	784	73.27
Boyle	9	1,944	1,300	66.87
Cootehill	9	1,564	1,056	67.52
Droichead Nua	9	9,561	4,170	43.61
Edenderry	9	2,936	1,686	57.43
Gorey	9	3,348	2,040	60.93
Granard	9	932	640	68.67
Greystones	9	8,434	3,670	43.51
Kilkee	9	1,183	818	69.15
Leixlip	9	9,767	4,240	43.41
Lismore	9	1,048	714	68.13
Loughrea	9	2,971	–	–
Mountmellick	9	2,528	1,519	60.09
Muinebheag	9	1,959	1,384	70.65
Mullingar	9	8,896	4,470	50.25
Passage West	9	3,133	1,764	56.30
Portlaoise	9	6,616	3,623	54.76
Shannon	9	6,433	3,004	46.70
Tramore	9	5,693	2,863	50.29
Tuam	9	4,733	2,886	60.98
Total	**234**	**102,727**	**53,202**	**51.79**
Overall Total	**744**	**477,469**	**255,746**	**53.56**

Source: Department of the Environment and Local Government

Appendix 8

Individual Incomes by Region and County*, 1995 and 2000

	Estimated total income per person (€)	
	1995	2000
Border, Midland and Western	*10,012*	*15,850*
Border	10,180	15,951
Cavan	10,135	15,483
Donegal	9,563	14,485
Leitrim	9,653	15,513
Louth	11,024	17,563
Monaghan	10,247	15,994
Sligo	10,443	17,302
Midlands	9,743	14,974
Laois	9,668	14,245
Longford	9,612	14,508
Offaly	9,165	14,353
Westmeath	10,408	16,386
West	9,973	16,231
Galway	10,616	17,475
Mayo	9,300	14,861
Roscommon	9,101	14,648

	Estimated total income per person (€)	
	1995	*2000*
Southern and Eastern	*11,723*	*19,036*
Dublin	13,260	21,941
Mid-East	10,970	18,239
Kildare	11,326	19,958
Meath	10,794	16,720
Wicklow	10,696	17,602
Mid-West	10,924	17,721
Clare	10,278	16,735
Limerick	11,258	18,631
Tipperary North	11,018	16,731
South-East	10,065	15,770
Carlow	9,501	15,076
Kilkenny	9,946	15,650
Tipperary South	9,548	14,820
Waterford	11,193	17,773
Wexford	9,729	15,004
South-West	10,902	16,950
Cork	11,283	17,637
Kerry	9,627	14,657
State	*11,267*	*18,196*

* The county estimates should be interpreted with caution because the underlying data are not always sufficiently robust – they should be regarded as indicative of relative levels rather than as accurate absolute estimates

Source: Central Statistics Office

Appendix 9

Regional Gross Value Added (GVA), 1995 and 2000

Region	Indices of GVA per person at basic prices (EU = 100)	
	1995	*2000*
Border, Midland and Western	*70.1*	*82.7*
Border	72.4	84.0
Midlands	67.2	80.8
West	69.0	82.3
Southern and Eastern	*101.3*	*126.6*
Dublin	121.9	152.9
Mid-East	83.5	92.7
Dublin plus Mid-East	*112.4*	*137.3*
Mid-West	86.9	106.3
South-East	79.3	92.5
South-West	97.4	134.3
State	*93.0*	*115.0*

Source: Central Statistics Office

Appendix 10

European Associations and Bodies Representing Local and Regional Government

Both the European Union and the Council of Europe have established bodies to represent local and regional interests. In addition to these structures, there are a number of groups of international and pan-European associations of local and regional authorities, with a membership of national associations of local authorities. These bodies also serve to represent the interests of their members vis-à-vis international and European organisations such as the UN and the EU.

The European Union

Within the EU's institutional structures, a formal body to represent local government interests was not established until the 1990s. In 1976, the international local government associations formed a Consultative Committee of Local and Regional Authorities of the Member Countries of the European Community, made up of representatives of the local government national associations within the CEMR and IULA as well as members from regional organisations. During the 1980s, CEMR campaigned to secure the official recognition of this consultative committee by the European Commission in particular. In response, the European Commission in 1988 agreed to form, with the international local government associations, a Consultative Council of Regional and Local Authorities. The commission appoints the members of this council on the joint nomination of CEMR and AER through their respective national memberships (with members being drawn equally between local and regional government).

Committee of the Regions (CoR)

The 1991 Maastricht Treaty on European Union provided for the establishment of a Committee of the Regions (CoR) on a statutory basis to facilitate a more formal representation of local and regional authorities within the EU's institutional framework. This body replaced the consultative council established in 1988.

The committee, which first met in 1994, consists of 222 members, of which nine come from Ireland. The Irish members are nominated by the Minister for the Environment and Local Government. The secretariat to the Irish delegation is based in the Dublin Regional Authority.

The committee must be consulted on draft EU legislation in a number of areas such as Structural Funds and regional policy, employment and social affairs, social exclusion, the environment, transport, culture, education and public health. The CoR can also draw up reports on its own initiative (which it frequently does) on issues of concern, which may or may not exert pressure on the other institutions to act in a particular area. However, the CoR's powers are advisory and the main EU institutions are not bound by its opinions.

The CoR meets in plenary, and also in a number of commissions (sub-committees). Opinions on draft legislation or specific issues are drafted by a single member and first debated in a commission and then referred to the plenary. Opinions from the CoR often reflect local government perspectives on the issue in question.

The CoR also organises seminars and conferences to disseminate its views amongst the wider public.

The Council of Europe

The Council of Europe was formed in 1949 to further the cause of European unity, with Ireland joining as a founding member. The Council of Europe now has some forty-five member countries, including many from Central and Eastern Europe. As a broader and more intergovernmental body, the Council of Europe is an entirely separate organisation to the EU.

In 1985, the Council of Europe agreed the European Charter of Local Self-Government, which outlines the basic principles of local democracy and acts as a benchmark for systems of local government (see appendix 1).

Congress of Local and Regional Authorities of Europe (CLRAE)

In 1957, a body called the European Conference of Local Authorities was established under the aegis of the Council of Europe to represent local interests. It was reconstituted as the Congress of Local and Regional Authorities of Europe (CLRAE) in 1994. The congress, which meets once a year in Strasbourg, is divided into two chambers: the Chamber of Local Authorities and the Chamber of Regions. Four members come from Ireland. The role of CLRAE is to:

- provide a forum where local and regional elected representatives can discuss problems, poll their experiences and express their views to governments
- advise other bodies within the Council of Europe (in particular those

representing national ministers and members of national parliaments) on all aspects of local and regional policy
- co-operate closely with national and international organisations representing local and regional government
- organise hearings and conferences to reach a wider public whose involvement is essential to a working democracy
- prepare regular country-by-country reports on the situation of local and regional democracy in all member countries and monitor how the principles of the European Charter of Local Self-Government are implemented. Based on these reports, a resolution is adopted. A report and resolution on the state of local and regional democracy in Ireland was prepared in 2001.

The congress also has committees covering issues such as culture and education, sustainable development and social cohesion. CLRAE often debates and comments on EU developments that are relevant to its membership and communicates regularly with the EU institutions. CLRAE, since 1989, has played a prominent role in supporting the development of local and regional democracy in Central and Eastern Europe through special programmes.

Other Representative Associations

International Union of Local Authorities (IULA)

The International Union of Local Authorities (IULA) was founded in 1913 in Ghent in Belgium – just before the outbreak of World War I. The organisation was quickly revived in the 1920s, eventually basing itself in The Hague in 1949. IULA's membership is largely based on national associations of local authorities and extends to over one hundred and ten countries worldwide.

Through their membership of national associations, individual local authorities are affiliated to IULA. The strategic aims of the organisation are to:

- develop and maintain a strong, democratic political organisation, managed to high professional standards in a global setting
- be the worldwide advocate and voice of democratic local government
- be the worldwide source of key information and intelligence regarding democratic local government
- be the worldwide source of learning, exchange and capacity-building programmes for democratic local government.

IULA adopted a World Wide Declaration on Local Self-Government in 1993 and is developing a World Charter of Local Self-Government in conjunction with other worldwide local government bodies and the UN. It is also making preparations to merge with a separate body, the United Towns Organisation (UTO/FMCU), to create a new world organisation of local government, to be known as United Cities and Local Governments, which will be established with its seat in Barcelona in 2004.

A co-ordinating body called the World Association of Cities and Local Authorities Coordination (WACLAC) was established in 1996 to co-ordinate the work of different global local government associations (such as IULA, UTO and Metropolis, a network of large cities) vis-à-vis the UN, reflecting the growing recognition within the international community of the work done by local government.

With a large number of associations joining after World War II, a number of regional sections were set up within IULA, for example covering North America, Latin America, Asia and the Pacific, and Africa. CEMR is the European section of IULA.

Council of European Municipalities and Regions (CEMR)

The Council of European Municipalities (CEM) was formed in 1951 in Geneva. Following the establishment of a regional tier of government in various European countries, the organisation's name was changed to the Council of European Municipalities and Regions (CEMR) in 1984. It was originally founded by a group of local government leaders who believed that a united Europe could only be built and rebuilt successfully though local action and the involvement of local communities. Although IULA and CEMR existed separately for some time, in 1990 an agreement was reached whereby CEMR would become the European section of IULA.

Membership of CEMR is largely based on national associations of local government. Some forty-two national associations of local and/or regional authorities from twenty-nine countries are affiliated to CEMR. The main objectives of CEMR are to:

- develop a European spirit among local and regional authorities in order to promote a federation of European states, based on the autonomy of these authorities and their participation in European construction
- contribute to the reflection of local and regional authorities on the EU's main political policies which affect them directly: reform of the institutions, subsidiarity and governance, employment, Charter of Fundamental Rights, equal opportunities
- encourage dialogue, exchange of experience and co-operation between its members, using all means (interregional and intermunicipal co-operation, partnership, twinning)
- disseminate to its members information from the EU institutions
- help make the voice of its members heard by the EU institutions and representative bodies.

CEMR has offices in both Brussels and Paris and undertakes representational activities on behalf of local and regional government throughout Europe. It co-ordinates its members' participation through various committees, made up of representatives from the relevant national associations, dealing with issues as varied as the environment and Local Agenda 21, regional policy and urban policy, employment and social affairs, transport, the information society, public procurement, town twinning and the concerns of female elected members. Through its committee structure, CEMR seeks to influence the EU institutions and contribute to draft EU legislation impacting on local government. In that context, it is regarded by the EU institutions as an important voice for local authorities.

CEMR also organises conferences on European topics and there is a meeting of a general assembly of members every three years. It also organises competitions and awards to reward and acknowledge best practice. At the time of writing, the President of CEMR is the former President of France and President of the Auvergne region, Valéry Giscard d'Estaing.

Assembly of European Regions (AER)

The Assembly of European Regions (AER) was created in 1985 (originally called the Council of European Regions) as a separate organisation to represent the specific interests of regional government. AER includes a number of grouping or regions with a common interest, including:

- Conference of Peripheral Maritime Regions (CPMR)
- Association of Regions of Traditional Industry (RETI)
- European Association of Border Regions (EABR)
- Union of Capital Regions (URCE)
- associations covering the Western, Central and Eastern Alps, the Jura and the Pyrenees mountain regions.

These specialised groupings retain their own identity within the more broadly based AER. AER also has working committees dealing with specific themes, such as: institutional affairs; social cohesion, social services and public health; regional policy; and culture, education, training and youth.

Eurocities

Other local government organisations include Eurocities, a grouping of over one hundred large cities from different European countries. Eurocities, established in 1986, lobbies the EU institutions on issues related to local government and acts as a network to share experience amongst its members, notably through a series of working groups based on particular themes (such as environment, economic development and urban regeneration and the information society). Dublin City Council and Belfast City Council are members of Eurocities.

Appendix 11

NUTS Classification and Administrative Levels within EU Member States in 2003

Note: NUTS stands for 'Nomenclature of Territorial Statistical Units', which is a system used by Eurostat and the European Commission to classify different regions across the EU for Structural Funds purposes. Until 1999, the whole of the Republic of Ireland was designated as a single NUTS II region

Source: adapted from Bollen (2001, p.38)

	NUTS I	n	NUTS II	n	NUTS III	n	NUTS IV	n	NUTS V	n
Belgium	Régions	3	Provincies	11	Arrondissementen	43	–		Gemeenten	589
Denmark	–	1	–	1	Amter	15	–		Kommuner	276
Germany	Länder	16	Regierungsbezirke	40	Kreise	441	–		Gemeinden	16,176
Greece	Groups of development regions	4	Development regions	13	Nomoi	51	Eparchies	150	Demoi/Koinotites	5,921
Spain	Agrupacion de comunidades autonomas	7	Comunidades autonomas + Ceuta y Melilla	17 / 1			Provincias + Ceuta y Melilla	50 / 2	Municipios	8,077
France	Z.E.A.T. + DOM	8 / 1	Régions + DOM	22 / 4	Départements + DOM	96 / 4	–		Communes	36,664
Ireland	–	1	Regional assemblies	2	Regional authorities	8	Counties and cities	34	DEDs/Wards	3,445
Italy	Gruppi di regioni	11	Regioni	20	Provincie	103	–		Communi	8,100
Luxembourg	–	1	–	1	–	1	Cantons	12	Communes	118
Netherlands	Landsdelen	4	Provincies	12	COROP regio's	40	–		Gemeenten	672
Austria	Gruppen von Bundesländern	3	Bundesländer	9	Gruppen von Politischen Bezirken	35	–		Gemeinden	2,351
Portugal	Continente + Regioes autonomas	1 / 2	Comissaoes de coordenaçao regional + Regioes autonomas	5 / 2	Grupos de Concelhos	30	Concelhos – municipios	305	Freguesias	4,208
Finland	Manner – Suomi/Ahvenanmaa	2	Suuralueet	6	Maakunnat	20	Seutukunnat	85	Kunnat	455
Sweden	–	1	Riksomräden	8	Län	21	–		Kommuner	286
UK	–	12	–	37	–	133	–	443	Wards	11,206
(England)	Government office regions	9	Counties (some grouped), inner and outer London	30	Upper tier authorities or groups of lower tier authorities (unitary authorities or districts)	93	Lower tier authorities (districts) or individual unitary authorities	354	Wards	8,512
(Wales)	Country	1	Groups of unitary authorities	2	Groups of unitary authorities	12	Individual unitary authorities	22	Wards	865
(Scotland)	Country	1	Groups of unitary authorities or LECs	4	Groups of unitary authorities or LECs (or parts thereof)	23	Groups of unitary authorities or LECs (or parts thereof)	41	Wards (or parts thereof)	1,247
(N. Ireland)	Country	1	Country	1	Groups of districts	5	Districts	26	Wards	582
EU 15		**78**		**211**		**1,093**		**1,029**		**98,544**

Bibliography

Administration (1976), vol. 24, no. 3, special issue on structures for regional development

Advisory Committee on Management Training (1988), *Managers for Ireland: The Case for the Development of Irish Managers*, Dublin: Government Publications

Advisory Expert Committee on Local Government Reorganisation and Reform (1991), *Local Government Reorganisation and Reform – Report of the Advisory Expert Committee*, Dublin: Government Publications [often referred to as the Barrington Report]

Ahearne, P. (1948), 'The Service State and Local Government', *Christus Rex*, vol. 2, no. 1

Ahern, M. G. (1982), 'The Evolution of the Limerick, Clare and Tipperary (NR) Regional Development Organisation', *The Engineers Journal*, vol. 35, nos 7 and 8

Alcock, P., S. Pearson and G. Craig (1996), 'Citizenship, Empowerment and the Poor – Local Government Anti-Poverty Strategies', *Local Government Policy-Making*, vol. 22, no. 4

Alderfer, H. (1964), *Local Government in Developing Countries*, London: McGraw Hill

Alexander, A. (1979), 'Local Government in Ireland', *Administration*, vol. 27, no. 1

Allen, H. (1974), 'The Relevance of Irish Local Government for Today's Third World', *Administration*, vol. 22, no. 4

Almy, T. A. (1980), 'The Development and Evolution of City/County Management in Ireland. An Illustration of Central–Local Administrative Relationships', *International Journal of Public Administration*, vol. 2, no. 4

An Chomhairle Leabharlanna (1999), *Joining Forces: Delivering Libraries and Information Services in the Information Age,* Dublin: An Chomhairle Leabharlanna/The Library Council

An Foras Forbartha (1972), *Dublin Transportation Study,* Dublin: An Foras Forbartha

An Foras Forbartha (1978), *Public Subventions to Housing in Ireland,* Dublin: An Foras Forbartha

An Foras Forbartha (1980), *Ireland in the Year 2000*, Dublin: An Foras Forbartha

An Foras Forbartha (1981), *Ireland in the Year 2000: Technology and the Infrastructure*, Dublin: An Foras Forbartha

An Foras Forbartha (1982), *Ireland in the Year 2000: Finance; Employment; Organisation*, Dublin: An Foras Forbartha

An Foras Forbartha (1983), *Ireland in the Year 2000: Issues and Perspectives*, Dublin: An Foras Forbartha

An Foras Forbartha (1984a), *Ireland in the Year 2000: Strategies for Employment*, Dublin: An Foras Forbartha

An Foras Forbartha (1984b), *Land Use Budgeting*, Development Plan Manual 7, Dublin: An Foras Forbartha

An Foras Forbartha (1985), *Ireland in the Year 2000: Urbanisation*, Dublin: An Foras Forbartha

Andrew, C. and M. Goldsmith (1998), 'From Local Government to Local Governance – And Beyond?', *International Political Science Review*, vol. 19, no. 2

Arts Council, The (2002), *The Arts Plan 2002–2006*, Dublin: The Arts Council

Asquith, A. and E. O'Halpin (1997), 'The Changing Roles of Irish Local Authority Managers', *Administration*, vol. 45, no. 4

Asquith, A. and E. O'Halpin (1998), 'Power with Responsibility: The Role of the Manager in Irish Local Government', in K. K. Klausen and A. Magnier (eds), *The Anonymous Leader – Appointed CEOs in Western Local Government*, Odense: Odense University Press

Audit Commission (1991), *A Rough Guide to Europe: Local Authorities and the EC*, London: HMSO

Bacon, P. (1998), *An Economic Assessment of Recent House Price Developments: Report Submitted to the Minister for Housing and Urban Renewal*, Dublin: Government Publications [often referred to as the Bacon Report]

Baker, T. J. and L. M. O'Brien (1979), *The Irish Housing System: A Critical Overview*, ESRI Broadsheet Series No. 17, Dublin: Economic and Social Research Institute

Ballymun Regeneration Ltd (1998a), *Integrated Area Plan under the Urban Renewal Scheme: Submitted to the Department of the Environment by Ballymun Regeneration Ltd*, Dublin: Ballymun Regeneration Ltd

Ballymun Regeneration Ltd (1998b), *Masterplan for the New Ballymun*, Dublin: Ballymun Regeneration Ltd

Bannon, M. J. (1979), 'Urban Land', in D. Gillmor (ed.), *Irish Resources and Land Use*, Dublin: Institute of Public Administration

Bannon, M. J. (1983), 'The Changing Context of Developmental Planning', *Administration*, vol. 31, no. 2

Bannon, M. J., K. J. Nowlan, K. Mawhinney and J. Hendry (1989), *Planning – The Irish Experience 1920–1988*, Dublin: Wolfhound Press

Barnes, M. (1975), 'Women in Local Politics', *Administration*, vol. 23, no. 1

Barrett, S. (1982), *Transport Policy in Ireland*, Dublin: IMI

Barrington, T. J. (1965), 'Public Administration, 1927–1936', *Administration*, vol. 13, no. 4

Barrington, T. J. (1971), 'The District, is there a Future for it?', *Administration*, vol. 19, no. 4

Barrington, T. J. (1973), 'Environment and the Quality of Life', *Administration*, vol. 21, no. 4

Barrington, T. J. (1975), *From Big Government to Local Government: The Road to Decentralisation*, Dublin: Institute of Public Administration

Barrington, T. J. (1976), 'Can there be Regional Development in Ireland?', *Administration*, vol. 24, no. 3

Barrington, T. J. (1980), *The Irish Administrative System*, Dublin: Institute of Public Administration

Barrington, T. J. (1985), 'A Ghastly Failure But Will We Learn?', *The Irish Times*, 7 January

Barrington, T. J. (1987a), 'Ireland: The Interplay of Territory and Function', in R. Rhodes and V. Wright (eds), *Tensions in the Territorial Politics of Western Europe*, London: Frank Cass

Barrington, T. J. (1987b), 'Ireland: The Interplay of Territory and Function', *West European Politics*, vol. 10, no. 4

Barrington, T. J. (1991a), 'Local Government in Ireland', in R. Batley and G. Stoker (eds), *Local Government in Europe*, Basingstoke: Macmillan

Barrington, T. J. (1991b), 'Local Government Reform: Problems to Resolve', in J. A. Walsh (ed.), *Local Economic Development and Administrative Reform*, Dublin: Regional Studies Association (Irish Branch)

Barrington, T. J. (1991c), 'The Crisis of Irish Local Government', in J. J. Hesse (ed.), *Local Government and Urban Affairs in International Perspective*, Baden-Baden: Nomos Verlagsgesellschaft

Barrington Report (1991), *Local Government Reorganisation and Reform – Report of the Advisory Expert Committee*, Dublin: Government Publications [Advisory Expert Committee on Local Government Reorganisation and Reform]

Barry, F., J. Bradley and A. Hannan (2001), 'The Single Market, the Structural Funds and Ireland's Recent Economic Growth', *Journal of Common Market Studies*, vol. 39, no. 3

Barry, M. A. (1982), 'Infrastructure in the South East Region', *The Engineers Journal*, vol. 35, no. 5

Batley, R. (1991), 'Comparisons and Lessons', in R. Batley and G. Stoker (eds), *Local Government in Europe*, Basingstoke: Macmillan

Batley, R. and G. Stoker (eds) (1991), *Local Government in Europe – Trends and Developments*, London: Macmillan

Bax, M. (1976), *Harpstrings and Confessions: Machine-Style Politics in the Irish Republic*, Assen/Amsterdam: Van Gorcum

Beetham, D. (1996), 'Theorising Democracy and Local Government', in D. King and G. Stoker (eds), *Rethinking Local Democracy*, London: Macmillan

Beirne, M. (1993), 'Out of the Bearpit', *Fortnight*, May

Bennett, D. (1983), 'Community Control of Crime', *Social Studies*, vol. 7, no. 2

Benoit, P. (1988), 'Allocation of Powers to the Local and Regional Levels of Government in the Member States of the Council of Europe', in Council of Europe, *Local and Regional Authorities in Europe*, Strasbourg: Council of Europe Study Series 42

Better Local Government – A Programme for Change (1996), Dublin: Government Publications [Department of the Environment]

Bewley, V. (1974), *Travelling People*, Dublin: Veritas Publications

Bird, T. H. (1932), 'Municipal Government of the City of Bombay, India', *Public Administration*, vol. x, no. 1 [contains comparative references to Irish system]

Birrell, D. (1993), 'Housing, North and South: A Comparative View', *Administration*, vol. 41, no. 3

Birrell, D. (1999), 'Cross-Border Co-operation between Local Authorities in Ireland', *Local Governance*, vol. 25, no. 2

Birrell, D. and A. S. Murie (1980), *Policy and Government in Northern Ireland: Lessons of Devolution*, Dublin: Gill and Macmillan

Black, R. and D. Collison (1960), *Economic Thought and the Irish Question, 1817–1870*, Cambridge: Cambridge University Press

Blackman, T. (1993), 'Tenant Participation or Community Development', *Administration*, vol. 41, no. 3

Blackwell, J. (1984), 'Housing Finance in Ireland in the 1980s', *Irish Banking Review*, December

Blackwell, J. (1986), *Some Issues in Housing Policy*, Dublin: UCD Resource and Environmental Policy Centre

Blackwell, J. (1988a), *A Review of Housing Policy,* Report No. 87, Dublin: National Economic and Social Council

Blackwell, J. (1988b), 'Paying for Housing: Policy Options', *Administration*, vol. 36, no. 4

Blackwell, J. and E. Brangan (1984), *Survey of the Housing Stock 1980: A Summary Report*, Dublin: An Foras Forbartha

Blackwell, J. and F. Convery (1989), *Replace or Retain: Irish Policies for Buildings Analysed*, Dublin: UCD Resource and Environmental Policy Centre

Blackwell, J. and H. van der Kamp (1987a), *Regional Planning in the 1990s. Review of the Planning System*, Discussion Paper 1, Dublin: An Foras Forbartha

Blackwell, J. and H. van der Kamp (1987b), *The Development Control System: A Survey of the Process*, Dublin: An Foras Forbartha

Blair, P. (1991), 'Trends in Local Autonomy and Democracy: Reflections from a European Perspective', in R. Batley and G. Stoker (eds), *Local Government in Europe – Trends and Developments*, Basingstoke: Macmillan

Blair, T. (1998), *Leading the Way: A New Vision for Local Government*, London: Institute for Public Policy Research

Blaney, N. T. (1965), 'The Role and Function of the Councillor', *Administration*, vol. 13, no. 2

Bollen, F. (2001), *Managing EU Structural Funds: Effective Capacity for Implementation as a Prerequisite*, Maastricht: European Institute of Public Administration

Bollen, F., I. Hartwig and P. Nicolaides (2000), *EU Structural Funds beyond Agenda 2000: Reform and Implications for Current and Future Member States*, Maastricht: European Institute of Public Administration

Bonner, K., M. O'Connell and D. Quigley (2002), *Estimates for Public Services 2003: Report of the Independent Estimates Review Committee to the Minister for Finance*, Dublin: Government Publications

Border, Midland and Western (BMW) Regional Assembly (2000), *Operational Programme for the Border, Midland and Western Region 2000 to 2006*, Ballaghaderreen: BMW Regional Assembly

Border, Midland and Western (BMW) Regional Assembly (2001), *Border, Midland and Western Regional Operational Programme 2000–2006: Programme Complement*, Ballaghaderreen: BMW Regional Assembly

Bowles, G. F. (1960), 'Environmental Sanitation, 4. The Health Inspector in the Field of Environmental Sanitation and Hygiene', *Administration*, vol. 8, no. 2

Boylan, T. A. (1986), 'Industrial Development in the West Region: Achievements and Prospects', *The Engineers Journal*, vol. 39, nos 7 and 8

Boylan, T. A. and M. P. Cuddy (1984), 'Regional Industrial Policy: Performance and Challenge', *Administration*, vol. 32, no. 3

Boyle, D. (1999), *A History of Meath County Council 1899–1999: A Century of Democracy in Meath*, Navan: Meath County Council

Boyle, O. (1987), *Waste Disposal in Ireland: A Discussion of the Major Issues*, Dublin: An Foras Forbartha

Boyle, R. (1986), *Local Government Management at a Time of Change – Trends and Implications*, Dublin: Institute of Public Administration

Boyle, R. (1995), *Towards a New Public Service*, Dublin: Institute of Public Administration

Boyle, R. (2000), *Performance Measurement in Local Government*, CPMR Discussion Paper 15, Dublin: Institute of Public Administration

Boyle, R. and P. C. Humphreys (2001), *A New Change Agenda for the Irish Public Service*, CPMR Discussion Paper 17, Dublin: Institute of Public Administration

Boyle, R., P. C. Humphreys, O. O'Donnell, J. O'Riordan and V. Timonen (2003), *Changing Local Government: A Review of the Local Government Modernisation Programme*, CPMR Research Report 5, Dublin: Institute of Public Administration

Boyle, T. (1999), *Kilkenny County Council: A Century of Local Government*, Kilkenny: Kilkenny County Council

Bradley, J., J. Fitzgerald, I. Kearney, G. E. Boyle, R. Breen, S. Shorthall, J. Durkan, A. Reynold-Feighan and E. O'Malley (1992), *The Role of the Structural Funds: Analysis of Consequences for Ireland in the Context of 1992,* Policy Research Series Paper No. 13, Dublin: Economic and Social Research Institute

Brady Shipman Martin (1984), *Development Strategy to 2004: Galway–Mayo Region*, Dublin: Brady Shipman Martin

Brady Shipman Martin (1986), *Donegal–Leitrim–Sligo: Regional Strategy*, Dublin: Brady Shipman Martin

Brady Shipman Martin (1999), *Strategic Planning Guidelines for the Greater Dublin Area*, Dublin: Brady Shipman Martin

Brady Shipman Martin (2000), *Strategic Planning Guidelines for the Greater Dublin Area, Review and Update*, Dublin: Brady Shipman Martin

Brady Shipman Martin (2001), *Strategic Planning Guidelines for the Greater Dublin Area, Review and Update*, Dublin: Brady Shipman Martin

Brangan, E. and R. Mulvihill (1989), *The Development Control System*, Dublin: Environmental Research Unit, Department of the Environment

Breen, R., D. Hannan, D. Rothman and C. Whelan (1990), *Understanding Contemporary Ireland: State, Class and Development in the Republic of Ireland,* London: Macmillan

Brennan, B. (1988), 'Construction, Maintenance and Management of Public Housing', *Administration*, vol. 36, no. 4

Brennan, L. (2000), *Count, Recount and Petition: Laois County Council Local Elections 1999*, Dublin: Institute of Public Administration

Brennan, S. and C. Murphy (eds) (1986), *Brennan's Key to Local Authorities*, Dublin: Landscape Press

Bresnihan, V. (1990), 'A Community Success Story: Connemara West', *Studies*, vol. 79, no. 313

Bristow, J. A. and A. A. Tait (eds) (1968), *Economic Policy in Ireland*, Dublin: Institute of Public Administration

Bristow, S. L. (1980), 'Women Councillors – An Explanation of the Under-Representation of Women in Local Government', *Local Government Studies*, vol. 6, no. 3

British Standards Institute (1998), *Guide to the Principles of the Conservation of Historic Buildings*, BSI 7913, London: British Standards Institute

Broe, T. F. (1964), 'Revenue and Expenditure of Local Authorities', *Administration*, vol. 12, no. 1

Bromage, A. W. (1954), 'Irish Councilmen at Work', *Administration*, vol. 2, no. 1

Bromage, A. W. (1961), 'The Council–Manager Plan in Ireland', *Administration*, vol. 9, no. 4

Brooke, R. (1989), *Managing the Enabling Authority*, Harlow: Longman

Brooke, S. and M. Norris (2002), *The Housing Management Initiatives Grants Scheme: An Evaluation*, Dublin: The Housing Unit

Buchanan and Partners, Colin (1968), *Regional Studies in Ireland*, Dublin: An Foras Forbartha [often referred to as the Buchanan Report]

Buckland, P. (1981), *A History of Northern Ireland*, Dublin: Gill and Macmillan

Buckley, J., J. Corcoran, J. Devlin, J. Feehily, F. Flanagan, D. McNally, M. O'Grady, J. Walsh and M. Whelan (1999), 'Integrating Performance Management in the Irish Civil Service: Performance and Human Resource Issues', *Administration*, vol. 47, no. 3

Busteed, W. A. (1968/9), 'The Belfast Region: Local Government in Need of Change', *Public Affairs*, vol. 1, no. 3

Busteed, W. A. (1970), 'Reshaping Belfast's Local Government', *Administration*, vol. 18, no. 3

Butlin, R. A. (ed.) (1977), *The Development of the Irish Town*, London: Croom Helm

Byrne, D. P., J. Fitzgerald and K. O'Sullivan (1992), *Local Government in Dublin: A New Beginning – The Reorganisation Report 1992*, Dublin: Fingal, South Dublin and Dún Laoghaire-Rathdown County Councils

Byrne, R. and W. Binchy (1982), *Annual Review of Irish Law*, Dublin: Round Hall Press

Byrne, R. and P. McCutcheon (1986), *The Irish Legal System: Cases and Materials*, Abingdon: Professional Books

Cabot, D. (1986), *EEC Environmental Legislation: A Handbook for Local Authorities*, Dublin: An Foras Forbartha

Cahill, C. (1984), *Handbook of Irish Case Law*, Dublin: Round Hall Press

Callan, T. (1991), *Property Tax: Principles and Policy Options,* Policy Research Series Paper No. 12, Dublin: Economic and Social Research Institute

Callanan, M. (2002a), *Local Government Act 2001*, Dublin: Thomson Round Hall

Callanan, M. (2002b), 'The White Paper on Governance: The Challenge for Central and Local Government', *Administration*, vol. 50, no. 1

Callanan, M. (forthcoming), 'Local and Regional Government', in N. Collins and T. Cradden (eds), *Political Issues in Ireland Today*, Manchester: Manchester University Press

Camblin, G. (1976), 'Structures for Development in Northern Ireland', *Administration*, vol. 24, no. 3

Campbell, M. J. (1968), 'Towards a Classification of Decentralised Systems', *Comparative Local Government*, vol. 2, no. 2

Canny, J. K. (2000), *The Law of Local Government*, Dublin: Round Hall Sweet and Maxwell

Carey, S. (1986), 'Role Perceptions among County Councillors', *Administration*, vol. 34, no. 3

Carmichael, P. (2002), 'Elections: Vote Early and Vote Often', in A. Aughey and D. Morrow (eds), *Northern Ireland Politics,* 2nd edn, Harlow: Longman

Carmichael, P. and C. Knox (1999), 'Towards a New Era? Some Development in Governance in Northern Ireland', *International Review of Administrative Sciences,* vol. 65, no. 1

Carroll, D. (2000), *Local Authorities: More than Service Providers*, Dublin: Institute of Public Administration

Carroll, W. G. and T. Byrne (1999), 'Regional Policy and Ireland', in J. Dooge and R. Barrington (eds), *A Vital National Interest: Ireland in Europe 1973–1998*, Dublin: Institute of Public Administration

Casey, T. A. (1983), 'Local Government (Water Pollution) Act 1977: The Kerry Experience', *The Engineers Journal*, vol. 37, no. 8

Casey, T. J. (1985), 'Discussion on Planning in Local Government: A Civil Engineering Viewpoint', a lecture to the annual conference of the County and City Engineers' Association, Kinsale, 29 October, Dublin: IPA Library Information File

Central Statistics Office (1997), *Census of Population 1996*, Dublin: Government Publications

Central Statistics Office (2000), *That Was Then, This Is Now, Change in Ireland, 1949–1999*, Dublin: Government Publications

Central Statistics Office (2003), *Census 2002: Preliminary Report*, Dublin: Government Publications

Central Statistics Office (various), *Census of Population of Ireland*, Dublin: Government Publications

Chambers of Commerce of Ireland (1999), *CCI Local Government Policy: From Local Administration to Real Local Government*, Dublin: Chambers of Commerce of Ireland

Chambers of Commerce of Ireland (2002), *Commercial Rates: The Forgotten Business Tax*, Dublin: Chambers of Commerce of Ireland

Chanan, G. (1997), *Active Citizenship and Community Involvement – Getting to the Roots*, Dublin: European Foundation

Chandler, J. A. and P. Lawless (1985), *Local Authorities and the Creation of Employment*, Aldershot: Gower

Chartered Institute of Public Finance and Accountancy (1997), *Councillors' Guide to Local Government Finance in Northern Ireland*, Belfast: CIPFA

Chavasse, M. (1961), *Terence Mac Swiney*, Dublin: Clonmore and Reynolds

Chubb, B. (1983), *A Source Book of Irish Government*, Dublin: Institute of Public Administration

Chubb, B. (1992), *The Government and Politics of Ireland*, 3rd edn, London: Longman

Clarke, M. (1998), 'Governance and the European Union: A Discussion of Co-Government', *Local Governance*, vol. 24, no. 1

Coakley, J. (1979), 'Spatial Units and the Reporting of Irish Statistical Data: The Evolution of Regional Divisions', *Administration*, vol. 27, no. 1

Coakley, J. (2001), 'Local Elections and National Politics', in M. E. Daly (ed.), *County and Town: One Hundred Years of Local Government in Ireland*, Dublin: Institute of Public Administration

Coakley, J. and M. Wolohan (1982), 'The Irish Local Elections of June 1979', *Administration*, vol. 30, no. 1

Cochrane, A. (1996), 'From Theories to Practices: Looking for Local Democracy in Britain', in D. King and G. Stoker (eds), *Rethinking Local Democracy*, London: Macmillan

Cole, M. (2002), 'The Role(s) of County Councillors: An Evaluation', *Local Government Studies*, vol. 28, no. 4

Colgan, J. (1991), 'Local Elections: Behind the Results', *Administration*, vol. 39, no. 4

Colivet, M. P. (1954), 'The Housing Board, 1932–1944', *Administration*, vol. 2, no. 3

Colleran, E. (1987), 'Perspectives on Planning', paper presented to the IPA/LAMA conference, Galway, 24/25 April, Dublin: IPA Library Information File

Collins, C. A. (1980), 'Local Political Leadership in England and Ireland', *Administration*, vol. 28, no. 1

Collins, C. A. (1985), 'Clientelism and Careerism in Irish Local Government: The Persecution of Civil Servants Revisited', *Economic and Social Review*, vol. 16, no. 4

Collins, J. (1953a), 'Notes on Local Government, 1. Beginnings of County Administration', *Administration*, vol. 1, no. 1

Collins, J. (1953b), 'Notes on Local Government, 2. Evolution of County Government', *Administration*, vol. 1, no. 2

Collins, J. (1953c), 'Notes on Local Government, 3. Local Government in Municipal Towns', *Administration*, vol. 1, no. 3

Collins, J. (1954a), *Local Government*, Dublin: Institute of Public Administration

Collins, J. (1954b), 'Notes on Local Government, 4. The Genesis of City and County Management', *Administration*, vol. 2, no. 2

Collins, J. (1954c), 'Notes on Local Government, 5. The Use of Committees', *Administration*, vol. 3, no. 1

Collins, N. (1985), 'Councillor/Officer Relations in Irish Local Government: Alternative Models', *Public Administration*, vol. 63, no. 3

Collins, N. (1986), 'The 1985 Local Government Elections in the Republic of Ireland', *Irish Political Studies*, vol. 1

Collins, N. (1987), *Local Government Managers at Work – The City and County Management System of Local Government in the Republic of Ireland*, Dublin: Institute of Public Administration

Collins, N. (1989), 'Regional Planning Structures under the National Development Plan for the Republic of Ireland', *Irish Political Studies*, vol. 4

Collins, N. and R. Haslam (1997), 'Trends Towards Decentralization in the Republic of Ireland', *Regional and Federal Studies*, vol. 7, no. 3

Collins, N. and M. O'Shea (2000), 'The Republic of Ireland', in J. A. Chandler (ed.), *Comparative Public Administration*, London: Routledge

Comhairle na Gaeilge (1971), *Local Government and Development Institutions for the Gaeltacht*, Dublin: Government Publications

Comhar – the National Sustainable Development Partnership (2002), *Principles for Sustainable Development*, Dublin: Comhar – the National Sustainable Development Partnership

Commins, P. (1985), 'Rural Community Development: Approaches and Issues', *Social Studies*, vol. 8, nos 3 and 4

Commission of Inquiry into the Municipal Corporations (1835), *Report*, London: HMSO, parliamentary papers XXIII and XXIV

Commission of the European Communities (1993), *Towards Sustainability: A European Community Programme of Policy and Action in Relation to the Environment and Sustainable Development*, OJ 1993 C138, Luxembourg: Office for Official Publications of the European Communities

Commission on Itinerancy (1963), *Report of the Commission on Itinerancy*, Dublin: Government Publications

Commission on Taxation (1985), *Fourth Report: Special Taxation*, Dublin: Government Publications

Commission on Technical Education (1927), *Report*, Dublin: Government Publications

Commission on the Relief of Sick and Destitute Poor (1927), *Report*, Dublin: Government Publications

Committee of Enquiry (1976), *Local Government Finance*, London: HMSO

Community Workers' Co-operative (2001), *Local Social Partnership Analysis*, Dublin: Community Workers' Co-operative

Computers' Survey Group (1970), *The Use of Computers in Local Government*, Dublin: Government Publications

Conlon, M. N. (1971), 'Local Government – Some Fundamental Principles', *Administration*, vol. 19, no. 4

Connolly, D. (1993), 'Housing in the 1990s', *Administration*, vol. 41, no. 3

Connolly, M. (1986), *Central–Local Government Relations in Northern Ireland. The Future Role and Organisation of Local Government*, Study Paper 5, Birmingham: University of Birmingham Institute of Local Government Studies

Connolly, M. and C. Knox (1988), 'Recent Political Difficulties of Local Government in Northern Ireland', *Policy and Politics,* vol. 16, no. 2

Convery, F. (1974), 'Concepts for Environmental Policy', *Administration*, vol. 22, no. 4

Convery, F. (1982), 'The Physical Environment', *Administration*, vol. 30, nos 2 and 3

Convery, F. (1988), 'Revitalizing Dublin', *Studies*, vol. 77, no. 306

Convery, F. and A. A. Schmid (1983), *Policy Aspects of Land-Use Planning in Ireland*, ESRI Broadsheet Series 22, Dublin: Economic and Social Research Institute

Conway, B. (2001), 'Housing and Social Inclusion: Democratising the Local Authority and the Tenant Community Relationship', *Administration*, vol. 49, no. 3

Cooney, T. A. M. (1982), 'An Aspect of Planning Appeal Procedures', *Irish Jurist*, vol. xvii

Copeland, J. and B. M. Walsh (1975), *Economic Aspects of Local Authority Expenditure and Finance*, Dublin: Economic and Social Research Institute

Corcoran, T. (1988), 'Government Policies Towards Public Housing', *Administration*, vol. 36, no. 4

Coughlan, M. and D. de Buitleir (1996), *Local Government Finance in Ireland*, Dublin: Institute of Public Administration

Council of Europe (1985a), *European Charter of Local Self-Government*, Strasbourg: Council of Europe

Council of Europe (1985b), *Local Authority Accounting in Europe*, Strasbourg: Council of Europe

Council of Europe (1997), *Draft European Charter of Regional Self-Government*, Recommendation 34 1997, Strasbourg: Council of Europe

Council of Europe (2000) – Steering Committee on Local and Regional Democracy (CDLR), *Participation of Citizens in Local Public Life*, Local and Regional Authorities in Europe No. 72, Strasbourg: Council of Europe Publishing

Council of Europe (2001) – Congress of Local and Regional Authorities of Europe, *Recommendation 97 (2001) on Local Democracy in Ireland*, Strasbourg: Council of Europe Publishing

Council of European Municipalities and Regions (CEMR) (1999), *White Paper on Consultation Procedures of Local and Regional Authorities in Europe*, Brussels: CEMR

Council of the European Union (2001), *Joint Report on Social Inclusion – Part I*, Document 15223/01, Brussels: Council of the European Union

County and City Managers' Association (1991), *City and County Management 1929–1990: A Retrospective*, Dublin: Institute of Public Administration

County and County Borough Electoral Area Boundaries Commission (1985), *Report of the Commission*, Dublin: Government Publications

Coyle, C. (1994), 'Administrative Capacity and the Implementation of EU Environmental Policy in Ireland', in S. Baker, K. Milton and S. Yearley (eds), *Protecting the Periphery: Environmental Policy and Peripheral Regions of the European Community*, special issue of *Regional Politics and Policy*, vol. 4, no. 1

Coyle, C. (1996), 'Local and Regional Administrative Structures and Rural Poverty', in C. Curtin, T. Hasse and H. Tovey (eds), *Poverty in Rural Ireland*, Dublin: Oak Tree Press

Coyle, C. (1997), 'European Integration: A Lifeline for Irish Local Authorities', in M. J. F. Goldsmith and K. K. Klausen (eds), *European Integration and Local Government*, Cheltenham: Edward Elgar Publishing

Coyle, C. (2001), 'The European Union and the Development of Local Government in Ireland', in M. E. Daly (ed.), *County and Town: One Hundred Years of Local Government in Ireland*, Dublin: Institute of Public Administration

Coyle, C. and R. Sinnott (1992), 'Regional Elites, Regional 'Powerlessness' and European Regional Policy in Ireland', *Regional Politics and Policy*, vol. 2, nos 1 and 2

Criminal Justice Review Group (2000), *Review of the Criminal Justice System in Northern Ireland*, Belfast: HMSO

Cromien, S. (2000), 'Serving in New Spheres', in R. O'Donnell (ed.), *Europe – The Irish Experience*, Dublin: Institute of European Affairs

Cronin, M. (1923), 'City Administration in Ireland', *Studies*, vol. xii

Crossman, V. (1994), *Local Government in Nineteenth-Century Ireland*, Belfast: Institute of Irish Studies, Queen's University Belfast

Cuddy, M. P. and T. A. Boylan (eds) (1987), *The Future of Regional Policy in the European Communities: Its Implications for Ireland*, Galway: UCG Social Sciences Centre

Cullinane, M. V. (1976), 'Administrative Structures for Regional Development: The Regional Development Authority Viewpoint', *Administration*, vol. 24, no. 3

Curtis, J. A. (2002), 'Advancing Waste Management Beyond Crisis', *Administration*, vol. 50, no. 3

Daemen, H. and L. Schaap (2000), *Citizen and City*, Delft: Eburon

Daly, J. P. (1988), 'Local Authority Waste Water Treatment Plants 1977–1987', *The Engineers Journal*, vol. 41, nos 1 and 2

Daly, M. E. (1997), *The Buffer State: The Historical Roots of the Department of the Environment*, Dublin: Institute of Public Administration

Daly, M. E. (2001), 'The County in Irish History', in M. E. Daly (ed.), *County and Town: One Hundred Years of Local Government in Ireland*, Dublin: Institute of Public Administration

Davies, R. and P. Hall (1978), *Issues in Urban Society*, Harmondsworth: Penguin Books

Davies, R. P. (1974), *Arthur Griffith and Non-Violent Sinn Féin*, Dublin: Anvil Books

Davis, G. (1997), 'Rethinking Policy Making: A New Role for Consultation?', *Administration*, vol. 45, no. 3

Davis, K. (1967), 'The Urbanisation of the Human Population', in *Cities, A Scientific America Book*, Harmondsworth: Penguin

de Buitleir, D. (1974), *Problems of Irish Local Finance*, Dublin: Institute of Public Administration

de Buitleir, D. (1991), 'Local Finance in Ireland – The Options', *Administration*, vol. 39, no. 4

de Buitleir, D. (2001), 'Local Government Finance in Ireland', in M. E. Daly (ed.), *County and Town – One Hundred Years of Local Government in Ireland*, Dublin: Institute of Public Administration

Demmke, C. and M. Unfried (2001), *European Environment Policy: The Administrative Challenge for the Member States*, Maastricht: European Institute of Public Administration

Dempsey, J. R. (1982), 'Administrative Reorganisation in Irish and American Contexts', *Administration*, vol. 30, no. 1

Department for Regional Development (2001), *Shaping our Future – Northern Ireland Regional Development Strategy 2025*, Belfast: Corporate Document Services

Department of Agriculture and Food (1996), *Operational Programme for the Implementation of the EU LEADER II Initiative in Ireland 1994–1999*, Dublin: Government Publications

Department of Agriculture, Food and Forestry (1995), *LEADER II Operating Rules*, Dublin: Department of Agriculture, Food and Forestry

Department of Agriculture, Food and Rural Development (1999), *Ensuring the Future – A Strategy for Rural Development in Ireland, A White Paper on Rural Development*, Dublin: Government Publications

Department of Arts, Culture and the Gaeltacht (1996), *Strengthening the Protection of the Architectural Heritage*, Dublin: Government Publications

Department of Arts, Heritage, Gaeltacht and the Islands (2002a), *Action on Architecture*, Dublin: Government Publications

Department of Arts, Heritage, Gaeltacht and the Islands (2002b), *National Heritage Plan*, Dublin: Government Publications

Department of Arts, Heritage, Gaeltacht and the Islands, Dúchas and Department of the Environment and Local Government (2001), *Architectural Heritage Protection: Guidelines for Planning Authorities* (Draft), Dublin: Government Publications

Department of Local Government (1948), *Housing: A Review of Past Operations and Immediate Requirements,* Dublin: Government Publications

Department of Local Government (annual), *Annual Report*, Dublin: Government Publications

Department of Local Government and Public Health (1925), *First Report (1922–25)*, Dublin: Government Publications

Department of Local Government and Public Health (1927), *Second Report (1925–27)*, Dublin: Government Publications

Department of Local Government and Public Health (1933), *Commission of Enquiry into the Sale of the Cottages and Plots Provided under the Labourers (Ireland) Acts: Final Report*, Dublin: Government Publications

Department of National Heritage (1994), *PPG 15: Planning in the Historic Environment*, London: Department of National Heritage

Department of Social, Community and Family Affairs (2002), *Building an Inclusive Society*, Dublin: Government Publications

Department of the Environment (1985a), *Financing of Housing – Ireland 1985*, Dublin: Department of the Environment

Department of the Environment (1985b), *Policy and Planning Framework for Roads*, Dublin: Government Publications

Department of the Environment (1985c), *The Reform of Local Government*, Dublin: Government Publications

Department of the Environment (1989), *Ireland: Road Development 1989–1993*, Dublin: Department of the Environment

Department of the Environment (1991), *A Plan for Social Housing*, Dublin: Government Publications

Department of the Environment (1993), *Memorandum on the Preparation of a Statement of Policy on Housing Management*, Dublin: Department of the Environment

Department of the Environment (1994), *Operational Programme for Environmental Services, 1994–1999*, Dublin: Department of the Environment

Department of the Environment (1995a), *Local Authorities and Sustainable Development – Guidelines on Local Agenda 21*, Dublin: Government Publications

Department of the Environment (1995b), *Social Housing – The Way Ahead*, Dublin: Department of the Environment

Department of the Environment (1996), *Better Local Government – A Programme for Change*, Dublin: Government Publications

Department of the Environment (annual), *Annual Report*, Dublin: Government Publications

Department of the Environment and Local Government (1997), *Strategic Policy Committees: Guidelines for Establishment and Operation*, Dublin: Government Publications

Department of the Environment and Local Government (1998a), *Branching Out – A New Public Library Service*, Dublin: Government Publications

Department of the Environment and Local Government (1998b), *Changing Our Ways: A Policy Statement on Waste Management by Noel Dempsey, Minister for the Environment and Local Government*, Dublin: Department of the Environment and Local Government

Department of the Environment and Local Government (1998c), *Focus on Strategic Policy Committees – Update March 1998: Guidelines and Seminar Proceedings*, Dublin: Government Publications

Department of the Environment and Local Government (1998d), 'Needs and Resources Study – Development of a Distribution Model', Dublin: Department of the Environment and Local Government, unpublished study

Department of the Environment and Local Government (1998e), *Report of the Task Force on the Integration of Local Government and Local Development Systems*, Dublin: Government Publications

Department of the Environment and Local Government (1998f), *The Road to Safety. Government Strategy for Road Safety 1998–2002*, Dublin: Department of the Environment and Local Government

Department of the Environment and Local Government (1999a), *Preparing the Ground: Guidelines for the Progress from Strategy Groups to County/City Development Boards*, Dublin: Government Publications

Department of the Environment and Local Government (1999b), *Residential Density, Guidelines for Planning Authorities*, Dublin: Government Publications

Department of the Environment and Local Government (1999c), *Strategic Policy Committees:*

Guidelines for Establishment and Operation, Dublin: Department of the Environment and Local Government

Department of the Environment and Local Government (2000a), *A Shared Vision for County/City Development Boards: Guidelines on the CDB Strategies for Economic, Social and Cultural Development*, Dublin: Government Publications

Department of the Environment and Local Government (2000b), 'Circular LG 9/00 – Service Indicators in Local Authorities', Dublin: Department of the Environment and Local Government, unpublished circular to local authorities

Department of the Environment and Local Government (2000c), *Homelessness – An Integrated Strategy*, Dublin: Department of the Environment and Local Government

Department of the Environment and Local Government (2000d), *ICT Vision for Local Government*, Dublin: Department of the Environment and Local Government

Department of the Environment and Local Government (2000e), *Local Elections, 1999*, vols 1 and 2, Dublin: Government Publications

Department of the Environment and Local Government (2000f), *Modernising Government: The Challenge for Local Government*, Dublin: Department of the Environment and Local Government

Department of the Environment and Local Government (2000g), *National Water Study*, Dublin: Department of the Environment and Local Government

Department of the Environment and Local Government (2000h), *Part V of the Planning and Development Act 2000 – Housing Supply: A Model Strategy and Step-by-Step Guide and Guidelines for Planning Authorities*, Dublin: Department of the Environment and Local Government

Department of the Environment and Local Government (2000i), *Service Indicators in Local Authorities*, Dublin: Department of the Environment and Local Government

Department of the Environment and Local Government (2001a), *Economic and Social Infrastructure Operational Programme: Programme Complement*, Dublin: Department of the Environment and Local Government

Department of the Environment and Local Government (2001b), *The National Spatial Strategy: Indications for the Way Ahead, Public Consultation Paper*, Dublin: Government Publications

Department of the Environment and Local Government (2001c), *Towards Sustainable Local Communities: Guidelines on Local Agenda 21*, Dublin: Government Publications

Department of the Environment and Local Government (2002a), *Making Ireland's Development Sustainable: Review, Assessment and Future Action* (National Report for Ireland for the Johannesburg World Summit on Sustainable Development), Dublin: Government Publications

Department of the Environment and Local Government (2002b), *The National Spatial Strategy 2002–2020: People, Places and Potential*, Dublin: Government Publications

Department of the Environment and Local Government (annual), *Annual Housing Statistics Bulletin*, Dublin: Department of the Environment and Local Government

Department of the Environment and Local Government (annual), *Annual Report*, Dublin: Government Publications

Department of the Environment and Local Government (annual), *Local Authority Estimates*, Dublin: Government Publications

Department of the Environment and Local Government (annual), *Returns of Local Taxation*, Dublin: Government Publications

Department of the Environment and Local Government (quarterly), *Environment Bulletin*, Dublin: Department of the Environment and Local Government

Department of the Environment and Local Government (quarterly), *Quarterly Bulletin of Housing Statistics*, Dublin: Government Publications

Department of the Environment and Local Government and Department of Public Enterprise (2001), *New Institutional Arrangements for Land Use and Transport in the Greater Dublin Area: Consultation Paper*, Dublin: Government Publications

Department of the Environment and Local Government and Government of Ireland (2001), *Economic and Social Infrastructure Operational Programme, 2000–2006*, Dublin: Government Publications

Department of the Taoiseach (1997), *A Review of the Efficiency of County Councils' Operations in the Non-National Roads Area*, Dublin: Department of the Taoiseach

Department of Transport (1985), *Transport Policy: A Green Paper*, Dublin: Government Publications

Departmental Committee on the Housing Conditions of the Working Classes in the City of Dublin (1914), *Report*, London: HMSO

Desmond, T. B. (1976), 'Sub-National Organisation of the Functions of Government', *Administration*, vol. 24, no. 3

Devlin Report (1969), *Report of the Public Services Organisation Review Group 1966–1969*, Dublin: Government Publications [Public Services Organisation Review Group]

Devolution Commission (1996), *Interim Report*, Dublin: Government Publications

Devolution Commission (1997), *Second Report*, Dublin: Government Publications

Dinan, D. (1999), *Ever Closer Union: An Introduction to European Integration*, 2nd edn, Basingstoke: Macmillan

Donnelly, B. (1999), *For the Betterment of the People: A History of Wicklow County Council*, Wicklow: Wicklow County Council

Donnelly, P. J. (1985), 'The Council–Manager System', background notes for the regional seminar for newly elected representatives held in Kilkenny, 9 November, Dublin: IPA Library Information File

Donnelly, S. (1992), *Poll Position – An Analysis of the 1991 Local Elections*, Dublin: S. Donnelly

Donnelly, S. (1998), *Elections '97*, Dublin: S. Donnelly

Donnelly, S. (2000), *Elections '99: All Kinds of Everything*, Dublin: S. Donnelly

Donnison, D. (1978), 'Urban Development and Social Policies', *Administration*, vol. 26, no. 1

Donoghue, D. (1985), 'Implications of Removal of Domestic Rates for Local Government', *Seirbhís Phoiblí*, vol. 6, no. 1

Dooge, J. C. I. (1952), 'Local Government from the Councillor's Point of View', *Public Administration*, vol. III

Dooney, S. and J. O'Toole (1998), *Irish Government Today*, Dublin: Gill and Macmillan

Downey, W. K. (1980), 'The Physical Environment and Implications for the Year 2000', in An Foras Forbartha, *Ireland in the Year 2000*, Dublin: An Foras Forbartha

Doyle, G. M. (1983), 'Community Policing', *Social Studies*, vol. 7, no. 2

Drury, B. (1970), 'Regionalism 1. Local Government', *Administration*, vol. 18, no. 3

Dublin City Council (2002), *Lord Mayor's Commission: Review of Future Funding Needs of Dublin City Council 2003–2006*, Dublin: Dublin City Council

Dublin Corporation (1999), *Housing in Dublin: A Strategic Review by the Dublin Local Authorities*, Dublin: Dublin Corporation

Dublin Corporation and Eastern Health Board (2000), *Many Peoples – One City, Policy for Promoting Racial Equality*, Dublin: Dublin Corporation and Eastern Health Board

Dublin Electoral Area Boundary Committee (1998), *Dublin Electoral Area Boundary Committee Report 1998*, Dublin: Government Publications

Dublin Inner City Partnership (1996), *Annual Report: Targeting the Long Term Unemployed*, Dublin: Dublin Corporation

Dublin Regional Authority (1996), *Dublin: A Regional Focus: A Regional Perspective and Strategic Vision for a Leading European Region*, Dublin: Dublin Regional Authority

Dublin Transportation Office (2001), *A Platform for Change. Strategy 2000–2016*, Dublin: Dublin Transportation Office

Duncan, R. (1999), 'Density Through Design', *Urban Design Quarterly*, no. 71

Dunleavy, P. (1981), *The Politics of Mass Housing in Britain 1945–1975: A Study of Corporate Power and Professional Influence on the Welfare State*, Oxford: Clarendon Press

Dunleavy, P. (1991), *Democracy, Bureaucracy and Public Choice*, Hemel Hempstead: Harvester Wheatsheaf

Dunsire, A. (1956), 'Accountability in Local Government', *Administration*, vol. 4, no. 3

Eames, R. (1993), 'Ruthless Loyalists', *Belfast Newsletter*, 18 January

Early, B. (1973), 'Dublin City Commissioners at Work', *Administration*, vol. 21, no. 4

Early, B. (1974), 'Local Government Reorganisation in Denmark – Some Comparisons with Ireland', *Administration*, vol. 22, no. 2

Eckstein, H. and D. Apter (eds) (1963), *Comparative Politics: A Reader*, New York: The Free Press

Edwards, R. D. and T. D Williams (eds) (1962), *The Great Famine: Studies in Irish History, 1845–1852*, Dublin: B & N

Elazar, D. (1996), 'From Statism to Federalism: A Paradigm Shift', *International Political Science Review*, vol. 17

Electoral Area Boundary Committee (1998), *Electoral Area Boundary Committee Report 1998*, Dublin: Government Publications

Environmental Protection Agency (2002), *Report on Water Quality in Ireland 1998–2000*, Dublin: Environmental Protection Agency

Ercole, E., M. Walters and M. Goldsmith (1997), 'Cities, Networks, Euregions, European Offices', in M. J. F. Goldsmith and K. K. Klausen (eds), *European Integration and Local Government*, Cheltenham: Edward Elgar Publishing

ESRI (1999), *National Investment Priorities 2000–2006*, Policy Research Series No. 33, Dublin: Economic and Social Research Institute

ESRI (quarterly), *Quarterly Economic Commentary*, Dublin: Economic and Social Research Institute

European Commission (2000), *Acting Locally for Employment – A Local Dimension for the European Employment Strategy*, COM 2000 196 final, Luxembourg: Office for Official Publications of the European Communities

European Commission (2001a), *Eighteenth Annual Report on Monitoring the Application of Community Law*, COM 2001 309 final, Luxembourg: Office for Official Publications of the European Communities

European Commission (2001b), *Environment 2010: Our Future, Our Choice – The Sixth Environment Action Programme*, COM 2001 31 final, Luxembourg: Office for Official Publications of the European Communities

European Commission (2001c), *Eurobarometer: Public Opinion in the European Union*, Report No. 54, Luxembourg: Office for Official Publications of the European Communities

European Commission (2001d), *European Governance: A White Paper*, COM 2001 428 final, Luxembourg: Office for Official Publications of the European Communities

European Commission (2001e), *A Sustainable Europe for a Better World: A European Union Strategy for Sustainable Development*, COM 2001 264 final, Luxembourg: Office for Official Publications of the European Communities

European Commission (2002), *Nineteenth Annual Report on Monitoring the Application of Community Law*, COM 2002 324 final, Luxembourg: Office for Official Publications of the European Communities

European Commission (2003), *Eurobarometer: Public Opinion in the European Union*, Report No. 58, Luxembourg: Office for Official Publications of the European Communities

European Foundation for the Improvement of Living and Working Conditions (1987), *Taking Action about Long-Term Unemployment in Europe. The Experience of 20 Locally Based Projects*, Luxembourg: Office for Official Publications of the European Communities

European Foundation for the Improvement of Living and Working Conditions (1988), *Locally Based Responses to Long-Term Unemployment*, Luxembourg: Office for Official Publications of the European Communities

European Industrial Relations Review (1986), 'Code of Practice in Security of Employment for Employee Grades in Local Authorities (Agreed November 1985)', *European Industrial Relations Review*, no. 148

European Union (2001), *Housing Statistics in the European Union, 2001,* Finland: Ministry of the Environment

Fahey, T. (1998), 'The Agrarian Dimension of the Irish Welfare State', Dublin: Economic and Social Research Institute, unpublished seminar paper

Fahey, T. (1999), 'Introduction', in T. Fahey (ed.), *Social Housing in Ireland: A Study of Success, Failure and Lessons Learned,* Dublin: Oak Tree Press

Falkiner, C. L. (1904), *Illustrations of Irish History and Topography, Mainly of the Seventeenth Century,* London: Longmans, Green and Company

Farrell Grant Sparks Consulting (2002), *Review of Fire Safety and Fire Services in Ireland: A Report Submitted to the Department of the Environment and Local Government,* Dublin: Government Publications

Farrell, B. (1970), 'The Drafting of the Irish Free State Constitution', *Irish Jurist,* vol. v

Farrell, B. (1971), 'The Drafting of the Irish Free State Constitution', *Irish Jurist,* vol. vi

Feeney, B. P. (1982), *Road Infrastructure Investment,* Dublin: An Foras Forbartha

Feeney, B. P. (1983), 'Paying for Road Damage', in J. Blackwell and F. Convery (eds), *Promise and Performance: Irish Environmental Policies Analysed,* Dublin: UCD Resource and Environmental Policy Centre

Feeney, B. P. and J. Devlin (1987), 'Developing an Economic Evaluation Procedure for Road Investments', *Irish Journal of Environmental Science,* vol. 4, no. 2

Fender, J. and P. A. Watt (2002), 'Should Central Government Seek to Control the Level of Local Authority Expenditures?', *Fiscal Studies,* vol. 23, no. 2

Fennell, D. (1976), 'Organising Connacht for Economic and Social Growth', *Administration,* vol. 24, no. 3

Ferriter, D. (1998), *A History of Limerick County Council 1898–1998,* Limerick: Limerick County Council

Fianna Fáil and Progressive Democrats (1997), *An Action Programme for the Millennium,* Dublin: Fianna Fáil and Progressive Democrats

Fine Gael, The Labour Party and Democratic Left (1994), *A Government of Renewal: A Policy Agreement between Fine Gael, The Labour Party, Democratic Left,* Dublin, December

Fitzgerald, E. (1988), 'A Housing Policy for Today's Needs', *Administration,* vol. 36, no. 4

FitzGerald, J. (2003), 'City Manager Queries Political Role in Rezoning', *The Irish Times,* 29 April

Fitzgerald, R. (1992), 'The 1991 Local Government Elections in the Republic of Ireland', *Irish Political Studies,* vol. 7

Fitzpatrick Associates (1997), *Mid-Term Evaluation: Regional Impact of the Community Support Framework for Ireland 1994–1999,* Dublin: Fitzpatrick Associates

Fitzpatrick, D. (1977), *Politics and Irish Life 1913–1921: Provincial Experience of War and Revolution,* Dublin: Gill and Macmillan

Flannery, M. (1961), 'Local Finance – An Outline', *Administration,* vol. 9, no. 1

Flannery, M. (1962), 'Some Current Road Problems', *Administration,* vol. 10, no. 2

Flannery, M. (1976), *Sanitation, Conservation and Recreation Services in Ireland,* Dublin: Institute of Public Administration

Flannery, M. (1978), 'One Hundred Years of Public Health', *Administration,* vol. 26, no. 4

Flannery, M. (1980), *Building Land Prices,* Birr: The Tribune Printing and Publishing Group

Fleming, T. (1989), 'Infrastructure in the Greater Cork Area in the Nineties', *The Engineers Journal,* vol. 42, nos 6 and 7

Flood, P. and J. Eising (1986), 'Bridge and Road Network Developments in the Galway Area', *The Engineers Journal,* vol. 39, nos 7 and 8

Flynn, T. (1997), 'Pop Concerts and Planning', *Irish Planning and Environmental Law Journal,* vol. 4, no. 4

Foley, D. (1953), 'The Public Libraries', *Administration,* vol. 1, no. 2

Fraser, M. (1996), *John Bull's Other Homes: State Housing and British Policy in Ireland, 1883–1922,* Liverpool: Liverpool University Press

Frazer, E. (1996), 'The Value of Locality', in D. King and G. Stoker (eds), *Rethinking Local Democracy*, London: Macmillan

Gailey, A. (1987), *Ireland and the Death of Kindness: The Experience of Constructive Unionism 1890–1905*, Cork: Cork University Press

Gale, P. (1834), *An Enquiry into the Ancient Corporate System of Ireland and Suggestions for its Immediate Restoration and General Extension*, London: Richard Bentley

Gallagher, M. (1989), 'Local Elections and Electoral Behaviour in the Republic of Ireland', *Irish Political Studies*, vol. 4

Gallagher, M. and L. Komito (1999), 'The Constituency Role of TDs', in J. Coakley and M. Gallagher (eds), *Politics in the Republic of Ireland*, London: Routledge

Galligan, E. (1997), *Irish Planning Law and Procedure*, Dublin: Round Hall Sweet and Maxwell

Gardiner, F. K. (1986), 'Community Security: The Irish Problem', *Economic and Social Review*, vol. 18, no. 1

Garvin, J. (1944), 'Public Assistance', in F. C. King (ed.), *Public Administration in Ireland*, vol. I, Dublin: Civics Institute

Garvin, J. (1949), 'Nature and Extent of Central Controls over Local Government Administration', in F. C. King (ed.), *Public Administration in Ireland*, vol. II, Dublin: Civics Institute

Garvin, J. (1955), 'Public Relations in Local Government', *Administration*, vol. 3, no. 1

Garvin, J. (1963), 'Local Government and its Problems', *Administration*, vol. 11, no. 3

Garvin, J. (1965), 'Problems and Prospects in Local Government', *Administration*, vol. 13, no. 1

Garvin, T. (2001), 'The Dáil Government and Irish Local Democracy 1919–23', in M. E. Daly (ed.), *County and Town – One Hundred Years of Local Government in Ireland*, Dublin: Institute of Public Administration

Gill, J. F. (1965), 'The Role and Function of the Councillor', *Administration*, vol. 13, no. 2

Gillman, D. A. (1986), 'Village Change', *Social Studies*, vol. 9, nos 1 and 2

Golden, T. P. (1977), *Local Authority Accounting in Ireland*, Dublin: Institute of Public Administration

Goldsmith, M. (1993), 'The Europeanisation of Local Government', *Urban Studies*, vol. 30, nos 4 and 5

Goldsmith, M. J. F. and K. K. Klausen (eds) (1997), *European Integration and Local Government*, Cheltenham: Edward Elgar Publishing

Gorham, M. (1961), 'Preserving Ireland', *Administration*, vol. 9, no. 3

Gould, F. and P. Zarkesh (1986), 'Local Government Expenditures and Revenues in Western Democracies 1960–1982', *Local Government Studies*, no. 12

Goulet, D. (1995), *Development Ethics: A Guide to Theory and Practice*, New York: Apex Press

Government of Ireland (1945), *The Powers and Functions of Elected Members and Local Bodies*, Dublin: Government Publications

Government of Ireland (1971), *Local Government Reorganisation – White Paper*, Dublin: Government Publications

Government of Ireland (1972), *Local Finance and Taxation – White Paper*, Dublin: Government Publications

Government of Ireland (1985a), *Reform of Local Government, A Policy Statement*, Dublin: Government Publications

Government of Ireland (1985b), *Serving the Country Better*, Dublin: Government Publications

Government of Ireland (1989), *National Development Plan 1989–1993*, Dublin: Government Publications

Government of Ireland (1991), *Programme for Economic and Social Progress*, Dublin: Government Publications

Government of Ireland (1993), *Ireland: National Development Plan 1994–1999*, Dublin: Government Publications

Government of Ireland (1994), *Operational Programme for Transport, 1994 to 1999*, Dublin: Government Publications

Government of Ireland (1995), *Operational Programme: Local, Urban and Rural Development 1994–1999*, Dublin: Government Publications

Government of Ireland (1996), *Partnership 2000, for Inclusion, Employment and Competitiveness*, Dublin: Government Publications

Government of Ireland (1997a), *National Anti-Poverty Strategy: Sharing in Progress*, Dublin: Government Publications

Government of Ireland (1997b), *Sustainable Development: A Strategy for Ireland*, Dublin: Government Publications

Government of Ireland (2000a), *National Development Plan 2000–2006*, Dublin: Government Publications

Government of Ireland (2000b), *National Development Plan – Economic and Social Infrastructure Operational Programme 2000–2006*, Dublin: Government Publications

Government of Ireland (2000c), *Programme for Prosperity and Fairness*, Dublin: Government Publications

Government of Ireland (2003), *Sustaining Progress*, Dublin: Government Publications

Gray, A. (1997), 'Challenges for Ireland in the Integrated European Union', in F. Ó Muircheartaigh (ed.), *Ireland in the Coming Times – Essays to Celebrate T. K. Whitaker's 80 Years*, Dublin: Institute of Public Administration

Gray, P. (1994), 'Housing in Northern Ireland', *Administration*, vol. 42, no. 3

Greater Dublin Commission of Inquiry (1926), *Report of the Greater Dublin Commission of Inquiry*, Dublin: Government Publications

Greer, J. (2000), 'Local Authority Cross-Border Networks: Lessons in Partnership and North-South Co-operation in Ireland', *Administration,* vol. 48, no. 1

Gribbin, E. (1998), 'Increasing Housing Densities', paper delivered at the Joint RIAI/IPI Conference, *The Housing Crisis, Is Higher Density a Solution?*, Dublin, 19 November

Grist, B. (1983), *Twenty Years of Planning. A Review of the System Since 1963*, Dublin: An Foras Forbartha

Grist, B. (1984), *Preparation of Development Plans. A Survey of the Process*, Dublin: An Foras Forbartha

Grist, B. (1999), *An Introduction to Irish Planning Law*, Dublin: Institute of Public Administration

Grist, B. (2001), 'Local Authorities and the Planning Process', in Mary E. Daly (ed.), *County and Town: One Hundred Years of Local Government in Ireland*, Dublin: Institute of Public Administration

Gwynn, D. (1928), *The Irish Free State 1922–1927*, London: Allen

Habermas, J. (1984), *Theory of Communicative Action*, vol. 1, Boston: Beacon Press

Habermas, J. (1987), *Theory of Communicative Action*, vol. 2, Boston: Beacon Press

Hall, P. A. (1980), 'Recent Developments in Transport Policy', *Administration*, vol. 28, no. 2

Harloe, M. (1995), *The People's Home: Social Rented Housing in Europe and America*, Oxford: Blackwell

Harloff, C. M. (1987), *The Structure of Local Government in Europe: Surveys of 29 Countries*, The Hague: International Union of Local Authorities

Harman, J. F. (1963), 'County Development Teams', *Administration*, vol. 11, no. 4

Hart, I. (1970), 'Public Opinion on Civil Servants and the Role and Power of the Individual in the Local Community', *Administration*, vol. 18, no. 2

Harvey, B. (1995), 'The Use of Legislation to Address a Social Problem: The Example of the Housing Act, 1998', *Administration,* vol. 43, no. 1

Harvey, S. (1989), 'The Local Enterprise Programme: A Strategy', *Irish Business and Administrative Research*, no. 10

Haslam, D. (2001), 'The County Manager', in M. E. Daly (ed.), *County and Town – One Hundred Years of Local Government in Ireland*, Dublin: Institute of Public Administration

Haslam, R. B. and N. Collins (1988), 'Local Government Finance in the Republic of Ireland: The Aftermath of Rates Abolition', in R. Paddison and S. Bailey (eds), *Local Government Finance: International Perspectives*, London: Routledge

Hayes, C. M. (1968), 'Local Government in Northern Ireland', *Léargas*, vol. 13

Hayes, M. N. (1967), 'Some Aspects of Local Government in Northern Ireland', in E. Rhodes (ed.), *Public Administration in Northern Ireland*, Derry: Magee University College

Healey, P. (1997), *Collaborative Planning: Shaping Places in Fragmented Societies*, London: Macmillan

Heanue, K. (1998), 'The Affordability Gap for Housing in Peripheral Rural Areas', *Administration*, vol. 46, no. 2

Hederman O'Brien, M. (1989), 'Whatever Happened to Rates? A Study of Irish Tax Policy on Domestic Dwellings', *Administration*, vol. 37, no. 4

Hegarty, D. A. (1944), 'An Outline of Local Government Administration', in F. C. King (ed.), *Public Administration in Ireland*, vol. I, Dublin: Civics Institute

Heichlinger, A. (1999), *A Regional Representation in Brussels: The Right Idea for Influencing EU Policy Making?*, Maastricht: European Institute of Public Administration

Henderson, P. and H. Salmon (1999), 'A Community Development Perspective on Local Governance', *Local Governance*, vol. 25, no. 2

Hendriks, F. (2001), 'The Netherlands: Reinventing Tradition in Local and Regional Democracy', in J. Loughlin (ed.), *Subnational Democracy in the European Union*, Oxford: Oxford University Press

Hesse, J. J. and L. J. Sharpe (1991), 'Local Government in International Perspective: Some Comparative Observations', in J. J. Hesse (ed.), *Local Government and Urban Affairs in International Perspective*, Baden-Baden: Nomos Verlagsgesellschaft

Hill, D. (1970), *Participating in Local Affairs*, Harmondsworth: Penguin

Hill, D. (1974), *Democratic Theory and Local Government*, London: George Allen and Unwin

HMSO (1970), *Review Body on Local Government in Northern Ireland, 1970*, London: HMSO

Holmes, M. and N. Rees (1995), 'Regions within a Region: The Paradox of the Republic of Ireland', in B. Jones and M. Keating (eds), *The European Union and the Regions*, Oxford: Clarendon Press

Honohan, P. (1997), *EU Structural Funds in Ireland – A Mid-Term Evaluation of the Community Support Framework 1994–99*, Policy Research Series Paper No. 31, Dublin: Economic and Social Research Institute

Horgan, J. J. (1920), 'City Management in America', *Studies*, vol. IX

Horgan, J. J. (1926), 'Local Government Developments at Home and Abroad', *Studies*, vol. XV

Horgan, J. J. (1929), *The Cork City Management Act: Its Origin, Provisions and Application*, Cork: Guy and Co.

Horgan, J. J. (1945), 'Growth of the Irish Manager Plan', *National Municipal Review*, vol. XXXIV, no. 6

Horgan, J. J. (1947), 'The Development of Local Government in Ireland', *Journal of the Social and Statistical Inquiry Society of Ireland*, vol. 17 (1942–47)

Hourihan, K. (1982), 'In-Migration to Irish Cities and Towns, 1970–1971', *Economic and Social Review*, vol. 14, no. 1

Hourihan, K. (1986a), 'Community Policy in Cork: Awareness, Attitudes and Correlates', *Economic and Social Review*, vol. 18, no. 1

Hourihan, K. (1986b), 'The Impact of Urbanisation on Municipal Government in Ireland', *Administration*, vol. 34, no. 2

Housing Management Group (1996), *First Report*, Dublin: Department of the Environment

Housing Management Group (1998), *Second Report*, Dublin: Department of the Environment and Local Government

Housing Welfare Section (1988), *Annual Report*, Dublin: Housing Welfare Section, Dublin Corporation

Howell, P. J. (1997), 'The Dual Staff Structure in Local Authorities', *Administration*, vol. 45, no. 1

Hughes, O. (1961), 'Rates Equalization', *Administration*, vol. 9, no. 2

Hughes, T. J. (1960), 'Administrative Divisions and their Development in Nineteenth-Century Ireland', *University Review*, vol. 3, no. 6

Humes, S. and E. Martin (1969), *The Structure of Local Government: A Comparative Survey of 81 Countries*, The Hague: International Union of Local Authorities

Humphreys, A. J. (1966), *New Dubliners: Urbanisation and the Irish Family*, London: Routledge and Kegan Paul

Hussey, M. O. (1966), 'Sir Richard Griffith – The Man and his Work', *Administration*, vol. 14, no. 4

Inquiry into Housing of Working Classes in the City of Dublin 1939–43 (1944), *Report*, Dublin: Government Publications

Institute of Engineers of Ireland (1984), *Value for Money in Infrastructural Development, Roads, Sanitary Services and Housing*, Dublin: Institute of Engineers of Ireland

Institute of Fiscal Studies (1992), *Rate Support Grant Distribution in Ireland*, Dublin: Government Publications

Institute of Public Administration (1971), *More Local Government: A Programme for Development*, Dublin: Institute of Public Administration

Institute of Public Administration (annual), *Administration Yearbook & Diary*, Dublin: Institute of Public Administration

Institute of Public Administration (quarterly), *Administration*, Dublin: Institute of Public Administration

Institute of Public Administration and Local Authority Members Association (1988), 'Financing Local Government. Is there a Better Way?', conference proceedings, Kilkenny, 8 and 9 April, Dublin: IPA Library Information File

Institute of Public Administration and Local Authority Members Association (1989), 'Financing Development – The Role of the Structural Funds', conference proceedings, Dundalk, 31 March and 1 April, Dublin: IPA Library Information File

Interdepartmental Committee on Local Finance and Taxation (1965), *Valuation for Rating Purposes: First Report of the Interdepartmental Committee on Local Finance and Taxation*, Dublin: Government Publications

Interdepartmental Committee on Local Finance and Taxation (1967), *Exemptions from and Remissions of Rates: Second Report of the Interdepartmental Committee on Local Finance and Taxation*, Dublin: Government Publications

Interdepartmental Committee on Local Finance and Taxation (1968), *Rates and Other Sources of Revenue for Local Authorities: Third Report of the Interdepartmental Committee on Local Finance and Taxation*, Dublin: Government Publications

Interdepartmental Task Force on the Integration of Local Government and Local Development Systems (1998), *Task Force on Integration of Local Government and Local Development Systems Report*, Dublin: Department of the Environment and Local Government

Iredale, R. (1999), 'Public Consultation and Participation in Policy Making', in G. Kiely, A. O'Donnell, P. Kennedy and S. Quin (eds), *Irish Social Policy in Context*, Dublin: UCD Press

Irish Academy of Engineering (2000), *Towards an Island Population of 6 Million, Implications for Spatial Development*, Dublin: Irish Academy of Engineering

Jackson, P. (1984), 'Training Schemes: A Dilemma for Community Work in Ireland', *Community Development Journal*, vol. 19, no. 2

Jeffrey, B. (1997), 'Creating Participatory Structures in Local Government', *Local Government Policy-Making*, vol. 23, no. 4

Jennings, R. (1980), 'Irish Housing Subsidies', *Administration*, vol. 28, no. 4

Jennings, R. (1983), 'Kerry Revisited: Can it Solve the Land Problem?', *Irish Journal of Environmental Science,* vol. 2, no. 2

Jennings, R. (1988), 'Housing Quality and Housing Choice', *Administration*, vol. 36, no. 4

Jennings, R. and B. Grist (1983), 'The Problem with Building Land', *Administration*, vol. 31, no. 3

John, P. (2001), *Local Governance in Western Europe*, London: Sage Publications

Johnson, T. (1944), 'Housing', in F. C. King (ed.), *Public Administration in Ireland*, vol. I, Dublin: Civics Institute

Joint Committee on Building Land (1985), *Report of the Joint Committee on Building Land*, Dublin: Government Publications

Jones, G. and J. Stewart (1985), *The Case for Local Government*, London: George Allen and Unwin

Jones, G. and J. Stewart (1997), 'What We Are Against and What We Are For', in G. Jones (ed.), *The New Local Government Agenda*, Hertfordshire: ICSA Publishing

Jones Hughes, T. (1959), 'The Origin and Growth of Towns in Ireland', *University Review*, vol. 2, no. 7

Joyce, L. and M. Daly (1987), *Towards Local Planning: An Evaluation of the Pilot COMTEC Programme,* Dublin: Institute of Public Administration

Kaim-Caudle, P. R. (1965), *Housing in Ireland: Some Economic Aspects*, Dublin: Economic and Social Research Institute

Kaim-Caudle, P. R. (1974), 'The Economic and Social Cost of Housing', *Administration*, vol. 22, no. 3

Keane, M. J. (1984), 'Accessibility and Urban Growth Rates: Evidence for the Irish Urban System', *Economic and Social Review*, vol. 15, no. 2

Keane, M. J. (1986), 'Using Lotteries to Pay for Roads: A Note of Caution', *Irish Journal of Environmental Science*, vol. 3, no. 2

Keane, R. (1982), *The Law of Local Government in the Republic of Ireland*, Dublin: The Incorporated Law Society of Ireland

Keane, R. (1983), 'Land Use, Compensation and the Community', *Irish Jurist*, vol. XVIII

Keane, R. (1987), 'The Constitution and Public Administration: Accountability and the Public Service, Administrative Law and Planning Law', *Administration*, vol. 35, no. 4

Keating, M. (1998), 'Is there a Regional Level of Government in Europe?', in P. Le Galès and C. Lequesne (eds), *Regions in Europe*, London: Routledge

Keating, M. (1999), *The Politics of Modern Europe*, 2nd edn, Cheltenham: Edward Elgar Publishing

Keating, M. and J. Loughlin (eds) (1997), *The Political Economy of Regionalism*, London: Frank Cass

Keating, S. (1976), 'Administrative Structures for Regional Development: The Local Authority Viewpoint', *Administration*, vol. 24, no. 3

Keating, S. (1987), 'Development Plans', paper presented to the IPA/LAMA annual conference, Galway, 24/25 April, Dublin: IPA Library Information File

Keegan, O. P. (1993), 'Social Housing: The Role of Housing Authorities – The View of the Lord Mayor's Commission on Housing', *Administration*, vol. 41, no. 3

Kelly, J. M. (1967), 'Local Authority Contracts, Tenders and Mandamus', *The Irish Jurist*, vol. II

Kelly, J. M. (1971), 'Judicial Review of Administrative Action: New Irish Trends', *The Irish Jurist*, vol. VI [deals with the case of Listowel Urban District Council *v.* McDonagh, a Traveller]

Kelly, P. J. (1985), 'The Role of the Councillor as Seen through the Eyes of a Councillor', address given at the LAMA conference for newly elected councillors, Ennis, 16 November, Dublin: IPA Library Information File

Kelly, V. (1987), 'Focus on Clients: A Reappraisal of the Effectiveness of TDs' Interventions', *Administration*, vol. 35, no. 2

Kenny, L. (ed.) (1999), *From Ballot Box to Council Chamber: A Guide to Ireland's County and Town Councillors*, Dublin: Institute of Public Administration

Keogan, J. F. and D. McKevitt (1999), 'Another Set of Strategy Statements: What is the Evidence of Implementation?', *Administration*, vol. 47, no. 1

Keogh, C. A. (1936), *Public Library Provision in the Irish Free State*, Athlone: Athlone Printing Works

Killen, J. (1979), 'Urban Transportation Problems and Issues in Dublin', *Administration*, vol. 27, no. 2

Knox, C. (1990), 'Sinn Féin and Local Elections – The Government's Response in Northern Ireland', *Parliamentary Affairs*, vol. 43, no. 4

Knox, C. (1996), 'The Emergence of Power Sharing in Northern Ireland: Lessons from Local Government', *The Journal of Conflict Studies*, vol. XVI, no. 1

Knox, C. (1998a), 'The European Model of Service Delivery: A Partnership Approach in Northern Ireland', *Public Administration and Development*, vol. 18, no. 1

Knox, C. (1998b), 'Local Government in Northern Ireland: Emerging from the Bearpit of Sectarianism?', *Local Government Studies*, vol. 24, no. 3

Komito, L. (1989), 'Voters, Politicians and Clientelism: A Dublin Survey', *Administration*, vol. 37, no. 2

KPMG (1996), *The Financing of Local Government in Ireland*, report commissioned by the Department of the Environment, Dublin: Government Publications

Labour Party, The (2000), *Visions of Ireland, Towards a National Spatial Plan 2000–2015*, Dublin: The Labour Party

Laffan, B. (1991), 'Government and Administration', in P. Keatinge (ed.), *Ireland and EC Membership Evaluated*, London: Pinter Publishers

Laffan, B. (1996), 'Ireland: A Region Without Regions – The Odd Man Out?', in L. Hooghe (ed.), *Cohesion Policy and European Integration: Building Multi-Level Governance*, Oxford: Oxford University Press

Laffan, B. (1999), 'The European Union and Ireland', in N. Collins (ed.), *Political Issues in Ireland Today*, Manchester: Manchester University Press

Laffan, B. (2000), 'Rapid Adaptation and Light Coordination', in R. O'Donnell (ed.), *Europe – The Irish Experience*, Dublin: Institute of European Affairs

Laffan, B. (2001), *Organising for a Changing Europe: Irish Central Government and the European Union*, Dublin: The Policy Institute

Laffan, B. and D. Payne (2001), *Creating Living Institutions – EU Cross-Border Cooperation after the Good Friday Agreement*, a report for the Centre for Cross Border Studies, Dublin: Institute for British–Irish Studies, UCD

LANPAG: Local Authority National Partnership Advisory Group (2002), *Deepening Partnership in Local Government*, strategic plan for 2003 to 2005, Dublin: LANPAG

Lawlor, J. (1996), 'The Use of Economic Instruments for Environmental Services in Irish Local Authorities', *Administration*, vol. 44, no. 1

Le Galès, P. (1998), 'Conclusion – Government and Governance of Regions: Structural Weaknesses and New Mobilisations', in P. Le Galès and C. Lequesne (eds), *Regions in Europe*, London: Routledge

Leach, S. and D. Wilson (2002), 'Rethinking Local Political Leadership', *Public Administration*, vol. 80, no. 4

Leach, S. and M. Wingfield (1999), 'Public Participation and the Democratic Renewal Agenda: Prioritisation or Marginalisation?', *Local Government Studies*, vol. 25, no. 4

Lee, J. (1993), 'Centralisation and Community', in M. R. O'Connell (ed.), *People Power: Proceedings of the Third Annual Daniel O'Connell Workshop*, Dublin: Institute of Public Administration on behalf of Daniel O'Connell Association Ltd

Leech, B., D. Cabot and S. Smyth (1985), *Job Creation Potential in Ireland Arising from Community and National Environmental Legislation*, 3 vols, Dublin: An Foras Forbartha

Library Association of Ireland (1999), *Public Libraries 2000: National Network–Local Service: Standards for the Public Library Services in the Republic of Ireland*, Dublin: Library Association of Ireland

Lichfield and Associates, Nathaniel (1965), *Limerick Regional Plan: Interim Report on the Economic, Social and Technical Problems of the Planning of the Limerick City–South Clare–Shannon Industrial Estate Complex*, Dublin: Government Publications

Local Authority Members Association (1985), 'Councillor/Manager Relations', paper presented at the LAMA conference for newly elected councillors, County Clare, 16 November, Dublin: IPA Library Information File

Local Authority News, Dublin: Nestron
Local Authority Times, Dublin: Institute of Public Administration
Local Government and Public Services Union (1972), 'Report to Minister for Local Government on: McKinsey Report', *Local and Public Forum*, vol. 3, no. 4
Local Government and Taxation in United Kingdom (1882), London: Cobden Club Essays; part VI, which relates to Ireland, is the work of Richard O'Shaughnessy, MP
Local Government (Dublin) Tribunal (1938), *Report*, Dublin: Government Publications
Local Government Reorganisation Commission (1996), *Towards Cohesive Local Government – Town and County: Report of the Reorganisation Commission*, Dublin: Government Publications
Local Government Staff Commission (1993), *The Councillor's Guide to Local Government in Northern Ireland*, Belfast: Local Government Training Group
Long, B. (1999), *Tipperary S.R. County Council 1899–1999 – A Century of Local Democracy*, Clonmel: Tipperary South Riding County Council
Lord Mayor's Commission on Housing (1993), *Report of the Lord Mayor's Commission on Housing*, Dublin: Dublin Corporation
Loughlin, J. (2001), *Subnational Democracy in the European Union*, Oxford: Oxford University Press
Loughlin, J. and B. G. Peters (1997), 'State Traditions, Administrative Reform and Regionalisation', in M. Keating and J. Loughlin (eds), *The Political Economy of Regionalisation*, London: Frank Cass
Loughran, G. F. (1965), 'The Problem of Local Government in Northern Ireland', *Administration*, vol. 13, no. 1
Lowndes, V., L. Pratchett and G. Stoker (2001a), 'Trends in Public Participation: Part 1 – Local Government Perspectives', *Public Administration*, vol. 79, no. 1
Lowndes, V., L. Pratchett and G. Stoker (2001b), 'Trends in Public Participation: Part 2 – Citizens' Perspectives', *Public Administration*, vol. 79, no. 2
Lucey, M. (1964), 'Rateable Valuation in Ireland', *Administration*, vol. 12, no. 1
Lucy, J. (1985), 'Planning in the Local Authority Service – The Engineering Involvement', a lecture to the annual conference of the County and City Engineers Association, Kinsale, 29 October, Dublin: IPA Library Information File
Lynch, M. (1988), 'Environmental Impacts of Planning Legislation', *The Environmentalist*, vol. II, no. I
Mac Cadáin, P. S. (1961), 'Internal Auditing in Local Authorities', *Administration*, vol. 9, no. 4
Mac Craith, S. (1967), 'Early Irish Local Government 1921–1927', *The Clonmel Nationalist*
Mac Greil, M. (1987), 'Housing: A Community Service and a Social Responsibility', *Social Studies*, vol. 9, nos 3 and 4
Mackenzie, W. J. M. (1961), *Theories of Local Government*, London: School of Economics and Political Science
Mac Manus, F. (ed.) (1967), *The Years of the Great Test 1926–1937*, Dublin: Mercier Press
Mac Niocaill, G. (1964), *Na Buirgéisi*, 2 vols, Dublin: Cló Morainn
Madden T., F. Griffin and T. Kelleher (1996), 'Social Work with Travellers in a Local Authority: The Dublin Corporation Experience', *Irish Social Worker*, vol. 14, no. 2
Maguire, B. (1999), *Irish Environmental Legislation,* Dublin: Round Hall Sweet and Maxwell
Malpass, P. and A. Murie (1999), *Housing Policy and Practice,* 5th edn, Basingstoke: Macmillan.
Manning, M. (1978), 'Women in Irish National and Local Politics 1922–27', in M. McCurtain and D. O'Corrain (eds), *Women in Irish Society: The Historical Dimension*, Dublin: Arlen House
Mansergh, N. (1934), *The Irish Free State, Its Government and Politics*, London: Macmillan
Mansergh, N. (1982), 'The Taxation of Development Land', *Administration,* vol. 30, no. 4
Marks, G., L. Hooghe and K. Blank (1996a), 'European Integration from the 1980s: State-Centric v. Multi-Level Governance', *Journal of Common Market Studies*, vol. 34, no. 3

Marks, G., F. Nielsen, L. Ray and J. E. Salk (1996b), 'Competencies, Cracks and Conflicts: Regional Mobilization in the European Union', *Comparative Political Studies*, vol. 29, no. 2

Marshall, A. H. (1967), *Local Government Administration Abroad*, vol. IV, London: HMSO

Marshall, A. H. (1969), *Local Government Finance*, The Hague: International Union of Local Authorities

Mawhinney, K. (1986), 'Local Authorities and Historical and Architectural Conservation', *Irish Journal of Environmental Science,* vol. 4, no. 1

McCarron, E. G. (1983), 'Planning for Living (in the Dublin Area)', *The Engineers Journal*, vol. 37

McCarthy, C. (2001), 'The Housing Situation Today: Social, Economic and Demographic Aspects', paper delivered at the *National Housing Conference: New Housing Challenges – Responding to the Changes*, Department of the Environment and Local Government and RIAI, Galway

McCashin, A. and M. Morrissey (1985), 'Housing Policy: North and South', *Administration*, vol. 33, no. 3

McColgan, J. (1983), *British Policy and the Irish Administration 1920–22*, London: Allen and Unwin

McDonagh, M. (1993), 'The Plan for Social Housing and the 1992 Housing Act: New Thinking on Social Housing?', *Administration*, vol. 41, no. 3

McDonald, F. (1990), 'Local Government: Does it Exist in Ireland?', [a two-part series of articles 'Where the Mandarins of Merrion St Rule' and 'Councils Powerless as Power is Whittled Away'], *The Irish Times*, 26 and 27 April

McDonald, F. (2000), *The Construction of Dublin*, Kinsale: Gandon Editions

McDowell, M. (1988), *Financing Local Authorities: The Questionable Viability of a Local Property Tax*, Economic Research Policy Paper 2, Dublin: UCD Centre for Economic Research

McDowell, R. B. (1964), *The Irish Administration 1801–1914*, London: Routledge and Kegan Paul

McElligott, C. C. (1955), 'The Problem of Revaluation', *Administration*, vol. 3, no. 1

McGilvray, J. (1962), 'The Economics of Roads', *Administration*, vol. 10, no. 2

McKay, P. (1987), 'Last Chance for Cork' [for the car ferry link between Cork and Wales], *Business and Finance,* 14 May

McKinsey and Company Incorporated (1971), *Strengthening the Local Government Service*, report prepared for the Minister for Local Government, Dublin: Government Publications

McManus, M. (1993), 'The Republic of Ireland', in J. A. Chandler (ed.), *Local Government in Liberal Democracies – An Introductory Survey*, London: Routledge

McNamara, B. (1977), 'Regional Development: Case Studies from France and Italy', *Administration*, vol. 25, no. 1

McNamara, T. (1989), 'Local Government is a Minority Interest', *The Irish Times,* 4 January

Meagher, G. A. (1954), 'Housing and the Taxpayer', *Administration*, vol. 2, no. 4

Meagher, G. A. (1959), 'Housing: Finance', *Administration*, vol. 7, no. 2

Meagher, G. A. (1965a), 'Planning and National Development', *Administration*, vol. 13, no. 4

Meagher, G. A. (1965b), 'The Role and Function of the Councillor', *Administration*, vol. 13, no. 2

Meghen, P. J. (1955), 'Building the Workhouses', *Administration*, vol. 3, no. 1

Meghen, P. J. (1957), 'Local Government and Central Control', *Administration*, vol. 5, no. 4

Meghen, P. J. (1958), 'The Administrative Work of the Grand Jury', *Administration*, vol. 6, no. 3

Meghen, P. J. (1960a), 'City and County Managers: The American Viewpoint', *Administration*, vol. 8, no. 1

Meghen, P. J. (1960b), 'The Development of Irish Local Government', *Administration*, vol. 8, no. 4

Meghen, P. J. (1964), 'Why Local Government?', *Administration*, vol. 12, no. 3

Meghen, P. J. (1965a), 'Central–Local Relationships in Ireland', *Administration*, vol. 13, no. 2

Meghen, P. J. (1965b), 'New Ways of Financing Local Government', *Administration*, vol. 9, no. 2

Meghen, P. J. (1965c), *Roads in Ireland*, Dublin: Institute of Public Administration

Meghen, P. J. (1968), 'Local Government Finance – 2', *Administration*, vol. 16, no. 3

Meghen, P. J. (1975), *Local Government in Ireland*, 5th edn (revised by D. Roche), Dublin: Institute of Public Administration

Mehra, M. (1997), *Towards Sustainable Development for Local Authorities: Approaches, Experiences and Sources*, Copenhagen: European Environment Agency

Miley, J. and F. C. King (1951), *Town and Regional Planning Law in Ireland*, Dublin: Browne and Nolan

Mill, J. S. (1975), *Three Essays: On Liberty, Representative Government, The Subjection of Women*, Oxford: Oxford University Press.

Minister for Local Government (1964), *Housing – Progress and Prospects*, Dublin: Government Publications

Monahan, P. (1954), 'Silhouette', *Administration*, vol. 2, no. 1

Monahan, P. (1959), 'Housing, 1. The Social Background', *Administration*, vol. 7, no. 2

Money, W. J. (1973), 'The Need to Sustain a Viable System of Local Democracy', *Urban Studies*, vol. 10

Morgan, D. G. and G. Hogan (1998), *Administrative Law in Ireland*, 3rd edn, London: Sweet and Maxwell

Moxon-Browne, E. and J. Munday (1984), 'Bridges and Chasms: Cross Cutting Attitudes among District Councillors in Northern Ireland', *Administration,* vol. 32, no. 1

Muintir na Tíre (1977), *Government at Sub-National Levels: Planning, Co-ordination, Local Participation*, Tipperary: Muintir na Tíre

Muintir na Tíre (1985), *Towards a New Democracy: Implications of Local Government Reform*, Dublin: Institute of Public Administration

Mullins, J. (2002), 'Public Libraries Enhancing Society: An Irish Perspective', *Administration*, vol. 50, no. 2

Murphy, D. A. (1994), *The Two Tipperarys*, Nenagh: Relay

Murphy, D. A. (1999), *Blazing Tar Barrels and Standing Orders: Tipperary North's First County & District Councils 1899–1902*, Nenagh: Relay

Murphy, T. (1960), 'Environmental Sanitation: Environment and Health', *Administration*, vol. 8, no. 2

Murray, C. H. (1966), 'National and Physical Planning', *Administration*, vol. 14, no. 4

Murray, P. (1978), 'Worker Participation in Local Authorities', *Administration*, vol. 26, no. 3

Nally, D. (1959), 'The Local Government Grant System', *Administration*, vol. 7, no. 4

National Economic and Social Council (1975), *Regional Policy in Ireland: A Review*, NESC Report No. 4, Dublin: National Economic and Social Council

National Economic and Social Council (1976), *Institutional Arrangements for Regional Economic Development*, NESC Report No. 22, Dublin: National Economic and Social Council

National Economic and Social Council (1977a), *Housing Subsidies*, NESC Report No. 23, Dublin: National Economic and Social Council

National Economic and Social Council (1977b), *Service-Type Employment and Regional Development*, NESC Report No. 28, Dublin: National Economic and Social Council

National Economic and Social Council (1978), *Rural Areas: Change and Development*, NESC Report No. 41, Dublin: National Economic and Social Council

National Economic and Social Council (1979), *Urbanisation and Regional Development in Ireland*, NESC Report No. 45, Dublin: National Economic and Social Council

National Economic and Social Council (1980), *Transport Policy*, NESC Report No. 48, Dublin: National Economic and Social Council

National Economic and Social Council (1981), *Urbanisation: Problems of Growth and Decay in Dublin*, NESC Report No. 55, Dublin: National Economic and Social Council

National Economic and Social Council (1983), *Housing Requirements and Population Change 1981–1991*, NESC Report No. 69, Dublin: National Economic and Social Council

National Economic and Social Council (1985a), *Designation of Areas for Industrial Policy*, NESC Report No. 81, Dublin: National Economic and Social Council

National Economic and Social Council (1985b), *The Financing of Local Authorities*, NESC Report No. 80, Dublin: National Economic and Social Council

National Economic and Social Council (1987), *Community Care Services: An Overview*, NESC Report No. 84, Dublin: National Economic and Social Council

National Economic and Social Council (1988), *A Review of Housing Policy*, NESC Report No. 87, Dublin: National Economic and Social Council

National Economic and Social Council (1989), *Ireland in the European Community: Performance, Prospects and Strategy*, NESC Report No. 88, Dublin: National Economic and Social Council

National Economic and Social Council (1994), *New Approaches to Rural Development*, NESC Report No. 97, Dublin: National Economic and Social Council

National Economic and Social Council (1996), *Strategy into the 21st Century*, NESC Report No. 99, Dublin: National Economic and Social Council

National Economic and Social Council (2002), *An Investment in Quality: Service, Inclusion and Enterprise*, NESC Report No. 111, Dublin: National Economic and Social Council

National Roads Authority (1998), *National Roads Needs Study*, Dublin: National Roads Authority

Nicholls, G. (1856), *A History of the Irish Poor Law in connection with the Condition of the People*, London: John Murray

Nolan, B., C. Whelan and J. Williams (1998), *Where are Poor Households? The Spatial Distribution of Poverty and Deprivation in Ireland,* Dublin: Oak Tree Press

Norris, M. (2001), 'Regenerating Run-Down Local Authority Estates: A Review of the Operation of the Remedial Works Scheme Since 1985', *Administration,* vol. 49, no. 1

Northern Ireland Executive (2001), *Programme for Government*, Belfast: Office of the Minister and Deputy First Minister

Norton, A. (1991), 'Western European Local Government in Comparative Perspective', in R. Batley and G. Stoker (eds.), *Local Government in Europe – Trends and Developments*, London: Macmillan

Norton, A. (1994), *International Handbook of Local and Regional Government*, Aldershot: Edward Elgar Publishing

Nowlan, K. I. (1999), *A Guide to Irish Planning Legislation*, Dublin: Law Society of Ireland

Nugent, N. (1999), *The Government and Politics of the European Union*, 4th edn, Basingstoke: Macmillan

Nurre, D. (1987), *Contracting Out of Local Services: Analysis of an Option for Local Authorities: The Case of Refuse Collection,* Dublin: Institute of Public Administration

O'Brien, G. (1921), *Economic History of Ireland from the Union to the Famine*, London: Longmans, Green and Company

O'Brien, W. P. (1878), *Local Government and Taxation (Ireland) Inquiry*, special report on local government in Ireland, London: HMSO, parliamentary papers XXIII

O'Byrne, M. (1968), 'Libraries and Librarianship in Ireland', *Administration*, vol. 16, no. 2

O'Carroll, J. P. (1985), 'Community Programmes and the Traditional View of Community', *Social Studies*, vol. 8, nos 3 and 4

O'Carroll, J. P. (1987), 'Strokes, Cute Hoors and Sneaking Regarders: The Influence of Local Culture on Irish Political Style', *Irish Political Studies*, no. 2

O'Cearbhaill, D. and M. S. O'Cinnéide (1986), 'Community Development in the West of Ireland: A Case Study of the Killala Area', *Community Development Journal*, no. 2

O'Cinnéide, S. (1985), 'Community Response to Unemployment', *Administration*, vol. 33, no. 2

O'Connell, C. (1993), 'Housing Trends and Issues: The Role of Social Housing', *Administration*, vol. 41, no. 3

O'Connell, C. (1994), 'Housing in the Republic of Ireland: A Review of Trends and Recent Policy Measures', *Administration*, vol. 42, no. 2

O'Connell, C. (1998), 'Tenant Involvement in Local Authority Estate Management: A New Panacea for Policy Failure?', *Administration*, vol. 46, no. 2

O'Connell, C. (1999), 'Local Authorities as Landlords', in T. Fahey (ed.), *Social Housing in Ireland: A Study of Success, Failure and Lessons Learned*, Dublin: Oak Tree Press

O'Connor, G. (1999), *A History of Galway County Council*, Galway: Galway County Council

O'Connor, J. and M. Daly (1983), *Transition and Change in the Mid West of Ireland: A Base Line Study of West Limerick*, 2 vols, Limerick: NIHE Social Research Centre

O'Connor, T. M. (1963), 'Local Government and Community Development', *Administration*, vol. 11, no. 4

O'Connor, T. M. (1972), 'Regional Industrial Planning', *Administration*, vol. 20, no. 1

O'Donnell, M. (1998), *Planning Law*, Dublin: Butterworths

O'Donoghue, M. (1989), 'Response to Dr O'Brien's "Study of Irish Tax Policy on Domestic Dwellings"', *Administration*, vol. 37, no. 4

O'Farrell, P. N. (1978), 'Regional Planning Policy – Some Major Issues', *Administration*, vol. 26, no. 2

O'Gorman, N. T. and T. A. O'Carroll (1986/7), 'The Dilemma of Irish Economic Development: Perspectives on the Evolution of Ireland's Public Finances and Economy from the Early 1960s to the Mid 1980s', *Journal of the Statistical and Social Inquiry Society of Ireland*, vol. xxv, no. IV

O'Hagan, J., P. McBride and P. Sanfey (1985), 'Local Government Finance: The Irish Experience', *British Tax Review*, vol. 4

O'Hagan, J., P. McBride and P. Sanfey (1986), 'Local Revenue Sources for Local Government: The Continuing Debate', *Administration*, vol. 34, no. 2

O'Halpin, E. (1991), 'The Origins of City and County Management', in J. Boland, R. Haslam, B. Johnston, B. Kiernan, J. O'Donnell and G. Ward (eds), *City and County Management 1929–1990: A Retrospective*, Dublin: Institute of Public Administration

O'Halpin, E. (2001), 'The System of City and County Management', in M. E. Daly (ed.), *County and Town – One Hundred Years of Local Government in Ireland*, Dublin: Institute of Public Administration

Ó hUiginn, P. (1960), 'Some Social and Economic Aspects of Housing – An International Comparison', *Administration*, vol. 8, no. 1

O'Keeffe, P. J. (1962a), 'Economic Aspects of Road Improvement in Ireland', *Administration*, vol. 10, no. 2

O'Keeffe, P. J. (1962b), 'Main Roads', *Administration*, vol. 10, no. 2

O'Neill, J. (1990), 'Local Government Reform: Lessons from Abroad', *Administration*, vol. 38, no. 3

O'Neill, T. P. (1962), 'The Administration of Relief', in R. D. Edwards and T. D. Williams (eds), *The Great Famine*, Dublin: B & N

O'Regan, J. (1983), 'Funding and the Current State of Irish Roads', *The Engineers Journal*, no. 37

O'Rourke, F. (1978), 'The Travelling People', *Administration*, vol. 26, no. 1

O'Shea, M. (2000), 'The 1999 Local Government Elections in the Republic of Ireland', *Irish Political Studies*, vol. 15

O'Sheil, K. (1921), 'County Councils, their Powers and their Possibilities', in Sinn Féin, *Irish Year Book*, Dublin: Sinn Féin

O'Sullivan, H. (2000), *A History of Local Government in the County of Louth from Earliest Times to the Present*, Dublin: Institute of Public Administration

O'Sullivan, P. and K. Shepherd (1984), *A Source Book on Planning Law in Ireland*, Abingdon: Professional Books [plus supplement, 1987]

O'Sullivan, P. and K. Shepherd (1991), *Irish Planning Law and Practice*, vols 1 and 2, London: Butterworths [loose-leaf, updated annually]

O'Sullivan P. and K. Shepherd (annual), *Irish Planning Law and Practice*, Dublin: Butterworths

OECD (1995), *Governance in Transition: Public Management Reforms in OECD Countries*, Paris: Organisation for Economic Co-operation and Development

OECD (1996), *Ireland: Local Partnerships and Social Innovation*, report prepared by Charles Sabel, Paris: Organisation for Economic Co-operation and Development

OECD (1997), *Managing Across Levels of Government*, Paris: Organisation for Economic Co-operation and Development

OECD (1999), *Revenue Statistics 1965/1998*, Paris: Organisation for Economic Co-operation and Development

OECD (2000), *Government of the Future*, Paris: Organisation for Economic Co-operation and Development

OECD (2001), *The Well-being of Nations: The Role of Human and Social Capital*, Paris: Organisation for Economic Co-operation and Development

Office of the Information Commissioner (annual), *Annual Report*, Dublin: Government Publications

Office of the Ombudsman (annual), *Annual Report*, Dublin: Government Publications

Oliver, J. (1978), *Working at Stormont*, Dublin: Institute of Public Administration

Osborne, D. and T. Gaebler (1992), *Reinventing Government: How the Entrepreneurial Spirit is Transforming the Public Sector*, Reading, MA: Addison-Wesley Publishing

Paddison, R. and S. Bailey (eds) (1988), *Local Government Finance: International Perspectives,* London: Routledge

Pakenham-Walsh, A. A. (1964), 'Financial Controls in Local Government', *Administration*, vol. 12, no. 1

Parker, A. J. (1982), 'The "Friends and Neighbours" Voting Effect in the Galway West Constituency, 1977', *Political Geography Quarterly*, vol. 1, no. 3

Parker, A. J. (1983), 'Localism and Bailiwicks: The Galway West Constituency in the 1977 General Election', *Proceedings Royal Irish Academy*, Dublin: Royal Irish Academy

Patten, C. (1999), *A New Beginning: Policing in Northern Ireland*, Belfast: Northern Ireland Office [often referred to as the Patten Report]

Pearson, P. (2000), *The Heart of Dublin: Resurgence of an Historic City*, Dublin: O'Brien Press

Peterson, J. (1994), 'Subsidiarity: A Definition to Suit Any Vision?', *Parliamentary Affairs*, vol. 47, no. 1

Pfretzschner, P. A. (1964), 'Development and Amenity', *Administration*, vol. 12, no. 3

Pfretzschner, P. A. (1965), *The Dynamics of Irish Housing*, Dublin: Institute of Public Administration

Philippovich, T. (1982), 'Organising for a Stronger Voice. The Role of Local Authority Associations', paper presented at the Irish Council for the European Movement seminar on *The Crisis in Local Government*, Dublin, 12/13 October

Pincus, A. (1973), *Social Work Practice: Model & Method*, Belmont, CA: F. E. Peacock

Pollitt, C. and G. Bouckaert (2000), *Public Management Reform*, Oxford: Oxford University Press

Power, A. (1993), *Hovels to High Rise: State Housing in Europe Since 1850*, London: Routledge.

Prescott, T. A. N. (1962), 'Road Services for a County', *Administration*, vol. 10, no. 2

Prior, D., J. Stewart and K. Walsh (1995), *Citizenship: Rights, Community and Participation*, London: Pitman Publishing

Public Library Service Review Group (1987), *Report of the Public Library Service Review Group*, Dublin: Government Publications

Public Services Organisation Review Group (1969), *Report of the Public Services Organisation Review Group 1966–1969*, Dublin: Government Publications [often referred to as the Devlin Report]

Putnam, R. (2001), 'Social Capital: Measurement and Consequences', *Canadian Journal of Policy Research*, vol. 2, no. 1

Pycroft, C. (1995), 'The Organisation of Local Authorities' European Activities', *Public Policy and Administration*, vol. 10, no. 4

Quinlivan, A. (2000), 'Local Government Bill 2000 – Implications for Municipal Authorities. Another False Pregnancy?', *Administration*, vol. 48, no. 3

Quinlivan, A. (2002), 'European Standards and Waste Management in Ireland – Examining the Local Implementation Deficit', *Administration*, vol. 50, no. 2

Quinn, B. and B. Foley (1999), *Towards Regionalisation and Regeneration: Report of the 15 County Committee for the Retention of Objective 1 Status*

Quinn, D. (1938), 'Anglo-Irish Local Government', *Irish Historical Studies*, vol. I

Rallings, C., M. Thrasher and D. Cowling (2002), 'Mayoral Referendums and Elections', *Local Government Studies*, vol. 28, no. 4

Raven, J. (1976), *Political Culture in Ireland: The Views of Two Generations*, Dublin: Institute of Public Administration

Rees, N. (1997), 'Inter-Regional Cooperation: An Effective Means Towards Sustained Economic Development?', Institute of Public Administration, *Inter-Regional Cooperation for European Development: An Evaluation for Future Policy*, conference proceedings, Dublin: Institute of Public Administration

Rees, N. and M. Farrows (1999), 'The Reform of the EU Structural Funds: Administrative Adaptation and the Prospects for Regionalisation in Ireland', draft paper presented at the Biennial Conference of the European Community Studies Association, Pittsburgh, USA

Reeves, E. (2000), 'Conflict and Co-operation in Contracting Out Local Authority Services in Ireland', *Administration*, vol. 48, no. 4

Reeves, E. and M. Barrow (2000), 'The Impact of Contracting Out on the Costs of Refuse Collection Services: The Case of Ireland', *The Economic and Social Review*, vol. 31, no. 2

Review Group on the Role of Supplementary Welfare Allowance in Relation to Housing (1995), *Report to the Minister for Social Welfare*, Dublin: Government Publications

Rhodes, R. A. W. (1996), 'The New Governance: Governing without Government', *Political Studies*, vol. XLIV

Rhodes, R. A. W. (1997), *Understanding Governance: Policy Networks, Governance, Reflexivity and Accountability*, Buckingham: Open University Press

Rice, T. P. (1982), 'The Revenue Finances of Local Authorities', *Administration*, vol. 30, no. 1

Ridley, F. F. (ed.) (1979), *Government and Administration in Western Europe*, Oxford: Martin Robertson

Rigal, J. (1989), 'Some Issues Concerning the Integration of Irish Travellers', *Administration*, vol. 37, no. 1

Rigney, P. (2001), *Social Dialogue & Lifelong Learning in Ireland*, Malmo: ETF Conference

Roberts, P. and T. Hart (1991), 'Local Authorities and 1992', in J. A. Walsh (ed.), *Local Economic Development and Administrative Reform*, Dublin: Regional Studies Association (Irish Branch)

Robertson, M. (1944), 'Town and Regional Planning', in F. C. King (ed.), *Public Administration in Ireland*, vol. I, Dublin: Civics Institute

Robins, J. A. (1961), 'The County in the Twentieth Century', *Administration*, vol. 19, no. 2

Robins, J. A. (1963), 'The Background to the First Irish Registration Acts', *Administration*, vol. 11, no. 3

Robins, J. A. (1972), 'Carlow Workhouse during the Famine Years', *Administration*, vol. 20, no. 2

Robinson, H. (1924a), *Further Memories connected with Local Government Administration in Ireland*, London: Cassell and Co.

Robinson, H. (1924b), *Memories Wise and Otherwise*, London: Cassell and Co.

Roche, D. (1965), 'The Future Role of Irish Local Government', *Administration*, vol. 13, no. 1

Roche, D. (1968), 'Local Government Finance', *Administration*, vol. 16, no. 3

Roche, D. (1982a), 'Local Government', *Administration*, vol. 30, nos 2 and 3

Roche, D. (1982b), *Local Government in Ireland*, Dublin: Institute of Public Administration

Roche, D. and R. F. Christopher (1973), *Consumer Protection: A Role for Local Government*, National Prices Commission, Occasional Paper No. 5, Dublin: Government Publications

Ronayne, L. (1987), 'The Public Library Authority: A Time for Reforms', *Irish Library*, vol. 4, no. 4

Rose, R. (1996), *What is Europe?*, New York: Harper Collins

Rowat, D. C. (ed.) (1980), *International Handbook on Local Government Re-organisation: Contemporary Developments*, London: Aldwych Press

Royal Commission on Local Government in England (1969), *Report*, 3 vols, London: HMSO

Royal Commission on Local Taxation (1902), *Reports and Minutes of Evidence*, London: HMSO

Royal Commission on the Housing of the Working Classes (1885), *Third Report, Ireland*, London: HMSO

Royal Commission on the Poor Law (1910), *Report*, London: HMSO

Royal Irish Academy and Department of the Environment (1982), *Housing in the Eighties, Proceedings of the 1981 National Housing Conference*, Dublin: An Foras Forbartha

Ryan, F. and T. McNamara (1983), *Local Authorities in Action: A Training Package and Educational Source Book*, Dublin: Institute of Public Administration

Sabel, C. (1996), *Ireland: Local Partnerships and Social Innovation*, Paris: Organisation for Economic Co-operation and Development

Sacks, P. M. (1976), *The Donegal Mafia: An Irish Political Machine*, New Haven/London: Yale University Press

SALA (Swedish Association of Local Authorities) and SFCC (Swedish Federation of County Councils) (2001), *Six Years in the EU – The Consequences for Sweden's Municipalities, County Councils and Regions 1995–2000*, Stockholm: SALA and SFCC

Saorstat Éireann (1931), *Commission of Inquiry into De-rating Reports*, Dublin: Government Publications

Scannell, Y. (1982a), *The Law and Practice Relating to Pollution Control in Ireland*, 2nd edn, London: Graham & Trotman

Scannell, Y. (1982b), 'Planning Control: Twenty Years On (Part I)', *Dublin University Law Journal*, no. 4

Scannell, Y. (1983), 'Planning Control: Twenty Years On (Part II)', *Dublin University Law Journal*, no. 5

Scannell, Y. (1995), *Environmental and Planning Law*, Dublin: Round Hall

Senior, D. (1976), 'Regional Devolution – Throughout the United Kingdom', *Administration*, vol. 24, no. 3

Shaffrey, P. (1975), *The Irish Town: An Approach to Survival*, Dublin: O'Brien Press

Shaffrey, P. (1983a), *Building of Irish Towns*, Dublin: O'Brien Press

Shaffrey, P. (ed.) (1983b), *Your Guide to Planning*, Dublin: O'Brien Press and An Taisce in association with the Irish Planning Institute

Sharpe, L. J. (1970), 'Theories and Values of Local Government', *Political Studies*, vol. 18

Sharpe, L. J. (ed.) (1993), *The Rise of Meso Government in Europe*, London: Sage Publications

Sheehy, E. T. (1962), 'Roads Administration', *Administration*, vol. 10, no. 2

Sheehy, E. T. (1965), 'A Study of the Law on Public Roads', *Administration*, vol. 13, no. 2

Sheehy, E. T. (1966), 'A Study of the Law on Motor Taxation', *Administration*, vol. 14, no. 1

Smiddy, T. A. (1930), 'The Present System of Municipal Government in the Irish Free State', *Public Administration*, vol. VIII, no. 3

Smith, G. and C. Wales (2000), 'Citizens' Juries and Deliberative Democracy', *Political Studies*, vol. 48, no. 1

Smyth, T. S. (1962), 'Municipal Charters of the Town of Cavan', *Administration*, vol. 10, no. 3

Southern & Eastern (S&E) Regional Assembly (2000), *Southern and Eastern Regional Operational Programme, 2000–2006*, Waterford: S&E Regional Assembly

Southern & Eastern (S&E) Regional Assembly (2001), *Southern and Eastern Regional Assembly, Operational Programme 2000–2006: Programme Complement*, Waterford: S&E Regional Assembly

Steering Committee on the Future Development of Higher Education (1995), *Report of the Steering Committee on the Future Development of Higher Education (Based on a Study of Needs to the Year 2015)*, Dublin: Higher Education Authority

Stevenson, C. P. (1984), 'Negotiated Planning: Circumventing The Planning System: I + II', *Irish Jurist*, no. XIX

Stewart, D. (1980), 'Urban Form', in An Foras Forbartha, *Ireland in the Year 2000*, Dublin: An Foras Forbartha

Stewart, J. (1990), 'The Enabling Authority', *Management Education and Development*, vol. 21, part 5

Stewart, J. (1995), 'A Future for Local Authorities as Community Government', in J. Stewart and G. Stoker (eds), *Local Government in the 1990s*, London: Macmillan

Stewart, J. (1997), 'The Local Authority as Regulator', *Local Government Policy-Making*, vol. 23, no. 4

Stewart, J. and H. Davis (1994), 'A New Agenda for Local Governance', *Public Money & Management*, vol. 14, no. 4

Stewart, J. J. (1985), 'Investment in Infrastructure – The Need and the Reality', *The Engineers Journal*, vol. 38, no. 5

Stoker, E. B. (1983), 'Cork Corporation, New Town Development at Mahon Peninsula', *The Engineers Journal,* vol. 37, no. 8

Stoker, G. (1996), 'Normative Theories of Local Government and Local Democracy', in D. King and G. Stoker (eds), *Rethinking Local Democracy*, London: Macmillan

Stout, R. (1985), *Administrative Law in Ireland*, Dublin: Institute of Public Administration

Strategic Planning Guidelines for the Greater Dublin Area (1999), prepared for Dublin Corporation, Dún Laoghaire-Rathdown County Council, Fingal County Council, Kildare County Council, Meath County Council, South Dublin County Council, Wicklow County Council and the Department of the Environment and Local Government, in conjunction with Dublin Regional Authority and Mid-East Regional Authority, by a consortium of consultants comprising Brady Shipman Martin, Kirk McClure Morton, Fitzpatrick Associates and Colin Buchanan and Partners, Dublin: Brady Shipman Martin [review and update published in 2000 and 2001]

Street, H. A. (1955), *The Law Relating to Local Government*, Dublin: Government Publications

Sullivan, M. (1987), 'Dublin City: Environment and Accessibility: A Traffic Engineer's View', *The Engineers Journal*, vol. 40, no. 4

Sullivan, P. (1978), *Irish Planning and Acquisition Law*, Dublin: Institute of Public Administration

Sutcliffe, J. C. (1963), 'The Public Image of the Public Servant', *Administration*, vol. 11, no. 2

Task Force on the Travelling Community (1995), *Report for the Task Force on the Travelling Community*, Dublin: Government Publications

The Arts Council (2002), *The Arts Plan 2002–2006*, Dublin: The Arts Council

The Environmentalist (1988), 'Local Government (Planning and Development) Act 1963–1976: Monaghan County Council v. Brendan Brogan and Patrick Brogan', *The Environmentalist*, vol. 11, no. 1

The Labour Party (2000), *Visions of Ireland, Towards a National Spatial Plan 2000–2015*, Dublin: The Labour Party

The Planning and Development Act 2000: Irish Planning Law and Practice Supplement (2001), annotated by the Environment and Planning Law Unit of A&L Goodbody, Solicitors, Dublin: Butterworth (Ireland) Ltd

Thompson, B. (1988), 'The Role of Housing Associations', *Administration,* vol. 36, no. 4

Threshold (1987), *Policy Consequences: A Study of the £5000 Surrender Grant in the Dublin Housing Area*, Dublin: Threshold

Tierney, M. (1982), *The Parish Pump: A Study of Efficiency and Local Government in Ireland*, Dublin: Able Press

Tomlinson, M. (1980), 'Relegating Local Government', in L. O'Dowd, B. Rolston and M. Tomlinson (eds), *Northern Ireland: Between Civil Rights and Civil War*, London: CSE Books

Tovey, M. (1985), '"Local Community": In Defence of a Much Criticised Concept', *Social Studies,* vol. 8, nos 3 and 4

Travelling People Review Body (1983), *Report of the Travelling People Review Body,* Dublin: Government Publications

Travers, P. (2001), 'A Bloodless Revolution: The Democratisation of Irish Local Government 1898–9', in Mary E. Daly (ed.), *County and Town: One Hundred Years of Local Government in Ireland,* Dublin: Institute of Public Administration

Tribunal of Inquiry [Flood Tribunal] (2002), *The Second Interim Report of the Tribunal of Inquiry into Certain Planning Matters and Payments,* Dublin: Government Publications

Turpin, D. (1954), 'Local Government Service 1: Achieving a Single Service', *Administration,* vol. 2, no. 4

Turpin, D. (1955), 'Local Government Service 2: Consolidating the Service', *Administration,* vol. 3, no. 1

Turpin, D. (1970), 'Regionalism – 2. Local Government', *Administration,* vol. 18, no. 3

UNDP (1994), *Human Development Report,* New York: Oxford University Press

United Nations (1948), *Universal Declaration of Human Rights,* text agreed by the General Assembly of the United Nations on 10 December 1948, New York: United Nations

United Nations (2002), *Report of the World Summit on Sustainable Development, Johannesburg, South Africa, 26 August – 4 September 2002,* New York: United Nations

United Nations Conference on Environment and Development (UNCED) (1993), *Agenda 21: Programme of Action for Sustainable Development – The Final Text of Agreements Negotiated by Governments at the United Nations Conference on Environment and Development (UNCED), 3–14 June, 1992, Rio de Janeiro, Brazil,* New York: United Nations

van der Kamp, H. (1987), *Regional Planning: A Review of Regional Studies,* Dublin: An Foras Forbartha

van der Kamp, H. (2001), 'Development of Infrastructure under the National Spatial Strategy', *Pleanáil (Journal of the Irish Planning Institute),* no. 15

Verdú, V. (1999), 'The Chinese Castle', *2G International Architecture Review,* no. 10

Vice-Regal Commission on Poor Law Reform in Ireland (1906), *Report,* vol. I, London: HMSO, CD 3202

Walker, D. (1962), *Local Government Finance in Ireland: A Preliminary Survey,* Paper No. 5, Dublin: Economic Research Institute

Walsh, A. (1988), 'The Role of the Local Authority' [in housing policy], *Administration,* vol. 36, no. 4

Walsh, B. M. (1978), 'National and Regional Demographic Trends', *Administration,* vol. 26, no. 2

Walsh, J. (1998), 'Local Development and Local Government in the Republic of Ireland: From Fragmentation to Integration?', *Local Economy,* vol. 12, no. 4

Walsh, J., S. Craig and D. McCafferty (1998), *Local Partnership for Social Inclusion,* Dublin: Oak Tree Press

Ward, G. (1983), 'Charging Users – Lessons from Local Authority Experience', in J. Blackwell and F. Convery (eds), *Promise and Performance: Irish Environmental Policies Analysed,* Dublin: UCD Resource and Environmental Policy Centre

Weafer, J. (1985), 'Urban Community: Dead or Alive', *Social Studies,* vol. 8, nos 3 and 4

Webb, J. J. (1918), *Municipal Government in Ireland: Medieval and Modern,* Dublin: Talbot Press

Webb, J. J. (1929), *The Guilds of Dublin,* Dublin: Sign of the Three Candles

Whelan, C. (1996), 'The Region and the Intellectuals', in L. O'Dowd (ed.), *On Intellectuals and Intellectual Life in Ireland,* Belfast: Institute of Irish Studies/Royal Irish Academy

Whelan, N. (1976), 'Considerations Relevant to Central Government', *Administration,* vol. 24, no. 3

Whelan, N. (2000), *Politics, Elections and the Law,* Dublin: Blackhall Publishing

White, R. H. (1954), 'Rateable Valuation', in F. C. King (ed.), *Public Administration in Ireland*, vol. III, Dublin: Civics Institute

Williams, B. and P. Shiels (2002), 'The Expansion of Dublin and the Policy Implications of Dispersal', *Journal of Irish Urban Studies*, vol. 1, no. 1

Wilson, D. (1999), 'Exploring the Limits of Public Participation in Local Government', *Parliamentary Affairs*, vol. 52, no. 2

Woodham-Smith, C. (1962), *The Great Hunger, Ireland, 1845–9*, London: Hamilton

Working Group on Cost Overruns on Public Construction Contracts (1983), *Report*, Dublin: Government Publications

Working Group on the Review of Rating Law (2001), 'Review of Rating Law: Report of the Working Group', Dublin: Department of the Environment and Local Government, unpublished report

Working Group on the Review of the Coroner Service (2000), *Review of the Coroner Service: Report of the Working Group*, Dublin: Government Publications

World Commission on Environment and Development (1987), *Our Common Future*, Oxford: Oxford University Press

Wright, M. (1967), *The Dublin Region: Advisory Plan and Final Report*, Dublin: Government Publications

Youth Employment Agency (1987), *Development of Community Enterprise in Ireland,* Dublin: Youth Employment Agency

Zimmerman, J. F. (1972a), 'Community Building in Large Cities', *Administration*, vol. 20, no. 2

Zimmerman, J. F. (1972b), 'Council–Manager Government in Ireland', *Studies in Comparative Local Government*, vol. 6, no. 1

Zimmerman, J. F. (1976), 'Role Perceptions of Irish City and County Councillors', *Administration*, vol. 24, no. 4

Zimmerman, J. F. (1978a), 'New Town Development in the Dublin Area', *Planning and Administration*, vol. 5, no. 1

Zimmerman, J. F. (1978b), 'Role Perceptions of Dual Office Holders', *Administration*, vol. 26, no. 1

Zimmerman, J. F. (1980), 'An Bord Pleanála (The Irish Planning Board)', *Administration*, vol. 28, no. 3

Zimmerman, J. F. (1982), 'Regional Governance Models: Greater Dublin and Greater London', *National Civic Review,* vol. 71, no. 2

Zimmerman, J. F. (1994), 'One County Becomes Three Counties', *Administration*, vol. 42, no. 4

Zimmerman, J. F. (2000), 'The Irish City and County Management System', *Home Rule & Civil Society*, no. 11

Index

litter, 256–8
miscellaneous, 264–5
noise pollution, 260
waste management, 254–6
water pollution, 258–9
sustainable development, 369–70,
371–80
voluntary groups, 500
Environmental Protection Agency Act,
1992, 78, 248, 260, 261, 266, 422
temporary dwellings, 264
Environmental Protection Agency Act,
1992 (Noise) Regulations, 1994,
248
Environmental Protection Agency (EPA),
77, 248, 254, 422, 458, 493
functions, 78, 247, 265–7
waste management, 255
water, 219, 220
equalisation, 455–7
fund, 337, 338, 343
equality, 309–10
racial, 399
Equality Act, 1998, 309
Equality Officers, 320
Esmonde, Sir Thomas, 27
estate duty, 191
estate improvement schemes, 180–1
ethics, 146–7, 318–19
registrar, 147
Ethics in Public Office Act, 1995, 146–7
ethnic minorities, 393, 394, 399
euro, introduction of, 410
Eurocities, 539
European Association of Border Regions
(EABR), 539
European Charter of Local Self-
Government, 3, 5, 13, 88–9, 444,
453, 483–4, 536, 537
text of, 509–15
European Commission, 99, 415, 431,
434, 481
co-funding, 214, 217
Committee of the Regions, 424–5
court of appeal, 411–12
Directives, 405

enforcement, 411
lobbying, 422–3
and local government, 418, 424, 428
regional assemblies, 67
role of, 406
White Paper on governance, 426–7
European Communities Act, 1972, 246,
405
European Communities (Environmental
Impact Assessment) Regulations,
1989, 246, 247
European Communities (Natural
Habitats) Regulations, 1997, 248
European Court of Auditors, 407
European Court of Justice, 99, 247,
405–6, 411
European Environment Agency, 266
European Parliament, 13, 99, 108, 406,
430, 465
European Regional Development Fund,
419
European Social Policy Forum, 296
European Spatial Development
Perspective, 410
European Statistical Agency (Eurostat),
436
European Union (EU), 161, 290, 430,
480, 494, 503. *see also* Cohesion
Funds; Structural Funds
architectural conservation, 387
area partnerships, 393
associations and bodies, 535–9
effects on sub-national structures, 400,
408–12, 418–22, 453
environment, 246–7, 259
Environmental Action Programme,
373–4, 375
funding, 413–15
influence of local government on,
424–7
infringement cases, 411–12
law and decision making, 254,
404–7
local authority response to, 422–4
and local economy, 415–18
local governance, 498

rural development, 1999, 362
social housing, 1991, 181–3, 327
Wicklow, County, 14, 360, 365, 440
Wicklow County Council, 199, 395, 440–1
Wicklow harbour, 65
Wicklow health area, 69
Wicklow Town, 358
'Wise Men,' Committee of, 212
women
  franchise, 35
  in Local Government Act, 1898, 27–8
  participation of, 110–11
women's groups, 500
Wood Quay, 135
worker participation, 320–2
Worker Protection (Regular Part-Time Employees) Act, 1991, 319
Workers Party, 104
workhouses, 21–3, 24, 29, 31
Working Time Directive, EU, 409

World Association of Cities and Local Authorities Coordination (WACLAC), 538
World Commission on Environment and Development, UN, 1983, 372
World Conservation Strategy, 373n
World Conservation Union, 373n
World Summit on Sustainable Development, 2002, 374, 380
World War I, 29, 37, 167, 169, 448
World War II, 74, 172, 176, 179, 195, 329, 443
World Wide Declaration on Local Self-Government, 537
World Wide Fund for Nature, 373n
Wyndham Act, 1903, 391

Y
Yeats, W.B., 455
Youghal, Co. Cork, 65